THE JERUSALEM TALMUD
THIRD ORDER: NAŠIM
TRACTATE *QIDDUŠIN*

STUDIA JUDAICA

FORSCHUNGEN ZUR WISSENSCHAFT DES JUDENTUMS

BEGRÜNDET VON
E. L. EHRLICH

HERAUSGEGEBEN VON
G. STEMBERGER

BAND XLIII

WALTER DE GRUYTER · BERLIN · NEW YORK

THE JERUSALEM TALMUD
תלמוד ירושלמי

THIRD ORDER: NAŠIM
סדר נשים
TRACTATE *QIDDUŠIN*
מסכת קידושין

EDITION, TRANSLATION, AND COMMENTARY

BY

HEINRICH W. GUGGENHEIMER

WALTER DE GRUYTER · BERLIN · NEW YORK

ISBN 978-3-11-068121-5
e-ISBN (PDF) 978-3-11-097126-2

This volume is text- and page-identical with the hardback published in 2008.

Library of Congress Control Number: 2020942831

Bibliographic information published by the Deutsche Nationalbibliothek
The Deutsche Nationalbibliothek lists this publication in the
Deutsche Nationalbibliografie;
detailed bibliographic data are available on the Internet at http://dnb.dnb.de.

© 2020 Walter de Gruyter GmbH, Berlin/Boston

Printing and binding: CPI books GmbH, Leck

www.degruyter.com

Preface

The present volume is the tenth in this series of the Jerusalem Talmud, the fifth in a five volume edition, translation, and Commentary of the Third Order of this Talmud. The principles of the edition regarding text, vocalization, and Commentary have been spelled out in detail in the Introduction to the first volume. The text in this volume is based on the manuscript text of the Yerushalmi edited by J. Sussman for the Academy of the Hebrew Language, Jerusalem 2001. The author has exercised his own independent judgment on what may or may not be corrupt in the text. The text essentially represents an outline, to be fleshed out by a teacher's explanation. The translation should mirror this slant; it should not endow the text with literary qualities which the original does not posses. In particular, the translation is not intended to stand separate from the Commentary.

The text contains many passages which are repeated in other Tractates of this Talmud. Occasionally in the Leiden manuscript, and quite frequently in the Genizah texts, the parallel text is not copied but after the first few words is replaced by a notice: "One continues this in Tractate A, Chapter X."[1] This proves that parallel passages in the Jerusalem Talmud are copies of one another. In the present edition, parallel passages in most

---

1   Cf. Chapter 3, Notes 147,162,166,192,259,280; Chapter 4, Note 171.

cases are considered as parallel sources and a full list of variant readings is given in every case. These readings show that in fact parallel passages are to be considered witnesses to the same original text, but it appears that a number of deviations cannot be explained as copyists' errors and that the scribe of the Leiden ms. copied different tractates from different mss. representing different histories of transmission and different stages of adaptation of Palestinian spelling (as represented by most Geniza fragments) to the Babylonian spelling with which the scribes were familiar.

The extensive Commentary is not based on emendations; where there is no evidence from manuscripts or early prints to correct evident scribal errors, the proposed correction is given in the Notes. As in the preceding volume, for each paragraph the folio and line numbers of the text in the Krotoschin edition are added. It should be remembered that these numbers may differ from the *editio princeps* by up to three lines. It seems to be important that a translation of the Yerushalmi be accompanied by the text, to enable the reader to compare the interpretation with other translations.

Again I wish to thank my wife, Dr. Eva Guggenheimer, who acted as critic, style editor, proof reader, and expert on the Latin and Greek vocabulary. Her own notes on some possible Latin and Greek etymologies are identified by (E. G.).

Contents

Introduction to Tractate Qiddušin 1

Qiddušin Chapter 1, האשה נקנית
    Halakhah 1 7
    Halakhah 2 45
    Halakhah 3 89
    Halahkah 4 108
    Halakhah 5 124
    Halakhah 6 141
    Halakhah 7 148
    Halakhah 9 174
    Halakhah 10 180

Qiddušin Chapter 2, האיש מקדש
    Halakhah 1 189
    Halakhah 2 215
    Halakhah 4 219
    Halakhah 5 220
    Halakhah 6 226
    Halakhah 7 231
    Halakhah 8 235
    Halakhah 9 245
    Halakhah 10 252

Qiddušin Chapter 3, האומר

Halakhah 1	257
Halakhah 2	272
Halakhah 3	282
Halakhah 4	289
Halakhah 5	294
Halakhah 6	301
Halakhah 7	306
Halakhah 10	309
Halakhah 13	318
Halakhah 14	321
Halakhah 15	339

Qiddušin Chapter 4, עשרה יוחסין

Halakhah 1	344
Halakhah 2	370
Halakhah 3	373
Halakhah 4	377
Halakhah 5	381
Halakhah 6	383
Halakhah 7	391
Halakhah 8	395
Halakhah 9	399
Halakhah 10	400
Halakhah 11	402
Halakhah 12	411

Indices

Sigla	415
Index of Biblical Quotations	415
Index of Talmudic Quotations	
Babylonian Talmud	418
Jerusalem Talmud	419

Mishnah	420
Tosephta	421
Midrashim	421
Rabbinical Literature	422
Index of Greek, Latin, and Hebrew words	422
Author Index	422
Subject Index	423

Introduction to Tractate Qiddušin

In most civilized societies, an actual marriage is preceded by a betrothal, a public statement by the parties that they are ready to contract marriage at a later date. Such betrothal is also found in medieval and later Jewish sources and is known either as תְּנָאִים "stipulations" or קְנָס "fine", since usually it was a contract for the marriage of two young persons detailing the promised monetary contributions by the parents of both parties to the new family and containing a clause stipulating the fine imposed on a party which would be backing out of the contract at a later time. Such a contract of betrothal is treated in the present Tractate under the Greek name of σύμφωνον "agreed upon, contract"; it has no parallel in the Babylonian Talmud, according to which in Babylonia property settlements on the young couple were settled orally.

It is a peculiarity of Jewish marriage law, accepted by all groups, that marriage must be executed in two steps. This is apparent from the Pentateuch, which in criminal law treats the betrothed girl as "one's neighbor's wife"[1] while she still is a virgin, and describes marriage as a two-step process[2]: "If a man (1) take a wife and (2) take possession of her." The verb לקח "to take' used in the description of the first step is the term

---

1   Deut. 22:24.
2   Deut. 24:1.

generally used to describe marriage in Genesis and other biblical books. The meaning "to buy, to acquire" in Hebrew only occurs in late texts, e. g., *Neh.* 5:2,3. Since the change of status of the prospective bride from single girl to married wife is relevant for criminal law, the point in time when this change occurs must be well defined by a legal action. Based on the interpretation of "to take" as "to acquire", the preliminary marriage must be an intentional act of acquisition by the groom. This act generally is called קִדּוּשִׁין "dedication"; the biblical root אָרַשׂ "to betrothe" is used only in quotes of or references to biblical texts. The real, definitive marriage, by which the bride enters the groom's house and lives with him, which activates all financial rights and obligations incidental to marriage, is called נִשׂוּאִין "carrying off"[3]. The modalities of the definitive marriage are discussed in Tractate *Ketubot*. In modern practice, preliminary and definitive marriage are performed consecutively in the same ceremony, following the Yerushalmi (*Ketubot* 1:1, Note 24).

Since preliminary marriage is structured as an act of acquisition, the first Chapter of the Tractate treats acquisitions in its diverse forms. This Chapter is by far the longest in all of the Jerusalem Talmud. The first Halakhah treats preliminary marriage. The Mishnah details the ways in which a man may acquire the exclusive right to marry a woman, both in original and levirate marriages, and the ways in which the wife may regain her status as single woman. Since the distinction between

---

3 It probably is an intended double-entendre that נשׂא is used in *Jud.* 21:23 to indicate that the Benjaminites both "carried off" and "married" the flute players in the vineyards of Shiloh. The only other biblical occurrence of נשׂא as "to marry" is *Ru.* 1:4, where the expression is used to emphasize the irregularity of marriages to unconverted Gentile women.

preliminary and definitive marriages is biblical, all the possibilities have to be shown to be valid by biblical standards. A side remark discusses the status of Gentile marriages in biblical law. The text quotes two opinions; the one which the New Testament follows that marriage can be contracted only by marital relations and is absolutely indissoluble, and the Roman one that marriage is a compact between two consenting parties which can be repudiated at will by either party. If the groom chooses to contract the preliminary marriage by a gift of money or valuables, the Houses of Hillel and Shammai disagree about the minimum amount involved. Talmudic theory does not take cognizance of inflation. According to the House of Hillel, the minimal amount is equal to the value of the smallest Hasmonean coin, the *perutah*, whose Roman equivalent had disappeared even under the Julio-Claudian emperors. The lengthy discussion about the subdivisions of the denar is an attempt, in post-Diocletian times, to reconstruct the Augustean monetary system. The Halakhah ends with a short discussion of divorce and levirate marriage, followed by an attempt to define the terms used in *Lev.* 19:20.

Halakhah Two is purely theoretical, dealing with the laws of the Hebrew slave. Since *Lev.* 25 connects Hebrew slavery with the institution of the Jubilee, the end of the latter at the latest with the fall of Samaria precluded any re-emergence of Hebrew slavery during or after the Second Commonwealth. This does not prevent the Talmudim from discussing at length the biblical laws of this by then hypothetical institution.

Halakhah Three deals with the acquisition and manumission of Gentile slaves. The manumission of Gentile slaves is a topic treated in Tractate *Gittin*. Here, only parallels to the Roman *manumissio inter amicos* and the Babylonian, Egyptian, and Byzantine *manumissio per epistulam* are treated, with an indication of the problems raised by partial manumission.

Halakhah Four treats the acquisition of livestock, Halakhah Five that of real estate and movables; it discusses deals involving both real estate and movables and the judicial status of suits involving composite transactions. Halakhah 6 covers barter.

The second part of the Chapter is introduced in Halakhah Seven, detailing the obligations of parents towards their children and of children towards their parents. The texts describing the obligations of children to honor and support their parents are copies of the relevant texts from *Peah*. The obligations of parents towards their children are really only obligations of the father's; this leads to a discussion of any biblical obligations not incumbent on women. Halakhah Nine similarly contains a discussion of those biblical obligations which are not relevant outside the Holy Land. The Chapter ends with a homily on the rewards awaiting the person who keeps his obligations.

Preliminary marriage, as a purely legal proceeding, is eminently suited to be performed by proxy. Chapters Two and Three deal with complications that might arise in preliminary marriage contracted by agent, or which is dependent on explicit or implicit stipulations, or executed by a gift of services. Chapter Two concludes with preliminary marriage executed by a gift of questionable value. The second part of Chapter Three treats preliminary marriages where either the identity of the woman is not clear or where the existence of such a marriage is itself a point of dispute between the parties.

The last part of the Chapter states the principle on which the qualifications for permitted marriages are based. There are two main problems. *Deut.* 23:3 prohibits the marriage of a bastard (the child from an adulterous or incestuous union) and any of his descendants with a regular member of the congregation. *Lev.* 21:7 restricts the marriage pool available to priests. In addition, priests of the Second Commonwealth disregarded the rule that prophetic utterances are invalid as bases of legal rules and, based on *Ez.* 44:22 forbade the marriage of priests with women proselytes. The children of priests from women forbidden to them are desecrated priests; their disability also is hereditary. The main rule stated in Mishnah 14 is that the children of a legal union belong to the marriage class of their father. This means that female bastards and female descendants of desecrated priests can remove their disabilities; bastards by marrying proselytes permitted to them, and female desecrated ones by marrying an Israel. In the last Halakhah it is indicated that male bastards can father non-bastard children by marrying an unconverted Gentile woman under Gentile rules and converting her children at birth. This makes the children proselytes, rather than bastards.

The last Chapter starts with detailing the different marriage classes, not all of which follow distinct rules. This is followed by a discussion of the rules applying to children with unknown paternity and foundlings, and the special rules applying to marriages of male and female members of the priestly clan. In the Halakhah, these latter rules are declared obsolete. The rules for marriages of desecrated priests and proselytes are discussed in passing.

The second part of Chapter Four deals with the power of the father to legitimize or delegitimize his children and the limits of this power, as well as the value of personal declarations in establishing family relationships. An appendix notes that a man may not be alone with a woman who neither is his wife nor a close relative forbidden to him by biblical incest rules; related rules forbid unmarried males to act as teachers and females to teach male children. In both cases the Halakhah notes that one does not suspect Jews to be either pedophiles or homosexuals but one is wary lest the teacher be attracted to one of the parents of the opposite sex.

The Chapter, Tractate, and Order closes with a lengthy homily on the merit of study of the Law and the rewards of such study.

The Tractate contains an above average number of passages borrowed from other Tractates, sometimes the same passage from different Chapters of the same Tractate. A complete list of the *sigla* used to characterise these parallels is given at the beginning of the Index. The critical notes also include the Geniza texts edited by Louis Ginzberg in his שְׁרִידֵי הַיְרוּשַׁלְמִי. They leave out three inedited Geniza fragments, for whose location I am indebted to Professor Jacob Sussman[4]. The first of these (Halakhot 3:1-3) contains only fragments of lines; short of a full publication of the text a list of the Galilean spellings (which otherwise confirm the Leiden text) would be very misleading. The interesting additions in the remaining short fragments in Halakhot 2:9, 3:1 have been given by Professor Sussman in his edition of the Leiden Text; these are duly noted in the text[5].

---

4   They are T.-S. NS 171.1 (at the Manuscript Department of the National and University Library in Jerusalem, reel 31347) and Cambridge University Library OR 1080.85a, 1080.452 (reel 19790).

5   Chapter 2, Notes 235, 236a; Chapter 3, Note 57.

הָאִשָּׁה נִקְנִית פֶּרֶק רִאשׁוֹן

משנה א: הָאִשָּׁה נִקְנֵית בְּשָׁלֹשׁ דְּרָכִים וְקוֹנָה אֶת עַצְמָהּ בִּשְׁתֵּי דְרָכִים. נִקְנֵית בְּכֶסֶף בִּשְׁטָר וּבְבִיאָה. בְּכֶסֶף בֵּית שַׁמַּאי אוֹמְרִים בְּדִינָר וּבְשָׁוֶה דִינָר וּבֵית הִלֵּל אוֹמְרִים בִּפְרוּטָה וּבְשָׁוֶה פְרוּטָה. וְכַמָּה הִיא פְרוּטָה אַחַת בִּשְׁמוֹנֶה בָּאִסָּר הָאִיטַלְקִי. וְקוֹנָה אֶת עַצְמָהּ בְּגֵט וּבְמִיתַת הַבַּעַל. הַיְבָמָה נִקְנֵית בְּבִיאָה וְקוֹנָה אֶת עַצְמָהּ בַּחֲלִיצָה וּבְמִיתַת הַיָּבָם.

Mishnah 1: A wife may be acquired[1] in three ways; she regains her autonomy in two ways. She is acquired by money[2], or by a document[3], or by intercourse[4]. By money, the House of Shammai say, by a denar[5] or a denar's value; but the House of Hillel say, by a *peruṭa* or a *peruṭa*'s value. How much is a *peruṭa*[6]? One eighth of an Italic *assarius*[7]. She regains her autonomy by a bill of divorce or by the husband's death. A sister-in-law[8] is acquired[9] by intercourse; she regains her autonomy by *ḥaliṣah* or by the brother-in-law's death[10].

1   In matters of criminal law, any relations the woman might have with another man would be adultery. The husband cannot live with his wife (and does not acquire any dowry she might bring with her) unless he accepts the financial responsibilities incumbent upon a husband in a public ceremony, attended by at least 10 witnesses (cf. Peah 6:2, Note 46). The acquisition, or betrothal, mentioned here only needs the presence of two witnesses.

2   The woman agrees to be preliminarily married for a monetary consideration given in the presence of two witnesses.

3   A written promise of marriage.

4   Attested to by two witnesses. It

is enough for the witnesses to confirm that the parties were together in a locked bedroom for a period of time sufficient for intercourse. Since one speaks of preliminary marriage, the couple is in principle forbidden to live together after such intercourse and before the definitive marriage. There is a midrashic doctrine that no woman can become pregnant from her first intercourse unless she had lesbian or autoerotic experiences [*Gen. rabba* 45(5), 51(11); *Pesiqta rabbati* 42, p. 177].

5   A Roman silver denar; under Augustus and his first successors about 3.5 g of silver.

6   The *peruṭa* was a small Hasmonean copper coin which disappeared with the end of the Jewish commonwealth, more than 100 years before the compilation of the Mishnah. Therefore, its value has to be defined in terms of Roman coins.

7   Corresponding to $1/192$ of a denar. *Assarius* is the old name of the Roman *as*. In rabbinic practice, a *peruṭa* is defined as half a grain ($1/960$ of a troy oz. or 0.0324 g) of sterling silver.

8   The widow of a brother who died childless; cf. Introduction to Tractate *Yebamot*.

9   In definitive marriage. By biblical standards there is no preliminary levirate marriage.

10   Before she entered the levirate marriage. Once she is married, she is a wife in all respects and regains her autonomy by divorce or widowhood.

(58b line 30) **הלכה א:** הָאִשָּׁה נִיקְנֵית בְּשָׁלֹשׁ דְּרָכִים כול'. כֵּינִי מַתְנִיתָא. אוֹ בְּכֶסֶף אוֹ בִשְׁטָר אוֹ בְּבִיאָה. וְתַנֵּי רִבִּי חִייָה כֵן. לֹא סוֹף דָּבָר בִּשְׁלָשְׁתָּן אֶלָּא אֲפִילוּ בְּאֶחָד מֵהֶן.

Halakhah 1: "A wife may be acquired in three ways," etc. So is the Mishnah: Either by money, or by document, or by intercourse. Rebbi Hiyya stated as follows: Not only by all three together, but even by any one of them.

(58b line 32) בְּכֶסֶף מְנַיִין. כִּי יִקַּח. מַגִּיד שֶׁנִּקְנֵית בְּכֶסֶף. בְּבִיאָה מְנַיִין. וּבְעָלָהּ. מַגִּיד שֶׁנִּקְנֵית בְּבִיאָה. הָיִיתִי אוֹמֵר. עַל יְדֵי זוֹ וְעַל יְדֵי זוֹ. כֶּסֶף בְּלֹא בִיאָה בִיאָה בְּלֹא כֶסֶף מְנַיִין. רִבִּי אַבָּהוּ בְּשֵׁם רִבִּי יוֹחָנָן. כְּתִיב. כִּי יִמָּצֵא אִישׁ שׁוֹכֵב עִם אִשָּׁה בְעוּלַת בַּעַל. הֲנַע עַצְמָךְ. אֲפִילוּ לֹא קְנָיָיהּ אֶלָּא בְבִיאָה אָמְרָה תוֹרָה הַבָּא אַחֲרָיו בְּחֶנֶק. לֹא סוֹף דָּבָר בְּכְדַרְכָּהּ אֶלָּא אֲפִילוּ שֶׁלֹּא כְדַרְכָּהּ. רִבִּי אַבָּהוּ בְּשֵׁם רִבִּי יוֹחָנָן. לֹא צְרִיכָה שֶׁלֹּא מִכְּדַרְכָּהּ. אִין תֵּימַר מִכְּדַרְכָּהּ. לָמָּה לִיהּ בְעָלָהּ. אֲפִילוּ אַחֵר. כַּיֵּי דְתַנִּינָן תַּמָּן. בָּאוּ עָלֶיהָ שְׁנַיִם. הָרִאשׁוֹן בִּסְקִילָה וְהַשֵּׁינִי בְּחֶנֶק.

By money, from where? "After he acquires," this tells you that she is acquired by money.[11] By marital relations, from where? "And has marital relations with her," this tells you that she is acquired by intercourse[12]. I would say, by both together. Money without intercourse and intercourse without money, from where? [13]Rebbi Abbahu in the name of Rebbi Johanan, it is written: "If a man is found lying with a woman having had intercourse with her husband." Think of it, even if he did only acquire her by intercourse, the one coming after him is [executed] by strangulation. Not only regular intercourse but even perverse[14]. Rebbi Abbahu in the name of Rebbi Johanan, it is necessary to mention perverse intercourse for if it were regular, why mention her husband[15]? As we have stated there[16]: "If she was raped by two men, the first is stoned, the second strangled[17]."

11   Babli 2a. In rabbinic Hebrew, לקח means "to buy". The Babli shows from *Gen.* 23:13 that לקח in biblical Hebrew may mean "to accept a deal involving money". By the talmudic doctrine of invariability of lexemes in biblical language, the same meaning must apply in all cases.

12   Babli 9b. *Deut.* 24:1: "After a man takes a wife and has marital relations with her" is the preamble to the rules of divorce. The verse is read

to mean: "After a man buys and/or has marital relations with a woman, if he desires to terminate the relationship he is required to follow the rules of divorce." Since there is no divorce without a preceding marriage, it follows that acquiring a wife by money and/or intercourse establishes marriage by biblical standards.

13   This elliptic statement is shortened from *Ketubot* 3:6 (Notes 88-92). The man who sleeps with a virgin preliminarily married to another man is stoned; one who sleeps with a married woman who is not a virgin is strangled. Since the verse mentions only intercourse, it is deduced that even if no money was given, the girl is legally bound to her husband and the seducer or rapist is executed for adultery.

14   Sex play which leads to satisfaction without penetration and ejaculation.

15   If the verse was simply intended to state that the punishment of the adulterer with a non-virgin is different from that with a virgin, it would not have mentioned "her husband". The husband makes his wife a non-virgin even by perverse intercourse, any other man only by penetration.

16   Mishnah *Sanhedrin* 7:15.

17   If the first one penetrated her.

(58b line 40) הָא לָמַדְנוּ בִּיאָה בְּלֹא כֶסֶף. כֶּסֶף בְּלֹא בִיאָה מְנַיִין. וְיָצְאָה חִנָּם אֵין כָּסֶף. אִם אַחֶרֶת יִקַּח לוֹ. מַה זוֹ בְּכֶסֶף אַף זוֹ בְּכֶסֶף.

So we learned intercourse without money. Money without intercourse, from where? "She shall go free, without money." "If he did acquire another one."[18] Since one was by money, so the other is by money[19].

18   *Ex.* 21:11,10, speaking of the "Hebrew slave girl", the underage girl sold by her father with the understanding that the buyer may use the amount he paid for the girl as bride-money in case he wants to marry her or give her to his son. This certainly is marriage by money. V. 11 notes that if she is not married either within 6 years or by the time she reaches adulthood, she goes free; the money given for her was to buy her working power. V. 10 states that once she is married, she cannot be treated differently from any other wife. It is inferred that as a matter of principle

her acquisition cannot be different from that of any other wife.

19   In *Mekhilta dR. Simeon bar Iohai* (p. 167) the argument is inverted: Since in general a woman may be acquired by a document, so Hebrew slave girls may be acquired by a document.

(58b line 41) בִּשְׁטָר. וְכָתַב לוֹ סֵפֶר כְּרִיתוּת וְנָתַן בְּיָדָהּ וְשִׁלְּחָהּ מִבֵּיתוֹ וְיָצְאָה מִבֵּיתוֹ וְהָלְכָה וְהָיְתָה לְאִישׁ אַחֵר. מַקִּישׁ הֲוָיָיתָהּ לִיצִיאָתָהּ. מָה יְצִיאָתָהּ בִּשְׁטָר אַף הֲוָיָיתָהּ בִּשְׁטָר.

By a document? "He shall write her a bill of divorce, hand it to her, and send her out of his house. If she left his house and went to be another man's.[20]" It brackets her being with her leaving[21]. Since her leaving was by a document, so her being is by a document.

20   *Deut.* 24:1.
21   Babli 5a, *Erubin* 15b, *Sukkah* 25a, *Ketubot* 47a, *Gittin* 21b; *Sifry Deut.* 269, end.

(58b line 44) אָמַר רִבִּי אָבִין וְתַנֵּי חִזְקִיָּה. וְכִי יִקַּח. מַגִּיד שֶׁנִּקְנֵית בְּכֶסֶף. וְדִין הוּא. מָה אִם עִבְרִיָּה שֶׁאֵינָהּ נִקְנֵית בְּבִיאָה נִקְנֵית בְּכֶסֶף. זוֹ שֶׁהִיא נִקְנֵית בְּבִיאָה אֵינוֹ דִין שֶׁנִּקְנֵית בְּכֶסֶף. יְבָמָה תּוֹכִיחַ. שֶׁהִיא נִקְנֵית בְּבִיאָה וְאֵינוֹ נִקְנֵית בְּכֶסֶף. אַף אַתָּה אַל תִּתְמַהּ עַל זוֹ שֶׁאַף עַל פִּי שֶׁהִיא נִקְנֵית בְּבִיאָה אֵינוֹ דִין שֶׁתִּקָּנֶה בְּכֶסֶף. תַּלְמוּד לוֹמַר כִּי יִקַּח. מַגִּיד שֶׁהִיא נִקְנֵית בְּכֶסֶף.

Rebbi Abin said that Hisqiah stated: [22]"After he acquires," which means that she is acquired by money[11]. Would it not be an argument *de minore ad majus*?[23] Since the Hebrew slave girl, who cannot be acquired by intercourse, can be acquired by money, would it not be logical that this one, who may be acquired by intercourse, should be acquired by money? This is proved[24] by the sister-in-law, who cannot be acquired by money but is acquired by intercourse[9]. Therefore you would not be astonished if this one, who may be acquired by intercourse, might not be acquired by money. The verse says, "after he acquires," this tells you that she is acquired by money[25].

22 *Sifry Deut.* 268; Babli 4b.
23 Then the verse would be redundant.
24 In these kinds of arguments, "proves" means "disproves the possibility of an argument *de minore ad majus*" because the rules are not comparable.
25 The verse is necessary to understand the rules.

(58b line 49) וּבְעָלָהּ. מַגִּיד שֶׁהִיא נִקְנֵית בְּבִיאָה. וְדִין הוּא. מָה אִם יְבָמָה שֶׁאֵינָהּ נִקְנֵית בְּכֶסֶף נִקְנֵית בְּבִיאָה. זוֹ שֶׁהִיא נִקְנֵית בְּכֶסֶף אֵינוֹ דִין שֶׁתִּקָּנֶה בְּבִיאָה. עִבְרִייָה תּוֹכִיחַ. שֶׁהִיא נִקְנֵית בְּכֶסֶף וְאֵינוֹ נִקְנֵית בְּבִיאָה. אַף אַתָּה אַל תִּתְמַהּ עַל זוֹ שֶׁאַף עַל פִּי שֶׁהִיא נִקְנֵית בְּכֶסֶף לֹא תִקָּנֶה בְּבִיאָה. תַּלְמוּד לוֹמַר כִּי יִקַּח. מַגִּיד שֶׁהִיא נִקְנֵית בְּכֶסֶף. וּבְעָלָהּ. מַגִּיד שֶׁהִיא נִקְנֵית בְּבִיאָה.

[26]"And has marital relations with her," this tells you that she is acquired by intercourse. Would it not be an argument *de minore ad majus*? Since the sister-in-law, who cannot be acquired by money, can be acquired by intercourse, would it not be logical that this one, who may be acquired by money, should be acquired by intercourse? The Hebrew slave girl proves[24], who cannot be acquired by intercourse but is acquired by money. You likewise do not wonder that this one, who may be acquired by money, might not be acquired by intercourse. The verse says, "after he acquires," this tells you that she is acquired by money; "and has marital relations with her," this tells you that she is acquired by intercourse.

26 *Sifry Deut.* 268; Babli 5a. The argument is completely parallel to that of the preceding paragraph.

(58b line 54) בִּשְׁטָר. מָה אִם הַכֶּסֶף שֶׁאֵינוֹ מוֹצִיא הֲרֵי הוּא מַכְנִיס. שְׁטָר שֶׁהוּא מוֹצִיא אֵינוֹ דִין שֶׁיַּכְנִיס. לֹא. אִם אָמַרְתָּ בַּכֶּסֶף שֶׁהוּא מוֹצִיא לְהַקְדֵּישׁ יְדֵי פִדְיוֹנוֹ. תֹּאמַר בִּשְׁטָר שֶׁאֵינוֹ מוֹצִיא לְהַקְדֵּשׁ יְדֵי פִדְיוֹנוֹ. נִשְׁבַּר קַל וָחוֹמֶר וְחָזַרְתָּה לַמִּקְרָא. לְפוּם כֵּן צָרַךְ מֵימַר וְכָתַב לָהּ סֵפֶר כְּרִיתוּת וְנָתַן בְּיָדָהּ וְשִׁלְּחָהּ מִבֵּיתוֹ וְיָצְאָה מִבֵּיתוֹ וְהָלְכָה וְהָיְתָה לְאִישׁ אַחֵר. הִקִּישׁ הֲוָיָתָהּ לִיצִיאָתָהּ. מָה יְצִיאָתָהּ בִּשְׁטָר אַף הֲוָיָתָהּ בִּשְׁטָר.

[22]By a document. Since money which does not send out permits to enter, would it not be logical that a document which sends out should permit to enter[27]? No If you speak about money which eliminates dedication through redemption[28], what can you say about a document which does not eliminate dedication through redemption[29]? The argument *de minore ad majus* is broken and you have to return to Scripture. Therefore, it was necessary to say: "He shall write her a bill of divorce, hand it to her, and send her out of his house. If she left his house and went to be another man's.[20]" It brackets her being with her leaving[21]. Since her leaving was by a document, so her being is by a document.

27 Money is used in preliminary marriage, to permit the woman to enter her husband's family. Money cannot be used for divorce; the wife cannot pay the husband as a formal means of divorce.

28 All valuables dedicated to the Temple regain their profane status by redemption when that money is given to the Temple treasury, and in no other way.

29 Dedications cannot be redeemed by an I.O.U.

(58b line 60) אָמַר רִבִּי יוּדָן. קַל וָחוֹמֶר לְבַת חוֹרִין שֶׁתִּקָּנֶה בַּחֲזָקָה. וְדִין הוּא. מָה אִם שִׁפְחָה כְּנַעֲנִית שֶׁאֵינָהּ נִקְנֵית בְּבִיאָה נִקְנֵית בַּחֲזָקָה. זוֹ שֶׁהִיא נִקְנֵית בְּבִיאָה אֵינוֹ דִין שֶׁתִּקָּנֶה בַּחֲזָקָה. תַּלְמוּד לוֹמַר וּבְעָלָהּ. בְּבִיאָה הִיא נִקְנֵית וְאֵינָהּ נִקְנֵית בַּחֲזָקָה. קַל וָחוֹמֶר בְּשִׁפְחָה כְּנַעֲנִית שֶׁתִּקָּנֶה בְּבִיאָה. וְדִין הוּא.

וּמַה אִם בַּת חוֹרִין שֶׁאֵינָהּ נִקְנֵית בַּחֲזָקָה נִקְנֵית בְּבִיאָה. זוֹ שֶׁהִיא נִקְנֵית בַּחֲזָקָה אֵינוֹ דִין שֶׁתִּקָּנֶה בְּבִיאָה. תַּלְמוּד לוֹמַר וְהִתְנַחַלְתֶּם אוֹתָם לִבְנֵיכֶם אַחֲרֵיכֶם לָרֶשֶׁת אֲחוּזָה וגו'. בַּחֲזָקָה הִיא נִקְנֵית וְאֵינָהּ נִקְנֵית בְּבִיאָה. הֲרֵי לָמַדְנוּ שֶׁהָאִשָּׁה נִקְנֵית בִּשְׁלֹשָׁה דְרָכִים. אוֹ בְכֶסֶף אוֹ בִשְׁטָר אוֹ בְבִיאָה.

Rebbi Yudan said, an argument *de minore ad majus* that a free woman should be acquired by actual possession[30]. Is it not logical that since a Gentile slave woman, who cannot be acquired by intercourse, can be acquired by actual possession, by an argument *de minore ad majus* a free woman, who can be acquired by intercourse, could be acquired by actual possession? The verse says, "and has marital relations with her." She can be acquired by intercourse but cannot be acquired by actual possession. An argument *de minore ad majus* that a Gentile slave woman should be acquired by intercourse: Is it not logical that since a free woman, who cannot be acquired by actual possession, can be acquired by intercourse, by an argument *de minore ad majus* a Gentile slave woman, who can be acquired by actual possession, could be acquired by intercourse? The verse[31] says, "you may leave them as inheritance to your sons after you, to inherit them as property." She is acquired by actual possession; she is not acquired by intercourse. So we inferred that a woman can be acquired in three ways: by money, or by document, or by intercourse.

30 His proof that arguments *de minore ad majus* are inappropriate here is explained at length in *Ketubot* 5:5, Note 100.

As a legal term, חֲזָקָה may have two very different meanings. What seems to be intended here is that ownerless property can be acquired by active actual possession (i. e., possession combined with use.) The idea seems to be that a woman, performing a wife's duty in a man's house, by this act should become his wife. The comparison is to a slave woman who belonged to a proselyte who failed to start a Jewish family and dies without heirs. Any Jew who gets hold of her and lets her perform a servile job for himself has acquired her in law.

A second meaning of חֲזָקָה is "permanence of the *status quo ante*," cf. *Giṭṭin* 3:3, Notes 81,89; *Nazir* 9:2, Note 90. This meaning is referred to, somewhat incongruously, in the verse quoted at the end; property is inherited by the permanence of the state of "belonging to".

A subcategory of "permanence of the *status quo ante*" is the validation of squatter's rights after three years of undisturbed possession, if accompanied by a claim of rightful acquisition.

31 Lev. 25:46.

(58b line 69) עַד כְּדוֹן בְּיִשְׂרָאֵל. בַּגּוֹיִם. רִבִּי אַבָּהוּ בְּשֵׁם רִבִּי אֶלְעָזָר. כְּתִיב הִנְּךָ מֵת עַל הָאִשָּׁה אֲשֶׁר לָקַחְתָּ וְהִיא בְעוּלַת בָּעַל. עַל רַבְעוּלוֹת הֵן חַיָּיבִין. וְאֵינָן חַיָּיבִין עַל הָאֲרוּסוֹת. מִילְתֵיהּ דְּרִבִּי אֶלְעָזָר אָמְרָה. וְהוּא שֶׁנִּתְכַּוֵּון לִקְנוֹתָהּ. מִילְתֵיהּ דִּשְׁמוּאֵל אָמְרָה. אֲפִילוּ לֹא נִתְכַּוֵּון לִקְנוֹתָהּ. דָּמַר רִבִּי יוֹנָה בְשֵׁם שְׁמוּאֵל. זוֹנָה עוֹמֶדֶת בַּחַלּוֹן. בָּאוּ עָלֶיהָ שְׁנַיִם. הָרִאשׁוֹן אֵינוֹ נֶהֱרָג וְהַשֵּׁנִי נֶהֱרָג עַל יָדָיו. וְכִי נִתְכַּוֵּון הָרִאשׁוֹן לִקְנוֹתָהּ.

So far for Israel. For the Gentiles? Rebbi Abbahu in the name of Rebbi Eleazar[32]: It is written[33] "you shall die because of the woman whom you took, since she is having marital relations with a husband." They are guilty for those having marital relations; they are not guilty for the betrothed[34]. The words of Rebbi Eleazar imply, only if he had intention of acquiring her; the words of Samuel imply, even if he had no intention of acquiring her; since Rebbi Jonah said in the name of Samuel[35]: "A prostitute stands in a window[36]. Two men sleep with her. The first one[37] is not killed, the second one is killed because of him[38]." But did the first one intend to acquire her[39]?

32 In *Gen. rabba* 18(8), a parallel source for this and the following paragraphs: R. Abbahu in the name of R. Johanan.

33 *Gen.* 20:3, speaking to the Gentile Abimelech.

34 Babli, *Sanhedrin* 57b.

35 In *Gen. rabba*: "Rebbi Samuel." For chronological reasons, and also because he is quoted after R. Eleazar, the reading of *Gen. rabba* is the only acceptable one.

36 To attract customers.

37 Who deflowers her. In R. Samuel's opinion, a Gentile marriage can be contracted only by intercourse and there is no divorce. Therefore, a free woman is automatically married to the man who deflowers her and any subsequent intercourse with any other man (during the first man's lifetime) is adultery.

38 As an adulterer. In his theory, a Gentile can sleep without guilt only with a wife whom he married as a virgin, or a chaste widow, or a servile prostitute who as a slave cannot marry.

39 According to R. Eleazar, Gentiles can be married only by mutual consent. Then they also can repudiate the marriage.

In *Gen. rabba* 18(8) only R. Samuel's opinion is quoted, with the addition that "for Gentiles, intercourse acquires automatically."

(58b line 74) אִישׁ. מַה תַּלְמוּד לוֹמַר אִישׁ אִישׁ. אֶלָּא לְהָבִיא אֶת הַגּוֹיִם שֶׁבָּאוּ עַל הָעֲרָיוֹת הָאוּמוֹת שֶׁיִּדּוֹנוּ בְּדִינֵי הָאוּמוֹת. וְאִם בָּאוּ עַל עֲרָיוֹת יִשְׂרָאֵל שֶׁיִּדּוֹנוּ אוֹתָם כְּדִינֵי יִשְׂרָאֵל. אָמַר רִבִּי לְעָזָר. מְכוּלָּם אֵין לָךְ אֶלָּא אֲרוּסַת יִשְׂרָאֵל בִּלְבַד. שֶׁאִם בָּא עַל אֲרוּסַת יִשְׂרָאֵל חַיָּיב. עַל אֲרוּסַת גּוֹיִם פָּטוּר. אִם בָּא עַל אֲרוּסַת יִשְׂרָאֵל חַיָּיבִין. בַּמֶּה הוּא מִתְחַיֵּיב. בְּדִינֵיהֶן בְּדִינֵי יִשְׂרָאֵל. אֵין תֵּימַר. בְּדִינֵי יִשְׂרָאֵל. בִּשְׁנֵי עֵדִים וּבְעֶשְׂרִים וּשְׁלֹשָׁה דַּיָּינִים זוֹ בְהַתְרָייָה וּבִסְקִילָה. וְאִין תֵּימַר. בְּדִינֵיהֶן. בְּעֵד אֶחָד וּבְדַיָּין אֶחָד וְשֶׁלֹּא בְהַתְרָייָה וּבְסַיָּף.

"A man." Why does the verse[40] say, "any man"? To include that Gentiles who committed adultery or incest[41] by Gentile rules should be judged by Gentile law, but if they committed adultery with a Jewish woman, one judges them by Jewish law. Rebbi Eleazar said, of all of them there is only the Jewish betrothed[42], for if he had intercourse with a Jewish preliminarily married woman he is guilty, with a betrothed Gentile woman he cannot be prosecuted. If he had intercourse with a Jewish preliminarily married woman he is guilty. How is he found to be guilty? By their rules or by Jewish rules? If you say by Jewish rules, by two witnesses[43], 23 judges[44], after warning[45], and by stoning. If you say by their rules, by one witness, one judge, without warning, and by the sword[46].

40 *Lev.* 18:5: "Any man to any blood relation shall not come to uncover nakedness." Parallel interpretations are in the Babli, *Sanhedrin* 57b; *Sifra Aḥare Pereq* 13(1).

41 עֶרְוָה "nakedness", abbreviated for גִּלּוּי עֶרְוָה "uncovering of nakedness", is the legal term for "incest and/or adultery".

42 The Gentile cannot commit incest with a Jewish partner since he has no family relationship with her. If he commits adultery with a married woman, he is guilty under Gentile law. The only case is intercourse with a preliminarily married woman, which is adultery in Jewish law but a relationship with an unmarried woman by Gentile standards.

In the Babli, *Sanhedrin* 57b, this also is a statement of R. Joḥanan.

43 *Deut.* 19:15.

44 Mishnah *Sanhedrin* 1:4.

45 Cf. *Soṭah* 3:4, Note 121.

(58c line 6) רִבִּי יוּדָה בַּר פָּזִי מוֹסִיף בְּחוֹנְקוֹ.[46] מִפְּנֵי עַצְמוֹ. מַה טַעַם. כִּי דָם בָּאָדָם.

[47]Rebbi Jehudah bar Pazi added one who strangles, as a separate offense. What is the reason? For "blood in a human."

46 Reading of the *editio princeps*. The corrector wrote בהונקו. No root הנק is known.

47 This does not belong here;

except for the name, it is the corrector's text taken from *Gen. rabba* 34(19) where from *Gen.* 9:6 it is inferred that Gentiles are executed by the sword. The verse reads: שׁוֹפֵךְ דַּם הָאָדָם בָּאָדָם דָּמוֹ יִשָּׁפֵךְ "He who spills a human's blood, by humans his blood shall be spilled." Then the question arises whether a murderer who kills by strangling can be prosecuted under Noahide law. To this, R. Jehudah *bar Simon* gives a positive answer by reading the verse as: "He who spills a human's blood *within a* human, his blood shall be spilled." [In the Babli, *Sanhedrin* 57b, R. Ismael is quoted as deducing that for a Gentile, the killing of a foetus, a "human within a human", is a capital crime. In rabbinic law, abortion is not prosecutable and is even required if the mother's life is at risk (Mishnah *Ahilut* 7:6).]

(58c line 7) אִין תֵּימַר בְּדִינֵי יִשְׂרָאֵל. וְנִתְגַּיֵּיר חַיָּיב. אִין תֵּימַר בְּדִינֵיהֶם. נִתְגַּיֵּיר פָּטוּר. דְּאָמַר רִבִּי חֲנִינָה. בֶּן נֹחַ שֶׁקִּילֵּל אֶת הַשֵּׁם נִתְגַּיֵּיר פָּטוּר. מִפְּנֵי שֶׁנִּשְׁתַּנָּה דִינוֹ. רִבִּי לְעָזָר בְּשֵׁם רִבִּי חֲנִינָה. מְנַיִּין שֶׁבְּנֵי נֹחַ מוּזְהָרִין עַל עֲרָיוֹת כְּיִשְׂרָאֵל. תַּלְמוּד לוֹמַר וְדָבַק בְּאִשְׁתּוֹ. וְלֹא בְאֵשֶׁת חֲבֵירוֹ. וְדָבַק בְּאִשְׁתּוֹ. וְלֹא בְזָכוֹר וְלֹא בִבְהֵמָה. רִבִּי שְׁמוּאֵל רִבִּי אַבָּהוּ רִבִּי לְעָזָר בְּשֵׁם רִבִּי חֲנִינָה. בֶּן נֹחַ שֶׁבָּא עַל אִשְׁתּוֹ שֶׁלֹּא כְדַרְכָּהּ נֶהֱרַג. מַה טַעַם. וְדָבַק בְּאִשְׁתּוֹ וְהָיוּ לְבָשָׂר אֶחָד. מִמָּקוֹם שֶׁשְּׁנֵיהֶן עוֹשִׂין בָּשָׂר אֶחָד.

If you say, by Jewish rules, he[48] is guilty if he converted. If you say, by their rules, he cannot be prosecuted if he converted, as Rebbi Ḥanina said, a descendant of Noah who blasphemed and then converted cannot be prosecuted since the law changed for him[49]. Rebbi Eleazar in the name of Rebbi Ḥanina: The descendants of Noah are warned about nakedness[41] as Jews are[50]; [51]the verse says, "he shall cling to his wife", not to somebody else's wife. "He shall cling to his wife", not to a male, nor to an animal[52]. Rebbi Samuel, Rebbi Abbahu, Rebbi Eleazar in the name of Rebbi Ḥanina: A descendant of Noah who had perverse intercourse[53] with his wife is killed. What is the reason? "He shall cling to his wife so they become one flesh," at the place where they together create one flesh[54].

48 The Gentile who had raped a preliminarily married virgin, mentioned in the paragraph before the last.

49 Nobody can be convicted under a law which did not apply to him at the moment the criminal act was committed. Since after conversion, Jewish law applies to him, he cannot be prosecuted for prior crimes. The Babli agrees, *Sanhedrin* 71b.

50 *Gen. rabba* 18(8), Babli *Sanhedrin* 58b.

51 *Gen.* 2:24. Cf. *Gen. rabba* 18(8), Babli *Sanhedrin* 57b.

52 In addition, it is deduced there that the wording "father and mother" prohibits incest of father with daughter or stepdaughter, and son with mother or father's wife. From *Gen.* 20:12 it is inferred that the uterine half-sister also is forbidden.

53 Any sex play which does not include penetration and ejaculation.

54 Any intercourse which excludes the possibility of creating a pregnancy is sinful, except regular intercourse with one's pregnant wife.

(58c line 14) רִבִּי יוֹסֵי בְּעָא. הַעֲרָיָיה בְּזָכוֹר מָה הִיא. הַעֲרָיָיה בַּבְּהֵמָה מָה הִיא. וְכָל־הָעֲרָיוֹת לֹא מִן הַנִּידָּה לָמְדוּ. זָכָר מִינָהּ. בְּהֵמָה מִינָהּ. עַד כְּדוֹן בְּיִשְׂרָאֵל. בַּגּוֹיִם. אָמַר רִבִּי מָנָא. לֹא מִינָהּ. וְדָבַק בְּאִשְׁתּוֹ. וְלֹא בְאֵשֶׁת חֲבֵירוֹ כָּל־שֶׁהוּא. וְדִכְוָותָהּ לֹא בְזָכוֹר וְלֹא בִבְהֵמָה אֲפִילוּ כָּל־שֶׁהוּא.

Rebbi Yose asked: What is the legal status of "touching"[55] a male? What is the legal status of "touching" an animal? Were not all incest prohibitions inferred from the menstruating woman[56]? The male is included; the animal is included. So far, for Israel. For Gentiles? Rebbi Mana said, not from this: "He shall cling to his wife"? Not in any way to somebody else's wife, not in any way to a male or an animal.

55 If the two persons' genitals are touching. This is the definition of a sex act for criminal and marriage laws (*Yebamot*, 4:2 Note 59; 6:1, Note 11 ff.)

56 Not the prohibition, but the technicalities which make the act prosecutable. It is spelled out in *Lev.* 20:18 that in the case of the menstruating woman, "touching" establishes the criminality of the act.

Therefore, for Jews "touching" is the equivalent of completed intercourse in criminal law. The Babli, *Yebamot* 54b, seems to reject the equation of bestiality with homosexual activity.

(58c line 19) הֲרֵי לָמַדְנוּ. גּוֹיִם אֵין לָהֶן קִידּוּשִׁין. מָהוּ שֶׁיְּהֵא לָהֶם גֵּירוּשִׁין. רַבִּי יוּדָה בֶּן פָּזִי וְרַבִּי חָנִין בְּשֵׁם רַבִּי חוּנָה רוֹבָה דְצִיפּוֹרִין. אוֹ שֶׁאֵין לָהֶן גֵּירוּשִׁין אוֹ שֶׁשְּׁנֵיהֶן מְגָרְשִׁין זֶה אֶת זֶה. רַבִּי יוֹחָנָן דְּצִפּוֹרִין רַבִּי אָחָא רַבִּי חִינְנָא בְּשֵׁם רַבִּי שְׁמוּאֵל בַּר נַחְמָן. כִּי שָׂנֵא שַׁלַּח אָמַר יי אֱלֹהֵי יִשְׂרָאֵל. בְּיִשְׂרָאֵל נָתַתִּי גֵּירוּשִׁין. לֹא נָתַתִּי גֵּירוּשִׁין בְּאוּמּוֹת הָעוֹלָם. רַבִּי חֲנַנְיָה בְּשֵׁם רַבִּי פִינְחָס. כָּל־הַפָּרָשָׁה כְּתִיב יי צְבָאוֹת. וְכָאן כְּתִיב אֱלֹהֵי יִשְׂרָאֵל. לְלַמְּדָךְ שֶׁלֹּא יִיחֵד הַקָּדוֹשׁ בָּרוּךְ הוּא שְׁמוֹ בְּגֵירוּשִׁין אֶלָּא בְּיִשְׂרָאֵל בִּלְבָד.

So we have established that Gentiles have no preliminary marriage. Do they have divorce? Rebbi Jehudah ben Pazi and Rebbi Ḥanin in the name of the great Rebbi Ḥuna of Sepphoris: Either they have no divorce, or either of them may divorce the other. Rebbi Joḥanan from Sepphoris, Rebbi Aḥa, Rebbi Ḥinena, in the name of Rebbi Samuel bar Naḥman: "For the divorcer is hateful, says the Eternal, Israel's God.[57]" In Israel I gave divorce, I did not give divorce among the nations of the world. Rebbi Ḥananiah in the name of Rebbi Phineas: In the entire paragraph it is written "the Eternal, Sabaot"; only here it is written "Israel's God." To teach you that the Holy One, praise to Him, did lend his name only to Jewish divorce.

57 *Mal.* 2:16, speaking of the person divorcing his first wife without necessity.

(58c line 25) מִילְּתֵיהּ דְּרַבִּי חִייָה רַבָּה אָמְרָה. גּוֹיִם אֵין לָהֶן גֵּירוּשִׁין. דְּתַנֵּי רַבִּי חִייָה כֵן. גּוֹי שֶׁגֵּירַשׁ אֶת אִשְׁתּוֹ וְהָלְכָה וְנִישֵּׂאת לְאַחֵר וְגֵירְשָׁהּ וְאַחַר כָּךְ נִתְגַּיְּירוּ

שְׁנִיהֶן. אֲנִי קוֹרֵא עָלֶיהָ לֹא יוּכַל בַּעֲלָהּ הָרִאשׁוֹן אֲשֶׁר שִׁלְּחָהּ לָשׁוּב לְקַחְתָּהּ. וְתַנֵּי כֵן. מַעֲשֶׂה בָא לִפְנֵי רַבִּי וְהִכְשִׁיר.

The word of the elder Rebbi Ḥiyya implies that Gentiles have no divorce[58], as Rebbi Ḥiyya stated in this matter[59]: A Gentile who divorced his wife, who herself then went and married another, when the latter divorced her and then both of them[60] converted, I do not read[61] for them: "Her first husband who had divorced her cannot return to marry her." It was stated in this matter: A case came before Rebbi and he approved[62].

58 Not that divorce were impossible for Gentiles but that Gentile divorce does not have the legal implications of Jewish divorce.

59 *Gen. rabba* 18(8).

60 The first husband and the wife.

61 Reading with *Gen. rabba* איני for אני

62 He lets the first husband remarry the divorced wife who, while Gentile, had another husband.

(58c line 29) בִּשְׁטָר. הָדָא דְתֵימַר. בִּשְׁטָר שֶׁאֵינוֹ יָפֶה שָׁוֶה פְּרוּטָה. אֲבָל בִּשְׁטָר שֶׁהוּא יָפֶה שָׁוֶה פְּרוּטָה כְּכֶסֶף הוּא. תַּנֵּי רִבִּי חִייָה כֵן. לֹא סוֹף דָּבָר בִּשְׁטָר שֶׁהוּא יָפֶה שָׁוֶה פְּרוּטָה. וַהֲלֹא מִתְקַדֶּשֶׁת הִיא הָאִשָּׁה בְּכָל־דָּבָר שֶׁהוּא יָפֶה שָׁוֶה פְּרוּטָר. אֶלָּא אֲפִילוּ כְּתָבוֹ עַל הַחֶרֶס אוֹ עַל נְיָיר וּנְתָנוֹ לָהּ הֲרֵי זוֹ מְקוּדֶּשֶׁת.

By a document. This means, by a document which is not worth a *peruṭah*[7], but a document which is worth a *peruṭah* is money's worth[63]. Rebbi Ḥiyya stated in this respect[64]: "Not only a document which is worth a *peruṭah* since a woman can have herself preliminarily married by anything which is worth a *peruṭah*. But even if he wrote it on an *ostrakon* or on papyrus[65] and gave it to her, she is preliminarily married."

63 Since betrothal by document is deduced from divorce by document (Note 21), if the document was invalid because it was not written for the

specific woman for whom it was used, the preliminary marriage would be effected if and only if the material used for the document was worth a *peruṭah* (interpretation of R. Nissim Gerondi).

64 Tosephta 1:2.

65 The document must only read: הרי את מקודשת לי "you are preliminarily married to me". It is possible to write it on a snippet of paper worth less than a penny.

(58c line 34) כְּתָבוֹ עַל דָּבָר שֶׁהוּא אִיסוּר הֲנָאָה. תַּנֵּי רִבִּי חָנִין. מַעֲשֶׂה בָא לִפְנֵי רִבִּי וְאָמַר. הֲרֵי זוֹ מְגוֹרֶשֶׁת. רִבִּי אֶלְעָזָר אָמַר. אֵינָהּ מְגוֹרֶשֶׁת. אָמַר רִבִּי זְעִירָא. הֲוַויָן רַבָּנִין פְּלִיגִין. מָן דְּאָמַר. אֵינָהּ מְקוּדֶּשֶׁת. אֵינָהּ מְגוֹרֶשֶׁת. וּמָן דָּמַר. מְקוּדֶּשֶׁת. מְגוֹרֶשֶׁת. חֲבֵרָיָיא אֳמָרִין לַחוּמְרִין. רִבִּי יוֹסֵי בְּעָא. מַהוּ לַחוּמְרִין. אֵינָהּ מְקוּדֶּשֶׁת מְגוֹרֶשֶׁת הַיְינוּ לַחוּמְרִין. אִילוּ אֵינָהּ מְגוֹרֶשֶׁת מְקוּדֶּשֶׁת הַיְינוּ לַחוּמְרִין. מַהוּ כְדוֹן. רַבָּנִין דְּקַיְסָרִין בְּשֵׁם רִבִּי יַעֲקֹב בַּר אֲחָא. מָאן דְּאָמַר. מְגוֹרֶשֶׁת. אִיסוּר הֲנָיָה מִדִּבְרֵיהֶם. וּמָן דָּמַר. אֵינָהּ מְקוּדֶּשֶׁת. אִיסוּר הֲנָיָה מִדְּבַר תּוֹרָה. הָא בְּאִיסוּר הֲנָיָה מִדִּבְרֵיהֶן מְקוּדֶּשֶׁת. אֵין תֵּימַר כֵּן לֵית הָדָא פְלִיגָא עַל רַב. דְּרַב אָמַר. דִּבְרֵי רִבִּי מֵאִיר. הַמְקַדֵּשׁ בְּחָמֵץ מִשֵּׁשׁ שָׁעוֹת וּלְמַעֲלָן לֹא עָשָׂה וְלֹא כְלוּם. וְחָמֵץ מִשֵּׁשׁ שָׁעוֹת וּלְמַעֲלָן טָב הוּא כְלוּם. תַּמָּן בְּגוּפוֹ קִידֵּשׁ. בְּרַם הָכָא בִּתְנָייִם שֶׁבּוֹ קִידֵּשׁ. מֵעַתָּה אֲפִילוּ בְּאִיסוּר הֲנָיָיה דְּבַר תּוֹרָה תְּהֵא מְקוּדֶּשֶׁת. מַה בֵּינָהּ לִשְׁטָר שֶׁאֵינוֹ יָפֶה שָׁוֶה פְרוּטָה. תַּמָּן אֵינוֹ רָאוּי לְהַשְׁלִים עָלָיו. בְּרַם הָכָא רָאוּי הוּא לְהַשְׁלִים עָלָיו.

If he wrote it[66] on material forbidden for usufruct? Rebbi Ḥanin[67] stated: A case came before Rebbi who said, she is divorced[68]. Rebbi Eleazar[69] said, she is not divorced[70]. Rebbi Ze'ira said, the rabbis disagree: For him who said, she is not preliminary married, she is not divorced. For him who said, she is preliminary married, she is divorced[21]. The colleagues say, for restrictions. Rebbi Yose asked, what means "for restrictions"? She is not preliminarily married but divorced, is this "for restrictions"? Or she is not divorced but preliminarily married, is this "for restrictions"? What about it? The rabbis of Caesarea in the name of Rebbi Jacob bar Aha: He who says that she is divorced, involving material forbidden for usufruct by their words[71]. But he who says that she is not divorced, involving material forbidden for usufruct by words of the Torah[72]. Therefore, by material forbidden for usufruct by their words she is preliminarily married. If you say so, does this not disagree with Rav? For Rav said, the words of Rebbi Meïr: A person who uses leavened material for preliminary marriage after noontime did not do anything. Is leavened material of any use after noontime[73]? There, he used the material for preliminary marriage[74], but here he effected the preliminary marriage by the [written] conditions. But then she should be preliminarily married even with material forbidden for usufruct by the Torah[75]! What is the difference between this and a document not worth a *perutah*? There, it cannot be used as filler. But here, it can be used as filler[76].

66   The declaration of marriage.

67   Rashba, *Responsa* vol. 1, #603, reads: *Zenon*.

68   Quoted as anonymous statement in the Babli, *Gittin* 20a, which also states as undisputed Galilean rule that a divorce document may be written on material forbidden for usufruct. By implication, a declaration of marriage also may be written on such material.

69   Rashba, *loc. cit.*, reads "R. Eliezer."

70   This opinion is not mentioned in the Babli. Rashba holds that the Babli, which simply quotes the rule without discussion, by reference incorporates the Yerushalmi discussion and decision.

71   Material permitted by biblical law, only forbidden by rabbinic rules.

72   Most material prohibited for ususfruct by biblical law must be burned or otherwise disposed of. It seems that the authorities quoted follow the opinion, not mentioned in the Yerushalmi and attributed in the Babli to R. Simeon as minority opinion

(*Pesaḥim* 12b, *Menaḥot* 79b,102b, *Keritut* 24b, *Temurah* 23a) that anything which must be burned by biblical command is legally considered ashes even if not burned.

73 According to everybody, leavened matter in possession of a Jew is forbidden for usufruct after noontime on Passover eve, the 14th of Nisan. For the majority, this is a biblical decree, derived from *Ex.* 23:18, 34:25. For R. Meïr it is a rabbinic decree; biblical prohibition of leavened matter only starts shortly before nightfall on the fourteenth (*Pesaḥim* 1:4, 27c l. 48 ff.). Why does R. Meïr invalidate a preliminary marriage document for which material was used which is only rabbinically prohibited for usufruct?

74 Since material rabbinically prohibited for usufruct has no monetary value, it cannot be used as a gift for preliminary marriage. It is possible that R. Meïr would validate a marriage by text written on paper sized with a solution of flour in water executed on Passover eve.

75 If used as writing material, rather than for its intrinsic worth.

76 Material not worth a *peruṭah* (in the Babli, *Giṭṭin* 20b, the example is a single leaf of an olive tree) can be used together with other materials as stuffing. Material forbidden for ususfruct cannot be used for anything.

(58c line 48) תַּמָּן תַּנִּינָן. שְׁבוּעַת הַדַּיָּינִין. הַטַּעֲנָה שְׁתֵּי כֶסֶף וְהַהוֹדָיָיה שָׁוֶה פְרוּטָה. הַטַּעֲנָה. בֵּית שַׁמַּי אוֹמְרִים. מָעָה. וּבֵית הִלֵּל אוֹמְרִים. שְׁתֵּי מָעִין. מַחְלָפָה שִׁיטָתְהוֹן דְּבֵית שַׁמַּי. תַּמָּן אִינּוּן אָמְרִין. כֶּסֶף דֵּינָר. וְכָא אִינּוּן אָמְרִין. כֶּסֶף מָעָה. מַחְלָפָה שִׁיטָתְהוֹן דְּבֵית הִלֵּל. תַּמָּן אִינּוּן אָמְרִין. כֶּסֶף פְּרוּטָה. וְכָא אִינּוּן אָמְרִין. כֶּסֶף שְׁתֵּי מָעִין. רִבִּי יַעֲקֹב בַּר אָחָא בְּשֵׁם רִבִּי חֲנִינָה. בֵּית שַׁמַּי לְמֵידִין מִתְּחִילַת מְכִירָתָהּ שֶׁלָּעִבְרִיָיה. מַה תְּחִילַת מְכִירָתָהּ בְּדֵינָר אַף קִידּוּשֶׁיהָ בְּדֵינָר. בֵּית הִלֵּל לְמֵידִין מִסּוֹף גֵּירוּעֶיהָ. מַה סּוֹף גֵּירוּעֶיהָ בִּפְרוּטָה אַף קִידּוּשֶׁיהָ בִּפְרוּטָה. מַה טַעֲמוֹן דְּבֵית שַׁמַּי. שֶׁנֶּאֱמַר וְיָצְאָה חִנָּם אֵין כָּסֶף. וְכִי אֵין אָנוּ יוֹדְעִים שֶׁאֵין כָּסֶף. מַה תַּלְמוּד לוֹמַר אֵין כָּסֶף. מִיכָּן שֶׁנִּמְכְּרָה בְּכֶסֶף יוֹתֵר מִכֶּסֶף. וְכַמָּה יוֹתֵר מִכֶּסֶף. דֵּינָר. אוֹ כֶסֶף פְּרוּטָה. יוֹתֵר מִכֶּסֶף שְׁתֵּי פְרוּטוֹת. סוֹף מַטְבֵּעַ כֶּסֶף מָעָה. וּתְהֵא מָעָה. רִבִּי בּוּן בְּשֵׁם רִבִּי יוּדָה בַּר פָּזִי.

שֶׁאָם בִּקְּשָׁה לִיגָּרַע. מְגָרַעַת בְּמָעָה בְּכָל־שָׁנָה וְיוֹצֵא וְתִגְרַע בִּפְרוּטָה. אָמַר רִבִּי בּוּן. הַגַּע עַצְמָךְ שֶׁאָם בִּקְּשָׁה לִיגָּרַע מִתְּחִילַת הַשָּׁנָה הַשִּׁשִׁית תְּחִילַת גֵּירוּעֶיהָ בִּפְרוּטָה וְסוֹף גֵּירוּעֶיהָ בִּפְרוּטָה. אֶלָּא תְּחִילַת גֵּירוּעֶיהָ בְּמָעָה וְסוֹף גֵּירוּעֶיהָ בִּפְרוּטָה. אִילּוּ נִשְׁתַּיֵּיר שָׁם אֶלָּא שָׁוֶה פְּרוּטָה שֶׁמָּא אֵינָה מְגָרַעַת וְיוֹצְאָה. כְּשֵׁם שֶׁסּוֹף גֵּירוּעֶיהָ בִּפְרוּטָה אַף קִידּוּשֶׁיהָ בִּפְרוּטָה. מַה טַּעֲמוֹן דְּבֵית הִלֵּל. מִמַּה שֶּׁסּוֹף גֵּירוּעֶיהָ בִּפְרוּטָה אַתְּ יוֹדֵעַ שֶׁקִּידּוּשֶׁיהָ בִּפְרוּטָה.

2 מעה ‏| ו‎ מעה כסף   3 שיטתהון ‏| ו‎ שיטתין   אינון ‏| ו‎ - (2 times)   4 שיטתהון ‏| ו‎ שיטתין   אינון ‏| ו‎ - (2 times)   5 שתי ‏| ו‎ תרין   6 למידין ‏| ו‎ אומ'   מכירתה שלעברייה ‏| ו‎ מכירת העבריה   7 בית ‏| ו‎ ובית   מה ‏| ו‎ ומה   אין ‏| ו‎ - שנמכרה בכסף ‏| ו‎ שנמכרת   10 יותר ‏| ו‎ היא יותר   11 בון ‏| ו‎ אבין   12 ליגרע ‏| ו‎ למיגרע במעה ‏| ו‎ מעה   ויוצא ‏| ו‎ ויוצאה   13 בון ‏| ו‎ אבין   תחילת גירועיה ‏| ו‎ מה תחילת השנה הששית גירועיה   14 וסוף גירועיה בפרוטה ‏| ו‎ עדף קידושיה בפרוטה   במעה ‏| ו‎ מעה   15 אילא נשתייר ... אף קידושיה בפרוטה ‏| ו‎ entire text missing

[77]There, we have stated: "A judicial oath[78], for a claim of two silver pieces and a judicial acknowlegdment of a *perutah*. The claim, the House of Shammai say, an obolus[79], but the House of Hillel say, two obols." The argument of the House of Shammai seems inverted. There[80], they say, "silver" is a denar, but here, they say that "silver" is an obolus. The argument of the House of Hillel seems inverted. There[80], they say, "money" is a *perutah*, but here, they say that "money" is two obols. Rebbi Jacob bar Aḥa in the name of Rebbi Ḥanina: The house of Shammai learn from the initial sale of a Hebrew girl[18]. Since her initial sale was by [at least] a denar, so her preliminary marriage is by [at least] a denar[81]. The House of Hillel learn from the end of her diminution[82]. Since the end of her diminution is a *perutah*, so her preliminary marriage is by a *perutah*[18]. What is the reason of the House of Shammai? As it is said: "She leaves gratis, without silver[83]." Would we not know that it is without

money? Why does the verse say, "without silver"[84]? From there, that she is sold for more than silver. And what is more than silver? A denar. But maybe "silver" is a *peruṭah*, more than silver two *peruṭot*? The smallest silver coin is an obolus[85]. So why is it not an obolus? Rebbi Abun in the name of Rebbi Judah bar Pazi: For if she wants to diminish, she diminishes every year by an obolus and leaves[86]. Could she not diminish by a *peruṭah*[87]? Rebbi Abun said, think of it. If she wanted to compute the diminution at the start of the sixth year, there would be a *peruṭah* left, and at the end of the sixth year, there would be a *peruṭah* left. But the start of the diminution must be an obolus, the end of the diminution a *peruṭah*. If there is only one *peruṭah* left, can she not pay the diminished amount and leave? Just as the last diminished amount is a *peruṭah*, so her preliminary marriage should be a *peruṭah*[88]! What is the reason of the House of Hillel? Since her last diminished amount is a *peruṭah*, you know that her preliminary marriage is by a *peruṭah*[81,89].

77 The original of this and the following paragraphs is in *Šebuot* 6:1 (36d, ll. 21-50, ‫ו‬).

78 The oath required by *Ex.* 22:8 for a person denying a claim when neither he nor the claimant have proof. The defendant can be made to swear only if he admits that at least one *peruṭah*'s worth of the claim is true; cf. *Ketubot* 2:1, Note 12 (*Mekhilta dR. Ismael, Neziqin* 2).

79 One sixth of a drachma identified with the imperial silver denar.

80 Miishnah *Qiddušin* 1:1. The formulation shows that the origin of the text is in *Ševuot*.

81 It is clear from the biblical text, *Ex.* 21:7-11, that the person buying an underage Hebrew girl is supposed to marry her when she grows up, or to marry her to his son. The money given for her services is at the same time the money for preliminary marriage. The House of Shammai hold that the original buying price, which later is

shown to be at least a silver denar, is the bridal money used for the legal acquisition of the girl as preliminarily wedded wife. The House of Hillel hold that only the amount not amortized by the girl's work in the meantime is bridal money. Since the master can marry the girl even on the last day of her servitude, he can marry her for a *peruṭah*'s worth and, as shown before, he can marry any other woman also for a *peruṭah*'s worth.

82 Since *Ex.* 21:8 states that "if she is bad in her master's eyes, who does not intend her for himself, let her be redeemed", it is concluded that the Hebrew girl-servant can be redeemed during her servitude, in contrast to the Hebrew indentured servant who has to serve his full six years. Since it is prescribed for the Hebrew servant of a Gentile master that he can be redeemed by paying off the proportion of his original price not amortized by the time spent in servitude (*Lev.* 25:50), the same must hold for the servant girl. As long as she still is a servant, the redemption price is at least a *peruṭah*.

83 *Ex.* 21:11. At the end of six years, the master cannot ask for money to let her go.

84 Since "gratis" means "without payment".

85 Even though in Achaemenid Persia, the silver half-obolus was currency (also minted in the province of Yehud), in later times, prior to the Roman conquest, the obolus was the smallest silver coin. In Roman currency, the denarius was the smallest silver coin.

86 Since she serves for six years, her price must be a six-fold multiple of a silver coin. This determines the drachma as the minimum price.

87 And be bought at the start for 6 *peruṭot*.

88 This argument is correctly missing in *Šebuot* since the House of Shammai consider the original sum as bride-money, cf. Note 81. The Yerushalmi's interpretation of the House of Shammai is explicitly rejected in the Babli, 12a.

89 The *Šebuot* text has here an additional text similar to the text used in *Qiddušin* in the discussion of the House of Shammai: הַגַּע עַצְמָךְ שֶׁאִם נִשְׁתַּיֵּר שָׁם שָׁוֶה פְּרוּטָה שֶׁמָּא אֵינָהּ מְגָרַעְתּוֹ וְיוֹצֵא. כְּשֵׁם שֶׁסּוֹף גֵּירוּעֶיהָ בִּפְרוּטָה אַף קִידּוּשֶׁיהָ בִּפְרוּטָה. "Think of it, if there is one *peruṭah*'s worth left, can she not pay the diminished amount and leave? Just as the last diminished amount is a *peruṭah*, so her preliminary marriage is a *peruṭah*."

(58c line 68) מַחְלְפָה שִׁיטַתְהוֹן דְּבֵית הֹלֵּל. כְּתִיב. כִּי יִתֵּן אִישׁ אֶל רֵעֵהוּ כֶּסֶף אוֹ כֵלִים לִשְׁמוֹר. אִם לְלַמֵּד שֶׁאֵין בֵּית דִּין נִזְקָקִין לְפָחוֹת מִשָּׁוֶה פְרוּטָה. כְּבָר כְּתִיב לְאַשְׁמָה בָהּ. פְּרָט לְפָחוֹת מִשָּׁוֶה פְרוּטָה. מַה תַּלְמוּד לוֹמַר אֵין כָּסֶף. מִיכָּן שֶׁיֵּשׁ כָּאן יוֹתֵר מִכֶּסֶף. וְכַמָּה הוּא יוֹתֵר מִכֶּסֶף. שְׁתֵּי מָעִין. אוֹ כֶסֶף פְּרוּטָה. יוֹתֵר מִכֶּסֶף שְׁתֵּי פְרוּטוֹת. סוֹף מַטְבֵּעַ כֶּסֶף מָעָה. וּתְהֵא מָעָה. אוֹ כֵלִים. מַה כֵּלִים שְׁנַיִם. אַף כֶּסֶף שְׁנַיִם. מַה מְקַיְּימִין בֵּית שַׁמַּי אוֹ כֵלִים. כְּהָדָא דְתַנֵּי. רִבִּי נָתָן אוֹמֵר. אוֹ כֵלִים. לְרַבּוֹת כֵּלִים הַרְבֵּה. שְׁמוּאֵל אָמַר. טְעָנוֹ שְׁנֵי מְחָטִים וְהוֹדָה לוֹ עַל אַחַת מֵהֶן. חַיָּיב. אָמַר רִבִּי חִינָּנָא. וְהוּא שֶׁיְּהוּ יָפוֹת כִּשְׁתֵּי פְרוּטוֹת. כְּדֵי שֶׁתְּהֵא הַטַּעֲנָה שָׁוֶה פְרוּטָה וְהַהוֹדָיָיה שָׁוֶה פְרוּטָה. וְאָתְיָיא כְּבֵית שַׁמַּי דְּלָא יַלְפֵי כֶסֶף מִכֵּלִים. בְּרַם כְּבֵית הֹלֵּל דְּאִינּוּן יָלְפִין כֶּסֶף מִכֵּלִים. מַה כֵּלִים שְׁנַיִם אַף כֶּסֶף שְׁנַיִם. וְדִכְוָותָהּ. מַה כֶּסֶף שְׁתֵּי מָעִים. אַף כֵּלִים שְׁתֵּי מָעִים.

1 כת' | ו - כסף או כלים לשמור | ו - 2 משוה פרוטה | ו מפרוטה 3 מה ת״ל אין כסף | ו - 4 יותר מכסף | ו - 6 בית שמי | ו דבית שמי 7 אומ' | ו - לרבות כלים הרבה | ו להביא כלי חרס 8 מחטים | ו מחטין על אחת | ו באחת והוא | ו והן 9 כשתי | ו שתי שוה | ו - (2 times) 10 ואתייה | ו אתיא דאינון ילפין | ו דילפי 11,12 מעים | ו מעין (2 times)

The argument of the House of Hillel seems inverted. It is written[90]: "If a person give to his neighbor money or vessels to watch over." If to teach that the court will not act on less that a *peruṭah*'s worth, is it not already written: "To incur liability for it"[91]? To exclude anything not worth a *peruṭah*. (Why does the verse say, "without silver"?)[92] From there, that it should be more than silver[93]. And what is more than silver? Two obols. But maybe "silver" is a *peruṭah*, more than silver two *peruṭot*? The smallest silver coin is an obolus[85]. So why is it not an obolus? "Or vessels"; since "vessels" are two[94], also "money" is two[95]. How do the House of Shammai interpret "or vessels"? As we have stated: Rebbi

Nathan says, "or vessels', to include all kinds of vessels[96]. Samuel said, if he claimed from him two needles and he admitted to one, he is guilty[97]. Rebbi Ḥinena said, only if they are worth two *perutot*, that the claim should be about a *peruṭah*'s worth and the confession about a *peruṭah*'s worth[98]. This follows the House of Shammai who do not learn money's worth from "vessels". But following the House of Hillel who learn money's worth from "vessels", since "vessels" are two, also "money" is two. Similarly, since "money" means two obols, also "vessels" means two oboli's worth.

90 *Ex.* 22:6. The verse is the introduction to the judicial oath prescribed in v 8 (cf. Note 78) and establishes the parameters of judicial intervention. The arguments in this paragraph are to some extent paralleled in *Mekhilta dR. Simeon ben Ioḥai*, ed. Epstein-Melamed, p. 199.

91 *Lev.* 5:26. One of the topics treated in *Lev.* 5:20-26 is the guilt of the person swearing falsely the oath required in *Ex.* 22:8. For the translation of the verbal root אשם as "to incur liability", cf. J. Milgram, *Leviticus 1-16*, Anchor Bible 1991, pp. 339-345 (the author does not refer to the rabbinic texts.) Since restitution is possible only by payment, anything worth less than the smallest coin cannot be restituted: There can be no oath for a residual claim not worth a *peruṭah* (*Sifra Wayyiqra Pereq* 23, end.)

92 This text is an intrusion from the parallel discussion in the preceding paragraph; it is correctly missing in *Šebuot*.

93 The argument seems to be that nobody will give a worthless thing to be watched over. If the verse emphasizes "silver" or "money", it must mean more than the minimum.

94 An indeterminate plural always means its minimum, 2. Cf. *Niddah* 2:5, Note 90.

95 Babli 11b, *Šebuot* 39b.

96 This argument can only be understood by reference to *Mekhilta dR. Simeon ben Ioḥai* (Note 90). There it is argued that since silver is mined from the earth, also "vessels" should be restricted to those made from terrestri-

al material, to exclude anything coming from the sea (either from seaweed or fish skin). R. Jehudah reads כֵּלִים as כְּלִי יָם "objects from the sea" (explanation of J. N. Epstein). E. Z. Melamed also reports there that J. N. Epstein, in his personal copy of the Yerushalmi, emended the parallel reading in *Šebuot*, כלי חרס "clay vessels", into כלי חרם "fisherman's netting", which might have been made from material grown in the sea. (The reading כלי חרס makes no sense, since clay vessels are always understood if "vessel" is used without qualifier in biblical texts and do not need to be defined through additions. In the Babli, *Zebaḥim* 22a, anything grown in water is considered water.) "All kinds of vessels" includes vessels made from marine material.

97 The Babli, *Šebuot* 40b, points out that Samuel must hold that the "vessels" quoted in the verse refer to any vessels, irrespective of their value.

98 Since otherwise the court could not take cognizance of the case, Note 91 (quoted in Tosephot *Šebuot* 39b, *s. v.* מה).

(58d line 4) אַף עַל פִּי שֶׁנֶּחְלְקוּ בֵּית שַׁמַּי וּבֵית הִלֵּל בְּצָרוֹת וּבָאֲחָיוֹת וּבְגֵט יָשָׁן וּבְסָפֵק אֵשֶׁת אִישׁ וּבִמְקַדֵּשׁ בְּשָׁוֶה פְּרוּטָה וְהַמְגָרֵשׁ אֶת אִשְׁתּוֹ וְלָנָה עִמּוֹ בְּפוּנְדָקִי וְהָאִשָּׁה מִתְקַדֶּשֶׁת בְּדֵינָר וּבְשָׁוֶה דֵינָר. לֹא נִמְנְעוּ בֵּית שַׁמַּי לִישָּׂא נָשִׁים מִבֵּית הִלֵּל וְלֹא בֵּית הִלֵּל מִבֵּית שַׁמַּי אֶלָּא נוֹהֲגִין בֶּאֱמֶת וּבְשָׁלוֹם. שֶׁנֶּאֱמַר וְהָאֱמֶת וְהַשָּׁלוֹם אֱהָבוּ. מַמְזֵרוּת בְּנָתַיִּים וְאַתְּ אָמַר הָכֵין. הֵיךְ עֲבִידָא. קִידֵּשׁ הָרִאשׁוֹן בְּשָׁוֶה פְּרוּטָה וְהַשֵּׁינִי בְּדֵינָר. עַל דַּעְתְּהוֹן דְּבֵית שַׁמַּי מְקוּדֶּשֶׁת לַשֵּׁינִי וְהַוְולָד מַמְזֵר מִן הָרִאשׁוֹן. עַל דַּעְתְּהוֹן דְּבֵית הִלֵּל מְקוּדֶּשֶׁת לָרִאשׁוֹן וְהַוְולָד מַמְזֵר מִן הַשֵּׁינִי. רִבִּי יַעֲקֹב בַּר אָחָא בְּשֵׁם יוֹחָנָן. מוֹדִים בֵּית שַׁמַּי לְבֵית הִלֵּל לְחוּמְרִין. מֵעַתָּה בֵּית שַׁמַּי יִשָּׂאוּ נָשִׁים מִבֵּית הִלֵּל דְּאִינּוּן מוֹדֵיי לוֹן. וּבֵית הִלֵּל לֹא יִשָּׂאוּ נָשִׁים מִבֵּית שַׁמַּי דְּלֵית אִינּוּן מוֹדֵיי לוֹן. רִבִּי יוֹחָנָן בְּשֵׁם רִבִּי יַנַּאי. אִילּוּ וְאִילּוּ כַּהֲלָכָה הָיוּ עוֹשִׂין. בְּדָא תַנִּינָן. שָׁלְחוּ בֵּית שַׁמַּי וּפְחָתוּהָ. שֶׁבֵּית שַׁמַּי אוֹמְרִים. עַד שֶׁיִּפָּחֲתוּ רוּבָּהּ. אָמַר רִבִּי יוֹסֵי בְּיִרְבִּי בּוּן. עַד שֶׁלֹּא בָּא מַעֲשֶׂה אֵצֶל בֵּית הִלֵּל הָיוּ בֵּית שַׁמַּי נוֹגְעִין בּוֹ. מִשֶּׁבָּא מַעֲשֶׂה אֵצֶל בֵּית הִלֵּל לֹא הָיוּ בֵּית שַׁמַּי נוֹגְעִין בּוֹ. אָמַר רִבִּי אַבָּא מָרִי. וְיָאוּת. מַה תַּנִּינָן. טִימְּאוּ

טָהֳרוֹת לְמַפְרֵעַ. לֹא מִיכָּן וְלָבָא. רִבִּי יוֹסֵי בֵּירבִּי בּוּן אָמַר. אִיתְפַּלְגוֹן רַב וּשְׁמוּאֵל. חַד אָמַר. אִילּוּ וְאִילּוּ כַּהֲלָכָה הָיוּ עוֹשִׂין. וְחָרָנָה אָמַר. אִילּוּ כְהִילְכָתָן וְאִילּוּ כְהִילְכָתָן. מַמְזֵירוּת בֵּינְתַיִים וְאַת אָמַר אָכֵין. הַמָּקוֹם מְשַׁמֵּר וְלֹא אִירַע מַעֲשֶׂה מֵעוֹלָם.

3 לישא | א מלישא   6 דעתהון | א דעתיה   7 דעתהון | א דעתיה   8 מודים | א מודין   9 לון | א להון   10 לון | א להון   ר' יוחנן בשם ר' ינאי | א ר' הילא בשם ר'   11 בדא | א אם כהלחכה היו עושין בדא   שלחו | א שלחו להן   12 רובה | א את רובה   14 אבא מרי | א אבמרי   15 מיכן ולבא | א מכן ולהבא   איתפלגון | א -   16 וחרנה | א וחד   17 ממזירות | א ממזרת   בינתים | א בינתיים   אכין | א הכין

99"Even though the House of Shammai and the House of Hillel disagreed about co-wives, and sisters, and an old bill of divorce, and a woman doubtfully married, and someone who gives *qiddushin* in the value of a *peruṭa*, and someone who divorces his wife and spends the night with her in a hostelry, and a woman who receives *qiddushin* for at least a *denar* or the value of a *denar*, the House of Shammai did not refrain from marrying women from the House of Hillel or the House of Hillel from the House of Shammai but they behave truthfully and in peace, as it is said: 'Love truth and peace.'" Bastardy is between them and you say so? How is that? If a first man gives her *qiddushin* for a *peruṭa* and a second [gives her afterwards)] for a *denar*, in the opinion of the House of Shammai she is betrothed to the second and her child by the first is a bastard. In the opinion of the House of Hillel she is betrothed to the first and her child by the second is a bastard. Rebbi Jacob bar Aḥa in the name of Rebbi Joḥanan: The House of Shammai concede to the House of Hillel as a restriction. In that case, the House of Shammai should marry women from the House of Hillel since they concede to them. But the House of Hillel should not marry women from the House of Shammai since they do not concede to them. Rebbi Johanan in the name of Rebbi Yannai: They all followed the same practice. If they followed the same practice, in this case we stated: "The House of Shammai sent and diminished it, since the House of Shammai say unless most of it is missing?" Rebbi Yose ben Rebbi Abun said, the House of Shammai acted before the question came before the House of Hillel. After a question came before the House of Hillel, the House of Shammai were not touching it. Rebbi Abba Mari said, that is correct. Did we not state: "They declared impure all purities from before", but not in the future. Rebbi Yose ben Rebbi Abun said, Rav and Samuel disagreed. One said both acted according to valid practice; the other said, each party followed their own practice. Bastardy is between them and you say so? The Omnipresent watched and no case ever happened.

99   The text of this paragraph and the one following is from *Yebamot* 1:6, Notes 243-261(א). It seems that the *Yebamot* text is the original.

(58d line 22) כְּהָדָא דְתַנֵּי. כָּל־הָרוֹצֶה לְהַחֲמִיר עַל עַצְמוֹ לִנְהוֹג כְּחוּמְרֵי בֵית שַׁמַּי וּכְחוּמְרֵי בֵית הֵלֵּל עַל זֶה נֶאֱמַר וְהַכְּסִיל בַּחוֹשֶׁךְ הוֹלֵךְ. כְּקוּלֵּי אִילוּ וּכְקוּלֵּי אִילוּ נִקְרָא רָשָׁע. אֶלָּא אוֹ כְדִבְרֵי בֵית שַׁמַּי כְּקוּלֵּיהֶם וּכְחוּמְרֵיהֶן. אוֹ כְדִבְרֵי בֵית הֵלֵּל כְּקוּלֵּיהֶן וּכְחוּמְרֵיהֶן. הָדָא דְתֵימַר עַד שֶׁלֹּא יָצְאַת בַּת קוֹל. מִשֶּׁיָּצְאַת בַּת קוֹל לְעוֹלָם הֲלָכָה כְדִבְרֵי בֵית הֵלֵּל. וְכָל־הָעוֹבֵר עַל דִּבְרֵי בֵית הֵלֵּל חַיָּיב מִיתָה. תַּנֵּי יָצְתָה בַת קוֹל וְאָמְרָה. אִילּוּ וְאִילּוּ דִבְרֵי אֱלֹהִים הֵן. אֲבָל הֲלָכָה כְּבֵית הֵלֵּל. אֵיכָן יָצְאַת בַּת קוֹל. רִבִּי בֵּיבַי בְּשֵׁם רִבִּי יוֹחָנָן. בְּיַבְנֶה יָצְאַת בַּת קוֹל.

2 וכקולי אילו | א ואילו   4 כקוליהן | א כקוליהם   משיצאת | א אבל משיצאת   5 כדברי בית | א כבית   6 יצתה | א יצאת   הן | א חיים הם   7 הלל | א הלל לעולם איכן | א באיכן   ר' ביבי | א רב ביבי   יוחנן | א יוחנן אמר

[99]In this matter, it was stated: "About anybody who wanted to take upon himself the stringencies both of the House of Shammai and the House of Hillel it was said: 'The silly one walks in darkness'. The leniencies of both of them, he is called wicked. Either following the words of the House of Shammai in their leniencies and stringencies, or following the words of the House of Hillel in their leniencies and stringencies." That is, before there came the disembodied voice. But after the disembodied voice was heard, "practice follows the House of Hillel forever." And any who transgress the words of the House of Hillel are deserving of death. It was stated: There came the disembodied voice and said: Both of them are the words of God, but practice follows the House of Hillel. Where was the disembodied voice heard? Rebbi Bebai in the name of Rebbi Joḥanan: The disembodied voice was heard at Yabneh.

(58d line 30) וְכַמָּה הִיא פְרוּטָה. אֶחָד מִשְּׁמוֹנֶה בְּאִסָּר הָאִיטַלְקִי. תַּנֵּי. הָאִיסָּר אֶחָד וְעֶשְׂרִים וְאַרְבָּעָה בְּדֵינָר כֶּסֶף. דֵּינָר כֶּסֶף אֶחָד מֵעֶשְׂרִים וְאַרְבָּעָה לְדֵינָר זָהָב. תַּנֵּי רִבִּי חִיָּיה. סִילְעָא אַרְבָּעָה דִינָרִין. שֵׁשׁ מָעָה כֶסֶף דֵּינָר. שְׁנֵי פוּנְדְּיוֹנִין מָעָה. מָעָה שְׁנֵי אִיסָּרִין. פוּנְדְּיוֹן שְׁנֵי מְסוּמִיסִין. אִיסָּר שְׁנֵי קַרְדְּיוֹנְטֵס. מְסוּמָס שְׁנֵי פְרוּטוֹת. קַרְדְּיוֹנְטֵס סָלְקִין אֶחָד מִשְּׁלֹשִׁים וּשְׁנַיִם לְמַעְלָה.

"How much is a *peruṭah*? One eighth of an Italic *as*." It was stated: [100]The *as* is $1/24$ of a silver denar; the silver denar is $1/24$ of a gold denar[101]. Rebbi Ḥiyya stated: "A tetradrachma is four *denarii*. Six silver *oboli* are in a denar. Two *dupondii* are an obolus. An *obolus*[102] is two *as*. A *pondius*[103] is two *semisses*. An *as*[104] is two *quadrantes*[105]. A *semis*[106] is two *peruṭot*. It turns out that a *quadrans* is $1/32$ of the above[107]."

100 Babli *Baba meṣia'* 44b, Tosephta *Baba batra* 5:11.

101 In Imperial coinage, the gold denar was usually counted for 25 silver denarii.

102 This has to read: "a *dupondius*".

103 This has to read: "an *as*."

104 This has to read: "a *semis*".

105 Greek κοδράντης, equivalent of Roman *quadrans*, $1/4$ of an *as*..

106 This has to read: "a *quadrans*". The final list reads: 1 denar = 6 *oboli* = 12 *dupondii* = 24 *as* = 48 *semisses* = 96 *quadrantes* = 192 *peruṭot* (confirming the tannaïtic standard of the *peruṭah* as $1/8$ of an *as*, Mishnah *Idiut* 4:7). In the Roman system, the obolus appears as a weight, rather than a coin: one-sixth of a denar of 3.6 g.

107 This has to read: "A *peruṭah* is $1/32$ of an obolus." In the entire list, the first entry in each sentence has to be replaced by the next smaller unit and מעה by למעלה.

(58d line 35) אָמַר רִבִּי זְעִירָא. בִּימֵי רִבִּי סִימַאי וְרַבּוֹתֵינוּ עָשׂוּ אוֹתָם אֶחָד מֵעֶשְׂרִים וְאַרְבָּעָה לְמַעֲלָה. וְתַנֵּי. רִבִּי שִׁמְעוֹן בֶּן גַּמְלִיאֵל אוֹמֵר. שְׁלֹשָׁה דוֹדְסִים מָעָה. שְׁנֵי בֵּיצִים דְּרוֹסָה. שְׁנֵי שְׂמִין נוֹתְנִין. שְׁנֵי פְּרוּטוֹת שְׂמִין. סָלְקוֹן אֶחָד מֵעֶשְׂרִים וְאַרְבָּעָה לְמָעָה.

Rebbi Ze'ira said, in the days of Rebbi Simai[108] and our teachers they made it[109] $1/24$ of an obolus, as it was stated: [100]"Rabban Simeon ben Gamliel says, three *dodrantes*[110] are an obolus, two *besses*[111] are a *dodrans*, two *semisses* are a *bes*, two *peruṭot* a *semis*. It results in $1/24$ of an obolus[112]."

108 Of the generation of transition between Tannaïm and Amoraïm. "Our teachers" therefore refers to Rebbi.

109 The *peruṭah*.

110 Latin for $3/4$ of any measure.

111 Latin for $2/3$ of any measure.

112 D. Sperber, *Roman Palestine 200-400, Money and Prices*, Ramat Gan 1974, pp. 78-80, conjectures that the change in computation of a *peruṭah* from $1/32$ to $1/24$ of an obolus was a rabbinic response to Caracalla's monetary reform which increased the ratio of silver to gold from 12:1 to 9:1.

The argument is purely theoretical since the *peruṭah* as a coin disappeared with the Jewish Commonwealth.

(58d line 38) רִבִּי חֲנִינָה וְרִבִּי מָנָא. רִבִּי חֲנִינָה אוֹמֵר. נְחָשָׁא בְּאַתְרֵיהּ קַייָם. כַּסְפָּא זְלִיל. כַּסְפָּא יְקִיר. רִבִּי מָנָא אָמַר. כַּסְפָּא בְּאַתְרֵיהּ קַייָם. נְחָשָׁא יְקִיר נְחָשָׁא זְלִיל. עַל דַּעְתֵּיהּ דְּרִבִּי חֲנִינָה לְעוֹלָם שֵׁשׁ נָשִׁים מִתְקַדְּשׁוֹת בְּאִיסָּר. עַל דַּעְתֵּיהּ דְּרִבִּי מָנָא פְּעָמִים שֵׁשׁ פְּעָמִים שְׁמוֹנֶה.

Rebbi Ḥanina and Rebbi Mana[113]. Rebbi Ḥanina says, bronze remained in its place[114], silver increased or decreased in value. Rebbi Mana said, silver remained in its place[114], bronze increased or decreased in value. In Rebbi Ḥanina's opinion, with one *as* six women always can contract a preliminary marriage. In Rebbi Mana's opinion, sometimes six, sometimes eight[115].

113 They probably are R. Ḥanania of Sepphoris and R. Mana I, of the last Amoraïm. After Diocletian's reform, with the gold standard universally accepted, they discuss the legal standard in the inflationary period of the last Severans and the following military anarchy when the government paid its debt in adulterated silver coin but required taxes to be paid in genuine silver coin.

114 I. e., is the monetary standard.

115 It is assumed that a man can deliver a coin to a goup of women as payment for his preliminary marriage to all of them (Mishnah *Qiadušin* 2:6-7). In R. Mana's opinion, the groom has to deliver merchandise (including copper coin considered as merchandise) in the actual value of a *peruṭah*. In terms of the silver *as*, not in circulation after Nero's time, he can use one silver coin for as many women as the *as* can buy *peruṭot*. In R. Ḥanina's opinion, since women cannot be expected to be cognizant of the current value of silver on the metals exchange, the women can be sure that the *as* represents the value promised them only at the historical minimum value of silver. (The explanations of the classical commentaries have to be rejected since

they require a switching of the names in addition to emending the text. The relation of coins to the mint standard, whether they are treated as money or merchandise, is the topic of *Baba meṣi'a*, Chapter 4.)

(58d line 42) חִילְפַּיי אָמַר. אַייתִיבוּנִי עַל גֵּיף נַהֲרָא. דְּלָא אֲפִיקִית מַתְנִיתָא דְרִבִּי חִיָיה רָבָא מִמַּתְנִיתִין זָרְקוּנִי לְנַהֲרָא. אָמְרִין לֵיהּ. וְהָא תַגֵּי רִבִּי חִיָּיה. סִילְעָא אַרְבַּע דֵּינָרִין. אָמַר לוֹן. אוּף אֲנָן תַּגִּינָתָהּ. כַּמָּה תְּהֵא הַסֶּלַע חֲסֵירָה וְלֹא יְהֵא בָהּ הוֹנָיָה. רִבִּי מֵאִיר אוֹמֵר. אַרְבַּע אִיסָרוֹת מֵאִיסָר לְדֵינָר. אָמְרִין לֵיהּ. וְהָתַגֵּי רִבִּי חִיָּיה. שֵׁשׁ מָעָה כֶסֶף דֵּינָר. אָמַר לֵיהּ. אוּף אֲנָא תַגִּינָתָא. הָאוֹנָאָה אַרְבַּע כֶּסֶף מֵעֶשְׂרִים וְאַרְבַּע כֶּסֶף לְסֶלַע שְׁתוּת לַמִּקָּח. אָמְרִין לֵיהּ. וְהָתַגֵּי רִבִּי חִיָּיה. שְׁנֵי פּוּנְדְּיוֹנִן מָעָה. אָמַר לוֹן. אוּף אֲנָן תַּגִּינָתָהּ. נוֹתֵן סֶלַע וּפוּנְדְּיוֹן לַשָּׁנָה. אָמְרִין לֵיהּ. וְהָתַגֵּי רִבִּי חִיָּיה. שְׁנֵי אִיסָרִין פּוּנְדְּיוֹן. אָמַר לוֹן. אוּף אֲנָן תַּגִּינָתָהּ. הַמֵּנִיחַ אִיסָר וְאָכַל עָלָיו חֶצְיוֹ וְהָלַךְ לוֹ לְמָקוֹם אַחֵר וַהֲרֵי הוּא יוֹצֵא בְּפוּנְדְּיוֹן. מוֹסִיף עָלָיו עוֹד אִיסָר. אָמְרִין לֵיהּ. וְהָתַגֵּי רִבִּי חִיָּיה. שְׁנֵי מְסוּמִיסִין אִיסָר. שְׁנֵי קָרְדְּיִנְטֵס מְסוּמָס. שְׁנֵי פְּרוּטוֹת קָרְדְּיִנְטֵס. אָמַר לוֹן. אוּף אֲנָן תַּגִּינָתָא. וְכַמָּה הִיא פְּרוּטָה אַחַת בִּשְׁמוֹנֶה בְּאִסָּר הָאִיטַלְקִי.

Ḥilfai said[116]: Bring me to the river's edge. If I cannot derive Rebbi Ḥiyya the Elder's *baraita*[117] from the Mishnah, throw me into the river. They said to him, did not Rebbi Ḥiyya state: "A tetradrachma are four denar." He said to them, we also have stated[118]: "By how much can a tetradrachma be deficient without being fraudulent? Rebbi Meïr said four *as*, one *as* per denar[119]." They said to him, did not Rebbi Ḥiyya state: "Six silver obols are a denar." He said to him, I also have stated it[120]: "Fraud[121] is four silver coins for twenty-four silver coins, a tetradrachma, one sixth of the selling price." They said to him, did not Rebbi Ḥiyya state: "Two *dupondii* are an obolus." He said to them, we also have stated thus[122]: "He gives a tetradrachma and a *dupondius* per year." They said to him, did not Rebbi Hiyya state: "Two *as* are a *dupondius*". He said to them, we also have stated thus[123]: "He who put aside an *as* and ate for half of its worth, then went to another place where it is worth a *dupondius*, has to eat another *as* for it." They said to him, did not Rebbi Hiyya state: "Two *semisses* are an *as*, two *quadrantes* are a *semis*, two *perutot* are a *quadrans*." He said to them, we also have stated thus[124]: "How much is a *perutah*? One eighth of an Italic *as*."

116 At many places, he is quoted as opposing the use of *baraitot* in talmudic discussions; cf. *Ketubot* 6:7, Note 113.

117 A paradigm for the later Tosephta, in the present case the two preceding *baraitot*.

118 Mishnah *Baba Meṣi'a* 4:4.

119 He accepts a coin as of full weight if it deviates from the standard by no more than $1/24$, i. e. 4.167%, in contrast to commercial contracts which are fraudulent only if the customer was overcharged by more than $1/6$, 16.667%. In any case, the Mishnah states clearly that the deficiency admissible for a tetradrachma is four times that of a denar. [Cf. Trimalchio's remark that the profession of banker is one of the most difficult since he must be able to recognize the inferior metal of a coin beneath its silver coating (E. G.)]

120 Mishnah *Baba Meṣi'a* 4:3. Since "silver coin" means "smallest silver coin", i. e., an obolus, and it was established that a denar was a quarter tetradrachma, it follows that a silver denar was 6 obols. These and smaller denominations had long disappeared from circulation in Hilfai's time, towards the middle of the Third Century. (Cf. Note 85.)

121 Overcharging or underpaying in commercial contracts.

122 Mishnah *'Arakhin* 7:1. If somebody dedicates his field to the Temple, Scripture prescribes that he redeem it proportional to the numbers of years to the next Jubilee. The full rate, for the entire 49 years of a Jubilee cycle, is 50 *šeqel* for a field on which a *ḥomer* (or *kur*, 30 *se'ah*) of barley can be sown (75'000 square cubits). Talmudic theory identifies the biblical *šeqel* with the Roman tetradrachma, which is slightly more than the

standard *šeqel* documented from First Kingdom times, 11.4 g. Since in the vernacular the *zūz*, the Babylonian half-*šeqel*, was identified with the Roman *denarius*, the "sheqel" was identified as two denar. This gave rise to the theory that the biblical "holy *šeqel*", which simply was "the king's weight" and still the Tyrian *šeqel* in Roman times, was twice the profane *šeqel*. The rate to be paid for the standard field per year therefore was $50/49 = 1^1/_{49}$ tetradrachma. The rate stated in the Mishnah is $1^1/_{48}$ tetradrachma. The small difference, $^1/_{48}$ - $^1/_{49}$ is *qolbon* (κόλλυβος, Latin *collybus, collubus*, "exchange of coins; rate of exchange"), the small coin paid as agio to the money-changer to convert the sum into actual coin. The Mishnah shows that a *dupondius* was $^1/_{48}$ of a tetradrachma or half an obolus.

123 Mishnah *Ma'aśer Šeni* 4:8, Note 130.

124 Mishnah 1:1. While the Mishnah does not state anything about the intermediate denominations, it clearly defines the relation between *peruṭah* and *as*.

(58d line 54) וְקוֹנָה אֶת עַצְמָהּ בְּגֵט. דִּכְתִיב וְכָתַב לָהּ סֵפֶר כְּרִיתוּת וְגו'. וּבְמִיתַת הַבַּעַל. דִּכְתִיב אוֹ כִי יָמוּת הָאִישׁ הָאַחֲרוֹן. עַד כְּדוֹן מִיתָתוֹ שֶׁלָּאַחֲרוֹן. מִיתָתוֹ שֶׁלָּרִאשׁוֹן. מָה אִם הָאַחֲרוֹן שֶׁאֵין הֶתֵּירוֹ הֶיתֵּר מְרוּבֶּה אַתְּ אוֹמֵר. מִיתָה מַתֶּרֶת. רִאשׁוֹן שֶׁהֶתֵּירוֹ הֶיתֵּר מְרוּבֶּה אֵינוֹ דִין שֶׁתְּהֵא הַמִּיתָה מַתֶּרֶת. אָמַר רִבִּי חוּנָה. קִרְיָיה אָמַר שֶׁהַמִּיתָה מַתֶּרֶת. דִּכְתִיב כִּי יֵשְׁבוּ אַחִים יַחְדָּיו וּמֵת אַחַד מֵהֶם וּבֵן אֵין לוֹ. הָא אִם יֵשׁ לוֹ בֵּן מִיתָה מַתֶּרֶת. אָמַר רִבִּי יוֹסֵי בֵּירִבִּי בּוּן. אִם אוֹמֵר אַתְּ שֶׁאֵין מִיתָה מַתֶּרֶת מִנָּן אֲנָן מַשְׁכְּחִין אַלְמָנָה לְכֹהֵן גָּדוֹל גְּרוּשָׁה וַחֲלוּצָה לְכֹהֵן הֶדְיוֹט. אָמַר רִבִּי יוֹחָנָן בַּר מַרְיָיה. תִּיפְתַּר בִּיבָמָה.

[125]"She regains her autonomy by a bill of divorce," as it is written[126]: "He shall write her a bill of divorce." "Or the husband's death," as it is written: "Or if the latter husband dies.[127]" So far, if the latter one dies, [what about] the death of the former[128]? Since the latter's death releases

her, even though his death does not cause a complete release[129], it is only logical that the former's death should release her since his death will cause a complete release[130]. Rebbi Huna said, the verse implies that death releases, as it is written: "If brothers live together and one of them dies childless, etc.[131]" Therefore, if he had a child, death releases. Rebbi Yose bar Abun said, if you would say that death does not release, how could we find a widow for a High priest, a divorcee or one who has received *haliṣah* for a common priest[132]? Rebbi Johanan bar Marius said, explain it for a sister-in-law[133].

125 A parallel but different discussion is in the Babli, 13b.

126 *Deut.* 24:1. The part not quoted and v. 2 make it clear that the divorcee is free to contract another marriage.

127 *Deut.* 24:3. Since the widow cannot remarry her first husband, it is clear that she can marry any other man.

128 Which is not mentioned in the verse.

129 The former husband becomes forbidden. He was permitted after his divorce and before her second marriage.

130 The divorcee is free to marry any man not forbidden to her by incest or holiness prohibitions.

131 *Deut.* 25:5. Since the verse prohibits remarriage of the widow outside the family, it implies that the widow of a man who had children is free to marry according to her wishes.

132 The statement about the common priest implies that a widow is permitted to a common priest even if he is not of her first husband's family.

133 If a brother of a High Priest dies childless, his widow is forbidden to the High Priest. The prohibition has to be stated even if in general a widow were not permitted to remarry.

(58c line 62) יְבָמָה יָבֹא עָלֶיהָ. זוֹ בִּיאָה. וּלְקָחָהּ לוֹ כְאִשָּׁה. זוֹ הַמַּאֲמָר. יָכוֹל כְּשֵׁם שֶׁהַבִּיאָה גּוֹמֶרֶת בָּהּ כָּךְ יְהֵא הַמַּאֲמָר גּוֹמֵר בָּהּ. תַּלְמוּד לוֹמַר וְיִבְּמָהּ. עִירָה כָּל־הַפָּרָשָׁה כּוּלָּהּ לְיִיבּוּם. הַבִּיאָה גּוֹמֶרֶת בָּהּ וְאֵין הַמַּאֲמָר גּוֹמֵר בָּהּ.

אִם כֵּן מַה מוֹעִיל בָּהּ מַאֲמָר. לְאוֹסְרָהּ עַל הָאַחִין.

רִבִּי שִׁמְעוֹן אוֹמֵר. הַמַּאֲמָר אוֹ קוֹנֶה אוֹ לֹא קוֹנֶה. מַה טַעֲמָא דְרִבִּי שִׁמְעוֹן. יְבָמָהּ יָבֹא עָלֶיהָ. זֶה הַבִּיאָה. וּלְקָחָהּ לוֹ לְאִשָּׁה. זֶה הַמַּאֲמָר. כְּשֵׁם שֶׁהַבִּיאָה גּוֹמֶרֶת בָּהּ כָּךְ יְהֵא הַמַּאֲמָר גּוֹמֵר בָּהּ. אוֹ יְבָמָהּ יָבֹא עָלֶיהָ וַהֲרֵי הִיא לְקוּחָה לוֹ. וְהַמַּאֲמָר לֹא הוֹעִיל בָּהּ כְּלוּם.

רִבִּי לְעָזָר בֶּן עֲרָךְ אָמַר. הַמַּאֲמָר קוֹנֶה קִנְיָין גָּמוּר בִּיבָמָה. מַה טַעֲמָא דְרִבִּי אֶלְעָזָר בֶּן עֲרָךְ. וּלְקָחָהּ לוֹ לְאִשָּׁה. הֲרֵי הוּא בְּקִידּוּשֵׁי אִשָּׁה. מַה קִידּוּשֵׁי אִשָּׁה קוֹנִין קִנְיָין גָּמוּר בִּיבָמָה. אַף הַמַּאֲמָר קוֹנֶה קִנְיָין גָּמוּר בִּיבָמָה. אֵי זֶהוּ מַאֲמָר בִּיבָמָה. הֲרֵי אַתְּ מְקוּדֶּשֶׁת לִי בְּכֶסֶף וּבְשָׁוֶה כֶסֶף.

1 זו | בה זה   זו | בה זה   יכול | ב יכול יהא   2 גומר בה | ה -   ויבמה | ה יבמה יבא עליה   3 עירה | ב עורה ה שרה   לייבום | ה ליבום   הביאה | ה מה הביאה   ואין | ה אף   4 אם כן | ה ואם כן   מועיל | בה הועיל   על האחין | בה לאחין   6 זה | ב זו לאשה | ה -   כשם | בה וכשם   7 יהא | בה -   יבא | ה יבוא   9 אמ' | בה אומ'   10 אלעזר | בה לעזר   בקידושי | בה כקידושי   11 ביבמה | בה -   ביבמה | ה -   אי זהו | ב אי זהו היא

[134]"Her levir shall come upon her", that is cohabitation. "And take her as a wife for himself", that is "bespeaking". I might think that just as cohabitation is final so "bespeaking" is final; the verse says "and take her in levirate." This directs the entire paragraph towards levirate. Cohabitation is final, "bespeaking" is not final. Then what is "bespeaking" good for? To forbid her to his brothers.

Rebbi Simeon says, "bespeaking" either acquires or does not acquire. What is the argument of Rebbi Simeon? "Her levir shall come upon her", that is cohabitation. "And take her for himself", that is "bespeaking". Just as cohabitation is final so "bespeaking" is final. Or "her levir shall come upon her", then she has been acquired by him and "bespeaking" was of no use to her.

Rebbi Eleazar ben Arakh says, "bespeaking" acquires a sister-in-law completely. What is the argument of Rebbi Eleazar ben Arakh? "And take her as a wife for himself", the same expression is used as for the preliminary marriage of a woman[19]. Just as preliminary marriage acquires completely, so "bespeaking" acquires a sister-in-law completely. What is the formula for "bespeaking" a sister-in-law? "You are betrothed to me by money or money's worth."

134 The text is from *Yebamot*, Chapter 2:1 (ב), explained there in Notes 12-20, and Chapter 5:1 (ה).

(58d line 74) רִבִּי יִצְחָק שָׁאַל. וְלָמָּה לִי נָן אָמְרִין. בֵּין בַּחֲלִיצָתָהּ בֵּין בַּחֲלִיצַת חֲבֶירְתָהּ. חָזַר וְאָמַר. מַה תַּנִּינָן. בַּחֲלִיצָתָהּ. לֹא חֲלִיצָתָהּ. וְהָכָא בֵּין בַּחֲלִיצָתָהּ בֵּין בַּחֲלִיצַת חֲבֶירְתָהּ. וְהָא תַּנִּינָן. בְּבִיאָה. אִית לָךְ מֵימַר. בֵּין בְּבִיאָתָהּ בֵּין בְּבִיאַת חֲבֶירְתָהּ. מַתְנִיתָא בִּיבָמָה אַחַת. מַה צְרִיכָה לֵיהּ בִּשְׁתֵּי יְבָמוֹת.

Rebbi Isaac asked: Why do we not say: "either by her own *haliṣah* or that of her co-wife?"[135] He turned around and said: Did we state "by her own *haliṣah*"? Not "by her own *haliṣah*"[136]! But here either by her own *haliṣah* or that of her co-wife. But did we not state, "by intercourse"? Can you say, either by her own intercourse or the intercourse of her co-wife[137]? The Mishnah speaks of one sister-in-law; the problem arises for two sisters-in-law.

135 This refers to the last sentence in the Mishnah, that the widow of the childless man can regain her autonomy by *haliṣah*. Mishnah *Yebamot* 4:1 states that for the House of Hillel the levirate marriage or *haliṣah* of one wife of the deceased childless brother forbids all her co-wives to the levir's brothers and,

therefore, frees the co-wives to marry any other man.

136   It is only stated "by *ḥaliṣah*," not indicating who performs it; it could be a co-wife.

137   One has to assume that the Mishnah is formulated in a uniform style. It is clear that a man cannot marry a group of women by sleeping with one of them, even though he could marry all women in the group by giving valuables to one of them if the others empower her to act for them (Note 115). If "intercourse" in the first case means a personal act, then *ḥaliṣah* in the last case also means a personal act.

(59a line 3) רִבִּי שְׁמוּאֵל בַּר רַב יִצְחָק בְּעָא. שִׁפְחָה חֲרוּפָה בַּמֶּה הִיא קוֹנָה אֶת עַצְמָהּ לְפוֹטְרָהּ מִן הַמַּלְקוּת וְלָבֹא עָלֶיהָ מִן הָאָשָׁם. פְּשִׁיטָא שֶׁאֵינָהּ יוֹצְאָה בַּגֵּט. דְּאָמַר רִבִּי חִייָה בְּשֵׁם רִבִּי יוֹחָנָן. מִי שֶׁחֶצְיוֹ עֶבֶד וְחֶצְיוֹ בֶּן חוֹרִין. קִידֵּשׁ אִשָּׁה אֵין חוֹשְׁשִׁין לְקִידּוּשָׁיו. וְדִכְוָותָא גֵירַשׁ אֵין חוֹשְׁשִׁין לְגֵירוּשָׁיו. פְּשִׁיטָא שֶׁהִיא יוֹצְאָה בַּגֵּט מִיהָא (דְּאָמַר רִבִּי חִייָה בְּשֵׁם רִבִּי יוֹחָנָן. מִי שֶׁחֶצְיוֹ עֶבֶד וְחֶצְיוֹ בֶּן חוֹרִין קִידֵּשׁ אִשָּׁה אֵין חוֹשְׁשִׁין לְקִידּוּשָׁיו. וְדִכְוָותָא גֵירַשׁ אֵין חוֹשְׁשִׁין לְגֵירוּשָׁיו. פְּשִׁיטָא שֶׁהִיא יוֹצְאָה בַּגֵּט מִיהָא) דְּאָמַר רִבִּי יוֹסֵי בְּשֵׁם רִבִּי יוֹחָנָן. תִּירְגֵּם עֲקִילַס הַגֵּר לִפְנֵי רִבִּי עֲקִיבָה. וְהִיא שִׁפְחָה נֶחֱרֶפֶת לְאִישׁ. בִּכְתוּשָׁה לִפְנֵי אִישׁ. כְּמָה דְאַתְּ אָמַר וַתִּשְׁטַח עָלָיו הָרִיפוֹת. אָמַר רִבִּי חִייָה בְּשֵׁם רִבִּי יוֹחָנָן. כָּךְ פֵּירְשָׁהּ רִבִּי לֶעָזָר בֵּירִבִּי שִׁמְעוֹן לִפְנֵי חֲכָמִים. וְהִיא שִׁפְחָה נֶחֱרֶפֶת לְאִישׁ. בִּכְתוּשָׁה לִפְנֵי אִישׁ. כְּמָה דְתֵימַר בְּתוֹךְ הָרִיפוֹת בַּעֲלִי.

Rebbi Samuel bar Rav Isaac asked: How can a *ḥăruphah* slave girl[138] acquire her autonomy in such a way that she would be freed from flogging, and [free] the one who had intercourse with her from a reparation sacrifice? It is obvious that she cannot leave by a bill of divorce since Rebbi Ḥiyya said in Rebbi Joḥanan's name: If a person who is half slave and half free entered a preliminary marriage, one does not consider his marriage[139]. In parallel, if he divorced one does not consider his divorce. It is obvious that she can leave by a bill of divorce at least since (Rebbi Ḥiyya said in Rebbi Joḥanan's name: If a person who is half slave and half free entered a preliminary marriage, one does not consider his marriage. In parallel, if he divorced one does not consider his divorce. It is obvious that she can leave by a bill of divorce at least)[140]. Rebbi Yose said in Rebbi Joḥanan's name: Aquila the proselyte translated before Rebbi Aqiba "and she is a slave girl נֶחֱרֶפֶת to a man"[141], by "one who was pounded before a man"[142], as you say, "she spread morsels on it[143]." Rebbi Ḥiyya said in Rebbi Joḥanan's name: So Rebbi Eleazar ben Rebbi Simeon explained it before the Sages. "And she is a slave girl נֶחֱרֶפֶת to a man", by "one who was pounded before a man", as you say, "in morsels by a pestle.[144]"

138   Cf. *Lev.* 19:20-22. The slave girl has a status approximating that of married woman but sleeps with another man. By rabbinic interpretation, the girl is whipped and the man has to bring a reparation sacrifice. The exact meaning of the root חרף is in doubt, in view of the multiple meanings of Arabic حرف or خرف; rabbinic interpretations are given at the end of this paragraph and the next. If she were an unattached slave, she could not marry and, therefore, could have guiltless sex with any man of her choosing. The Jewish man who slept with her would be guilty of violating *Deut.* 23:18 for which he could be whipped if the act was observed by two witnesses, but no sacrifice would be due.

139   *Giṭṭin* 4:5, Notes 140-141. In this interpretation the girl is partially manumitted and engaged to be married by a free Jewish man after her complete manumission. Since in her present state she cannot be legally married, neither can she be divorced.

140   The meaning of this sentence is unclear. The text in parentheses is dittography inserted by the corrector.

141   *Lev.* 19:20.

142   She was betrothed by intercourse.

143   *2S.* 17:19. The identification of

ה and ח is routine in rabbinic derivations but etymologically unfounded. Modern dictionaries treat הרפות, הריפות as derived from a hypothetical root ריף, not הרף.

144 *Pr.* 17:19. Aquila translates בְּחוֹךְ הָרִיפוֹת by ἐν μέσῳ ἐμπτισσομένων "in the midst of pounded things". Both verses are quoted in the same sense in the Babli, *Keritut* 11a, that a man who sleeps with a *ḥaruphah* slave girl is guilty only if the girl had previously slept with her assignee, not if she is a virgin. (This agrees with the derivation of נחרפת, accepted by Gesenius, from Accadic *ḫarāpu*, Arabic خرف "to pluck, to harvest", that the slave girl "had been plucked by a man," *Lev.* 19:20.) The tradent there is R. Isaac; Aquila is not mentioned [since in the Babli's tradition he did not translate following R. Aqiba but R. Eliezer and R. Joshua, one generation earlier (*Megillah* 3a).] {One is tempted to find in חרף the root of Greek Χάρυβδις, a dangerous whirlpool between Italy and Sicily, personified as a dangerous female being who "plucks men" (E. G.).}

(59a line 15) מָהוּ שֶׁתִּקְנֶה עַצְמָהּ בְּמִיתַת רַבָּהּ וּבְהַשְׁלִים שֵׁשׁ. מַה צְרִיכָה לֵיהּ. כְּרִבִּי עֲקִיבָה. דְּרִבִּי עֲקִיבָה אָמַר. בְּשֶׁחֶצְיָיהּ שִׁפְחָה וְחֶצְיָיהּ בַּת חוֹרִין בִּמְאוֹרֶסֶת לְבֶן חוֹרִין הַכָּתוּב מְדַבֵּר. בְּרַם כְּרִבִּי יִשְׁמָעֵאל צְרִיכָה לֵיהּ. דְּרִבִּי יִשְׁמָעֵאל אָמַר. שִׁפְחָה כְּנַעֲנִית הַנְּשׂוּאָה לְעֶבֶד עִבְרִי הַכָּתוּב מְדַבֵּר. אִם נִשּׂוּאֵי תּוֹרָה הֵן אִם אֲדֹנָיו יִתֶּן לוֹ אִשָּׁה. לֹא צוֹרְכָה דְּלֹא. מָהוּ שֶׁתִּקְנֶה עַצְמָהּ בְּמִיתַת רַבָּהּ וּבְהַשְׁלִים שֵׁשׁ. וּכְמָאן דְּאָמַר. אֵין עֶבֶד עִבְרִי עוֹבֵד אֶת הַיּוֹרֵשׁ.

Can she[145] regain her autonomy through her master's death or by the end of six [years]? What is the problem? Following Rebbi Aqiba? But Rebbi Aqiba said that the verse speaks about a woman half slave and half free engaged to be married by a free man[146]. Therefore, his problem is following Rebbi Ismael, since Rebbi Ismael said that the verse speaks about a Canaanite[147] slave girl married to a Hebrew slave, since this is marriage sanctioned by the Torah: "If his master give him a wife.[148]" But his problem is whether she regains her autonomy through her master's death or by the end of six [years] for him who says that the Hebrew slave does not serve the heir[149].

145 The *ḥarupnah* slave girl, to be able to sleep with whomever she pleases.

146 Babli *Keritut* 11a. Her situation can be remedied only by her full manumission, Mishnah *Giṭṭin* 4:5.

147 Meaning: originally Gentile.

148 *Ex.* 21:4. Since the children born from this union are slaves, the woman cannot be a Hebrew slave girl. Since the woman is called "wife", she is required to be faithful by biblical standards. The question is whether this kind of marriage is terminated automatically, without any formality, at the moment the Hebrew slave regains his freedom. At the same moment, the slave woman becomes forbidden to him since any sexual relations between people who could not legally be married is qualified as *qādēš* (*Deut.* 23:18).

149 As explained in the next Halakhah. The question is not answered since it can never arise in the future (Note 152).

(fol. 58a) **משנה ב:** עֶבֶד עִבְרִי נִקְנֶה בְּכֶסֶף וּבִשְׁטָר וְקוֹנֶה אֶת עַצְמוֹ בַּשָּׁנִים וּבַיּוֹבֵל וּבְגִרְעוֹן כֶּסֶף. יְתֵירָה עָלָיו אָמָה הָעִבְרִיָּה שֶׁקּוֹנָה אֶת עַצְמָהּ בַּסִּימָנִים. הַנִּרְצָע נִקְנֶה בָּרְצִיעָה וְקוֹנֶה אֶת עַצְמוֹ בַּיּוֹבֵל וּבְמִיתַת הָאָדוֹן.

Mishnah 2: A Hebrew slave[150] is acquired by money or a document; he regains his autonomy by years[151], or the Jubilee[152], or reduction of the amount[153]. The Hebrew slave girl[154] in addition regains her autonomy by indicators of puberty[155]. The pierced slave is acquired by piercing[156]; he regains his autonomy in the Jubilee or by the master's death[157].

150 The rules are based on *Ex.* 21:2-6, *Lev.* 25:39-43, *Deut.* 15:12-18. The *Lev.* source clearly refers to the person who sells himself as indentured servant

because he cannot fend for himself. *Ex.* 22:2 provides for judicial sale of the thief who cannot pay the required double restitution.

Separate rules for the Hebrew slave acquired by a Gentile are given in *Lev.* 25:47-54. In that case, the slave regains his freedom automatically only in the Jubilee year but the family can force his redemption by repaying the portion of his buying price not amortized by the time passed (*Lev.* 25:50).

151 The maximum time of a contract of an indentured servant was 6 years; *Ex.* 21:2, *Deut.* 15:12.

152 *Lev.* 25:40. Since the Jubilee brings back everybody to his ancestral land, everybody is presumed to be able to feed himself. The dependence of the rules of the Hebrew slave on the Jubilee implies that Hebrew slavery disappeared with the Jubilee; it never existed during the Second Commonwealth and is not to be re-instituted in the times of the Messiah (*Ševi'it* 10:3, Notes 83-88; *Giṭṭin* 4:3, Note 65). The discussion about the rules of Hebrew male slavery are a purely theoretical reconstruction of the past whose interest is not in statements but in the rules of inference.

153 If the slave or his family buy his freedom, the master is required to accept payment proportional to the time not yet served.

154 While the rules for the Hebrew slave girl are not tied to the Jubilee, the verses *Deut.* 15:12,17 equate the rules for male and female slaves. Therefore, all the detailed rules developed in this Halakhah are purely theoretical interpretations of the biblical text; they never were operational within the rabbinic framework.

155 While a father can forcibly marry off his daughter until she has reached adulthood (12 years six months and one day) he cannot sell her into slavery beyond adolescence (12 years and a day if she shows signs of puberty). He cannot sell her to work for longer than he had the right to sell.

156 The slave who does not want to regain his freedom after six years, whose earlobe is pierced (*Ex.* 21:6, *Deut.* 15:17).

157 *Ex.* 21:5, *Deut.* 15:16 make it clear that the relationship of the "pierced" slave to his master is a personal one, not transferable to his heirs.

HALAKHAH 2

הלכה ב: עֶבֶד עִבְרִי נִקְנֶה בְּכֶסֶף כול'. כְּתִיב כִּי יִמָּכֵר לְךָ אָחִיךָ (59a line 21) הָעִבְרִי אוֹ הָעִבְרִיָּה. הִקִּישׁ עִבְרִי לָעִבְרִיָּה. מָה עִבְרִיָּה נִקְנֵית בַּכֶּסֶף וּבִשְׁטָר. אַף עִבְרִי נִקְנֶה בְּכֶסֶף וּבִשְׁטָר. נִיחָא בַּכֶּסֶף. דִּכְתִיב וְיָצְאָה חִנָּם אֵין כָּסֶף. בִּשְׁטָר מִנָּלָן. עִבְרִיָּה לְמֵידָה מִבַּת חוֹרִין. וְעִבְרִי לְמֵידָה מֵעִבְרִיָּה. [158]נִמְצָא לָמֵד מִלָּמֵד. עַד כְּדוֹן כְּרִבִּי עֲקִיבָה. דְּאִית לֵיהּ לָמֵד מִן הַלָּמֵד. כְּרַבִּי יִשְׁמָעֵאל. דְּלֵית לֵיהּ לָמֵד מִן הַלָּמֵד. אַשְׁכָּח תַּנֵּי רִבִּי יִשְׁמָעֵאל לְהָא מִילָּה וְחָפְשָׁה מִלָּה חָפְשִׁי מֵחוּפְשָׁה. בְּכָל־אֲתָר לֵית לְרִבִּי יִשְׁמָעֵאל לָמֵד מִן הַלָּמֵד וְהָכָא אִית לֵיהּ רִבִּי יִשְׁמָעֵאל. תַּנֵּי לָהּ בְּשֵׁם חֲכָמִים. מִנָּן תֵּיהִי רִבִּי יִשְׁמָעֵאל. שִׁילּוּחַ שִׁילּוּחַ. מַה שִׁילּוּחַ שֶׁנֶּאֱמַר לְהַלָּן בִּשְׁטָר אַף כָּאן בִּשְׁטָר. וְלֹא דַמְיָא. תַּמָּן לְהַקְנוֹת לְעַצְמָהּ. בְּרַם הָכָא לְהִיקָּנוֹת לַאֲחֵרִים. אָמַר רִבִּי מַתַּנְיָּה. מְכִירָה מְכִירָה. מַה מְכִירָה שֶׁנֶּאֶמְרָה לְהַלָּן בִּשְׁטָר אַף כָּאן בִּשְׁטָר. אִי מַה לְהַלָּן בַּחֲזָקָה אַף כָּאן בַּחֲזָקָה. אָמַר רִבִּי חִיָּיה בַּר אָדָא. הוּא עִבְרִי הוּא עִבְרִיָּה.

5 דאית ליה A - | 6 להא A לה | 9 דמיא A דמיה | 10 חהיקנות A להקנות | מתניה A מתניתה | 11 או A אי | 12 אדא A אבא

Halakhah 2: "A Hebrew slave is acquired by money," etc. It is written: "If your Hebrew brother or sister be sold to you," he bracketed the male Hebrew with the female[159]. Since the female Hebrew can be acquired by money or contract, also the male Hebrew can be acquired by money or contract. One understands money since it is written[160]: "She leaves gratis, without money [due]." From where by contract? The female Hebrew is inferred from the free woman[161], and the male Hebrew from the female. This is a combination of inferences. That follows Rebbi Aqiba who accepts combination of inferences[162]. Following Rebbi Ismael who rejects combination of inferences? It was found that Rebbi Ismael stated: In the case of the word חָפְשָׁה, "free" is inferred from חָפְשָׁה[163]. Everywhere Rebbi Ismael rejects combination of inferences and here, he accepts combination of inferences? Rebbi Ismael stated it in the name of the

Sages[164]. From where is it derived for Rebbi Ismael? "Sending away, sending away." Since "sending away" mentioned there means by a contract, also "sending away" here means by a contract[165]. But it does not compare. There it is to gain autonomy, here it is to be acquired by others! Rebbi Mattaniah[166] said, "sale, sale"[167]. Since "sale" mentioned there means by a contract, "sale" here also means by a contract. But since there[168] it is possible by possession, then here it should be possible by possession. Rebbi Ḥiyya bar Ada[169] said, the male Hebrew is like the female Hebrew[170].

158 From here on there exists a parallel text of an Ashkenazi ms. edited with partial variant readings by J. Sussman in *Kobez al Yad* xii (xxii), Jerusalem 1994, pp. 112 ff. In the Notes, this text will be referred to as A, the Leiden ms. as L.

159 *Deut.* 15:12. The Babli, 14b, points out that the verse only covers persons sold by others, the girl by her father and the man by the court, not the person who sells himself. *Sifry Deut.* 118 disputes the entire argument and holds that the female had to be mentioned separately from the male since the rules of her acquisition and liberation are distinct from those of the male. (E. g., the female cannot sell herself; the adult female cannot be a Hebrew slave.)

160 *Ex.* 21:11. Since after six years, or after she reached adulthood, she leaves without payment, it follows that her work was worth money; cf. Note 18.

161 *Ex.* 21:10 equates the marriage of the Hebrew slave girl to her master to the latter's marriage with another, free, woman. (Babli 16a; *Mechilta dR. Šimon b. Jochai*, ed. Epstein-Melamed, p. 167).

162 Except for texts based on *Lev.* For the intricacies of his position, cf. H. Guggenheimer, *Über ein bemerkenswertes logisches System aus der Antike*, Methodos 1951, pp. 150-164; *Logical Problems in Jewish Tradition*, in: Confrontations with Judaism, ed. Ph. Longworth, London 1966, pp. 171-196.

The problem before the rabbis of the second and third generations of Tannaïm was to derive a consistent legal system which intellectually could compete with the Roman law from the scattered remarks offered in the Biblical text. R. Ismael allows no more than one intermediate step between biblical text and legal statement.

163 The expression מָשַׁל is used in *Ex.* 21:2,5 in reference to the male Hebrew slave. In R. Ismael's opinion, the *ḥâruphah* slave girl is a former Gentile who needs manumission (Notes 147,148) and חֻפְשָׁה mentioned in *Lev.* 19:20 is her bill of manumission. Since the Gentile slave girl can be manumitted by a document, it is concluded that the Hebrew slave can be acquired by a document. As noted later, this is a *non sequitur*.

164 This translation follows the sentence structure of A.

165 Divorce, which requires a written document, is called "sending away" (of the wife) in *Deut.* 24:1. Therefore, the "sending away" of the Hebrew slave (*Deut.* 15:12,13) also refers to a written document. As noted immediately, this only would prove that the master can terminate the indenture by a written document, not that he could acquire the Hebrew's services by a document.

166 In A: "Rebbi said a *baraita*." This reading is preferable since a fifth-generation Amora is unlikely to appear in a Tannaïtic discussion.

167 In *Lev.* 25:42 it is stated that a Hebrew "shall not be sold as in the sale of a [Gentile] slave." In *Deut.* 15:12 it says, "If your Hebrew brother or sister be sold to you." It is an accepted principle (*Sifry Deut.* 72, Yerushalmi *Baba batra* 8:5 (16b), Babli *Temurah* 5a) that if the verse notes that "something shall not be done." if it is done it is sinful but legally valid since an invalid action does not have to be forbidden. Since the Gentile slave can be bought by contract (Mishnah 3), the Hebrew slave also can be bought by contract. The question remains whether he can be bought by contract without the buyer sinning.

168 Since the laws regarding Gentile slaves in general follow the rules of real estate, undisturbed possession for three years accompanied by a claim of rightful acquisition legally establishes ownership. Nobody claims that the same holds for Hebrew slaves.

169 A: R. Ḥiyya bar Abba (an Amora of the third generation). The reading of L is the only one acceptable, referring to R. Ḥiyya bar Ada I, of the generation of transition between Tannaïm and Amoraïm.

170 This essentially is the argument

(59a line 34) בְּכָסֶף. וְהָיָה כֶסֶף מִמְכָּרוֹ. בַּכֶּסֶף הוּא נִגְאָל וְאֵינוֹ נִגְעָל לֹא בַּתְּבוּאָה וְלֹא בַכֵּלִים. בְּכָל־אָתָר אַתְּ עָבֵד שָׁוֶה כֶסֶף כְּכֶסֶף. וְהָכָא לֵית אַתְּ עָבִיד שָׁוֶה כֶסֶף כְּכֶסֶף. אָמַר רִבִּי אַבָּא מָרִי. שַׁנְיָיא הִיא. שֶׁשָּׁנָה[171] עָלָיו הַכָּתוּב כֶּסֶף בְּכָסֶף. אוּף רִבִּי חִייָה בַּר אָדָא יוֹדֶה שֶׁאִם בִּיקֵּשׁ לִגְרוֹעַ. שֶׁמְּגָרֵעַ וְיוֹצֵא אֲפִילוּ בִתְבוּאָה וַאֲפִילוּ בְכֵלִים. אָמַר רִבִּי יוּדָן אָבוֹי דְרִבִּי מַתַּנְיָיה. הָדָא דְתֵימַר בְּשֶׁלֹּא עָשָׂאָן דָּמִים. אֲבָל אִם עֲשָׂאָן דָּמִים כְּכֶסֶף הוּא.

1 לא A - ‎ 3 שוה כסף ככסף A | כסף בשווה כסף שנייא A | שנייה ששנה A | ששינה ‎ 4 בכסף A | כסף אוף ר' חייה בר אדא יודה A | א' ר' חייה בר אדא שמגרע ויוצא A | מגרע ויצא ‎ 5 ואפי' A | אפי' הדא דתימר A | ההח דתמר

"By money". "The money of his sale price shall be;"[172] he can be redeemed by money, not by produce nor by vessels[173]. Everywhere you treat money's worth like money, but here you do not treat money's worth like money. Rebbi Abba Mari said, there is a difference, because the verse repeated "money, of money"[174]. Rebbi Ḥiyya bar Ada said[175], but if he wants to reduce, he can leave for the reduced amount even for produce, even for vessels[176]. Rebbi Yudan, Rebbi Mattaniah's father, said that this is only if he did not give them their money's worth[176]. But if he gave them their money's worth, it is like money.

171 In L the word is partially vocalized שִׁשָּׁנה, by the rules of grammar it should be שֶׁשָּׁנָה. The vocalization is intended to show that the translation should be "because it repeated", to exclude the reading of A (and uncorrected L) ששינה "because it changed".
172 Lev. 25:50, speaking of the redemption of a Hebrew slave from his Gentile master by his family.

173 Babli 8a, *Sifra Behar Pereq* 8(4).

174 The first כסף is from *Lev.* 25:50, the second (read מכסף for בכסף) *Lev.* 25:52, about the same subject. The repetition shows that the redemption can be forced only by payment in cash.

175 Text of A: א״ר חייא בר אדא preferred over L: "Even R. Ḥiyya bar Ada will agree."

176 The cash requirement applies only to redemption by his family. If the slave himself buys his freedom, he can offer valuables instead of money.

177 If the parties agree on a fixed monetary value for the objects given in payment, it counts as cash payment. In the Babli (8a, argument of Rav Joseph; 16a, a *baraita*) this is the interpretation of *Lev.* 25:52, against the Yerushalmi (Note 174).

(59a line 40) בִּשְׁטָר. רִבִּי אַבָּהוּ אָמַר. בִּשְׁטָר שֶׁלְּכֶסֶף. הָא בִשְׁטָר שֶׁל מַתָּנָה לֹא. שֶׁמָּא יַחֲזוֹר בּוֹ הֶעָבֶד. מֵעַתָּה אֲפִילוּ בִּשְׁטָר שֶׁלְּכֶסֶף יָכוֹל הוּא לַחֲזוֹר בּוֹ. אָמַר לוֹ. שֶׁמָּא תָבוֹא שְׁנַת רְעָבוֹן וְיַחֲזוֹר בּוֹ רַבּוֹ.

2 העבד A | בעבד   3 תבוא A | תבא

"By a document." Rebbi Abbahu said, by a money document[178]; therefore not by a gift document[179], since maybe he would renege. But then, could he not renege even with a money document? He said to him[180], maybe there comes a year of famine and his master reneges[181].

178 A written contract which promises the slave a fixed sum of money, presumably at the end of his period of service.

179 The slave agrees to serve without remuneration.

180 R. Abbahu to the person raising the question.

181 It is not a problem of the prospective slave's reneging, but his master's. If in a year of famine the cost of the slave's upkeep exceeds the value of his work, the master might be tempted to get rid of the slave. But if there is an IOU in the slave's hand, he can be sure to be kept for the full period. Therefore, with a money document the slave has the intent from the start to be acquired by the master.

(59a line 43) סֵדֶר מְכִירָה כָּךְ הוּא. אֲנִי פְלוֹנִי מָכַרְתִּי בִתִּי לִפְלוֹנִי. סֵדֶר קִידּוּשִׁין כָּךְ הוּא. אֲנִי פְלוֹנִי קִידַּשְׁתִּי בִתִּי לִפְלוֹנִי. רִבִּי חַגַּיי בְּעָא קוֹמֵי רִבִּי יוֹסֵי. הֶחֱלִיף וְאָמַר. אֲנִי פְלוֹנִי לָקַחְתִּי בִּתּוֹ שֶׁלִּפְלוֹנִי. אֲנִי פְלוֹנִי קִידַּשְׁתִּי בִּתּוֹ שֶׁלִּפְלוֹנִי. אָמַר לֵיהּ. וּמַה בְכָךְ. אֲבָל אִם הֶחֱלִיף לְשׁוֹן מְכִירָה בִּלְשׁוֹן קִידּוּשִׁים אוֹ לְשׁוֹן קִידּוּשִׁין בִּלְשׁוֹן מְכִירָה לֹא עָשָׂה כְּלוּם.

1 הוא A היא | לפלוני A' לפלני 2 הוא A היא 3 יוסי A יוסה 4 קידושים A קידושין

The order of sale[182] is the following: I X sold my daughter to Y. The order of preliminary marriage is the following: I X gave my daughter to Y in preliminary marriage. Rebbi Ḥaggai asked before Rebbi Yose: If he switched and said, I Y acquired X's daughter, I Y took X's daughter in preliminary marriage? He said to him, what is the difference[183]? But if he changed the language of sale to that of preliminary marriage or vice-versa, he did not do anything.

182 The required text in a contractual sale or marriage of an underage girl by her father. This is the only relevant case possible in law after the disestablishment of the Jubilee.

183 The marriage of the underage girl is purely a matter of contract between two adults; the girl is not involved and it does not matter which party writes the contract. This is in contrast to the marriage of an adult woman where a text "I, X, am taking you, Y, as preliminarily wedded wife" is valid, but "I, Y, am agreeing to be your, X's, preliminarily wedded wife" is invalid.

(59a line 48) כְּתִיב שֵׁשׁ שָׁנִים יַעֲבֹד. כֵּיצַד עוֹבֵד. יָכוֹל יוֹצֵא בְסוֹף שֵׁשׁ. תַּלְמוּד לוֹמַר וּבַשְּׁבִיעִית יֵצֵא. יָכוֹל יֵצֵא בְסוֹף שֶׁבַע. תַּלְמוּד לוֹמַר שֵׁשׁ שָׁנִים יַעֲבֹד. הָא כֵּיצַד. עוֹבֵד כָּל־שֵׁשׁ וְיוֹצֵא בִּתְחִילַּת שֶׁבַע. וּבַשְּׁבִיעִית יֵצֵא. שְׁבִיעִית שֶׁלַּמְּכִירָה לֹא שְׁבִיעִית שֶׁלָּעוֹלָם. אַתָּה אוֹמֵר. שְׁבִיעִית שֶׁלַּמְּכִירָה אוֹ אֵינָהּ אֶלָּא שְׁבִיעִית שֶׁלָּעוֹלָם. כְּשֶׁהוּא אוֹמֵר. שֵׁשׁ שָׁנִים יַעֲבֹד. הֲרֵי שֵׁשׁ שָׁנִים אֲמוּרוֹת. הָא מָה אֲנִי

מְקַיְּיֵם וּבַשְּׁבִיעִית יֵצֵא. שְׁבִיעִית שֶׁלַּמְּכִירָה לֹא שְׁבִיעִית שֶׁלְּעוֹלָם. אֵימָא חֲלִיף. אָמַר רִבִּי זְעִירָא בְשֵׁם רַב הוּנָא. וּבַשְּׁבִיעִית וּבַשְּׁבִיעִית כָּתַב. אָמַר רִבִּי חוּנָה. אִם אוֹמֵר אַתְּ. שְׁבִיעִית שֶׁלַּ184 עוֹלָם. אִם כֵּן מָה הַיּוֹבֵל בָּא וּמוֹצִיא. אָמַר רִבִּי יוֹחָנָן בַּר מַרְיָיה. אַתְיָיא כְּמָאן דְּאָמַר. אֵין הַיּוֹבֵל עוֹלֶה מִמִּנְיָין שְׁנֵי שָׁבוּעַ. בְּרַם כְּמָאן דְּאָמַר. הַיּוֹבֵל עוֹלֶה מִמִּנְיָין שְׁנֵי שָׁבוּעַ. פְּעָמִים שֶׁהוּא בָא בְּאֶמְצַע שְׁנֵי שָׁבוּעַ. רַבָּנִין דְּקַיְסָרִין אָמְרִין. אֲפִילוּ כְּמָאן דְּאָמַר. הַיּוֹבֵל עוֹלֶה מִמִּנְיָין שְׁנֵי שָׁבוּעַ יָכְלִין אֲנָן מַפְקִין לָהּ מִן הָכָא. שְׁבִיעִית מוֹצִיאָה אֶת הָעֲבָדִים וְיוֹבֵל אֶת הַנִּרְצָעִים.

1 יעבוד A | תעבד. הא יכול יוצא A | כל שש 2 הא A | - 4 לא A | ולא 5 כשהוא A | ומה שהוא יעבד A | יעבד 6 יצא A | יצא לחפשי לא A | ולא אימא חליף A | או חילוף 7 אמ' ר' זעירא A | ר' זעירה הונא A | הונה 9 אתייא A | אתייה ממניין A | ממיניין 10 ממניין A | ממיניין 11 אמרין A | אמרי 13 את A | מוציא את

It is written: "Six years he shall work[135]." How much does he work? I could think that he leaves at the end of six [years]. The verse says, "and in the seventh he shall leave[185]." I could think that he leave at the end of seven [years][186]. The verse says, "six years he shall work." How is that? He works the entire six and leaves at the start of the seventh. "And in the seventh he shall leave." The seventh from the sale and not the Seventh of the world[187]. Do you say, the seventh from the sale and not the Seventh of the world? Since it says, "six years he shall work," this spells out six years. How can I confirm "and in the seventh he shall leave?" The seventh from the sale and not the Seventh of the world. Say it is the opposite. Rebbi Ze'ira said in the name of Rav Huna: It is written: "and in the seventh," "and in the seventh[188]". Rebbi Huna said, if you say, in the Seventh of the world, what would the Jubilee free[189]? Rebbi Johanan bar Marius said, this follows him who said that the Jubilee does not become part of a Sabbatical period[190]. But following him who said that the Jubilee becomes part of a Sabbatical period, sometimes it falls in the middle of a Sabbatical period[191]. The rabbis of Caesarea say, even following him who said that the Jubilee becomes part of a Sabbatical period, we could deduce from here that the Sabbatical year frees the slaves and the Jubilee the pierced ones[192].

---

184 Vocalization of the ms. (As usual in Medieval European texts, *pataḥ* takes the place of *qāmaṣ*)

185 *Ex.* 21:2.

186 In *Mekhilta dR. Šim'on b. Jochai* (ed. Epstein-Melamed) p. 160 the argument is made that the slave should leave only at the end of the year since debts are remitted only at the end of the Sabbatical. A similar argument is presupposed here.

187 The Sabbatical year. *Mekhilta dR. Ismael* (ed. Horovitz-Rabin p. 249).

188 It seems that the correct interpretation is the one given by *Qorban Ha'edah*: One has to read the word וּבַשְּׁבִיעִת as if it were written twice with two different meanings. "Six years he shall work, including the Sabbatical; but in the seventh he shall leave."

189 Since the 49th year of a cycle is a Sabbatical, if the slaves left then, nobody would be freed in the 50th, the Jubilee.

190 The Sabbatical period following the first Jubilee starts only in year 51; there is a Jubilee in every year which is a multiple of 50 in the Jubilee calendar; Babli *Nedarim* 61a. This is the calendar also underlying the Saducee Jubilee.

191 Since year 49 was a Sabbatical, the next Sabbatical is in year 55, and the next Jubilee in year 100 is in year 2 of the Sabbatical cycle. The Jubilee in year $n\cdot 50$ falls on year n (mod 7) of a Sabbatical cycle, it will eventually fall on any of the years of the cycle.

192 The preceding argument cannot be used to prove that the "seventh' mentioned in the verse is not the Sabbatical; the argument at the start of the paragraph is the only valid one. (The emendation of this sentence by the classical commentaries has to be rejected since the text is confirmed by A.)

HALAKHAH 2

(59ᵉ line 62) מִנַּיִין אֲפִילוּ חָלָה. תַּלְמוּד לוֹמַר וּבַשְּׁבִיעִית יֵצֵא לַחָפְשִׁי חִנָּם. יָכוֹל אֲפִילוּ בָּרַח. תַּלְמוּד לוֹמַר שֵׁשׁ שָׁנִים יַעֲבֹד. מָה רָאִיתָ לְרַבּוֹת אֶת זֶה וּלְהוֹצִיא אֶת זֶה. אַחַר שֶׁרִיבָּה הַכָּתוּב מִיעֵט. מַרְבֶּה אֲנִי אֶת זֶה שֶׁהוּא בִרְשׁוּתוֹ וּמוֹצִיא אֶת זֶה שֶׁאֵינוֹ בִרְשׁוּתוֹ. רִבִּי בּוּן בַּר חִיָּיה אָמַר. רַב הוֹשַׁעְיָה בְּעָא. נִיחָא חָלָה וְאַחַר כָּךְ בָּרַח בָּרִיךְ מַשְׁלֵם. בָּרַח וְאַחַר כָּךְ חָלָה. אָמַר רִבִּי חִיָּיה בַּר אָדָא. נִישְׁמְעִינָהּ מִן הָדָא. הַמּוֹרֶדֶת עַל בַּעֲלָהּ כּוֹתְבִין לוֹ אִיגֶּרֶת מֶרֶד עַל כְּתוּבָּתָהּ. וְהִתְנֵי רִבִּי חִיָּיה נִדָּה וַחוֹלָה וַאֲרוּסָה וְשׁוֹמֶרֶת יָבָם כּוֹתְבִין לוֹ אִיגֶּרֶת מֶרֶד עַל כְּתוּבָּתָהּ. מָה אֲנָן קַייָמִין. אִם בְּשֶׁמֶּרְדָה עָלָיו וְהִיא נִידָה. הַתּוֹרָה הִמְרִידָתָהּ עָלָיו. אֶלָּא כֵן אֲנָן קַייָמִין בְּשֶׁמֶּרְדָה עָלָיו עַד שֶׁלֹּא בָּאת נִידָה וּבָאת לַנִידָה. הֲרֵי אֵינָהּ רְאוּיָה לִמְרוֹד וְאַתְּ אוֹמֵר. כּוֹתֵב. אַף הָכָא בָּרַח וְאַחַר כָּךְ חָלָה מַשְׁלֵם. דּוּ יָכִיל מֵימַר לֵיהּ. אִילּוּ הֲוֵית גַּבַּאי לָא אַבְאֲשָׁתָא. אָמַר רִבִּי חִינְנָא. אֲפִילוּ עַל קַדְמִיתָא אַתְיָיא הִיא. חָלָה וְאַחַר כָּךְ בָּרַח מַשְׁלֵם. דּוּ יָכִיל מֵימַר לֵיהּ. אִילּוּ הֲוֵיתָה גַּבַּאי אִינְשַׁמַּת בְּפָרִיעַ.

2 יעבד A | יעבוד 4 בעא A | בעה ניחא A | ניחה 7 התתני A | הא תני נדה A נידה ארוסה A | וארוסה 9 נידה A | לנידה 10 אף A | אוף 11 ליה A | לית הוית גבאי A | החויתה גב אבאשתא A | איבאשתא חינא A | חננא 13 גבאי A | לגבי אינשמת בפריע A | אי נשמתה בו פריע

From where even if he fell ill¹⁹³? The verse says¹⁸⁵, "in the seventh year he shall leave into freedom gratis." I could think, even if he fled; the verse says¹⁸⁵, "six years he shall work.¹⁹⁴" What did you see to include this and to exclude that? After the verse included, it excluded. I am including the one who remains in his power and am exluding the one who is not in his power. Rebbi Abun bar Ḥiyya said that Rav Hoshaia asked: I understand that if he fell ill and fled afterwards, he has to make up [the time lost]. If he fled and then fell ill? Rebbi Ḥiyya bar Ada said, let us hear from the following: "If a woman rebels against her husband, one writes him a bill of rebellion on her *ketubah*."¹⁹⁵ And Rebbi Ḥiyya stated:

One writes a bill of rebellion on the *ketubah* of a menstruating woman or a sick one, a preliminarily married one and one waiting for her levir[196]. Where do we hold? If she rebelled against him while she was menstruating, the Torah instructed her to rebel[197]. But we must hold that she rebelled when she was not menstruating and then started menstruating. Here she is unable to rebel, nevertheless you say, one writes[198]. Here also, if he rebelled and then fell ill he has to make up. For he can say to him, if you had stayed with me, you would not have become sick. Rebbi Ḥinena said, that argument even works in the first case. If he fell ill and fled afterwards[199], he has to make up, since he can say to him, if you had stayed with me, you would have recuperated sooner.

193 He could not work the entire six years. Nevertheless, he leaves on time. The same argument in the Babli, 17a. In *Mekhilta dR. Šim'on b. Jochai*, p. 161, the word "gratis" is interpreted to mean that the master has no regress on the slave for his medical costs.

194 Babli 16b; *Massekhet 'Avadim* 1.

195 A rewording of Mishnah *Ketubot* 5:9, Notes 199-100. The wife refuses marital relations with her husband; the court deducts from her future claim of *ketubah*.

196 *Ketubot* 5:10, Babli *Ketubot* 63b.

197 Since sexual relations with menstruating women are forbidden.

198 Once she refused marital relations, one fines her by reducing the sum due from her *ketubah* the entire time she had no relations, irrespective of the cause. By analogy, the runaway slave has to make up the time lost, including the time he was ill and could not have worked while in his master's house.

199 If he was ill when he fled, he has to make up even the times of his sickness.

(59a line 76) וְקוֹנֶה אֶת עַצְמוֹ בַּשָּׁנִים. אִית תַּנָּיֵי תַּנֵּי. נִמְכָּר בְּפָחוֹת מִשֵּׁשׁ וְאֵינוֹ נִמְכָּר יוֹתֵר עַל שֵׁשׁ. וְאִית תַּנָּיֵי תַּנֵּי. אֵינוֹ נִמְכָּר לֹא בְּפָחוֹת מִשֵּׁשׁ וְלֹא יוֹתֵר

HALAKHAH 2

(עַל)²⁰⁰ שֶׁבַע. אָמַר רִבִּי יִרְמְיָה. טַעֲמֵיהּ דְּהָדֵין תַּנָּיָיא פְּעָמִים שְׁתַּיִם אוֹ שָׁלֹשׁ שָׁנִים לִפְנֵי הַיּוֹבֵל וְהַיּוֹבֵל בָּא ומוציאו עַל כָּרְחוֹ.

1 תניי A | תני   2 תנייא A | תני   יותר על A | יתר

"He regains his autonomy by years." Some *Tannaïm* state: He may be sold for less than six [years], but he cannot be sold for more than six. But some *Tannaïm* state: He may not be sold for less than six [years] or more than to [year] seven. Rebbi Jeremiah said, the reason of that Tanna: Sometimes he is sold two or three years before the Jubilee; then the Jubilee arrives and frees him automatically²⁰¹.

200 Word missing in A. If the word is accepted in the text, "seven" would have to be corrected to "six." But the reading "seven" is confirmed by A.

201 Even though formally he was sold for six years. Babli 15a; *Sifra Behar Pereq* 7(4) in the name of the Tanna R. Eliezer ben Jacob.

(59b line 4) וּבַיּוֹבֵל. דִּכְתִיב וּבַיּוֹבֵל יֵצֵא. וּבְגִרְעוֹן כָּסֶף. דִּכְתִיב אִם עוֹד רַבּוֹת בַּשָּׁנִים. וְאִם מְעַט נִשְׁאַר בַּשָּׁנִים. וְכִי אֵין אָנוּ יוֹדְעִין שֶׁאִם יֵשׁ רוֹב אֵין מִיעוּט. שֶׁאִם יֵשׁ מִיעוּט אֵין רוֹב. אָמַר רִבִּי הִילָא. פְּעָמִים שֶׁהַשָּׁנִים מְרוּבּוֹת עַל הַשָּׂכָר. וּפְעָמִים שֶׁהַשָּׁנִים מְעוּטוֹת מִן הַשָּׂכָר. מִנַיִין אַתָּה אוֹמֵר. נִמְכַּר מִמֶּנָּה מָנֶה וְהִשְׁבִּיחַ וַהֲרֵי הוּא יָפֶה מִמָּאתַיִם מָאתָיִם. מִנַיִין שֶׁאֵינוֹ מְחַשֵּׁב עִמּוֹ אֶלָּא מִמֶּנָּה מָנֶה. תַּלְמוּד לוֹמַר כְּפִי שָׁנָיו יָשִׁיב אֶת גְּאוּלָּתוֹ. לָמַדְנוּ בְּנִמְכַּר לְגוֹי כְּשֶׁהוּא נִגְאָל יָדוֹ לָעֶלְיוֹנָה. מִנַיִין בְּנִמְכַּר לְיִשְׂרָאֵל כְּשֶׁהוּא נִגְאָל יָדוֹ לָעֶלְיוֹנָה. שָׂכִיר שָׂכִיר לִגְזֵירָה שָׁוָה. מַה שָׂכִיר הָאָמוּר לְגוֹי כְּשֶׁהוּא נִגְאָל יָדוֹ לָעֶלְיוֹנָה. אַף שָׂכִיר הָאָמוּר לְיִשְׂרָאֵל כְּשֶׁהוּא נִגְאָל יָדוֹ לָעֶלְיוֹנָה. רִבִּי אוֹמֵר. מַה תַּלְמוּד לוֹמַר. יִגְאָלֶנּוּ יִגְאָלֶנּוּ שְׁלֹשָׁה פְּעָמִים. לְרַבּוֹת כָּל־הַגְּאוּלוֹת שֶׁיְּהוּ כְּסֵדֶר הַזֶּה.

2 יודעק A | יודעים   4 מנה A -   5 מאתים A -   מנה A -   6 בנמכר A כשנמכר   8 אף שכיר האמור ליש׳ כשהוא נגאל ידו לעליונה | A -   9 יגאלנו יגאלנו | A יגאלינו יגאלנו

"Or the Jubilee," as it is written, "in the Jubilee he shall leave."[202] "Or reduction of the amount," as it is written: "If there still are many years[203]." Do we not know that if there are many there are not few, and if there are few there are not many? Rebbi Hila said, sometimes the years are worth more than the wages, sometimes the wages are worth more than the years. How do you explain the following? If he was sold for a *mina*[204] each and improved so that now he is worth 200 each, from where that one computes for him only by a *mina* each? The verse says, "according to the years he shall compute his redemption[205]." We learned that one sold to a Gentile is advantaged[206] when he comes to be redeemed. From where that one sold to an Israel is advantaged when he comes to be redeemed? "Hireling, hireling"[207] for an equal cut. Since the hireling is advantaged in redemption when he is sold to a Gentile, so too the hireling is advantaged in redemption when he is sold to an Israel. Rebbi says, why does the verse say "he shall be redeemed, he shall be redeemed," three times? To add all redemptions that they have to follow this order[209].

202 *Lev.* 25:31. This quote does not make sense since it refers to real estate transactions. The correct quotes are *Lev.* 25:40 for the slave sold to an Israel and *Lev.* 25:53 for the one sold to a Gentile. Babli 16a.

203 *Lev.* 25:51-52; *Sifra Behar Pereq* 8(5). The biblical text is unusually wordy, stating that the redemption price is high if many years of service remain and low if few years remain.

204 The Greek Μνᾶ of 100 drachmas each, not the Babylonian מָנֶה of 60 *šeqel*.

205 *Lev.* 25:52. In the Babli 20a and *'Arakhin* 30a, the proof is from v. 51: "He shall compute the amount of his redemption from the amount for which he was bought." There is an additional text: From where that if he was sold for 200 denars each but now he is worth only a *mina*, one computes a

mina per year, the verse says "according to the years he shall compute his redemption." If this passage also was in the Yerushalmi text, it must have disappeared already from the common source of A and L.

206   In that his redemption price is determined by law from the original sale price; there can be no haggling over the amount.

207   The slave has to be treated like a hireling; *Lev.* 25:53 for the one sold to a Gentile, *Lev.* 25:40 for the one sold to an Israel *Sifra Behar Pereq* 8(6).

208   *Lev.* 25:48 once, v. 49 twice. The entire list of relatives who might force a redemption on an unwilling master could have been written in one sentence.

209   *Sifra Behar Pereq* 8(3), an anonymous statement.

(59b line 15) וְאִם לֹא יִגָּאֵל בְּאֵלֶּה. רִבִּי יוֹסֵי הַגָּלִילִי אוֹמֵר. בְּאֵלֶּה לְשִׁחְרוּר וּבִשְׁאַר כָּל־אָדָם לְשִׁיעְבּוּד. רִבִּי עֲקִיבָה אוֹמֵר. בְּאֵלֶּה לְשִׁיעְבּוּד וּבִשְׁאַר כָּל־אָדָם לְשִׁיחְרוּר. רִבִּי אַבָּהוּ בְשֵׁם רִבִּי יוֹחָנָן. וּשְׁנֵיהֶן בְּמִקְרָא אֶחָד דּוֹרְשִׁין וְאִם לֹא יִגָּאֵל בְּאֵלֶּה. רִבִּי יוֹסֵי הַגָּלִילִי דָּרִישׁ. וְאִם לֹא יִגָּאֵל בְּאֵלֶּה אֶלָּא בָּאֲחֵרִים מְשַׁעְבֵּד וְיוֹצֵא. רִבִּי עֲקִיבָה דָּרִישׁ. וְאִם לֹא יִגָּאֵל בְּאֵלֶּה אֶלָּא בְיוֹצֵא מַשְׁלִים וְיוֹצֵא. דִּבְרֵי חֲכָמִים. רִבִּי יָסָא בְשֵׁם רִבִּי יוֹחָנָן. בֵּין זֶה וּבֵין זֶה לְשִׁחְרוּר. וְתַנֵּי כֵן. וְהִשִּׁיגָה יָדוֹ. יַד עַצְמוֹ. וּמָצָא כְּדֵי גְאוּלָּתוֹ. מַה הַשָּׁגַת יָד שֶׁלְּעַצְמוֹ אַף הַשָּׁגַת יְדֵי אֲחֵרִים לְעַצְמוֹ.

1 יוסי A | יוסה   2 עקיבר A | עקיבא   3 ושניהן A | ושניהם   4 יוסי A | יוסה
5 אלא ביוצא A | באלה   8 לעצמו A | לעצמן

"If he be not redeemed by these[210]." [211]Rebbi Yose the Galilean says, by these to freedom, by all others to servitude[212]. Rebbi Aqiba says, by these to servitude, by all others to freedom. Rebbi Abbahu in the name of Rebbi Johanan: Both interpret the same verse: "Unless he be redeemed by these." Rebbi Yose the Galilean interprets: "Unless he be redeemed by these" but by others he is made to serve before he leaves[213]. Rebbi Aqiba interprets: "Unless he be redeemed by these", by these he completes[213a] before he leaves. The words of the Sages? Rebbi Yasa[214] in the name of Rebbi Joḥanan: In both cases to freedom[215]. It was stated thus: "If his hand achieves,[216]" his own hand[217]. "Or he found for *his* redemption[216]." Since his own hand achieves for himself, what others achieve also is for himself.

210   Lev. 25:54.

211   Babli 15b, *Sifra Behar Pereq* 9(1).

212   "These" are the family members mentioned in vv. 48-49, who are required to buy him back from the Gentile. If he is bought from the Gentile by an unrelated Jew, he has to serve as a Hebrew slave either for six years or until the Jubilee,

213   The verse reads: "Unless he be redeemed by these, he leaves in the Jubilee year." If "these" are the modalities of redemption detailed in vv. 48-52, then the meaning is that the Hebrew slave of the Gentile leaves his service in the Jubilee year. But if "these" are persons, then there must be a case when the slave is redeemed from the Gentile and nevertheless has to serve until the Jubilee.

213a   The translation follows A.

214   In the Babli: R. Ḥiyya bar Abba.

215   They read "these" as the modalities of his redemption, Note 213.

216   Lev. 25:26, referring to the right of a farmer to buy back his ancestral land for the prorated price the buyer had paid.

217   *Sifra Behar Pereq* 5(2).

(59b line 23) רִבִּי יַעֲקֹב בַּר אָחָא בְּשֵׁם רִבִּי יוֹחָנָן. כְּדִבְרֵי מִי שֶׁאוֹמֵר לְשִׁיעְבּוּד מֻשְׁלָם וְיוֹצֵא. וְהָתַנֵּי. אִם מִשֶּׁגְּאָלוֹ הֲרֵי כְנִמְכָּר לוֹ מְשֻׁעְבָּד וְיוֹצֵא. אָמַר רִבִּי אַבָּא מָרִי. לֵית כָּאן מְשֻׁעְבָּד וְיוֹצֵא אֶלָּא מַשְׁלִים וְיוֹצֵא. רָצוּ קְרוֹבָיו שֶׁלָּרִאשׁוֹן לִיגָּאֵל גּוֹאֲלִין לָהֶן. רָצוּ קְרוֹבָיו שֶׁלַּשֵּׁנִי לִיגָּאֵל אֵין גּוֹאֲלִים לָהֶם. רִבִּי יָסָא בְּשֵׁם רִבִּי יוֹחָנָן. אָתְיָיא כְּמָאן דְּאָמַר. בְּאֵלֶּה לְשִׁחְרוּר וּבִשְׁאָר כָּל־אָדָם לְשִׁיעְבּוּד.

1 כדברי | A ברי   לשיעבוד | A לשעבר ? לשעבד ?   2 כנמכר | A כנמר   4 ליגאל גואלין להן | A הגאל מגאילין לחם   ליגאל | A להיגאל   גואלים | A מגאילין   5

HALAKHAH 2

אתייא A | אתייה

Rebbi Jacob bar Aḥa in the name of Rebbi Joḥanan: Following him, who said "for servitude"[218], he makes up before he leaves[219]. But was it not stated: After he redeemed him it is as if he were sold to him, he enslaves him before he leaves[220]. Rebbi Abba Mari said, there is no "enslaves him before he leaves", only "he makes up before he leaves." If his relatives want to redeem him from the first [master's], they redeem. If his relatives want to redeem him[221] from the second [master's], they cannot redeem[222]. Rebbi Yose in the name of Rebbi Joḥanan: That follows him[223] who said: "by these to freedom, by all others to servitude."

218 Either R. Yose the Galilean or R. Aqiba.

219 He serves until the Jubilee or until he has served a total of six years.

220 This seems to mean that he has to serve the Jew who buys him a full six years, irrespective of how long he served the Gentile.

221 It would be reasonable to vocalize active לִגְאֹל but ms. A clearly reads niph'al לְהִגָּאֵל. Yerushalmi Hebrew usually avoids qal, replacing it in general by pi'el, sometimes by niph'al.

222 There is no verse authorizing the premature release of a Hebrew slave from a Hebrew master.

223 R. Yose the Galilean; but the authorized interpretation is that of the Sages.

(59b line 28) שְׁמוּאֵל בַּר אַבָּא בְּעָא קוֹמֵי רִבִּי יָסָא. הָכָא כְּתִיב וְחִשַּׁב וְהָכָא כְּתִיב וְחִשַּׁב. הָכָא אַתְּ מְחַשֵּׁב חֳדָשִׁים וְשָׁנִים וְיוֹצֵא. וְהָכָא לֵית אַתְּ מְחַשֵּׁב חֳדָשִׁים וְשָׁנִים וְיוֹצֵא. אֲמַר לֵיהּ. שַׁנְיָא הִיא. שֶׁהִקְשִׁיתָהּ תּוֹרָה לִשְׂכִיר. מַה זֶּה מְחַשֵּׁב חֳדָשִׁים וְשָׁנִים וְיוֹצֵא אַף זֶה מְחַשֵּׁב חֳדָשִׁים וְשָׁנִים וְיוֹצֵא.

1 והכא A | ולהלן   2 הכא A | הכה   והכא לית את מחשב חדשים ויוצא A | -   3 שהקשיתה A | הקישתו   תורה A | התירה

Samuel bar Abba asked before Rebbi Yose: There it is written "he computes" and here it is written "he computes"[224]. Here you compute months and years so he may leave, there you do not compute months and years so he may leave. He said to him, the difference is that the Torah compared him to the hireling[225]. Since the latter computes months and years and leaves, so this one computes months and years and leaves.

224 The person who sells of his ancestral property until the Jubilee "computes the years of sale" when he buys the property back (*Lev.* 25:27). Since sale of agricultural property is a sale of harvests (*Lev.* 25:15) it is clear that the right of redemption can be exercised only between harvest and the next sowing. Only full years are counted. But the redemption of the Hebrew slave of a Gentile is possible at all times and, therefore, the amount due changes every month.

225 *Lev.* 25:53, even though the verse refers to "a hireling on a yearly contract."

(59b line 32) וְיָצְאָה חִנָּם. אֵילוּ יְמֵי הַבַּגְרוּת. אֵין כָּסֶף. אֵילוּ הַסִּימָנִין. וְיֹאמַר בְּאַחַת מֵהֶם. אֵילוּ נֶאֱמַר בְּאַחַת מֵהֶן הָיִיתִי אוֹמֵר. אִם בְּסִימָנִים הִיא יוֹצְאָה לֹא כָּל־שֶׁכֵּן בִּימוֹת הַבֶּגֶר. אֵילוּ כֵן הָיִיתִי אוֹמֵר. הֵן הֵן יְמוֹת הַבֶּגֶר. וְהַדִּין נוֹתֵן. הוֹאִיל וְהִיא יוֹצְאָה מֵרְשׁוּת הָאָב וְיוֹצְאָה מֵרְשׁוּת הָאָדוֹן. מַה מֵּרְשׁוּת הָאָב אֵינָהּ יוֹצְאָה אֶלָּא בְסִימָנִין. אַף מֵרְשׁוּת הָאָדוֹן לֹא תֵצֵא אֶלָּא בְסִימָנִין. לְפוּם כָּךְ צָרַךְ מֵימַר. וְיָצְאָה חִנָּם. אֵילוּ יְמֵי הַבֶּגֶר. אֵין כָּסֶף. אֵילוּ הַסִּימָנִין. אוֹ חֲלִיף. רִבִּי תַנְחוּמָא בְּשֵׁם רִבִּי חוּנָה. אֵין כָּסֶף. בְּכָל־מָקוֹם שֶׁיֵּשׁ כֶּסֶף לָאָב אֵין כֶּסֶף לָאָדוֹן.

2 באחת A | כאחת אילו נא' באחת מהן | A - | אם בסימנים A | בסימנין 3 הבגר | A הבגרים 6 ימי A | ימות 7 חליף A | חילוף תנחומא A | תנחומה

[226]"She leaves gratis,[227]" these are the days of adulthood[228]; "without money[227]," these are the indicators [of adolescence.] Could He not have mentioned only one of them[229]? If only one of them were mentioned,

would I not have said that if she leaves with indicators [of adolescence], then certainly in the days of adulthood? But in that case I would have said that they are identical with the days of adulthood. Would this not be logical? She is emancipated from the power of the father and she is emancipated from the power of the master; since she is emancipated from the power of the father by some indicators [of adulthood][230], she is emancipated from the power of the master by the same indicators. Therefore, it was necessary to say, "she leaves gratis," these are the days of adulthood, "without money," these are the indicators [of adolescence.] Or maybe the other way around? Rebbi Tanḥuma in the name of Rebbi Huna: "Without money." At a place where there is money for the father, there is no money for the master[231].

---

226   *Mekhilta dR. Ismael, Neziqin* 3; *Mekhilta dR. Šim'on b. Jocḥai* p. 168; *Midrash Wehizhir Mišpaṭim* p. 130; alluded to in Babli *Qiddušin* 4a.

227   *Ex.* 21:11. Here starts the discussion of the rules for the girl sold by her father.

228   The indicators of adolescence are two pubic hairs after the girl has reached the age of 12 years and one day (cf. *Nedarim* 10:1, Note 1.) An adolescent is legally responsible for her actions but still under her father's authority (cf. *Yebamot* 1:2, Note 159). She becomes an independent adult six months after becoming an adolescent. (A male becomes an adult only at age 13 years and one day if he did grow two pubic hairs.) Since the adult girl is not under her father's authority, she cannot be under the authority of a master to whom she was given by her father even though she remains legally married by biblical standards if she was married off by her father when underage or adolescent. The double expression in the verse is taken to mean that the master's authority ends when she reaches the stage of adolescent.

229   When the text of the laws was given to Moses.

230   It would be reasonable to emend סימנין to בגר to keep unity of style

(*Qorban Ha'edah*), but A confirms the text as it stands.

231 Babli *Ketubot* 46b, as proof that the father retains the right to marry off his daughter and pocket the valuables offered for the preliminary marriage, even though the master's authority already expired at the girl's adolescence.

(59b line 32) אֲשֶׁר לֹא יְעָדָהּ וְהֶפְדָּהּ. מְלַמֵּד שֶׁאֵינוֹ מִיָּעֲדָהּ לוֹ עַד שֶׁיְּהֵא בַּיּוֹם כְּדֵי לִפְדּוֹתָהּ וּבְמַעֲשֵׂה יָדֶיהָ שָׁוֶה פְרוּטָה וּבְגֵירוּעֶיהָ שָׁוֶה פְרוּטָה. דִּבְרֵי רִבִּי יוֹסֵי בֵּירִבִּי יְהוּדָה. וַחֲכָמִים אוֹמְרִים. מִיָּעֵד וְהוֹלֵךְ עַד דְּמִדּוּמֵי חַמָּה. אָמַר רִבִּי חִייָה בַּר אָדָא. הַכֹּל מוֹדִין בְּעֶבֶד עִבְרִי עַד שֶׁיְּהֵא שָׁם שָׁוֶה פְרוּטָה. יָאוּת אָמַר רִבִּי יוֹסֵי בֵּירִבִּי יְהוּדָה. מַה טַעֲמוֹן דְּרַבָּנִין. כֶּסֶף אֵין כָּאן מַעֲשֵׂה יָדַיִם אֵין כָּאן. בַּמֶּה הוּא מִיָּעֲדָהּ. אָמַר רִבִּי זְעִירָא. מִיָּעֲדָהּ בִּדְבָרִים.

1 לא A | לו   2 כדי A | כדי שהות   ובגירועיה A | ובגירועית   3 יוסי ביר' A | יוסה בר   עד A | אפילו עד   4 אדא A | אבא   מודין A | מודים   5 יוסי ביר' A | יוסה בר   6 מייעדה A | מיעדה (twice)   זעירא A | זעירה

"If he did not allot her, he must let her be redeemed[232]." This teaches that he cannot allot her for himself unless there is time for her handywork to be worth a *perutah* and that a *perutah* be left to be deducted, the words of Rebbi Yose ben Rebbi Jehudah[233]. But the Sages say, he allots any time until sundown[234]. Rebbi Ḥiyya bar Ada[235] said, everybody agrees that for a Hebrew slave only if a *perutah*'s worth is left. Rebbi Yose ben Rebbi Jehudah says it correctly, what is the rabbis' reason? There is no money left, there is no handiwork left? Rebbi Ze'ira said, he allots her by speech[236].

232 *Ex.* 21:8. *Mekhilta dR. Šim'on b. Jochai* p. 166; Babli 19a. "Allotment" is the legal term for the preliminary marriage of the slave girl to her master or his son.

233 If he wants to marry her but first extract the maximum of work from the girl, he must divide the money

he paid by the number of days of her prospective servitude and marry her as long as at least a *peruṭah* is not worked off by her. (Since she works at most 6 years, at most 2190 days, if the buying price was at least 11.5 denars he can marry her early on the last day of her servitude.)

234 On the last day of her servitude;
Babli 19b.

235 In A: "Abba". Cf. Note 169.

236 The money he paid to the father was *not* given for preliminary marriage but to acquire the right to make her his wife by declaration (Interpretation of Maimonides; cf. S. Z. Brauda, בגדרי יעוד, *Moriah* 23 fasc. 6-7, 2000, p. 100-107.)

(59b line 46) תַּנִּי רִבִּי הוֹשַׁעְיָה. כֵּיצַד הוּא מִייַעֲדָהּ. אוֹמֵר לָהּ בִּפְנֵי שְׁנַיִם. הֲרֵי אַתְּ מְיוּעֶדֶת לִי. עַל דַּעְתֵּיהּ דְּרִבִּי יוֹסֵי בֵּירִבִּי יְהוּדָה בְּסוֹף נוֹתֵן לָהּ כֶּסֶף לִייעוּדִים. עַל דַּעְתּוֹן דְּרַבָּנִין מִשָּׁעָה רִאשׁוֹנָה נִיתַּן כֶּסֶף לִייעוּדִים. מַה נַּפְקָא מִבֵּינֵיהוֹן. מַעֲשֵׂה יָדֶיהָ. מָאן דְּאָמַר. בְּסוֹף נָתַן לָהּ כֶּסֶף שֶׁלִּייעוּדִים. מַעֲשֵׂה יָדֶיהָ שֶׁלְּבַעְלָהּ. מָאן דְּאָמַר. מִשָּׁעָה רִאשׁוֹנָה נִיתַּן כֶּסֶף לִייעוּדִים. מַעֲשֵׂה יָדֶיהָ שֶׁלְּאָבִיהָ. אֲפִילוּ כְּמָאן דְּאָמַר. מִשָּׁעָה רִאשׁוֹנָה נִיתַּן כֶּסֶף לִייעוּדִים. מַעֲשֵׂה יָדֶיהָ שֶׁלְּבַעְלָהּ. נַעֲשֶׂה כְּאוֹמֵר לְאִשָּׁה. הֲרֵי אַתְּ מְקוּדֶּשֶׁת לִי עַל מְנָת שֶׁמַּעֲשֵׂה יָדַיִיךְ שֶׁלִּי.

2 יוסי ביר׳ | A יוסה בר   3 לייעודים | A ליעודים   ניתן | A נותן   מה נפקא מביניהון. מעשה ידיה. מאן דאמ׳. בסוף נתן לה כסף לייעודים | A -   5 לייעודים | A של ייעודים   7 שמעשה | A מעשה

Rebbi Hoshaia stated: How does he allot her? He tells her in front of two [witnesses] "You are allotted to me.[237]" In Rebbi Yose ben Rebbi Jehudah's opinion, he gives her[238] money for the allotment at the end. In the rabbis' opinion, the money for allotment was given at the first hour[239]. What is the difference between them? Her earning power. For him who says, he gives her money for the allotment at the end, her earning power belongs to her husband[240]. For him who says, the money for allotment was given at the first hour, her earning power belongs to her father[241].

Even for him who says, the money for allotment was given at the first hour, her earning power belongs to her husband. It is as if he said: "You are preliminarily married to me on condition that your earning power belong to me.242"

237 Babli 19b, an anonymous tannaïtic statement. Since "allotment" legally is preliminary marriage, it has to follow the latter's formal rules.

238 This word, לָהּ, is correctly missing in A and in the quote of this passage in Rashba's *Novellae* to Qiddušin, 19b. The money was not given to her but to her father.

239 At the moment of the original sale.

240 From the moment of "allotment", she has to be treated as fiancee and can no longer be used as a slave. But anything she completed before this moment rightfully belongs to her master who now is her husband, since he paid for it.

241 Since it turns out that the money was not given for her work but for *qiddušin*, the father should have the right to claim the proceeds of anything she earned during her years of servitude, since the earnings of the daughter belong to the father until either she is married or becomes an adult (*Ketubot* 4:2, Note 30). That would create an impossible situation.

242 The father, by agreeing to the sale, agreed to the stipulation.

(59b line 53) הָיָה נָשׂוּי אֶת אֲחוֹתָהּ וּמֵתָה. מָאן דְּאָמַר. בְּסוֹף נִיתַּן כֶּסֶף לְיִיעוּדִים. צְרִיכָה כֶּסֶף אַחֵר. וּמָאן דְּאָמַר. מִשָּׁעָה רִאשׁוֹנָה נִיתַּן כֶּסֶף לְיִיעוּדִים. אֵינָהּ צְרִיכָה כֶּסֶף אַחֵר. אֲפִילוּ כְּמָאן דְּאָמַר. מִשָּׁעָה רִאשׁוֹנָה נִיתַּן כֶּסֶף לְיִיעוּדִים צְרִיכָה כֶּסֶף אַחֵר. לָמָּה. כָּל־עַמָּא מוֹדֵיי שֶׁאֵין קִידּוּשִׁין תּוֹפְסִין בַּעֲרָיוֹת.

2 דאמ' A | דמר   3 כמאן דאמ' A | כמן דמר   4 למה A | -

If he was married to her sister who died243. For him who says, he gives money for the allotment at the end, she needs additional money. For him who says, the money for allotment was given at the first hour, she does not need additional money. Even for him who says, the money for allotment was given at the first hour, she needs additional money. Why? Everybody agrees that preliminary marriage is impossible in an incestuous relationship[244].

243 At the moment of sale, the future master could not possibly think of allotting her for himself since she was forbidden to him, *Lev.* 18:18. Therefore, the money was given only for her services as a slave.

244 The master could not have acquired the right of allotment from the father while the girl was forbidden to him by an incest prohibition; he has to buy this right after the death of his first wife.

(59b line 58) מִיסְבַּר סָבִיר רִבִּי יוֹסֵי בֵּירִבִּי יְהוּדָה. אִילַּין יְיעוּדִין דְּהָכָא קִידּוּשֵׁי תּוֹרָה הֵן. אָמַר רִבִּי אָבוּן. אַתְיָיא דְּרִבִּי יוֹסֵי בֵּירִבִּי יְהוּדָה כְּרִבִּי שִׁמְעוֹן בֶּן אֶלְעָזָר. דְּתַנֵּי. בְּפִיקְדוֹן שֶׁיֵּשׁ לִי בְּיָדְךָ. וְהָלְכָה וּמְצָאַתּוּ שֶׁנִּגְנַב אוֹ שֶׁאָבַד. אִם נִשְׁתַּיֵּיר שָׁם שָׁוֶה פְרוּטָה מְקוּדֶּשֶׁת וְאִם לָאו אֵינָהּ מְקוּדֶּשֶׁת. מִלְוָה שֶׁיֵּשׁ לִי בְיָדְךָ. וְהָלְכָה וּמְצָאָתָהּ שֶׁנִּגְנְבָה אוֹ שֶׁנֶּאֶבְדָה. אֲפִילוּ לֹא נִשְׁתַּיֵּיר שָׁם שָׁוֶה פְרוּטָה מְקוּדֶּשֶׁת. רִבִּי שִׁמְעוֹן בֶּן אֶלְעָזָר מִשּׁוּם רִבִּי מֵאִיר. מִלְוָה כְפִקְדוֹן. אִם נִשְׁתַּיֵּיר שָׁם שָׁוֶה פְרוּטָה מְקוּדֶּשֶׁת וְאִם לָאו אֵינָהּ מְקוּדֶּשֶׁת. כְּמָה דְּרִבִּי שִׁמְעוֹן בֶּן אֶלְעָזָר עֲבִיד מִלְוָה כְפִיקְדוֹן כֵּן רִבִּי יוֹסֵי בֵּירִבִּי יְהוּדָה עֲבִיד יִיעוּדִים כְּמִלְוָה.

1 מיסבר A | מסבור   סביר A | סבר   יוסי ביר׳ יהודה A | יוסה בר יודה   דהכא A | דהכה   2 אתייא A | אתיא   יוסי ביר׳ יהודה A | יוסה בר׳ יודה   3 שיש לי בידך A | שישליך בידי   ומצאתו A | ומצאתה   5 בידך A | בידיך   שנאבדה A | שאבדה   שם A | שם אלא   6 למקודשת A | הרי זו מקודשת   7 כפקדון A | כפיקדון   כמה A | במה   8 יוסי ביר׳ יהודה A | יוסה בר׳ יודה   ייעודים A | ייעוד

Is Rebbi Yose ben Rebbi Jehudah of the opinion that the "allotment" discussed here is preliminary marriage by biblical standards[245]? Rebbi Abun said, it turns out that Rebbi Yose ben Rebi Jehudah agrees with

Rebbi Simeon ben Eleazar. As it was stated[246]: By the deposit you hold for me[247]; if she went and found that it was stolen or lost, if there was a *peruṭah*'s worth left, she is preliminarily married; otherwise, she is not preliminarily married. By the loan you are holding from me, if she went and found that it was stolen or lost, even if there was no *peruṭah*'s worth left, she is preliminarily married[248]. Rebbi Eleazar ben Rebbi Simeon says in the name of Rebbi Meïr, a loan is like a deposit: If there was a *peruṭah*'s worth left, she is preliminarily married; otherwise, she is not preliminarily married[249]. Just as Rebbi Eleazar ben Rebbi Simeon equates loan and deposit, so Rebbi Yose ben Rebbi Jehudah equates "allotment" and loan[250].

245 Does R. Yose ben R. Jehudah require that a *peruṭah* be left in the end because he holds that "allotment" not only *is* preliminary marriage but also must follow all rules of preliminary marriages? Then it is difficult to understand why separate biblical rules are given in this case.

246 Babli 47a, Tosephta 3:1.

247 There should be an initial clause: "You are preliminarily married to me for the value of . . . " It is assumed that the deposit was given on condition that she would be responsible only if she misused it, not if it was lost without her fault or stolen. If nothing was left, she received nothing and could not possibly be married.

248 Since she does not have to repay the loan, she received value and is married.

249 As the Babli explains, 47a, a loan is given to be spent. For R. Meïr, nobody can marry except by offering some tangible value.

250 He considers the purchase price as a loan to the father which is going to be repaid by the daughter's work. Therefore she cannot be married if she is not freed from a *peruṭah*'s worth of work by the "allotment".

HALAKHAH 2

(59b line 66) וְאִם לִבְנוֹ יִיעָדֶנָּה. לִבְנוֹ מִייַעֲדָהּ. אֵינוּ מִייַעֲדָהּ לְאָחִיו. וְיִיעֲדִינָהּ לְאָחִיו מִקַּל וָחוֹמֶר. מַה אִם הַבֵּן שֶׁאֵינוֹ קָם תַּחְתָּיו לַחֲלִיצָה יְלִיבּוּם הֲרֵי הוּא מְייַעֲדָהּ לוֹ. אָחִיו שֶׁהוּא קָם תַּחְתָּיו לַחֲלִיצָה וְלְיִיבּוּם אֵינוּ דִין שֶׁייַעֲדִינָה לוֹ. לֹא. אִם אָמַרְתָּ בְּבֵן שֶׁהוּא קָם תַּחְתָּיו בִּשְׂדֵה אֲחוּזָה. תֹּאמַר בְּאָחִיו שֶׁאֵינוֹ קָם תַּחְתָּיו בִּשְׂדֵה אֲחוּזָה דִין הוּא שֶׁייַעֲדֶנָּה לוֹ. תַּלְמוּד לוֹמַר וְאִם לִבְנוֹ יִיעָדֶנָּה. לִבְנוֹ הוּא מְייַעֲדָהּ וְאֵינוּ מְייַעֲדָהּ לְאָחִיו.

1 לבנו | י לבנו הוא אינו A ואינו לאחיו | י לאחין וייעדינה A | ייעדינה וייעדנה 2 לאחיו | י לאחין מה A. ומה להליצה A | בחליצה 3 אחיו A לאחיו שייעדינה | י שייעדנה A שיעדנה לו. | י לו. ת״ל לו. ואם לבנו ייעדנה. הוא מייעדה אינו מייעדה לאחיו. 5 דין הוא | י הואיל ואים קם תחתיו בשדה אחוזה אינו דין שייעדנה A | שייעדנה 6 מייעדה A | מיעדה (2 times)

252"If he allots her to his son." He allots her to his son but may not allot her to his brother. He should be able to allot her to his brother by an argument *de minore ad majus*! If he may allot her to his son who may not take his place for *ḥaliṣah* and levirate, should it not be logical that he may allot her to his brother who may take his place for *ḥaliṣah* and levirate? No. If you would accept the son since he will take [the father's] place in a field of inheritance, what can you say about his brother who will not take his place in a field of inheritance? Would it be reasonable that he may allot her to him? The verse says, "if he allots her to his son." He allots her to his son but may not allot her to his brother.

252 This and the following paragraphs are paralleled in *Yebamot* 10:14   (י), explained there in Notes 178–210.

(59b line 72) וְאִם לִבְנוֹ יִיעָדֶנָּה. וְאֵינוּ מִייַעֲדָהּ לְבֶן בְּנוֹ. שְׁמוּאֵל בַּר אַבָּא בְּעָא קוֹמֵהּ רִבִּי זְעִירָא. בְּפָרָשַׁת נְחָלוֹת אַתְּ עָבִיד בֶּן בֶּן כְּבֵן וְהָכָא לֵית אַתְּ עָבִיד בֶּן בֶּן כְּבֵן. אָמַר רִבִּי זְעִירָא. מָאן דְּאָמַר לִי הָדָא מִילְּתָא אֲנָא מַשְׁקֵי לֵיהּ

קוֹנְדִּיטוֹן. הֵתִיב רִבִּי נָחוּם. הֲרֵי פָרָשַׁת נְחָלוֹת. הֲרֵי עֲשִׂיתָה אָח כְּבֵן וּשְׁאָר כָּל־הַקְּרוֹבִין כְּבֵן אַתְּ עוֹשֶׂה בֶן בֶּן כְּבֵן. וְכָאן שֶׁלֹּא עֲשִׂיתָ אָח כְּבֵן וּשְׁאָר כָּל־הַקְּרוֹבִין כְּבֵן אֵין אַתְּ עוֹשֶׂה בֶן בֶּן כְּבֵן. מְתִיבִין רַבָּנִין דְּקַיסָרִין. הֲרֵי פָרָשַׁת הַטּוּמְאָה. הֲרֵי עֲשִׂיתָ אָח כְּבֵן וּשְׁאָר כָּל־הַקְּרוֹבִין כְּבֵן. וְאֵין אַתְּ עוֹשֶׂה בֵן בֶּן כְּבֵן. אָמְרִין. אֲזִיל קוֹנְדִּיטוֹן.

1 - | י לבנו הוא מייעדה A לבנו מייעדה   שמואל A ר' שמואל   בעא A | בעה   2 קומה A|י קומי   עביד A|י עבד   זעירא A|י זעירה   והכא A|והכה   את עביד|י עבד   3 זעירא A|י זעירה   דאמר|י דמר   הדא A|הדה   אנא A|היא אנא   4 נחום|י תנחום   עשיתה A|עשית   כבן|י מבן   5 הקרובין|י A הקרובים   וכאן A|וכן   עשית A|עשיתה   את עושה בן בן כבן. וכאן שלא עשית אח כבן ושאר כל הקרובין כבן   אין|י ואין   6 הקרובין A|הקרובים   מתיבין|י A התיבון   רבנין|י רבנן   7 הטומאה|י טמאות   עשית A|י עשיתה   הקרובין|י A הקרובים   את A|אתה   8 אזיל A|י הא אזיל

"If he allots her to his son;" but he may not allot her to his grandson. Samuel bar Abba asked before Rebbi Ze'ira: In matters of inheritance you recognize the grandson like a son but here you do not recognize the grandson like a son? Rebbi Ze'ira said, if anybody explains this matter, I shall pour him spiced wine. Rebbi Naḥum answered: In matters of inheritance where the brother can take the place of a son and all others can take the place of the son, the grandson takes the place of a son. But here, where neither the brother nor any other relative can take the place of a son, the grandson cannot take the place of a son. The rabbis of Caesarea answered: In matters of impurity you consider a brother like a son and all [near] relatives like a son but not a grandson like a son. They said, there went the spiced wine.

(59c line 5) וְאִם לִבְנוֹ יִיעָדֶנָּה. לְדַעַת. אָמַר רִבִּי יוֹחָנָן. לֵית כָּאן לְדַעַת. אָמַר רִבִּי יַעֲקֹב בַּר אָחָא. אִית כָּאן כְּרִבִּי יוֹסֵי בֵּירִבִּי יְהוּדָה. אָמַר רִבִּי שְׁמוּאֵל בַּר

אֲבְדוֹמָא. אֲפִילוּ תֵּימָא אִית כָּאן כְּרִבִּי יוֹסֵי בֵּירִבִּי יְהוּדָה. וְלֹא קָטָן הוּא. וְאִם לִבְנוֹ יְיעֲדֶנָּה. לְדַעַת. רִבִּי יוֹחָנָן אָמַר. מְיָיעֲדָהּ בֵּין לִבְנוֹ גָדוֹל בֵּין לִבְנוֹ קָטָן בֵּין לְדַעַת בֵּין שֶׁלֹא לְדַעַת. רִבִּי שִׁמְעוֹן בֶּן לָקִישׁ אָמַר. אֵינוֹ מְיָיעֲדָהּ אֶלָּא לִבְנוֹ גָדוֹל. וּבִלְבַד לְדַעַת.

2 אחא | י אחא כי יוסי A | יוסה יחידה A | יודה 3 תימא A | יתימר כאן A | כן יוסי A | יוסה ואם | י אם 4 מייעדה | י מייעדנה גדול י הגדול קטן | י הקטן 6 גדול | י הגדול ובלבד | י בלבד

"If he allots her to his son;" with [the girl's] agreement. Rebbi Johanan said, there is no agreement here. Rebbi Jacob bar Aha said so, the statement follows Rebbi Yose ben Rebbi Jehudah. Rebbi Samuel bar Eudaimon said, even if you say the statement follows Rebbi Yose ben Rebbi Jehudah, is he not a minor? "If he allots her to his son;" with [the latter's] agreement. Rebbi Johanan said, he allots her to his minor or adult son, with or without the latter's agreement. Rebbi Simeon ben Laqish said, he allots her only to his adult son with the latter's agreement.

(59c line 10) בֶּן תֵּשַׁע שָׁנִים וְיוֹם אֶחָד עוֹשֶׂה אַלְמָנָה לְכֹהֵן גָדוֹל גְרוּשָׁה וַחֲלוּצָה לְכֹהֵן הֶדְיוֹט. עַל דַּעְתֵּיהּ דְּרִבִּי שִׁמְעוֹן בֶּן לָקִישׁ דּוּ פָּתַר לָהּ בְּנִישּׂוּאִין תְּהֵא פְטוּרָה מִן הַחֲלִיצָה וּמִן הַיִּיבּוּם. וְתַנִּינָן נָשָׂא אִשָּׁה וּמֵת הֲרֵי זוֹ פְטוּרָה. אָמַר רִבִּי אָבוּן. אַתְיָיא דְּרִבִּי שִׁמְעוֹן בֶּן לָקִישׁ כְּרִבִּי יוֹסֵי בֵּירִבִּי יוּדָה. דְּתַנֵי. בֶּן תֵּשַׁע שָׁנִים וְיוֹם אֶחָד וְעַד בֶּן שְׁתֵּים עֶשְׂרֵה שָׁנִים וְיוֹם אֶחָד שֶׁהֵבִיא שְׁתֵּי שְׂעָרוֹת הֲרֵי זוֹ שׁוּמָא. רִבִּי יוֹסֵי בֵּירִבִּי יְרוּדָה אוֹמֵר. הֲרֵי אֵילוּ סִימָנִין. רִבִּי יַעֲקֹב בֵּירִבִּי בּוּן בְּשֵׁם רִבִּי יוֹסֵי בֶּן חֲנִינָה. וְהֵן שֶׁעָמְדוּ בוֹ בִּשְׁעַת סִימָנִין.

2 - | י על דעתיה דר' יוחנן דהוא פתר לה בייעודין ניחא ייעודין שיש לו קניין בה עושה אלמנה לכהן גדול גרושה וחלוצה לכהן הדיוט דו | י דהוא 3 ותנינן | י והתנינן ומת | י ומתה 4 אבון | י אבין אתייא | י אתיא יודה | י יהודה דתני | י ותני כן 5 שנים | י שנה 6 יהודה A | יודה 7 ביר' בון A | בר בון יוסי בן A | יוסה בר'

"A male nine years and one day old makes a widow for the High Priest or a divorcee or one who performed *ḥaliṣah* for a common priest." In the opinion of Rebbi Simeon ben Laqish who must explain this for a marriage, she should also be free from levirate or *ḥaliṣah*, as we have stated: "If he married a woman, that one is free from levirate or *ḥaliṣah*." Rebbi Abin said, following Rebbi Simeon ben Laqish it comes following Rebbi Yose ben Rebbi Jehudah, as it was stated so: If a male nine years and one day old up to twelve years and one day old grew two pubic hairs, they are warts. Rebbi Yose ben Rebbi Jehudah said, they are indicators [of puberty]. Rebbi Jacob ben Rebbi Abun in the name of Rebbi Yose ben Ḥanina: Only if they were still there at the time of indicators.

(59c line 17) רְבִּי יוֹסֵי בָּעֵי. עָמְדוּ בוֹ בִשְׁעַת סִימָנִין. לְמַפְרֵיעוֹ הוּא נַעֲשָׂה אִישׁ אוֹ מִכָּן וְלָבָא. אָמַר לֵיהּ רְבִּי אָבוּן. פְּשִׁיטָא לֵיהּ לְמַפְרֵיעוֹ הוּא נַעֲשָׂה אִישׁ כָּל־שֶׁכֵּן לָבָא. דּוּ פָתַר לָהּ הָדָא דְּרְבִּי שִׁמְעוֹן בֶּן לָקִישׁ כְּרְבִּי יוֹסֵי בֵּירְבִּי יוּדָה. וְלָמָה לֵית רְבִּי יוֹסֵי פָתַר הָדָא דְּרְבִּי שִׁמְעוֹן בֶּן לָקִישׁ כְּרְבִּי יוֹסֵי בֵּירְבִּי יְהוּדָה. אָמַר רְבִּי מָנָא. דְהוּא צְרִיכָה לֵיהּ. רְבִּי יוֹסֵי בָּעֵי קוֹמֵי. עָמְדוּ לוֹ בִשְׁעַת סִימָנִין. לְמַפְרֵיעוֹ הוּא נַעֲשָׂה אִישׁ אוֹ מִכָּן וְלָבָא. נִיחָא אַלְמָנָה. וּגְרוּשָׁה. תִּיפְתָּר שֶׁבָּא עָלֶיהָ מִשֶּׁהִגְדִּיל. נָתַן לָהּ גֵּט. חֲלִיצָה. תִּיפְתָּר שֶׁבָּא עָלֶיהָ וָמֵת וְחָלְצוּ לָהּ אַחִים וְעַל יָדָם הִיא נַעֲשֵׂית חֲלוּצָה. מֵעַתָּה אֲפִילוּ פָּחוֹת מִבֶּן תֵּשַׁע. אָמַר רְבִּי שְׁמוּאֵל בַּר אַבְדּוֹמָא. וְכֵינִי. אֶלָּא בְּגִין דְּתַנָּא כּוּלְהוֹן תֵּשַׁע. תַּנָּא אַף הוּא עִמְּהוֹן.

1 יוסי | יוסה   2 אמר ליה | י -   למפריעו | A למפריע   3 דו פתר לה | י די פתר
A דופתר הדה   יודה | י יהודה   5 קומי | י -   6 הוא נעשה | י נעשה   ולבא | י ולהבא   7 גט | י גיטי   8 אחים | י אחין   מבן תשע | י מתשע

Rebbi Yose asked: When they remained until the time of indicators, does he retroactively become a man or from that time onward? For

Rebbi Abun it is obvious that he becomes a man retroactively, so certainly also for the future, for he explains the position of Rebbi Simeon ben Laqish[253] by Rebbi Yose ben Rebbi Jehudah. Why does Rebbi Yose not explain the position of Rebbi Simeon ben Laqish by Rebbi Yose ben Rebbi Jehudah since he asked, when they remained until the time of indicators, does he retroactively become a man or from that time onward? Rebbi Mana said, because he had difficulty. Rebbi Yose asked before me: When they remained until the time of indicators, does he retroactively become a man or from that time onward? One understands the case of a widow. But a divorcee? Explain it if he copulated with her after he became an adult and divorced her. *Ḥaliṣah*? Explain it if he copulated with her, died, and the [adult] brothers performed *ḥaliṣah*; she had *ḥaliṣah* because of him. In that case, even if he was younger than nine [years]! Rebbi Samuel ben Eudaimon said, that is correct. But because in all cases one stated "nine", one stated this with them.

253   Here ends fragment A.

(59c line 26) רִבִּי יְהוּדָה בֶּן פָּזִי בְּשֵׁם רִבִּי יְהוֹשֻׁעַ בֶּן לֵוִי. מֵאָחָז לָמַד רִבִּי יוֹסֵי בְּיִרְבִּי יְהוּדָה. דְּתַנֵּי. אָחָז הוֹלִיד בֶּן תֵּשַׁע וְהָרָן בֶּן שֵׁשׁ וְכָלֵב בֶּן עֶשֶׂר. וּכְמָאן דְּאָמַר. הוּא כָּלֵב בֶּן חֶצְרוֹן הוּא כָּלֵב בֶּן יְפוּנֶּה.

1 יהודה | י יודה   וכמאן | י כמאן   3 דאמר | י דמר

Rebbi Jehudah ben Pazi in the name of Rebbi Joshua ben Levi: Rebbi Yose ben Jehudah learned from Aḥaz, as it was stated: Aḥaz produced a child at age nine, Haran at age six, and Caleb at age ten following him who identifies Caleb ben Ḥeṣron with Caleb ben Yephuneh.

(59c line 29) מְכָרָהּ לָזֶה וְקִידְּשָׁהּ לָזֶה שִׂיחֵק הָאָב בָּאָדוֹן. דִּבְרֵי רִבִּי יוֹסֵי בֵּירִבִּי יְהוּדָה. וַחֲכָמִים אוֹמְרִים. לֹא שִׂיחֵק הָאָב בָּאָדוֹן. נַעֲשָׂה כְאוֹמֵר לְאִשָּׁה. הֲרֵי אַתְּ מְקוּדֶּשֶׁת לִי לְאַחַר שְׁלֹשִׁים יוֹם. אִילּוּ הָאוֹמֵר לְאִשָּׁה. הֲרֵי אַתְּ מְקוּדֶּשֶׁת לִי לְאַחַר שְׁלֹשִׁים יוֹם. וּבָא אַחֵר וְקִידְּשָׁהּ לְאַחַר שְׁלֹשִׁים יוֹם שֶׁמָּא אֵינָהּ מְקוּדֶּשֶׁת לַשֵּׁינִי. מֵעַכְשָׁיו לְאַחַר שְׁלֹשִׁים יוֹם. אִילּוּ הָאוֹמֵר לְאִשָּׁה. הֲרֵי אַתְּ מְקוּדֶּשֶׁת לִי מֵעַכְשָׁיו לְאַחַר שְׁלֹשִׁים יוֹם וּבָא אַחֵר וְקִידְּשָׁהּ בְּתוֹךְ שְׁלֹשִׁים יוֹם שֶׁמָּא אֵינָהּ מְקוּדֶּשֶׁת לִשְׁנֵיהֶן. מִכְּבָר לִכְשֶׁיִּרְצֶה. הַכֹּל מוֹדִין שֶׁאִם הִשִּׂיאָהּ שֶׁשִּׂיחֵק הָאָב בָּאָדוֹן.

If he[254] sold her to one and gave her in preliminary marriage to another, the father played with the master[255], the words of Rebbi Yose ben Rebbi Jehudah; but the Sages say that the father did not play with the master[256]. It is as if somebody said to a woman, "you are preliminarily married to me after 30 days," since if somebody said to a woman, "you are preliminarily married to me after 30 days," and another came and married her preliminarily (after)[257] 30 days, is she not preliminarily married to the second man[258]? "From now after 30 days." Since if somebody said to a woman, "you are preliminarily married to me from now after 30 days," and another came and married her preliminarily within the 30 days, is she not preliminarily married to both of them?[259] From then when he wants[260]. Everybody agrees that if he definitively married her off, the father played with the master[261].

254 The father. The same statement is in the Babli, 19b.

255 She is preliminarily married to the other man and the master lost his right of allotment.

256 The master did not lose his right of allotment.

257 This should read: "Within".

258 Mishnah 3:1. Since R. Yose ben R. Jehudah holds that the money paid for the services of the girl is not given for preliminary marriage but only to

acquire the right of allotment, the girl was not married at the time the second man gave money for preliminary marriage. Since nobody can marry an already married woman, the master has lost his right of allotment.

259 Mishnah 3:1. The Sages hold that the original price was given for preliminary marriage at the time chosen by the master. If another man gives her money for preliminary marriage before the master exercises his right of allotment, both have equal rights to her and neither can marry her without the other writing a bill of divorce. A third man can marry her only if both divorce her.

260 It is the Sages' interpretation of the sale contract, that the buyer can activate his right of allotment any time he chooses.

261 If the second man combined preliminary and definitive marriage at the same time, nothing can undo a definitive marriage except divorce or death. However, this statement is problematic both for R. Yose ben R. Jehudah and for the Sages.

A reasonable interpretation of the position of R. Yose ben R. Jehudah would be that the sales contract, by which the master acquires the right of allotment, implies that the father surrendered his right to marry off his daughter. One must assume that the contract explicitly excluded this interpretation.

For the Sages it really should not make any difference whether preliminary and definitive marriages are performed together or not; the potential preliminary marriage of the master in any case precedes any action by the second man. One must assume that the Yerushalmi holds that in addition to the cases mentioned in the Mishnah, definitive marriage frees the girl from the ownership of her master (cf. Note 279). In that case, even though the act of preliminary marriage created the impossible situation described in the text, the definitive marriage solved the problem by eliminating the master's ownership and with it his right of allotment. The only recourse the master has is to sue the father for the value of services lost. (Explanation of S. Z. Brauda, *loc. cit.* Note 236)

(59c line 38) לְאָמָה. לְאָמָה בִּלְבָד. מְלַמֵּד שֶׁהוּא מוֹכְרָהּ לוֹ וּמַתְנֶה עִמּוֹ עַל מְנָת שֶׁלֹּא יְהוּ עָלֶיהָ יִיעוּדִין. דִּבְרֵי רִבִּי מֵאִיר. וַחֲכָמִים אוֹמְרִים. לֹא עָשָׂה כְלוּם.

שֶׁהִתְנָה עַל מַה שֶׁכָּתוּב בַּתּוֹרָה. וְכָל־הַמַּתְנֶה עַל מַה שֶׁכָּתוּב בַּתּוֹרָה תְּנָיָיו בָּטֵל. וְלֵית לְרִבִּי מֵאִיר כָּל־הַמַּתְנֶה עַל מַה שֶׁכָּתוּב בַּתּוֹרָה תְּנָיָיו בָּטֵל. אִית לֵיהּ תְּנַיי אֶיפְשָׁר לוֹ לְקַיְימוֹ בְסוֹפוֹ. וְזֶה אֶיפְשָׁר לוֹ לְקַיְימוֹ בְסוֹפוֹ. וְלֵית לֵיהּ לְרַבָּנִין תְּנַיי אֶיפְשָׁר לְקַיְימוֹ בְסוֹפוֹ. אִית לוֹן תְּנַיי מָמוֹן. וְזֶה תְּנַיי גּוּף הוּא. וְהָא תַּנֵּי. נוֹשֵׂא אָדָם אִשָּׁה וּמַתְנֶה עִמָּהּ עַל מְנַת שֶׁלֹּא יְהֵא לָהּ עָלָיו לֹא שְׁאֵר וְלֹא כְסוּת וְלֹא עוֹנָה. נִיחָא שְׁאֵר וּכְסוּת. וְעוֹנָה לֹא תְנַיי גּוּף הוּא. אָמַר רִבִּי חִיָּיה בַּר אָדָא. תִּיפְתָּר בִּקְטַנָּה. מַה מְקַיֵּים הָדָא תַנָּיָיא לְאָמָה. מוֹכְרָהּ אַלְמָנָה לְכֹהֵן גָּדוֹל גְּרוּשָׁה וַחֲלוּצָה לְכֹהֵן הֶדְיוֹט. מַה מְקַיֵּים הָדֵין תַּנָּיָיה לְאָמָה. אָמַר רִבִּי יוֹסֵי בֵּירִבִּי בּוּן. תִּיפְתָּר בְּאַלְמָנָה מִן הָאֵירוּסִין. וְהָא תַּנֵּי. מוֹכֵר הוּא אָדָם אֶת בִּתּוֹ לְאִישׁוּת וְשׁוֹנֶה. לְשִׁפְחוּת וְשׁוֹנֶה. לְאִישׁוּת אַחַר שִׁפְחוּת. אֲבָל לֹא לְשִׁפְחוּת אַחַר אִישׁוּת. אָמַר רִבִּי יוֹחָנָן. תַּנָּיִין אִינּוּן. מָאן דְּאִית לֵיהּ אַלְמָנָה לְכֹהֵן גָּדוֹל אִית לֵיהּ שִׁפְחוּת אַחַר אִישׁוּת. מָאן דְּלֵית לֵיהּ אַלְמָנָה לְכֹהֵן גָּדוֹל לֵית לֵיהּ שִׁפְחוּת אַחַר אִישׁוּת. מַה מְקַיֵּים הָדֵין תַּנָּיָיא לְאָמָה. אָמַר רִבִּי מַתַּנְיָיה. תִּיפְתָּר שֶׁהָיָה נָשׂוּי לָאֲחוֹתָהּ.

[262]"As a slave girl.[263]" Only as a slave girl: this teaches that he may sell her on condition that he not have the right of allotment over her, the words of Rebbi Meïr. But the Sages say, he did not do anything, for he stipulated against what is written in the Torah, "and the stipulation of anybody who stipulates against what is written in the Torah is invalid."[264] But does Rebbi Meïr not agree that "the stipulation of anybody who stipulates against what is written in the Torah is invalid"[265]? He accepts it if it is impossible to keep the stipulation in the end, but here it is possible to keep the stipulation in the end[266]. Do the rabbis not agree about a stipulation which it is possible to keep in the end? They agree to it in money matters[267], but this is a personal matter. But did we not state: A person may marry a woman and stipulate with her that she have no claim

on him for food, clothing, or marital relations[268]? One understands food and clothing. But are marital relations not a personal matter? Rebbi Hiyya bar Ada said, explain it for an underage girl[269]. How can that Tanna explain "as a slave girl"[270]? He may sell her as a widow to the High Priest, as a divorcee or one who received *ḥaliṣah* to a common priest[271]. How can that Tanna explain "as a servant"? Rebbi Yose ben Rebbi Abun said, explain it by a widow from preliminary marriage[272]. But was it not stated: A person may sell his daugher into marriage[273] and repeat, into servitude and repeat, into marriage after servitude, but not into servitude after marriage[274]? Rebbi Johanan said, these are different Tannaïm. He who states "a widow to the High Priest" agrees to servitude after marriage; he who does not state "a widow to the High Priest" does not agree to servitude after marriage. How does the latter Tanna explain "as a servant"[275]? Rebbi Mattaniah said, explain it if [the master] was married to her sister[271].

262 Babli 19b; *Mekhilta dR. Šim'on b, Jochai*, p. 165.
263 *Ex.* 21:7
264 Mishnah *Baba meṣi'a* 7:14.
265 Since the Mishnah is anonymous and is based on R. Meïr's compilation, it is assumed that it represents R. Meïr's position.
266 This is explicitly stated in *Baba meṣi'a* 7:14. Since the master is not required to marry his servant, he will not infringe on any biblical obligation by agreeing not to marry her. Every-body will agree that if a man marries a woman on condition that she be freed from levirate or *ḥaliṣah* if he should die childless, the stipulation is invalid since it infringes on obligatory biblical law.
267 For which it is formulated in Mishnah *Baba meṣi'a* 7:14; cf. *Ketubot* 5:10 Note 227 where all references are given.
268 In the Babli, 19b, it reads: "A person may marry a woman and stipulate with her that she have no

claim on him for food, clothing, or marital relations; she is married and the stipulations are void, the words of R. Meïr; R. Jehudah says, in money matters his stipulation is valid." As noted in *Ketubot* 5:10 Note 227, R. Jehudah's opinion is accepted in the Yerushalmi as generally valid.

269   Who does not expect sexual relations.

270   R. Meïr who denies the ability of the father to exclude allotment.

271   The father may sell her to a person unable to marry her by biblical law (Babli 19b; *Mekhilta dR. Šim'on b, Jochai*, p. 165).

272   Since an underage girl is emancipated from her father by definitive marriage (*Ketubot* 4:3, Note 42), the girl sold as a widow or divorcee must be a widow or divorcee after preliminary marriage only. The mention of ḥaliṣah is a slip of the pen because of the usual combination of the terms; for the House of Hillel ḥaliṣah is possible only after definitive marriage (*Yebamot* 1:6, Note 192).

273   Preliminary, not definitive.

274   Babli 18a; *Massekhet 'Avadim* 1.

275   As servant only, excluding the possibility of marriage; cf. Note 243.

(59c line 55) תַּנֵּי רַבִּי שִׁמְעוֹן בֶּן יוֹחַי. כְּשֵׁם שֶׁאֵינוֹ מוֹכְרָהּ לְשִׁפְחוּת אַחַר אִישׁוּת אַף לֹא שִׁפְחוּת אַחַר שִׁפְחוּת. מַה טַעֲמֵיהּ דְּרַבִּי שִׁמְעוֹן בֶּן יוֹחַי. בְּבִגְדוֹ בָהּ. פַּעַם אַחַת הוּא בוֹגֵד בָּהּ וְאֵינוֹ בוֹגֵד בָּהּ פַּעַם שְׁנִיָּה. מַה מְקַיְּימִין רַבָּנָן טַעֲמָא דְּרַבִּי שִׁמְעוֹן בֶּן יוֹחַי. בְּבִגְדוֹ בָהּ. מִכֵּיוָן שֶׁפִּירֵשׂ טַלִּיתוֹ עָלֶיהָ עוֹד אֵין לְאָבִיהָ בָּהּ רְשׁוּת.

Rebbi Simeon ben Yoḥai stated: Just as he cannot sell her into servitude after marriage, so not into servitude after servitude[276]. What is Rebbi Simeon ben Ioḥai's reason? "By his being unfaithful to her.[277]" Once he can be unfaithful to her, he cannot be unfaithful to her a second time. How do the rabbis explain Rebbi Simeon ben Ioḥai's reason? "She being in his garment[278];" from the moment that [her master] spread his garment on her, her father no longer has any power over her.

HALAKHAH 2

276 Babli 18b. In *Mekhilta dR. Ismael, Neziqin* 3, this is ascribed to R. Yose the Galilean and derived from the singular used in *Ex.* 21:7.

277 He reads בְּבִגְדוֹ as verbal form derived from the root בגד "to be unfaithful, traitorous", referred to the father. In the Babli, 18b, this is R. Aqiba's opinion.

278 He reads בְּבִגְדוֹ as nominal form derived from בגד "garment", referring to the master as husband. They hold that the girl sold into servitude is emancipated even by preliminary marriage. In the Babli this is the position taken by R. Eliezer; anonymous in *Mekhilta dR. Šim'on b, Jochai*, p. 166.

(59c line 59) רַבִּי שִׁמְעוֹן בֶּן לָקִישׁ בָּעָא קוֹמֵי רַבִּי יוֹחָנָן. אָמָה הָעִבְרִיָּיה יוֹצְאָה בְּנִשּׂוּאִים מִקַּל וָחוֹמֶר. מָה אִם הַסִּימָנִין שֶׁאֵינָן מוֹצִיאִין אוֹתָהּ מֵרְשׁוּת הָאָב הֲרֵי הֵן מוֹצִיאִין אוֹתָהּ מֵרְשׁוּת הָאָדוֹן. נִשּׂוּאִין שֶׁהֵן מוֹצִיאִין מֵרְשׁוּת הָאָב אֵינוֹ דִין שֶׁיּוֹצִיאוּ אוֹתָהּ מֵרְשׁוּת הָאָדוֹן. אֲמַר לֵיהּ. אֲנִי אֵין לִי אֶלָּא שֶׁלְּמִשְׁנָה. יְתֵירָה עָלָיו אָמָה הָעִבְרִיָּיה. שֶׁהִיא קוֹנָה אֶת עַצְמָהּ בַּסִּימָנִין. בַּר פְּדָיָיה אָמַר. אָמָה הָעִבְרִיָּיה יוֹצְאָה בְּמִיתַת רַבָּהּ. מָה טַעֲמָא. וְאַף לַאֲמָתְךָ תַּעֲשֶׂה כֵּן וּכְתִיב וְהָיָה לְךָ עֶבֶד עוֹלָם. הִקִּישׁ אָמָה עִבְרִיָּיה לַנִּרְצָע. מָה הַנִּרְצָע יוֹצֵא בְּמִיתַת רַבּוֹ. אַף אָמָה עִבְרִיָּה יוֹצְאָה בְּמִיתַת רַבָּהּ. וְאָתְיָיא דְבַר פְּדָיָיה כְּהָדֵין תַּנָּיָיא דְתַנֵּי. עֶבֶד עִבְרִי עוֹבֵד אֶת הַבֵּן וְאֵינוֹ עוֹבֵד אֶת הַבַּת. אָמָה הָעִבְרִיָּיה עוֹבֶדֶת אֶת הַבַּת וְאֵינָהּ עוֹבֶדֶת אֶת הַבֵּן. אִית תַּנָּיֵי תַּנֵּי. בֵּין עִבְרִיָּה בֵּין עִבְרִי אֵינָן עוֹבְדִין לֹא אֶת הַבֵּן וְלֹא אֶת הַבַּת. מַה מְקַיֵּים הָדֵין תַּנָּיָה וְאַף לַאֲמָתְךָ תַּעֲשֶׂה כֵּן. פָּתַר לָהּ בְּהַעֲנָק. דְּתַנֵּי. אֵילּוּ שֶׁמַּעֲנִיקִין לָהֶם. הַיּוֹצֵא בַּשָּׁנִים וּבַיּוֹבֵל וְאָמָה הָעִבְרִיָּה שֶׁהִיא קוֹנָה אֶת עַצְמָהּ בַּסִּימָנִין. אֲבָל הַיּוֹצֵא בְּגֵירָעוֹן כֶּסֶף וּבְמִיתַת הָאָדוֹן אֵין מַעֲנִיקִין לָהֶן.

Rebbi Simeon ben Laqish asked before Rebbi Johanan: Should not the Hebrew slave girl leave by definitive marriage, by an argument *de minore ad majus*? Since indications [of puberty] which do not emancipate her from her father's power, free her from her master's power[279], is it not logical that definitive marriage, which emancipates her from her father's power, shall free her from her master's power? He said to him, I have only the Mishnah: "The Hebrew slave girl in addition regains her autonomy by indicators of puberty[155]." Bar Pedaiah[280] said, the Hebrew slave girl leaves at the death of her master. What is the reason? "Also your slave girl you shall treat in the same way;" and it is written: "He shall be *for you* a permanent slave.[281]" He bracketed the Hebrew slave girl with the "pierced slave". Since the "pierced slave" leaves at his master's death, the Hebrew slave girl also leaves at her master's death[282]. It turns out that Bar Pedaiah parallels the following Tanna, as it was stated: The Hebrew slave[283] serves the son but not the daughter; the Hebrew slave girl serves the daughter but not the son[284]. Some Tannaïm state: The Hebrew slave girl as well as the Hebrew slave[285] serve neither the son nor the daughter. How does the Tanna confirm "your slave girl you also shall treat in the same way"? He explains it about the allowance[286], as it was stated: The following are given allowances: The one who leaves after six years or in the Jubilee, and the Hebrew slave girl who becomes autonomous by indicators of puberty. But one does not give allowances to one who leaves by the reduction of the amount[287] or following the master's death[288].

279 An adolescent girl remains in her father's power for six months after her formal puberty (*Nedarim* 10:1, Note 1) but leaves servitude at the actual onset of puberty.

280 In the Babli, 17b, "R. Pada".

281 *Deut.* 15:17, making it clear that the servitude of the "pierced slave" is personally to his master; cf. Note 157. By consensus of all sources, the final clause of that verse, speaking of the Hebrew slave girl, cannot refer to the piercing of the earlobe since this would contradict *Ex.* 21:5.

282 Babli 17b; *Sifry Deut.* #122; *Mekhilta dR. Ismael, Neziqin* 2; *Mekhilta dR. Šim'on b. Jochai* p. 164.
283 The one indentured for six years, not the "pierced slave" (parallel sources cf. Note 282).
284 In the Babli 17b: Neither son nor daughter.
285 The "pierced slave", not the one indentured for six years. This is Bar Pedaiah's statement.
286 A supply of produce, required to be given the departing slave by *Deut.* 15:14. This is the standard interpretation (Babli 17b; *Sifry Deut.* #122).
287 Who buys his freedom by repaying the amount given for his services reduced proportionally to the time served.
288 In the Babli, 16b, and *Sifry Deut.* #119, the person leaving at his master's death is entitled to an allowance. The Yerushalmi restricts allowances to persons serving a predetermined period. (In *Masekhet 'Avadim* 2, allowances are given only to those sold by the court.)

(59c line 74) כְּתִיב וְהִגִּישׁוֹ אֲדוֹנָיו אֶל הָאֱלֹהִים וְרִגְּשׁוֹ אֶל הַדֶּלֶת וְגוֹ'. הָא כֵיצַד. זֶה שֶׁהוּא נִמְכַּר בְּבֵית דִּין וְהִגִּישׁוֹ אֲדוֹנָיו אֶל הָאֱלֹהִים. וְזֶה שֶׁהוּא מוֹכֵר אֶת עַצְמוֹ וְהִגִּישׁוֹ אֶל הַדֶּלֶת. רִבִּי אִמִּי בָּעָא. פְּשִׁיטָא זֶה שֶׁהוּא נִמְכַּר בְּבֵית דִּין בֵּית דִּין כּוֹתְבִין שְׁטָרוֹ. זֶה שֶׁהוּא מוֹכֵר אֶת עַצְמוֹ מִי כוֹתֵב אֶת שְׁטָרוֹ. כְּתִיב לֹא יִקְשֶׁה בְעֵינֶיךָ בְּשַׁלֵּחֲךָ אוֹתוֹ חָפְשִׁי מֵעִמָּךְ כִּי מִשְׁנֶה שְׂכַר שָׂכִיר עֲבָדְךָ שֵׁשׁ שָׁנִים. שָׂכִיר עוֹבֵד בַּיּוֹם וְאֵינוֹ עוֹבֵד בַּלַּיְלָה. עֶבֶד עִבְרִי עוֹבֵד בֵּין בַּיּוֹם בֵּין בַּלַּיְלָה. כְּתִיב לֹא יִרְדֶּנּוּ בְּפֶרֶךְ לְעֵינֶיךָ. וְאַתְּ אוֹמֵר אָכֵן. רִבִּי אִמִּי בְּשֵׁם רִבִּי יוֹחָנָן. רַבּוֹ מַשִּׂיאוֹ אִשָּׁה כְּנַעֲנִית וְנִמְצָא עוֹבֵד בֵּין בַּיּוֹם בֵּין בַּלַּיְלָה. רִבִּי בָּא בַּר מָמָל בָּעָא קוֹמֵי רִבִּי אִמִּי. הַגַּע עַצְמָךְ שֶׁהָיָה קוֹנֶה כֹּהֵן. אָמַר לֵיהּ. וְיִשְׂרָאֵל לֹא הִיתֵּר מִכְּלָל אִיסּוּר הוּא. כְּרִבִּי שִׁמְעוֹן רִבִּי בָּא בַּר מָמָל כָּאן חָזַר בֵּיהּ.

It is written: "His master shall bring him to the judges, or he shall bring him to the door²⁸⁹." How is that? The one who was sold by the court, "his master shall bring him to the judges." The one who sold himself, "or he shall bring him to the door."²⁹⁰ Rebbi Immi asked: It is obvious that the court writes the contract for him who was sold by the court. Who is writing the contract for him who sells himself?[291] It is written: "It shall not be hard in your eyes to send him away free from you; for twice the hire of a hireling he served you for six years." The hired hand works during the day; he does not work in the night. The Hebrew slave works both day and night. It is written: "He shall not treat him harshly before your eyes[292]," and you say so[293]? Rebbi Immi in the name of Rebbi Joḥanan: His master marries him to a Canaanite slave; it turns out that he serves him day and night[294]. Rebbi Abba bar Mamal asked before Rebbi Immi: Think of it, if he was buying a Cohen[295]! He answered him: Would the case of an Israel not also be permission of something prohibited following Rebbi Simeon[296]? Rebbi Abba bar Mamal here changed his mind.

288 *Ex.* 21:6.

290 *Mekhilta dR. Ismael Neziqin* 2; but in *Mekhilta dR. Šim'on b. Jochai* p. 163 (*Midrash Haggadol Deut.* 15:17) even the private act of piercing needs a public act in court.

291 No answer is given since in a private transaction any one of the parties may write the contract.

292 *Lev.* 25:53.

293 It certainly is forbidden to ask more than a full day's work from any slave, whether Hebrew or not.

294 Since in the night he produces slave children for his master.

295 Since a Cohen may not marry a divorcee, certainly a slave woman is forbidden to him.

296 The slave woman is not more strictly forbidden to the Cohen than she is to the Israel. According to R. Simeon, children of a Gentile father and a Jewish mother have no family relationship with their father; children of a Jewish father and Gentile mother have no family relationship with their father; the latter statement includes slave women who as yet are not fully Jewish (cf. *Yebamot* 4:15,7:6 Note 135). Therefore, if the slave woman is temporarily permitted to the Israel, she also is temporarily permitted to the

Cohen slave. The woman is not married to the slave in legal terms since at the moment when the slave regains his freedom she automatically becomes forbidden to him and permitted to others without a bill of divorce.

In the Babli, 21b, only Rav holds that the Canaanite woman was permitted to the Cohen while Samuel disagrees.

(59d line 9) דָּרַשׁ רִבִּי יְהוּדָה בֵּירִבִּי בּוּן. הַמִּילָת הַזֶּה נִרְצָע. שֶׁלֹּא יְהֵא כֹהֵן וְיִפָּסֵל. רִבִּי מֵאִיר אוֹמֵר. מִן חַסְחוּס הָיָה נִרְצָע. מִיכָּן הָיָה רִבִּי מֵאִיר אוֹמֵר. אֵין הַכֹּהֵן נִרְצָע. שֶׁמָּא יֵיעָשֶׂה בַּעַל מוּם וְיִפָּסֵל מִן הָעֲבוֹדָה. וְיֵירָצַע חַסְחוּס פָּחוּת מִן הַכַּרְשִׁינָה. שֶׁמָּא יָבוֹא לִידֵי כַרְשִׁינָה. וְיָבוֹא לִידֵי כַרְשִׁינָה. הַתּוֹרָה אָמְרָה וְשָׁב לַאֲחוּזָתוֹ. בְּעַיָּינוּ. כְּלוּם הָיָה נִרְצָע אֶלָּא אִם כֵּן הָיוּ לוֹ אִשָּׁה וּבָנִים. בַּמַּרְצֵעַ. אֵין לִי אֶלָּא בַּמַּרְצֵעַ. מְנַיִין אֲפִילוּ בָסוֹל אֲפִילוּ בְקוֹץ אֲפִילוּ בִזְכוּכִית. תַּלְמוּד לוֹמַר וְרָצַע. עַד כְּדוֹן כְּרִבִּי עֲקִיבָה.

Rebbi Jehudah ben Rebbi Abun[297] preached: The earlobe was pierced, lest a Cohen become disqualified. Rebbi Meïr says, he was pierced at his cartilage. Therefore, Rebbi Meïr says that a Cohen cannot be pierced lest he become blemished and be disqualified for service[298]. Could not the cartilage be pierced less than the size of a vetch seed? Maybe it would result in the size of a vetch seed. Let it be the size of a vetch! The Torah said, "he shall return to his inheritance[299]," as he was. He cannot be pierced unless he had a wife and children[300]. "By an awl"[301]. Not only an awl, from where even a buck-thorn, even a thorn, even glass? The verse says, "he pierces"[302]. This follows Rebbi Aqiba.

297 In the Babli, 21b, and *Sifry Deut.* #122, he seems to be identified as R. Jehudah (bar Ilai); explicitly so in *Mekhilta dR. Ismael Neziqin* 2. The opinion ascribed here to R. Meïr there is that of the anonymous Sages.

298 Mishnah *Bekhorot* 6:1 notes that both sacrificial animal and priest are

disqualified for Divine service if the cartilage of their ears be punctured in the size of a vetch seed.

299   *Lev. 25:27.* This is the wrong quote since it refers to real estate returned to its original owner in the Jubilee. The verse referring to the Hebrew slave released in the Jubilee is v. 41, "he shall return to his family, to his forefathers' inheritance he shall return." The inheritance of a priest is the Divine service (*Num.* 18:20).

300   A Jewish wife and children, whom he is unable to support by himself. *Mekhilta dR. Ismael Neziqin 2, dR. Šim'on b. Jochai* p. 163.

301   *Ex. 21:6.*

302   This interpretation seems to be the reason for the masoretic accents which introduce a dividing accent: "he shall pierce his ear, with an awl", taking "as an awl" as an afterthought. The Babli, 21b, refers to *Deut* 15:17: "You shall take the awl," anything that can be used to serve as an awl.

(59d line 16) כְּרִבִּי יִשְׁמָעֵאל. תַּנֵּי רִבִּי יִשְׁמָעֵאל. בִּשְׁלֹשָׁה מְקוֹמוֹת הַתּוֹרָה עוֹקֶפֶת לְמִקְרָא וּבְמָקוֹם אַחֵר לְמִדְרָשׁ. הַתּוֹרָה אָמְרָה בַּסֵּפֶר. וַהֲלָכָה אָמְרָה בְּכָל־דָּבָר שֶׁהוּא בְּתָלוּשׁ. הַתּוֹרָה אָמְרָה בְּעָפָר. וַהֲלָכָה אָמְרָה בְּכָל־דָּבָר שֶׁהוּא מְגַדֵּל צְמָחִים. הַתּוֹרָה אָמְרָה בַּמַּרְצֵעַ. וַהֲלָכָה אָמְרָה אֲפִילוּ בְסוֹל אֲפִילוּ בְקוֹץ אֲפִילוּ בִזְכוּכִית. וּבְמָקוֹם אֶחָד לְמִדְרָשׁ. תַּנֵּי רִבִּי יִשְׁמָעֵאל. וְהָיָה בַּיּוֹם הַשְּׁבִיעִי יְגַלַּח אֶת כָּל־שְׂעָרוֹ כְּלָל. אֶת רֹאשׁוֹ וְאֶת זְקָנוֹ וְאֶת גַּבֹּת עֵינָיו פְּרָט. וּכְשֶׁהוּא אוֹמֵר וְאֶת כָּל־שְׂעָרוֹ יְגַלֵּחַ חָזַר וְכָלָל. כְּלָל וּפְרָט וּכְלָל אֵין אַתָּה דָן אֶלָּא כְעֵין הַפְּרָט. לוֹמַר לָךְ. מָה הַפְּרָט מְפוֹרָשׁ שֶׁהוּא מְקוֹם כִּינּוּס שֵׂיעָר וּבְנִרְאֶה. אַף אֵין לִי אֶלָּא מְקוֹם כִּינּוּס שֵׂיעָר וּבְנִרְאֶה. וַהֲלָכָה אָמְרָה יְגַלְּחֶנּוּ כִּדְלַעַת. בַּמַּרְצֵעַ. מָה מַרְצֵעַ שֶׁהוּא שֶׁלְּמַתֶּכֶת. רִבִּי אוֹמֵר. זֶה מַקְדֵּחַ גָּדוֹל. רִבִּי יוֹסֵי בֵּירִבִּי יוּדָה אוֹמֵר. זֶה הַפְּסִילָה. וְהִגִּישׁוֹ אֶל הַדֶּלֶת. יָכוֹל אֲפִילוּ מוּטָּל. תַּלְמוּד לוֹמַר אוֹ אֶל הַמְּזוּזָה. מָה הַמְּזוּזָה עוֹמֶדֶת. אַף הַדֶּלֶת יְהֵא עוֹמֵד. גְּנַאי לוֹ גְנַאי לְמִשְׁפַּחְתּוֹ.

Following Rebbi Ismael? Rebbi Ismael stated[303]: At three places teaching circumvents Scripture and at another place the interpretation.

The Torah said, "in a scroll[304]", but practice said on anything separated from the ground. The Torah said, "in dust"[305], but practice said in anything on which plants grow[306]. The Torah said, "with an awl", but practice said, even a buck-thorn, even a thorn, even glass. And at one place the interpretation[307]: Rebbi Ismael stated: "It shall be on the seventh day that he shave all his hair[308]," inclusion. "His head, his beard, and his eyebrows," detail. Since it continues "and all his hair he shall shave," it repeats inclusion. Inclusion, detail, and inclusion is judged only by what is similar to the detail[309]. Since the detail is explained as place of bunching and exposed, it should refer only [hair growing] in bunches at exposed places. But practice is that he shaves to be like a gourd[310]. "With an awl", since an awl is made of metal, so anything made of metal[311]. Rebbi Yose said, this is a large drill[312]. Rebbi Yose ben Rebbi Jehudah says, that is the engraving-knife. "He shall bring him to the door.[313]" I could think, even if it was lying flat. The verse says, "or to the door-post". Since the door-post is upright, so also the door has to be upright[314]: a shame to him and to his family[315].

303 Babli *Soṭah* 16b; *Sifry Deut.* #122.

304 This is a wrong quote, referring to *Num.* 6:23, the text of the incantations required in the rite of the wife suspected of infidelity. But that text has to be written on a scroll; cf. *Soṭah* 2:4, Notes 143-144. Here, it should say סֵפֶר "book", referring to the divorce document mentioned in *Deut.* 24:1 which can be written on anything not connected to the ground; Mishnah *Giṭṭin* 2:3. The quote is correct in the sources quoted in the preceding Note.

305 *Lev.* 17:13. The blood of slaughtered wild animals or birds has to be covered "in dust".

306 Mishnah *Ḥulin* 6:6.

307 R. Ismael's own hermeneutical rules.

308 *Lev.* 14:9, speaking of the ritual purification of the healed sufferer

from skin disease. All the quotes are from this verse.

309 By the seventh hermeneutical rule one has to try to find an intensional definition of the properties common to the examples given as detail; these then are the properties referred to by the inclusions.

310 Shaving completely every exposed hair; Mishnah *Nega'im* 14:4. (*Sifra Meṣora' Pereq* 2 disagrees with the *baraita* here and the Mishnah and holds that the insistence on the shaving of *all* hair in both inclusions requires that any single one of the properties mentioned in the analysis of the detail, hair growing in bunches *or* visible, has to be shaved but nothing else. The Tanna of *Sifra* holds that practice follows interpretation closely.)

311 In Babylonian sources, Babli 21b, *Mekhilta dR. Ismael Neziqin* 2, *Sifry Deut* # 122, this is an argument of Rebbi, in *Mekhilta dR. Šim'on b. Jochai*,

of R. Yose ben Jehudah: Any metal implement which can be used for piercing is called "awl". The most detailed analysis of the verse is in the Babli, 21b, (*Midrash Haggadol Deut.* 15:17) where the inclusion-exclusion methodology of R. Ismael is shown to lead to the admissibility of any metal piercing instrument and the addition-subtraction methodology of R. Aqiba to the inclusion of all mechanical and the exclusion of chemical means.

312 In *Sifry Deut* # 122, *Midrash Haggadol Deut.* on *Deut.* 15:17: This is the large awl. The Yerushalmi text seems to be the original.

313 *Ex.* 21:6; cf. *Deut.* 15:17.

314 Babli 22b, *Mekhilta dR. Ismael Neziqin* 2, *Mekhilta dR. Šim'on b. Jochai* p. 163.

315 They violated their obligation to support their relative when he could not fend for himself.

(59d line 30) תַּנֵּי. רִבִּי אֱלִיעֶזֶר בֶּן יַעֲקֹב אוֹמֵר. וְלָמָה אֶל הַדֶּלֶת. שֶׁעַל יַד דֶּלֶת יָצְאוּ מֵעַבְדוּת לַחֵירוּת. שֶׁאֲלוּ הַתַּלְמִידִים אֶת רַבָּן יוֹחָנָן בֶּן זַכַּאי. מָה רָאָה הָעֶבֶד הַזֶּה לִירָצַע בְּאָזְנוֹ יוֹתֵר מִכָּל־אֵיבָרָיו. אָמַר לָהֶן. אוֹזֶן שֶׁשָּׁמְעָה מֵהַר סִינַי לֹא יִהְיֶה לְךָ אֱלֹהִים אֲחֵרִים עַל פָּנַי וּפֵירְקָה מֵעָלֶיהָ עוֹל מַלְכוּת שָׁמַיִם וְקִיבְּלָה עָלֶיהָ עוֹל בָּשָׂר וְדָם. אוֹזֶן שֶׁשָּׁמְעָה לִפְנֵי הַר סִינַי כִּי לִי בְנֵי יִשְׂרָאֵל עֲבָדִים. וְהָלַךְ זֶה וְקָנָה אָדוֹן אַחֵר. לְפִיכָךְ תָּבוֹא הָאוֹזֶן וְתֵירָצַע. לְפִי שֶׁלֹּא שָׁמַר מַה שֶּׁשָּׁמְעָה אָזְנוֹ.

It was stated: Rebbi Eliezer ben Jacob says, why at the door? Because by the door they went from servitude to freedom[316]. [317]The students asked Rabban Johanan ben Zakkai: Why should the slave be pierced in his ear rather than in any of his other body parts? He said to them, the ear which heard at Mount Sinai: "You shall have no other powers besides Me," and removed from himself the yoke of the Kingdom of Heaven but accepted the yoke of flesh and blood; the ear which heard before Mount Sinai: "For the Children of Israel are My servants," and went and acquired another master; therefore the ear should come and be pierced for he[317a] did not follow what his ear heard.

316 By the blood of the Passover sacrifice on the doorposts in Egypt, *Ex.* 12:7.

317 Babli 22b; *Mekhilta dR Ismael Neziqin* 2.

317 The slave.

(59d line 36) אָזְנוֹ. מָה אָזְנוּ שֶׁנֶּאֱמַר לְהַלָּן יְמָנִית אַף כָּאן יְמָנִית. וְאִם אָמוֹר יֹאמַר הָעֶבֶד. שְׁתֵּי אֲמִירוֹת. אַחַת בְּסוֹף שֵׁשׁ וְאַחַת בִּתְחִילַּת שֶׁבַע. אַחַת בְּסוֹף שֵׁשׁ. עַד שֶׁהוּא בָּעֲבוֹדָתוֹ. וְאַחַת בִּתְחִילַּת שֶׁבַע. לֹא אֵצֵא חָפְשִׁי. אָהַבְתִּי אֶת אֲדוֹנִי אֶת אִשְׁתִּי וְאֶת בָּנָי. מְלַמֵּד שֶׁאֵינוֹ נִרְצָע עַד שֶׁיִּהֱא לוֹ אִשָּׁה וּבָנִים וּלְרַבּוֹ אִשָּׁה וּבָנִים. עַד שֶׁיִּהֱא אוֹהֵב אֶת רַבּוֹ וְרַבּוֹ אוֹהֲבוֹ. עַד שֶׁיִּתְבָּרְכוּ הַנְּכָסִים עַל יָדוֹ. שֶׁנֶּאֱמַר כִּי טוֹב לוֹ עִמָּךְ.

"His ear[318]." Since "his ear" mentioned there[319] means the right ear, also here the right ear[320].

"If the slave says saying[321]", two sayings, one at the end of the sixth year and one at the start of the seventh year[322]. One at the end of the sixth year, while he still is in his servitude and one at the start of the seventh year, "I will not go free.[323]"

"I love my master, my wife, and my children.³²⁴" This teaches that he cannot be pierced unless he have a wife and children, unless he love his master and his master love him; unless the property be blessed because of him³²⁵ as it is said: "For he feels well with you³²⁴."

318 *Ex.* 21:6.

319 This may refer either to the induction ceremony of the priests (*Lev.* 8:23,24) or the purification of the sufferer from skin disease (*Lev.* 14:14,17,25,28). In both cases, it is spelled out that blood was given on the *right* ear's cartilage.

320 *Mekhilta dR. Ismael, Neziqin* 2; *Sifry Deut.* #122.

321 *Ex.* 21:5. The interpretation of the emphatic infinitive construction as additional condition is characteristic of R. Aqiba's interpretation; it is rejected by R. Ismael who considers it a regular feature of biblical syntax.

322 The slave has to give notice of his intention to remain in his servile state while he still is indentured and has to repeat it at the moment he should become free again. Babli 22a, *Mekhilta dR. Ismael, Mišpaṭim* 2; *Mekhilta dR. Šim'on b. Jochai* p. 162; *Sifry Deut.* #121.

323 This is the statement required at the time of his planned release.

324 *Ex.* 21:5.

325 *Mekhilta dR. Ismael, Mišpaṭim* 2; *Mekhilta dR. Šim'on b. Jochai* p. 162; *Sifry Deut.* #121; *Midrash Tannaïm* preserved in *Midrash Haggadol Deut.* 15:17. The last source is the only one which explicitly refers the mention of "the wife" to the Canaanite slave given to him by his master (cf. Rashi to *Ex.* 21:5), not to the Jewish wife and her children who also have to be sustained by his master (*Ex.* 21:3).

(59d line 42) וְקוֹנֶה אֶת עַצְמוֹ בַּיוֹבֵל. דִּכְתִיב וְיָצָא בַּיוֹבֵל הוּא וּבָנָיו עִמּוֹ. וּבְמִיתַת הָאָדוֹן. דִּכְתִיב וְהָיָה לְךָ עֶבֶד עוֹלָם. כָּל־יְמֵי עוֹלָמוֹ שֶׁלָּאָדוֹן.

"He regains his autonomy in the Jubilee," as it is written: "He leaves in the Jubilee together with his children³²⁶." "Or at the master's death," as it is written: "He shall be for you a perpetual slave,³²⁷" all the days of his master's lifetime.

326 *Lev.* 25:54. The text is misquoted; it reads וְיָצָא בִּשְׁנַת הַיֹּבֵל "he leaves in the Jubilee year."

327 *Deut.* 15:17. In contrast to the slave indentured for six years, the "pierced slave" does not serve the son. *Mekhilta dR. Ismael Neziqin* 2, end; *Mekhilta dR. Šim'on b. Jochai* p. 164; *Sifry Deut.* #121.

(fol. 58a) **משנה ג:** עֶבֶד כְּנַעֲנִי נִקְנֶה בְּכֶסֶף וּבִשְׁטָר וּבַחֲזָקָה. וְקוֹנֶה אֶת עַצְמוֹ בְּכֶסֶף עַל יְדֵי אֲחֵרִים וּבִשְׁטָר עַל יְדֵי עַצְמוֹ דִּבְרֵי רִבִּי מֵאִיר. וַחֲכָמִים אוֹמְרִים אַף בְּכֶסֶף עַל יְדֵי עַצְמוֹ וּבִשְׁטָר עַל יְדֵי אֲחֵרִים וּבִלְבַד שֶׁיְּהֵא הַכֶּסֶף מִשֶּׁל אֲחֵרִים.

Mishnah 3: A Canaanite slave[328] is acquired by money, or contract, or possession[329]. He gains his autonomy by money through a third party[330] or a document by himself[331], the words of Rebbi Meïr. But the Sages say, by money also by himself[332] or a document through a third party[333], if only the money comes from a third party.

328 Any Gentile slave is called "Canaanite" since Canaan was called "a slave of slaves to his fellow men" (*Gen.* 9:25).

329 A slave who becomes ownerless by the death of his intestate owner who dies without heirs can be acquired by anybody who makes him perform a slave's duties for himself. Also, a person who claims to have bought a slave from another party will have his ownership confirmed by the court if he can show three years of uncontested ownership. Cf. *Ketubot* 5:5, Note 100.

330 R. Meïr holds that any property of the slave's is his master's. If the slave receives monies from other people on condition that they not be his master's property, the condition is not operative. The slave cannot buy his freedom with his master's money.

331 By manumission, the slave (who had been circumcised as a Jew's slave) becomes a full Jew. As such, he is

permitted to marry a Jewish partner but is prohibited promiscuity. R. Meïr holds that people prefer promiscuity to the discipline of marriage; for him, manumission has detrimental aspects. Since nobody can legally act to another person's detriment without that person's authorization, a third party cannot accept a document of manumission without the slave's authorization.

332   If a slave receives money on condition that it not be his master's, the condition is valid. The slave may use that money to buy his freedom.

333   They hold that the prohibition of promiscuity is a small price to pay for freedom and the possibility of marriage. Since a person can legally act to another person's benefit without that person's authorization, a third party can accept a document of manumission without the slave's authorization.

(59d line 45) **הלכה ג**: עֶבֶד כְּנַעֲנִי נִקְנֶה בְּכֶסֶף כול׳. כְּתִיב וְהִתְנַחַלְתֶּם אוֹתָם לִבְנֵיכֶם אַחֲרֵיכֶם לָרֶשֶׁת אֲחוּזָּה. הִקִּישׁ עֲבָדִים לַאֲחוּזָּה. מָה אֲחוּזָּה נִקְנֵית בְּכֶסֶף וּבִשְׁטָר וּבַחֲזָקָה. אַף עֶבֶד כְּנַעֲנִי נִקְנֶה בְּכֶסֶף וּבִשְׁטָר וּבַחֲזָקָה.

Halakhah 3: "A Canaanite slave is acquired by money," etc. It is written[334]: "They shall be inherited by your children after you, to be possessed as inheritance" This brackets slaves with landed property. Since real estate can be acquired by money, or contract, or possession, so a Canaanite slave can be acquired by money, or contract, or possession.

334   *Lev.* 25:46, speaking of Gentile slaves. The same argument in the Babli, 22b, *Bekhorot* 13a; *Sifra Behar Parašah* 6(4).

(59d line 48) מְנַיִין שֶׁאֲחוּזָּה נִקְנֵית בְּכֶסֶף וּבִשְׁטָר וּבַחֲזָקָה. שָׂדוֹת בַּכֶּסֶף יִקְנוּ וְכָתוֹב בַּסֵּפֶר וְחָתוֹם וְהָעֵד עֵדִים. וְחָתוֹם אֵילוּ עֵידֵי שְׁטָר. וְהָעֵד עֵדִים אֵילוּ עֵידֵי חֲזָקָה. אוֹ אֵינָן אֶלָּא עֵידֵי שְׁטָר. כְּבָר כָּתוּב וְכָתוֹב בַּסֵּפֶר וְחָתוֹם.

[335]From where that landed property is bought by money, or contract, or possession? "Fields will be bought by money, writing on a scroll and signing, and testifying of witnesses.[336]" "And signing", these are the witnesses on the contract. "And testifying of witnesses," these are the witnesses to possession. Or maybe these are only the witnesses on the contract? These are already written: "Writing on a scroll and signing."

335   Cf. Babli 26a.
    A parallel text for this and the following paragraphs is in Halakhah 5 (Note 479); variants are noted there.
336   *Jer.* 32:44. A prophetic text cannot really serve as legal source but it can demonstrate practice. Since the speaker in this verse is God, the practice is accepted by Heaven.

(59d line 51) רִבִּי יָסָא בְּשֵׁם רִבִּי מָנָא רִבִּי תַנְחוּם רִבִּי אַבָּהוּ בשם רִבִּי יוֹחָנָן. אֵין קַרְקַע נִקְנֶה בְּפָחוֹת מִשְּׁוֶה פְרוּטָה. מַה טַעֲמָא. שָׂדוֹת בַּכֶּסֶף יִקְנוּ. וּפְלִיג עַל הַהִיא דְּאָמַר רִבִּי חֲנִינָר. כָּל־שְׁקָלִים שֶׁכְּתוּבִים בַּתּוֹרָה סְלָעִים וּבַנְּבִיאִים לִיטְרִין וּבַכְּתוּבִים קִינְטִירִין. אָמַר רִבִּי יוּדָה בַּר פָּזִי. חוּץ מִשִּׁיקְלֵי עֶפְרוֹן דְּהַוְיָין קִנְטִירִין. מַה טַעֲמָא. בְּכֶסֶף מָלֵא יִתְּנֶנּוּ לִי. וְלֹא דַמְיָא. תַּמָּן כְּתִיב כֶּסֶף וְהָכָא כְּתִיב שְׁקָלִים. הָתִיבוּן. הֲרֵי הָאוֹנֶס הֲרֵי אֵין כָּתוּב בּוֹ אֶלָּא כֶּסֶף וְאַתְּ אָמַר שְׁקָלִים.

Rebbi Yasa in the name of Rebbi Mana[337]; Rebbi Tanḥum, Rebbi Abbahu in the name of Rebbi Joḥanan: Real estate cannot be bought for less than a *peruṭah*. What is the reason? "Fields will be bought by money[338]." This disagrees with what Rebbi Ḥanina said[339]: Any *šeqalim* mentioned in the Torah are tetradrachmas[122], in the Prophets pounds[340], and in the Hagiographs *centenarii*[341]. Rebbi Jehudah bar Pazi said, except for the *šeqalim* paid to Ephron[342], which were *centenarii*. What is the reason? "For full money he shall give it to me." There is no comparison since here it is written "money" but there "*šeqalim*". They objected, is there not the rapist[343], for whom "money" is written and you say "*šeqalim*"?

337 R. Mana I.

338 Anything less than the smallest coin is not money.

339 Babli *Bekhorot* 50a. There, the statement of R. Jehudah bar Pazi is ascribed to R. Ḥanina. In *Gen. rabba* 58(9), the statement of R. Jehudah bar Pazi is in the name of R. Yudan.

340 A Roman *libra*, Greek λίτρα, of 96 *denarii* or 24 tetradrachmas.

341 A noun, meaning "100 pieces" formed in vulgar Latin from the classical adjective *centenarius*, "consisting of a hundred", in this case 100 *librae*. The same meaning, 100 lb., is found in Middle High German *zëntenære, zëntner*.

342 Paid by Abraham for the Makhpela cave, *Gen.* 23:9.

343 *Deut.* 23:29; the extra fine the rapist of a virgin pays is "50 silver pieces"; cf. *Ketubot* 3:1, Note 1.

(59d line 57) וּדְלֹא כְרִבִּי לְעָזֶר. דְּרִבִּי לְעָזֶר אָמַר. הִילֵּךְ קָנָה. דְּתַנֵּי. הִילֵּךְ בְּשָׂדֶה לְאוֹרְכָּהּ וּלְרָחְבָּהּ קָנָה עַד מָקוֹם שֶׁהִילֵּךְ. דִּבְרֵי רִבִּי אֱלִיעֶזֶר. וַחֲכָמִים אוֹמְרִים. לֹא קָנָה עַד שָׁעָה שֶׁיַּחֲזִיק. הַכֹּל מוֹדִין בְּמוֹכֵר שְׁבִיל לַחֲבֵירוֹ כֵּיוָן שֶׁהִילֵּךְ בּוֹ קְנָייוֹ. מַה טַעֲמָא. קוּם הִתְהַלֵּךְ בָּאָרֶץ לְאוֹרְכָּהּ וּלְרָחְבָּהּ כִּי לְךָ אֶתְּנֶנָּה.

This does not follow Rebbi Eliezer, for Rebbi Eliezer said that walking acquires, as it was stated: [344]If one walked across a field in length and breadth, he acquired up to the place he walked to, the words of Rebbi Eliezer. But the Sages say that he did not acquire up to the moment he acted in possession[345]. Everybody agrees that if somebody sells a path to another, when the latter went, he acquired. What is the reason? "Arise, walk in the Land in length and breadth, for I shall give it to you.[346]"

344 Babli *Baba batra* 100a. One assumes either that the field is ownerless or that the acquirer has a claim of possession that would give him squatter's rights; cf. *Ketubot* 5:5, Note 100.

In R. Eliezer's opinion, the rules of acquisition of a Canaanite slave are not identical with those for real estate; he will reject deriving legal rules from a verse in the Prophets.

345 He performed some agricultural work on the property.

346 *Gen.* 13:17.

(59d line 61) אִית מַתְנִיתָא אָמְרָה. עֲבָדִים כְּקַרְקָעוֹת. אִית מַתְנִיתָא אָמְרָה. כִּמְטַלְטְלִין. אִית מַתְנִיתָא אָמְרָה. לֹא כְּקַרְקָעוֹת וְלֹא כְמִטַלְטְלִין. מַתְנִיתָא אָמְרָה. עֲבָדִים כְּקַרְקָעוֹת. דְּתַנִּינַן תַּמָּן. חֶזְקַת בָּתִּים בּוֹרוֹת שִׁיחִין וּמְעָרוֹת מֶרְחֲצָאוֹת וְשׁוֹבָכוֹת בֵּית הַבַּדִּים וּבֵית הַשְׁלָחִין וַעֲבָדִים. אִית מַתְנִיתָא אָמְרָה. עֲבָדִים אֵינָן כִּמְטַלְטְלִין. דְּתַנֵּי. אֵי זוֹ הִיא חֶזְקַת עֲבָדִים. נָעַל לוֹ מִנְעָלוֹ. וְהִתִּיר לוֹ מִנְעָלוֹ. נָטַל לְפָנָיו לְמֶרְחָץ. רַבִּי שִׁמְעוֹן אוֹמֵר. אִם הִגְבִּיהוֹ הֲרֵי זוֹ חֲזָקָה. הִגְבִּיהַּ הוּא אֶת רַבּוֹ אֵין חֲזָקָה גְדוֹלָה מִזּוֹ. מִילֵּיהוֹן דְּרַבָּנִין אָמְרִין. עֲבָדִים כִּמְטַלְטְלִין. דָּמַר רַבִּי יוֹסֵי בְּשֵׁם רַבָּנִין. אֵין שִׁיעְבּוּד לְמַתָּנָה. אֵין גּוֹבִין מִן הָעֲבָדִים כְּקַרְקָעוֹת. אָמַר רַבִּי מָנָא לְרַבִּי שַׁמַּי. כָּאן אִינוּן רַבָּנִין. אָמַר לֵיהּ. רַבִּי יִצְחָק וְרַבִּי אִימִי. אַרְמַלְתָּא תְּפָסַת אֲמָתָא. אָתָא עוֹבְדָא קוֹמֵי רַבִּי יִצְחָק. אָמַר. תְּפָסַת תְּפָסַת. רַבִּי אִימִי מַפִּיק מִינָהּ. דְּהִיא סָבְרָה דְּהִיא דִידָהּ וְלֵית הִיא דִידָהּ. וְלֹא בְקַרְקָעוֹת. דְּתַנֵּי. קַרְקָעוֹת וַעֲבָדִים הֶחֱזִיק בַּקַּרְקָעוֹת. אִם אוֹמֵר אַתְּ. עֲבָדִים כְּקַרְקָעוֹת. כֵּיוָן שֶׁהֶחֱזִיק בַּקַּרְקָעוֹת הֶחֱזִיק בָּעֲבָדִים. דְּאָמַר רַבִּי יָסָא בְּשֵׁם רַבִּי יוֹחָנָן. הָיוּ לוֹ שְׁתֵּי שָׂדוֹת אַחַת בִּיהוּדָה וְאַחַת בַּגָּלִיל. הֶחֱזִיק בְּזוֹ שֶׁבִּיהוּדָה לִזְכּוֹת בְּזוֹ שֶׁבַּגָּלִיל אוֹ בְזוֹ שֶׁבַּגָּלִיל לִזְכּוֹת בְּזוֹ שֶׁבִּיהוּדָה. קָנָה. לֹא בִמְטַלְטְלִין. אִם אוֹמֵר אַתְּ. עֲבָדִים כִּמְטַלְטְלִין. כֵּיוָן שֶׁהֶחֱזִיק בִּמְטַלְטְלִין הֶחֱזִיק בָּעֲבָדִים. דְּתַנִּינַן תַּמָּן. שֶׁהַנְּכָסִין שֶׁאֵין לָהֶן אַחֲרָיוּת זוֹקְקִין אֶת הַנְּכָסִים שֶׁיֵּשׁ לָהֶן אַחֲרָיוּת לִישָׁבַע עֲלֵיהֶן.

A Mishnah says that slaves follow the rules of real estate. A *baraita* states, the rules of movables. A *baraita* states, neither the rules of real estate nor the rules of movables.

A Mishnah says that slaves follow the rules of real estate, as we have stated there[347]: "Possession of houses, cisterns, ditches, and caves, bath houses, and dovecots, olive presses, and irrigated fields, and slaves."

A *baraita* states, slaves do not follow the rules of movables. As it is stated: What is possession of a slave[30,348]? He tied his shoe for him, or untied his shoe, carried his things to the bath. Rebbi Simeon says, if he lifted him, that is possession. If he lifted his master, there is no stronger possession than this.

A statement of the rabbis says that slaves follow the rules of movables. For Rebbi Yose said in the name of rabbis, there is no lien for a gift[349]; one does not collect from slaves as from real estate[350]. Rebbi Mana asked Rebbi Shammai, who are those rabbis? He told him, Rebbi Isaac and Rebbi Immi. [351]A widow took a slave girl. The case came before Rebbi Isaac who said, what she took, she took. Rebbi Immi took her away, for she thought that she was hers but she was not hers.

Not of real estate, as it was stated: Real estate and slaves[352]; he took possession of the real estate. If you say that slaves follow the rules of real estate, when he took possession of the real estate he would have taken possession of the slaves, since Rebbi Yasa said in the name of Rebbi Joḥanan: If he had two fields, one in Judea and one in Galilee. If he took possession of the one in Judea with intention to take possession also of that in Galilee, or of the one in Galilee with intention to take possession also of that in Judea, he acquired[353].

Not of movables. If you say that slaves follow the rules of movables, when he took possession of the movables he would have taken possession of the slaves, since we did state there: "For property that is not guaranteed[354] will cause guaranteed properties to be objects of swearing about them.[355]"

347   Mishnah *Baba batra* 3:1. The Mishnah discusses how to establish title in the absence of a deed.

348   Babli 22b; Tosephta 1:5. Movables are acquired by actually taking them. Similarly, ownerless slaves are acquired by having them carry the new master's property.

349   This statement has no connection with the remainder of the text. If real estate is sold, the seller accepts responsibility to indemnify the buyer if the latter should lose the real estate because of foreclosure of a pre-existing lien, whether or not this is spelled out in the sale contract. For a gift of real estate, the donor accepts responsibility only if this is so stated in the deed. In the Babli, *Baba batra* 128a, this is a matter in dispute; the ultimate authority Rav Nahman agrees with the ruling of the Yerushalmi.

350   While slaves can be given in chattel mortgage, they are not subject to blanket liens which cover all the debtor's real estate. In particular, at places where a woman's *ketubah* is a lien only on her husband's real estate, the *ketubah* cannot be collected by the widow or divorcee by taking slave girls from the estate.

351   *Ketubot* 9:3, Notes 111-112.

352   Like Ptolemaic and Roman laws, rabbinic civil law is based on the distinction between ownership and possession. Paying for an acquisition conveys ownership but the transfer of property rights and liabilities requires an act of possession (cf. Halakhot 4,5). Taking possession by use (cf. Note 30) of a piece of real estate establishes possession of all real estate and movables included in one sale contract. Similarly, movables are taken into possession by moving one piece; this simultaneously gives possession of all items included in the sale. Since taking possession of slaves is by individual action only, in this respect they follow neither the rules of real estate nor those of movables. Taking possession of slaves does not induce possession of either estate or movables covered by the same sales contract; Babli *Baba qama* 12a.

253   In the Babli, *Baba qama* 12a,

this is a statement of Samuel, the Babylonian expert on civil law.

354 I. e., movables which have no title guarantee.

355 Mishnah 1:5; *Šebuot* 6:5.

Property claims about real estate and slaves, in contrast to movables, cannot be adjudicated by having the parties swear about ownership and responsibility.

(60a line 4) בְּכֶסֶף. רִבִּי יִרְמְיָה אָמַר. מֵאַחֵר לְרַבּוֹ. הָא מֵרַבּוֹ לְאַחֵר לֹא. אָמַר רִבִּי זְעִירָא. אֲפִילוּ מֵרַבּוֹ לְאַחֵר. מָהוּ מוֹצִיא. מֵרַבּוֹ לְעַצְמוֹ. רִבִּי יִרְמְיָה בְּעָא קוֹמֵי רִבִּי זְעִירָא. הֵילָךְ כֶּסֶף זֶה שֶׁתְּהֵא שָׂדְךָ לְחֵירוּת. אָמַר לֵיהּ. יָצָאת. שֶׁתְּהֵא שָׂדְךָ לְהֶבְקֵר. אָמַר לֵיהּ. לֹא יָצָאת. מַה בֵּין זֶה לָזֶה. זֶה זִיכָּה לְבֶן דַּעַת וְזֶה לֹא זִיכָּה לְבֶן דַּעַת. הַגַּע עַצְמָךְ שֶׁהָיָה חֵרֵשׁ. אָמַר לֵיהּ אִישׁ. הַגַּע עַצְמָךְ שֶׁהָיָה קָטָן. אָמַר לֵיהּ דַּרְכּוֹ לְהַגְדִּיל. אָמַר רִבִּי יוֹנָה. אַתְיָיא דְּרִבִּי זְעִירָא כְּרִבִּי שִׁמְעוֹן בֶּן אֶלְעָזָר. דְּתַנֵּי. רִבִּי שִׁמְעוֹן בֶּן אֶלְעָזָר אוֹמֵר מִשּׁוּם רִבִּי מֵאִיר. אַף בִּשְׁטָר עַל יְדֵי אֲחֵרִים. לֹא עַל יְדֵי עַצְמוֹ. מָהוּ בִּשְׁטָר עַל יְדֵי אֲחֵרִים לֹא עַל יְדֵי עַצְמוֹ. לֹא רַבּוֹ נוֹתֵן שְׁטָר לַאֲחֵרִים שֶׁיֵּצֵא עַבְדּוֹ לְחֵירוּת. אוּף הָכָא רַבּוֹ נוֹתֵן כֶּסֶף לַאֲחֵרִים שֶׁתְּהֵא שָׂדֵהוּ לְהֶבְקֵר.

"By money.[356]" Rebbi Jeremiah said, from another person to his master, therefore not from his master to another person[357]. Rebbi Ze'ira said, even from his master to another person. What brings this? From his master to himself[358]. Rebbi Jeremiah asked before Rebbi Ze'ira: "Here you have money that your field shall be unencumbered[359]." He answered, it is unencumbered. "That it be ownerless[360]"? He answered, it is not ownerless[361]. What is the difference between the cases? Here he advantaged a thinking person, there he did not advantage any thinking person. Think of it, if he[362] was deaf-mute[363]? He said to him, "a man.[364]" Think of it, if he[362] was underage? He said to him, one usually grows up[365]. Rebbi Jonah said, Rebbi Ze'ira follows Rebbi Simeon ben Eleazar, since Rebbi Simeon ben Eleazar says in the name of Rebbi Meïr:

Even with a contract through others, not by himself[366]. Does not his master deliver a document to others that his slave regain his freedom? Here also, his master gives money to others that his field become ownerless[367].

356 Here starts the discussion of the manumission of a slave according to R. Meïr.

357 A third party gives money to the master to buy the slave's freedom. This works even if the transaction is purely symbolic and only a *peruṭah* changes hands. But the master cannot give a *peruṭah* to a third person as a symbol of the slave's manumission.

358 The result of the transaction between master and third party is the freedom of the ostensibly uninvolved slave.

359 A third party can give money to a creditor to satisfy the mortgage on a field since even R. Meïr will agree that a person can legally act to another person's benefit without that person's authorization.

Some commentators are emending "field" to "slave" in the entire paragraph.

360 A person gives money to the owner of a piece of real estate for the latter to renounce his ownership. It is clear that if the former owner renounces his ownership by explicit declaration, the land becomes ownerless. Here the money is given without the owner's saying a word.

361 The action is not valid in law.

362 The beneficiary of a sane person's action.

363 Who is unable to act in law; cf. *Ketubot* 1:2 Note 134, *Yebamot* 14:1.

364 In *Lev.* 25:17, the word "man" is used to describe the agent in a real estate transaction. The deaf-mute is a man even if he is unable to act in law.

365 Only a minority of children die before reaching puberty. (The Babli would reject this argument since it insists that R. Meïr requires rules also to be valid for a minority. For the rabbis who dispute R. Meïr's position, a minor can acquire but not renounce ownership; *Sukkah* 46b.)

366 He disagrees with the Mishnah. Since R. Meïr states that the hand of the slave is the hand of his master (see below and *Ketubot* 6:1, Note 10), a document delivered by the master to the slave is a document delivered by

the master to himself and cannot have any validity. The bill of manumission must be delivered through the agency of a third person whose acceptance of the bill sets the slave free. The Tanna of the Mishnah holds that "he receives simultaneously his hand and his freedom." The Babli, 24a, reports a similar opinion of R. Simeon bar Eleazar in the name of R. Meïr regarding a wife's ability to contract without her husband.

367 This justifies R. Ze'ira's earlier remark that a slave can be manumitted by his master's giving a coin to a third party.

(60a line 14) אָמַר רִבִּי אָבוּן. אַתְיָיא כְּרִבִּי. דְּרִבִּי אָמַר. אָדָם מְשַׁחְרֵר חֲצִי עַבְדּוֹ. וְלֵית לְרַבָּנִין אָדָם מְשַׁחְרֵר חֲצִי עַבְדּוֹ. אִית לוֹן בְּעֶבֶד שֶׁלְּשׁוּתָפוּת. אֲבָל בְּעֶבֶד שֶׁכּוּלוֹ שֶׁלּוֹ שַׁנְיָיא הִיא. שֶׁהוּא כְּזָכָה מִימִינוֹ לִשְׂמֹאלוֹ. וְלֵית לְרִבִּי שֶׁהוּא כְּזָכָה מִימִינוֹ לִשְׂמֹאלוֹ. אִית לֵיהּ בְּמִזַּכֶּה לוֹ עַל יְדֵי אַחֵר. וְלֵית לְרַבָּנִין בְּמִזַּכֶּה לוֹ עַל יְדֵי אַחֵר. סָבְרִין רַבָּנִין. הָרָאוּי לִזְכּוֹת עַל יְדֵי עַצְמוֹ רָאוּי לִזְכּוֹת עַל יְדֵי אַחֵר. וְשֶׁאֵינוֹ רָאוּי לִזְכּוֹת עַל יְדֵי עַצְמוֹ אֵינוֹ רָאוּי לִזְכּוֹת עַל יְדֵי אַחֵר. רִבִּי אוֹמֵר. אַף עַל פִּי שֶׁאֵינוֹ רָאוּי לִזְכּוֹת עַל יְדֵי עַצְמוֹ רָאוּי לִזְכּוֹת לוֹ עַל יְדֵי אֲחֵרִים.

Rebbi Abun said, it[368] follows Rebbi, since Rebbi said that a person can free half of his slave[369]. But do the rabbis not hold that a person can free half of his slave? They admit it for a slave held in partnership[370]. But there is a difference for a slave who entirely belongs to him, for it is as if he gave something from his right into his left hand[371]. Does Rebbi hold that it is not as if he gave something from his right into his left hand? He admits it if he gave to him through a third party. Do the rabbis not hold that he may give to him through a third party? The rabbis hold that one who can acquire by himself can acquire through a third party; one who cannot acquire by himself cannot acquire through a third party. Rebbi says, even though he cannot acquire by himself, he can acquire through third parties.

368 The statement of R. Simeon ben Eleazar that R. Meïr requires the intervention of a third party in the manumission of a slave by document.

369 Babli *Giṭṭin* 23b, 41b; in *Temurah* 25b ascribed to R. Meïr. It is clear that "half of his slave" means "any part of his slave." Why would anybody want to partially emancipate his slave? By Mishnah *Giṭṭin* 4:5, the master is then forced to emancipate the slave completely and the slave has to write an IOU for the part of him that was not manumitted. If the slave is not worth his upkeep, the slave has no interest in being freed but his master is interested in getting rid of him and even having the chance of collecting some money from the IOU. (In Roman law, partial emancipation is accepted by Ulpian I 18 but rejected by most other earlier authorities. The Mishnaic law also appears in Egyptian sources and is incorporated in Justinian's Code; cf. R. Taubenschlag, *The Law of Greco-Roman Egypt in the Light of the Papyri*, New York 1944, p. 75.)

370 Since the partial owner eliminates all of his ownership in the slave.

371 Since for R. Meïr the slave's hand is his master's hand.

(60a line 21) הִגְבִּיהַּ אֶת הַמְצִיאָה וְאָמַר. עַל יְדֵי שֶׁאֶזְכֶּה בָּהּ אֲנִי וְלֹא רַבִּי. עַל כּוֹרְחוֹ זָכָה הוּא וְרַבּוֹ אוֹ זָכָה הוּא וְלֹא רַבּוֹ. נִישְׁמְעִינָהּ מִן הָדָא. הַמּוּדָּר הֲנָייָה מֵחֲתָנוֹ וְהוּא רוֹצֶה לָתֵת לְבִתּוֹ מָעוֹת. אוֹמֵר לָהּ. הֲרֵי הַמָּעוֹת הָאִילּוּ נְתוּנִין לָךְ מַתָּנָה. וּבִלְבַד שֶׁלֹּא יְהֵא לְבַעְלֵיךְ רְשׁוּת בָּהֶן אֶלָּא מַה שֶׁאַתְּ נוֹתֶנֶת לְפִיךְ. תַּנֵּי. וְלֹא לֵיהּ. אָמַר רַבִּי זְעִירָא. מָאן תַּנָּא. וְלֹא לֵיהּ. רַבִּי מֵאִיר. דְּרַבִּי מֵאִיר עָבִיד יַד עֶבֶד כְּיַד רַבּוֹ. בְּמַתָּנָה כְּרַבִּי מֵאִיר הוּא יַד הָאִשָּׁה כְּיַד בַּעְלָהּ. בִּמְצִיאָה כְּרַבָּנִין. אָמַר רַבִּי זְעִירָא קוֹמֵי רַבִּי מָנָא. שַׁנְייָא הִיא. שֶׁהוּא כְּזָכָה מִדַּעַת אַחֵר. אָמַר לֵיהּ. יְלֹא כָל־שֶׁכֵּן הִיא. מָה אִם שֶׁהִיא כְּזָכָה מִדַּעַת אַחֵר אַתְּ אוֹמֵר. זָכַת הָאִשָּׁה זָכָה בַעְלָהּ. כָּאן שֶׁהוּא כְּזָכָה מִדַּעַת עַצְמוֹ לֹא כָל־שֶׁכֵּן זָכָה הָעֶבֶד יִזְכֶּה רַבּוֹ.

4 נותנת לפיך | נ נושא ונותנת בפיך   5 ר' זעירא | נ ר'   6 עביד | נ עבד   עבד | נ העבד   8 היא | נ הוא

If he[372] picked up a find and said, for the purpose that I own it rather than my master. Does he and his master own it automatically[373] or does he own it but not his master? Let us hear from the following[374]: "If a person is by a vow prevented from benefitting his son-in-law but wants to give money to his daughter, he says to her: These coins are given to you as a gift on condition that your husband have no claim to them, except what you put into your mouth." It was stated: "Neither do you[375]". Rebbi Ze'ira said, who stated "neither do you"? Rebbi Meïr since Rebbi Meïr makes the hand of a slave the hand of his master. For a gift [we follow] Rebbi Meïr that the wife's hand is her husband's hand[376]; for a find [do we follow] the rabbis? Rebbi Ze'ira[377] said before Rebbi Mana, is there not a difference, for he is as if he acquired by somebody else's opinion[378]? He said to him, is it not a case *a fortiori*? Since in her case, when she would acquire by somebody else's opinion[379], you say that what a wife acquired, her husband acquired: here where he acquires by his own opinion, *a fortiori* what the slave acquired his master must acquire.

372 The slave picks up something that was lost in the public domain and, therefore, is ownerless. By the act of lifting, the finder acquires as property (Mishnah *Baba meṣia'* 1:1.)

373 Mishnah *Baba meṣia'* 1:5 gives the master ownership of the finds of his Cannanite slave. The question is whether this is always the case automatically or whether it is only the default option, valid unless the slave stipulates that it be his own property before he picks up the object. The question has to be asked for the anonymous majority who hold that a third party may give something to a slave on condition that his master have no part in it.

374 Mishnah and Halakhah *Nedarim* 11:5 (ג), Notes 69-70.

375 Everything remains the father's property until the food is eaten. But for the rabbis, a wife can acquire independent from her husband; Babli

376 Since the Mishnah is formulated anonymously, it represents practice.
377 The name probably should be "Ezra".
378 If the person who lost the article realizes his loss and gives up hope of recovery, he implicitly agrees to transfer his property rights to the finder.
379 A conscious transfer of property by the father.

(60a line 31) וְלָמָּה לֹא תַנִּינָן. בְּרָאשֵׁי אֵיבָרִים שֶׁאֵינָן חוֹזְרִין. אָמַר רִבִּי יוֹחָנָן בֶּן מַרְיָיה. מִפְּנֵי הַמַּחֲלוֹקֶת. אִית תַּנָּיֵי תַנֵּי. צָרִיךְ גֵּט שִׁחְרוּר. אִית תַּנָּיֵי תַנֵּי. אֵין צָרִיךְ גֵּט שִׁחְרוּר.

Why did we not state: By important limbs that do not regenerate[380]? Rebbi Joḥanan ben Marius said, because of the disagreement. Some Tannaïm[381] state that he needs a bill of manumission; some Tannaïm state that he does not need a bill of manumission[382].

380 *Ex.* 21:26-27 prescribes that a slave who lost an eye or a permanent tooth by his master's action must be given his freedom. "Tooth and eye" is generalized as "permanent deficiency involving a visible essential limb." (*Mekhilta dR. Ismael Neziqin* 9).
381 R. Ismael in Babli *Gittin* 42b, R. Eliezer in *Mekhilta dR. Ismael Neziqin* 9; an anonymous Tanna in *Mekhilta dR. Šim'on b. Jochai*, p. 177. For this Tanna, the freedom of the injured slave is "freedom by document", covered by the Mishnah. The omission in the Mishnah is an implicit indication that practice requires a bill of manumission.
382 R. Meïr in Babli *Gittin* 42b; cf. *Gittin* 4:4, Note 100.

(60a line 33) פְּשִׁיטָא שֶׁהָעֶבֶד מְקַבֵּל מַתָּנָה מֵאַחֵר לְאַחֵר. מֵאַחֵר לְרַבּוֹ. לְעַצְמוֹ לֹא. מֵאַחֵר לְעַצְמוֹ מַחֲלוֹקֶת רִבִּי מֵאִיר וַחֲכָמִים. אוֹמֵר. הָא לָךְ כֶּסֶף זֶה שֶׁלֹּא יְהֵא לְרַבָּךְ רְשׁוּת בָּהֶן. זָכָה הָעֶבֶד זָכָה רַבּוֹ. דִּבְרֵי רִבִּי מֵאִיר. וַחֲכָמִים אוֹמְרִים. זָכָה הָעֶבֶד זָכָה רַבּוֹ. מַה צְּרִיכָה לֵיהּ. מֵרַבּוֹ לְאַחֵר. כְּשֵׁם שֶׁהָעֶבֶד זָכָה מֵאַחֵר לְרַבּוֹ כָּךְ הוּא זוֹכֶה מֵרַבּוֹ לְאַחֵר. נִישְׁמְעִינָהּ מִן הָדָא.

הַשּׁוֹאֵל אֶת הַפָּרָה וְשִׁילְּחָהּ לוֹ בְיַד עַבְדּוֹ בְּיַד בְּנוֹ בְּיַד שְׁלוּחוֹ. לֵית הָדָא אֲמְרָה שֶׁהָעֶבֶד זָכָה מֵרבּוֹ לְאַחֵר. אָמַר רִבִּי אֶלְעָזָר. תִּיפְתָּר בְּעֶבֶד עִבְרִי. אָמַר רִבִּי יוֹחָנָן. תִּיפְתְּרִינֵיהּ בְּעֶבֶד כְּנַעֲנִי. תִּיפְתָּר בְּאוֹמֵר לוֹ. פְּתַח לָהּ וְהִיא בָאָה מֵאֵילֶיהָ. וְתַנִּינָן. הִנְהִיגָהּ הַמְשִׁיכָהּ קָרָא לָהּ וּבָאת אַחֲרוֹן מִתְחַיֵּיב בָּהּ כְּשׁוֹאֵל. רִבִּי זְעִירָא שְׁמַע לָהּ מִן הָדָא. אֲבָל אֵינוֹ מְזַכֶּה לֹא עַל יְדֵי בְנוֹ וּבִתּוֹ הַקְּטַנִּים וְלֹא עַל יְדֵי עַבְדּוֹ וְשִׁפְחָתוֹ הַכְּנַעֲנִים מִפְּנֵי שֶׁיָּדָן כְּיָדוֹ. לֵית הָדָא אֲמְרָה שֶׁאֵין הָעֶבֶד זוֹכֶה מֵרבּוֹ לְאַחֵר. תִּיפְתָּר כְּרִבִּי מֵאִיר. דְּרִבִּי מֵאִיר עָבַד יַד הָעֶבֶד כְּיַד רַבּוֹ. וְהָתַנֵּי. אִשְׁתּוֹ. דְּרִבִּי מֵאִיר עָבַד יַד הָאִשָּׁה כְּיַד בַּעֲלָהּ. רִבִּי חֲנִינָה בְּשֵׁם רִבִּי פִּינְחָס. תִּיפְתָּר כִּהֲדֵין תַּנְיָיא דְתַנֵּי. אִשְׁתּוֹ אֵינָהּ פּוֹדָה לוֹ מַעֲשֵׂר שֵׁינִי. הָדֵין תַּנְיָיא דְרִבִּי שִׁמְעוֹן בֶּן אֶלְעָזָר אָמַר מִשּׁוּם רִבִּי מֵאִיר. אִשְׁתּוֹ פּוֹדָה לוֹ מַעֲשֵׂר שֵׁינִי. וְהָדֵין תַּנְיָיא דְרִבִּי מֵאִיר עָבִיד יַד הָעֶבֶד כְּיַד רַבּוֹ וְלֹא יַד הָאִשָּׁה כְּיַד בַּעֲלָהּ.

It is obvious that a slave may accept a gift by one third party to another[383], by a third party to his master, [but] not from his master to himself[384]. From a third party to himself is in dispute between Rebbi Meïr and the Sages. If one said: Here [I am giving] you this money on condition that your master have no power over it, the slave acquired it and with him his master, the words of Rebbi Meïr. But the Sages say, the slave acquired it [but not][385] his master[386]. What is the problem? From his master to a third party. Since the slave may receive from a third party for his master, may he receive from his master for a third party? Let us hear from the following[387]: [388]"If somebody borrowed a cow and [the lender] sent her to him through his slave, his son, or his agent." Does this not mean that the slave is able to transfer rights from his master to a third party? Rebbi Eleazar said, explain it for a Hebrew slave. Rebbi Johanan said, you have to explain if for a Canaanite slave; explain it that he said, open [the gate] for her and she will come by herself, as we have stated: "If he led her, drew her to himself, called her and she followed him, he is responsible as a borrower." Rebbi Zeïra understood it from here: 'But he cannot make them acquire through his underage son or daughter or his Canaanite male or female slave, because their hand is not like his hand." Does this not imply that a slave is not able to transfer rights from his master to another person? Explain it following Rebbi Meïr since Rebbi Meïr makes the hand of the slave the hand of his master. But did we not state "his wife"? Rebbi Meïr holds that the hand of the wife is the hand of her husband! Rebbi Hananiah said in the name of Rebbi Phineas, explain it following the Tanna who stated: "His wife cannot redeem Second Tithe for him. Rebbi Simeon ben Eleazar says in the name of Rebbi Meïr, his wife can redeem Second Tithe for him." For that Tanna, Rebbi Meïr makes the hand of the slave the hand of his master but not the hand of the wife the hand of her husband! Rebbi Zeïra understood it from here: "But he cannot make them acquire through his underage son or daughter or his Canaanite male or female slave, because their hand is not like his hand." Does this not imply that a slave is not able to transfer rights from his master to another person? Explain it following Rebbi Meïr since Rebbi Meïr makes the hand of the slave the hand of his master. But did we not state "his wife"? Rebbi Meïr holds that the hand of the wife is the hand of her husband! Rebbi Ḥananiah said in the name of Rebbi Phineas, explain it following the Tanna who stated: "His wife cannot redeem Second Tithe for him. Rebbi Simeon ben Eleazar says in the name of Rebbi Meïr, his wife can redeem Second Tithe for him." For that Tanna, Rebbi Meïr makes the hand of the slave the hand of his master but not the hand of the wife the hand of her husband!

383 Since gifts can be given without the recipient's knowledge, the master A could accept B's gift to C without asking C. Therefore, the slave can do the same in his master's stead.

384 A direct gift from the master to his slave is "a gift from the master's right to his left hand" (Note 371).

385 Word missing in ms., corrected in *editio princeps*.

386 Quoted but in the end rejected in the Babli, 23b. The only gift which the Babli removes from the master is one given to the slave for the purpose of buying the latter's freedom. Since the slave did not acquire the money, his master has no claim.

387 Mishnah *Baba meṣia'* 8:4. The borrower of livestock is responsible if the animal is injured or dies while in his custody (*Ex.* 22:13). The responsibility of the borrower starts at the moment when he takes control of the animal. As long as the animal is driven by the owner's slave, it is in the owner's hand and the borrower is not responsible. But (as stated in the part of the Mishnah not quoted here) if the borrower said, send it to me through your slave and something happens on the way, the borrower is responsible.

388 The text from here to the end of the paragraph is from *Ma'aśer Šeni* 4:4 (**מ**, Notes 91-97), *Erubin* 7, **ע**.

389 The reading in *Qiddušin* is a scribal error, not translated.

390 The normal Yerushalmi spelling.

(60a line 50) רִבִּי זְעִירָא וְרִבִּי חִייָה בְּשֵׁם רִבִּי יוֹחָנָן. נְרָאִין דְּבָרִים שֶׁיִּזְכֶּה הָעֶבֶד בְּגֵט שִׁיחְרוּר שֶׁיֵּשׁ לוֹ גֵט שִׁיחְרוּר. וְאַל יִזְכֶּה בְּגֵט אִשָּׁה שֶׁאֵין לוֹ גֵט אִשָּׁה. אֵין

תֵּימַר. מַתְנִיתָא הִיא. הֲרֵי אַתְּ שִׁפְחָה וּוְלָדָךְ בֶּן חוֹרִין. אִם הָיְתָה עוּבָּרָה זָכַת לוֹ. עוּבָּרָה עָשׂוּ אוֹתוֹ כְּאֶחָד מֵאֵיבָרֶיהָ. רִבִּי בָּא בַּר חִייָה בְּשֵׁם רִבִּי יוֹחָנָן. נִרְאִין דְּבָרִים שֶׁיְּקַבֵּל הָעֶבֶד גֵּט שִׁחְרוּר וְאַל יְקַבֵּל גֵּט כְּנָתִין. אִין תֵּימַר. מִשְׁנָה קוֹדֶמֶת. הֲרֵי אַתְּ שִׁפְחָה וּוְלָדָךְ בֶּן חוֹרִין. אִם הָיְתָה עוּבָּרָה זָכַת לוֹ. עוּבְרָהּ עָשׂוּ אוֹתוֹ כְּאֶחָד מֵאֵיבָרֶיהָ.

Rebbi Ze'ira and Rebbi Ḥiyya in the name of Rebbi Joḥanan. It is reasonable that a slave be able to accept a bill of manumission[391] since a bill of manumission applies to him. But he should not be able to accept a bill of divorce[392] since a bill of divorce does not apply to him. If you say, is that not a *baraita*? "Your are a slave but your child is free; if she was pregnant, she acquired for him." They considered her fetus as one of her limbs[393]. Rebbi Abba bar Ḥiyya in the name of Rebbi Joḥanan[394]: It is reasonable that a slave be able to accept a bill of manumission but he should not be able to accept a bill of his equal[395]. If you say, the preceding *baraita*? "You are a slave but your child is free; if she was pregnant, she acquired for him." They considered her fetus as one of her limbs.

391 The bill of manumission of another owner's slave, even following R. Meïr. Babli *Giṭṭin* 23b.

392 *Giṭṭin* 2:6, Notes 129,130; Babli 23b.

393 As explained below, this rule follows Rebbi who permits partial manumission, but R. Joḥanan claims that his statement is accepted by everybody. Therefore, the *baraita* is no support for the first statement of R. Joḥanan; Babli *Giṭṭin* 23b, *Temurah* 25a.

394 He presents an alternate version of what R. Joḥanan said.

395 A slave cannot accept the bill of manumission of a fellow slave of the same master since his hand is his master's hand. It is necessary to emphasize that the slave can validly receive only the bill of another master's slave.

(60a line 57) פְּלָנִית שִׁפְחָתִי עוֹשָׂה אֲנִי לָהּ כְּתָב שֶׁלֹּא תִּשְׁתַּעְבֵּד. רבִּי לָעֶזָר וְרבִּי שׁמְעוֹן בֶּן יָקִים אֲעָלוּן עוֹבְדָא קוֹמֵי רבִּי יוֹחָנָן. אָמַר. לֹא הַכֹּל מִמֶּנּוּ לְשַׁעְבֵּד. בָּנֶיהָ מָה הֵם. עֲבָדִים. מָה שִׁיֵּיר בָּהּ. מַעֲשֵׂה יָדֶיהָ. רבִּי אַבָּא וְרבִּי יוֹסֵי תְּרֵיהוֹן אָמְרִין. דְּרבִּי הִיא. דְּרבִּי אָמַר. אָדָם מְשַׁחְרֵר חֲצִי עַבְדּוֹ. כָּתַב כָּל־נְכָסָיו לִשְׁנֵי עֲבָדָיו כְּאַחַת. שְׁנֵיהֶן יָצְאוּ לְחֵירוּת וּשְׁנֵיהֶן צְרִיכִין לְשַׁחְרֵר זֶה אֶת זֶה. רַב יְהוּדָה בְּשֵׁם שְׁמוּאֵל רבִּי אַבָּהוּ בְּשֵׁם רבִּי יוֹחָנָן. דְּרבִּי הִיא. דְּרבִּי אָמַר. אָדָם מְשַׁחְרֵר חֲצִי עַבְדּוֹ. אָמַר רבִּי זְעִירָא לְרבִּי בָּא. לֵית הָדָא אֲמָרָה שֶׁהָעֶבֶד זָכָה מֵרַבּוֹ לְאַחֵר. אָמַר לֵיהּ. מָה אַתְּ סָבַר. מִשֶּׁזָּכוּ בִּנְכָסִים יָצְאוּ לְחֵירוּת. אֶלָּא כְּאַחַת עֲבָדִים וּנְכָסִים יָצְאוּ לְחֵירוּת.

"For my slave girl X I want a document that she should not be enslaved.[396]" Rebbi Eleazar and Rebbi Simeon ben Yaqim brought a case before Rebbi Joḥanan. He said, he[397] has no power to enslave. What are her children[398]? Slaves. What did he retain for her? Her earnings[399]. Rebbi Abba and Rebbi Yose both said, this follows Rebbi who said that a person frees half of his slave. If he wrote all his possessions jointly to two of his slaves, both are free and both have to free one another[400]. Rav Jehudah in the name of Samuel, Rebbi Abbahu in the name of Rebbi Joḥanan: This follows Rebbi who said that a person frees half of his slave. Rebbi Ze'ira said to Rebbi Abba: Does this not imply that one slave accepts from his master for another one[401]? He answered, what do you think? Since they acquired the properties they went free? No, simultaneously slaves and properties went free[402].

396 A man writes in his will that the girl who cared for him cannot be used for servile tasks by his heirs. The heirs have to support her but cannot require any work from her. (The Babli, *Giṭṭin* 40a, disagrees and holds that the slave girl must be freed by the heirs. Only if the testator said that "she should be treated well", she remains a slave but cannot be forced to do any work she

dislikes.)

397 The heir.

398 Born after her original master's death. The Babli, *loc. cit.*, agrees.

399 She pockets all she earns while being supported by the heir.

400 Babli *Giṭṭin* 42a, which notes that if the properties were not given jointly but half to one and half to the other, they would remain slaves and get nothing since they could not free one another.

401 If the two slaves have to free one another, it seems to imply that by accepting the will each of them was instrumental in freeing half of the other. This would contradict the earlier statement that a slave cannot be part of the manumission of another slave of the same master.

402 The argument proposed in the previous Note is impossible since a half-free slave is unable to act in law. As the Babli formulates it, "his bill of manumission and his hand are simultaneous." The *baraita* can only be satisfactorily explained following the rabbis who oppose R. Meïr and hold that a slave can accept his own bill since by the bill he is able to act in law.

(60a line 66) הֲרֵי אַתְּ בַּת חוֹרִין וּוְלָדֵךְ עֶבֶד. וּוְלָדָהּ כְּיוֹצֵא בָהּ. דִּבְרֵי רִבִּי יוֹסֵי הַגְּלִילִי. וַחֲכָמִים אוֹמְרִים. לֹא עָשָׂה כְלוּם. אָמַר רִבִּי אֶלְעָזָר. כָּךְ פֵּירְשָׁהּ רִבִּי הוֹשַׁעְיָה אָב הַמִּשְׁנָה. שְׁנֵיהֶן בֶּן חוֹרִין. רִבִּי אִימִי בְשֵׁם רִבִּי יוֹחָנָן. שְׁנֵיהֶן עֲבָדִים. עַל דַּעְתֵּיהּ דְּרִבִּי יוֹחָנָן נִיחָא מַחֲלוֹקֶת. עַל דַּעְתֵּיהּ דְּרִבִּי אֶלְעָזָר מַה אִיכָּא מַחֲלוֹקֶת. אֶלָּא כֵינֵי. דְּבָרָיו קַיָּימִין. דִּבְרֵי רִבִּי יוֹסֵי הַגְּלִילִי. וַחֲכָמִים אוֹמְרִים. לֹא עָשָׂה כְלוּם. מָהוּ לֹא עָשָׂה כְלוּם. אָמַר רִבִּי אֶלְעָזָר. כָּךְ פֵּירְשָׁהּ רִבִּי הוֹשַׁעְיָה אֲבִי הַמִּשְׁנָה. שְׁנֵיהֶן בֶּן חוֹרִין. רִבִּי אִימִי בְשֵׁם רִבִּי יוֹחָנָן. שְׁנֵיהֶן עֲבָדִים. וּכְרִבִּי. דְּרִבִּי אָמַר. אָדָם מְשַׁחְרֵר חֲצִי עַבְדּוֹ.

"You are free but your child[403] will be a slave,' her child is like her[404], the words of Rebbi Yose the Galilean. But the Sages say, he did not do anything. Rebbi Eleazar said, so did Rebbi Hoshaia, the father of the Mishnah[405], explain: Both are free. Rebbi Immi in the name of Rebbi Johanan: Both are slaves. According to Rebbi Johanan, it is understandable; there is a disagreement. What is the disagreement following Rebbi Eleazar? But it must be so[406]: His words stand, the words of Rebbi Yose the Galilean[407]. But the Sages say, he did not do anything. What means "he did not do anything"? Rebbi Eleazar said, so did Rebbi Hoshaia, the father of the Mishnah, explain: Both are free. Rebbi Immi in the name of Rebbi Johanan: Both are slaves[408]. Following Rebbi, since Rebbi said that a person can free half of his slave[407].

403 The unborn child.

404 In this version (the only one quoted in the Babli, *Temurah* 25b), R. Yose the Galilean disagrees with Rebbi and holds that a slave partially freed is totally freed. He also holds that the fetus is part of the mother; the opposing view, that a fetus has a life of its own, is only found in the Babli (*loc. cit.* Note 393).

405 He reputedly was one of the first collectors of the Tosephta, illustrating the Mishnah.

406 Corrected version of the *baraita*.

407 As mentioned at the end of the paragraph, he follows Rebbi and admits freeing a slave limb by limb.

408 Following the Sages who admit partial manumission only in the case of a slave jointly owned by several persons, Note 370.

משנה ד: בְּהֵמָה גַסָּה בִּמְסִירָה וְהַדַּקָּה בְּהַגְבָּהָה דִּבְרֵי רַבִּי מֵאִיר וְרַבִּי אֶלְעָזָר. וַחֲכָמִים אוֹמְרִים בְּהֵמָה דַקָּה נִקְנֵית בִּמְשִׁיכָה. (fol. 58a)

Mishnah 4: Large animals by handing over[409] and small[410] by lifting, the words of Rebbi Meïr and Rebbi Eleazar. But the Sages say, small animals are taken possession of by drawing near[411].

409 Actual possession of cattle or horses is obtained by the buyer grasping either the animal's hair or any saddle, bridle, or belt tied to it.

Talmudic civil law, in parallel to Ptolemaic law in Egypt, is based on the distinction between ownership and possession. Ownership can be acquired by a monetary transaction but possession, including transfer of responsibility, requires a separate act. While acquisition, as a private act between consenting adults, is essentially unregulated, taking possession must follow specific rules.

410 Sheep and goats.

411 By making the animal walk according to the buyer's will, but also by lifting the animal.

(60a line 74) **הלכה ד**: בְּהֵמָה גַסָּה נִקְנֵית בִּמְסִירָה כול׳. רִבִּי הוּנָא אָמַר. אֵין מוֹסִירָה קוֹנָה אֶלָּא בְנִכְסֵי הַגֵּר. רַב חִזְקִיָּה רִבִּי בָּא רִבִּי לְעָזָר שָׁאַל. הָיוּ לוֹ עֲשָׂרָה גְמַלִּים קְשׁוּרִים זֶה בָזֶה. מָסַר לוֹ מוֹסִירָה שֶׁלְּאַחַת מֵהֶן. כּוּלְּהֶם קָנָה אוֹ לֹא קָנָה אֶלָּא אוֹתוֹ שֶׁמָּסַר לוֹ בִּלְבָד. רַב חִסְדָּא אָמַר. מְשׁוֹךְ אֶת הַבְּהֵמָה זוֹ לִקְנוֹתָהּ. קָנָה. לִקְנוֹת וּוְלָדוֹתֶיהָ. לֹא קָנָה. לִקְנוֹתָהּ הִיא וּוְלָדוֹתֶיהָ. קָנָה. אִילּוּ הָאוֹמֵר לַחֲבֵירוֹ. מְשׁוֹךְ אֶת הַבְּהֵמָה זוֹ שֶׁתִּקְנֶה מַשּׂוּי שֶׁלָּהּ שֶׁמָּא לֹא קָנָה. אָמַר רִבִּי יוֹסֵי. הָדָא דְתֵימַר בְּשֶׁלֹּא הָיְתָה הַבְּהֵמָה עוֹבָרָה. אֲבָל אִם הָיְתָה עוֹבָרָה עָשׂוּ אוֹתָהּ כְּמַשָּׂאָהּ.

Halakhah 4: "Large animals are taken possession of by handing over," etc. Rebbi Huna said, the halter gives possession only for property of the proselyte[412]. Rav Ḥizqiah, Rebbi Abba: Rebbi Eleazar asked, if there were ten camels tied one to another and he handed him the halter of one of them. Did he take possession of all of them or only of the one of which he handed him [the halter][413]? Rav Ḥisda said: "Draw[414] this animal to take possession of it, he took possession. To take possession of its offspring, he did not take possession[415]. To take possession of it together with its offspring, he took possession[416]." If somebody said to another person, draw this animal close to take possession of its load, would he not take possession[417]? Rebbi Yose said, that is, if the animal was not pregnant[418]. But if it was pregnant, they considered it as if carrying a load[419].

412 Who failed to start a Jewish family and whose property becomes ownerless at his death; cf. Note 30. In the Babli, *Baba meṣia'* 8b, *Rav* Huna states: that "a halter from another person takes possession except in case of a find and property of a proselyte." On basis of this quote, all commentators and editors delete אֶלָּא "only" in the present text. The deletion is unjustified; the texts in Yerushalmi and Babli are not comparable.

In the Babli, the formulation makes it clear that the buyer either receives the animal's halter from the seller or is instructed to take it. Since both a lost article and the estate of an intestate heirless person are ownerless, there is nobody who could hand over the halter or authorize its use. Therefore, only actual moving of the animal can be an act of simultaneous acquisition and taking in possession. While the text of the Babli is beyond doubt, confirmed by Rashi's translation of מוסירה by *chevêtre*, it is quoted in Tosaphot *Baba batra* 75b, *s. v.* אחזה, as מְסִירָה מֵחֲבֵירוֹ, "handing over by another person", which is correct in meaning if not in text. By contrast, neither handing over nor third person is mentioned in the Yerushalmi. The Yerushalmi asserts that in acquiring and taking possession of ownerless property, taking up the halter is enough, but not in course of formal taking possession of property acquired from a prior owner.

413 It is assumed that even if the first camel took a step under the influence of its new owner, the other nine did not move.

414 The seller instructs the buyer to proceed to take possession of the animal he bought.

415 Moving an animal which he did not buy does not give possession. In the parallel *Baba batra* 3:1, fol. 13d l. 66, "he took possession." The reading of *Baba batra* is incomprehensible.

416 In taking possession of a group of animals, it is enough to move one of them. This answers R. Eleazar's question. In *Baba batra*: "He did not take possession," cf. Note 415.

417 If he also bought the animal, moving it moves the load and all is taken in possession. The Babli, *Baba meṣia'* 9b, disagrees.

418 If the offspring are already born, they are independent animals which must be acquired by themselves.

419 In *Baba batra* (Note 415), R. Nasa notes that a fetus is part of his mother's body (Note 404).

(60b line 6) רִבִּי אַבָּא רַב הוּנָא בְּשֵׁם רַב. הָהֵן דִּנְגִיד בְּזֵקָה וְהִיא מִבַּזְעָא בְּיָדֵיהּ לֹא חַיָּיב בָּהּ. אָמַר רִבִּי יוֹסֵי בֵּירִבִּי בּוּן. לָכֵן צְרִיכָה. אֲפִילוּ לְמַעֲלָה לְגוֹ חָנוּתָא דְּלָא אִיתְכַּוֵּון אֶלָּא דְלָא יִסְבָּהּ בַּר חוֹרִין. מָהוּ שֶׁתִּקָּנֶה בְּשַׁעַר הַפָּחוֹת. אָמַר רִבִּי חַגַּיי בְּשֵׁם רִבִּי יוֹסֵי. מַתְנִיתָא אָמְרָה שֶׁאֵינָהּ נִיקְנֵית בְּשַׁעַר הַפָּחוֹת. דְּתַנִּינָן תַּמָּן. הַמּוֹכֵר יֵינוֹ לְנָכְרִי. פָּסַק עַד שֶׁלֹּא מָדַד דָּמָיו מוּתָּרִין. מָדַד עַד שֶׁלֹּא פָסַק דָּמָיו אֲסוּרִין. אִם אוֹמֵר אַתְּ אֶת שֶׁתִּקָּנֶה לִי בְּשַׁעַר הַפָּחוֹת אֲפִילוּ מָדַד עַד שֶׁלֹּא פִיסֵק. וְיֵיעָשֶׂה כְּמִי שֶׁפִּיסֵק עַד שֶׁלֹּא מָדַד וְיִהְיוּ דָּמָיו מוּתָּרִין.

1 דנגיד | ז דנגד   בזקה | ז בזיקא   מבזעא | ז מיבזעא   2 למעלה | ז מעיל   לגו | ז גו
3 דלא | ז ולא   יסבה בר חורין | ז יזכה בה חורון   בשער | ז לו כשר   4 בשם | ז קומי
בשער | ז כשר   6 או' את | ז אתה או'   שתקנה לי | ז לקנות לו   בשער | ז כשר
7 וייעשה | ז ייעשה

⁴²⁰Rebbi Abba, Rav Huna in the name of Rav: One who handles a wine-skin⁴²¹ and it splits in his hand is not responsible for it. Rebbi Yose ben Rebbi Abun, it is necessary even if he takes it in the store when he had no other intention than that no other person should take it⁴²². Can he take possession at a minimal rate⁴²³? Rebbi Haggai said in the name of Rebbi Yose: A Mishnah says that it cannot become his possession at a minimal rate, as we have stated there⁴²⁴: "If somebody sells his wine to a Non-Jew⁴²⁵. If he fixed the price before he measured, the proceeds are permitted⁴²⁶; if he measured before he fixed the price, the proceeds are forbidden⁴²⁷." If you say that it can come into his possession at a minimal rate⁴²⁸, even if he measured before he fixed the price, it should be as if he fixed the price before he measured⁴²⁹ and the proceeds would be permitted.

420 A parallel is in 'Avodah zarah 5:10 (ט).

421 When no price had been agreed upon. Therefore, handling of the wine skin by the prospective buyer cannot be taking possession.

422 It was handled in preparation of a buy.

423 Is it possible to take possession now of a commodity whose price will be determined at a future rate, e. g., the lowest price at which the commodity will be traded in the market (the commodities exchange) during the next 30 days. This is a futures contract which cannot be enforced (cf. *Ketubot* 5:5, Note 116.

424 Mishnah *'Avodah zarah* 5:10.

425 The Non-Jew is assumed to use his wine for libations, among other things. Since a libation makes the wine an instrument of pagan worship, it will be forbidden to a Jew and all proceeds received for it are forbidden (*Deut.* 13:18).

426 The Non-Jew owed the price to the Jew before he went and took possession of the wine. What the Jew sold was wine, not an article of pagan worship.

427 If the Non-Jew handled the wine before the price was fixed, the Jew sold an article of pagan worship.

428 Or any rate to be determined in the future.

429 Since he could have transferred possession to the Non-Jew before the latter handled the wine. The Babli, *'Avodah zarah* 72a, rejects the argument since it may be that the seriousness of the prohibition of pagan worship might override rules of contracts.

(60b line 13) שְׁמוּאֵל אָמַר. הָהֵין דִּנְסַב כְּזָנִיתָא וְהִיא מִתְחַטְּפָא מִי חַיָּיב בָּהּ. אָמַר רִבִּי שְׁמוּאֵל בַּר אֲבוּדָמָא. הָדָא דְתֵימַר כְּצוֹר וַחֲבֵירוֹתֶיהָ כְּקַיְסָרִין וַחֲבֵירוֹתֶיהָ. בְּרַם הָכָא עַד כְּדוֹן אוֹרְחֵיהּ מְחַזְרָה לְמִתְקְלָא.

Samuel said, if somebody take a small gold vessel and it be snatched, who is responsible for it[430]? Rebbi Samuel ben Eudaimon said, that is at Tyre or a similar place, at Caesarea[431] or a similar place. But here, so far it usually would be recovered.

HALAKHAH 4

430 If the person handling the vessel was not the owner.

431 Big cities where thieves easily find fences.

(60b line 16) רִבִּי שִׁמְעוֹן בֶּן לָקִישׁ בְּשֵׁם רִבִּי יַנַּאי. הַמּוֹכֵר צֹאן לַחֲבֵירוֹ כֵּיוָן שֶׁמָּסַר לוֹ מַשְׁכּוֹכִית קָנָה. מָהוּ מַשְׁכּוֹכִית. אִית דְּאָמְרִין. חוּטְרָא. וְאִית דְּאָמְרִין. שַׁרְקוּקִיתָא. וְאִית דְּאָמְרִין. נְגָדְתָּא.

Rebbi Simeon ben Laqish in the name of Rebbi Yannai: If somebody sold a flock[432] to another person, when [the seller] delivered the *maškokît*, [the buyer] took possession. What is *maškokît*? Some say, the shepherd's staff. But some say, a whistle. And some say, the bell-wether[433].

432 Of sheep or goats.

433 It is difficult to explain the feminine form chosen for 'bell-wether'. In the parallel *Baba batra* 3:1 (13d l. 43), the bell-wether is called תַּיָּישָׁא רַבָּא "the large ram", and instead of "whistle" one has πανδοῦρα, Latin *pandura*, a three-stringed musical instrument, invented by Pan. [Also compare Latin *pandus, -a, -um* "bent, crooked, curved" as reference to shephard's crook? (E. G.)] In the Babli, *Baba qama* 52a, only tambourine and bell-wether ("the ram at the head of the flock") are offered as explanations of *maškokît*.

(60b line 18) רִבִּי יַעֲקֹב בַּר אָחָא רִבִּי שִׁמְעוֹן בַּר אַבָּא בְּשֵׁם רִבִּי יְהוֹשֻׁעַ בֶּן לֵוִי. הַמּוֹכֵר בּוֹר לַחֲבֵירוֹ כֵּיוָן שֶׁמָּסַר לוֹ דְּלָיוֹ קָנָה. רִבִּי אִמִּי בְּשֵׁם רִבִּי יוֹחָנָן. הַמּוֹכֵר בַּיִת לַחֲבֵירוֹ כֵּיוָן שֶׁעָבַר לְתוֹכוֹ קְנָייוֹ. רִבִּי יוּדָה בֶּן פָּזִי בָּעֵי. מָסַר לוֹ אֶת הַמַּפְתֵּחַ מָהוּ. אָמַר רִבִּי זְכַרְיָה חַתְנֵיהּ דְּרִבִּי לֵוִי. מַחֲלוֹקֶת רִבִּי שִׁמְעוֹן וַחֲכָמִים. דְּתַנִּינָן תַּמָּן. הַמּוֹסֵר מַפְתֵּחַ לְעַם הָאָרֶץ הַבַּיִת טָהוֹר. שֶׁלֹּא מָסַר לוֹ אֶלָּא שְׁמִירַת הַמַּפְתֵּחַ. תַּנֵּי. רִבִּי שִׁמְעוֹן מְטַמֵּא.

Rebbi Jacob bar Aḥa, Rebbi Simeon bar Abba in the name of Rebbi Joshua ben Levi: If somebody sell a cistern, when he handed over its pail [the buyer] took possession[434]. Rebbi Immi in the name of Rebbi Joḥanan:

If somebody sell a house, when [the buyer] stored there, he took possession. Rebbi Jehudah ben Pazi asked, what if he handed over the key[435]? Rebbi Zachariah, son-in-law of Rebbi Levi, said: This is a disagreement between Rebbi Simeon and the Sages, as we have stated there[436]: "If somebody hand over the key to his house to an *'am ha'areṣ*[437], the house is pure since he handed to him only the guarding of the key." It was stated[438]: "Rebbi Simeon declares impure."

434 The Babli, *Baba qama* 51b, requires a declaration by the seller that the pail is handed over for possession.

435 In the Babli, *Baba qama* 51b/52a, handing over the key as sign of transfer of possession is undeniably a valid action.

436 Mishnah *Ṭahorot* 7:1.

437 A person who does not keep the rules of ritual purity. If he did enter the house, any movables (food and vessels) he touches there would become impure.

438 Tosephta *Ṭahorot* 8:1. He implies, against the othet Tanna, that handing over the key implies permission to use the house.

(60b line 24) רִבִּי אַבָּהוּ בְּשֵׁם רִבִּי שִׁמְעוֹן בֶּן לָקִישׁ. הַמּוֹכֵר מַעְשְׂרוֹת שָׂדֵהוּ לַחֲבֵירוֹ לֹא עָשָׂה כְלוּם. וְלַד שִׁפְחָתוֹ שֶׁל חֲבֵירוֹ לֹא עָשָׂה כְלוּם. עוֹבְרֵי בְהֶמְתּוֹ לַחֲבֵירוֹ לֹא עָשָׂה כְלוּם. אֲוֵיר חֲרֵבָתוֹ לַחֲבֵירוֹ לֹא עָשָׂה כְלוּם. אֶלָּא מוֹכֵר שָׂדֵהוּ וּמְשַׁיֵּיר מַעְשְׂרוֹתֶיהָ. מוֹכֵר לוֹ שִׁפְחָה וּמְשַׁיֵּיר לוֹ וְלָדָהּ. מוֹכֵר לוֹ בְהֵמָה וּמְשַׁיֵּיר לוֹ וְלָדָהּ. מוֹכֵר לוֹ חוֹרְבָה וּמְשַׁיֵּיר לוֹ אֲוִירָהּ. וְהֵיאַךְ אִיפְשָׁר לָאָדָם לִמְכּוּר אֲוֵיר חֲרֵבָתוֹ לַחֲבֵירוֹ. תִּיפְתָּר בְּאוֹמֵר לוֹ. תְּלוּשׁ מִן הֶחָרֵבָה הַזּוֹ שֶׁהִקְנָה אֶחָד מֵעֶשֶׂר שֶׁבָּהּ. וְכָא קַרְקַע לְפָנָיו שֶׁהוּא אוֹמֵר לוֹ. תְּלוּשׁ מִן הַקַּרְקַע הַזֶּה שֶׁיָּקְנֶה לָךְ אֶחָד מֵעֶשֶׂר שֶׁבּוֹ.

2 ולד | ד וולדי   של חבירו | ד לחבירו   3 חרבתו | ד חורבתו   4 שדהו | ד לו שדה
משייר | ד משייר לו   5 וולדה | ד עוברה   6 חרבתו | ד חורבתו   חרבה | ד חורבה
7 אחד מעשר שבה | ד לך אוירה   8 שיקנה לך | ד שתקנה   מעשר | ד מעשרה

[439]"Rebbi Abbahu said in the name of Rebbi Simeon ben Laqish: He who sells the tithes of his field to another person did not do anything; the future children of his slave girl to another person[440], he did not do anything; the fetus of his animal to another person, he did not do anything; the airspace of his dry land to another person, he did not do anything. But he may sell him a field and reserve the tithes for himself; a slave girl and reserve her children for himself; an animal and reserve her fetus for himself. Is it not impossible for a person to sell the airspace of his dry land to another person? Explain it if he tells him, tear out some grasses from that dry land to acquire its airspace[441]. And here there is real estate before him and he says, pluck something from the ground so that one tenth of it be acquired by you.

439   This paragraph is from *Demay* 6:3 (ז), Notes 79-83, which has an intelligible text.

440   Translation of the text in *Demay*. The text here reads: "The children of another person's slave girl" which does not make sense.

441   Translation of the text in *Demay*. The text here reads: "A tenth of its surface area", which is inappropriate.

(60b line 32) רִבִּי שְׁמוּאֵל וְרִבִּי זְעִירָא רִבִּי חִייָה בַר אַשִׁי בְשֵׁם רַב. אֵין מְשִׁיכָה קוֹנָה בְחָצֵר שֶׁאֵינָהּ שֶׁלִּשְׁנֵיהֶן. תַּנֵּי רִבִּי חִייָה וּפָלִיג. אֵימָתַי אָמְרוּ. הַמִטַּלְטְלִין נִיקְנִין בִּמְשִׁיכָה. בִּרְשׁוּת הָרַבִּים אוֹ בְחָצֵר שֶׁאֵינָהּ שֶׁלִּשְׁנֵיהֶן. אֲבָל בִּרְשׁוּת הַלּוֹקֵחַ כֵּיוָן שֶׁקִּיבֵּל עָלָיו זָכָה. בִּרְשׁוּת הַמּוֹכֵר לֹא קָנָה אֶלָּא עַד שָׁעָה שֶׁיַּגְבִּיהַּ אוֹ עַד שָׁעָה שֶׁיִּמְשׁוֹךְ וְיוֹצֵא חוּץ רְשׁוּת הַבְּעָלִים. בִּרְשׁוּת זֶה שֶׁהֵן מוּפְקָדִים אֶצְלוֹ לֹא קָנָה עַד שֶׁיִּזְכֶּה הוּא בָהֶן אוֹ עַד שֶׁיַּשְׂכִּיר לוֹ אֶת מְקוֹמוֹ.

[442]Rebbi Samuel, Rebbi Ze'ira, Rebbi Hiyya bar Ashi said in the name of Rav: Drawing close does not acquire in a courtyard which belongs to

neither of them. But Rebbi Hiyya stated in disagreement: "Under which circumstances did they say that movables are acquired by drawing close? In the public domain or in a courtyard which belongs to neither of them. But in the buyer's domain he acquired the moment he accepted it. In the seller's domain he does not acquire unless either he lifts it up or moves it out of its prior owner's domain. In a domain where it was deposited he does not acquire unless he either is explicitly empowered or he leases its place."

442 *Gittin* 8:1, Notes 17-21.

(60b line 38) וַחֲכָמִים אוֹמְרִים. בְּהֵמָה דַקָּה נִקְנֵית בִּמְשִׁיכָה. מַה טַעֲמוֹן דְּרַבָּנִין. מִשְׁכוּ וּקְחוּ לָכֶם צֹאן לְמִשְׁפְּחוֹתֵיכֶם. כִּי הָא דְּרַב יְהוּדָה שָׁלַח לִשְׁאוֹל. בְּהֵמָה גַסָּה בְּמָה הִיא נִקְנֵית. אֲמַר לֵיהּ. בִּמְסִירָה. אֲמַר לֵיהּ. וְלֹא מַתְנִיתָא הִיא. בְּהֵמָה גַסָּה נִקְנֵית בִּמְסִירָה. אִית תַּנָּיֵי תַּנֵּי מִיחְלַף. רַב יְהוּדָה שָׁאַל לְרִבִּי אֶלְעָזָר. בְּכוֹר שֶׁנִּטְרַף בְּתוֹךְ שְׁלֹשִׁים. אֲמַר לֵיהּ. כַּמָּה שָׁמֵת וּפָטוּר מֵחָמֵשׁ סְלָעִים שֶׁלַּבֵּן. רַב יְהוּדָה שָׁלַח שָׁאַל לְרִבִּי אֶלְעָזָר. שִׁילְיָיא שֶׁיָּצָאת מִקְצָתָהּ הַיּוֹם וּמִקְצָתָהּ לְמָחָר. אֲמַר לֵיהּ. אִם לְדָם טָהוֹר מוֹנֶה מִיּוֹם הָרִאשׁוֹן. וְאִם לְדָם טָמֵא מוֹנֶה מִיּוֹם שֵׁנִי. אֲמַר רִבִּי מַתַּנְיָיה. הֲדָא דְּתֵימַר בְּשֶׁלֹּא יָצָא עִמָּהּ וָלָד. אֲבַל אִם יָצָא עִמָּהּ וָלָד בֵּין לְדָם טָהוֹר בֵּין לְדָם טָמֵא אֵינָהּ מוֹנָה אֶלָּא מִשְׁעַת יְצִיאַת הַוָּלָד.

"But the Sages say, small animals are taken possession of by drawing near." What is the reason of the rabbis? "Draw near and take for yourselves small animals for your families[443]." As Rav Jehudah sent to ask[444]: By what means is possession of large animals established? He answered, by handing over; and asked, is that not the Mishnah? There are Tannaïm who switch the attributions[445]. Rav Jehudah asked Rebbi

Eleazar: If a firstborn became "torn" within thirty days[446]? He answered, he is as if dead[447] and free from the five tetradrachmas of a son. [448]Rav Jehudah sent and asked Rebbi Eleazar: A placenta which was delivered partially today and partially tomorrow? He answered, for pure blood she counts from the first day, for impure blood from the second day. Rebbi Mattaniah said, that is, if no child was produced with it. But if there was a child, both for pure and impure blood she counts only from the moment of birth of the child.

443   Ex. 12:21.

444   As the later text shows, probably one should read here: "To ask R. Eleazar." According to the Babli, Baba qama 11b, the messenger was Ulla.

445   Obviously, Rav Jehudah was supposed to have studied the Mishnah. But he was not sure about the references to large and small domesticated animals and asked for the correct text from the Babylonian R. Eleazar in Galilee where the latter had access to the traditions of the school of Rebbi.

446   A firstborn son has to be redeemed (Ex. 13:13,34:20); this is specified in Num. 3:40,47 to apply to firstborn sons above the age of one month and the redemption money, 5 biblical šeqalim (Note 122), has to be given to a priest. A human who develops a defect which makes his long-term survival impossible is called "torn", a term used in parallel with the talmudic interpretation of "torn" animals forbidden as food (Ex. 22:30).

447   This parallels the rabbinic theory that a person who kills a "torn" human cannot be convicted of first-degree murder (Babli Sanhedrin 78a). In the Babli, Menaḥot 37a/b, the rule is derived from Num. 18:15 (cf. also Sifry Num. #118.)

448   Niddah 3:4, Notes 103-104; the parallel in the Babli is Baba qama 11a.

(60b line 38) רַב יְהוּדָה שָׁלַח לְרִבִּי אֶלְעָזָר. שׁוֹמֵר שֶׁמָּסַר לְשׁוֹמֵר. אָמַר לֵיהּ. הָרִאשׁוֹן חַיָּיב. רִבִּי יוֹחָנָן אָמַר. הַשֵּׁינִי חַיָּיב. רִבִּי שִׁמְעוֹן בֶּן לָקִישׁ אָמַר. הַשֵּׁינִי

חַיָּב. תַּמָּן תַּנִּינָן. הַשּׂוֹכֵר פָּרָה מֵחֲבֵירוֹ וְהִשְׁאִילָהּ לְאַחֵר וּמֵתָה כְּדַרְכָּהּ. יִשָּׁבַע הַשּׂוֹכֵר שֶׁמֵּתָה כְדַרְכָּהּ. הַשּׁוֹאֵל מְשַׁלֵּם לַשּׂוֹכֵר. אָמַר רִבִּי יוֹסֵה. כֵּיצַד הֲלָה עוֹשֶׂה סְחוֹרָה בְּפָרָתוֹ שֶׁלָּזֶה. אֶלָּא תַחֲזוֹר פָּרָה לַבְּעָלִים. רִבִּי אִילָא בְשֵׁם רִבִּי יַנַּאי. וְהוּא שֶׁנָּתַן לוֹ רְשׁוּת לְהַשְׁאִיל. אֲבָל אִם לֹא נָתַן רְשׁוּת לְהַשְׁאִיל לֹא בְדָא. וְתַנֵּי רִבִּי חִייָה כֵּן. אֵין הַשּׁוֹאֵל רַשַּׁאי לְהַשְׁאִיל. וְלֹא הַשּׂוֹכֵר רַשַּׁאי לְהַשְׁכִּיר. וְלֹא הַשּׁוֹאֵל רַשַּׁאי לְהַשְׁכִּיר. וְלֹא הַשּׂוֹכֵר רַשַּׁאי לְהַשְׁאִיל. וְלֹא מִי שֶׁהוּפְקַד אֶצְלוֹ רַשַּׁאי לְהַפְקִיד אֵצֶל אַחֵר. אֶלָּא אִם כֵּן נָטְלוּ רְשׁוּת מִן הַבְּעָלִים. וְכוּלָּן שֶׁשִּׁינּוּ שֶׁלֹּא מִדַּעַת הַבְּעָלִים חַיָּיבִין. וְשׁוֹאֵל אֲפִילוּ לֹא שִׁינָּה חַיָּב. אֶלָּא בְגִין דְּתַנִּינָן תַּמָּן. מַתְּנָה שׁוֹמֵר חִנָּם לִהְיוֹת פָּטוּר מִשְּׁבוּעָה וְהַשּׁוֹאֵל לִהְיוֹת פָּטוּר מִלְּשַׁלֵּם. אָתָא מֵימַר לָךְ אֲפִילוּ הִתְנָה עִמּוֹ שֶׁהוּא פָּטוּר חַיָּב. בִּיקֵּשׁ לְהַשְׁבִּיעַ אֶת הַשּׁוֹאֵל. נִשְׁבַּע מִן הָדָא. כָּתַב לָהּ. נֶדֶר וּשְׁבוּעָה אֵין לִי עָלַיִךְ. אֵינוֹ יָכוֹל לְהַשְׁבִּיעָהּ. אֲבָל מַשְׁבִּיעַ הוּא אֶת יוֹרְשֶׁיהָ וְאֶת הַבָּאִים בִּרְשׁוּתָהּ. הָדָא אָמְרָה שֶׁאִם בִּקֵּשׁ אֶת הַשּׁוֹאֵל שֶׁהוּא מַשְׁבִּיעוֹ. וְהִיא יַלְפָה מִן הָדָא. שֶׁאִם בִּקֵּשׁ לְהַשְׁבִּיעַ אֶת הַאִשָּׁה שֶׁהוּא מַשְׁבִּיעָהּ. אָמַר רִבִּי חֲנִינָה. לָא צְרִיכָה מֵילַף הָדָא מִן הַהִיא. וּמַה צְּרִיכָה מֵילַף. הַהִיא מִן הָדָא. כַּיי דָּמַר רִבִּי הִילָא בְשֵׁם רִבִּי יַנַּאי. וְהוּא שֶׁנָּתַן לוֹ רְשׁוּת לַשּׁוֹאֵל. וְהָכָא שֶׁנָּתַן לָהּ רְשׁוּת שֶׁיְּהוּ בָנֶיהָ אֶפִּיטְרוֹפִּין. אָמַר רִבִּי יוֹסֵה. צָרִיךְ לְהַעֲלוֹת לוֹ שָׂכָר כָּל־זְמָן שֶׁהִיא שְׁכוּרָה אֶצְלוֹ. רִבִּי זְעִירָא שָׁאַל לְרִבִּי אֲבִינָא. שְׁאָלוּהָ הַבְּעָלִים וָמֵתָה. אָמַר לֵיהּ. כֵּן אֲנַן קַיָּימִין. אֲפִילוּ אֲכָלוּהָ. אָמַר רִבִּי יוֹסֵי בֵּירִבִּי בּוּן. שְׁלָהֶם אֲכָלוּ. רִבִּי זְעִירָא בְעָא קוֹמֵי רִבִּי יָסָא. הֵיךְ עָבְדִין עוֹבְדָא. אָמַר לֵיהּ. תְּרֵי כָלְקֳבֵל אַרְבְּעָה לָא עָבְדִין עוֹבְדָא בְסוּגְיָיא. אָמַר לֵיהּ. תְּרֵי כָלְקֳבֵל תְּרֵי אִינּוּן. רִבִּי לָעְזָר תַּלְמִידֵיהּ דְּרִבִּי חִייָה רוֹבָא רִבִּי יוֹחָנָן תַּלְמִידֵיהּ דְּרִבִּי יַנַּאי.

Rav Jehudah sent to Rebbi Eleazar: If a keeper give to another keeper[449]. He answered, the first is responsible. Rebbi Joḥanan said, the second[450] is responsible. Rebbi Simeon ben Laqish said, the second is responsible. [451]There, we have stated: "If somebody leases a cow from another person and lends it to a third party; if it died naturally, the lessee has to swear that it died naturally and the borrower has to pay to the lessee. Rebbi Yose said, how can this person make a deal with another's cow? But the cow's [price] has to be restituted to the owner." Rebbi Hila in the name of Rebbi Yannai: Only if he gave permission to lend to others. Also Rebbi Hiyya stated thus: "The borrower cannot lend, nor the lessee lease, nor the borrower lease, nor the lessee lend, nor the trustee give to another unless they received permission from the owners. And all who changed the titles without the owners' knowledge are liable. But the borrower is liable even if he did not change." But it is because we stated: "An unpaid watchman can stipulate to be exempt from an oath and the borrower may stipulate that he not have to pay." This means that even if he stipulated to be exempt he is obligated. What if he wanted to let the borrower swear? Let us hear[452] from the following: "If he wrote to her: 'I have no vow or oath against you,' he cannot make her swear, but he can ask an oath from the heirs or her business associates." This implies that if he wanted to make the borrower swear, he can force him to swear. The second case teaches about the first, that if he wants to force the wife to swear, he can make her swear. Rebbi Hanina said, it is not necessary to derive the first case from the second, and what does one learn for the second case from the first? Following what Rebbi Hila said in the name of Rebbi Yannai: Only if he gave permission to lend to others. And here, only if he gave permission to let her sons be stewards. Rebbi Yose said, he has to pay the lease the entire time it is leased to him. Rebbi Ze'ira asked Rebbi Abinna: If the owners borrowed it and it died? He said to him, we hold that they ate it. Rebbi Yose bar Abun said, if they ate it, they ate their own property. Rebbi Ze'ira asked before Rebbi Yasa: How does one act? He said to him, there are two against four; one does not act following the argument. He said to him, they are two against two! Rebbi Eleazar is the Elder Rebbi Ḥiyya's student; Rebbi Joḥanan is Rebbi Yannai's student.

449 And something happens to the object to be kept, who is responsible?

450 This must read: "The first", as shown by the last statement in the paragraph and shown in *Ketubot* 9:5, Note 144.

451 From here to the end of the paragraph, the text is from *Ketubot* 9:5, Notes 128-146 (variant readings given there).

452 Translation of נשמעינה in the *Ketubot* text, instead of נשבע "been made to swear" which does not fit here.

(60b line 73) רַב יְהוּדָה שָׁלַח שָׁאַל לְרִבִּי לְעָזָר. הָאַחִין שֶׁחָלְקוּ וְאַחַר כָּךְ יִיבֵּם אֶחָד מֵהֶן. אָמַר לֵיהּ. כְּנִכְסֵי כוּלָם כְּנִכְסֵי הַמֵּת. עוּלָא בַּר יִשְׁמָעֵאל אָמַר. מְצוּיַת דַּעְתֵּיהּ דְּרִבִּי לְעָזָר. וְלֹא שַׁנְיָיא. הִיא שֶׁחָלְקוּ וְאַחַר כָּךְ יִיבֵּם אֶחָד מֵהֶן. הוּא שֶׁיִּיבֵּם אֶחָד מֵהֶן וְאַחַר כָּךְ חָלְקוּ. זָכוּ כּוּלָן בְּנִיכְסֵי הַמֵּת. וְלָמָּה אָמַר לֵיהּ. מַה דִּשְׁאָלֵיהּ אֲגִיבֵהּ. וְלָמָּה לֹא שָׁאֲלוּ לָהּ דְּאָמַר רִבִּי אֲבִינָא בְּשֵׁם רִבִּי אַסִּי. בְּכוֹר שֶׁחָלַק כִּפְשׁוּט חֲזָקָה וִיתֵּר.

Rav Jehudah sent asking from Rebbi Eleazar: If brothers split [the estate] and then one of them entered a levirate marriage[453]? He answered, the property of the deceased is like common property[454]. Ulla bar Ismael said, it is found that in Rebbi Eleazar's opinion there is no difference whether they split and then one of them entered a levirate marriage or one of them entered a levirate marriage and then they split, but all of them share[455] in the property of the deceased. Why did he not say so? He answered what was asked of him. And why did he not ask?

Because of what Rebbi Abinna said in the name of Rebbi Assi[456]: If a first-born shared as a common son, it is *prima facie* evidence that he renounced his prerogative[457].

453 The father died and then one of the brothers died childless. The brother who married the widow inherits the childless brother's property. If the deceased brother was not married, it is clear that the father's inheritance is distributed among the surviving brothers. The problem is whether the brother who marries the widow only gets the deceased brother's property or also has a claim to the share the brother would have had if he had not died.

454 The estate of the deceased brother has no claim on the father's inheritance.

455 Equally.

456 Babli *Baba batra* 126a; Yerushalmi *Ketubot* 4:13, Notes 257-258.

457 The claim to a double portion. Similarly, if the brother who married the widow did not put forth his deceased brother's claim at the moment of distribution, he is presumed to have waived his claimt.

(60c line 3) רַב יְהוּדָה שָׁלַח שָׁאַל לְרִבִּי לָעְזָר. הָאַחִין שֶׁחָלְקוּ. אָמַר לֵיהּ. חוֹלְקִין מַה שֶׁעֲלֵיהֶן וְאֵין חוֹלְקִין לֹא מַה שֶׁעַל בְּנֵיהֶן וְלֹא מַה שֶׁעַל בְּנוֹתֵיהֶן. רִבִּי אִימִּי אוֹמֵר. הָעוֹשֶׂה שׁוּם לְבֵיתוֹ מְבִיאִין שׁוּם לְעַצְמָן לָאֶמְצַע וְחוֹלְקִין. הָעוֹשֶׂה קַטְלָא לְבֵיתוֹ אֵין מְבִיאִין לָאֶמְצַע וְחוֹלְקִין. בִּרְאוּיָה לְהִשְׁתַּמֵּשׁ בַּחוֹל. אֲבָל בִּרְאוּיָה לְהִשְׁתַּמֵּשׁ בָּרֶגֶל מְבִיאִין לָאֶמְצַע וְחוֹלְקִין. רִבִּי מָנָא אָמַר. כְּלֵי רֶגֶל חוֹלְקִין. כְּלֵי שַׁבָּת צְרִיכָא. רִבִּי אָבִין פְּשִׁיטָא לֵיהּ. בֵּין כְּלֵי רֶגֶל בֵּין כְּלֵי שַׁבָּת מְבִיאִין לָאֶמְצַע וְחוֹלְקִין. רִבִּי זְעִירָא בְּעָא קוֹמֵי רִבִּי מָנָא. אִילֵין בּוֹלָסַיָּיא. אָמַר לֵיהּ. חֲכִים אַתְּ דְּאִית לָךְ בּוֹלָסַיִּין סַגִּין. אָמַר לֵיהּ. מְבִיאִין וְחוֹלְקִין.

Rav Jehudah sent and asked Rebbi Eleazar: Brothers who split[458]? He answered, they divide what they are wearing but not what their sons and daughters are wearing[459]. Rebbi Immi said, if one makes an appraisal[460] for his wife, this is counted for himself and becomes part of the common estate to be distributed. If one makes a necklace[460a] for his wife, this is not of the common estate to be distributed if it is to be used on weekdays[461]. But if it is made to be used on holidays. it becomes part of the common estate to be distributed. Rebbi Mana said, holiday dresses are distributed[462]. Sabbath dresses are problematic. It is obvious for Rebbi Abin that both holiday and Sabbath dresses become part of the common estate and are distributed. Rebbi Ze'ira[377] asked before Rebbi Mana: What about spherules[463]? He answered, you understand this since you own many spherules. He said to him, they become part of the common estate to be distributed.

458 Brothers who all were living and working together on the father's estate. During their father's lifetime, they had no independent income. Sometime after the father's death they decided to split the estate.

459 Since all they have came from the father's estate, even what they are wearing is part of the estate. However, their children's clothing is property of the children and cannot be counted in the estate. The Babli *Baba qama* 11b agrees. It notes that if the oldest brother had been made to wear more distinguished clothing in order to represent the entire family before the authorities, the extra expenditure was made on behalf of the estate and cannot be debited to the brother.

460 It is difficult to understand what is meant. The word שום has two meanings, (1) appraisal (of real estate, of dowry, etc.), (2) mole (on the skin). Neither of the meanings is appropriate here. It seems that meaning (1) is derived from Accadic *šāmum* "buy, object of acquisition; price of object". Following the first meaning of the Accadic word, one speaks of clothing which one of the brothers bought for his wife with his father's money, as distinct from clothing made by home manufacture. In making an inventory of the estate, these clothes are debited

to the brother.
460a Latin *catella*.
461 Small jewellery objects become property of the women and are not to be counted.
462 They are not distributed but are counted as part of the husband's part in the estate.
463 Greek βῶλοι, Latin *boloe*, "spherules" of glass or metal beads, used for jewellery, also kind of precious stones.

(60c line 12) רַב יְהוּדָה שָׁלַח שָׁאַל לְרִבִּי לְעָזָר. מַהוּ לִגְבּוֹת מִן הָעֲבָדִים בְּקַרְקָעוֹת. אֲמַר לֵיהּ. גּוֹבִין מִן הָעֲבָדִים בְּקַרְקָעוֹת. הוֹרֵי רִבִּי לְעָזָר לְאִילֵּין דְּבֵית רִבִּי יַנַּאי לִגְבּוֹת מִן הָעֲבָדִים בְּקַרְקָעוֹת.

Rav Jehudah sent and asked Rebbi Eleazar: May one foreclose slaves with real estate? He answered, one may foreclose slaves with real estate[464]. Rebbi Eleazar instructed those from the House of Rebbi Yannai to foreclose slaves with real estate[465].

464 Since mortgages usually were written as liens on the entire real estate of the debtor (the Byzantine mortgage *omnium bonorum*, derived from Ptolemaic Egyptian practice), not on a specific parcel, the question arises whether slaves can be treated as real estate since for them the rules of possession are derived from the rules of real estate. In the Babli, *Baba batra* 128a, the Babylonian Rav Naḥman rules against the Yerushalmi rule, represented there by the Galilean Rebbi Abba. (The Galilean rule could not be based on Egyptian precedents since mortgages in Egypt had to be registered with the registrar of deeds, restricted to real estate.)
465 His ruling was in practice, not only theoretical.

(60c line 14) רַב יְהוּדָה שָׁלַח שָׁאַל לְרִבִּי אֶלְעָזָר. הָאַנָּס וְהַגּוֹזְלָן וְהַגַּנָּב. אֲמַר לֵיהּ. חֲזָקָה שֶׁאֵין הַבְּעָלִים מִיטַּפְּלִין בְּמֵיתָה. וּמְנַיָּין שֶׁאֵין הַבְּעָלִים מִיטַּפְּלִים בְּמֵיתָה. אָמַר רִבִּי בָּא בַּר מָמָל. חַיִּים שְׁנַיִם יְשַׁלֵּם. וְלֹא מֵתִים. עַד כְּדוֹן גְּנֵיבָה. גְּזֵילָה. אָמַר רִבִּי אָבוּן. וְהֵשִׁיב אֶת הַגְּזֵילָה אֲשֶׁר גָּזָל. בְּעֵינָהּ.

Rav Jehudah sent and asked Rebbi Eleazar: The extortionist, and the robber, and the thief[466]? He answered, it is assumed that the owners do not deal with the dead animal[467]. From where that the owners do not deal with the dead animal? Rebbi Abba bar Mamal said, "alive, he shall pay double[468]," but not dead animals. That refers to theft; for robbery? Rebbi Abun said, "he shall return the robbed object which he robbed[469]," as it was.

466 The owner obtained a court order of restitution for anything taken unlawfully. If the thing was broken in the meantime or if it was livestock it died (cf. *Ex.* 21:35), is the thief or robber obligated to pay for the entire damage or may he return the damaged object and pay only the difference between the original value and the amount recoverable from sale of the damaged object?

467 In the Babli, *Baba qama* 11a, Ulla in the name of R. Eleazar represents the opposite opinion. The opinion expressed here is accepted by the Babylonian authorities as judicial practice. The paragraph is discussed in Tosaphot *Baba meṣia'* 96b/97a, *s. v.* זיל.

468 *Ex.* 22:3, speaking of the thief of livestock.

469 *Lev.* 5:23.

(fol. 58a) **משנה ה**: נְכָסִים שֶׁיֵּשׁ לָהֶן אַחֲרָיוּת נִקְנִין בְּכֶסֶף וּבִשְׁטָר וּבַחֲזָקָה. וְשֶׁאֵין לָהֶן אַחֲרָיוּת אֵינָן נִקְנִין אֶלָּא בִּמְשִׁיכָה. נְכָסִים שֶׁאֵין לָהֶן אַחֲרָיוּת נִיקְנִין עִם נְכָסִים שֶׁיֵּשׁ לָהֶן אַחֲרָיוּת בְּכֶסֶף וּבִשְׁטָר וּבַחֲזָקָה. וְשֶׁאֵין לָהֶן אַחֲרָיוּת זוֹקְקִין אֶת הַנְּכָסִים שֶׁיֵּשׁ לָהֶם אַחֲרָיוּת לִישָּׁבַע עֲלֵיהֶן.

Mishnah 5: Guaranteed properties[470] can be acquired by money, or contract, or possession[329]. Not guaranteed properties[471] can be acquired only by drawing close[472]. Not guaranteed properties can be acquired together with guaranteed properties by money, or contract, or possession[473]. Not guaranteed properties can force [the owner of] guaranteed properties to swear about them[474].

470 Real estate which normally is sold with a title guarantee.

471 Movables.

472 For this Tanna, there is no transfer of possession of movables except by delivery.

473 Taking possession of a piece of real estate transfers possession of all things included in the sale.

474 Monetary claims which cannot be proven or disproved are settled by an oath taken by the defendent. The verse, *Ex.* 22:8, specifies that the oath is required for "ox, donkey, sheep, garment, or anything lost," excluding real estate (Mishnah *Šebuot* 6:7). But if the dispute was about both movables and real estate, since one party has to swear about the movables, it can also be made to include a statement about the real estate.

(60c line 18) **הלכה ח**: נְכָסִים שֶׁיֵּשׁ לָהֶן אֲחֵרָיוּת כול'. בָּרִאשׁוֹנָה הָיוּ קוֹנִין בִּשְׁלִיפַת הַמִּנְעָל. הָדָא הִיא דִכְתִיב וְזֹאת לְפָנִים בְּיִשְׂרָאֵל עַל הַגְּאוּלָה וְעַל הַתְּמוּרָה שָׁלַף אִישׁ נַעֲלוֹ וגו'. תַּמָּן אָמְרִין. רַב וְלֵוִי. חַד אָמַר. הַקּוֹנֶה. וְחַד אָמַר. הַמַּקְנֶה. וְאַתְיָין אִילֵּין פְּלוּגְוָתָא כְּאִינּוּן פְּלוּגְוָתָא. דְּתַנֵּי. בּוֹעַז נוֹתֵן לַגּוֹאֵל. רִבִּי יְהוּדָה אוֹמֵר. הַגּוֹאֵל נָתַן לְבוֹעַז.

Halakhah 5: "Guaranteed properties," etc. In earlier times, transfer of possession was effected by taking off a shoe. That is what is written[475]: "This was earlier in Israel about redemption and exchange, a person would take off his shoe." Who took it off? There, they say Rav and Levi[476], one said the acquirer, and one said the transferer. It turns out that this disagreement parallels the following disagreement which was stated: Boaz was giving to the redeemer; Rebbi Jehudah said that the redeemer gave to Boaz.

475 *Ruth* 4:7.

476 In the Babli, *Baba meṣia'* 47a, the first opinion is attributed to Rav, the second to Levi. In the Babli, the transaction is not considered as archaic but as current practice, meaning that claims can be validly transferred following Rav when the transferrer moves some of the acquirer's movable property.

(60c line 23) חָזְרוּ לִהְיוֹת קוֹנִין בִּקְצָצָה. מָהוּ בִקְצָצָה. בְּשָׁעָה שֶׁהָיָה אָדָם מוֹכֵר שָׂדֵה אֲחוּזָתוֹ הָיוּ קְרוֹבָיו מְבִיאִין חָבִיּוֹת וּמְמַלִּין אוֹתָן קְלָיוֹת וֶאֱגוֹזִים וְשׁוֹבְרִין לִפְנֵי הַתִּינוֹקוֹת. וְהַתִּינוֹקוֹת מְלַקְטִין וְאוֹמְרִים. נִקְצַץ פְּלוֹנִי מֵאֲחוּזָתוֹ. וּבְשָׁעָה שֶׁהָיְתָה מַחֲזִירָהּ לוֹ הָיוּ עוֹשִׂין כָּךְ וְאוֹמְרִים. חָזַר פְּלוֹנִי לַאֲחוּזָתוֹ.⁴⁷⁷ אָמַר רִבִּי יוֹסֵה בֵּירִבִּי בּוּן. אַף מִי שֶׁהוּא נוֹשֵׂא אִשָּׁה שֶׁאֵינָהּ הוֹגֶנֶת לוֹ הָיוּ קְרוֹבָיו מְבִיאִין חָבִיּוֹת וּמְמַלִּין אוֹתָן קְלָיוֹת וֶאֱגוֹזִים וְשׁוֹבְרִין לִפְנֵי הַתִּינוֹקוֹת. וְהַתִּינוֹקוֹת מְלַקְטִין וְאוֹמְרִים. נִקְצַץ פְּלוֹנִי מִמִּשְׁפַּחְתּוֹ. וּבְשָׁעָה שֶׁהָיָה מְגָרְשָׁהּ הָיוּ עוֹשִׂין כֵּן וְאוֹמְרִים. חָזַר פְּלוֹנִי לְמִשְׁפַּחְתּוֹ.

1 בקצצה] כ בקציצת   2 שדה] כ את שדה   קרוביו מביאין חביות וממלין אותן] כ קרובין ממלין   4 שהיה מחזירה] כ שהיתה חוזרת   כד] כ לו כן   5 יוסה] כ יוסי שהוא] כ שהיה   קרוביו מביאין חביות וממלין אותן] כ קרובין ממלין   7 כן] כ לו כן

Then they changed it to clipping. ⁴⁷⁸What is clipping? If a man sold his inherited field, his relatives brought amphoras, filled them with roasted kernels and nuts and broke them before children. The children were collecting them and saying, X was clipped from his inheritance. When he brought it back, they were doing the same and saying, X returned to his inheritance. Rebbi Yose ben Rebbi Abun said, also if a man married an unsuitable woman, his relatives brought amphoras, filled them with roasted kernels and nuts and broke them before children. The children were collecting them and saying, X was clipped from his family. When he divorced her, they were doing the same and saying, X returned to his family.

| 477 In the ms: לאחזותו, a metathesis not detected by the corrector. | 478 This paragraph is from *Ketubot* 2:1 (כ), Notes 201-203. |

(60c line 31) חָזְרוּ לִהְיוֹת קוֹנִים בְּכֶסֶף וּבִשְׁטָר וּבַחֲזָקָה. בְּכֶסֶף. שָׂדוֹת בַּכֶּסֶף יִקְנוּ. זֶה הַכֶּסֶף. וְכָתוֹב בַּסֵּפֶר וְחָתוֹם אֵילוּ עֵידֵי הַשְּׁטָר. וְהָעֵד עֵדִים. אֵילוּ עֵידֵי חֲזָקָה. אוֹ אֵינָן אֶלָּא עֵידֵי הַשְּׁטָר. כְּבָר כָּתוּב וְכָתוֹב בַּסֵּפֶר וְחָתוֹם.

2 יקנו. זה הכסף | ק - וחתום אילו | ק וחתום והעד עדים. וחתום אילו   3 אלא עידי השטר | ק אלא אילו עידי שטר

Then they changed it to acquisition by money, by document, or by possession. By money: [479]"Fields will be bought by money," that is money. "Writing on a scroll and signing", these are the witnesses on the contract. "And testifying of witnesses," these are the witnesses to possession. Or maybe these are only the witnesses to the contract? These are already written: "Writing on a scroll and signing."

| 479 This and the following two paragraphs are from Halakhah 3 (ק), | Notes 335-346. |

(60c line 34) רִבִּי יָסָא בְּשֵׁם רִבִּי מָנָא בַּר תַּנְחוּם רִבִּי אַבָּהוּ בְּשֵׁם רִבִּי יוֹחָנָן. אֵין קַרְקַע נִקְנָה בְּפָחוֹת מִשְּׁוֵה פְרוּטָה. מַה טַעְמָא. שָׂדוֹת בַּכֶּסֶף יִקְנוּ. וּפְלִיג עַל הַהִיא דְּאָמַר רִבִּי חֲנִינָה. כָּל־שְׁקָלִים שֶׁכְּתוּבִים בַּתּוֹרָה סְלָעִים. וּבַנְּבִיאִים לִיטְרִין. וּבַכְּתוּבִים קִינְטִירִין. חוּץ מִשִּׁיקְלֵי עֶפְרוֹן. בְּכֶסֶף מָלֵא יִתְּנֶנּוּ לִי. וְלֹא דָמְיָיא. תַּמָּן כְּתִיב כֶּסֶף וְהָכָא כְּתִיב שְׁקָלִים. הַתִּיבוּן. הֲרֵי אוֹנֵס. הֲרֵי אֵין כָּתוּב כָּאן אֶלָּא כֶּסֶף וְאַתְּ אָמַר שְׁקָלִים.

1 מנא בר תנחום | ק מנא ר' תנחום   4 חוץ | ק אמ' | ק יודה בר פזי. חוץ   מה | ק דהויין קינטירין. מה   6 אונס | ק האונס

Rebbi Yasa in the name of Rebbi Mana bar Tanḥum, Rebbi Abbahu in the name of Rebbi Joḥanan: Real estate cannot be bought for less than a *peruṭah*. What is the reason? "Fields will be bought by money." This disagrees with what Rebbi Ḥanina said: All *šeqalim* mentioned in the Torah are tetradrachmas, in the Prophets pounds, and in the Hagiographs *centenarii*, except for the *šeqalim* paid to Ephron. What is the reason? "For full money he shall give it to me." There is no comparison since here it is written "money" but there "*šeqalim*". They objected, is there not the rapist, for whom "money" is written and you say "*šeqalim*".

(60c line 41) וְלֹא כְרִבִּי לִיעֶזֶר. דְּרִבִּי לִיעֶזֶר אוֹמֵר. הִילּוּךְ קוֹנֶה. דְּתַנֵּי. הִילֵּךְ בְּשָׂדֶה לְאוֹרְכָּהּ וּלְרָחְבָּהּ קָנָה עַד מָקוֹם שֶׁהִילֵּךְ. דִּבְרֵי רִבִּי אֱלִיעֶזֶר. וַחֲכָמִים אוֹמְרִים. לֹא קָנָה עַד שֶׁיַּחֲזִיק. הַכֹּל מוֹדִין בְּמוֹכֵר שְׁבִיל לַחֲבֵירוֹ כֵּיוָן שֶׁהִילֵּךְ בּוֹ קְנָייוֹ. מַה טַעֲמָא. קוּם הִתְהַלֵּךְ בָּאָרֶץ וגו'.

1 ולא כר' ליעזר | **ק** ודלא כר' לעזר   ליעזר | **ק** לעזר   הילוך | **ק** הילך   3 שיחזיק | **ק** שעה שיחזיק   4 וגו' | **ק** לאורכה ולרחבה כי לך אתננה

This does not follow Rebbi Eliezer, for Rebbi Eliezer said that walking acquires. If one walked across a field in length and breadth, he acquired up to the place he walked, the words of Rebbi Eliezer. But the Sages say that he did not acquire up to the moment he acted in possession. Everybody agrees that if somebody sells a path to another, when the latter went, he acquired. What is the reason? "Arise, walk in the Land, etc."

(60c line 45) בִּשְׁטָר. רִבִּי יִרְמְיָה סְבַר מֵימַר. בִּשְׁטָר עַל מְנָת שֶׁלֹּא לִיתֵּן כֶּסֶף. אֲבָל בִּשְׁטָר עַל מְנָת לִיתֵּן כֶּסֶף לֹא קָנָה עַד שֶׁיִּתֵּן כֶּסֶף. רִבִּי יוֹנָה וְרִבִּי יוֹסֵה תְּרֵיהוֹן אָמְרִין. אֲפִילוּ לֹא נָתַן כֶּסֶף קָנָה. מַתְנִיתָא מְסַייְעָה לְרִבִּי יוֹנָה וְרִבִּי יוֹסֵה. מָכַר לוֹ עֶשֶׂר שָׂדוֹת כְּאַחַת כֵּיוָן שֶׁהֶחֱזִיק בְּאַחַת מֵהֶן הֶחֱזִיק בְּכוּלָּם. אֲבָל אִם לֹא נָתַן לוֹ אֶלָּא דְּמֵי אַחַת מֵהֶן אוֹ שֶׁלֹּא כָתַב לוֹ אוֹנוֹ אֶלָּא עַל אַחַת מֵהֶן לֹא קָנָה אֶלָּא אוֹתָהּ שֶׁמָּכַר לוֹ בִּלְבַד. וְכִי יֵשׁ אוֹנִי בְּלֹא כֶסֶף. אֵין תֵּימַר.

בִּשְׁנָתַן לוֹ דְמֵי כּוּלָם אֲנָן קַייָמִין. לֹא אָמַר אֶלָּא. דְמֵי אֶחָד מֵהֶן. אֶלָּא אוֹ הָדָא אוֹ הָדָא.

By document. Rebbi Jeremiah thought to say, by a contract without obligating money[480], but with a contract obligating money he did not acquire until he paid. Rebbi Jonah and Rebbi Yose both said, he acquired even if he did not pay[481]. A *baraita* supports Rebbi Jonah and Rebbi Yose: [482]"If he sold him ten fields together, when he took possession of one of them, he took possession of all of them. But if he only paid the amount for one *or* wrote the deed[483] only for one of them he acquired only the one which was sold to him." Does there exist a deed without money[484]? If you say, we hold that he paid for all of them, did it not say: "the amount of one"? It must be one or the other[485].

480 The deed of a gift transfers possession but a sales contract does not. The Babli, 26a, endorses this opinion in the name of Samuel.

481 If the document mentions the transfer of possession; cf. *Sefer Ha'ittur* I, p. 13a, Note 7.

482 Babli 27a; Tosephta *Baba batra* 2:12. These texts do not refer to a sale document in the Greek style.

483 Greek ὠνή cf. *Giṭṭin* 4:6, Note 167. The Hellenistic ὠνή was a transfer of title; cf Taubenschlag (Note 369), pp. 155, 206. It is asserted here that if the transfer was made conditional upon payment, the transfer of title was restricted to the amount paid.

484 There does, in the transfer of real estate from living parents to children in the form of a fictitious sale; cf. Taubenschlag p. 155. This practice is discussed in the next paragraph.

485 The *or* in the second sentence is an exclusive "or"; the second clause is independent of the first. It follows that if the contract was written for all properties, it transfers possession of all of them.

(60c line 52) בְּכֶסֶף. רִבִּי בָּא סְבַר מֵימַר. בְּכֶסֶף עַל מְנָת שֶׁלֹּא יִכְתּוֹב אוֹנִי. אֲבָל בְּכֶסֶף עַל מְנָת לִכְתּוֹב לוֹ אוֹנִי לֹא קָנָה עַד שָׁעָה שֶׁיִּכְתּוֹב אוֹנִי. רִבִּי יוֹנָה וְרִבִּי יוֹסֵי פְּלִיגִין. אַתְיָיא דְּרִבִּי בָּא כִּשְׁמוּאֵל וּדְרַב הוּנָא כְּרִבִּי יוֹחָנָן. דְּרִבִּי בָּא כִּשְׁמוּאֵל. שְׁמוּאֵל שָׁאַל לְרַב חוּנָה. שׁוֹחֵט וְנִתְעַסֵּק בַּקֳּדָשִׁים. אֲמַר לֵיהּ. לִרְצוֹנְכֶם. פְּרָט לְמִתְעַסֵּק. כָּתַב מַתָּנָה בִּלְשׁוֹן קְנִיָּין. אֲמַר לֵיהּ. אַרְכְּבֵיהּ אַתְּרֵי רִיכְשֵׁי. אֲמָרָהּ רִבִּי בָּא וְלֹא קִיבְלָהּ שְׁמוּאֵל. מָהוּ אַרְכְּבֵיהּ עַל תְּרֵין רִיכְשֵׁי בְּרָקֵי. סָבְרִין מֵימַר. מַייְתֵי תְּרֵין סוּסְיָוָן שַׁטְיֵי וּמְרַכְּבִין לֵיהּ עַל תְּרֵיהוֹן וְהַהוּא אֲזִיל בְּדָא וְהַהֵין אֲזַל בְּדָא לֹא אַשְׁכַּח גַּבֵּי כְּלוּם. אָמַר רִבִּי יוֹסֵי מַמְלְחָיָּיא. יִיפָּה כוֹחוֹ בִּשְׁנֵי דְבָרִים. שֶׁיֵּשׁ שִׁיעְבּוּד לִמְכִירָה וְאֵין שִׁיעְבּוּד לְמַתָּנָה. שֶׁהַמּוֹכֵר לֹא מָכַר אֶת הַכֹּל וְהַנּוֹתֵן מַתָּנָה נָתַן אֶת הַכֹּל. וּדְרַב חוּנָה כְּרִבִּי יוֹחָנָן. חַד בַּר נַשׁ מִי דְמִיךְ אָמַר. יַנְּתְנוּ כָּל־נְכָסַיי לִפְלוֹנִי. חָזַר וְאָמַר. כִּתְבוּ וּתְנוּ. רִבִּי לֶעְזָר וְרִבִּי שִׁמְעוֹן בַּר יָקִים אַעֲלוֹן עוֹבְדָא קוֹמֵי רִבִּי יוֹחָנָן. אָמַר. אִם אָמַר. לִזְכוּתוֹ. דְּבָרָיו הַכֹּל זָכָה. וְאִם לְזַפּוֹתוֹ בִּכְתָב. כָּל־עַמָּא מוֹדֵיי שֶׁאֵין אָדָם זוֹכֶה לְאַחַר מִיתָה. מִי מוֹדִיעַ. אֶת רְבוֹ. תִּיפְתָּר שֶׁהָיוּ שָׁם עֵדִים יוֹדְעִין. הִגַּע עַצְמָךְ שֶׁאֵין שָׁם עֵדִים יוֹדְעִים. אָמַר רִבִּי יוֹסֵי. לְעוֹלָם הַשָּׂדֶה בְחֶזְקַת בְּעָלֶיהָ וּמוֹצִיא מֵחֲבֵירוֹ עָלָיו הָרְאָיָיה.

"By money." Rebbi Abba was of the opinion, by money if there was no intention to write a deed. But if money was given with the intention to write a deed for him, possession was transferred only when the deed was written[486]. Rebbi Jonah and Rebbi Yose disagree[487]. It follows that Rebbi Abba parallels Samuel and Rav Huna Rebbi Johanan.

Rebbi Abba parallels Samuel. Samuel asked Rav Huna: He was slaughtering sacrifices while being occupied[488]? He answered, "for your intention[489]," this excludes one otherwise occupied. If one wrote a gift in the language of a sale[490]? He answered, he made it ride on two racing horses; Rebbi Abba[491] said this; Samuel did not accept it. What means "he made it ride on two shining racing horses"? They wanted to say, one brings two crazy horses and makes it ride on both. One goes in one direction and the other in another; he has nothing in his hand[492]. Rebbi Yose from Mamelia said, he doubly empowered him, for there is a title guarantee in a sale but none for a gift[493]; the seller did not sell everything but the giver of a gift gave everything[494].

And Rav Huna parallels Rebbi Johanan. A person, when he lay dying, said: my property should be given to X. Afterwards he said: write and deliver. Rebbi Eleazar and Rebbi Simeon bar Yaqim brought the case before Rebbi Johanan who said: If he said to transfer to him, everybody agrees that he entered into possession[495]. If the transfer was to be in writing, everybody agrees that nobody transfers rights in writing after his death[496]. Who would notify the greatness[497]? Explain it if witnesses know. Think of it, if no witnesses know it? Rebbi Yose said, the field remains in the hand of its proprietors[498]; the burden of proof is on the claimant[499].

486 Since proving title is difficult without a written deed, the buyer has no intention of accepting title without the deed. Therefore, transfer of possession is possible only by delivery of the deed unless one explicitly stipulates otherwise. In the Babli, 26a, this is a statement of Rav (Rebbi Abba bar Ayvo).

487 Since they are the collectors of the material in the Yerushalmi, their opinion is accepted as practice; it is not mentioned in the Babli for whom Samuel is the deciding authority in civil law.

488 He was occupied in slaughtering profane animals when he also slaughtered an animal dedicated as sacrifice without realizing it. Is this valid slaughter? The scenario is really impossible since the slaughter of profane animals is forbidden in the holy precinct, as is the slaughter of sacrifices outside. A Temple slaughterer has to

learn his trade outside the holy precinct.

489 Lev. 22:19. Babli *Ḥulin* 13a

490 Is a deed valid if it formulates a gift in the language of a fictitious sale? Starting here there is a shortened version, formulated differently, in *Baba batra* 8:5.

491 Since Rav was Rav Huna's teacher, this reference must be to Rav, in whose name the expression is quoted in Babli *Baba batra* 152a.

492 Since sale and gift follow different rules, a gift formulated as sale is invalid.

493 The seller is required to indemnify the buyer if the latter loses his land because of foreclosure of a mortgage owed by the seller. A gift is given without such guarantee.

494 A sale document is interpreted minimally: the seller of a parcel is not presumed to have sold a cistern or any other building on the parcel unless it be mentioned in the deed (Mishnah *Baba batra* 4:2; cf Tosaphot *Qiddušin* 26a *s. v.* ולמה), but a gift document is interpreted maximally. In this interpretation of Rav, confirmed by the Babli *Baba batra* 152a, the holder of the deed is doubly privileged. In the Babli, Samuel is quoted as being unable to decide whether the deed is judged as sale or gift. Since Samuel is quoted as disagreeing, he must hold with R. Abba that if a deed is intended, only the deed will transfer possession.

495 If the first time he stated that the person designated should be his heir, the latter will inherit if the dying person made it clear that the deed will only be written as proof of title, not as means of transfer of property.

496 If the document was a deed, not a will, intended to convey possession but not delivered during the donor's lifetime, it cannot be delivered after death (Babli *Baba batra* 135b).

497 If the donor intended his orally conveyed gift to convey possession, how can the recipient prove his title?

498 In this case, the legal heirs.

499 *Baba qama* 5:1 (21b l. 70), Babli *Baba qama* 27b,46b, *Baba batra* 92b.

(60c line 69) מִנַּיִין לִנְכָסִים שֶׁאֵין לָהֶן אַחֲרָיוּת שֶׁהֵן נִקְנִין עִם נְכָסִים שֶׁיֵּשׁ לָהֶם אַחֲרָיוּת בְּכֶסֶף וּבִשְׁטָר וּבַחֲזָקָה. רִבִּי יוֹסֵי בְּשֵׁם חִזְקִיָּה רִבִּי יוֹנָה רִבִּי חֲנִינָא תִּרְתֵּיָּה בְּשֵׁם חִזְקִיָּה. כְּתִיב וַיִּתֵּן לָהֶם אֲבִיהֶם מַתָּנוֹת רַבּוֹת לְכֶסֶף וּלְזָהָב וּלְמִגְדָּנוֹת עִם עָרִים בְּצוּרוֹת בִּיהוּדָה. עַד כְּדוֹן כְּשֶׁהָיוּ קַרְקָעוֹת וּמְטַלְטְלִין

בְּמָקוֹם אֶחָד. הָיוּ קַרְקָעוֹת בְּמָקוֹם אֶחָד וּמִטַּלְטְלִין בְּמָקוֹם אַחֵר. אָמַר רִבִּי בּוּן בַּר חִייָה. נִשְׁמְעִינָהּ מִן הָדָא. אָמַר לָהֶן רִבִּי אֱלִיעֶזֶר. מַעֲשֶׂה בִּמְרוֹנִי אֶחָד שֶׁהָיָה דָר בִּירוּשָׁלֵם וְהָיוּ לוֹ מִיטַּלְטְלִין הַרְבֵּה וּבִיקֵּשׁ לְחַלְּקָן. אָמְרוּ לוֹ אֵין אַתְּ יָכוֹל אֶלָּא אִם כֵּן קָנִיתָ קַרְקַע. מֶה עָשָׂה. הָלַךְ וְקָנָה סֶלַע אֶחָד בְּצַד יְרוּשָׁלֵם. אָמַר. חֲצָיָיהּ צְפוֹנִי אֲנִי נוֹתֵן לִפְלוֹנִי עִם מֵאָה חָבִיּוֹת שֶׁל יַיִן. חֲצָיָיהּ דְּרוֹמִית אֲנִי נוֹתֵן לִפְלוֹנִי עִם מֵאָה חָבִיּוֹת שֶׁלְּשֶׁמֶן. וּבָא מַעֲשֶׂה לִפְנֵי חֲכָמִים וְקִייְמוּ אֶת דְּבָרָיו. אָמַר רִבִּי חֲנַנְיָה קוֹמֵי רִבִּי מָנָא. וְלֹא שְׁכִיב מְרַע הוּא. לְפִי שֶׁבְּכָל־מָקוֹם אֵין אָדָם מְזַכֶּה אֶלָּא בִּכְתָב. וְכָאן אֲפִילוּ בִדְבָרִים. לְפִי שֶׁבְּכָל־מָקוֹם אֵין אָדָם מְזַכֶּה עַד שֶׁיְּהוּ קַרְקָעוֹת וּמִטַּלְטְלִין בְּמָקוֹם אֶחָד. וְכָאן אֲפִילוּ קַרְקָעוֹת בְּמָקוֹם אֶחָד וּמִטַּלְטְלִין בְּמָקוֹם אַחֵר. אָמַר לֵיהּ. לֹא כְרִבִּי לִיעֶזֶר הוּא. שַׁנְיָיא הִיא שְׁכִיב מְרַע דְּרִבִּי לִיעֶזֶר הוּא שְׁכִיב מְרַע דְּרַבָּנִין. אָמַר לֵיהּ. שְׁכִיב מְרַע דְּרִבִּי לִיעֶזֶר כִּבְרִיא דְּרַבָּנִין.

1 שהן נכנין | פ שהם נקנים　4 כשהיו | פ כשהיה　5 ומטלטלין | פ עם המטלטלין אחר | פ אחד　7 דר | פ -　- | פ לחלקן | פ לחלקן ליתנן במתנה　9 אמ' | פ ואמ' דרומית | פ דרומי　11 ולא | פ ולאו　15 כר' ליעזר | פ ר' אליעזר　שכיב מרע דר' ליעזר כשכיב מרע דרבנן. אמ' ליה | פ -　16 ליעזר | פ אליעזר　דרב:ין | פ דרבנן

[500]From where that non-guaranteed property may be acquired together with guaranteed property, by money, document, or by possession? Rebbi Yose in the name of Ḥizqiah; Rebbi Jonah, Rebbi Ḥanina Tortaya in the name of Ḥizqiah, it is written (*2Chr.* 21:3): "Their father gave them many gifts, silver and gold and delicacies, with fortified cities in Jehudah." So far real estate and movables were at the same place. If real estate was at one place and movables elsewhere? Rebbi Abin bar Ḥiyya said, let us hear from the following: Rebbi Eliezer said to them, it happened that a man from Meron was dwelling in Jerusalem, who was rich in movables. He wanted to distribute them, to give them as gifts. They said to him, you cannot do that except if you acquire real estate. What did he do? He

went and bought a rock near Jerusalem and said: The Northern part I give to X with a hundred amphoras of wine, the Southern part I give to Y with a hundred amphoras of oil. The matter came before the Sages and they upheld his words.

Rebbi Ḥananiah said before Rebbi Mana: But was he not bedridden? For in general a person might give property rights only in writing, and here even orally. In general, a person might give only if real estate and movables are at the same place; here, however, the real estate was at one place and the movables elsewhere. He said to him: But is there a difference for Rebbi Eliezer? Is not the sick person for Rebbi Eliezer like the sick person for the rabbis? He said to him: The sick person for Rebbi Eliezer is like the healthy person for the rabbis.

500 This paragraph and the following are from *Peah* 3:8, Notes 134-147 (**פ**). The second paragraph has no connection to the topics discussed here; this shows that the original place of the texts was in *Peah*.

(60d line 9) תַּמָּן תַּנִּינָן. קַרְקַע כָּל־שֶׁהוּא חַיָּיב בְּפֵיאָה וּבְבִיכּוּרִים דִּבְרֵי רִבִּי עֲקִיבָה. קַרְקַע כָּל־שֶׁהוּא מַהוּ טָב. אָמַר רִבִּי מַתַּנְיָיה. תִּיפְתָּר שֶׁהָיָה שָׁם מָקוֹם שִׁיבּוֹלֶת אַחַת וּמַרְגָּלִית טְמוּנָה בּוֹ.
1 קרקע | פ ר' עקיבה או'. קרקע דברי ר' עקיבה | פ -

There, we have stated: "Any real estate is subject to *peah* and first fruits, the words of Rebbi Aqiba." What is the use of "any" real estate? Rebbi Mattaniah said, explain it if it had space for one stalk but a pearl was hidden in it.

(60d line 9) רִבִּי יָסָא בְּשֵׁם רִבִּי יוֹחָנָן. הָיוּ לוֹ שְׁתֵּי שָׂדוֹת אַחַת בִּיהוּדָה וְאַחַת בְּגָלִיל. הֶחֱזִיק בְּזוֹ שֶׁבִּיהוּדָה לִזְכוֹת בְּזוֹ שֶׁבְּגָלִיל. אוֹ בְּזוֹ שֶׁבְּגָלִיל לִזְכוֹת בְּזוֹ

HALAKHAH 5

שֶׁבִּיהוּדָה. קָנָה. וּבְנִכְסֵי הַגֵּר לֹא קָנָה אֲפִילוּ מֵיצַר בֵּינְתַיִים. רִבִּי זְעִירָא בְעָא קוֹמֵי רִבִּי יָסָא. נִתְכַּוֵּון לִקְנוֹת מִן הַמֵּיצַר וּשְׁרַע מִינֵּיהּ. רַב חִסְדָּא אָמַר. נִכְסֵי הַגֵּר. הֶחֱזִיק בִּצְפוֹנָן עַל מְנָת לִזְכּוֹת בִּדְרוֹמָן. בִּדְרוֹמָן עַל מְנָת לִזְכּוֹת בִּצְפוֹנָן לֹא נִתְכַּוֵּון לִקְנוֹת בְּאֶמְצָעִיתָן. לֹא קָנָה עַד שָׁעָה שֶׁיִּתְכַּוֵּין לִקְנוֹת בְּאֶמְצָעִיתָן. מַתְנִיתָא פְלִיגָא עַל רַב חִסְדָּא. גֵּר שֶׁמֵּת וּבְזָזוּ יִשְׂרָאֵל אֶת נְכָסָיו. הַמַּחֲזִיק בַּקַּרְקַע חַיָּיב בַּכֹּל. הַמַּחֲזִיק בַּקָּמָה חַיָּיב בְּלֶקֶט שִׁכְחָה וּפֵיאָה וּפָטוּר מִן הַמַּעְשְׂרוֹת. וְאֵין אֲוֵיר מַפְסֶקֶת בֵּין שִׁיבּוֹלֶת לְשִׁיבּוֹלֶת. תַּמָּן תַּנִּינָן. אִם הָיָה מְחוּבָּר לְקַרְקַע וְתָלַשׁ כָּל־שֶׁהוּא קָנָה. שְׁמוּאֵל אָמַר. לֹא קָנָה אֶלָּא אוֹתוֹ קֶלַח בִּלְבָד. וְהָתָנַן[501] אִם הָיָה מְחוּבָּר לַקַּרְקַע וְתָלַשׁ כָּל־שֶׁהוּא קָנָה. אָמַר רִבִּי יוֹסֵי. קַיְּימָהּ רִבִּי אֲבוּדוּמָא נְחוּתָא מוֹדֶה שְׁמוּאֵל בְּנִכְסֵי הַגֵּר.

Rebbi Yasa in the name of Rebbi Joḥanan: If two fields were involved[502], one in Judea and one in Galilee. If he took possession of the one in Judea with the intent of taking possession of the one in Galilee, or the one in Galilee with the intent of taking possession of the one in Judea, he took possession. But in [the case of] property of a proselyte[503] he did not acquire even the boundary strip between them[504]. Rebbi Ze'ira asked before Rebbi Yasa: If he intended to acquire starting from the boundary strip and below[505]? Rav Ḥisda said, property of a proselyte which he took possession of in the North with the intent of also acquiring that in the South, or in the South with the intent of acquiring also that in the North, but did not have the intent of acquiring the strip in the middle[506], he did not acquire unless he also intended to acquire the middle part[507]. A *baraita*[508] disagrees with Rav Ḥisda: If a proselyte died and Jews plundered his property, if one takes possession of the ground he is obligated for everything[509]. If he took possession of standing grain, he is obligated for fallen stalks, forgotten sheaves, and *peah* but freed from tithes. Does not the air separate between stalks[510]? There, we have stated[511]: "If he tore off anything connected to the ground, he took possession." Samuel said, he took possession only of that leaf. But did we not state: "If it was connected to the ground and he tore off anything, he took possession"? Rebbi Yose said, Rebbi Eudaimon the emigrant[512] confirmed it: Samuel will agree, for proselyte's property[513].

501 This is Babli terminology, for Yerushalmi תניין. The sentence was added by the corrector; obviously it was added as an (unnecessary) emendation of the text, not from a different ms.

502 In a real estate transaction; the seller expects the buyer to take possession of both fields; cf. Note 345.

503 Who dies intestate without Jewish heirs and whose property now is ownerless. The rules of taking possession of ownerless property are more strict than those of taking possession of what was bought since the agreement of the seller to the transfer of the property is missing.

504 If the proselyte owned two adjacent fields; the Jew took possession of both of them by doing some agricultural work on both but he did not walk the boundary strip with the intent of acquiring it; the strip is not automatically acquired with the fields since it is not subject to agricultural activities such as ploughing, weeding, or harvesting; cf. Note 353.

505 The question is not answered; cf. *Peah* 2:1, Note 16. In the Babli, *Baba batra* 52b, the question is undecided, i. e., anybody laying claim to the strip would have to prove his claim by other means.

506 I. e., the boundary strip in between.

507 Also quoted in *Baba batra* 3:1 (13d l. 55). In the Babli, *Baba batra* 55a, R. Johanan states that the boundary strip separates properties of the intestate proselyte. He also states Rav Hisda's position even for commercial real estate transactions (*Baba batra* 53a/b).

508 Tosephta *Peah* 2:10.

509 Tithes and all obligatory gifts to the poor.

510 Since single stalks can be picked up by the owner, not subject to the law

of gleanings reserved for the poor, if the air separates the ownerless stalks the entire crop would be exempt from that law. This contradicts Rav Hisda who holds that any ground not taken in possession separates properties of the intestate proselyte.

511 Mishnah *Baba batra* 5:9, speaking of a transaction involving a field of flax.

512 He emigrated from Galilee to Babylonia.

513 A proselyte's standing crop cannot be acquired by harvesting a single stalk, but only by taking the entire crop. Otherwise, it can be acquired only by taking possession of the land and paying taxes on it. In the Babli, *Baba batra* 87a, Rav Sheshet explains the problem away by postulating that the seller of the crop also sold a *peruṭah*'s worth of ground and that the movable crop was taken as possession together with the fictitious real estate.

(60d line 25) רִבִּי יוֹחָנָן בָּעֵי. הַמְטַלְטְלִין מָהוּ שֶׁיִּקְנוּ בִּגְרִירָה. אָמַר רִבִּי בָּא בַּר מָמָל. מַה צְּרִיכָה לֵיהּ. בְּעוֹרוֹת הַקָּשִׁים. אָבָל בְּעוֹרוֹת הָרַכִּים לֹא קָנָה עַד שֶׁיַּגְבִּיהַּ. מַתְנִיתָא פְלִיגָא עַל רִבִּי בָּא בַּר מָמָל. הַגּוֹנֵב כִּיסוֹ שֶׁלַּחֲבֵירוֹ וְהוֹצִיאוֹ בַשַּׁבָּת חַייָב. שֶׁכְּבָר נִתְחַייֵב בִּגְנֵיבָתוֹ שֶׁלְּכִיס עַד שֶׁלֹּא קִידְשָׁה עָלָיו הַשַּׁבָּת. אֲבָל אִם הָיָה גּוֹרֵר בּוֹ וְיוֹצֵא פָטוּר. מִפְּנֵי שֶׁחָלָה עָלָיו מִיתָה וְתַשְׁלוּמִין כְּאַחַת. הָא אִם לֹא חָלָה עָלָיו מִיתָה וְתַשְׁלוּמִין כְּאַחַת חַייָב. אָמַר רִבִּי מַתַּנְיָה. תִּיפְתָּר בְּאִילֵּין כִּיסַיָּיא רַבְרְבַיָּיא דְּאוּרְחֵיהוֹן מִתְגְּרָרָה.

Rebbi Johanan asked: Can movables be taken into possession by dragging? Rebbi Abba bar Mamal said, what is his problem? With hard hides[514]. But soft hides are not taken into posession until lifted[515]. A *baraita* disagrees with Rebbi Abba bar Mamal: If somebody steals another person's pouch and removes it on the Sabbath, he is obligated since he already is obligated for the theft of the wallet before he comes in conflict with the holiness of the Sabbath[516]. But if he was dragging it until he left, he is free since the obligations of capital crime and restitution fall on him simultaneously[517]. Therefore, if the obligations of capital crime and restitution do not fall on him simultaneously he is obligated[518]. Rebbi Mattania said, explain it with large pouches which usually are dragged[518].

---

514 Which are too heavy to be lifted.

515 Movables which can be lifted are taken into possession only by being picked up and then moved; heavy movables can be taken into possession simply by being moved on the ground.

516 Tosephta *Baba qama* 9:19. A person committing two crimes simultaneously can be prosecuted only for the more serious crime even if this prosecution is impossible because of external circumstances (for example, if the rabbinic court has only civil but no criminal jurisdiction, or if the civil offense can be proven by the standards of civil procedure but the criminal act cannot be proven by the stricter standards of criminal law; cf. Terumot 7:1, Notes 51-71, paralleled in *Ketubot* 3:1, Note 30.)

Since the thief incurred the liabilities for his theft the moment he took the pouch in his victim's room but he violated the Sabbath prohibition only when he left and transported the pouch from a private to the public domain, the capital crime of violating the Sabbath is not connected with the theft. Paralleled in Babli *Šabbat* 91a, *Ketubot* 31a, where some unconnected problems are raised about the Sabbath prohibition of moving between domains; *Baba batra* 86a, *Sanhedrin* 72a; a different version in *Baba qama* 3:4 (3c l. 58ff.).

517 Dragging a person's pouch in that person's domain does not transfer possession to the person dragging.

518 If the theft happened on a weekday and the thief only dragged, never lifted, the pouch, he nevertheless is obligated for double restitution. He cannot be liable for double restitution unless he took possession. This seems to contradict R. Abba bar Mamal.

519 And therefore acquired by dragging. In *Baba batra* 86a, in the name of Rav Ada bar Mattanah.

(60d line 32) מְנַיִין לָמְדוּ לְגִילְגוּל שְׁבוּעָה. מִסּוֹטָה. אָמֵן מֵאִישׁ זֶה. אָמֵן מֵאִישׁ אַחֵר. עַד כְּדוֹן דְּבָרִים שֶׁהֵן רְאוּיִין לְהַשְׁבִּיעַ. דְּבָרִים שֶׁאֵינוֹ רָאוּי לְהַשְׁבִּיעַ אָמַר רִבִּי יוֹסֵי בֵּירִבִּי בּוּן. נִישְׁמְעִינָהּ מִן הָדָא. אָמֵן שֶׁלֹּא סָטִיתִי אֲרוּסָה וּנְשׂוּאָה שׁוֹמֶרֶת יָבָם וּכְנוּסָה. אֲרוּסָה וְשׁוֹמֶרֶת יָבָם רָאוּי הוּא לְהַשְׁבִּיעַ. אַתְּ אָמַר מְגַלְגְּלִין. וְהָכָא מְגַלְגְּלִין.

1 אמן | ס ואמרה האשה אמן אמן. אמי   מאיש | ס עם איש (2 times)   2 שהן | ס שהוא   ראויין | ס ראוי   4 להשביע | ס להישבע   את אמר | ס ותימר

[520]From where did they learn rollover of oaths? From the suspected wife: Amen from this man, Amen from any other man. That refers to subjects he is able to make her swear about. What about subjects he is not able to make her swear about? Rebbi Yose ben Rebbi Abun said, let us hear from the following: "Amen that I was not deviant preliminarily married and married, waiting for the levir and taken in." Can he make her swear when she is preliminarily married or waiting for the levir? Nevertheless one rolls over.

520 This paragraph and the next are from *Sotah* 2:5 (פ, Notes 166-174). In the Babli, the parallel is *Qiddušin* 27b.

(60d line 37) אִית תַּנָּיֵי תַנֵּי. מַה זוֹ בְּאָלָה וּבִשְׁבוּעָה אַף כָּל־הַנִּשְׁבָּעִין בְּאָלָה וּבִשְׁבוּעָה. אִית תַּנָּיֵי תַנֵּי. בְּזוֹ אָלָה וּשְׁבוּעָה וְאֵין כָּל־הַנִּשְׁבָּעִין בְּאָלָה וּבִשְׁבוּעָה. הָוָון בָּעֵיי מֵימַר. מָאן דְּאָמַר. מַה זוֹ בְּאָלָה וּבִשְׁבוּעָה אַף כָּל־הַנִּשְׁבָּעִין בְּאָלָה וּבִשְׁבוּעָה נִיחָא. מָאן דְּאָמַר. זוֹ בְּאָלָה וּבִשְׁבוּעָה וְאֵין כָּל־הַנִּשְׁבָּעִין בְּאָלָה וּבִשְׁבוּעָה. לְגִילְגּוּל אַתְּ לָמֵד וְלִשְׁבוּעָה אֵין אַתְּ לָמֵד. אִית תַּנָּיֵי תַנֵּי. מַה זוֹ בְּאָמֵן וּבְאָמֵן. אַף כָּל־הַנִּשְׁבָּעִין בְּאָמֵן וּבְאָמֵן. אִית תַּנָּיֵי תַנֵּי. זוֹ בְּאָמֵן וּבְאָמֵן. אֵין כָּל־הַנִּשְׁבָּעִין בְּאָמֵן וּבְאָמֵן. הָוָון בָּעֵיי מֵימַר. מָאן דְּאָמַר. מַזוֹ בְּאָמֵן וּבְאָמֵן אַף כָּל־הַנִּשְׁבָּעִין בְּאָמֵן וּבְאָמֵן. נִיחָא. וּמָאן דְּאָמַר. זוֹ בְּאָמֵן וּבְאָמֵן

וְאֵין כָּל־הַנִּשְׁבָּעִין בְּאָמֵן וּבְאָמֵן. כְּלוּם לָמְדוּ לְגִילְגּוּל שְׁבוּעָה אֶלָּא מִסּוֹטָה. לְגִילְגּוּל אַתְּ לָמֵד. וּלְאָמֵן אָמֵן אִי אַתְּ לָמֵד.

2 אית | ס ואית   בזו אלא ושבועה | ס זו באלא ובשבועה   3 הוון | ס הוו   דאמ' | ס
דמר   4 דאמ' | ס דמר   5 ולשבועה | ס לאלה ולשבואה   אין | ס ואין   6 ובאמן
| ס ואמן (3 times)   7 ובאמן | ס ואמן (2 times)   הוון | ס הוו   דאמ' | ס דמר   מזו | ס
זו   דאמ' | ס דמר   8 ובאמן | ס ואמן (2 times)   ומאן דאמ' | ס מאן דמר   9
ובאמן | ס ואמן   לגילגול | ס גילגול   אלא | ס לא   10 אמן | ס ואמן   אי | ס אין

Some Tannaïm state: Since this one is subject to curse and oath, so also all who have to swear are under curse and oath. Some Tannaïm state: This one is subject to curse and oath, but no others who have to swear are under curse and oath. They wanted to say, the one who said, since this one is subject to curse and oath, so also all who have to swear are under curse and oath, is understandable. The one who said, this one is subject to curse and oath, but no others who have to swear are under curse and oath, can you infer for rollover only but not for oath? Some Tannaïm state: Since this one is subject to Amen, Amen, so also all who have to swear are under Amen, Amen. Some Tannaïm state: This one is subject to Amen, Amen, but no others who have to swear are under Amen, Amen. They wanted to say, the one who said, since this one is subject to Amen, Amen, so also all who have to swear are under Amen, Amen, is understandable. The one who said, this one is subject to Amen, Amen, but no others who have to swear are under Amen, Amen, did one not infer rollover of oaths from the suspected wife? Can you infer for rollover only but not for Amen, Amen?

(fol. 58b) **משנה ו**: כָּל־הַנַּעֲשָׂה דָּמִים בְּאַחֵר כֵּיוָן שֶׁזָּכָה זֶה נִתְחַיֵּיב זֶה בַּחֲלִיפָיו. כֵּיצַד הֶחֱלִיף שׁוֹר בְּפָרָה אוֹ חֲמוֹר בְּשׁוֹר כֵּיוָן שֶׁזָּכָה זֶה נִתְחַיֵּיב לָזֶה בַּחֲלִיפָיו. רְשׁוּת הַגָּבוֹהַּ בְּכֶסֶף וּרְשׁוּת הַהֶדְיוֹט בַּחֲזָקָה. אֲמִירָתוֹ לַגָּבוֹהַּ כִּמְסִירָתוֹ לַהֶדְיוֹט.

Mishnah 6: If anything is given instead of money, if one entered in possession, the other is obligated for its exchange[521]. How is this? If an ox was exchanged for a cow, or a donkey for an ox, if one entered in possession, the other is obligated for its exchange. Possession of Heaven is by money[522], possession of an individual by taking hold. A promise to Heaven is like delivery to an individual[523].

521 If property is acquired by payment in kind, only one of the parties has to execute an act of taking possession. The other party then automatically is in possession and also assumes liability. This is not simple barter but exchange of money's worth against money's worth.

522 For the Temple, possession comes together with ownership by payment; it does not need a separate act on entering into possession.

523 Anything vowed to Heaven is as if delivered; the promise cannot be retracted.

(60d line 47) **הלכה ו**: כָּל־הַנַּעֲשָׂה דָּמִים בְּאַחֵר כול׳. תַּמָּן תַּנִּינָן. זֶה הַכְּלָל. כָּל־הַמִּיטַּלְטְלִין קוֹנִין זֶה אֶת זֶה. רִבִּי בָּא רַב חוּנָה בְּשֵׁם רַב. אֲפִילוּ צִבּוּר בְּצִיבּוּרִין. אָמַר לֵיהּ רִבִּי לְעָזָר. לֹא שָׁנִינוּ אֶלָּא כָּל־הַנַּעֲשָׂה דָּמִים בְּאַחֵר בִּלְבַד. דָּבָר שֶׁהוּא צָרִיךְ לְשׁוּם. אַתְיָיא דְרַב חוּנָה כְּרִבִּי יוֹחָנָן וְרִבִּי לְעָזָר כְּשִׁיטָתֵיהּ. דְּתַנִּינָן תַּמָּן. הָאַחִין הַשּׁוּתָּפִין שֶׁחַיָּיבִין בְּקוֹלְבּוֹן פְּטוּרִין מִמַּעֲשֵׂר בְּהֵמָה. וְשֶׁחַיָּיבִין בְּמַעֲשֵׂר בְּהֵמָה פְּטוּרִין מִן הַקּוֹלְבּוֹן. אָמַר רִבִּי לְעָזָר. וְהֵן שֶׁחָלְקוּ גְּדָיִים כְּנֶגֶד תְּיָישִׁים וּתְיָישִׁים כְּנֶגֶד גְּדָיִים. אֲבָל אִם חָלְקוּ גְּדָיִים כְּנֶגֶד גְּדָיִים וּתְיָישִׁים כְּנֶגֶד תְּיָישִׁים הוּא חֶלְקוֹ מִשָּׁעָה רִאשׁוֹנָה. אָמַר רִבִּי יוֹחָנָן. וַאֲפִילוּ חָלְקוּ גְּדָיִים כְּנֶגֶד גְּדָיִים וּתְיָישִׁים כְּנֶגֶד תְּיָישִׁים כִּלְקוּחוֹת הֵן. דְּתַנִּינָן תַּמָּן. הַלָּקוּחַ וְהִנִּיתָּן לוֹ מַתָּנָה פָּטוּר מִמַּעֲשֵׂר בְּהֵמָה. הָאַחִין הַשּׁוּתָּפִין שֶׁחַיָּיבִין

בְּקוֹלְבּוֹן פְּטוּרִין מִמַּעֲשֵׂר בְּהֵמָה. בְּשֶׁחָלְקוּ וְחָזְרוּ וְנִשְׁתַּתְּפוּ. כְּשֶׁחַיָּיבִין בְּמַעֲשֵׂר בְּהֵמָה וּפְטוּרִין מִן הַקּוֹלְבּוֹן. בְּשֶׁלֹּא חָלְקוּ.

Halakhah 6: "If anything is given instead of money," etc. There, we have stated[524]: "This is the principle: All movables acquire one another." Rebbi Abba, Rav Huna in the name of Rav: Even heaps among heaps[525]. Rebbi Eleazar said to him, we have stated only: "If anything is given *instead of money*," anything that needs estimation. It turns out that Rebbi Abba follows Rebbi Johanan and Rebbi Eleazar his own opinion, as we have stated there[526]: "Brothers having common property who are obligated for agio[527] are free from animal tithe[528], but if they are obligated for animal tithe they are free from agio[529]." Rebbi Eleazar said, only if they exchanged kid goats against rams and rams against kid goats. But if they exchanged kid goats against kid goats and rams against rams, that was [the recipient's] part from the first moment[530]. Rebbi Johanan said, even if they exchanged kid goats against kid goats and rams against rams, they are buyers[531]. But we have stated there: "The buyer and the recipient of a gift are free from animal tithe. Brothers having common property who are obligated for agio are free from animal tithe." When they split and then joined again. "But if they are obligated for animal tithe they are free from agio." If they never split.

524 Mishnah *Baba mesia'* 4:1. Legal tender coin is not "movables" (Babli 28a/b); payment transfers ownership but not possession. The exchange of movables transfers both ownership and possession.

525 A heap of grain at one place may be exchanged for a heap of grain at another place even if it is impossible to assign an exact price to either of them.

526 Mishnah *Šeqalim* 1:7, *Hulin* 1:7, *Bekhorot* 9:3. Tradition held that firstlings are sanctified only if they

belong to a single owner. The same is stated for animal tithe (*Lev.* 27:32); it is due only if the herd belongs to a single individual.

527 Cf. Note 122. The annual Temple tax, half a *holy šeqel* (cf. Note 353) per person, had to be given as a coin (*Šeqalim* 1:6, 46 l. 32; cf. all sources quoted in *Tanhuma Buber Ky Tiśśa* 7, Note 46.) If payment was not made in the correct coin, an agio had to be paid to the Temple's collectors. Only one agio was due per household, when the father paid the tax for himself and all adult males in his house. (Liddell and Scott compare the Greek word κόλλυβος to Hebrew חלף, "exchange, substitution".)

528 If brothers are obligated to pay separate agios, they do not form a household. The flock they own as inheritance from their father therefore is held in partnership and is free from the duty of animal tithe.

529 If their father's inheritance was not distributed, they still form their father's family, pay the Temple tax together, and are obligated for animal tithe.

530 It turns out that it was his from the moment of the father's death. Then the animals never had multiple owners. In the Babli, *Bekhorot* 52b, the opinion attributed here to R. Eleazar is ascribed to Rav Anan; R. Eleazar there requires that not all brothers receive the same number of animals.

531 In all cases of liquidation of an inheritance with multiple heirs. This principle is accepted in the Babli in R. Johanan's name (*Beṣah* 37b, *Giṭṭin* 25a,48a, *Baba qama* 69b, *Bekhorot* 52b,57a).

(60d line 60) רִבִּי בָּא בְשֵׁם רַב יְהוּדָה בְשֵׁם שְׁמוּאֵל. לָזֶה פָרָה וְלָזֶה חֲמוֹר. הֶחֱלִיפוּ אֶת שֶׁלָּזֶה לָזֶה וְאֶת שֶׁלָּזֶה לָזֶה. מָשַׁךְ בַּעַל הַחֲמוֹר אֶת הַפָּרָה וּבָא בַּעַל הַפָּרָה לִמְשׁוֹךְ אֶת הַחֲמוֹר וְנִמְצָא שֶׁמֵּתָה הַחֲמוֹר. בַּעַל הַחֲמוֹר צָרִיךְ לְהָבִיא רְאָיָיה שֶׁהָיְתָה חֲמוֹרוֹ קַייֶמֶת בְּשָׁעָה שֶׁמָּשַׁךְ אֶת הַפָּרָה. שֶׁכָּל־הַמּוֹצִיא מֵחֲבֵירוֹ עָלָיו הָרְאָיָיה חוּץ מִן הַחֲלִיפִין. וּמַאן דְּלָא סָבַר דָּא מִילְּתָא לָא סָבַר בִּנְזִיקִין כְּלוּם. אָמַר רִבִּי זְעִירָא. וַאֲנָא לֵית נָא סָבַר לָהּ. אָמַר רִבִּי בָּא לְרִבִּי זְעִירָא. מַתְנִיתָא פְלִיגָא עַל שְׁמוּאֵל. הָיוּ בָהּ מוּמִין וְעוֹדָהּ בְּבֵית אָבִיהָ. הָאָב צָרִיךְ לְהָבִיא רְאָיָיה. לֹא הַבַּעַל צָרִיךְ לְהָבִיא רְאָיָיה לְהוֹצִיא קִידּוּשִׁין מֵרְשׁוּת הָאָב.

תַּלְמִידוֹי דְּרִבִּי יוֹנָה אָמְרִין. תִּיפְתָּר בְּקִידּוּשִׁים קְטַנִּים. דְּלֹמָא. רִבִּי חוּנָה וְרִבִּי פִּינְחָס וְרִבִּי חִזְקִיָּה סָלְקִין מִישְׁאוֹל בִּשְׁלָמֵיהּ דְּרִבִּי יוֹסֵף לְמֵילַף מִינֵיהּ. אָמְרוּ לֵיהּ. מַתְנִיתָא מְסַיְּיעָא לִשְׁמוּאֵל. נִכְנְסָה לִרְשׁוּת הַבַּעַל. הַבַּעַל צָרִיךְ לְהָבִיא רְאָיָיה. וְלֹא הָאָב צָרִיךְ לְהָבִיא רְאָיָיה לְהוֹצִיא כְּתוּבָה מֵרְשׁוּת הַבַּעַל. אָמַר לוֹן. לֹא מוֹדֶה שְׁמוּאֵל שֶׁאִם מָשַׁךְ בַּעַל הַפָּרָה אֶת הַחֲמוֹר שֶׁהוּא צָרִיךְ לְהָבִיא רְאָיָיה שֶׁהָיוּ בָהּ מוּמִין אֵילוּ עַד שֶׁלֹּא תִיכָּנֵס לִרְשׁוּתוֹ. וְזֶה כֵּיוָן שֶׁכָּנַס כְּמִי שֶׁמָּשַׁךְ.

[532]Rebbi Abba in the name of Rav Jehudah in the name of Samuel: One has a cow and one a donkey. They exchanged one for the other. The donkey's owner took the cow[533]. When the cow's owner came to take the donkey and found that it had died, the donkey's owner has to bring proof that his donkey was alive at the moment he took the cow. For the burden of proof is on the claimant[499] except for barter[534]. And anybody who does not agree to this does not know anything about civil law. Rebbi Ze'ira said, I do not agree[535]. Rebbi Abba said to Rebbi Ze'ira: A Mishnah[536] disagrees with Samuel. "If she had bodily defects, as long as she is in her father's house, the father has to prove." Not the husband has to prove to regain the [money given] for preliminary marriage from the father[537]. The students of Rebbi Jonah said, explain it if little money was involved[538]. An example: Rebbi Huna, Rebbi Phineas, and Rebbi Hizqiah went to visit Rebbi Yosef[539] to learn from him. They said to him, the Mishnah supports Samuel: "Once she entered the husband's domain, the husband has to prove." Would not the father have to prove, to extract the *ketubah* from the husband's possession[540]? He answered them, does not Samuel agree that if the cow's owner took possession of the donkey, he has to prove that it was defective before it came into his possession[541]? And this one, when he took her in it is as if he drew close[542].

532 Shortened versions of this paragraph are in *Baba meṣia'* 4:1 (9c l. 36), Babli *Ketubot* 67a/b.

5323 Then automatically the donkey became the possession of its new owner.

534 In case one party had no opportunity to inspect the object given in barter before the transfer of possession.

535 For him, the burden of proof is always on the claimant, without exception. In *Baba meṣia'*, he is reported to note that apparently he does not understand civil law.

536 *Ketubot* 7:9. The husband divorces his wife because of bodily defects without paying the *ketubah*. If the defects are discovered between preliminary and definitive marriages, the father (of the underage bride) has to prove that at the moment of preliminary marriage the girl was without blemish in order to collect the *ketubah*. After definitive marriage, the husband has to prove that she was defective even before the preliminary marriage in order to avoid paying the *ketubah*.

537 The Babli, *loc. cit.*, notes that it is not obvious that money given for preliminary marriage can be recovered, even if the marriage was entered into under false premises.

538 Not worth the bother of a court battle. Then only the father's claim on the husband for the *ketubah* money remains; the father is the claimant who has to bring proof.

539 In *Baba qama*: R. Yose.

540 The question is, who is considered the claimant? The husband, who wants to avoid paying the *ketubah* which became due at the moment of divorce, or the father who would have to collect the money.

541 Since possession implies not only rights but also liabilities, the act of taking possession eliminates the liabilities of the previous owner. The owner of the cow should have inspected the donkey before moving the cow; afterwards he certainly is the claimant.

542 In this respect, definitive marriage of a woman entails transfer of liabilities to the husband, parallel to the transfer of liabilities for livestock by taking possession.

(60d line 75) רִבִּי בָּא רַב הַמְנוּנָא רַב אָדָא בַּר אַחֲוָה בְשֵׁם רַב. מְכָרָה לוֹ פָּרָה בְדָמִים. דַּחֲזָקִיָּה אָמַר לֵיהּ. הַב לִי אִינוּן פְּרִיטַיָּא. אָמַר לֵיהּ. מָה אַתְּ בְּעִי מִינְּהוֹן. אָמַר לֵיהּ. מִיזַבִּין לֵיהּ חֲמוֹר. מָשַׁךְ בַּעַל הַפָּרָה אֶת הַחֲמוֹר לֹא נִקְנֵית הַפָּרָה. חֲמוֹר מָהוּ שֶׁיִּקָּנֶה. רִבִּי בָּא אָמַר. נִקְנֵית. רִבִּי יוֹסֵי אָמַר. אֵינָהּ נִקְנֵית. סָבַר רִבִּי בָּא דְּאִינּוּן חֲלִיפִין. וְלֵית אִינוּן חֲלִיפִין. רִבִּי מָנָא בְּשֵׁם רִבִּי יוֹסֵי. פְּעָמִים שֶׁתְּחִילַּת מֶקַח לָזֶה וּתְחִילַּת מֶקַח לָזֶה. הֵיךְ עֲבִידָא. מְכָרָה לוֹ פָּרָה בְדָמִים. סְמִיכָה גַּבֵּי חָדָא פְּרִיטַיָּא. לְמָחָר אַשְׁכְּחֵיהּ קָאִים תַּמָּן. אָמַר לֵיהּ. מָה אַתְּ עָבִיד קַיָּים הָכָא. אָמַר לֵיהּ. בְּעָא אִינוּן פְּרִיטַיָּא. אָמַר לֵיהּ. מָה אַתְּ בְּעִי מִינְּהוֹן. אָמַר לֵיהּ. מִיזַבִּין לִי חַד חֲמוֹר. אָמַר לֵיהּ. הֲרֵי חֲמוֹר לְפָנֶיךָ. מָשַׁךְ זֶה לֹא קָנָה זֶה. מָשַׁךְ זֶה לֹא קָנָה זֶה. אֶלָּא זֶה קָנָה לְעַצְמוֹ וְזֶה קָנָה לְעַצְמוֹ.

Rebbi Abba, Rav Hamnuna, Rav Ada bar Ahawa in the name of Rav[543]: If he[544] sold a cow for money, then grabbed him[545] and said, give me that money. He[545] answered, for what do you need it? He said, to buy a donkey for him[self][546]. If the owner of the cow took possession of the donkey, the cow was not taken into possession[547]. Was the donkey taken into possession[548]? Rebbi Abba said, it was taken into possession. Rebbi Yose said, it was not taken into possession. Rebbi Abba thought that this was barter, but it was not barter. Rebbi Mana in the name of Rebbi Yose: Sometimes it is a new deal for one party and a new deal for the other party. How is that? He[544] sold him[545] a cow for money; he left the money standing with him. The next day, he[545] found him[544] standing there and said, what are you doing here? He[544] said, I want to collect the money. He[545] answered, for what do you want it? He[544] said, to buy myself a donkey. He[545] answered, there is a donkey before you. If either one of them drew[549], the other one did not enter into possession; each one has to take possession separately.

543 In the Babli, *Baba meṣi'a* 47a, Rav Ada bar Ahava has a similar statement which however refers to true barter.

544 The seller of the cow.

545 The buyer of the cow.

546 Obviously, something is missing in this sentence. The seller stated that he needed the money to buy a donkey, the buyer sold him a donkey for the money he owed him. Then sale of the cow and purchase of the donkey are two unrelated operations.

547 If the deal had be agreed upon but was not yet executed.

548 If the buyer of the cow took possession of it.

549 He drew the animal close to himself in order to take possession. Since there are two separate deals, it needs two separate actions to take possession.

(61a line 9) מַתְנִיתָא. רְשׁוּת הַגָּבוֹהַּ בְּכֶסֶף וּרְשׁוּת הַהֶדְיוֹט בַּחֲזָקָה. כֵּיצַד. גִּיזְבָּר שֶׁנָּתַן מָעוֹת הֶקְדֵּשׁ בְּמִטַּלְטְלִין קָנָה הֶקְדֵּשׁ בְּכָל־מָקוֹם שֶׁהוּא. שֶׁנֶּאֱמַר לַיי הָאָרֶץ וּמְלוֹאָהּ תֵּבֵל וְיוֹשְׁבֵי בָהּ.

The Mishnah: "Possession of Heaven is by money, possession of any individual by taking hold." How? If the treasurer paid with Temple money for movables, they are in the Temple's possession anywhere they are[550], for it is written[551]: "The Eternal's are the earth and what fills it, dry land and its inhabitants."

550 Without a separate act of taking possession. The seller cannot retract the sale. Babli 28b; Tosephta *Qiddušin* 1:9, *Baba qama* 4:3, *'Arakhin* 4:4.

551 Ps. 24:1.

(61a line 11) אֲמִירָתוֹ לַגָּבוֹהַּ כִּמְסִירָתוֹ לַהֶדְיוֹט. כֵּיצַד. לָקַח פָּרָה מִן הַהֶקְדֵּשׁ בְּמָאתַיִם. לֹא הִסְפִּיק לְהָבִיא מָאתַיִם עַד שֶׁעָמַד בְּמָנֶה. מֵבִיא מָאתַיִם. הָדָא הִיא אֲמִירָתוֹ לַגָּבוֹהַּ כִּמְסִירָתוֹ לַהֶדְיוֹט. פָּרָה מִן הַהֶקְדֵּשׁ בְּמָנֶה. לֹא הִסְפִּיק לְהָבִיא מָנֶה עַד שֶׁעָמַד בְּמָאתַיִם. מֵבִיא מָאתַיִם. הָדָא הִיא דִכְתִיב וְיָסַף חֲמִישִׁית כֶּסֶף עֶרְכְּךָ עָלָיו וְקָם לוֹ. הָא אִם יוֹסִיף הֲרֵי הוּא קָם לוֹ וְאִם לָאו

אֵינוֹ קָם לוֹ. שׁוֹר זֶה עוֹלָה וּבַיִת זֶה קָרְבָּן. קָנָה הֶקְדֵּשׁ בְּכָל־מָקוֹם שֶׁהוּא. דִּכְתִיב לַיִי הָאָרֶץ וּמְלוֹאָהּ וגו'. וּבְהֶדְיוֹט לֹא קָנָה עַד שֶׁיַּחֲזִיק.

"A promise to Heaven is like delivery to an individual." How? If he bought a cow from the Temple for 200. If he did not have occasion to pay the 200 until the going rate was a *mina*, he has to pay 200. That means, a promise to Heaven is like delivery to an individual. A cow from the Temple for a *mina*. If he did not have occasion to pay the *mina* until the going rate was 200, he has to pay 200. That is what is written[552]: "He has to add a fifth of its estimated value, then it is delivered to him." Therefore, if he adds, it is delivered to him; if he does not add, it is not delivered to him. [553]"'This steer as elevation offering, or this house as a *qorbān*,' they are in the Temple's possession wherever they are, for it is written: "The Eternal's are the earth and what fills it," etc. But among private persons one obtains possession only be taking hold."

552   *Lev.* 27:19.   553   Babli 28b, Tosephta 1:9.

(fol. 58b) **משנה ז**: כָּל־מִצְוַת הָאָב עַל הַבֵּן הָאֲנָשִׁים חַיָּיבִין וְהַנָּשִׁים פְּטוּרוֹת. כָּל־מִצְוַת הַבֵּן עַל הָאָב אֶחָד אֲנָשִׁים וְאֶחָד נָשִׁים חַיָּיבִין. כָּל־מִצְוַת עֲשֵׂה שֶׁהַזְּמָן גְּרָמָא הָאֲנָשִׁים חַיָּיבִין וְהַנָּשִׁים פְּטוּרוֹת. כָּל־מִצְוַת עֲשֵׂה שֶׁלֹּא הַזְּמָן גְּרָמָא אֶחָד אֲנָשִׁים וְאֶחָד נָשִׁים חַיָּיבִין. כָּל־מִצְוָה בְלֹא תַעֲשֶׂה בֵּין שֶׁהַזְּמָן גְּרָמָא בֵּין שֶׁלֹּא הַזְּמָן גְּרָמָא אֶחָד אֲנָשִׁים וְאֶחָד נָשִׁים חַיָּיבִין חוּץ מִבַּל תַּשְׁחִית וּבַל תַּקִּיף וּבַל תִּיטַּמֵּא לַמֵּתִים.

Mishnah 7: For any commandment a father has to fulfill towards his son, men are obligated but women are free. For any commandment the son has to fulfill towards his father, men and women are equally obligated. For any positive commandment activated by time[554], men are obligated but women are free. For any positive commandment not activated by time[555], men and women are equally obligated. For any prohibition, whether or not activated by time, men and women are equally obligated except for "do not destroy", "do not shear,"[556] and "do not become impure for the dead.[557]"

[554] Which either depends on the time of day or the calendar date. This rule admits of quite a few exceptions.

[555] E. g., the obligation to give charity and do charitable work.

[556] Not to destroy one's beard or shear the sideburns, Lev. 19:27, inappropriate for women.

[557] Lev. 21:1. In general, holiness prohibitions valid for priests do not apply to their daughters and only partially to their wives.

משנה ח: הַסְּמִיכוֹת וְהַתְּנוּפוֹת הַהַגָּשׁוֹת הַקְּמִיצוֹת הַהַקְטָרוֹת וְהַמְּלִיקוֹת הַהַזָּאוֹת וְהַקַּבָּלוֹת נוֹהֲגוֹת בָּאֲנָשִׁים וְאֵינָן נוֹהֲגוֹת בַּנָּשִׁים חוּץ מִמִּנְחַת סוֹטָה וּנְזִירָה שֶׁהֵן מְנִיפוֹת.

Mishnah 8: Leanings[558] and weavings[559], presentations[560], taking of fistfuls[561], burnings[562] and neck breakings[563], sprinklings[564] and receptions[565] apply to men but not to women except for the flour offerings of the suspected wife and the *nezirah;* those do weave.

[558] The obligatory leaning on the head of the sacrifice (Lev. 1:4, 3:2,8, 13; 4:4,15,24,29,33).

[559] The prescribed motions for selected sacrifices of purification (Lev. 8:27; 14:12,24; Num. 5:25; 6:19).

[560] Presentations to the altar, mainly of flour offerings (Lev. 2:6; 6:7).

[561] The fistful burned on the altar of flour offerings; Lev. 6:8.

[562] Bringing meat, flour, or incense and putting it in the fire on the altar.

[563] Of bird sacrifices; Lev. 1:15, 5:8.

[564] Of blood on the walls of the altar, Lev. 1:5,11; 3:2,8,13; 4:6,7,17,18, 25,30,34; 5:9.

[565] Receiving the blood of slaughtered sacrifices in a sanctified vessel. All these actions are restricted to male Aharonides except for leanings and weavings, which are prescribed for the public.

(61a line 18) **הלכה ז**: כָּל־מִצְוֹת הָאָב עַל הַבֵּן כול׳. מִצְוֹת שֶׁהָאָב חַיָּיב לַעֲשׂוֹת לִבְנוֹ. לְמוֹהֲלוֹ לִפְדּוֹתוֹ לְלַמְּדוֹ תוֹרָה וּלְלַמְּדוֹ אוּמָנוּת לְהַשִּׂיאוֹ אִשָּׁה. רִבִּי עֲקִיבָה אוֹמֵר. אַף לְלַמְּדוֹ לָשׁוּט עַל פְּנֵי הַמַּיִם. לְמוֹהֲלוֹ. בַּיּוֹם הַשְּׁמִינִי יִמּוֹל בְּשַׂר עָרְלָתוֹ. לִפְדּוֹתוֹ דִּכְתִיב וְכָל־בְּכוֹר אָדָם בְּבָנֶיךָ תִּפְדֶּה. לְלַמְּדוֹ תוֹרָה. וְלִמַּדְתֶּם אוֹתָם אֶת בְּנֵיכֶם. לְלַמְּדוֹ אוּמָנוּת. תַּנֵּי רִבִּי יִשְׁמָעֵאל. וּבָחַרְתָּ בַּחַיִּים. זוֹ אוּמָנוּת. לְהַשִּׂיאוֹ אִשָּׁה. וְהוֹדַעְתָּם לְבָנֶיךָ וְלִבְנֵי בָנֶיךָ. אֵימָתַי אַתָּה זוֹכֶה לְבָנֶיךָ וְלִבְנֵי בָנֶיךָ. בְּשָׁעָה שֶׁאַתְּ מַשִּׂיא אֶת בָּנֶיךָ קְטַנִּים. רִבִּי עֲקִיבָה אוֹמֵר. אַף לָשׁוּט עַל פְּנֵי הַמַּיִם. דִּכְתִיב לְמַעַן תִּחְיֶה אַתָּה וְזַרְעֶיךָ. מַה. לְמִצְוָה אוֹ לְעִיכּוּב. נִישְׁמְעִינָהּ מִן הָדָא. בַּר תְּרִימָה אֲתָא לְגַבֵּי רִבִּי אִימִּי. אֲמַר לֵיהּ. פַּייֵס לְאַבָּא דְּיַסְּבֵינִי אִתָּא. פַּייְסֵיהּ וְלָא קַבִּיל עֲלוֹי. הָדָא אָמְרָה לְמִצְוָה. אִין תֵּימַר לְעִיכּוּב. הֲוָה לֵיהּ לְכוּפְנֵיהּ. מִנַּיִין שֶׁאִם לֹא עָשָׂה לוֹ אָבִיו שֶׁהוּא חַיָּיב לַעֲשׂוֹת לְעַצְמוֹ. תַּלְמוּד לוֹמַר אָדָם תִּפְדֶּה. וּנְמַלְתֶּם אוֹתָם. וְלִמַּדְתֶּם אוֹתָם. וְהוֹדַעְתָּ אַתָּה. לְמַעַן תִּחְיֶה אַתָּה.

Halakhah 7: "Any commandment the father has to fulfill towards his son," etc. [566]"To circumcise him, to redeem him, to teach him Torah, to teach him a trade, and to marry him to a wife. Rebbi Aqiba says, also to teach him to swim in water." To circumcise him, "on the eighth day, he shall circumcise the flesh of his foreskin.[567]" "To redeem him," as is written: "Any firstborn human among your sons you shall redeem.[568]" To teach him Torah, "you shall teach them to your sons.[569]" To teach him a trade, Rebbi Ismael stated: "Choose life[570]," that is a trade. To marry him to a wife, "make it known to your children and grandchildren[571]." When do you have children and grandchildren: if you marry off your sons when young. Rebbi Aqiba says, also to swim in water. "That you shall live together with your descendants[570]." How is this? Is it a commandment[572] or is it obligatory? Let us hear from the following: Bar Tarima came to Rebbi Immi and said to him, talk to my father that he should marry me to a woman. He talked to [the father], but the latter refused. That means it is a commandment, for if it were obligatory, he should have forced him. From where that if his father did not do these things for him, he is required to do them himself? The verse says a human you shall redeem[568], "you shall circumcise" them[573], "you shall study them[574]", "you shall know[571]" yourself, "that you shall live[570]."[575]

566 Babli 29a,30b; Tosephta 1:11; *Mekhilta dR. Ismael, Pisḥa* 18.

567 *Lev.* 12:3. The masculine form of the verb implies that the father, who otherwise is not mentioned in the paragraph, is obligated to circumcise his son.

568 *Ex.* 13:13.

569 *Deut.* 11:19. Cf. *Berakhot* 2:3. Note 110, where the verse is quoted to show that daughters do not have to be instructed in Torah (Babli 29b).

570 *Deut.* 30:19.

571 *Deut.* 4:9.

572 A meritorious deed.

573 *Gen.* 17:11.

574 *Deut.* 4:9; reading וְלִמַּדְתָּם instead of וְלִמַּדְתֶּם

575 The Babli, 29a-30a, in most cases quotes different verses to the same effects.

(61a line 31) תַּמָּן תַּנִּינָן. הָאָב זָכָה לַבֵּן בְּנוֹי בַּכֹּחַ בָּעוֹשֶׁר וּבַחָכְמָה וּבַשָּׁנִים. בְּנוֹי מִנַּיִין יֵירָאֶה עַל עֲבָדֶיךָ פָּעֳלֶיךָ וַהֲדָרְךָ עַל בְּנֵיהֶם. בַּכֹּחַ. גִּיבּוֹר בָּאָרֶץ יִהְיֶה זַרְעוֹ וגו'. בָּעוֹשֶׁר. נַעַר הָיִיתִי וְגַם זָקַנְתִּי וְלֹא רָאִיתִי צַדִּיק נֶעֱזָב וְזַרְעוֹ מְבַקֶּשׁ לָחֶם. בַּחָכְמָה. וְלִמַּדְתֶּם אוֹתָם אֶת בְּנֵיכֶם לְדַבֵּר בָּם. בַּשָּׁנִים. לְמַעַן יִרְבּוּ יְמֵיכֶם וִימֵי בְנֵיכֶם. וּכְשֵׁם שֶׁהוּא זָכָה לוֹ בַּחֲמִשָּׁה דְבָרִים כָּךְ הוּא חַיָּיב לוֹ בַּחֲמִשָּׁה דְבָרִים. וְאֵילּוּ הֵן מַאֲכָל וּמַשְׁקֶה מַלְבִּישׁ מַנְעִיל מַנְהִיג. הָדָא הוּא דִכְתִיב חָחוּלוּ עַל רֹאשׁ יוֹאָב. זָב וּמְצוֹרָע וּמַחֲזִיק בַּפֶּלֶךְ וְנוֹפֵל בַּחֶרֶב וַחֲסַר לֵב. זָב תָּשִׁישׁ. וּמְצוֹרָע עָזִיב. יִמַּחֲזִיק בַּפֶּלֶךְ בּוֹרָיי. נוֹפֵל בַּחֶרֶב קְצַר יָמִים. וַחֲסַר לֶחֶם מִסְכֵּן. כַּד אֲתָא שְׁלֹמֹה מִיקְטוֹל לְיוֹאָב אֲמַר לֵיהּ. אָבִיךְ גָּזַר עָלַי חָמֵשׁ גְּזֵירוֹת. קַבְּלִין וַאֲנָא מִיתְקַטִּיל. וְקַבְּלִין. וְכוּלְּהוֹן קָמִין מִן דְּבֵית דָּוִד. זָב הָיָה רְחַבְעָם. וְהַמֶּלֶךְ רְחַבְעָם הִתְאַמֵּץ לַעֲלוֹת בַּמֶּרְכָּבָה לָנוּס לִירוּשָׁלִָם. מָאן דְּאָמַר. זָב. וּמָאן דְּאָמַר. אִיסְטְנֵיס. מְצוֹרָע זֶה עֻזִּיָּהוּ. וַיְהִי עֻזִיָּהוּ הַמֶּלֶךְ

מצוֹרָע עַד יוֹם מוֹתוֹ. מַחֲזִיק בַּפֶּלֶךְ זֶה יוֹאָשׁ. וְאֶת יוֹאָשׁ עָשׂוּ שְׁפָטִים. תַּנֵּי רַבִּי יִשְׁמָעֵאל. מְלַמֵּד שֶׁהֶעֱמִידוּ עָלָיו בִּירְנִיּוֹת קָשִׁים שֶׁלֹּא הִכִּירוּ אִשָּׁה מִימֵיהֶם וְהָיוּ מְעַנִּין בּוֹ כְּדֶרֶךְ שֶׁמְּעַנִּין אֶת הָאִשָּׁה. הֲדָא הוּא דִכְתִיב וְעָנָה גְאוֹן יִשְׂרָאֵל בְּפָנָיו. וְעִינָה גְאוֹן יִשְׂרָאֵל בְּפָנָיו. וְנוֹפֵל בַּחֶרֶב זֶה יֹאשִׁיָּהוּ. דִכְתִיב וַיֹּרוּ הַמּוֹרִים לַמֶּלֶךְ יֹאשִׁיָּהוּ. וְאָמַר רִבִּי יוֹחָנָן. מְלַמֵּד שֶׁעָשׂוּ גּוּפוֹ כִּכְבָרָה. תַּנֵּי רַבִּי יִשְׁמָעֵאל. שְׁלֹשׁ מֵאוֹת חִיצִים יוֹרוּ בִּמְשִׁיחַ ה'. וַחֲסַר לָחֶם. זֶה יוֹיָכִין. וַאֲרוּחָתוֹ אֲרוּחַת תָּמִיד נִתְּנָה לוֹ וגו'.

There, we have stated[576]: "The father bestows on his son beauty, strength, riches, wisdom, and years." From where beauty? "May Your deeds appear on Your servants, and Your glory on their sons.[577]" Strength, "strong on earth will be his descendants.[578]" Riches, "I was young and became old, but never saw a just man abandoned and his descendants in need of bread.[579]" Wisdom, "you shall teach your sons to argue about them.[569]" Years, "that your and your sons' days be many.[580]" And just as he inherits five qualities, so he owes him the following five things. He feeds him, he gives him to drink, he clothes him, he puts on his shoes, he leads him[581]. That is what is written[582]: "This should fall on Joab's head: sufferer from flux and from skin disease, holding the distaff, falling by the sword, and senseless.[583]" Sufferer from flux, weak. From skin disease, abandoned[584]. Holding the distaff, uneducated. Falling by the sword, short lived. Without bread, poor. [585]When Solomon came to kill Joab, he said to him: Your father gave me five sentences; accept them and I can be killed. He accepted them and all of them came to pass on the House of David. Sufferer from flux was Rehabeam: "King Rehabeam with difficulty climbed on his chariot to flee to Jerusalem;[586]" some say, he suffered from flux; some say, he was weak. Suffering from skin disease was Uziahu: "King Uziahu suffered from skin disease until the day of his death[587]." Holding the distaff was Joash: "They punished Joash[588]."

Rebbi Ismael stated: [589]This teaches that they gave him over to hardened hoodlums who had never known a woman and they raped him the way women are raped. That is what is written: "Israel's pride will testify against it,[590]" Israel's pride will be raped in its face. Falling by the sword, this is Josiah, as is written: "The archers shot at king Josia,[591]" and Rebbi Joḥanan said, this teaches that they made his body like a sieve[592]. Rebbi Ismael stated: 300 arrows were shot at the Eternal's anointed. Without bread, that is Jehoiachin: "And his meal, a permanent meal was given to him,[593]."

576 Mishnah *Idiut* 2:9.
577 *Ps.* 90:16.
578 *Ps.* 112:2.
579 *Ps.* 37:25.
580 *Deut.* 11:21.
581 *Peah* 1:1, Note 119; Babli 31b.
582 *2S.* 3:29.
583 This is a slip of the pen; later it is quoted in the language of the verse, "without bread".
584 Cf. *Lev.* 13:46.
585 The Babylonian version is in the Babli, *Sanhedrin* 48b, and *Num. rabba* 23(13).

586 *1K.* 12:18.
587 *2Chr.* 26:21.
588 *2Chr.* 24:24.
589 *Mekhilta dR. Ismael, Amaleq* 1; *Tanḥuma Bešallaḥ* 25
590 *Hos.* 5:5, repunctuating עָנָה to עָנָה.
591 *2Chr.* 35:23. In the text: הַיֹּרִים.
592 Babli *Mo'ed qaṭan* 28b; *Thr. rabbati* on 1:18.
593 *2K.* 25:30. He never had any money of his own. A completely different interpretation of the verse in *Midrash Shemuel* 18(5).

(61a line 50) תַּמָּן תַּנִּינָן. אִם הִתְחִילוּ אֵין מַפְסִיקִין. הִתְחָלַת הַמֶּרְחָץ אֵי זוֹ הִיא. רִבִּי זְרִיקָן בְּשֵׁם רִבִּי חֲנִינָה. מִשֶּׁיַּתִּיר אֵיזוֹרוֹ. רַב אָמַר. מִשֶּׁיַּתִּיר מִנְעָלוֹ. רִבִּי יְהוֹשֻׁעַ בֶּן לֵוִי הֲוָה יְלִיף שְׁמַע פַּרְשָׁתָה דְּבַר בְּרֵיהּ בְּכָל־עֲרוּבַת שׁוּבְתָּא. חַד זְמָן אִינְשֵׁי וְעָאל מִיסְחֵי בְּהָהֵין דֵּימוֹסִין דְּטִיבֶּרְיָא. וַהֲוָה מִסְתַּמִּיךְ עַל כַּתְפֵי דְרִבִּי חִייָה בַּר בָּא. אֲנְחַר וּנְפַק לֵיהּ מִן דֵּימוֹסָא. אָמַר. כָּךְ הֲוָה. רִבִּי לְעָזָר בַּר יוֹסֵי אָמַר. שְׁלִיחַ מָטֵי. אָמַר לֵיהּ רִבִּי חִייָה בַּר בָּא. לֹא כֵן אַלְפָן רִבִּי. אִם

הִתְחִילוּ אֵין מַפְסִיקִין. אָמַר לֵיהּ. חִיָּיה בְנִי. וְקַלָּה הִיא בְעֵינֶיךָ. שֶׁכָּל־מִי שֶׁהוּא שׁוֹמֵעַ פָּרָשָׁה מִבֶּן בְּנוֹ כְּאִילּוּ הוּא שׁוֹמְעָהּ מֵהַר סִינַי. מַאי טַעְמָא. וְהוֹדַעְתָּם לְבָנֶיךָ וְלִבְנֵי בָנֶיךָ וגו'. יוֹם אֲשֶׁר עָמַדְתָּ לִפְנֵי י"י אֱלֹהֶיךָ בַּחוֹרֵב. כְּיוֹם אֲשֶׁר עָמַדְתָּ לִפְנֵי י"י אֱלֹהֶיךָ בַּחוֹרֵב. רִבִּי חִזְקִיָּה בַּר יִרְמִיָה רִבִּי חִייָה בְשֵׁם רִבִּי יוֹחָנָן. אִם יָכוֹל אַתְּ לְשַׁלְשֵׁל שְׁמוּעָה עַד משֶׁה שַׁלְשְׁלָהּ. וְאִם לָאו תְּפוֹשׂ אוֹ רִאשׁוֹן אוֹ אַחֲרוֹן אַחֲרוֹן. גִּידּוּל אָמַר. כָּל־הָאוֹמֵר שְׁמוּעָה מִשּׁוּם אוֹמְרָהּ יְהֵא רוֹאֶה בְעַצְמוֹ כְּאִילּוּ בַעַל הַשְּׁמוּעָה עוֹמֵד לְפָנָיו. מַה טַעְמָא. אַךְ בְּצֶלֶם יִתְהַלֶּךְ אִישׁ וגו'. רַב אָדָם יִקְרָא אִישׁ חַסְדּוֹ וְאִישׁ אֱמוּנִים מִי יִמְצָא. זֶה רִבִּי זְעִירָא. דְּאָמַר רִבִּי זְעִירָא. לֵית אֲנַן חָשִׁין עַל שְׁמוּעָתָהּ דְּרַב שֵׁשֶׁת דְּהוּא גַבְרָא מַפְתְּחָא. וְאָמַר רִבִּי זְעִירָא לְרִבִּי יָסָא. חַכִּים רִבִּי לְבַר פְּדָיָיה דְּאַתְּ אָמַר שְׁמוּעָתָא מִן שְׁמֵיהּ. אָמַר לֵיהּ. רַב אָדָא בַּר אֲחָוָה אֲמָרִין בִּשְׁמוֹ.

2 חנינה | ש חנינא אמ'   איזורו | ש חגורו   3 ר' יהושע | ש כהדא ר' יהושע   דבר | ש מן בר   שובתא | ש שובא   4 מיסתמיד | ש מסתמיך   כתפיה | ש כתפתיה   5 חייה | ש חייא   אנהר | ש אינהר דלא שמע מן בר בריה וחזר   מן דימוסא | ש -   אמ'. כך הוה | ש ר' דרוסי אמ'. כך הוה   בר | ש ביר'   6 מטי | ש מנוי הוה   חייה בר בא | ש חייא בר אבא   לא | ש ולא   7 וקלה | ש קלה   8 שהוא שומע | ש השומע   מבן | ש מן בן מאי | ש מה   9 וגו' | ש -   כיום אשר אמדת לפני י"י אלהיך בחורב | ש -   10 בר ירמיה | ש ר' ירמיה   חייה | ש חייא   12 אחרון | ש אחרון. מה טעמ' והודעתם לבניך ולבני בניך יום אשר עמדת. עד יום אשר אמדת לפני י"י אלהיך בחורב   משום | ש מפי 13 בעצמו כאילו בעל השמועה | ש בעל השמועה כאילו הוא   מה | ש ומה   14 וגו' | ש - רב | ש כת' רב   אמונים | ש אמונות   15 זה ר' זעירא | ש רב אדם יקרא איש חסדו זה שאר כל אדם. ואיש אמונים מי ימצא. זה ר' זעירא   חשין | ש צריכין חששין   על שמועתה | ש לשמועתיה   16 ואמ' | ש אמ'   חכם | ש חכים   פדייה | ש פדיה   17 רב אדא בר אחוה אמרין בשמו | ש ר' יוחנן אמרן משמו. אמר ר' זעירא לר' בא בר זבדא. חכים ר' לרב דאת אמר שמועתא מן שמיה. אמ' ליה. רב אדא בי אהבא אמרן משמו.

[594]There, we have stated: "If they started[595], one does not interrupt." What is the start of bathing? Rebbi Zeriqan in the name of Rebbi Ḥanina: When he opened his belt. Rav said, when he took off his shoe. Rebbi Joshua ben Levi used to hear the lesson[596] of his grandson every Friday. Once he forgot and went bathing in the public baths of Tiberias; he was

leaning on Rebbi Hiyya bar Abba's shoulder. He remembered[597] and left the public bath. [598]He said, so it was: Rebbi Eleazar bar Yose said, he had taken off [his clothes][599]. Rebbi Hiyya bar Abba said to him, did our teacher not teach us, "if they started, one does not interrupt"? He said to him, Hiyya my son, is that unimportant in your eyes? For anyone who hears the lesson from his grandson is as if he heard it from Mount Sinai. What is the reason? "[600]You shall make them known to you sons and grandsons," etc., [601]"the day when you stood before the Eternal, your God, at Horeb." Like the day when you stood before the Eternal, your God, at Horeb. Rebbi Hizqiah bar[602] Jeremiah, Rebbi Hiyya in the name of Rebbi Johanan: If you can link the tradition back to Moses, link it. Otherwise take either the very first or the very last [source][603]. Giddul said, anybody who quotes somebody should consider it as if the author of the quote stood before him. What is the reason? "Only in image a man wanders.[604]" "Many a man professes good will, but where will you find one you can trust?" [605]That is Rebbi Ze'ira, as Rebbi Ze'ira said, we do take the traditions of Rav Sheshet into account since he is blind. [606]And Rebbi Ze'ira said to Rebbi Yasa, does the Rabbi know Bar Pedaiah, that you quote in his name? He said to him, Rav Ada bar Ahawa said it in his name.

594 The origin of this text is in Šabbat 1, to Mishnah 2.

595 The Mishnah contains a list of things one should not do on Friday afternoon, but if one started one does not have to interrupt. One of these is going to the public bathhouse.

596 The portion of the Torah to be read on the Sabbath.

597 In Šabbat: He remembered that he had not heard the lesson from his grandson, returned and left.

598 In Šabbat: How was it? Rebbi Derose said, he was anointing himself. Rebbi Eleazar . . .

599 For Šabbat, instead of the unintelligible מטי written here.

600 Deut. 4:10.

601 Missing in *Šabbat*, probably correctly.

602 In *Šabbat*: R. Ḥizqiah, R. Jeremiah, R. Ḥiyya. This is the only correct text.

603 In *Šabbat* added: What is the reason? "The day when you stood," Up to the day when you stood before the Eternal, your God, at Horeb. (Referring to the verse quoted earlier, Note 600. Since Moses was speaking to the second generation, not present at Sinai, it proves that a person can be present at Sinai by connecting with the teachings from Sinai.)

604 *Ps.* 39:7.

605 This is a *non sequitur*. The intelligible text is in *Šabbat*: "Many a man professes good will," these are all other people, "but where will you find one you can trust?" That is R. Ze'ira.

606 This text is unacceptable for reasons of chronology. The correct text is in *Šabbat*: "He said to him, R. Joḥanan said it in his name. R. Ze'ira asked R. Abba bar Zavda: Did you know Rav (a chronological impossibility), that you are quoting in his name? He answered, Rav Ada bar Ahava said it in his name."

(61a line 67) מִצְוֹת שֶׁהַבֵּן חַיָּב לַעֲשׂוֹת לְאָבִיו. אֵי זֶהוּ מוֹרָא. לֹא יוֹשֵׁב בִּמְקוֹמוֹ. וְלֹא מְדַבֵּר בִּמְקוֹמוֹ. וְלֹא סוֹתֵר אֶת דְּבָרָיו. אֵי זֶהוּ כִּיבּוּד. מַאֲכִיל וּמַשְׁקֶה מַלְבִּישׁ וּמְכַסֶּה וּמַנְעִיל מַכְנִיס וּמוֹצִיא. מִן דְּמַאן. הוּנָא בַּר חִייָה אָמַר מִשֶּׁלְּזָקֵן. וְאִית דְּבָעֵי מֵימַר. מִשֶּׁלּוֹ. לֹא כֵן אָמַר רִבִּי אַבָּהוּ בְּשֵׁם רִבִּי יוֹסֵי בְּרִבִּי חֲנִינָה. מִנַּיִן אֲפִילוּ אָמַר לוֹ אָבִיו. הַשְׁלֵךְ אֶת הָאַרְנְקִי הַזּוֹ לַיָּם. שְׁשׁוֹמֵעַ לוֹ. בְּהַהוּא דְּאִית לֵיהּ חוֹרָנִין וּבְעוֹשֶׂה הֲנָחַת רוּחַ שֶׁלְּאָבִיו. אֶחָד הָאִישׁ וְאֶחָד הָאִשָּׁה. אֶלָּא שֶׁהָאִישׁ סְפִּיקָה בְיָדוֹ. הָאִשָּׁה אֵינָהּ סְפִיקָה בְיָדָהּ מִפְּנֵי שֶׁיֵּשׁ רְשׁוּת לַאֲחֵרִים עָלֶיהָ. נִתְאַרְמְלָה אוֹ נִתְגָּרְשָׁה כְּמִי שֶׁהִיא סְפִיקָה בְיָדָהּ לַעֲשׂוֹת.

2 דבריו R | דבריו ולא מכריעו   3 ומכסה | פR -   חייה | פR חייא   5 בר' | פ בן הארנקי הזו | פ הארנק   6 חורנין | פ חורין   7 האשה אינה | פR והאשה אין

Commandments which the son is obligated to fulfill towards his father. 607What is fear? He may not sit in his place and may not speak in his stead nor contradict his words. What is honor? He feeds and gives him to drink, clothes him, covers him, and puts on his shoes, leads him out and in. From whose money? Huna bar Ḥiyya said, from the old man's. Some want to say, from his own. Did not Rebbi Abbahu say in the name of Rebbi Yose bar Ḥanina: From where do we know that even if his father tells him to throw the wallet into the sea that he should obey him? That is, if he has another one and if it helps to quiet his father's spirit. Both men and women. Only the man has the power in his hand, but the woman does not have the power in her own hand because others have disposition over her. If she is widowed or divorced, the power is in her own hand.

607 This is from *Peah* 1:1, Notes 117-124. Leiden ms. text ⅌, Rome ms. R. This is a quote out of context, repeated in the following paragraphs which copy *Peah* 1:1, Notes 98-137.

A few sentences from *Peah* which are missing in the text have been given in brackets.

(61a line 75) עַד אֵיכָן הוּא כִּיבּוּד אָב וָאֵם. אָמַר לָהֶן. וְלִי אַתֶּם שׁוֹאֲלִין. לְכוּ וְשַׁאֲלוּ אֶת דָּמָה בֶּן נְתִינָה. דָּמָה בֶּן נְתִינָה רֹאשׁ פַּטְרְכוּלִי הָיָה. פַּעַם אַחַת הָיְתָה אִמּוֹ מְסַטַּרְתּוֹ בִּפְנֵי כּוּלֵי שֶׁלּוֹ וְנָפַל קוּרְדְקָסִין שֶׁלָּהּ מִיָּדָהּ וְהוֹשִׁיט לָהּ שֶׁלֹּא תִצְטַעֵר. אָמַר רִבִּי חִזְקִיָּה. הַגּוֹי אַשְׁקְלוֹנִי הָיָה וְרֹאשׁ פַּטְרְכוּלִי הָיָה. וְאֶבֶן שֶׁיָּשַׁב עָלֶיהָ אָבִיו לֹא יָשַׁב עָלֶיהָ מִיָּמָיו. וְכֵיוָן שֶׁמֵּת עָשָׂה אוֹתָהּ יִרְאָה מִשֶּׁלּוֹ. פַּעַם אַחַת אָבְדָה יָשְׁפֶה שֶׁלְּבִנְיָמִין. אָמְרוּ מַאן דְּאִית לֵיהּ טָבָא דִּכְוָותָהּ. אָמְרִין דְּאִית לְדָמָה בֶּן נְתִינָה. אָזְלוּן לְגַבֵּיהּ וּפָסְקוּ עִמֵּיהּ בְּמֵאָה דֵּינָרִין. סְלִיק בְּעֵי מַיְיתִיתָא לְהוֹן וְאַשְׁכַּר לְאָבוּי דָּמַךְ. וְאִית דַּאֲמְרִין מַפְתָּחָא דְּתֵיבוּתָא הֲוָה יְתִיב גּוֹא אֶצְבְּעָתֵיהּ דְּאָבוּהַ. וְאִית דַּאֲמְרִין רִיגְלֵיהּ הֲוַת פְּשִׁיטָא עַל תֵּיבוּתָא. נְחַת לְגַבֵּיהוֹן. אָמַר לוֹן. לָא יְכִילִית מַיְיתִיתֵיהּ לְכוֹן. אָמְרִין. דִּילְמָא דְהוּא בְּעֵי פְּרִיטִין תּוּבָן. אַסְקִינְיֵהּ לְמָאתַיִם. אַסְקִינְיֵהּ לְאָלֶף. כֵּיוָן דְּאִיתְעִיר אָבִיו מִן שִׁינְתֵּיהּ סְלַק וְאַיְיתוּתֵיהּ לְהוֹן. בְּעוֹ מִתַּן לֵיהּ כְּדַפְסְקוֹ לֵהּ לְאַחֲרַיָּיא לָא קַבִּיל. אָמַר. מָה אֲנָא מְזַבְּנָא לְכוֹן אִיקָרָא דְּאֲבָהָתִי בִּפְרִיטִין. אִינִּי נֶהֱנֶה מִכְּבוֹד אֲבוֹתַי כְּלוּם. מַה פָּרַע לוֹ הַקָּדוֹשׁ בָּרוּךְ הוּא שָׂכָר. אָמַר רִבִּי יוֹסֵי בֵּי רִבִּי בּוּן. בּוֹ בַלַּיְלָה יָלְדָה פָרָתוֹ אֲדוּמָה. וְשָׁקְלוּ לוֹ יִשְׂרָאֵל מִשְׁקָלָהּ זָהָב וּשְׁקָלוּהָ. אָמַר רִבִּי שַׁבְּתַי. כְּתִיב וּמִשְׁפָּט וְרַב צְדָקָה לֹא יְעַנֶּה. אֵין הַקָּדוֹשׁ בָּרוּךְ הוּא מַשְׁהֶא מַתַּן שְׂכָרָן שֶׁל עוֹשֵׂי מִצְוֹת בַּגּוֹיִים.

1 עד איכן | פ שאלו את ר' אליעזר. עד היכן 3 כולי שלו | פ כל בולי שלי   קורדקסין |
פ קורדקון   4 הגוי | פ גוי   5 שמת | פ שמת אביו   משלו | פ שלו   6 דאית | פ
אית   אמרין | פ אמרו   8 מייתיתא | פ מייתה   דמך | פ דמיך   9 יתיב R | פ יהיב
גוא | פ גו   דאבוה | פ דאבוי   דאמרין | פ דמרין   ריגליה | פ ריגלה דאבוה   10
לגביהון | פ לגבון   מייתיתיה | פ מייתותיה   דהוא | פ דו   11 תובן | פ טובן   אביו | פ
אבוה   12 להון | פ לון   כדפסקו לה לאחרייא | פ כפסיקוליה אחרייא   קביל | פ
קביל עלוי   13 מזבנא | פ מזבין   15 אדומה | פ פרה אדומה

[They asked Rebbi Eliezer,] how far does honoring father and mother go? He said to them, you are asking me? Go and ask Dama ben Netinah. Dama ben Netinah was the head of the city council. Once his mother was slapping him in front of the entire council and a slipper fell from her hand, and he handed it back to her so that she should feel no inconvenience. Rebbi Ḥizqiah said: He was a Gentile from Ascalon and the head of the city council. He never sat on the stone on which his father used to sit and when his father died, he worshipped the stone. Once the jaspis of Benjamin was lost. They inquired, who would have one of similar quality? They were informed that Dama ben Netinah did. They went to him and agreed on 100 denars. He went to the upper floor to bring it and found his father sleeping. Some say that the key to the chest was in his father's fingers; some say his father's foot was resting on the chest. He descended to them and told them: I could not bring it to you. They thought, maybe he wants more money, and raised the price to two hundred, then to a thousand. When his father woke up from his sleep, he went up and brought it to them. They wanted to give him according to the amount last mentioned, but he refused. He said: Do I sell my father's honor for money? I will not have any advantage from honoring my father. What reward did the Holy One, praise to Him, give him? Rebbi Yose bar Abun said: The following night, his cow gave birth to a red heifer and Israel gave him its weight in gold and took it. Rebbi Sabbatai said (*Job* 37:23), it is written: "Justice and much charity He will not suppress." The Holy One, praise to Him, will not wait to give the reward for good deeds to the Gentiles.

(61b line 18) אִמּוֹ שֶׁלְּרִבִּי טַרְפוֹן יָרְדָה לְטַיֵּיל לְתוֹךְ חֲצֵירָהּ בְּשַׁבָּת וְנִפְסַק קוֹרְדִּיָּקִין שֶׁלָּהּ. וְהָלַךְ רִבִּי טַרְפוֹן וְהִנִּיחַ שְׁתֵּי יָדָיו תַּחַת פַּרְסוֹתֶיהָ וְהָיְתָה מְהַלֶּכֶת עֲלֵיהֶן עַד שֶׁהִגִּיעָה לְמִיטָתָהּ. פַּעַם אַחַת נִכְנְסוּ חֲכָמִים לְבַקְּרוֹ. אָמְרָה לָהֶן. הִתְפַּלְלוּ עַל טַרְפוֹן בְּנִי שֶׁהוּא נוֹהֵג בִּי בְּכָבֵד יוֹתֵר מִדַּאי. אָמְרִין לָהּ מַהוּ עֲבִיד לֵיךְ. וְתַנִּיַת לְהוֹן עוּבְדָא. אָמְרִין לָהּ. אֲפִילוּ עוֹשֶׂה כֵן אֶלֶף אֲלָפִים אֲדַיִין לַחֲצִי הַכִּיבּוּד שֶׁאָמְרָה הַתּוֹרָה לֹא הִגִּיעַ.

1 ונפסק קורדייקין שלה | פ -   3 נכנסו | פ חלה ונכנסו   4 בכיבוד | פ כבוד   6 הכיבוד | פ הכבוד   התורה | פ תורה

Rebbi Tarphon's mother went to promenade in her backyard on the Sabbath when her slipper broke. Rebbi Tarphon went and put his two hands under her feet and she walked on them until she got to her couch. Once the Sages came to visit him. She told them: Pray for my son Tarphon because he honors me too much. They asked her, what did he do for you? She told them what had happened. They said to her, even if he did this a million times, he did not yet reach even half of the honor that the Torah requires.

(61b line 25) אִמּוֹ שֶׁלְּרִבִּי יִשְׁמָעֵאל בָּאת וְאָמְרָה וְקֵבְלָה עָלָיו לְרַבּוֹתֵינוּ. אָמְרָה. גְּעוּרוּ בְּיִשְׁמָעֵאל בְּנִי שֶׁאֵינוֹ נוֹהֵג בִּי כָבוֹד. בְּאוֹתָהּ שָׁעָה נִתְכַּרְכְּמוּ פְּנֵיהֶן שֶׁלְּרַבּוֹתֵינוּ. אָמְרִין. אִיפְשַׁר לֵית רִבִּי יִשְׁמָעֵאל נוֹהֵג בִּכְבוֹד אֲבוֹתָיו. אָמְרוּ לָהּ. מָה עֲבִיד לֵיךְ. אָמְרָה. כַּד נָפִיק מִבֵּית וַעֲדָה אֲנָא בְּעָיָא מְשָׁזְגָא רִיגְלוֹי וּמִישְׁתֵּי מֵהֵן וְלָא שָׁבֵק לִי. אָמְרִין. הוֹאִיל וְהוּא רְצוֹנָהּ הוּא כִּיבּוּדָהּ.

1 באת ואמרה | פ באה   2 אמ' | פ אמ' להן   כבו־ | פ בכבוד   3 אמרין | פ אמרו   4 עביד | פ עבד   כד | פ כדו   5 שבק | פ שביק   אמרין | פ אמרו לו   כיבודה | פ כבודה

Rebbi Ismael's mother came, spoke, and complained to our teachers about him. She said to them: Scold my son Ismael because he does not honor me! At that, the faces of our teachers became saffron colored. They said, is it possible that Rebbi Ismael does not honor his parents? They said to her, what did he do to you? She said, when he comes from the house of assembly, I want to wash his feet and drink from it, and he refuses. They said, since it is her wish it is her honor.

(61b line 30) אָמַר רִבִּי מָנָא. וְיָאוּת אִילֵּין טְחוֹנַיָּיא אָמְרִין. כָּל־בַּר נַשׁ וּבַר נַשׁ זְכווָתֵיהּ גּוֹ קוּפָתֵיהּ. אִימֵּיהּ דְּרִבִּי טַרְפוֹן אָמְרָה לוֹן אָכֵין וַאֲגִיבוּנְתָהּ אָכֵין. אִימֵּיהּ דְּרִבִּי יִשְׁמָעֵאל אָמַר לוֹן אָכֵן וַאֲגִיבוּנָהּ אָכֵן. רִבִּי זְעִירָא הֲוָה מִצְטַעֵר וַאֲמַר. הַלְוַאי הֲוָה לִי אַבָּא וְאִימָּא דְּאוֹקְרִינוֹן וְאִירַת גַּן עֵדֶן. כַּד שְׁמַע אִילֵּין תְּרֵין אוּלְפָנַיָּיא אֲמַר. בְּרִיךְ רַחְמָנָא דְּלֵית לִי לָא אַבָּא וְלָא אִימָּא. לָא כְּרִבִּי טַרְפוֹן הֲוִינָא יָכִיל עֲבִיד וְלָא כְּרִבִּי יִשְׁמָעֵאל הֲוִינָא מְקַבְּלָהּ עֲלָי. אָמַר רִבִּי אָבוּן. פָּטוּר אֲנִי מִכִּבּוּד אָב וְאֵם. אָמְרִין. כַּד עֲבָרַת אִימֵּיהּ מַיְית אֲבוֹהִי. כַּד יַלְדְתֵיהּ מֵיתַת.

1 ויאות | פ יאות   טחונייא | פ טחוניא   2 זכוותיה | פ זכותיה   לון | פ הכון ואגיבונתיה | פ ואגינוניה   4 דאוקרינון | פ דאיקרינהון   ואירת | פ דנירת   5 תרין | פ תרתין   ולא | פ -   6 הוינא יכיל | פ הוה יכילנא   7 עברת | פ עברת ליה   מיית אבוהי | פ מית אבוי

Rebbi Mana said: The millers are correct when they say that each and every person has in his chest that which is appropriate for him. Rebbi Tarphon's mother said so and they answered her appropriately, Rebbi Ismael's mother said so and they answered her appropriately. Rebbi Zeïra was sorry and said, if only I had father or mother that I could honor them and inherit paradise. When he heard these two instructions, he said: Praise to the All-Merciful that I have neither father nor mother. I could not have done as Rebbi Tarphon did and I could not accept what Rebbi

HALAKHAH 7

Ismael accepted. Rebbi Abun said, I am free from honoring father and mother. They said, his father died when his mother was pregnant and she died in giving birth.

(61b line 38) יֵשׁ שֶׁהוּא מַאֲכִיל אֶת אָבִיו פְטוּמוֹת וְיוֹרֵשׁ גֵּהִנָּם. וְיֵשׁ שֶׁהוּא כּוֹדְנוֹ לָרֵחַיִם וְיוֹרֵשׁ גַּן עֵדֶן. כֵּיצַד הוּא מַאֲכִיל אֶת אָבִיו פְטוּמוֹת וְיוֹרֵשׁ גֵּהִנָּם. חַד בַּר נָשׁ הֲוָה מַייכֵל לְאָבוֹי תַּרְנְגוֹלִין פְּטִימָן. חַד זְמָן אֲמַר לֵיהּ אֲבוֹי. בְּרִי. אִילֵּין מְנָן לָךְ. אֲמַר לֵיהּ. סַבָּא סַבָּא. אֲכוֹל וַאֲדִישׁ. דְּכַלְבַּיָּיא אָכְלִין וּמַדְשִׁין. נִמְצָא מַאֲכִיל אֶת אָבִיו פְטוּמוֹת וְיוֹרֵשׁ גֵּהִנָּם. כֵּיצַד כּוֹדְנוֹ בָּרֵחַיִם וְיוֹרֵשׁ גַּן עֵדֶן. חַד בַּר נַשׁ הֲוָה טְחִין בְּרֵיחַיָּא. אָתַת מִצְוָותָא לַטְחוֹנִייָא. אֲמַר לֵיהּ. אַבָּא. עוּל וּטְחוֹן תַּחְתַּי. אִין מָטַת מִבְזַיָּיהּ טַב לִי אֲנָא וְלָא אַתְּ. אִין מָטַת מִילְקִי טַב לִי אֲנָא וְלָא אַתְּ. נִמְצָא כּוֹדְנוֹ לָרֵחַיִם וְיוֹרֵשׁ גַּן עֵדֶן.

2 לרחים | פ ברחים   הוא | פ -   3 מייכל | פ מייכיל   פטימן | פ פטימין   4 דכלבייא | פ דכלביא   5 ברחים | פ לרחים   6 טחין | פ איטחין   מצוותא | פ צמות   7 מבזייה | פ מבזייא   8 לרחים | פ בריחים

Some person might serve his father fattened meat and inherit hell. Some person might bind his father to the grindstone and inherit paradise. How does one serve his father fattened meat and inherit hell? A person used to serve his father fattened chickens. One day, his father said to him: My son, from where do you get the money for these? He said to him: Old man, old man, eat and shut up just as dogs eat and are silent. It turns out that he serves his father fattened meat and inherits hell. How does one bind his father to the grindstone and inherits paradise? A person was a miller at a grindstone; there came a requisition for millers. He said: Father, go and grind in my stead. If it should come to pass that anyone be degraded, it is better that it should happen to me rather than to you. If it should come to pass that anyone be beaten, it is better that it should happen to me rather than to you. It turns out that he binds his father to the grindstone and inherits paradise.

(61b line 47) אִישׁ אִמּוֹ וְאָבִיו תִּירָאוּ וְנֶאֱמַר אֶת ה' אֱלֹהֶיךָ תִּירָא. הִקִּישׁ מוֹרָא אָב וָאֵם לְמוֹרָא הַמָּקוֹם. נֶאֱמַר וּמְקַלֵּל אָבִיו וְאִמּוֹ מוֹת יוּמָת. וְנֶאֱמַר אִישׁ אִישׁ כִּי יְקַלֵּל אֱלֹהָיו וְנָשָׂא חֶטְאוֹ. הִקִּישׁ קִילְלַת אָב וָאֵם לְקִלְלַת הַמָּקוֹם. אֲבָל אֵי אֶיפְשָׁר לוֹמַר מַכֶּה כְּלַפֵּי לְמַעֲלָה. וְכֵן בְּדִין מִפְּנֵי שֶׁשְּׁלָשְׁתָּן שׁוּתָּפִין בּוֹ.

1 איש | פ נאמר איש   תירא | פ תירא ואותו תעבוד   2 המקום | פ שמים. נאמ' כבד את אביך ואת אמך ונאמ' כבד את ה' מהונך. הקיש כיבוד אב ואם לכיבוד המק':   4 למעלה | פ למעלן

It is said (*Lev.* 19:3): "Everybody must fear his mother and his father," and it is said (*Deut.* 6:13): "You must fear the Eternal, your God, and serve Him." This brackets the fear of father and mother with the fear of the Omnipresent. [It is said (*Ex.* 20:12): "Honor your father and your mother," and it is said (*Prov.* 3:9): "Honor the Eternal with your property." This brackets the honor of father and mother with the honor of the Omnipresent.] Is is said (*Ex.* 21:17): "He who curses his father or his mother shall be put to death," and it is said (*Lev.* 24:19): "Everybody who curses his God must bear his sin." This brackets cursing father and mother with cursing the Omnipresent. It is impossible to speak about hitting relative to the Deity. All this is logical since all three of them are partners in him.

(61b line 51) אֵי זֶהוּ מוֹרָא. לֹא יוֹשֵׁב בִּמְקוֹמוֹ. וְלֹא מְדַבֵּר בִּמְקוֹמוֹ. וְלֹא סוֹתֵר אֶת דְּבָרָיו. אֵי זֶהוּ הַכִּיבּוּד. מַאֲכִיל וּמַשְׁקֶה מַלְבִּישׁ וּמַנְעִיל מַכְנִיס וּמוֹצִיא. מִן דְּמַאן חוּנָא בַּר חִיָּיא אָמַר.

[608]What is fear? He may not sit in his place and may not speak in his stead nor contradict his words. What is honor? He feeds and gives him to drink, clothes him and puts on his shoes, leads him out and in. From whose money? Huna bar Ḥiyya said.

608   This is a truncated repetition of the text at Note 607.

(61b line 54) מִילְתֵיהּ דְּרִבִּי חִיָּיה בַּר בָּא פְלִיגָא. דְּאָמַר רִבִּי חִיָּיה בַּר בָּא. תַּנִּי רִבִּי יוּדָן בַּר בְּרַתֵּיהּ דְּרִבִּי שִׁמְעוֹן בֶּן יוֹחַי. דְּתַנִּי רִבִּי שִׁמְעוֹן בֶּן יוֹחַי. גָּדוֹל הוּא כִּיבּוּד אָב וָאֵם שֶׁהֶעֱדִיפוֹ הַקָּדוֹשׁ בָּרוּךְ הוּא יוֹתֵר מִכְּבוֹדוֹ. נֶאֱמַר כָּאן כַּבֵּד אֶת אָבִיךָ וְאֶת אִמֶּךָ. וְנֶאֱמַר לְהַלָּן כַּבֵּד אֶת יי מֵהוֹנֶךָ. בַּמֶּה אַתְּ מְכַבְּדוֹ מֵהוֹנֶךָ. מַפְרִישׁ לֶקֶט שִׁכְחָה וּפֵיאָה. מַפְרִישׁ תְּרוּמָה וּמַעֲשֵׂר רִאשׁוֹן וּמַעֲשֵׂר שֵׁנִי וּמַעֲשֵׂר עָנִי וְחַלָּה. וְעוֹשֶׂה סוּכָּה וְלוּלָב שׁוֹפָר וּתְפִילִּין וְצִיצִית. מַאֲכִיל אֶת הָרְעֵיבִים וּמַשְׁקֶה אֶת הַצְּמֵאִים. אִם יֵשׁ לָךְ אַתְּ חַיָּיב בְּכָל־אֵילּוּ. וְאִם אֵין לָךְ אֵין אַתְּ חַיָּיב בְּאַחַת מֵהֶן. אֲבָל כְּשֶׁהוּא בָא אֵצֶל כִּיבּוּד אָב וָאֵם בֵּין שֶׁיֵּשׁ לָךְ בֵּין שֶׁאֵין לָךְ כַּבֵּד אֶת אָבִיךָ וְאֶת אִמֶּךָ. אֲפִילוּ אַתְּ מְסַבֵּב עַל הַפְּתָחִים.

1 בא פליגא | פ ווא   דאמר ר' חייה בר בא תני | פ אמ' תנא   2 בר ברתי | פ בן דורתי יוחי | פ יוחי היא   יוחי | פ יוחי או'   3 הקב״ה | פ הק'   כאן | פ -   4 להלן | פ - במה | פ ממה   מהונך | פ משיחננך   6 ולולב | G לולב   שופר | G ושופר   ותפילין | G תפילין   את הרעיבים | פ את העניים ואת הרעיבים G הרעיבים   7 את הצמיאים | G הצמאים   את | G אתה   לך | פ לך הון (2 times)   9 אפי' | פ ואפי'

The words of Rebbi Ḥiyya bar Abba disagree, for Rebbi Ḥiyya bar Abba said that Rebbi Yudan, son of Rebbi Simeon bar Ioḥai's daughter, stated that Rebbi Simeon bar Ioḥai stated: Honoring father and mother is great because the Holy One, praise to Him, preferred it over His own honor. It is said (*Ex.* 20:12): "Honor your father and your mother," and it is said (*Prov.* 3:9): "Honor the Eternal with your property." How do you honor Him? From your property! [609]One gives gleanings, forgotten sheaves, and *peah*, one gives *terumah*, the First and Second Tithes and the tithe for the poor, *ḥallah*, one makes a *sukkah*, and *lulav*, *shofar*, and *tefillin*, and *ẓiẓit*, one feeds the hungry and gives to drink to the thirsty. If you have the wherewithal, you are obliged for all of these; if you have nothing, you are not obliged even for one of them. But when it comes to honoring father and mother, whether you own property or you do not, you must honor father and mother, even if you are a beggar at people's doors.

609 From here on there exists a Genizah fragment of the text (G). It is fragmentary in this paragraph, continuous in the following.

(61b line 63) רִבִּי אָחָא בְשֵׁם רִבִּי אַבָּא בַּר כַּהֲנָא. כְּתִיב אוֹרַח חַיִּים פֶּן תְּפַלֵּס נָעוּ מַעְגְּלוֹתֶיהָ וְלֹא תֵדָע. טִילְטֵל הַקָּדוֹשׁ בָּרוּךְ הוּא מַתַּן שְׂכָרָן שֶׁלְּעוֹשֵׂי מִצְוֹת כְּדֵי שֶׁיְּהוּ עוֹשִׂין אוֹתָם בֶּאֱמוּנָה. רִבִּי אָחָא בְשֵׁם רִבִּי יִצְחָק. כְּתִיב מִכָּל־מִשְׁמָר נְצוֹר לִבֶּךָ כִּי מִמֶּנּוּ תוֹצְאוֹת חַיִּים. מִכָּל־מַה שֶּׁאָמַרְתִּי לָךְ בַּתּוֹרָה תִּשְׁמוֹר. שֶׁאֵין אַתְּ יוֹדֵעַ מֵאֵי זֶה מֵהֶן יוֹצֵא לָךְ חַיִּים. אָמַר רִבִּי אַבָּא בַּר כַּהֲנָא. הִשְׁוָה הַכָּתוּב מִצְוָה קַלָּה שֶׁבַּקַּלּוֹת לְמִצְוָה חֲמוּרָה מִן הַחֲמוּרוֹת. מִצְוָה קַלָּה שֶׁבַּקַּלּוֹת זוֹ שִׁילּוּחַ הַקָּן. וּמִצְוָה חֲמוּרָה שֶׁבַּחֲמוּרוֹת זוֹ הִיא כִּיבּוּד אָב וְאֵם. וּבִשְׁתֵּיהֶן כְּתִיב וְהַאֲרַכְתָּ יָמִים. אָמַר רִבִּי אָבוּן. מָה אִם דָּבָר שֶׁהוּא כִּפְרִיעַת הַחוֹב כְּתִיב בּוֹ לְמַעַן יִיטַב לָךְ וּלְמַעַן יַאֲרִיכוּן יָמֶיךָ. דָּבָר שֶׁיֵּשׁ בּוֹ חִסָּרוֹן כִּיס וְסִיכּוּן נְפָשׁוֹת לֹא כָל־שֶׁכֵּן. אָמַר רִבִּי לֵוִי וְהַהִיא דְרַבָּנָא גָדוֹל הוּא דָּבָר שֶׁהוּא כִּפְרִיעַת חוֹב מִדָּבָר שֶׁאֵינוֹ כִּפְרִיעַת חוֹב. תַּנֵּי. רִבִּי שִׁמְעוֹן בֶּן יוֹחַי אוֹמֵר. כְּשֵׁם שֶׁמַּתַּן שְׂכָרָן שָׁוֶה כָּךְ פּוּרְעָנוּתָן שָׁוֶה. עַיִן תִּלְעַג לְאָב וְתָבוּס לִקְּהַת אֵם. עַיִן שֶׁהִלְעִיגָה עַל כִּיבּוּד אָב וְאִם וּבִיזָּת לֹא תִקַּח הָאֵם עַל הַבָּנִים יִקְּרוּהָ עוֹרְבֵי נַחַל. יָבוֹא עוֹרֵב שֶׁהוּא אַכְזָרִי וְיִקְּרִינָה וְלֹא יֵהֲנֶה מִמֶּנָּה. וְיֹאכְלוּהָ בְנֵי נֶשֶׁר. יָבוֹא נֶשֶׁר שֶׁהוּא רַחֲמָן וְיֹאכְלֶנָּה וְיֵהֲנֶה מִמֶּנָּה.

2 מצות G | מצוה ‎3 אותם ‎| פ אותן ‎4 שאמרתי ‎| פ שאמרו תשמור G‎ | פ השמר שאין את ‎| ג שאינך ‎5 אבא G | בא ‎6 שבקלות - G (2 times) ‎| מן החמורות ‎| פ שבחמורות - G. ‎7 ומצוה חמורה שבחמורות G | וחמורה ‎8 אבון G | אבין כפריעת | פ פריעת G בפריעת ‎10 והחיא דרבנא | פ והוא דרבה מנה G והחיא דרב מנה כפריעת | פ בפריעת ‎11 אומר - G | פ ‎12 ותבוס לקהת אם G | וגו' הלעיגה G הילעיגה על | פ - G | ‎13 כיבוד G בכיבוד ‎14 ולא | פ ואל

Rebbi Aḥa in the name of Rebbi Abba bar Cahana: It is written (*Prov.* 5:6): "She does not smooth the way of life, her tracks deviate and you will not notice it." The Holy One, praise to Him, moved the rewards of those who fulfill the commandments (to the future world) so that they should act in faith. Rebbi Aḥa in the name of Rebbi Isaac: It is written (*Prov.*

4:23): "Observe carefully everything which must be kept, for from it comes life," observe carefully all the things you were told in the Torah, for you do not know from which of them life will come to you. Rebbi Abba bar Cahana said, the verse equals the easiest commandment with the most difficult one. The easiest commandment is sending away [the mother] from the nest. The most difficult one is honoring father and mother. For both of them it is written: "Your days will be lengthened." Rebbi Abun said, if for anything that is repayment of debt it is written (*Deut.* 5:16): "That you shall be well and that your days shall be lengthened," so much more something that involves monetary loss and personal danger. Rebbi Levi said, this one is greater; repaying a debt is greater than fulfilling an obligation that does not involve repaying a debt. Rebbi Simeon ben Iohai stated: Just as their rewards are the same, so their punishments are identical. (*Prov.* 30:17) "The eye that scoffs at the father and despises to obey the mother," the eye that scoffs about honoring father and mother and despises the commandment not to take the mother with the chicks, "the river ravens should pick it out," the cruel raven should come, pick it out, and not have any enjoyment from it, "the sons of the eagle should eat it," the merciful eagle should come and enjoy it.

(61c line 3) רִבִּי יַנַּאי וְרִבִּי יוֹנָתָן הֲווֹן יְתִיבִין. אֲתָא חַד בַּר נָשׁ וּנְשַׁק רִיגְלוֹי דְּרִבִּי יוֹנָתָן. אֲמַר לֵיהּ רִבִּי יַנַּאי. מַה טִיבוּ הוּא שְׁלָם לָךְ מִן יוֹמוֹי. אֲמַר לֵיהּ. חַד זְמַן אֲתָא קָבַל לִי עַל בְּרֵיהּ דִּיזוֹנִינֵיהּ. וַאֲמָרִית לֵיהּ. אֵיזִיל צוֹר כְּנִישְׁתָּא עֲלוֹי וּבְזֵיתֵיהּ. וַאֲמַר לֵיהּ. וְלָמָּה לָא כְפַתּוּנֵיהּ. אֲמַר לֵיהּ. וְכוֹפִין. אֲמַר לֵיהּ. וַאֲדַיִין אַתְּ לְזוֹ. אֲמַר לוֹן. חָזַר בֵּיהּ רִבִּי יוֹנָתָן וְקָבְעָהּ שְׁמוּעָה מִשְּׁמֵיהּ. אֲתָא רִבִּי יַעֲקֹב בַּר אָחָא רִבִּי שְׁמוּאֵל בַּר נַחְמָן בְּשֵׁם רִבִּי יוֹנָתָן. שֶׁכּוֹפִין אֶת הַבֵּן לָזוּן אֶת הָאָב. אֲמַר רִבִּי יוֹסֵי הַלְוַאי הֲוַיִין כָּל־שְׁמוּעֲתַי בְּרִיָּין לִי כְּהָדָא שֶׁכּוֹפִין אֶת הַבֵּן לָזוּן אֶת הָאָב.

1 ר' ינאי ור' יונתן | פ ר' יונתן ור' ינאי G ר' ינייי ור' יונתן   הוון | G פ הוו   ריגלוי | G רגלי
2 דר' יונתן | G ר' יונתן   ינאי | G פ ינייי   טיבו | G טבו   הוא | - G .   מן יומוי | - G . ³
דיזונייניה | G דיזיינייניה   ואמרית | G ואמרת   איזיל | G אזל   4 ואמר | G פ אמר
כפתונייה | G פ כפיתינייה   וכופין | פ וכופין ליה   ⁵אמר לון | פ - G .   ביה | - G .   משמיה |
פ מן שמיה G מקמוי   6 את | - G .   ⁷ יוסי | פ G יוסי ביר' בון   הויין | פ הוון
שמועתי | פ שמועתא   ברייין | פ ברירין G ברירן   כהדא | G כהדה   שכופין | G כופין
את | - G (2 times)

Rebbi Yannai and Rebbi Jonathan were sitting together. There came a man and kissed Rebbi Jonathan's foot. Rebbi Yannai said to him: What kindness did he pay you back for from former days? He said to him: He once came and complained to me about his son that he should support him and I told him, go, assemble a congregation and humiliate him[609a]. He said to him, why did you not force him? He said to him, does one force him? He said to him, you still have questions about that? One said, Rebbi Jonathan changed his opinion and fixed it as a tradition in his own name. The result is: Rebbi Jacob bar Aḥa, Rebbi Samuel bar Naḥman in the name of Rebbi Jonathan, one forces the son to feed his father. Rebbi Yose bar Abun said, if only all my traditions were so clear to me as this one: One forces the son to feed his father.

[609a] S. Assaf (*Responsa Geonica* 1942, p. 105; *Courts and their organization*, Jerusalem 1924, p. 25-26) reads: "Go, arrest the congregation and humiliate him." He sees here a reference to the practice known from Galilean and Medieval Ashkenazic sources (rejected by Babylonian Geonim) that a person whose grievances are not addressed by the court may publicly request the congregation to stop their prayers until his complaint is heard (in Ashkenazic practice before the *Qaddiš* which introduces the main prayer.)

(61c line 11) אֵי זוֹ הִיא מִצְוַת עֲשֵׂה שֶׁהַזְּמָן גְּרָמָא. כְּגוֹן סוּכָּה וְשׁוֹפָר וְלוּלָב וּתְפִילִּין. וְאֵי זוֹ הִיא מִצְוַת עֲשֵׂה שֶׁלֹּא הַזְּמָן גְּרָמָא. כְּגוֹן אֲבֵידָה וְשִׁלּוּחַ הַקֵּן

HALAKHAH 7   167

וּמַעֲקֶה וְצִיצִית. רַבִּי שִׁמְעוֹן פּוֹטֵר אֶת הַנָּשִׁים מִן הַצִּיצִית שֶׁהוּא מִצְוַת עֲשֵׂה שֶׁהַזְּמַן גְּרָמָא. אָמַר לָהֶן רַבִּי שִׁמְעוֹן. אֵין אַתֶּם מוֹדִין לִי שֶׁהִיא מִצְוַת עֲשֵׂה שֶׁהַזְּמַן גְּרָמָא. שֶׁהֲרֵי כְסוּת לַיְלָה פָּטוּר מִן הַצִּיצִית. אָמַר רַבִּי הִילָא. טַעֲמוֹן דְּרַבָּנִין שֶׁכֵּן אִם הָיוּ מְיוּחָדוֹת לוֹ לְיוֹם וּלְלַיְלָה שֶׁהִיא חַיֶּבֶת בְּצִיצִית.

1 איזו היא G ‖ איזהו   גרמא GR ‖ גרמה   ושופר ולולב ‖ GR= לולב שופר   2 ואי זו היא G ‖ איזהו   שלא ת שאין   גרמא GR ‖ גרמה   3 ומעקה ת מעקה   מן הציצית ‖ ב ממצוה ציצית   שהוא GR ‖ שהיא   גרמא GR ‖ גרמה   4 א' להם ר' שמעון. אין אתם מודין לי שהיא כצות עשה שהזמן גרמא ‖ ב - R ‖ גרמה G אינבם מודים, גרמה   5 פטור ‖ G פטורין   הילא ת לייא   ב דרבנן ‖ 6 דרבנין ‖ ב דרבנן   היו ת היתה   מיוחדות ‖ RG ת מיוחדת

610"What is a positive commandment that is activated by time? For example *sukkah,* and *shofar,* and *lulab,* and *tefillin*. What is a positive commandment that is not activated by time? For example lost articles, sending away the [mother from the] nest, railing, and *ẓiẓit*611. Rebbi Simeon exempts women from *ẓiẓit* because it is a positive commandment activated by time." Rebbi Simeon said to them: Do you not agree with me that it is a positive commandment activated by time? Because a nightgown is exempt from *ẓiẓit*. Rebbi Hila said: The reason of the rebbis is that, if a garment is designated both for daytime and for night, it needs *ẓiẓit*.

610 Here begins the discussion of the second half of the Mishnah. Except for a sentence which has disappeared from the Leiden ms. and *editio princeps*, this paragraph is from *Berakhot* 3:3, Notes 143-146. The ms. text there is noted ת, the Rome ms. R. The text in quotation marks is from Tosephta 1:10.

611 The Babli, *Qiddušin* 33b, does not mention *ẓiẓit*, cf. *Berakhot*, Note 146; it is quoted *Menahot* 43a.

(61c line 17) אָמַר רַבִּי לְעָזָר. פִּסְחָן שֶׁלְּנָשִׁים רְשׁוּת וְדוֹחִין עָלָיו אֶת הַשַּׁבָּת. רַבִּי יַעֲקֹב בַּר אָחָא בְּשֵׁם רַבִּי לְעָזָר. פִּסְחָן שֶׁלְּנָשִׁים וְשֶׁלַּעֲבָדִים רְשׁוּת. כָּל־שֶׁכֵּן

דּוֹחִין עָלָיו אֶת הַשַּׁבָּת. מַצָּתָן מָהוּ. אָמַר לֵיהּ. חוֹבָה. רִבִּי זְעִירָה אָמַר. מַחֲלוֹקֶת. רִבִּי הִילָא אָמַר. דִּבְרֵי הַכֹּל. מַתְנִיתָא מְסַייְעָא לְדֵין וּמַתְנִיתָא מְסַייְעָה לְדֵין. מַתְנִיתָא מְסַייְעָה לְרִבִּי זְעִירָא. חֲזֶרֶת מַצָּה וּפֶסַח לַיְלָה הָרִאשׁוֹן חוֹבָה וּשְׁאָר כָּל־הַיָּמִים רְשׁוּת. מַתְנִיתָא מְסַייְעָא לְרִבִּי הִילָא. נֶאֱמַר לֹא תֹאכַל עָלָיו חָמֵץ. וְנֶאֱמַר שִׁבְעַת יָמִים תֹּאכַל עָלָיו מַצּוֹת לֶחֶם עוֹנִי. אֶת שֶׁהוּא בְּבַל תֹּאכַל חָמֵץ הֲרֵי הוּא בְּקוּם אֱכוֹל מַצָּה. וְנָשִׁים הֲרֵי הֵן בְּבַל תֹּאכַל חָמֵץ הֲרֵי הֵן בְּקוּם אֱכוֹל מַצָּה. וְהָא תַנִּינָן. כָּל־מִצְוַת עֲשֵׂה שֶׁהַזְּמַן גְּרָמָא הָאֲנָשִׁים חַייָבִין וְהַנָּשִׁים פְּטוּרוֹת. אָמַר רִבִּי מָנָא. הוּא מִצְוַת עֲשֵׂה שֶׁהִיא בָאָה מִכֹּחַ בְּלֹא תַעֲשֶׂה.

1 פסחן | G פסח ▪ פיסחן שלנשים | G נשים את | G - 2 לעזר | ▪ אלעזר | פסחן | G פסח ▪ פיסחן שלנשים ושלעבדים | G נשים ועבדין 3 את | G - מצתן | G מצאתן מהו | G מחוא ▪ מהיא זעירה זעירא | G ▪ זעירא 4 מחלוקת | ▪ רשות לדין ומתניתא מסייעה לדין. מתניתא | G לדן ולדן 5 מסייעה ▪G מסייעא (2 times) זעירא | G זעירה ראשון | G▪ הראשון 6 מתניתא | G - תאכל | G תאכלו 7 מצות לחם עוני | G וגו' 8 הרי | G הואיל והרי ▪ הואיל והן בבל | G בלא 9 גרמא | G גרמה האנשים חייבין והנשים | G נשים הוא | G▪ חומר היא 10 שהיא באה | G שבאה בלא | G לא

⁶¹²Rebbi Eleazar said: The Passover sacrifice of women is voluntary⁶¹³ but one pushes the Sabbath away for it⁶¹⁴. Rebbi Jacob bar Aḥa in the name of Rebbi Eleazar: The Passover sacrifice by women and slaves⁶¹⁵ is voluntary; certainly one does push the Sabbath away for it. What is their *mazzah*⁶¹⁶? He said to him⁶¹⁷, it is obligatory. Rebbi Ze'ira said, this is in dispute. Rebbi Hila said, it is everybody's [opinion]. A *baraita* supports the one and a *baraita* supports the other. A *baraita* supports Rebbi Ze'ira: Lettuce, *mazzah* and Passover sacrifice are obligatory in the first night; on all other days they are voluntary⁶¹⁸. A *baraita* supports Rebbi Hila: It was said: "Do not eat leavened matter with it⁶¹⁹," and it was said: "For seven days you shall eat with it *mazzot*, the bread of deprivation⁶¹⁹,⁶²⁰." Anybody under the prohibition of leavened matter is

under the obligation to eat *mazzah*, and women, being under the prohibition of leavened matter, are under the obligation to eat *mazzah*[621]. But did we not state: "For any positive commandment triggered by time, men are obligated but women are free'? Rebby Mana said, [622]it is a positive commandment which is implied by a prohibition[623].

612 The origin of this paragraph is *Pesahim* 8:1 (35d L 35 ff.), noted ﬨ.

613 This sentence contradicts everything a student of the Babli would expect. Most commentators either emend the passage or explain it away. But since there are three witnesses to the text, emendation is not an acceptable option. In the Babli, 91b, R. Eleazar declares a woman to be obligated for Passover like men. However, this statement is obtained by an editorial re-interpretation of R. Eleazar's statement.

In the Babli and its related texts, it is taken for granted that women present in Jerusalem on Passover eve are obligated to take part in the Passover meal, based on *Ex.* 12:4 which designates the participants as "persons", not "men" (*Mekhilta dR. Ismael, Pisha* 3, *Mekhilta dR. Šim'on b. Jochai* p. 10; cf. Mishnah *Peschim* 8:1,7, Tosephta *Pesahim* 8:10; Babli *Pesahim* 91a/b.) But it is to be noted that missing the sacrificial meal is a deadly sin only for men (*Num.* 9:13); only men are required (and permitted) to make up the missed sacrifice on the 14th of Iyar (*Num.* 9:13; Tosephta *Pisha* 8:10).

The statement means that an unaffiliated female, living neither in her father's nor a husband's house, is not obligated to seek a group with which to celebrate Passover. It would be considered most inappropriate if a single woman would join a group of men unrelated to her. But since she is included in the circle of celebrants of Passover by biblical law, if she alone or a group of similarly situated women want to organize their own Passover sacrifice and meal, they are authorized to do so.

614 If the 14th of Nisan is a Sabbath, the public Passover sacrifice has precedence over the Sabbath (Mishnah *Pesahim* 6:1). Since women are biblically empowered to celebrate Passover, the rule applies also to groups of women.

615 Circumcised slaves are included in the group of Passover celebrants in *Ex.* 12:44. The owner of uncircumcised

slaves is prohibited from celebrating Passover.

616   Are women and slaves obligated to eat *maẓẓah*, a commandment triggered by the calendar?

617   R. Eleazar (the Amora) to R. Jacob bar Aḥa.

618   *Pesaḥim* Tosephta 2:22, Babli 91b. The Passover sacrifice is forbidden after the first night. The Tanna who holds that women are obligated for the sacrifice will hold that they are obligated to eat *maẓẓah*; he who holds that their Passover celebration is voluntary (R. Simeon in the Tosephta)

must hold that their eating *maẓẓah* is voluntary.

619   *Deut.* 17:3.

620   Rules stated in the same verse must be of one and the same category.

621   In the Babli, 91b, this is a statement of R. Eleazar, probably the Tanna. In *Sifry Deut.* 130, its contrapositive is a statement of R. Simeon.

622   The other two sources add: It is more weighty since . . . That probably is the correct text.

623   And therefore follow the rules of prohibitions, obligatory for women; Note 620.

(61c line 28) וְאָתְיָיא כְּמָאן דְּאָמַר פִּסְחָן שֶׁלַּנָּשִׁים רְשׁוּת. תַּנֵּי. הָאִשָּׁה עוֹשָׂה פֶסַח הָרִאשׁוֹן לְעַצְמָהּ וְהַשֵּׁנִי טְפֵילָה לָאֲחֵרִים. דִּבְרֵי רִבִּי מֵאִיר. רִבִּי יוֹסֵי אוֹמֵר הָאִשָּׁה עוֹשָׂה פֶסַח שֵׁנִי לְעַצְמָהּ אֵין צָרִיךְ לוֹמַר הָרִאשׁוֹן. רִבִּי אֶלְעָזָר בֵּירִבִּי שִׁמְעוֹן אוֹמֵר הָאִשָּׁה עוֹשָׂה פֶסַח רִאשׁוֹן טְפֵילָה לָאֲחֵרִים וְאֵינָהּ עוֹשָׂה פֶסַח שֵׁנִי. מַה טַעֲמָא דְּרִבִּי מֵאִיר. אִישׁ שֶׂה לְבֵית אָבוֹת. וְאִם רָצוּ לַבָּיִת. מַה טַעֲמָא דְּרִבִּי יוֹסֵי. אִישׁ שֶׂה לְבֵית אָבוֹת. כָּל־שֶׁכֵּן לַבָּיִת. מַה טַעֲמָא דְּרִבִּי אֶלְעָזָר בֵּירִבִּי שִׁמְעוֹן אִישׁ וְלֹא אִשָּׁה. מַה מְּקַייְמִין רַבָּנִין אִישׁ. פְּרָט לְקָטָן. אָמַר רִבִּי יוֹנָה. אֲפִילוּ כְּמָאן דְּאָמַר חוֹבָה שְׁנִייָא הִיא שֶׁהַדָּבָר מְסוּיָּים. שֶׁלֹּא יִקְבַּע הַדָּבָר חוֹבָה.

1 ואתייא G | ואתייה ב ואתיא   כמאן G | כמן   2 והשיני G | והשני   לאחרים G | לאחרון   יוסי ב G | יוסה   3 אין | ב ואפילו בשבת ואין ח אפילו בשבת ואין   צריך | ח צריכה   אלעזר ביר' שמעון | ח שמעון בן אלעזר   האשה G | אשה   שיני לעצמה . . .   שיני G | שני⁶²⁵   5 ואם ב G | אם   רצו לבית | ח רצה שה לבית   6 יוסי G | יוסה   7 אלעזר ב G | לעזר   ביר' | G בר'   אלעזר ביר' שמעון | ח שמעון בן אלעזר   לא | ח ולא   8 אפי' | ח אפי ואפי'   כמאן G | כמן   חובה | ב פסחים שלנשים רשות   שנייא G | שנייה   מסויים G | מסוים   שלא | ח שמא   9 חובה G | לחובה

HALAKHAH 7

[624]Does it follow him who says the *Pesaḥ* of women is voluntary? It was stated: "A woman may make the First *Pesaḥ* by herself and the Second joining others, the words of Rebbi Meïr. Rebbi Yose says, a woman may make the Second *Pesaḥ* by herself, and certainly the First. Rebbi Eleazar ben Rebbi Simeon says, a woman may make the First *Pesaḥ* joining others but does not make the Second." What is the reason of Rebbi Meïr? (*Ex.* 12:3) "Every man a sheep for the family," if they want "a sheep for the house." What is the reason of Rebbi Yose, "Every man a sheep for the family," *a fortiori* "a sheep for the house." What is the reason of Rebbi Eleazar ben Rebbi Simeon? "Every man", not woman. How do the rabbis uphold "man"? A man, not a minor. Rebbi Jonah said, even according to him who says it is an obligation, it is different here since the occasion was news, lest it become an obligation.

624 This paragraph is not only in *Pesahim* (ס) but also in *Ḥallah* 4:12, Notes 194-202 (ח) and refers to Mishnah *Ḥallah* 4 12 which states that a certain Joseph Hakohen was refused permission to celebrate the Second Passover with his wife and children.

625 The entire quote referring to R. Eleazar ben R. Simeon is missing in G.

(61c line 36) חוּץ מִבַּל תַּשְׁחִית וּבַל תַּקִּיף וּמִבַּל תִּטַּמֵּא לַמֵּתִים. אִיסִּי אוֹמֵר. אַף לֹא מִשּׁוּם לֹא יִקְרְחוּ קָרְחָה. מַה טַעְמָא. לֹא יִקְרְחוּ קָרְחָה. אֶת שֶׁיֶּשְׁנוֹ בִּפְאַת זָקָן יֶשְׁנוֹ בְקָרְחָה. וְנָשִׁים שֶׁאֵין לָהֶן זָקָן פְּטוּרוֹת מִן הַקָּרְחָה. וְעוֹד מִן הָדָא בָּנִים. וְלֹא בָנוֹת. אָמַר רִבִּי לָעְזָר. נָשִׁים חַייָבוֹת בְּקָרְחָה מַה טַעְמָא. כִּי עַם קָדוֹשׁ אַתָּה לַיי אֱלֹהֶיךָ. אֶחָד אֲנָשִׁים וְאֶחָד נָשִׁים. מַה מְקַייֵם רִבִּי לָעְזָר בָּנִים. בְּשָׁעָה שֶׁיִּשְׂרָאֵל עוֹשִׂין רְצוֹנוֹ שֶׁלְּהַקָּדוֹשׁ בָּרוּךְ הוּא קְרוּאִים בָּנִים. וּבְשָׁעָה שֶׁאֵין יִשְׂרָאֵל עוֹשִׂין רְצוֹנוֹ שֶׁלְּהַקָּדוֹשׁ בָּרוּךְ הוּא אֵינָן קְרוּיִין בָּנִים. רַב מְפַקֵּד לְאִילֵּין דְּבֵי רַב אֲחֵי רַב הַמְנוּנָא מְפַקֵּד לַחֲבֵרַיָּא. פַּקְדוּן לִנְשֵׁיכוֹן כַּד הָוְויָן בַּייְמִין עַל מֵיתַיָּא דְּלָא לִיהַוְיָן מִתְלַּשִׁין בְּשַׂעֲרֵיהוֹן שֶׁלֹּא יָבוֹאוּ לִידֵי

קָרְחָה. עַד כַּמָּה הִיא קָרְחָה. אִית תַּנָּיֵי תַגֵּי. כָּל־שֶׁהוּא. וְאִית תַּנָּיֵי תַגֵּי. כִּגְרִיס. מָאן דָּמַר כָּל־שֶׁהוּא. מְמַשְׁמַע קָרְחָה כָּל־שֶׁהוּא. מָאן דְּאָמַר כִּגְרִיס. נֶאֱמַר כָּאן קָרְחָה וְנֶאֱמַר לְהַלָּן קָרְחָה. מַה קָרְחָה הָאֲמוּרָה לְהַלָּן כִּגְרִיס אַף כָּאן כִּגְרִיס. רִבִּי יוֹסֵי בַּר מָמָל. כֹּהֶנֶת מוּתֶּרֶת לָצֵאת חוּצָה לָאָרֶץ. מַאי טַעֲמָא. אֱמוֹר אֶל הַכֹּהֲנִים. לֹא אֶל הַכֹּהֲנוֹת. דְּלֹא כֵן מָה אֲנָן אֲמָרִין. הוֹאִיל וְהִיא בִכְלָל גְּזִירָה לֹא תֵצֵא. אִם אוֹמֵר אַתְּ כֵּן נִמְצֵאתָ דּוֹחֶה פָּרָשַׁת טְמֵאוֹת.

1 תשחית G | תקיף תשחית G | תקיף תיטמא למתים G | תטמא למתין איסי G | אסי 2 לא G | בל שישנו בפאת G | שיש פאת 3 ישנו בקרחה G | דקרחה זקן | G - מן הקרחה G | קרחה מן הדא G | מהדה 4 חייבות G | חיבות 5 לי' אלהיך G | - מקיים G | מקים 6 רצונו של | G - קרויים G | - 7 שלהק״בה | G - קרואין G | קרוין לאילין G | לאילן 8 אתי G | אחי לחברייא G | לחברייה לנשיכון G | נשיכון 8-9 כד הוויין קיימין על מיתיא דלא ליהויין מתלשן בשעריהון | G דלא יתלשון שעריהון על מיתייא 9 עד G | ועד 10 דמר G | דא' 11 שהוא | G שהו 12 האמורה G | שנא' אף G | אוף 13 ממל G | ממל חייה ר' אחא בש' ר' לעזר כהנת G | כוהנות מותרת G | מותרות מאי G | מה 14 הכהנות G | הכוהנות גזירה | G - 15 נמצאת G | נמצאתה דוחה G | מדחה

"Except 'do not destroy', 'do not shear,[556]' and 'do not become impure for the dead'." Issy says, also because of "do not make a bald spot.[626]" What is the reason? "They shall not make a bald spot[627]." One subject to the rules of the beard is subject to the rules of the bald spot; women who have no beard are free from the rules of the bald spot[628]. And also from the following: "sons[626]," not daughters. Rebbi Eleazar said, women are obligated by the rules of the bald spot. What is the reason? "For you are a holy people for the Eternal, your God.[629]" Both men and women. How does Rebbi Eleazar explain "sons"? When they do the will of the Holy One, praise to Him, they are called sons, but when they do not do the will of the Holy One, praise to Him, they are not called sons[630]. Rav was ordering his students, there came Rav Hamnuna ordering the colleagues: Order you wives not to tear out their hair when standing by a deceased, that they should not make a bald spot. What is a bald spot? There are Tannaïm who stated: Any size. There are Tannaim who state: The size of a peeled grain. The one who says, any size, because the meaning of "bald spot" is of any size. The one who says, a peeled grain, for it is said here "to make a bald spot", and it says there, a bald spot[631]. Since "bald spot" mentioned there means in the size of a peeled grain, here also it means the size of a peeled grain. Rebbi Yose bar Mamal[632]: A Cohenet is permitted to leave the Land[633]. What is the reason? "Say to the Cohanim[634]," not to the Cohanot. If it were otherwise, what would we say? Since she is included in the decision[635], she may not leave[636]. If you say so, you push aside the paragraph of impurities.

626 *Deut.* 14:1: "You are children of the Eternal, your God; do not injure yourselves, do not make a bald spot between your eyes for a deceased." The same argument in the Babli, 35b.

627 *Lev.* 21:5, speaking of Cohanim: "They may not make a bald spot on their head; the sideburn of their beard they shall not shave."

628 What is missing here is an argument why rules promulgated for Cohanim are valid for all Israelites; cf. *Sifry Deut.* 96; *Sifra Emor Pereq* 1(3).

629 *Deut.* 14:2. The expression "people" applies to both men and women, even hermaphrodites and the sexless.

630 Babli 36a. In this interpretation, when Jesus insists on his being the Father's son, he implies that the rest of the people do not obey God's will.

631 *Lev.* 13:42,43. As with all skin diseases, the disease at a bald spot is diagnosed as such once it has reached the size of a peeled grain; Mishnah *Nega'im* 4:5,6.

632 In the Genizah text, the rule is traced to R. Eleazar, in line with the other rules of this section.

633 Since the "Land of the Gentiles" is impure, a Cohen is not permitted to leave the Land of Israel except in extraordinary circumstances. But the special laws for Cohanim promulgated in *Lev.* 21 do not apply to their wives and daughters, who cannot serve in the Sanctuary.

634 *Lev.* 21:1.

635 It is difficult to know what this means; the word is missing in the

Genizah text. Probably one should read גְּדִידָה "inflicting injury on oneself", or in Rashi's words *esgratiner* (*égratigner*), "to slit", forbidden in *Deut.* 14:1 to all of Israel.

636 Since the general prohibition of *Deut.* 14:1, applicable also to women, is also the particulat prohibition of *Lev.* 21:5, one might think that all special rules of *Lev.* 21 apply to everybody. Then the special position of Cohanim in rules of impurity would be abolished.

(61c line 52) וְכֹהֵן מֵנִיחַ יָדוֹ תַחְתֶּיהָ וּמְנִיפָהּ. אֵין הַדָּבָר כָּאוּר. מֵבִיא מַפָּה. וְאֵינוּ חוֹצֵץ. מֵבִיא כֹהֵן זָקֵן. וַאֲפִילוּ תֵימַר. כֹּהֵן יֶלֶד. שֶׁאֵין יֵצֶר הָרַע מָצוּי לְשָׁעָה. תַּנֵּי רִבִּי חִייָה. מָצוּי. סוֹטָה גִידֶּמֶת שְׁנֵי כֹהֲנִים מְנִיפִין עַל יָדֶיהָ.

1 אין | ס ואין   2 מביא | ס ומביא   ילד | G בחור

[637]"The Cohen puts his hands under hers and performs the weave." Does the Cohen put his hands under hers? Is that not objectionable? He brings a kerchief. Does that not separate? He brings an elderly Cohen. You may even say, a young man, since bad inclinations do not happen at that hour. Rebbi Ḥiyya stated: It happens. If the suspected wife has no hands, two priests weave in her stead.

637 This refers to Mishnah 8, speaking of the flour offering of the suspected wife. The text is from *Soṭah* 3:1 (ט), Notes 8-14.

(fol. 58b) **משנה ט:** כָּל־מִצְוָה שֶׁאֵינָהּ תְּלוּיָה בָאָרֶץ נוֹהֶגֶת בֵּין בָּאָרֶץ בֵּין בְּחוּצָה לָאָרֶץ. וְכָל־שֶׁהִיא תְלוּיָה בָאָרֶץ אֵינָהּ נוֹהֶגֶת אֶלָּא בָאָרֶץ חוּץ מִן הָעָרְלָה וְהַכִּלְאַיִם. רִבִּי אֱלִיעֶזֶר אוֹמֵר אַף הֶחָדָשׁ.

Mishnah 9: Any commandment which does not refer to the Land is obligatory both in the Land and outside the Land. But any commandment which does refer to the Land is obligatory only in the Land, except *'orlah*[638] and *kilaim*[639]. Rebbi Eliezer says, also new grain[640].

[638] Even though the commandment is formulated with a reference to the Land (*Lev.* 19:23), it has to be applied in a modified form outside the Land; cf. Mishnah *'Orlah* 3:9.

[639] The prohibitions of cross-breeding of animals and wearing a mixture of wool and linen (a prerogative of the priests serving in the Sanctuary) do not refer to the Land. The prohibition of *kilaim* in agriculture outside the Land is rabbinic in character.

[640] The prohibition of grain of the new harvest before the *'Omer* sacrifice, while referring to the Land, is written in the holiday catalogue of *Lev.* 23 which is presumed not to be bound to the Land. In Mishnah *'Orlah* 3:8, the obligation of *'orlah* outside the Land is tradition, not Holy Writ.

(61c line 55) **הלכה ט:** כָּל־מִצְוָה שֶׁאֵינָהּ תְּלוּיָה בָאָרֶץ כּוֹל'. כְּתִיב אֵלֶּה הַחוּקִים וְהַמִּשְׁפָּטִים אֲשֶׁר תִּשְׁמְרוּן לַעֲשׂוֹת בָּאָרֶץ. בָּאָרֶץ אַתֶּם חַיָּיבִין לַעֲשׂוֹת. אֵין אַתֶּם חַיָּיבִין בְּחוּצָה לָאָרֶץ. אֲדַיִּין אָנוּ אוֹמְרִים. מִצְוֹת הַתְּלוּיוֹת בָּאָרֶץ אֵינָן נוֹהֲגוֹת אֶלָּא בָאָרֶץ. יָכוֹל אֲפִילוּ מִצְוֹת שֶׁאֵינָן תְּלוּיוֹת בָּאָרֶץ לֹא יְהוּ נוֹהֲגוֹת אֶלָּא בָאָרֶץ. תַּלְמוּד לוֹמַר הִשָּׁמְרוּ לָכֶם פֶּן יִפְתֶּה לְבַבְכֶם וְחָרָה אַף יי וגו'. וְשַׂמְתֶּם אֶת דְּבָרַי אֵלֶּה. אֲפִילוּ גוֹלִים. וְשַׂמְתֶּם אֶת דְּבָרַי אֵלֶּה עַל לְבַבְכֶם וְעַל נַפְשְׁכֶם. מָה אִית לָךְ. כְּגוֹן תְּפִילִּין וְתַלְמוּד תּוֹרָה. מַה תְּפִילִּין וְתַלְמוּד תּוֹרָה שֶׁאֵינָן תְּלוּהִין בָּאָרֶץ נוֹהֲגִין בָּאָרֶץ וּבְחוּצָה לָאָרֶץ. אַף כָּל־דָּבָר שֶׁאֵינוֹ תָלוּי בָּאָרֶץ יְהֵא נוֹהֵג בֵּין בָּאָרֶץ בֵּין בְּחוּצָה לָאָרֶץ.

3 אין אתם | ש ואי אתם G ואינכם | בחוצה G חוץ | אנו אומ' G אני או' | 4 אפי' מצות שאינן תלויות G אפלו שאינן תלייות | 6 דבריי G דברי | אלא | ש אלא על לבבכם וגו' | G - | 7 תפילי G תפלין | 9 בין בארץ בין בחוצה | Gש בארץ ובחוצה

Halakhah 9: "Any commandment which does not refer to the Land," etc.[641] It is written (*Deut.* 12:1): "These are the statutes and the rules of law which you will be required to follow in the Land." In the Land you are required to follow them but not outside the Land. Still we say obligations depending on the Land only apply in the Land, but we might think that obligations not depending on the Land also should only apply in the Land. The verse says (*Deut.* 11:16-18) "Be careful, lest your heart be seduced . . . and the Eternal's rage be inflamed against you, etc. Put these words on your hearts,". Even if you are exiled. (*Deut.* 11:18) "Put these words on your hearts and your persons." You have to say, for example *tefillin* and the study of Torah. Just as *tefillin* and the study of Torah do not depend on the Land and apply both in the Land and outside the Land, so everything not depending on the Land applies both in the Land and outside the Land.

641 This entire Halakhah except the last paragraph is from *Ševi'it* 6:1 (Notes 4-20); readings given by שׁ. The Genizah text is again indicated by G.

(61c line 64) מֵעַתָּה מִשֶּׁנִּגְאֲלוּ יְהוּ פְטוּרִין. כְּתִיב וַיַּעֲשׂוּ כָל־הַקָּהָל הַשָּׁבִים בִּימֵי יֵשׁוּעַ. וְלָמָּה יֵשׁוּעַ. הִילֵּל בְּרֵיהּ דְּרִבִּי שְׁמוּאֵל בַּר נַחְמָן אָמַר. פָּגַם הַכָּתוּב כְּבוֹד צַדִּיק בַּקֶּבֶר מִפְּנֵי כְּבוֹד צַדִּיק בְּשַׁעְתּוֹ. הִקִּישׁ בִּיאָתָן בִּימֵי עֶזְרָא לְבִיאָתָן בִּימֵי יְהוֹשֻׁעַ. מַה בִּיאָתָן בִּימֵי יְהוֹשֻׁעַ פְּטוּרִין הָיוּ וְנִתְחַיְּיבוּ. אַף בִּיאָתָן בִּימֵי עֶזְרָא פְּטוּרִין הָיוּ וְנִתְחַיְּיבוּ. מִמַּה נִתְחַיְּיבוּ. רִבִּי יוֹסֵי בֵּירִבִּי חֲנִינָה אָמַר. מִדְּבַר תּוֹרָה נִתְחַיְּיבוּ. הָדָא הִיא דִכְתִיב וֶהֱבִיאֲךָ יי אֱלֹהֶיךָ אֶל הָאָרֶץ אֲשֶׁר יָרְשׁוּ אֲבוֹתֶיךָ וִירִשְׁתָּהּ. הִקִּישׁ יְרוּשָׁתְךָ לִירוּשַׁת אֲבוֹתֶיךָ. מַה יְרוּשַׁת אֲבוֹתֶיךָ מִדְּבַר תּוֹרָה. אַף יְרוּשָׁתְךָ מִדְּבַר תּוֹרָה. וְהֵטִיבְךָ וְהִרְבְּךָ מֵאֲבוֹתֶיךָ. פְּטוּרִין הָיוּ וְנִתְחַיְּיבוּ. וְאַתֶּם פְּטוּרִין הֱיִיתֶם וְנִתְחַיַּיבְתֶּם. אֲבוֹתֶיךָ לֹא הָיָה עֲלֵיהֶם עוֹל מַלְכוּת. וְאַתֶּם אַף עַל פִּי שֶׁיֵּשׁ עֲלֵיכֶם עוֹל מַלְכוּת. אֲבוֹתֵיכֶם לֹא נִתְחַיְּיבוּ אֶלָּא לְאַחַר אַרְבַּע עֶשְׂרֵה שָׁנָה. שֶׁבַע שֶׁכִּיבְּשׁוּ וְשֶׁבַע שֶׁחִילְּקוּ. אֲבָל אַתֶּם רִאשׁוֹן רִאשׁוֹן קוֹנֶה וּמִתְחַיֵּיב.

1 משנגאלו | שׁ משגלו   השבים בימי ישוע | G שׁ הבאים מן השבי סוכות שׁ ויעשו סוכות כי לא עשו מימי ישוע בן נון   2 הילל | שׁ ר' הילל   דר' שמואל | שׁ דשמואל   5 ממה | G מה   ביר' | G בן   6 נתחייבו | G -   הדא היא דכת' | G -   היא | שׁ הוא   8

HALAKHAH 9

פטורין | שׁ אבותיך פטורין   עול 9-10 | G - (2 times)   אבל אתם | Gשׁ כיון 11
שנכנסתם נתחייבתם. אבותיכם לא נתחיבו עד שעה שקנו :ולה. אבל אתם

If it is so, they should have been freed once they were redeemed. It is written (*Neh.* 8:17): "All the congregation coming from captivity ... since the days of Joshua bin Nun." Why Joshua? Rebbi Hillel, the son of Samuel ben Naḥmani: The verse damaged the reputation of the just person in his grave for the reputation of the just person in his time; it compares their coming in the days of Ezra to the coming in the days of Joshua. As at the coming in the days of Joshua they had been free and became obligated, also at the coming in the days of Ezra they had been free and became obligated. How did they become obligated? Rebbi Yose ben Ḥanina said, they became obligated by the words of the Torah; that is what is written (*Deut.* 30:5): "The Eternal, your God, will bring you to the Land that your fathers inherited and you will inherit it." Just as the inheritance of your fathers was by the words of the Torah, so your inheritance is by the words of the Torah. "He will be good to you and give increase to you more than to your forefathers." Your fathers had been free and became obligated, also you had been free and became obligated. On your fathers there was no yoke of government, but you [are obligated] even though there is on you the yoke of government. Your fathers did become obligated only after fourteen years, seven they conquered and seven they distributed, but you became obligated [immediately when you entered. Your fathers did become obligated only after they had acquired all, but you become obligated][642] for every single piece at the moment you acquire it.

642 The Genizah text shows that this argument from *Ševi'it* belongs to the text here also. The text here is an abbreviation of the original from *Ševi'it*.

(61d line 1) אָמַר רִבִּי אֶלְעָזָר. מֵאֲלֵיהֶן קִיבְּלוּ עֲלֵיהֶן אֶת הַמַּעְשְׂרוֹת. מַה טַעַם וּבְכָל־זֹאת אֲנַחְנוּ כּוֹרְתִים אֲמָנָה וְחוֹתְמִים. מַה מְקַיֵּים רִבִּי לְעָזָר וְאֶת בְּכוֹרוֹת בְּקָרֵינוּ וְצֹאנֵינוּ. מִכֵּיוָן שֶׁקִּיבְּלוּ עֲלֵיהֶן דְּבָרִים שֶׁלֹּא הָיוּ חַיָּיבִין עֲלֵיהֶם אֲפִילוּ דְּבָרִים שֶׁהֵן חַיָּיבִין עֲלֵיהֶם הֶעֱלָה הַמָּקוֹם כְּאִילוּ מֵאֲלֵיהֶן קִיבְּלוּ עֲלֵיהֶם.

אלעזר | ש G לעזר   קיבלו | G קיבלה   המעשרות   G מעשרות   2 וחותמים | ש
וכותבים ועל החתום שרינו לוייני וכהנינו (G lacuna)   3 וצאננו | G וגו'   מכיון | G
וכיון   עליהן | ש עליהם   עליהם | ש G עליהן   4 שהן חייבין | ש שהיו חייבין | G
שחייבין   חייבין | ש G חייבין עליהן   עליהם | ש G עליהן   כאילו | G כילו   קיבלו
עליהם | ש קיבלו עליהן G קיבלום

Rebbi Eleazar said, they accepted the tithes voluntarily. What is the reason? (*Neh.* 10:1) "In view of all this, we execute a contract and sign." How does Rebbi Eleazar uphold (10:37): "The first-born of our cattle and flock"? Since they accepted upon themselves matters they were not obligated for, even matters they were obligated for the Omnipresent credited to them as if they were accepted voluntarily.

(61d line 6) מַה מְקַיֵּים רִבִּי יוֹסֵי בֵּירִבִּי חֲנִינָה וּבְכָל־זֹאת אֲנַחְנוּ כּוֹרְתִים אֲמָנָה וְחוֹתְמִים. מִכֵּיוָן שֶׁקִּיבְּלוּ עֲלֵיהֶן בְּסֵבֶר פָּנִים יָפוֹת הֶעֱלָה עֲלֵיהֶן הַמָּקוֹם כְּאִילוּ מֵאֲלֵיהֶן קִיבְּלוּ עֲלֵיהֶן אֶת הַמַּעְשְׂרוֹת. מַה מְקַיֵּים רִבִּי לְעָזָר מֵאֲבוֹתֶיךָ. פָּתַר לָהּ לֶעָתִיד לָבוֹא. דְּאָמַר רִבִּי חֶלְבּוֹ שִׁמְעוֹן בַּר בָּא בְּשֵׁם רִבִּי יוֹחָנָן. אֲבוֹתֶיךָ יָרְשׁוּ אֶרֶץ שִׁבְעָה עַמְמִים. וְאַתֶּם עֲתִידִין לִירַשׁ אֶרֶץ שֶׁלְּעֶשֶׂר עַמְמִים. תְּלָתֵי אַחֲרָנְיָיתָא אִילֵּין אִינּוּן אֶת הַקֵּינִי וְאֶת הַקְּנִזִּי וְאֶת הַקַּדְמוֹנִי. רִבִּי יוּדָה אָמַר. שַׁלְמָאָה שְׁכִינָה נַבָּטַיָּה. רִבִּי שִׁמְעוֹן אוֹמֵר אַסְיָא וְאִסְטַטְיָה וְדַרְמֶשֶׂק. רִבִּי לִיעֶזֶר בֶּן יַעֲקֹב אוֹמֵר אַסְיָיא וְקַרְתִּיגְנִי וְתוֹרְקִי. רִבִּי אוֹמֵר אֱדוֹם וּמוֹאָב וְרֵאשִׁית בְּנֵי עַמּוֹן. מֵאֲבוֹתֶיךָ. אֲבוֹתֶיךָ אַף עַל פִּי שֶׁנִּגְאֲלוּ חָזְרוּ וְנִשְׁתַּעְבְּדוּ. אֲבָל אַתֶּם מִשֶּׁאַתֶּם נִגְאָלִין עוֹד אֵין אַתֶּם מִשְׁתַּעְבְּדִין. מַה טַעֲמָא. שַׁאֲלוּ נָא וּרְאוּ אִם יוֹלֵד זָכָר. כְּשֵׁם שֶׁאֵין הַזָּכָר יוֹלֵד כָּךְ אַתֶּם מִשֶּׁאַתֶּם נִגְאָלִין אֵין אַתֶּם מִשְׁתַּעְבְּדִין.

1 יוסי G | יוסה ביר' | ש בר G בן   רנינה | ש חנינא   אנחנו כורתים אמנה וחותמים | ש
G -   2 שקיבלו עליהן | G שקיבלום   המקום | ש הכת'   3 עליהן את המעשרות | ש
עליהן G המעשרות   4 לבוא | G לבא   5 שבעה | ש שלשבעה זֹ G שלעשר   G שלי
תלתי G | זֹ   6 אחרנייתא | שֹ G חורנייתא   את הקני ואת הקניזי ואת הקדמוני | G
הקני והקנזי והקדמוני   7 שלמאה שכייה נבטייה | ש ערכייא שלמייא נבטייא G ..
שלמייה נבטייה   ואסטטיה ודרמשק | ש ואספמיא ודמשק G ואספנניה ודרמסק   8
קרתיגיני ותורקי | G וקרטריגינה ותריקי   11 אין | ש עוד אין

How does Rebbi Yose bar Ḥanina explain "In view of all this, we execute a contract and sign"? Since they accepted [the obligations] with good grace, the verse credits it to them as if they had accepted it voluntarily. How does Rebbi Eleazar explain "more than your forefathers?" He explains it for the future since Rebbi Ḥelbo, Simeon bar Abba said in the name of Rebbi Joḥanan: Your forefathers inherited the land of seven peoples, but you will in the future inherit the land of ten peoples. The three others are (*Gen.* 15:19) "the Qenites, the Qenizites and the Qadmonites." Rebbi Jehudah said, [these are] Arabia, Salmaia and Nabataea. Rebbi Simeon says, Asia, Spain, and Damascus. Rebbi Eliezer ben Jacob says, Asia, Cartagena, and Thrace. Rebbi says, Edom, Moab, and the best of Ammon. "More than your forefathers": Your forefathers, even though they were redeemed, were later subjugated again. But you when you are redeemed will not be subjugated again. What is the reason? (*Jer.* 30:6) "Inquire and see whether a male gives birth." Just as a male cannot give birth so you, after you are redeemed, will not be subjugated again.

(61d line 17) חוּץ מִן הָעָרְלָה וּמִן הַכִּלְאַיִם. רִבִּי אֱלִיעֶזֶר אוֹמֵר אַף הֶחָדָשׁ. מָה טַעֲמָא דְּרִבִּי אֱלִיעֶזֶר. בְּכָל־מוֹשְׁבוֹתֵיכֶם. בֵּין בָּאָרֶץ בֵּין בְּחוּצָה לָאָרֶץ. מָה מְקַייְמִין רַבָּנָן בְּכָל־מוֹשְׁבוֹתֵיכֶם. בֶּחָדָשׁ שֶׁבּוֹ שֶׁיָּצָא לְחוּצָה לָאָרֶץ. רִבִּי יוֹנָה בָּעָא. וְלָמָה לֹא תַנִּינָן. אַף הַחַלָּה. אָמַר לֵיהּ רִבִּי יוֹסֵי. לֹא תַנִּינָן אֶלָּא דְבָרִים

שֶׁנּוֹהֲגִין בְּיִשְׂרָאֵל וְנוֹהֲגִין בַּגּוֹיִם. וְחַלָּה נוֹהֶגֶת בְּיִשְׂרָאֵל וְאֵינָהּ נוֹהֶגֶת בַּגּוֹיִם. מַה טַעַם. רֵאשִׁית עֲרִיסוֹתֵיכֶם. וְלֹא שֶׁלְּגוֹיִם.

1 אליעזר | ל G ליעזר   2 אליעזר | ל G ליעזר   3 רבנן | ל G רבנין   בכל | ל טע' דר' ליעזר בכל   שבו | ל G שכן   לחוצה לארץ | ל בחוץ G חוץ לארץ   4 בעא | ל בעי קומי ר' יוסי G בעי   החלה | ל החלה עמהן G החלף   ר' יוסי | ל -   לא תנינן | ל G לא אתינן מתני   דברים שנוהגין | ל דבר שהוא נוהג   5 ונהגין בגויים | ל G ובגויים   נוהגת בישראל ואינה נוהגת בגוים | ל אינה נוהגת אלא בישראל G בישראל נוהגת בגוים אינה נוהגת   6 מה טע' | ל דכת'

⁶⁴³"Rebbi Eliezer says, also new grain." What is the reason of Rebbi Eliezer? (*Lev.* 23:14) "In all your dwelling places," both inside and outside the Land. How do the rabbis explain the reason of Rebbi Eliezer, "in all your dwelling places"? New grain from here which was exported. Rebbi Jonah asked: Why did we not state *hallah* with these? Rebbi Yose said to him, our Mishnah only deals with something which applies to Israel and the Gentiles. But *hallah* only applies to Israel, not to Gentiles. What is the reason? (*Num.* 15:20): The first of *your* dough," not of Gentiles.

643   This text is from '*Orlah* 3:8 (62b, line 37) (**ל**); Notes 158-160.

(fol. 58b) **מִשְׁנָה י:** כָּל־הָעוֹשֶׂה מִצְוָה אַחַת מְטִיבִין לוֹ וּמַאֲרִיכִין אֶת יָמָיו וְנוֹחֵל אֶת הָאָרֶץ. וְכָל־שֶׁאֵינוֹ עוֹשֶׂה מִצְוָה אַחַת אֵין מְטִיבִין לוֹ וְאֵין מַאֲרִיכִין אֶת יָמָיו וְאֵינוֹ נוֹחֵל אֶת הָאָרֶץ. וְכָל־שֶׁאֵינוֹ לֹא בַּמִּקְרָא וְלֹא בַּמִּשְׁנָה וְלֹא בְדֶרֶךְ אֶרֶץ אֵין זֶה מִן הַיִּשּׁוּב וְהַמַּחֲזִיק בִּשְׁלָשְׁתָּן עָלָיו הַכָּתוּב אוֹמֵר וְהַחוּט הַמְשֻׁלָּשׁ לֹא בִמְהֵרָה יִנָּתֵק.

Mishnah 10: Everybody who keeps one commandment they⁶⁴⁴ treat well and prolong his life; he will inherit the Land⁶⁴⁵. But everybody who does not keep one commandment they do not treat well, do not prolong his life, and he does not inherit the Land. [646]Anybody who knows neither Scripture nor Mishnah nor a trade[647] is not part of civilization, but about one who holds on to these three, the verse says[648]: "The triple cord will not easily break."

644 The Heavenly court.

645 This probably is the Future World, in Psalms called "the Lands of Life."

646 Of this part of the Mishnah there exist versions widely differing in text but identical in meaning.

647 Which lets him earn an honest living.

648 Eccl. 4:12. The person studying Scripture and tradition, and earning an honest living, will not easily sin. This formulation is that of the Tosephta, 1:17.

(61d line 23) **הלכה י:** כָּל־הָעוֹשֶׂה מִצְוָה אַחַת מְטִיבִין לוֹ כוּל. הָא כָּל־הַיּוֹשֵׁב וְלֹא עָבַר עֲבִירָה נוֹתְנִין לוֹ שָׂכָר כְּעוֹשֵׂה מִצְוָה. וְאַתְּ אָמַרְתְּ אָכֵן. אֶלָּא כֵן אֲנָן קַיָּימִין בִּמְחוּצָה. עָשָׂה מִצְוָה אַחַת מְטִיבִין לוֹ וּמַאֲרִיכִין אֶת יָמָיו וְנוֹחֵל אֶת הָאָרֶץ. וְהָעוֹבֵר עֲבֵירָה אַחַת אֵין מְטִיבִין לוֹ וְאֵין מַאֲרִיכִין אֶת יָמָיו וְאֵינוֹ נוֹחֵל אֶת הָאָרֶץ. תַּמָּן תַּנִּינָן. הָא כָּל־הַיּוֹשֵׁב וְלֹא עָבַר עֲבִירָה נוֹתְנִין לוֹ שָׂכָר כְּעוֹשֵׂה מִצְוָה. אָמַר רִבִּי זְעִירָה. מִי שֶׁבָּאת לְיָדוֹ סְפֵק עֲבֵירָה וְלֹא עֲשָׂאָהּ. אָמַר רִבִּי יוֹסֵי בֵּירִבִּי בּוּן. מִי שֶׁיִּיחֵד לוֹ מִצְוָה וְלֹא עָבַר עָלֶיהָ מִיָּמָיו. מָה אִית לָךְ. אָמַר רִבִּי מַר עוּקְבָּן. כְּגוֹן כִּיבּוּד אָב וָאֵם. אָמַר רִבִּי מָנָא. אַשְׁרֵי תְמִימֵי דָרֶךְ הַהֹלְכִים בְּתוֹרַת יי. כְּהוֹלְכִים בְּתוֹרַת יי. אָמַר רִבִּי אָבוּן. אַף לֹא פָעֲלוּ עַוְלָה בִּדְרָכָיו הָלָכוּ. כִּבְדְרָכָיו הָלָכוּ. אָמַר רִבִּי יוֹסֵי בֵּירִבִּי בּוּן. מַה כְּתִיב. אַשְׁרֵי הָאִישׁ אֲשֶׁר לֹא הָלַךְ בַּעֲצַת רְשָׁעִים. מִכֵּיוָן שֶׁלֹּא הָלַךְ בַּעֲצַת רְשָׁעִים כְּמִי שֶׁהָלַךְ בַּעֲצַת צַדִּיקִים.

1 הא G | תנינן הא   2 אלא כן אנן | א"א כינן   3 לו G | לו כל   את | G - (2   4 והעובר G | וכל העובר   את | G - (times   5 את | G -   ולא עבר עבירה | G   ואינו חוטא   6 זעירה G | זעורה   7 מימיו - G | ר' - G | 9 ההולכים בתורת יי G | וגו'   כהלכים G | כהולכין   אבון G | אבין   10 בדרכיו הלכו G | וגו'   כבדרכיו G

כבדרכו יוסי G ‏| יוסה אשרי G ‏| אשר הלך בעצת צדיקים לית כת׳ אלא אשרי

Halakhah 10: "Everybody who keeps one commandment they treat well," etc. [649]"Therefore anybody who is passive and refrains from sinning they reward like one who fulfills a commandment," and you say so[650]? But we hold with one who is 50-50[651]. If he keeps one commandment, they treat him well and prolong his life; he will inherit the Land. But if he commits one sin, they do not treat him well, do not prolong his life, and he does not inherit the Land. There[649], we have stated: "Therefore anybody who is passive and refrains from sinning they reward like one who fulfills a commandement." Rebbi Ze'ira said, one who had occasion to commit a possible sin and did not act[652]. Rebbi Yose ben Rebbi Abun said, one who chose one commandment which he never violated in his lifetime. What kind? Mar Uqban said, for example the honor of father and mother[653]. Rebbi Mana said, "Happy are those on a straight path, who walk in the Eternal's Torah[654]," as if they did walk in the Eternal's Torah. Rebbi Abun said, "Also they did no evil, in His path they went," as if they went in His path[655]. Rebbi Yose ben Rebbi Abun said, what is written? "[656]Happy the man who did not walk in the council of the wicked;" since he did not walk in the council of the wicked it is as if he walked in the council of the just.

649 Mishnah *Makkot* 3:17.

650 Mishnah *Makkot* contradicts the Mishnah here since there one is rewarded for not sinning while here one is only rewarded for doing good.

651 In the Heavenly accounting, he collected as many merits as demerits. If he now collects one merit, he is one of the Just and takes his place in Paradise; if he sins once he is of the sinners and has lost his share in the Future Life. If he does not do anything, his fate remains suspended; cf. Babli 39b.

652 He refrained from acting out of religious scruple when there was a possibility that the intended act was permitted because possibly it was

forbidden. His inaction is a very meritorious act.

653 Which is extremely difficult to keep at all times; cf. Halakhah 7.

654 *Ps.* 119:1. If they walk in the Eternal's Torah, they certainly are on the right path. The verse can only mean that somebody choosing the right path, even if he is far from being perfect, is considered walking totally in the Eternal's Torah. This gives a biblical source for the Mishnah.

655 *Ps.* 119:3. In order to be counted with those who walk in the Eternal's way it is enough to refrain from evil; this explains the Mishnah in *Makkot*.

656 *Ps.* 1:1. The argument is better in the Genizah text: "It does not say, 'Happy the man who walks in the council of the just,' but..."

(61d line 35) דָּרַשׁ בֶּן עַזַּאי. זְבוּבֵי מָוֶת יַבְאִישׁ יַבִּיעַ שֶׁמֶן רוֹקֵחַ. אִילוּ זְבוּב אֶחָד שֶׁמֵּת שֶׁמָּא אֵינוֹ מַבְאִישׁ שֶׁמֶן רוֹקֵחַ. וְזֶה עַל יְדֵי חֵטְא שֶׁחָטָא אִיבֵּד כָּל־זְכֻיּוֹת שֶׁבְּיָדוֹ. דָּרַשׁ רַבִּי עֲקִיבָה. לָכֵן הִרְחִיבָה שְׁאוֹל נַפְשָׁהּ וּפָעֲרָה פִיהָ לִבְלִי חֹק. לִבְלִי חוּקִּים אֵין כָּאן כָּתוּב אֶלָּא לִבְלִי חוֹק. לְמִי שֶׁאֵין בְּיָדוֹ מִצְוָה אַחַת שֶׁיְּסַיֵּיעַ לוֹ לְכַף זְכוּת. הָדָא דְאַתְּ אָמַר לָעוֹלָם הַבָּא. אֲבָל בָּעוֹלָם הַזֶּה אֲפִילוּ תְּשַׁע מֵאוֹת וְתִשְׁעִים וְתִשְׁעָה מַלְאָכִים מְלַמְּדִין עָלָיו חוֹבָה וּמַלְאָךְ אֶחָד מְלַמֵּד עָלָיו זְכוּת הַקָּדוֹשׁ בָּרוּךְ הוּא מַכְרִיעוֹ לְכַף זְכוּת. וּמַה טַעַם. אִם יֵשׁ עָלָיו מַלְאָךְ מֵלִיץ אֶחָד מִנִּי אָלֶף לְהַגִּיד לְאָדָם יָשְׁרוֹ. וַיְחֻנֶּנּוּ וַיֹּאמֶר פְּדָעֵהוּ מֵרֶדֶת שַׁחַת מָצָאתִי כוֹפֶר. אָמַר רַבִּי יוֹחָנָן. אִם שָׁמַעְתָּ דָּבָר מֵרַבִּי לִיעֶזֶר בְּנוֹ שֶׁלְּרַבִּי יוֹסֵי הַגְּלִילִי נְקַב אָזְנְךָ כְּאַפַּרְכֶּסֶת הַזּוֹ וּשְׁמַע. דְּאָמַר רַבִּי יוֹחָנָן. רַבִּי לִיעֶזֶר בְּנוֹ שֶׁלְּרַבִּי יוֹסֵי הַגְּלִילִי אוֹמֵר. אֲפִילוּ תְּשַׁע מֵאוֹת וְתִשְׁעִים וְתִשְׁעָה מַלְאָכִים מְלַמְּדִין עָלָיו חוֹבָה וּמַלְאָךְ אֶחָד מְלַמֵּד עָלָיו זְכוּת הַקָּדוֹשׁ בָּרוּךְ הוּא מַכְרִיעוֹ לְכַף זְכוּת. וְלֹא סוֹף דָּבָר כָּל־אוֹתוֹ הַמַּלְאָךְ אֶלָּא אֲפִילוּ תְּשַׁע מֵאוֹת וְתִשְׁעִים וְתִשְׁעָה צְדָדִין מֵאוֹתוֹ כַּמַּלְאָךְ מְלַמְּדִין עָלָיו חוֹבָה וְצַד אֶחָד מֵאוֹתוֹ הַמַּלְאָךְ מְלַמֵּד עָלָיו זְכוּת הַקָּדוֹשׁ בָּרוּךְ הוּא מַכְרִיעוֹ לְכַף זְכוּת. מַה טַעַם. אִם יֵשׁ עָלָיו מַלְאָךְ אֶחָד מֵאָלֶף אֵין כָּתוּב כָּאן אֶלָּא אֶחָד מִנִּי אָלֶף. מֵאֳלָפִי לִצְדָדִין שֶׁלְּאוֹתוֹ מַלְאָךְ. מַה כְּתִיב בַּתְרֵיהּ. וַיְחֻנֶּנּוּ וַיֹּאמֶר פְּדָעֵהוּ מֵרֶדֶת שַׁחַת מָצָאתִי כוֹפֶר. פְּדָעֵהוּ בְּיִיסּוּרִין. מָצָאתִי כוֹפֶר. מָצָא כוֹפֶר לְעַצְמוֹ. הָדָא דְאַתְּ אָמַר בָּעוֹלָם

הַזֶּה. אֲבָל לְעוֹלָם הַבָּא [657]רוּבּוֹ זְכִיּוֹת יוֹרֵשׁ גַּן עֵדֶן. רוּבּוֹ עֲבֵירוֹת יוֹרֵשׁ גֵּיהִנָּם. הָיָה מֶחֱצָיָין. רִבִּי יוֹסֵי בֶּן חֲנִינָה אָמַר. נוֹשֵׂא עָוֹן. רִבִּי אַבָּהוּ אָמַר. נוֹשֵׂא כְּתִיב. מָה הַקָּדוֹשׁ בָּרוּךְ הוּא עוֹשֶׂה. חוֹטֵף אֶחָד מֵחוֹבוֹתָיו וּזְכִיּוֹתָיו מַכְרִיעוֹת. אָמַר רִבִּי לְעָזָר. וּלְךָ יי חָסֶד כִּי אַתָּה תְשַׁלֵּם לְאִישׁ כְּמַעֲשֵׂהוּ. וְאִין לֵית אַתְּ יָהִיב לֵיהּ מִן דִּידָךְ. הִיא דַעְתֵּיהּ דְּרִבִּי אֶלְעָזָר. דְּרִבִּי אֶלְעָזָר אָמַר. וּלְךָ יי חָסֶד מְלַמֵּד שֶׁהוּא מַטֶּה כְּלַפֵּי חֶסֶד.

1 עזאי G | עזיי רוקח G | - .G 2 שמת G | שימות על ידי G | למען חט אחד שחטא איבד G | שאובד 3 שבידו G | - .G נפשה ופערה פיה לבלי חוק G | - .G 4 חוקים G | חקים חוק G | חק 5 שיסייע G | שיכריע הדא G | הדא 6 תשע מאות ותשעים ותשע G | תתקצ״ט ומלאך אחד G | ואחד 8 מלאך מליץ אחד מני אלף להגיד לאדם יושרו G | וגו' פדעהו מרדת שחת מצאתי כופר G | וגו' 10 כאפרכס הזו G | כזו האפרכס דאמ' G | ואמ' 11 תשע מאות ותשעים ותשע G | תתקצ״ט מלאכים G | מלאכין 12 מלמד עליו G | - .G 13 אפילו G | אפלו תשע מאות ותשעים ותשע G | תתקצ״ט 14 מאותו המלאך G | ממלאך ההוא 17 פדעהו מרדת שחת מצאתי כופר G | - .G 18 הדא G | הדה 19 רובו G | רבו היה G | הוה פ - (erased by corrector) 20 מחציין | מעויין (also text of Peah before erasure by the corrector) ר' יוסי | פן אמ' ר' יוסי חנינה | פ חנינא אמר. נושא עון. ר' אבהו אמ'. נושא כת' | פן נושא עוונות אין כת' כאן אלא נושא עון 21 מה הקב״ה עושה | פן הקב״ה אחד מחובותיו פן שטר ... וזכיותיו | פס והזכיות 22 כי אתה תשלם לאיש כמעשהו ואין לית ליה את יהיב ליה מן דידך. היא דעת' דר' אלעזר. דר' אלעזר אמ' | G - .ו כי אתה תשלם לאיש כמעשהו. מעשהו אין כת' כאן אלא כמעשהו. 24 מלמד שהוא | פן -

Ben Azai preached: "A dead fly will permanently spoil perfumer's oil.[658]" Does not one dead fly spoil perfumer's oil? And this person[659] by one sin spoiled all merits he had. Rebbi Aqiba preached: "[660]So the abyss opened wide and its mouth swallowed the one without law." It does not say "without laws", but "without law", him who has not a single merit that should help him on the scale of merit[661]. That is, for the Future World. But in this world, even if 999 angels plead for his conviction and one angel pleads for his acquittal, the Holy One, praise to Him, lends His weight to the scale of merit. What is the reason? "If there is for him one angel out of a thousand, to tell a man his straightness. He will act with him in grace and say, let him be redeemed, not go down to destruction; I found weregilt[652]." Rebbi Johanan said, if you find a saying of Rebbi Eliezer, son of Rebbi Yose the Galilean, bend your ear like this funnel and listen, since Rebbi Johanan reported that Rebbi Eliezer, the son of Rebbi Yose the Galilean, said: Even if 999 angles plead for his conviction and one angel pleads for his acquittal, the Holy One, praise to Him, lends His weight to the scale of merit. Not only this entire angel, but if 999 aspects of that angel plead for conviction and one aspect for acquittal, the Holy One, praise to Him, lends His weight to the scale of merit. What is the reason? It does not say, 'if there is for him one angel of a thousand," but "one *out* of a thousand", one aspect out of a thousand aspects of that angel. What is written afterwards? "He will act with him in grace and say, let him be hurt, not go down to destruction; I found weregilt." "Let him be hurt," by suffering[663]. "I found weregilt," he found means to redeem himself. That is, in this world. But in the Future World, if he has a majority of merits, he inherits paradise; a majority of sins, he inherits hell. If he was 50-50. Rebbi Yose ben Hanina said, "he carries his iniquity.[664]" Rebbi Abbahu said, it is written: "He carries." What does the Holy One, praise to Him, do? He grabs one of his demerits, and the merits decide[665]. [666]Rebbi Eleazar said: 'You, Eternal, are acting in grace, for You will complete for everybody according to his deeds.[667]" And if he has none, You will give him from Yours. That is Rebbi Eleazar's opinion, for Rebbi Eleazar said, "You, Eternal, are acting in grace," this teaches that He turns to the aspect of grace[668].

657 From here to the end of the Halakhah, there are parallel texts in *Peah* 1:1 (Notes 209-213, 16b l. 43 ff., פ) and *Sanhedrin* 10:1 (27c l. 41 ff., ץ)

The introduction is missing in both texts; this indicates that the original place of the text is here in *Qiddušin*.

658   *Eccl.* 10:1; the translation follows Ibn Ezra.

659   Who has exactly as many merits as he has demerits. The Babylonian sources, Babli 40b, Tosephta 1:14, base a formally similar agument on *Eccl.* 9:18; but the Babli does not make the difference between the Worlds that are the main thrust of this paragraph.

660   *Is.* 5:14.

661   The image is always that the deeds of a person are weighed on scales in Heavenly court; the person is found innocent if the scale containing his merits tilts the balance in his favor. A different interpretation is in the Babli, *Sanhedrin* 111a.

662   *Job* 33:23-24.

663   R. Eliah Wilna points out that the Talmud reads פְּדָעֵהוּ as Aramaism, equivalent to Hebrew פְּצָעוֹ (cf. Onqelos and Pseudo-Jonathan to *Ex.* 21:25).

664   *Ex.* 34:7, *Micah* 7:18. R. Yose ben R. Ḥanina holds that the person with an equal number of merits and demerits is found guilty. But in *Peah* 1:1, *Sanhedrin* 10:1, and the Babli, *Roš Haššanah* 17a, R. Yose ben R. Ḥanina is credited with the opinion attributed here to R. Abbahu, who is not mentioned in the other sources. Everybody seems to agree that in the Heavenly Court, no more than one transgression will be forgiven.

665   R. Abbahu holds that the person with an equal number of merits and demerits is found not guilty.

666   Babli *Roš Haššanah* 17b.

667   *Ps.* 62:13.

668   He also holds that the person with an equal number of merits and demerits is found not guilty.

(61d line 60)   רַב יִרְמְיָה אָמַר רִבִּי שְׁמוּאֵל בַּר רַב יִצְחָק בְּעָא. צְדָקָה תְּצֹּר תָּם דָּרֶךְ וְרִשְׁעָה תְּסַלֵּף חַטָּאת. חַטָּאִים תְּרַדֵּף רָעָה וְאֶת צַדִּיקִים יְשַׁלֶּם טוֹב. רַגְלֵי חֲסִידָיו יִשְׁמוֹר וּרְשָׁעִים בַּחוֹשֶׁךְ יִדָּמּוּ וגו'. אִם לַלֵּצִים הוּא יָלִיץ וְלַעֲנָוִים יִתֶּן חֵן. כְּבוֹד חֲכָמִים יִנְחָלוּ וּכְסִילִים מֵרִים קָלוֹן. וְסִייְגִּין סִייְגָא וְתִרְעִין תְּרִיעָה. וּבֵינֵי סִייְגָא וְתִרְעִין תְּרִיעָה. אֶלָּא בָּעֵי רִבִּי יִרְמְיָה בְּשֵׁם רִבִּי שְׁמוּאֵל בַּר רַב יִצְחָק. שׁוֹמֵר עַצְמוֹ מִן הָעֲבִירָה פַּעַם רִאשׁוֹנָה וּשְׁנִייָה וּשְׁלִישִׁית מִיכָּן וָהֵילַךְ הַקָּדוֹשׁ בָּרוּךְ הוּא מְשַׁמְּרוֹ. מַה טַּעַם. הֶן כָּל־אֵלֶּה יִפְעַל אֵל פַּעֲמַיִם שָׁלֹשׁ עִם גָּבֶר.

1 רב | מ ר' בעא | פ בעי | ן בעה 2-3 רגלי חסידיו ישמור ורשעים בחושך ידמו וגו'. 4 אם ללצים הוא יליץ ולענוים יתן חן. בוד חכמים ינחלו וכסילים מרים קלון | G - 4 סייגין | פס סיגין 4 סייגא | G סייגה וביני | G וכני | אלא כימי 5 סייגא | G סייגין | סייגה וביני סייגין סייגא ותרעין תריעה. אלא בעי | פ - 6 שומר | G שומר אדן ראשונה ושנייה ושלישית | G א' וב' והילך | G ואילך 7 אל | G איל

Rebbi[669] Jeremiah said that Rebbi Samuel bar Rav Isaac asked about: "Justice watches over the one ambling in simplicity but evil falsifies sin[670]." "Evil pursues the sinners but He well rewards the just."[671] "He watches over the feet of His pious, but the wicked will be silenced in darkness, etc.[672]" "If He scoffs with the scoffers, but to the meek He gives kindness.[673]" "Sages inherit honor, but shame lifts the silly.[674]" Fencing makes a fence, and doors entry[675]. And so it is, fencing makes a fence and a door entry. But Rebbi Jeremiah asked in the name of Rebbi Samuel bar Rav Isaac: If somebody guards himself once, twice, and three times from a sin, from then on the Holy One, praise to Him, will guard him[676]. What is the reason? "Lo, all this God will work, twice or three times with a man."

668 For chronological reasons, this title from פ is the only correct one.

669 *Prov.* 13:6. This and the following verses seem to imply that a person is just not by his own merit but only by God's grace, whereas the wicked are destined to be wicked. This kind of predestination certainly contradicts the doctrine of personal responsibility which rabbinic interpretation finds in *Deut.* 11:26-28, 30:15-20.

670 *Prov.* 13:21.

671 *1S.* 2:9. This and the following verses are not in the Genizah fragment. In *Peah*, the order of the verses is slightly different.

672 *Prov.* 3:34.

673 *Prov.* 3:35.

674 A popular adage to the effect that a good fence warns away potential trespassers but an open door invites thieves. If the just are fenced in from the start but the wicked left open to sin, there is no personal merit in good behavior.

675   If a person from personal initiative guards himself a few times from sinning in a particular way, then it becomes an automatic habit and in the future will not require additional will power. In the Babli, *Yoma* 86b, the Tanna R. Yose ben R. Jehudah is quoted as inferring that the same kind of sin is forgiven by the Heavenly Court a maximum of three times. *Šabbat* 104a, *Yoma* 38b, R. Simeon ben Laqish quotes *Prov.* 3:34 to the effect that Heaven will make it easy for the just to be just, for the wicked to be wicked.

(61d line 68) אָמַר רִבִּי זְעִירָא וּבִלְחוּד דְּלָא יְתוּב לֵיהּ. וְהַחוּט הַמְשׁוּלָשׁ לֹא לְעוֹלָם יִנָּתֵק. אֵין כְּתִיב כָּאן אֶלָּא לֹא בִּמְהֵרָה יִנָּתֵק. אִין מִטְרַחַת עֲלוֹי מִיפְסָק הוּא. רִבִּי חוּנָא בְּשֵׁם רִבִּי אַבָּהוּ. הַקָּדוֹשׁ בָּרוּךְ הוּא אֵין לְפָנָיו שִׁכְחָה. הָא מִפְּנֵי יִשְׂרָאֵל נַעֲשָׂה שׁוֹכְחָן. מַה טַּעַם מִי אֵל כָּמוֹךָ נֹשֵׂא עָוֹן וְעֹבֵר עַל פֶּשַׁע. נוֹשֵׁא כְּתִיב. וְכֵן דָּוִד הוּא אוֹמֵר נָשָׂאתָ עֲוֹן עַמֶּךָ כִּסִּיתָ כָל חַטָּאתָם סֶלָה.

1 זעירא G זעורא⁶⁷⁷ יתוב | **פן** יתיב והחוט | **פ** מה טעם | והחוט | והחוט טע׳. והחוט
2 מטרחת | **ן** אטרחת 3 מיפסק הוא | **ן** הוא מיפסק חונא | **ן** הונא הקב״ה | **פ** הק׳
4 הא | **ן** כביכול הא מפני | **פן** בשביל שוכחן | **ן** שכחן מי אל כמוך נושא עון ועובר על פשע. נושא | **פן** נושא עוון 5 הוא | **פ** -

Rebbi Zeïra said, but only if the person does not revert⁶⁷⁸. What is the reason? It does not say "The triple thread will never snap" but rather "The triple thread will not quickly snap." If you work on it, it will split. Rebbi Ḥuna said in the name of Rebbi Abbahu: There is no forgetting before the Holy One, praise to Him, but for Israel He becomes forgetful. What is the reason? It is written⁶⁶⁴ "He *forgets*⁶⁷⁹ sin." And so David says⁶⁸⁰: "You *forgot* Your people's sin, You covered up all their misdeeds, Selah."

677   Here ends the Genizah fragment.

678   Here begins the discussion of the quote at the end of the Mishnah

679   Replacing נשא "to lift, carry" by נשה "to forget".

680   *Ps.* 85:3.

האיש מקדש פרק שני

(fol. 62a) **משנה א**: הָאִישׁ מְקַדֵּשׁ בּוֹ וּבִשְׁלוּחוֹ וְהָאִשָּׁה מִתְקַדֶּשֶׁת בָּהּ וּבִשְׁלוּחָהּ. הָאִישׁ מְקַדֵּשׁ אֶת בִּתּוֹ כְּשֶׁהִיא נַעֲרָה בּוֹ וּבִשְׁלוּחוֹ. הָאוֹמֵר לָאִשָּׁה הִתְקַדְּשִׁי לִי בִּתְמָרָה זוֹ הִתְקַדְּשִׁי לִי בָּזוֹ אִם יֵשׁ בְּאַחַת מֵהֶן שָׁוֶה פְרוּטָה מְקוּדֶּשֶׁת וְאִם לָאו אֵינָהּ מְקוּדֶּשֶׁת. בָּזוֹ וּבָזוֹ אִם יֵשׁ בְּכוּלָּן שָׁוֶה פְרוּטָה מְקוּדֶּשֶׁת. הָיְתָה אוֹכֶלֶת רִאשׁוֹנָה רִאשׁוֹנָה אֵינָהּ מְקוּדֶּשֶׁת עַד שֶׁיְּהֵא בְּאַחַת מֵהֶן שָׁוֶה פְרוּטָה.

Mishnah 1: A man may contract a premininary marriage either in person or through an agent[1], and a woman may be taken in preliminary marriage either in person or through an agent. A man may give away his adolescent daughter[2] in preliminary marriage himself or through his agent. If a man say to a woman: Be married to me preliminarily by this date fruit, be preliminarily married by that one, she is preliminarily married if one of them was worth a *perutah*, otherwise she is not preliminarily married[3]. By this and by that one, she is preliminarily married if together they are worth a *perutah*[4], but if she was eating immediately[5] what she received, she is not preliminarily married unless one of them was worth a *perutah*.

1 Since the groom is not permitted to live with the bride before the definitive marriage, the preliminary marriage is a legal, not a personal, act and may be executed either by the principal or by his duly appointed representative. For the same reason, a woman may appoint a representative to agree on her behalf to the stipulations proposed by the groom.

2 Who still can be married off by her father without necessarily being

asked, while she is able to act in law in other respects; cf. Chapter 1, Note 228, *Yebamot* 1:2, Note 159.

3 Two separate gifts of less than a *peruṭah* each do not add up to one gift of a *peruṭah*.

4 If the entire gift was given, or at least promised, as a whole, it does not matter of how many individual pieces it is composed.

5 If the dates were not promised as a bunch but given as "this and this and this" and the first date was already eaten by the time the second was received, they cannot be counted together since a nonexisting object cannot be counted together with an existing one. But if ten dates were promised at the outset in so many words and the prospective bride ate each one as soon as she received it, she is preliminarily married as soon as together they had represented a *peruṭah*'s worth.

(62a line 46) **הלכה א:** הָאִישׁ מְקַדֵּשׁ בּוֹ וּבִשְׁלוּחוֹ כול׳. מְנַיִין שֶׁשְּׁלוּחוֹ שֶׁלְּאָדָם כְּמוֹתוֹ. אָמַר רִבִּי לְעָזָר. וְשָׁחֲטוּ אוֹתוֹ כֹּל קְהַל עֲדַת יִשְׂרָאֵל בֵּין הָעַרְבָּיִם. וְכִי כּוּלָּן שׁוֹחֲטִין אוֹתוֹ. וַהֲלֹא אֶחָד הוּא שֶׁהוּא שׁוֹחֵט עַל יְדֵי כוּלָּם. אֶלָּא מִיכָּן שֶׁשְּׁלוּחוֹ שֶׁלְּאָדָם כְּמוֹתוֹ. וְיַידָא אָמַר דָּא. וְיִקְחוּ לָהֶם אִישׁ שֶׂה לְבֵית אָבוֹת שֶׂה לַבָּיִת. וְכִי כוּלָּם הָיוּ לוֹקְחִין. וַהֲלֹא אֶחָד הוּא שֶׁהוּא לוֹקֵחַ עַל יְדֵי כוּלָּם. אֶלָּא מִיכָּן שֶׁשְּׁלוּחוֹ שֶׁל אָדָם כְּמוֹתוֹ. אָמַר רִבִּי יוֹסֵי. שַׁנְייָא הִיא שֶׁאָדָם שׁוֹחֵט פִּסְחוֹ שֶׁלַּחֲבֵירוֹ שֶׁלֹּא מִדַּעְתּוֹ. אֵין תֵּימַר. אָדָם מַפְרִישׁ פִּסְחוֹ שֶׁלַּחֲבֵירוֹ שֶׁלֹּא מִדַּעְתּוֹ לֵית יְכִיל. דְּאָמַר רִבִּי זְעִירָא בְּשֵׁם רִבִּי לְעָזָר. אָדָם שׁוֹחֵט פִּסְחוֹ שֶׁלַּחֲבֵירוֹ שֶׁלֹּא מִדַּעְתּוֹ אֲבָל אֵינוֹ מַפְרִישׁוֹ שֶׁלֹּא מִדַּעְתּוֹ.

Halakhah 1: "A man may contract a premininary marriage either in person or through an agent," etc. From where that a person's agent may act in his stead[6]? Rebbi Eleazar said: "The entirety of the assembly of the congregation of Israel shall slaughter it in the evening.[7]" But do all of them slaughter[8]? Does not one slaughter for the many? From here [it follows that] a person's agent may act in his stead[9]. And that would be the same as: "Everybody should take for himself a sheep for the family, a sheep to a house[10]." Did everyone take? Did not one take for the many[11]? From here [it follows that] a person's agent may act in his stead. Rebbi Yose said, there is a difference, for a person may slaughter the Passover sacrifice of another without the latter's knowledge[12]. If you wanted to say that a person may separate the Passover sacrifice for another without the latter's knowledge, you cannot say so, for Rebbi Ze'ira said in the name of Rebbi Eleazar that a person may slaughter the Passover sacrifice of another without the latter's knowledge, but nobody may separate the Passover sacrifice for another without the latter's knowledge[13].

6 Since preliminary marriage is an act prescribed by biblical standards, one has to ascertain that agency is admissible in the fulfilment of biblical decrees. {Agency always is direct representation as in Egyptian and Roman law (cf. R. Taubenschlag, *The Law of Greco-Roman Egypt in the Light of the Papyri*, New York 1944, §37). Indirect representation is authorized only if it unquestionably is to the benefit of the person represented; cf. *Giṭṭin* 1:6, Note174.}

7 *Ex.* 12:6.

8 Since the Passover sacrifice is not an individual but a family affair, it is obvious that only one person can slaughter for his entire family.

9 *Mekhilta Bo, Masekhet Depisḥa* Chap. 5 (ed. Horovitz-Rabin, p. 17) as tannaïtic statement; in the Babli attributed to R. Joshua ben Qorḥa. The parallel discussion in the Babli, 41a-42a, is a long-winded, possibly Saboraic, affair.

10 *Ex.* 12:3. The same argument applies as for the other verse. Then the question arises, at least for the school of R. Aqiba, why the same rule has to be expressed by two separate verses. This contradicts R. Aqiba's axiom that the Torah text admits of no redundancies.

11 In *Mekhilta Bo, Masekhet Depisḥa* Chap. 3 (ed. Horovitz-Rabin, p. 11) this also is a tannaïtic statement, not the subject of a discussion

12 The people participating in the Passover meal do not have to know who prepared it. Therefore, the

slaughterer does not have to be the agent of every participant; the verse *Ex.* 12:6 does not prove the thesis for which it was quoted.

13 *Pesaḥim* 8:1 (35d l. 13), Babli *Nedarim* 36a. A person who was not inscribed beforehand in the list of participants cannot join the Passover celebration; Mishnah *Zebaḥim* 5:8. Only *Ex.* 12:3 is a proof; there is no redundancy.

(62a line 55) בֵּית שַׁמַּי אוֹמְרִים. אֵין הַשָּׁלִיחַ עוֹלֶה מִשֶׁם עֵד. וּבֵית הִלֵּל אוֹמְרִים. הַשָּׁלִיחַ עוֹלֶה מִשֶׁם עֵד. הֵיךְ עֲבִידָא. שִׁילַח שְׁנַיִם. עַל דַּעְתּוֹן דְּבֵית שַׁמַּי שָׁלִיחַ וּשְׁנֵי עֵדִים. עַל דַּעְתּוֹן דְּבֵית הִלֵּל שְׁלָשְׁתָּן שְׁלוּחִין וּשְׁלָשְׁתָּן עֵדִים. אָמַר רִבִּי אָבוּן בַּר חִיָּיה. נִרְאִין דְּבָרִים בְּשֶׁקִּידְּשָׁהּ בִּשְׁטָר. אֲבָל אִם קִידְּשָׁהּ בְּכֶסֶף נַעֲשָׂה כְנוֹגֵעַ בְּעֵדוּתוֹ. אָמַר רִבִּי יוֹסֵי. מִכֵּיוָן שֶׁהֶאֱמִינָתוֹ הַתּוֹרָה אֲפִילוּ קִידְּשָׁהּ בְּכֶסֶף אֵינוֹ כְנוֹגֵעַ בְּעֵדוּתוֹ. אָמַר רִבִּי בָּא. אָתָא עוֹבְדָא קוֹמֵי רַב וְעָשָׂה שָׁלִיחַ עֵד. חַד בַּר נָשׁ אַפְקִיד גַּרְבּוֹי גַּבֵּי קַרְפֵּיפָא דְחַבְרֵיהּ וְכָפַר בֵּיהּ. אָמַר רִבִּי פִּינְחָס. אָתָא עוֹבְדָא קוֹמֵי רִבִּי יִרְמְיָה וְעָשָׂה שָׁלִיחַ עֵד וְחִיְּיבוֹ שְׁבוּעָה עַל יְדֵי הַכַּתָּף.

The House of Shammai say, an agent may not testify as witness. But the House of Hillel say, an agent may testify as witness[14]. How is that? If he sent two[15], in the opinion of the House of Shammai there is an agent and two witnesses[16]. In the opinion of the House of Hillel, all three can be agents and all three can be witnesses[17]. Rebbi Abun bar Ḥiyya said, the matter is reasonable if the preliminary marriage was executed by document. But if he executed the preliminary marriage by money, he became an interested party in his testimony[18]. Rebbi Yose said, since the Torah made him trustworthy[19], even if he executed the preliminary marriage by money, he did not become an interested party in his testimony. Rebbi Abba said, there came a case before Rav who admitted the agent as witness[20]. A person deposited his amphoras in another's corral; [the latter] reneged[21]. The case came before Rebbi Jeremiah who admitted the agent as witness and made him swear [by the testimony of] the porter[22].

14 In the Babli, 43a, the tannaïtic tradition is declared to be unclear. The problem is that if an agent acts instead of the principal, he should be disqualified from acting as a witness if the principal is unable to testify. Since relatives are disqualified as witnesses and everybody is a relative of himself, an agent should be disqualified in any suit involving the principal's money.

15 In the quote of this *baraita* in the Babli, 43a, "three". *Qorban Ha'edah* reads the statement as "two [in addition to the agent]".

16 Only one of the three may be appointed as agent to reserve the option of proving a case in court by witnesses.

17 At the same time agents and witnesses.

18 If he did not deliver the money to the prospective bride, he would have to pay back the consignor; his testimony is self-serving and therefore barred.

19 All commentators have great difficulty with this statement, from *Tosaphot* (43b *s. v.* וכן) and Rashba (*Novellae*, 43a *s. v.* ירושלמי) to the commentators of Maimonides (*ad Iššut* 3:16) and the standard commentators of the Yerushalmi (שיירי קרבן and מראה פנים *ad loc.*). In fact, R. Yose's remark is incompatible with the Babli's treatment of the subject in 43a/b. R. Yose seems to argue that the monetary aspect is irrelevant. The main consequence of preliminary marriage is to forbid the woman to any man other than her fiancé; this is not a matter of civil law. It is a principle in both Talmudim that in matters of prohibitions a single witness has standing by biblical law (cf. *Soṭah* 6:2, Note 26). Since the agent has standing in biblical law to force her to go to court if she wants to marry any other man, he also has standing to join another witness in the related financial case.

20 Since the normal case is preliminary marriage by money, it must be assumed that the case before Rav was of this kind. Since Rav was the foremost authority in Babylonia, his decision was obligatory precedent in Babylonia.

21 He said that all amphoras in his corral were his own property. This is a purely financial case, where R. Yose's argument is irrelevant.

22 The person hired to deliver the amphoras to the corral was admitted as witness in court, even though his testimony was partly self-serving since he would have been liable as a thief had he failed to deliver the amphoras.

Since R. Jeremiah had a low opinion of everything Babylonian, it follows that the rule admitting an agent as witness is accepted both in Babylonia and in Galilee.

(62a line 64) אִית מַתְנִיתָא אָמְרָה שֶׁשְּׁלוּחוֹ שֶׁל אָדָם כְּמוֹתוֹ. וְאִית מַתְנִיתָא אָמְרָה שֶׁאֵין שְׁלוּחוֹ שֶׁל אָדָם כְּמוֹתוֹ. וְאִם הָמֵר יְמִירֶנּוּ. יָפֵר יְפִירֶנּוּ. הֲוֵינָן סָבְרִין מֵימַר שֶׁאֵין שְׁלוּחוֹ שֶׁל אָדָם כְּמוֹתוֹ אֶלָּא שֶׁמִּיעֵט הַכָּתוּב. וְסָמַךְ יָדוֹ וְלֹא יַד בְּנוֹ וְלֹא יַד עַבְדּוֹ וְלֹא יַד שְׁלוּחוֹ. הֲוֵינָן סָבְרִין מֵימַר שֶׁשְּׁלוּחוֹ שֶׁלְאָדָם כְּמוֹתוֹ אֶלָּא שֶׁמִּיעֵט הַכָּתוּב. וְרָצַע אֲדוֹנָיו אֶת אָזְנוֹ בַּמַּרְצֵעַ. אֲדוֹנָיו וְלֹא בְנוֹ. אֲדוֹנָיו וְלֹא שְׁלוּחוֹ. הֲוֵינָן סָבְרִין מֵימַר שֶׁשְּׁלוּחוֹ שֶׁל אָדָם כְּמוֹתוֹ אֶלָּא שֶׁמִּיעֵט הַכָּתוּב. אִית תַּנָּיֵי תַנֵּי. וְרָצַע. לְרַבּוֹת אֶת הַשָּׁלִיחַ. עַד כְּדוֹן כְּרַבִּי עֲקִיבָה. כְּרַבִּי יִשְׁמָעֵאל. אֲדוֹנָיו. כָּל־שֶׁהוּא בָא מַחֲמַת אֲדוֹנָיו.

Some *baraita* implies that the agent of a person acts in his stead, and some *baraita* implies that the agent of a person does not act in his stead[23]. "If he definitively will substitute[24], if he himself will dissolve[25]." We may hold that a person's agent cannot act in his stead because Scripture excluded him. "He shall lean his hand,[26]" not the hand of his son nor the hand of his slave nor the hand of his agent[27]. We may hold that a person's agent can act in his stead but [in this case] Scripture excluded him. "His master shall pierce his ear with an awl[28];" "his master" but not the latter's son, "his master" but not the latter's agent[29]. We may hold that a person's agent can act in his stead but Scripture excluded him. Some Tannaïm state: "He shall pierce", to include the agent. This follows Rebbi

Aqiba. Following Rebbi Ismael? "His master", anybody acting on his master's authority[30].

23 Everybody agrees that there exist situations in which an agent acts with the full authority of a principal and others where only the person himself can act. The question is, what is the normal case and what is the exception?

24 This seems to be a quote from *Lev.* 27:10, but there the masoretic text is הָמֵר יָמִיר. If the word יְמִירֶנּוּ is not a slip of the scribe's pen, the reference might be to יַחֲלִיפֶנּוּ ("he himself may exchange it") in the same verse. There is no explicit *baraita* in rabbinic literature which would invalidate substitution by agent; the double expression is always interpreted as an addition in R. Aqiba's system. In *Sifra Behuqqotay Pereq* 9(6), the double expression is interpreted to include a woman for her own sacrifice and an heir for an inherited one. Since the agent is not mentioned, he is excluded. In the Babli, *Temurah* 2a, the statement of *Sifra* is characterized as R. Meïr's.

25 *Num.* 30:14. This does not refer to an infinitive construction but to the use of the word יְפֵרֶנּוּ instead of the simple יָפֵר. In R. Aqiba's system, suffixes always carry a special meaning. The argument is explicit in the Babli, *Nazir* 12b, where the Tanna R. Joshia quotes *Num.* 30:14 to prove that a husband cannot delegate his power over his wife's vows to an attorney. R. Jonathan holds that an agent always can act for his principal.

26 *Lev.* 1:4;3:2,8,13;4:24,29,33, a necessary action to validate a sacrifice. The repetition of *his hand* in all these verses is taken in the Babli, *Menahot* 93b, as proof that any agency is impossible for animal sacrifices.

27 This formulation is in *Sifra Wayyiqra Pereq* 4(2).

28 *Ex.* 21:6, speaking of the Hebrew slave; cf. Chapter 1:2.

29 *Mekhilta dR. Ismael, Neziqin* 2 (ed. Horovitz-Rabin p. 253), *dR. Simeon ben Iohai Mišpatim* 6:6.

30 This opinion is not found in any parallel source.

(62a line 74) תַּמָּן תַּנִּינָן. נַעֲרָה הַמְאוֹרָסָה הִיא וְאָבִיהָ מְקַבְּלִין אֶת גִּיטָהּ. רֵישׁ לָקִישׁ אָמַר. כְּמַחֲלוֹקֶת בְּגִיטִּין כֵּן מַחֲלוֹקֶת בְּקִידּוּשִׁין. אָמַר רִבִּי יוֹחָנָן. הַכֹּל

מוֹדִין בְּקִידּוּשִׁין שֶׁאָבִיהָ מְקַדְּשָׁהּ. לֹא הָיָה מוֹדֶה רֵישׁ לָקִישׁ בְּנִישּׂוּאִין שֶׁלֹּא הַכֹּל מִמֶּנָּה לְהַשִּׂיא עַצְמָהּ לְהַפְסִיד מַעֲשֵׂה יָדֶיהָ עַל אָבִיהָ. עַל דַּעְתֵּיהּ דְּרִבִּי יוֹחָנָן אֵין לָהּ דַּעַת אֵצֶל אָבִיהָ וְאֵינָהּ עוֹשָׂה שָׁלִיחַ. עַל דַּעְתֵּיהּ דְּרִבִּי שִׁמְעוֹן בֶּן לָקִישׁ יֵשׁ לָהּ דַּעַת אֵצֶל אָבִיהָ וְהִיא עוֹשָׂה שָׁלִיחַ. מַתְנִיתָא פְּלִיגָא עַל רִבִּי יוֹחָנָן. הָאִישׁ מְקַדֵּשׁ בּוֹ וּבִשְׁלוּחוֹ וְהָאִשָּׁה מִתְקַדֶּשֶׁת בָּהּ וּבִשְׁלוּחָהּ. פָּתַר לָהּ בִּגְדוֹלָה. וְהָתַנִּינָן. קְטַנָּה שֶׁאָמְרָה. הִתְקַבֵּל לִי גִּיטִּי. אֵינוֹ גֵט עַד שֶׁיַּגִּיעַ הַגֵּט לְיָדָהּ. פָּתַר לָהּ בִּיתוֹמָה. וְהָתַנִּינָן. אִם אָמַר לוֹ אָבִיהָ. צֵא וְהִתְקַבֵּל לְבִתִּי גִּיטָּהּ. אִם רָצָה לְהַחֲזִיר לֹא יַחֲזִיר. פָּתַר לָהּ לְצִדָּדִין. הָא מַתְנִיתָהּ פָּתַר לָהּ רֹאשָׁהּ בִּיתוֹמָה וְסוֹפָהּ בְּשֶׁיֵּשׁ לָהּ אָב. מַתְנִיתָא פְּלִיגָא עַל רִבִּי שִׁמְעוֹן בֶּן לָקִישׁ. הָאִישׁ מְקַדֵּשׁ אֶת בִּתּוֹ כְּשֶׁהִיא נַעֲרָה בּוֹ וּבִשְׁלוּחוֹ. פָּתַר לָהּ כְּרִבִּי יוּדָה. דְּרִבִּי יוּדָה אָמַר. אֵין שְׁתֵּי יָדַיִם זוֹכוֹת כְּאַחַת. אָמַר רִבִּי אַסִּי. חַד רַב נְפַק מִן בֵּית וַעֲדָא. אָמַר. נְפַק עוֹבְדָא כְּרִבִּי יוֹחָנָן. וְסָמְכוּן עֲלוֹי. לָא דַהֲוָה צוֹרְכָא מִיסְמַךְ עֲלוֹי אֶלָּא דַהֲוָת מִן יַמָּא לְטִיגְנָא.

[31] We have stated: "A preliminarily married adolescent girl, or her father, can accept her bill of divorce." Rebbi Simeon ben Laqish said, like the disagreement about divorce is the disagreement about preliminary marriage. Rebbi Johanan said, everybody agrees about preliminary marriage that her father contracts but not she herself. Rebbi Simeon ben Laqish agrees about a definitive marriage that she is not empowered to marry herself off and to let her father lose her earnings. In the opinion of Rebbi Johanan she has no legal standing relative to her father and cannot appoint an agent. In the opinion of Rebbi Simeon ben Laqish she does have legal standing relative to her father and can appoint an agent. A Mishnah disagrees with Rebbi Johanan: "A man contracts a preliminary marriage either in person or through his agent and a woman contracts a preliminary marriage either in person or through her agent." He explains

it about an adult woman. But did we not state: "If an underage girl said, accept the bill of divorce for me, it is no valid bill of divorce until it reaches her hand." He explains it about an orphan. But did we not state: "If her father said to [an agent]: Go and receive my daughter's bill of divorce, if [the husband] wants to retract he cannot retract." He explains that the Mishnah deals with cases; the first part about an orphan and the second part if she has a father. A Mishnah disagrees with Rebbi Simeon ben Laqish. "A man may contract a preliminary marriage for his adolescent daughter either by himself or by his agent." He explains that following Rebbi Jehudah, since Rebbi Jehudah said, "no two hands can acquire together." Rebbi Yose said, a rabbi came out from the assembly and said, a case was decided following Rebbi Johanan. Can one rely on that? It was no question of relying on him since it was as from the sea to the frying pan.

31 From *Gittin* 6:2, Notes 55-69. Variant readings are given there.

(62b line 13) רַב הַמְנוּנָא בְּשֵׁם רִבִּי אַסִי. קְטַנָּה שֶׁקִּידְשָׁה אֶת עַצְמָהּ בִּשְׁתֵּי שְׂעָרוֹת אָבִיהָ מְמָאֵן לֹא הִיא. לֹא אַתְיָיא לֹא כְרִבִּי יוֹחָנָן וְלֹא כְרִבִּי שִׁמְעוֹן בֶּן לָקִישׁ. אִין כְּרִבִּי יוֹחָנָן אֵין כָּאן מֵיאוּן. אִין כְּרִבִּי שִׁמְעוֹן בֶּן לָקִישׁ. נִישׂוּאֵי תוֹרָה הֵן. לֹא אַתְיָיא אֶלָא כְּרִבִּי יוֹחָנָן. אַף עַל גַּב דְּרִבִּי יוֹחָנָן אָמַר. הַכֹּל מוֹדִין בְּקִידּוּשִׁין שֶׁאָבִיהָ מְקַדְּשָׁהּ לֹא הִיא. מוֹדֶה בָהּ אָבִיהָ יְמָאֵן עַל יָדֶיהָ.

Rav Hamnuna in the name of Rebbi Assi[32]: If an underage girl married herself off preliminarily with two pubic hairs[33], her father repudiates the marriage[34] but not she herself. This follows neither Rebbi Johanan nor Rebbi Simeon ben Laqish. If following Rebbi Johanan, there is no place for repudiation[35]. If following Rebbi Simeon ben Laqish, the marriage is valid by biblical standards[36]. It follows only Rebbi Joḥanan. Even though Rebbi Joḥanan says that everybody agrees about preliminary marriage that her father contracts but not she herself, he agrees in this case that the father repudiates on her behalf[37].

32 The Babylonian, Rav Assi in the Babli.

33 This statement seems to be a contradiction in terms. The definition of an underage girl is a female who does not yet have two pubic hairs. The interpretation can be either that she contracted the marriage when she was underage but now, when the case comes to court, she already became an adolescent (R. Moses Margalit) or, preferably, that she is an adolescent (Chapter 1, Note 228) who, while legally responsible, still is under her father's authority in marital matters (R. David Fraenckel). In either case it is presumed that the father was not informed of the preliminary marriage at the time it was contracted.

In the Babli, 46a, Rav Assi's statement is that only the father has the right to annul her marriage but not she herself, since she unlawfully arrogated to herself the rights of an adult. In the Babli, practice is decided following Rav that both her father and herself have the right to unilaterally terminate the irregular preliminary marriage.

34 Repudiation of a marriage is possible only for an orphan girl who was married off by her mother or brothers, who can walk out of a marriage by a simple declaration as long as she is formally underage, i. e., did not grow two pubic hairs (*Yebamot* Chapter 13). In the present case, the expression "repudiates" would seem to be inappropriate but it is justified in the Babli (46a) by reference to *Ex.* 22:16 which uses the verb מאן to describe the father's veto of the marriage of his daughter to her seducer.

35 Since only the father has the right to contract the marriage of his underage or adolescent daughter, there is no marriage and the transaction does not have to be nullified.

36 Since he holds that there is an opinion which gives the adolescent girl the right to marry on her own, he would have to require a valid bill of divorce to dissolve the marriage.

37 R. Johanan agrees that the marriage contracted by an adolescent on her own is valid if it is not countermanded by her father. She herself cannot walk out of a union contracted by herself as an adolescent. Since this statement cannot hold for a marriage contracted by an underage girl without her father's knowledge, it seems that the interpretation of R. Moses Margalit cannot be sustained.

(62b line 18) רִבִּי בָּא בַּר כַּהֲנָא וְרִבִּי יַעֲקֹב בַּר אִידִי בְּשֵׁם רִבִּי יְהוֹשֻׁעַ בֶּן לֵוִי. קִידְּשָׁהּ לַדַּעַת וְהִכְנִיסָהּ שֶׁלֹּא לַדַּעַת. זֶה הָיָה מַעֲשֶׂה וּבָא אָבִיהָ וְהוֹצִיאָהּ מִגְּנוּנָהּ. רִבִּי יַעֲקֹב בַּר אָחָא בְּשֵׁם רִבִּי יְהוֹשֻׁעַ סִימָן הֲוָה לוֹ. דַּהֲוָה רִבִּי יְהוֹשֻׁעַ בֶּן לֵוִי פְּלִיג עַל רִבִּי שִׁמְעוֹן בֶּן לָקִישׁ. לֵית הִיא פְלִיגָא. הֵיךְ מַה דְּרִבִּי שִׁמְעוֹן בֶּן לָקִישׁ אָמַר תַּמָּן. לֹא הַכֹּל מִמֶּנָּה לְהַשִּׂיא אֶת עַצְמָהּ וּלְהַפְסִיד מַעֲשֵׂה יָדֶיהָ לְאָבִיהָ. כֵּן רִבִּי יְהוֹשֻׁעַ בֶּן לֵוִי אָמַר הָכָא. לֹא הַכֹּל מִמֶּנָּה לְהַשִּׂיא אֶת עַצְמָהּ וּלְהַפְסִיד מַעֲשֵׂה יָדֶיהָ עַל אָבִיהָ. אָתָא רִבִּי אַבָּא בַּר כַּהֲנָא רִבִּי יַעֲקֹב בַּר אִידִי בְּשֵׁם רִבִּי יְהוֹשֻׁעַ בֶּן לֵוִי. קִידְּשָׁהּ שֶׁלֹּא לַדַּעַת וּכְנָסָהּ שֶׁלֹּא לַדַּעַת. זֶה הָיָה מַעֲשֶׂה וּבָא אָבִיהָ וְעָקַר קִידּוּשֶׁיהָ.

Rebbi Abba bar Cahana and Rebbi Jacob bar Idi in the name of Rebbi Joshua ben Levi: If she[38] was preliminarily married with agreement[39] but definitively married without agreement there was such a case and the father came and removed her from the bridal chamber[40]. Rebbi Jacob bar Aha in the name of Rebbi Joshua[41]: He[42] had an indication that Rebbi Joshua ben Levi disagreed with Rebbi Simeon ben Laqish. But this does not disagree. Just as Rebbi Simeon ben Laqish said there[43], she is not empowered to marry herself off and let her father lose her earnings, so Rebbi Joshua ben Levi said here, she is not empowered to marry herself off and let her father lose her earnings[44]. Rebbi Abba bar Cahana and Rebbi Jacob bar Idi came in the name of Rebbi Joshua ben Levi: If she was preliminarily married without agreement and was being definitively married without agreement: there was such a case and the father came and annulled her preliminary marriage[45].

38 An underage or adolescent girl.

39 The father's agreement.

40 Even an adolescent is emancipated from her father's power only by definitive marriage, not by the preliminary. Therefore, she cannot contract the definitive marriage on her own.

41 This name probably is corrupt.

42 R. Abba bar Cahana justified himself for quoting R. Joshua ben Levi whom he could not have known by quoting an attached lemma to the effect that the latter ruled differently from what R. Simeon ben Laqish would expound a generation later.

43 Two paragraphs earlier.

44 Her earnings are her father's before and her husband's after definitive marriage. Therefore, it is understandable that the father will want to give his adolescent daughter in preliminary marriage, for which he is paid, but refuse to let her enter definitive marriage before she reaches adulthood and he anyhow loses the right to her earnings.

45 Then automatically the definitive marriage cannot proceed.

(62b line 27) קִידְּשָׁהּ לַדַעַת וּכְנָסָהּ שֶׁלֹּא לַדַעַת מָהוּ שֶׁתֹּאכַל בַּתְּרוּמָה. רַב אָמַר. אוֹכֶלֶת. וּשְׁמוּאֵל אָמַר. אֵינָהּ אוֹכֶלֶת. אָמַר רִבִּי מָנָא. טַעְמָא דְרַב מִכֵּיוָן שֶׁקִּידְּשָׁהּ לַדַעַת חֲזָקָה שֶׁכְּנָסָהּ לַדַעַת. אָמַר רבִּי יוֹסֵי בֵּירִבִּי בּוּן. טַעְמָא דְרַב שֶׁכֵּן מִשְׁנָה רִאשׁוֹנָה אֲרוּסָתוֹ בַת יִשְׂרָאֵל אוֹכֶלֶת בַּתְּרוּמָה. מַה נָפַק מִבֵּינֵיהוֹן. מַעֲשֶׂה יָדֶיהָ. עַל דַּעְתֵּיהּ דְּרִבִּי מָנָא כְּרַב מַעֲשֶׂה יָדֶיהָ לְבַעֲלָהּ. עַל דַּעְתֵּיהּ דְּרִבִּי יוֹסֵי בֵּירִבִּי בּוּן כְּרַב מַעֲשֶׂה יָדֶיהָ לְאָבִיהָ. מֵתָה מִי יוֹרְשָׁהּ. עַל דַּעְתֵּיהּ דְּרִבִּי מָנָא כְּרַב בַּעֲלָהּ יוֹרְשָׁהּ. עַל דַּעְתֵּיהּ דְּרִבִּי יוֹסֵי בֵּירִבִּי בּוּן כְּרַב. מֵתָה בַּעֲלָהּ יוֹרְשָׁהּ. אָתָא רבִּי יוֹסֵי בֵּירִבִּי בּוּן כְּרַב. קִידְּשָׁהּ שֶׁלֹּא לַדַעַת וְהִכְנִיסָהּ שֶׁלֹּא לַדַעַת מָהוּ שֶׁתֹּאכַל בַּתְּרוּמָה. שְׁמוּאֵל אָמַר. אוֹכֶלֶת. אִיתָא חֲמִי. אִילּוּ קִידְּשָׁהּ לַדַעַת וּכְנָסָהּ שֶׁלֹּא לַדַעַת שְׁמוּאֵל אָמַר. אֵינָהּ אוֹכֶלֶת. וְהָכָא אָמַר. אוֹכֶלֶת. שְׁמוּאֵל עֲבַד לָהּ כִּיתוֹמָה.

If she[38] was preliminarily married with agreement[39] but definitively married without agreement, may she eat heave[46]? Rav said, she does eat; but Samuel said, she may not eat. Rebbi Mana said, Rav's reason is that if she was preliminarily married with agreement, the permanence of the status quo implies the assumption that he definitively married her with agreement[47]. Rebbi Yose ben Rebbi Abun said, Rav's reason is that by the earlier Mishnah[48], a preliminarily married daughter of an Israel may eat heave[49]. What is the difference between them? Her earnings. According to Rebbi Mana, for Rav her earnings belong to her husband[50]; according to Rebbi Yose ben Rebbi Abun, for Rav her earnings belong to her father[51]. If she should die, who inherits from her? According to Rebbi Mana, for Rav her husband inherits; according to Rebbi Yose ben Rebbi Abun, for Rav her father inherits if she dies[52]. Rebbi Yose ben Rebbi Abun stated, for Rav her husband inherits if she dies[53]. If she was preliminarily married without agreement and definitively married without agreement, may she eat heave? Samuel said, she does eat[54]. Come and see: If she was preliminarily married with agreement and definitively married without agreement, Samuel says that she may not eat; here he says she may eat? Samuel treats her as an orphan[55].

46 If the bride was an Israel but the groom a Cohen. The wife of a Cohen is a member of his family and as such entitled to eat heave (*Num.* 18:11).

47 The father's agreement to the preliminary marriage implies his acquiescence in a definitive marriage unless he explicitly objects. A definitive marriage without consent or objection by the father is marriage with consent. The treatment of this topic in the Babli, 45b, is not comparable to the argument here since the Babli distinguishes between a marriage in the presence of the father and one contracted when the father

was on a far away trip. The Babli notes that Rav in a real case followed Samuel's opinion, attributed in the Babli to Rav Assi.

48   Only the preliminary marriage is an act of acquisition which brings the bride into the husband's family; cf. *Ketubot* 5:3, Note 66. The denial of heave to the bride before the definitive marriage is a later rabbinic institution; Mishnah *Ketubot* 5:4.

49   By biblical standards, definitive marriage is irrelevant for the bride to be able to eat heave.

50   Since the earnings are the husband's from the moment of definitive marriage which for R. Mana is valid unless vetoed explicitly.

51   One would have to say that the father might have the right to the earnings, since R. Yose ben R. Abun does not say that the definitive marriage is invalid, only that its status is irrelevant.

52   For the wife's estate, the same rules apply as for the wife's earnings.

53   The prior speculation about the difference between the two arguments attributed to Rav is false; R. Yose ben R. Abun also will agree that the definitive marriage is valid unless explicitly vetoed by the father. He only stated that the problem of validity of the definitive marriage is irrelevant for the problem of heave.

54   In the Babli, 45b, this is attributed to Rav Huna.

55   Since everything was done without consulting the father, one may assume that the latter would have indicated his disapproval had he disapproved. His silence therefore is considered as formal approval and the underage girl is emancipated from him; she becomes "an orphan during the father's lifetime" (cf. *Gittin* 6:1, Note 20). The same argument is given in the Babli.

(62b line 39) מַתְנִיתָא. הִתְקַדְּשִׁי לִי בִּתְמָרָה זוֹ וכל. מַתְנִיתָא בְּשֶׁאָמְרָה. אִי אֵיפְשִׁי בָּזוֹ אֶלָּא בָזוֹ. אִי אֵיפְשִׁי בָּזוֹ אֶלָּא בָזוֹ. בָּזוֹ וּבָזוֹ וּבָזוֹ. מָאן תַּנָּא וָוִין. רִבִּי יוּדָה. בְּרַם כְּרִבִּי מֵאִיר אוֹ בָזוֹ אוֹ בָזוֹ אוֹ בָזוֹ.

Mishnah: "Be married to me preliminarily by this date fruit," etc. The Mishnah [presents the case] that she said, I cannot accept this one, try that one; I cannot accept this one, try that one[56]. "By this and by that one and by that one.⁵⁷" Who is the Tanna of *Wawim*? Rebbi Jehudah. But for Rebbi Meïr, either this or this or that one⁵⁸.

56 In this interpretation, if the man said: Be preliminarily married to me by this, by that one, etc., she would be married if all dates together were worth a *perutah*. If the preliminary marriage must be mentioned every time, it must be that the proposal was rejected in between. Then not *any* date but specifically the last one must be worth a *perutah*.

57 The triple mention is the version of the Mishnah in the Babli and most independent Mishnah mss.

58 The positions of Rebbis Jehudah and Meïr about the interpretation of conjunctions in multiple statements are discussed in *Gittin* 9:7, Notes 92-101.

(62b line 42) רִבִּי יִרְמְיָה בְּשֵׁם רַב. הִתְקַדְּשִׁי לִי בְּסֶלַע זוֹ לְאַחַר שְׁלֹשִׁים. אוֹכֶלֶת (בִּתְרוּמָה)⁵⁹ בְּתוֹךְ שְׁלֹשִׁים הֲרֵי זוֹ מְקוּדֶּשֶׁת. אוֹף רִבִּי שִׁמְעוֹן בֶּן אֶלְעָזָר מוֹדֶה בָהּ. מַה בֵּינָהּ לְמִלְוָה. מִלְוָה לֹא נִיתְּנָה לְשֵׁם קִידּוּשִׁין. קִידּוּשִׁין לְכָךְ נִיתְּנוּ מִשָּׁעָה רִאשׁוֹנָה. וְהָא תַּנִּינָן. הָיְתָה אוֹכֶלֶת רִאשׁוֹנָה אֵינָהּ מְקוּדֶּשֶׁת עַד שֶׁיְּהֵא בְּאַחַת מֵהֶן שָׁוֶה פְּרוּטָה. מֵעַתָּה אֲפִילוּ לֹא נִשְׁתַּיֵּיר שָׁם שָׁוֶה פְּרוּטָה תְּהֵא מְקוּדֶּשֶׁת. פָּתַר לָהּ עַל רִאשָׁהּ. וְאֵין עַל רִאשָׁהּ בְּדָא תַּנִּינָן. הָיְתָה אוֹכֶלֶת רִאשׁוֹנָה רִאשׁוֹנָה אֵינָהּ מְקוּדֶּשֶׁת עַד שֶׁיְּהֵא בְּאַחַת מֵהֶן שָׁוֶה פְּרוּטָה. אָמַר רִבִּי אֶלְעָזָר. דְּרִבִּי שִׁמְעוֹן בֶּן אֶלְעָזָר הִיא. דְּתַנֵּי. הִתְקַדְּשִׁי לִי בְּפִקָּדוֹן שֶׁיֵּשׁ לִי בְּיָדָךְ. וַהֲלָכָה וּמְצָאַתּוּ שֶׁנִּגְנַב אוֹ שֶׁאָבַד. אִם נִשְׁתַּיֵּיר שָׁם שָׁוֶה פְּרוּטָה מְקוּדֶּשֶׁת וְאִם לָאו אֵינָהּ מְקוּדֶּשֶׁת. בְּמִלְוָה שֶׁיֵּשׁ לִי בְּיָדָךְ. וַהֲלָכָה וּמְצָאָתָהּ שֶׁנִּגְנְבָה אוֹ שֶׁאָבָד. אֲפִילוּ לֹא נִשְׁתַּיֵּיר שָׁם שָׁוֶה פְּרוּטָה מְקוּדֶּשֶׁת. רִבִּי שִׁמְעוֹן בֶּן אֶלְעָזָר אוֹמֵר מִשּׁוּם רִבִּי מֵאִיר. מִלְוָה כְּפִקָּדוֹן. אִם נִשְׁתַּיֵּיר שָׁם שָׁוֶה פְּרוּטָה מְקוּדֶּשֶׁת וְאִם לָאו אֵינָהּ מְקוּדֶּשֶׁת. אָמַר רִבִּי לְעָזָר. אַתְיָא דְּרִבִּי שִׁמְעוֹן בֶּן אֶלְעָזָר כְּרִבִּי מֵאִיר. כְּמָה דְּרִבִּי מֵאִיר אָמַר. כָּל־הַמַּשְׁנֶה מִדַּעַת הַבְּעָלִים נִקְרָא גּוֹזְלָן. כֵּן רִבִּי שִׁמְעוֹן בֶּן אֶלְעָזָר אָמַר הָכָא. כָּל־הַמַּשְׁנֶה מִדַּעַת הַבְּעָלִים נִקְרָא גּוֹזְלָן. דְּהוּא פָּתַר לָהּ בְּמִלְוָה שֶׁהַלַּוֶוה אָמַר לוֹ. קַח לִי חִטִּים. וְלָקַח לוֹ שְׂעוֹרִים.

וְקַשְׁיָא. וּמְקַדְּשִׁין בִּגְזֵילָה. רִבִּי יוֹסֵי בָּעָא. נִיחָא אָדָם שָׁוֶה נוֹתֵן פְּרוּטָה עַל דִּינָר שֶׁמָּא נוֹתֵן שָׁוֶה פְּרוּטָה עַל שָׁוֶה פְּרוּטָה. אִית תַּנָּיֵי תַּנֵּי. מְקַדְּשִׁין בִּגְזֵילָה. וְאִית תַּנָּיֵי תַנֵּי. אֵין מְקַדְּשִׁין בִּגְזֵילָה. אָמַר רִבִּי מָנָא. מָאן דְּאָמַר. מְקַדְּשִׁין בִּגְזֵילָה. בִּגְזֵילָה שֶׁהוּא יָכוֹל לְהַצִּילָהּ מִיָּדוֹ. מָאן דְּאָמַר. אֵין מְקַדְּשִׁין בִּגְזֵילָה. בִּגְזֵילָה שֶׁאֵינוֹ יָכוֹל לְהוֹצִיאָהּ מִיָּדָהּ. רִבִּי יוֹסֵי בֵּירִבִּי בּוּן בְּשֵׁם רִבִּי שְׁמוּאֵל בַּר רַב יִצְחָק. מָאן דְּאָמַר. מְקַדְּשִׁין בִּגְזֵילָה. בִּגְזֵילָה שֶׁנִּתְיִיאֲשׁוּ הַבְּעָלִים מִמֶּנָּה. וּמָאן דְּאָמַר. אֵין מְקַדְּשִׁין בִּגְזֵילָה. בִּגְזֵילָה שֶׁלֹּא נִתְיִיאֲשׁוּ הַבְּעָלִים מִמֶּנָּה.

Rebbi Jeremiah[60] in the name of Rav: "'Be preliminarily married to me by this tetradrachma after thirty [days].' Even if she spent it within the thirty [days], she is preliminarily married; also Rebbi Simeon ben Eleazar[61] will agree to this." What is the difference between this and a loan[62]? A loan was not given for preliminary marriage[63], while this was given from the start for preliminary marriage. But did we not state: "If she was eating right away she is not preliminarily married unless one of them was worth a *perutah*"? Then even if a *perutah*'s worth was not left, she should be preliminarily married[64]! He explains that as earlier[65]. If it refers to the earlier statement, did we not state: "If she was eating immediately she is not preliminarily married unless one of them was worth a *perutah*"[66]? Rebbi Eleazar said, it[67] follows Rebbi Simeon ben Eleazar, as it was stated[68]: "Be preliminarily married to me by the deposit you hold for me; if she went and found that it was stolen or lost, if there was a *perutah*'s worth left, she is preliminarily married; otherwise, she is not preliminarily married. By the loan you are holding from me, if she went and found that it was stolen or lost, even if there was no *perutah*'s worth left, she is preliminarily married. Rebbi Eleazar ben Rebbi Simeon says in the name of Rebbi Meïr, a loan is like a deposit: If there was a *perutah*'s worth left, she is preliminarily married; otherwise, she is not preliminarily married." Rebbi Eleazar said, Rebbi Simeon ben Eleazar follows Rebbi Meïr[69]. Just as Rebbi Meïr said that anybody who deviates from the orders of the owner is called a robber[70], so Rebbi Simeon ben Eleazar says here, anybody who deviates from the orders of the owner is called a robber. For he explains it[71] to be for a loan when the lender said[72], buy wheat for me, but he bought barley for him[73]. That is difficult: can one pay for a preliminary marriage with robbed money? Rebbi Yose asked: One understands that a person may invest a *perutah* to gain a denar; would he invest a *perutah* to gain a *perutah*[74]? Some Tannaïm state: One may preliminarily marry with a robbed item; some Tannaïm state: One cannot preliminarily marry with a robbed item. Rebbi Mana said, the one who said that one may preliminarily marry with a robbed item refers to an item which he has a chance to recoup from her hand. The one who said that one cannot preliminarily marry with a robbed item refers to an item which he has no chance to remove from her hand[75]. Rebbi Yose ben Rebbi Abun in the name of Rebbi Samuel bar Rav Isaac: the one who said that one may preliminarily marry with a robbed item refers to an item which the owner gave up hope to recover. The one who said that one cannot preliminarily marry with a robbed item refers to an item which the owner did not give up hope to recover[76].

59 This word is an echo of the preceding text. Instead of אוֹכֶלֶת בִּתְרוּמָה one should read either active אֹכְלָה or passive נֶאֱכֶלֶת.

60 Rav Jeremiah, the colleague of Rav.

61 Whose opinion will be discussed later in this paragraph.

62 If the creditor forgives a loan to his prospective bride, she receives real value. Nevertheless, RR. Meïr and Simeon ben Eleazar hold that there is

no marriage if nothing of the original loan is left in the fiancée's hand. But if the money was given specifically for preliminary marriage, there is no restriction on its use. The Babli agrees, 59a, in the names of both Rav and Samuel. The Babli raises the additional problem, whether the woman may have second thoughts and return the money's worth before the end of the thirty days if at the start she accepted it.

63 Forgiving the loan, while it might involve considerable value, is only invalidating a sheet of paper which in itself is not worth a *peruṭah*.

64 If all dates were given for the preliminary marriage and all were eaten, in what is this different from the tetradrachma which was spent before the marriage entered into force?

65 In the preceding paragraph; the woman explicitly rejected every gift as inadequate.

66 Even if the dates were referred to as given together.

67 The Mishnah, while formulated anonymously, only represents the opinion of R. Simeon ben Eleazar.

68 Halakhah 1:1, Notes 246-249.

69 In asserting that Mishnah 2:1 follows R. Simeon ben Eleazar in Tosephta 3:1, R. Eleazar holds that both can be analyzed in the same way.

70 *Baba meṣi'a* 6:3 (11a l. 13), Babli 78a/b. If raw wool was given to the dyer to be died red and he died it black, for R. Meïr the dyer acquired the wool as a robber and has to pay the value of the raw wool to his client. R. Jehudah holds that the wool remains the property of the consignor but the dyer is paid only an amount which protects the consignor from loss. (Mishnah *Baba qama* 9:6)

71 The Tosephta quoted from 1:2.

72 It would be natural to read the text as לוֶֹה "the borrower". This is the reading of the commentaries who are led to extraordinary intellectual acrobatics to make sense of the text. If לווה is read as a verbal noun derived from *pi'el*, parallel to Babylonian מַלְוֶה, everything becomes simple.

73 R. Simeon ben Eleazar follows R. Meïr only in a very special case. He will agree in general with the anonymous majority that forgiving a loan represents enough monetary value to create a valid marriage. He only holds that if the borrower violated the terms of the loan, there no longer exists a loan but rather lender's money in the borrower's hand, i. e., a deposit.

74 This question is asked against R. Meïr's position in general. It is understandable that for the anonymous

majority the woman is married, since the profit she gains from not having to repay the entire loan is certainly worth an extra *peruṭah*. Therefore, even if we note that a loan was given to be spent and cannot retroactively be given as a marriage present, the additional profit for the woman makes her marriage worthwhile. But for R. Meïr, who holds that only the unspent part of the loan can be a marriage gift, there is no additional profit for the woman and one may ask why R. Meïr does not have a general statement that forgiving a loan can never be a valid marriage present.

75   He refers to the situation described by R. Eleazar, that the loan given to the woman turned into robbed property in her hand. If the prospective groom has documents to prove his case in court, the woman is a robber and he has a good chance to recoup his property in court, he offers her real value and the marriage is valid. But if all he has is a moral claim, that has no monetary value and cannot be used as a marriage present.

76   This opinion does not disagree with R. Mana's but refers to a different situation: The man is a robber and offers his prospective bride an object which he obtained by robbery. He can use the object for a preliminary marriage if and only if it is his both in ownership and in possession. The robber, who is in possession by the act of robbing, becomes owner at the moment the prior owners give up hope of recovery (cf. *Giṭṭin* 4:4 Note 88, 5:6 Note 169).

(62b line 67) רִבִּי אַבָהוּ בְּשֵׁם רִבִּי יוֹחָנָן. מַתְנִיתָא בְּשֶׁאָמַר לָהּ. בְּפִיקָּדוֹן שֶׁיֵּשׁ לִי בְיָדֵךְ. אֲבָל אִם אָמַר לָהּ. בְּכָל־מַה שֶׁהִפְקַדְתִּי בְּיָדֵךְ. אֵינָה מְקוּדֶּשֶׁת עַד שֶׁיְּהוּ כּוּלָּן קַיָּימִין. מַה בֵּינָן לְמִלְוָה. מִלְוָה נִיתְּנָה לְהוֹצִיאָהּ וְזֶה לֹא נִיתַּן לְהוֹצִיאוֹ. וְהָתַנִּינָן. הָיְתָה אוֹכֶלֶת רִאשׁוֹנָה רִאשׁוֹנָה אֵינָה מְקוּדֶּשֶׁת עַד שֶׁיְּהֵא בְּאַחַת מֵהֶן שָׁוֶה פְרוּטָה. מֵעַתָּה אֲפִילוּ נִשְׁתַּיֵּיר שָׁם שָׁוֶה פְרוּטָה לֹא תְּהֵא מְקוּדֶּשֶׁת עַד שֶׁיְּהוּ כּוּלָּן קַיָּימִין. פָּתַר לָהּ עַל רֹאשָׁהּ. וְאֵין עַל רֹאשָׁהּ בְּדָא תַנִּינָן. הָיְתָה אוֹכֶלֶת רִאשׁוֹנָה רִאשׁוֹנָה אֵינָהּ מְקוּדֶּשֶׁת עַד שֶׁיְּהֵא בְּאַחַת מֵהֶן שָׁוֶה פְרוּטָה. אָמַר רִבִּי אָבוּן. לֹא כֵן סָבְרִינָן מֵימַר. מָאן תַּנָּא וָיִין. רִבִּי יוּדָה. אָמַר רִבִּי יוֹחָנָן. דִּבְרֵי רִבִּי יוּדָה. נִכְלָלִין בְּקָרְבָּן אֶחָד וְנִפְרָטִין בִּשְׁלֹשָׁה

קָרְבָּנוֹת. כְּמָא דְהוּא אָמַר תַּמָּן. נִכְלָלִין בְּקָרְבָּן אֶחָד וְנִפְרָטִין בִּשְׁלֹשָׁה קָרְבָּנוֹת. כֵּן הוּא אָמַר הָכָא. נִכְלָלִין בְּקִידּוּשׁ אֶחָד וְנִפְרָטִין בִּשְׁלֹשָׁה קִידּוּשִׁין.

Rebbi Abbahu in the name of Rebbi Johanan: The *baraita*[71] if he said to her, by the deposit you are holding for me. But if he said, by *everything* which I deposited with you, she is not preliminarily married unless all of it is available[77]. What is the difference between this and a loan? A loan was given to be spent[78]; this was not given to be spent[79]. But did we not state: "If she was eating right away she is not preliminarily married unless one of them was worth a *perutah*." Then even if a *perutah*'s worth was left, she should not be preliminarily married unless all of them were available! He explains that as earlier[65]. If it refers to the earlier statement, did we not state: "If she was eating immediately she is not preliminarily married unless one of them was worth a *perutah*"[66,80]? Rebbi Abun said, were we not of the opinion to say, who is the Tanna of *Wawim*? Rebbi Jehudah[58]. Rebbi Johanan said: The words of Rebbi Jehudah imply comprehensive one sacrifice, in detail three sacrifices[81]. Just as he says there, comprehensive one sacrifice, in detail three sacrifices, so he says here, comprehensive one preliminary marriage, in detail three preliminary marriages[82].

77 Since he insists that everything shall be her property, she cannot be married if anything does not become her property because it is lost.

78 Babli 47a; *Mo'ed qatan* 2:3 (81b l. 27).

79 It is at the disposal of the depositor at any moment.

80 If the dates were stated as given together, the marriage should be possible if all of them come into the woman's hand together.

81 Cf. *Gittin* 9:7. If A sues B for wheat, barley, and spelt, and B denies falsely in court that he owes any, he has to atone by one sacrifice. But if he

enters three separate denials, he owes three separate sacrifices.

82 As explained earlier, the Mishnah is explained to refer to the case that the woman rejects all dates except the last. Then each is given as a separate gift; one cannot require that all of them should have been together.

(62c line 3) הִתְקַדְּשִׁי לִי בְּסֶלַע זוֹ. וְאָמְרָה. הַשְׁלִיכָהּ לַיָם אוֹ לַנָּהָר. אֵינָהּ מְקוּדֶּשֶׁת. תְּנֵיהָ לְעָנִי. הֲרֵי זוֹ מְקוּדֶּשֶׁת. מִכָּל־מָקוֹם לֹא נִכְנַס לְתוֹךְ יָדָהּ כְּלוּם הָכָא אַתְּ אָמַר. מְקוּדֶּשֶׁת. וְהָכָא אַתְּ אָמַר. אֵינָהּ מְקוּדֶּשֶׁת. אָמַר רִבִּי אַבָּהוּ בְּשֵׁם רִבִּי יוֹחָנָן. רוֹצָה הִיא מְקוּדֶּשֶׁת וְתֵרָאֶה עוֹשָׂה טוֹבָה לֶעָנִי. אָמַר רִבִּי פִּינְחָס. וְאַתְיָא אוֹ כְרִבִּי זְעִירָא אוֹ כְרִבִּי אִילָא.

83דְּתַנֵּי. אוֹמֵר הוּא אָדָם לְפוֹעֵל. הֵילָךְ דֵּינָר זֶה אֱכוֹל בּוֹ. הֵילָךְ דֵּינָר זֶה שְׁתֵה בּוֹ. וְאֵין חוֹשְׁשִׁין עַל שְׂכָרוֹ לֹא מִשּׁוּם שְׁבִיעִית וְלֹא מִשּׁוּם מַעְשְׂרוֹת וְלֹא מִשּׁוּם יַיִן נֶסֶךְ. אֲבָל אִם אָמַר לוֹ. צֵא וְקַח לָךְ בְּכַר וַאֲנִי נוֹתֵן לָךְ דָּמָיו. צֵא וְקַח לָךְ רְבִיעִית שְׁלָיַּיִן וַאֲנִי נוֹתֵן לָךְ דָּמֶיהָ. חוֹשְׁשִׁין עַל שְׂכָרוֹ מִשּׁוּם שְׁבִיעִית וּמִשּׁוּם מַעְשְׂרוֹת וּמִשּׁוּם יַיִן נֶסֶךְ. אָמַר רִבִּי זְעִירָא. נַעֲשָׂה הַחֶנְוָנִי שְׁלוּחוֹ שֶׁלְבַּעַל הַבַּיִת לְזַכּוֹת לַפּוֹעֵל. [אָמַר רִבִּי הִילָא פּוֹעֵל] זָכָה לְבַעַל הַבַּיִת מִשֶּׁל חֶנְוָנִי וְחוֹזֵר זָכָה לְעַצְמוֹ.

1 דתני | ד׳ תני   2 ואין חוששין | ד ואינו חושש   3 וקח | ד ולקח (2 times)   דמיו | ד דמים   4 דמיה | ד דמים   6 - | ד אמ׳ ר׳ הילא פועל   זכה | ד וזוכה

אוֹף הָכָא עַל דַּעְתֵּיהּ דְּרִבִּי זְעִירָא הַבַּעַל נַעֲשָׂה שְׁלוּחוֹ שֶׁלָאִשָּׁה לְזַכּוֹת לְעָנִי. אָמַר רִבִּי הִילָא. הֶעָנִי זָכָה לָאִשָּׁה מִשֶּׁלְבַּעֲלָהּ וְחוֹזֵר וְזוֹכֶה לְעַצְמוֹ.

84מָה נָפַק מִבֵּינֵיהוֹן. הָיָה הַחֶנְוָנִי חֵרֵשׁ. עַל דַּעְתֵּיהּ דְּרִבִּי זְעִירָא לֹא חָשַׁשׁ. שֶׁאֵין שְׁלִיחוּת לְחֵרֵשׁ. עַל דַּעְתֵּיהּ דְּרִבִּי הִילָא חָשַׁשׁ.

2 חשש | ד חושש

הָיָה הַפּוֹעֵל חֵרֵשׁ. עַל דַּעְתֵּיהּ דְּרִבִּי הִילָא לֹא חָשַׁשׁ. שֶׁאֵין זְכִיּוֹת לְחֵרֵשׁ. עַל דַּעְתֵּיהּ דְּרִבִּי זְעִירָא חָשַׁשׁ.

"Be preliminarily married to me by this tetradrachma," and she said, "throw it into the sea or the river," she is not married.[86] "Give it to a poor person," she is married[87]. In either case nothing came into her hand; in one case you say, she is married; in the other case you say, she is not married! Rebbi Abbahu said in the name of Rebbi Johanan: She wants to be married and be seen as benefiting the poor. Rebbi Phineas said, this can be interpreted either following Rebbi Ze'ira or Rebbi Ila.

[83]As it was stated: "One may say to his worker: Here you have a denar, use it for food, here you have a denar, use it for drink, and not be worried about either the Sabbatical year, tithes, or wine for libations. But if he told him, go and buy yourself a loaf and I shall give you the money, go and buy yourself a *reviit* of wine and I shall give you the money, he has to worry because of the Sabbatical year, tithes, and wine used for libations." Rebbi Ze'ira said, the grocer becomes the agent of the employer to let the worker acquire. [85][Rebbi Hila said, the worker] acquired for the employer from the grocer and then acquires it himself.

Here also, in the opinion of Rebbi Ze'ira the husband becomes the wife's agent[88] to benefit the poor. Rebbi Hila said, the poor person acquired it for the wife from her husband[87] and afterwards acquired it for himself.

[84]What is the difference between them? If the grocer was deaf-mute. According to Rebbi Ze'ira, he does not have to worry because a deaf-mute cannot become an agent; according to Rebbi Hila, he does have to worry.

If the worker was deaf-mute. According to Rebbi Hila, he does not have to worry[89] because a deaf-mute cannot acquire; according to Rebbi Ze'ira, he does have to worry.

83 This text is from *Demay* 6:12, Notes 205-214 (ד). The insert given in the next paragraph shows that this is a genuine quote, not a copy.

84 This also is from *Demay*.
85 Text missing here, added from *Demay*.
86 A superficially similar text is in the Babli, 8b, and Tosephta, 2:8. The big difference is that in the Babylonian texts the woman took the coin and threw it into the sea whereas in the Yerushalmi the woman never touched the coin. It is a recognized principle that actions speak louder than words; if a marriage gift is offered to a woman and she reacts by throwing it away, she certainly is not married. This has nothing to do with the problem treated in the present paragraph.
87 From the moment the coin was given as charity.
88 Therefore, the coin became the woman's property in her future husband's hand; the objection raised at the start is baseless.
89 But then the woman is not married if the coin is given to a deaf-mute beggar.

(62c line 20) חָטַף הַסֶּלַע מִיָּדָהּ וּנְתָנוֹ לָהּ. בִּשְׁעַת מַתָּנָה אָמַר לָהּ. הֲרֵי אַתְּ מְקוּדֶּשֶׁת לִי. הֲרֵי זוֹ מְקוּדֶּשֶׁת. בַּמֶּה קִידְּשָׁהּ. רִבִּי חַגַּיי בְּשֵׁם רִבִּי פְדָת. רוֹצָה הִיא שֶׁתְּהֵא מְקוּדֶּשֶׁת לוֹ וְיהֵא חַיָּיב לָהּ סֶלַע. אָמַר רִבִּי יוֹסֵי. אִילּוּ אִיתְּמַר כְּלִי יָאוּת. סֶלַע דַּרְכָּהּ לְהִתְחַלֵּף.

If he grabbed a tetradrachma from her hands, returned it to her and at the moment of delivery said to her: "You are preliminarily married to me", then she is preliminarily married. By what was she preliminarily married[90]? Rebbi Ḥaggai in the name of Rebbi Pedat: She wants to be preliminarily married[91] to him and he would owe her a tetradrachma[92]. Rebbi Yose said, if this had been formulated for a vessel, it would be understandable. A tetradrachma can be exchanged[93].

90 Since it was her money, she did not receive anything. In addition, it is questionable whether one may use robbed property as marriage gift.
91 In the Babli, 13a, she is only married if she had previously agreed to be married to him.
92 She accepts the coin as a

marriage gift, not as return of stolen goods. Therefore, the husband now owes her another tetradrachma.

93 Nobody insists that payment be made with a particular coin. He disputes that the husband owes another coin. The fact that she does not have to go to court to retrieve her coin is worth a *peruṭah*.

(62c line 23) כִּינְסִי לִי סֶלַע זוֹ. וּבִשְׁעַת מַתָּנָה אָמַר לָהּ. הֲרֵי אַתְּ מְקוּדֶּשֶׁת לִי. הֲרֵי זוֹ מְקוּדֶּשֶׁת. אִם מְשֶׁנְּתָנָהּ לָהּ. רָצָת מְקוּדֶּשֶׁת. לֹא רָצָת אֵינָהּ מְקוּדֶּשֶׁת. הֵילָךְ סֶלַע זוֹ שֶׁאֲנִי חַיָּיב לָךְ. וּבִשְׁעַת מַתָּנָה אָמַר לָהּ. הֲרֵי אַתְּ מְקוּדֶּשֶׁת לִי. רָצָת מְקוּדֶּשֶׁת. וְאִם לָאו אֵינָהּ מְקוּדֶּשֶׁת. אִם מְשֶׁבָּאת לְתוֹךְ יָדָהּ אָמְרָה לָהּ. הֲרֵי אַתְּ מְקוּדֶּשֶׁת לִי. אַף עַל פִּי שֶׁשְּׁנֵיהֶן רוֹצִין אֵינָהּ מְקוּדֶּשֶׁת. כֵּיצַד יַעֲשֶׂה. יְטִילֶנּוּ מִמֶּנָּה וְיַחֲזוֹר וְיִתְּנֶינּוּ לָהּ וְיֹאמַר לָהּ. הֲרֵי אַתְּ מְקוּדֶּשֶׁת לִי. הִתְקַדְּשִׁי לִי בְּמָנֶא זוֹ. וְנִמְצָא חָסֵר דֵּינָר. אֵינָהּ מְקוּדֶּשֶׁת. הָיָה בּוֹ דֵּינָר רַע הֲרֵי זוֹ מְקוּדֶּשֶׁת. וְהוּא שֶׁיַּחֲלִיף. הָיָה מוֹנֶה רִאשׁוֹן רִאשׁוֹן וּמַשְׁלִיךְ לְתוֹךְ יָדָהּ יְכוֹלָה הִיא שֶׁתַּחֲזוֹר בָּהּ עַד שָׁעָה שֶׁיַּשְׁלִים. רִבִּי לְעָזָר אוֹמֵר. מְקוּדֶּשֶׁת בָּרִאשׁוֹן וְהַשְּׁאָר עַל תְּנָאי. רִבִּי יוֹחָנָן אָמַר. לִכְשֶׁיַּשְׁלִים. אָמַר דֵּין חָזַר בֵּיהּ רִבִּי יוֹחָנָן.

[94]"'Hold this tetradrachma for me' and at the moment of delivery he said, 'lo, you are preliminarily married to me,' she is preliminarily married[95]. After delivery, if she agrees[96], she is preliminarily married, otherwise she is not preliminarily married. 'Here is the tetradrachma which I owe you,' and at the moment of delivery he said, 'lo, you are preliminarily married to me,' if she agrees[96], she is preliminarily married, otherwise she is not preliminarily married. If after delivery he said, 'lo, you are preliminarily married to me,' she is not preliminarily married even if both parties agree. What can he do? He should take the coin back, deliver it again and say, 'lo, you are preliminarily married to me.' 'Be preliminarily married to me by this *mina*,' if it turns out that a denar was missing, she is not preliminarily married[97]. If one denar was bad[98], she is

preliminarily married if he replaces it. If he was counting the coins into her hand, she can change her mind any time before he finishes." Rebbi Eleazar said, she is preliminarily married by the first [coin]; the remainder is a condition[99]. Rebbi Joḥanan said, only after he completes [the count.][100] It was said that Rebbi Joḥanan changed his mind about this.

94 Tosephta 2 7-9; Babli 12b, 13a, 8a.	that he asked the woman to be married by *a* mina, not *this* mina. Then the first coin establishes the marriage, the remainder is the husband's debt to be liquidated.
95 Unless she objects in word or deed. She is married if she remains silent.	
96 But not if she remains silent.	100 He seems to hold that the start of delivery is an obligation to finish it at that time. This opinion is not mentioned in the Babli since it is retracted here.
97 Since there is no *mina* given to her.	
98 Counterfeit or underweight.	
99 Babli 8a, 47a. It is understood	

(62c line 34) חַד בַּר נָשׁ עֵרְבוֹנָא יְהִיב לְחַבְרֵיהּ וְכָפַר בָּהּ חַבְרֵיהּ. רִבִּי בָּא וְרִבִּי הִילָא וְרִבִּי יַעֲקֹב בַּר אָחָא בַּר תְּלָתֵירוֹן אָמְרִין. זֶרַע פִּשְׁתָּן הָיָה יִמְקְצָת דָּמִים נָתַן לָהּ. אָתָא עוֹבְדָא קוֹמֵי רִבִּי יוֹחָנָן. אָמַר. אוֹ יִתֵּן לוֹ בְכָל־מִקְחוֹ אוֹ יִמְסוֹר אוֹתוֹ לְמִי שֶׁפָּרַע. רִבִּי חִיָּיה בַּר יוֹסֵף אָמַר. אוֹ יִתֵּן לוֹ בְכָל־עֵרְבוֹנוֹ אוֹ יִמְסוֹר אוֹתוֹ לְמִי שֶׁפָּרַע. מוֹדֶה רִבִּי חִיָּיה בַּר יוֹסֵף לְרִבִּי יוֹחָנָן בְּמִקַּח שֶׁאֵין דַּרְכּוֹ לְהִיקָּנוֹת חֲצָיִים כְּגוֹן פָּרָה וְטַלִּית. וְאִשָּׁה דַרְכָּהּ לְהִיקָּנוֹת חֲצָיָן. רִבִּי חַגַּי וְרִבִּי יוּדָן תְּרֵיהוֹן אָמְרִין. מִקַּח דַּרְכּוֹ לְהִיקָּנוֹת חֲצָיָין וְאִשָּׁה אֵין דַּרְכָּהּ לְהִיקָּנוֹת חֲצָיָין.

[101]A person gave a pledge to another; the other reneged on it[102]. Rebbi Abba, Rebbi Hila, and Rebbi Jacob bar Aḥa all three say it was a deal about flax seed[103] and he had given partial payment. The case came before Rebbi Joḥanan[104], who said: Either he delivers the entire contract

or one may turn him over to "Him Who exacted retribution.[105]" Rebbi Hiyya bar Joseph said, either he delivers for the amount of the pledge or ome may turn him over to "Him Who exacted retribution.[106]" Rebbi Hiyya bar Joseph agrees with Rebbi Johanan in a sale which is not usually split, such as of a cow or a stole[107]. Is a woman usually acquired split? Rebbi Haggai and Rebbi Yudan both said, a sale usually may be split, the acquisition of a wife cannot be split[108].

101   A different version is in *Baba meṣi'a* 4:2 (9c).

102   In *Baba meṣi'a*: A person made a down payment, the seller then annulled the contract. Here also "reneged" does not mean that the seller claimed not to have received a pledge, but that he refused to honor the contract.

103   In *Baba meṣi'a*: "silk".

104   In *Baba meṣi'a*: Before R. Hiyya bar Joseph and R. Johanan. This also is required by the context here.

105   It was stated in Mishnah 1:5 that possession of movables is obtained only by an act of moving. The buyer does not acquire possession by paying the price for the object bought. It is possible for the seller to take the money but then to renege on the deal, not deliver the merchandise but return the money. The injured buyer cannot force the execution of the contract but Mishnah *Baba meṣi'a* 4:2 states that he can go to court and have the court declare that "He Who exacted retribution from the generation of the Flood and of the generation of the Tower of Babylon will in the future exact retribution from him who does not keep his word."

106   R. Johanan here decides following R. Eleazar in the previous paragraph: Even a partial payment validates the entire deal. He should hold that the woman who starts to accept partial payment for the promised marriage gift is married. R. Hiyya bar Joseph represents the position first ascribed to R. Johanan, that financial deals are not completed until the entire debt be paid.

107   A down payment for a cow requires the delivery of the entire cow.

108   The position of R. Eleazar in the preceding paragraph is universally accepted.

HALAKHAH 2

(fol. 62a) **משנה ב:** הִתְקַדְּשִׁי לִי בְּכוֹס זֶה שֶׁל יַיִן וְנִמְצָא שֶׁל דְּבַשׁ. שֶׁל דְּבַשׁ וְנִמְצָא שֶׁל יַיִן. בְּדִינָר זֶה שֶׁל כֶּסֶף וְנִמְצָא שֶׁל זָהָב. שֶׁל זָהָב וְנִמְצָא שֶׁל כֶּסֶף. עַל מְנָת שֶׁאֲנִי עָנִי וְנִמְצָא עָשִׁיר. עָשִׁיר וְנִמְצָא עָנִי. אֵינָהּ מְקוּדֶּשֶׁת. רַבִּי שִׁמְעוֹן אוֹמֵר. אִם הִטְעָהּ לְשֶׁבַח הֲרֵי זוֹ מְקוּדֶּשֶׁת.

Mishnah 2: "Be preliminarily married to me by this cup of wine," but it turned out to be honey; "of honey" but it turned out to be wine; "by this silver denar," but it turned out to be of gold, "gold denar" but it turned out to be of silver; "on condition that I be poor", but he turned out to be rich; "rich" but he turned out to be poor; she is not preliminarily married. Rebbi Simeon said, if he tricked her by understatement she is preliminarily married[109].

משנה ג: עַל מְנָת שֶׁאֲנִי כֹהֵן וְנִמְצָא לֵוִי. לֵוִי וְנִמְצָא כֹהֵן. נָתִין וְנִמְצָא מַמְזֵר. מַמְזֵר וְנִמְצָא נָתִין. בֶּן עִיר וְנִמְצָא בֶּן כָּרַךְ. בֶּן כְּרַךְ וְנִמְצָא בֶּן עִיר. עַל מְנָת שֶׁבֵּיתִי קָרוֹב לַמֶּרְחָץ וְנִמְצָא רָחוֹק רָחוֹק וְנִמְצָא קָרוֹב. עַל מְנָת שֶׁיֵּשׁ לִי בַת אוֹ שִׁפְחָה מְגוּדֶּלֶת וְאֵין לוֹ. עַל מְנָת שֶׁאֵין לִי וְיֵשׁ לוֹ. עַל מְנָת שֶׁאֵין לִי בָנִים וְיֵשׁ לוֹ. עַל מְנָת שֶׁיֵּשׁ לִי וְאֵין לוֹ. וְעַל כּוּלָּם אַף עַל פִּי שֶׁאָמְרָה בְּלִבִּי הָיְתָה לְהִתְקַדֵּשׁ לוֹ אַף עַל פִּי כֵן אֵינָהּ מְקוּדֶּשֶׁת. וְכֵן הִיא שֶׁהִיטְעַתּוּ.

Mishnah 3: "On condition that I be a Cohen," and he turned out to be a Levite; "a Levite" and he turned out to be a Cohen[110]; "a Gibeonite" and he turned out to be a bastard, "a bastard" and he turned out to be a Gibeonite[111]; "a villager[112]" and he turned out to be from a walled city; "from a walled city" and he turned out to be from a village; "on condition that my house be close to the public baths" and it turned out to be far, "far" and it turned out to be close; "on condition that I have a grown-up daughter or slave-girl[113]" and it turned out that he had none, "on condition that I have not" and it turned out that he did have; "on condition that I have children" and it turned out that he had none, "on condition that I not have children" and it turned out that he did have[114]. In all these cases she is not preliminarily married even if she says, I had the intention to be preliminarily married to him regardless. The same holds if she misinformed him.

109 If he gave a gold denar pretending it was of silver or pretended to be poor when he was rich.

110 A Cohen has many more rights than a Levite but a Cohen's wife is subject to many more restrictions than a Levite's.

111 For Gibeonites, cf. Chapter 4, Notes 48ff.; *Yebamot* 2:4, Note 72. Both Gibeonites and bastards (children of adulterous or incestual unions) are precluded from marrying in the congregation.

112 In rabbinic Hebrew, any unwalled place is called עִיר.

113 She can do the household chores. In some Mishnah mss. one reads גַדֶּלֶת, "hairdresser."

114 If the husband already has children, the second wife is not in danger of a levirate marriage. But the existence of children from a prior marriage may cause trouble.

(62c line 42) **הלכה ב:** הִתְקַדְּשִׁי לִי בְּכוֹס זֶה שֶׁלְּיַיִן כוּל'. בְּכוֹס זֶה. וּבַמֶּה שֶׁבְּתוֹכוֹ שָׁוֶה פְּרוּטָה מִתְקַדֶּשֶׁת. וְאִם לָאו אֵינָהּ מִתְקַדֶּשֶׁת. זְכֵה בּוֹ וּבַמֶּה שֶׁבְּתוֹכוֹ. אִם יֵשׁ בְּמַה שֶׁבְּתוֹכוֹ שָׁוֶה פְּרוּטָה מִתְקַדֶּשֶׁת וְאִם לָאו אֵינָהּ מִתְקַדֶּשֶׁת. לֹא זָכַת אֶלָּא בְּמַה שֶׁבְּתוֹכוֹ בִּלְבָד.

Halakhah 2: "Be preliminarily married to me by this cup of wine," etc. If this cup and its contents together have the value of a *peruṭah*, she is preliminarily married; otherwise she is not preliminarily married. "Acquire it and its contents," if its contents are worth a *peruṭah*, she is preliminarily married; otherwise she is not preliminarily married; she acquired only its contents[115].

115 This text seems to be elliptic. It probably should be understood following the text of Tosephta 2:3:

הִתְקַדְּשִׁי לִי בְּכוֹס זֶה. אִם יֵשׁ בּוֹ וּבְמָה שֶׁבְּתוֹכוֹ שָׁוֶה פְּרוּטָה מְקוּדֶּשֶׁת. וְאִם לָאו אֵינָהּ מְקוּדֶּשֶׁת. זָכַת בּוֹ וּבְמָה שֶׁבְּתוֹכוֹ. בְּמָה שֶׁיֵּשׁ בְּכוֹס זֶה. אִם יֵשׁ בְּמָה שֶׁבְּתוֹכוֹ שָׁוֶה פְּרוּטָה מְקוּדֶּשֶׁת וְאִם לָאו אֵינָהּ מִתְקַדֶּשֶׁת. וְלֹא זָכַת אֶלָּא בְּמָה שֶׁבְּתוֹכוֹ בִּלְבָד.

"Be preliminarily married to me by this cup of wine. *If it* and its contents together are worth a *perutah*, she is preliminarily married; otherwise she is not preliminarily married; *she acquired it and its contents*. "By its contents," if its contents are worth a perutah, she is preliminarily married; otherwise she is not preliminarily married; she acquired only its contents."

The Babli, 48b, notes that every statement has to interpreted in context. If the cup was filled with water, it is understood that the cup was given. If wine, only the contents are intended. If any fluid used as spice, not intended to be used immediately, both cup and contents are given.

(62c line 45) רִבִּי שִׁמְעוֹן אוֹמֵר. אִם הִטְעָהּ לַשֶּׁבַח מְקוּדֶּשֶׁת[116]. אָמַר רִבִּי יוֹחָנָן. מוֹדֶה רִבִּי שִׁמְעוֹן שֶׁאִם הִטְעָהּ לַשֶּׁבַח יְחָסִים אֵינָהּ מְקוּדֶּשֶׁת. אָמַר רִבִּי יוֹסֵה. מַתְנִיתָא אָמְרָה כֵן עַל מְנָת שֶׁאֲנִי כֹהֵן וְנִמְצָא לֵוִי.

"Rebbi Simeon said, if he tricked her by understatement she is preliminarily married." Rebbi Johanan said, Rebbi Simeon agrees that she is not preliminarily married if he tricked her by misstating his personal status[117]. Rebbi Yose said, the Mishnah says this: "'On condition that I be a Cohen,' and he turned out to be a Levite.[118]"

116 This shorter version is that of the Mishnah in the Babli.

117 In the Babli, 49a, and the Tosephta, 2:5, this is a tannaïtic statement.

118 R. Simeon disagrees only in Mishnah 2, about monetary affairs, not in Mishnah 3, in matters of personal status.

(62c line 48) נִיחָא כֹּהֵן וְנִמְצָא לֵוִי. לֵוִי וְנִמְצָא כֹהֵן. יְכוֹלָה הִיא מֵימַר. לָא הֲוֵינָא בְּעָיָיא דִי רוּחֵיהּ רַבָּא עֲלַי. בֶּן כָּרַךְ וְנִמְצָא בֶּן עִיר. בֶּן עִיר וְנִמְצָא בֶּן כָּרַךְ. יְכוֹלָה הִיא מֵימַר. בְּעָיָיא הֲוֵינָא מִצְטַנְּעָא. עַל מְנָת שֶׁבֵּיתִי קָרוֹב לַמֶּרְחָץ וְנִמְצָא רָחוֹק. נִיחָא קָרוֹב וְנִמְצָא רָחוֹק. רָחוֹק וְנִמְצָא קָרוֹב. יְכוֹלָה הִיא מֵימַר. בְּעָיָיא הֲוֵינָא מְטַרְפְּסָא אֲזָלָה מְטַרְפְּסָא אַתְיָיא. עַל מְנָת שֶׁיֵּשׁ לִי בַת אוֹ שִׁפְחָה גּוֹדֶלֶת. וְאֵין לוֹ. נִיחָא. עַל מְנָת שֶׁיֵּשׁ לִי. וְאֵין לוֹ. הַגַּע עַצְמָךְ שֶׁהָיָה לוֹ בְּסוֹף הָעוֹלָם. אָמַר רִבִּי בָּא בַּר מָמָל. כֵּינִי מַתְנִיתָא. בַּת לְגוּדְלָתֵיהּ וְשִׁפְחָה לְשַׁמָּשׁוּתֵיהּ.

One understands "Cohen and he turns out to be a Levite.[119]" "Levite and he turns out to be a Cohen[120]"? She may say, I do not want one who is haughty towards me[121]. One understands "from a walled city" and he turned out to be a villager; "from a village" and he turned out to be from a walled city? She may say, I want to be in a quiet place. "On condition that my house be close to the public baths" and it turned out to be far. One understands "close and it turned out to be far." "Far and it turned out to be close"? She can say, I want to take a walk[122] going and returning. "On condition that I have a daughter or slave-girl hairdresser" and it turned out that he had none, that one understands. "On condition that I have" and it turned out that he did not have? Think of it, if he had one at the end of the world[123]! Rebbi Abba bar Mamal said, so is the Mishnah: "A daughter to dress your hair, and a slave-girl to serve you.[124]"

119 If he is less than he represented himself to be, there is no reason to validate the marriage.

120 Why can we not assume that normally a woman will be glad to get a husband of higher social standing than he represented himself to be.

121 In the Babli, 49a, this argument is attributed to Ulla.

122 This translation is pure speculation. It does not seem that this טרפס is identical to טפס as asserted by

the dictionaries and commentators. In Arabic, طرف means "look through almost closed eyelids; put on many garments; be dark (night)". Perhaps cf. ظرف "to be beautiful".

123 What difference would it make to the woman?

124 The Babli, 49a, notes that while this looks like a monetary stipulation, it is one of personal service and R. Simeon is correct in not objecting.

(fol. 62a) **משנה ד:** הָאוֹמֵר לִשְׁלוּחוֹ צֵא וְקַדֵּשׁ לִי אִשָּׁה פְלוֹנִית בְּמָקוֹם פְּלוֹנִי וְהָלַךְ וְקִידְּשָׁהּ בְּמָקוֹם אַחֵר אֵינָהּ מְקוּדֶּשֶׁת. הֲרֵי הִיא בְמָקוֹם פְּלוֹנִי וְקִידְּשָׁהּ בְּמָקוֹם אַחֵר הֲרֵי זוֹ מְקוּדֶּשֶׁת.

Mishnah 4: Somebody said to his agent: "Go and marry me preliminarily to woman X at place Y"; if he went and married him preliminarily at another place, she is not preliminarily married. "She is at place Y;" if he married him preliminarily at another place, she is preliminarily married[125].

125 The geographical information is not part of the instruction of agency but an indication where the agent may discharge his commission.

(62c line 56) **הלכה ד:** הָאוֹמֵר לִשְׁלוּחוֹ צֵא וְקַדֵּשׁ לִי אִשָּׁה פְלוֹנִית כול׳. מַתְנִיתָא דְּלָא כְרִבִּי לְעָזָר. בְּרַם כְּרִבִּי לְעָזָר לְעוֹלָם הִיא מְקוּדֶּשֶׁת עַד שֶׁיֹּאמַר לוֹ. אַל תַּקְדִּישֶׁינָּהּ לִי אֶלָּא בְּמָקוֹם פְּלוֹנִי. וְהָלַךְ וְקִידְּשָׁהּ בְּמָקוֹם אַחֵר.

Halakhah 4: "Somebody said to his agent: "Go and marry me preliminarily to woman X," etc. The Mishnah does not follow Rebbi Eleazar[126]. But following Rebbi Eleazar she is preliminarily married unless [the husband] tells [the agent]: Do not preliminarily marry me to her except at place X[84] and he went and executed the preliminary marriage at another place.

הֲרֵי זוֹ מְקוּדֶּשֶׁת. אוֹף רִבִּי לֶעְזָר מוֹדֶה בָהּ. שֶׁאֵינוֹ אֶלָּא כְּמַרְאֶה לָהּ מָקוֹם. אוֹף רַבָּנִין מוֹדֵיי בָהּ. שֶׁאֵינוֹ אֶלָּא כְּמַרְאֶה לָהּ מָקוֹם.

"She is preliminarily married," Rebbi Eleazar agrees that he only indicates a place; the rabbis agree that he only indicates a place[127].

126 Both paragraphs parallel *Gittin* 6:4, Notes 83-84. The statement of the Tanna R. Eleazar is in Mishnah *Gittin* 6:5.

127 The Babli agrees, 59a.

(fol. 62a) **משנה ה:** הַמְקַדֵּשׁ אֶת הָאִשָּׁה עַל מְנָת שֶׁאֵין עָלֶיהָ נְדָרִים וְנִמְצְאוּ עָלֶיהָ נְדָרִים אֵינָהּ מְקוּדֶּשֶׁת. כְּנָסָהּ סְתָם וְנִמְצְאוּ עָלֶיהָ נְדָרִים תֵּצֵא שֶׁלֹּא בִכְתוּבָה. שֶׁכָּל־הַמּוּמִין הַפּוֹסְלִין בַּכֹּהֲנִים פּוֹסְלִין בַּנָּשִׁים.

Mishnah 5: If somebody performed preliminary marriage with a woman on condition that she had no obligation of vows on her and it turns out that she had vows to fulfill, she is not preliminarily married. If he married her definitively without inquiry and she had vows to fulfill, she should leave without *ketubah*. For all defects which disqualify a priest disqualify a woman[128].

128 This Mishnah is severely truncated. It is identical to Mishnah *Ketubot* 7:8 (Notes 101-105). The missing part, which explains the last sentence, reads: "If somebody performed preliminary marriage with a woman on condition that she had no bodily defects and it turned out that she did have bodily defects, she is not preliminarily married. If he married

her definitively without inquiry and she had bodily defects, she should leave without *ketubah*." The following Halakhah is from *Ketubot* 7:9, Notes 110-143. The minor differences in readings are noted there.

(62c line 60) **הלכה ה**: הַמְקַדֵּשׁ אֶת הָאִשָּׁה כול'. תַּנִּינָן מוּמִין. בְּאֵילוּ נְדָרִים אָמְרוּ. רִבִּי יוֹחָנָן בְּשֵׁם רִבִּי שִׁמְעוֹן בֶּן יוֹצָדָק. נָדְרָה שֶׁלֹּא לוֹכַל בָּשָׂר וְשֶׁלֹּא לִשְׁתּוֹת יַיִן וְשֶׁלֹּא לִלְבּוֹשׁ בִּגְדֵי צִבְעוֹנִין. אָמַר רִבִּי זְעִירָא. כְּלֵי פִשְׁתָּן הַדַּקִּים הַבָּאִין מִבֵּית שְׁאָן כִּכְלֵי צְבוּעִין הֵן. אָמַר רִבִּי יוֹסֵי. מַתְנִיתָא בְּשֶׁאָמַר לָהּ. עַל מְנָת שֶׁאֵין עָלַיִךְ נְדָרִים. אֲבָל אִם אָמַר לָהּ. עַל מְנָת שֶׁאֵין לִיךְ נֶדֶר. אֲפִילוּ נָדְרָה שֶׁלֹּא לֶאֱכוֹל חָרוּבִין נֶדֶר הוּא.

Halakhah 5: "If somebody performed preliminary marriage with a woman etc. We have stated defects. Which vows? Rebbi Johanan in the name of Rebbi Simeon ben Yosadaq: If she vowed not to eat meat, or not to drink wine, or not to wear dyed garments. Rebbi Ze'ira said, the fine linen garments which come from Bet She'an have the status of dyed garments. Rebbi Yose said, the Mishnah deals with the case that he said to her, "on condition that you have no obligation of vows on you." But if he said to her, "on condition that you have no vow on you," then even if she made a vow not to eat carob fruit it is a vow.

(62c line 66) הָלְכָה אֵצֶל הַזָּקֵן וְהִתִּיר לָהּ הֲרֵי זוֹ מְקוּדֶּשֶׁת. אֵצֶל הָרוֹפֵא וְרִיפְּאָהּ אֵינָהּ מְקוּדֶּשֶׁת. מַה בֵּין זָקֵן וּמַה בֵּין רוֹפֵא. זָקֵן עוֹקֵר אֶת הַנֶּדֶר מֵעִיקָּרוֹ. רוֹפֵא אֵינוֹ מְרַפֵּא אֶלָּא מִיכָּן וּלְהַבָּא. אִית תַּנָּיֵי תַנֵי. אֲפִילוּ הָלְכָה אֵצֶל הַזָּקֵן וְהִתִּיר לָהּ אֵינָהּ מְקוּדֶּשֶׁת. מַתְנִיתָא דְּרִבִּי לֶעְזָר. אָמַר רִבִּי לֶעְזָר. בְּדִין הָיָה אֲפִילוּ נֶדֶר שֶׁהוּא צָרִיךְ חָכָם שֶׁהַזָּקֵן עוֹקֵר הַנֶּדֶר מֵעִיקָּרוֹ. וְלָמָּה אָסְרוּ נֶדֶר שֶׁהוּא צָרִיךְ חֲקִירַת חָכָם. מִפְּנֵי נֶדֶר שֶׁאֵינוֹ צָרִיךְ חֲקִירַת חָכָם. אִית תַּנָּיֵי תַנֵּי. מוּתֶּרֶת לְהִינָּשֵׂא בְלֹא גֵט. וְאִית תַּנָּיֵי תַנֵּי. אֲסוּרָה לְהִינָּשֵׂא בְלֹא

גט. הֲוֹון בָּעֵיי מֵימַר. מָאן דָּמַר. מוּתֶּרֶת לְהִינָּשֵׂא בְלֹא גֵט. רִבִּי לְעָזָר. וּמָאן דָּמַר. אֲסוּרָה לְהִינָּשֵׂא בְלֹא גֵט. רַבָּנִין. כּוּלָּהּ רַבָּנִין. מָאן דְּאָמַר. אֲסוּרָה לְהִינָּשֵׂא בְלֹא גֵט. רַבָּנִין. מָאן דְּאָמַר. מוּתֶּרֶת לְהִינָּשֵׂא בְלֹא גֵט. שֶׁמִּתּוֹךְ שֶׁהִיא יוֹדַעַת שֶׁאִם הוֹלֶכֶת הִיא אֵצֶל הַזָּקֵן וְהוּא מַתִּיר לָהּ אֶת נִדְרָהּ וְהִיא אֵינָהּ הוֹלֶכֶת. לְפוּם כֵּן מוּתֶּרֶת לְהִינָּשֵׂא בְלֹא גֵט. מַאי טַעֲמָא דְמָאן דָּמַר. אֲסוּרָה לְהִינָּשֵׂא בְלֹא גֵט. שֶׁלֹּא תֵלֵךְ אֵצֶל הַזָּקֵן וְיַתִּיר לָהּ אֶת נִדְרָהּ וְקִידּוּשִׁין חָלִין עָלֶיהָ לְמַפְרֵעַ וְנִמְצְאוּ בָנֶיהָ בָּאִין לִידֵי מַמְזֵירוּת. לְפוּם כֵּן אֲסוּרָה לְהִינָּשֵׂא בְלֹא גֵט.

"If she went to an Elder and he dissolved her vow, she is preliminarily married. To a doctor and he healed her, she is not preliminarily married." What is the difference between the Elder and the doctor? The Elder uproots the vow from its start; the doctor heals only for the future. Some Tannaïm state: Even if she went to an Elder and he dissolved her vow, she is not preliminarily married. The *baraita* follows Rebbi Eleazar, as we have stated there: "Rebbi Eleazar said, it would have been logical about a vow which has to be investigated by a Sage, because the Elder uproots the vow from its start. Why did they forbid a vow which has to be investigated by a Sage? Because of a vow which does not have to be investigated by a Sage. Some Tannaïm state: She is allowed to marry without a bill of divorce. Some Tannaïm state: She is forbidden to marry without a bill of divorce. They wanted to say that he who says, she is allowed to marry without a bill of divorce is Rebbi Eleazar, and he who says, she is forbidden to marry without a bill of divorce are the rabbis. Everything follows the rabbis. He who says, she is forbidden to marry without a bill of divorce, the rabbis. He who says, she is allowed to marry without a bill of divorce: Since she knows that if she went to an Elder, he would dissolve her vow, since she does not go therefore she can be married without a bill of divorce. What is the reason of him who says, she is forbidden to marry without a bill of divorce, that she should not go to an Elder who would dissolve her vow, then the preliminary marriage would become retroactively valid for her and it would turn out that her children became bastards. Therefore she is forbidden to marry without a bill of divorce.

(62d line 6) כְּנָסָהּ סְתָם. רַבִּי שִׁמְעוֹן בֶּן לָקִישׁ אָמַר. מַתְנִיתָא בְּשֶׁקִּידְּשָׁהּ עַל תְּנַאי וּכְנָסָהּ סְתָם. אֲבָל אִם קִידְּשָׁהּ סְתָם וּכְנָסָהּ סְתָם יֵשׁ לָהּ כְּתוּבָּה. רַבִּי יוֹחָנָן אָמַר. אֲפִילוּ קִידְּשָׁהּ סְתָם וּכְנָסָהּ סְתָם אֵין לָהּ כְּתוּבָּה. וְאָמַר רַבִּי חִייָה בְּשֵׁם רַבִּי יוֹחָנָן. וּצְרִיכָה מִמֶּנּוּ גֵט אֲפִילוּ קִידְּשָׁהּ עַל תְּנַאי וּכְנָסָהּ עַל תְּנַאי. רַבִּי זְעוּרָא בָּעָא קוֹמֵי רַבִּי מָנָא. קִידְּשָׁהּ סְתָם וְגֵירְשָׁהּ מִן הָאֵירוּסִין מָה אָמַר בָּהּ רַבִּי שִׁמְעוֹן בֶּן לָקִישׁ. נִישְׁמְעִינָהּ מִן הָדָא. הָיוּ בָהּ מוּמִין וְעוֹדָהּ בְּבֵית אָבִיהָ הָאָב צָרִיךְ לְהָבִיא רְאָיָיה. הָא אִם הֵבִיא רְאָיָיה יֵשׁ לָהּ כְּתוּבָּה. מַה חֲמִית לְמֵימַר. בְּשֶׁקִּידְּשָׁהּ סְתָם וְגִירְשָׁהּ מִן הָאֵירוּסִין. מָה אֲנָן קַייָמִין מִן דְּבַתְרָהּ. בַּמֶּה דְּבָרִים אֲמוּרִים. בְּמוּמִין שֶׁבַּסֵּתֶר. אֲבָל בְּמוּמִי' שֶׁבַּגָּלוּי אֵינוֹ יָכוֹל לִטְעוֹן. וְאִים בְּמַתְנָה אַף בְּמוּמִין שֶׁבַּגָּלוּי טוֹעֵן הוּא. אָמְרִין חַבְרַייָא קוֹמֵי רַבִּי יוֹסֵה. אֱמוֹר דְּבַתְרָהּ וּתְהֵא פְּלִיגָא עַל רַבִּי שִׁמְעוֹן בֶּן לָקִישׁ. נִכְנְסָה לִרְשׁוּת הַבַּעַל הַבַּעַל צָרִיךְ לְהָבִיא רְאָיָיה. הָא אִם הֵבִיא הַבַּעַל רְאָיָיה אֵין לָהּ כְּתוּבָּה. וְהֵיךְ רַבִּי שִׁמְעוֹן בֶּן לָקִישׁ אָמַר. יֵשׁ לָהּ כְּתוּבָּה. רַבִּי לֹהֵן בְּשֵׁם רַבָּנִין דְּקֵיסָרִין. מַתְנִיתָא בְּשֶׁקָּנַס וְלֹא בָעַל. מַה דְּאָמַר רַבִּי שִׁמְעוֹן בֶּן לָקִישׁ בְּשֶׁכָּנַס וּבָעַל. אֲנִי אוֹמֵר. נִתְרַצָּה לוֹ בִּבְעִילָה.

"If he married her definitively without inquiry". Rebbi Simeon ben Laqish said, the Mishnah deals with the case that he married her preliminarily conditionally but definitively silently. But if he married her preliminarily silently and definitively silently, she can claim her *ketubah*. Rebbi Johanan said, even if he married her preliminarily silently and definitively silently, she has no *ketubah*. Rebbi Hiyya in the name of Rebbi Johanan: But she needs a bill of divorce from him even if he married her preliminarily conditionally but definitively silently. Rebbi Ze'ira asked before Rebbi Mana: In case he married her preliminarily silently and divorced her after the preliminary marriage, what does Rebbi Simeon ben Laqish say? Let us hear from the following: "If she had bodily defects, as long as she is in her father's house, the father has to prove." This implies that if he proved his case, she can claim her *ketubah*. What do you see to say, if he married her preliminarily silently and divorced her after the preliminary marriage! Where do we hold? Since afterwards [it is stated]: "When was this said? For hidden defects, but he has no claim about visible defects." If he. made it conditional, could he not also claim for visible ones? But did not the colleagues say before Rebbi Yose: Should we say that the following statement disagrees with Rebbi Simeon ben Laqish? "Once she entered her husband's domain, the husband has to prove." This implies that if the husband proved his case, she has no claim to *ketubah*. But by the statement of Rebbi Simeon ben Laqish, she has a claim to *ketubah*. Rebbi Cohen in the name of the rabbis of Caesarea: The Mishnah deals with the case that he definitively married her but did not sleep with her; Rebbi Simeon ben Laqish speaks about the case that he definitively married her and slept with her; I am saying that she was acceptable to him since he took her to bed.

(62d line 20) שֶׁכָּל־הַמּוּמִין הַפּוֹסְלִים בַּכֹּהֲנִים פּוֹסְלִין בַּנָּשִׁים. הוֹסִיפוּ עֲלֵיהֶן בָּאִשָּׁה רֵיחַ הַפֶּה וְרֵיחַ הַזִּיעָא שׁוּמָא שֶׁאֵין בָּהּ שֵׂיעָר. רִבִּי חָמָא בַּר עוּקְבָא בְשֵׁם רִבִּי יוֹסֵי בֶּן חֲנִינָה. בְּעוֹר הַפָּנִים שָׁנוּ. וְהָתַנִּינָן. בַּמֶּה דְבָרִים אֲמוּרִים. בְּמוּמִין שֶׁבַּסֵּתֶר. אֲבָל בְּמוּמִין שֶׁבַּגָּלוּי אֵינוֹ יָכוֹל לִטְעוֹן. וְזוֹ לֹא מִן הַמּוּמִין שֶׁבַּגָּלוּי הוּא. תִּיפְתָּר בְּהַהִיא דְמִטַּמְרָה לָהּ תַּחַת קֶלְסִיתָהּ דְרֹאשָׁהּ. תַּנֵּי. שׁוּמָא שֶׁיֵּשׁ לָהּ שֵׂיעָר בֵּין גְּדוֹלָה בֵּין קְטַנָּה בֵּין בַּגּוּף בֵּין בַּפָּנִים הֲרֵי זֶה מוּם. וְשֶׁאֵין בָּהּ שֵׂיעָר. בַּפָּנִים מוּם. בַּגּוּף אֵינוֹ מוּם. בַּמֶּה דְבָרִים אֲמוּרִים. בִּקְטַנָּה. אֲבָל בִּגְדוֹלָה בֵּין בַּגּוּף בֵּין בַּפָּנִים הֲרֵי זֶה מוּם. עַד כַּמָּה הִיא גְדוֹלָה. רַבָּן שִׁמְעוֹן בֶּן גַּמְלִיאֵל אוֹמֵר. עַד כְּאִיסָּר הָאִיטַלְקִי. רִבִּי לְעָזָר בְּשֵׁם רִבִּי חֲנִינָה. כְּגוֹן הָדֵין דֵּינָרָא קוּרְדִּייָנָא שִׁיעוּרוֹ כַחֲצִי זָהוֹב כָּל־שֶׁהוּא. רִבִּי רְדִיפָה רִבִּי יוֹנָה רִבִּי יִרְמְיָה שָׁאַל. אִשָּׁה קָרַחַת וְשִׁיטָה שֶׁלְּשֵׂיעָר מַקֶּפֶת מֵאוֹזֶן לָאוֹזֶן. בָּעֵי מִישְׁמַעִינָהּ מִן הָדָא. הוֹסִיפוּ עֲלֵיהֶן בָּאִשָּׁה רֵיחַ הַפֶּה וְרֵיחַ הַזִּיעָא וְשׁוּמָא שֶׁאֵין בָּהּ שֵׂיעָר. וְלֹא אַדְכְּרוֹן קָרְחָה. סָבְרִין מֵימַר שֶׁאֵינוֹ מוּם. אֲתָא רִבִּי שְׁמוּאֵל בְּרֵיהּ דְּרִבִּי יוֹסֵי בֵּירִבִּי בּוּן בְּשֵׁם רִבִּי נִיסָא. מוּם הוּא. לָא אֲתִינַן מִיתְנֵי אֶלָּא דָּבָר שֶׁהוּא כְעוּר בָּזֶה וּבָזֶה מוּם בָּזֶה וְאֵין מוּם בָּזֶה. אֲבָל דָּבָר שֶׁהוּא נוֹי בָּזֶה וּמוּם בָּזֶה כְּגוֹן הָדָא קָרַחְתָּא אַף עַל גַּב דְּהוּא מוּם לֹא תַנִּינָתָהּ. תֵּדַע לָךְ שֶׁהִיא כֵן. הֲרֵי זָקָן הֲרֵי נוֹי בָּאִישׁ וּמוּם בָּאִשָּׁה. וְלֹא תַנִּינָן. יֵתֵר עֲלֵיהֶן בָּאִשָּׁה זָקָן. הֲרֵי דַדִּים הֲרֵי נוֹי בָּאִשָּׁה וּמוּם בָּאִישׁ. וְלֹא תַנִּינָן. יֵתֵר עֲלֵיהֶן בָּאִישׁ דַּדִּים.

"And all defects which disqualify a priest disqualify a woman. They added to them for women mouth odor, sweat odor, and a hairless mole." Rebbi Ḥamai bar Uqba in the name of Rebbi Yose ben Ḥanina: They taught this about the skin of the face. But did we not state: "When was this said? For hidden defects, but he has no claim about visible defects." Is this not of the visible defects? Explain it if she hid it under her headgear. It was stated: "A mole with hairs is a defect, whether it be large or small, whether it be on the body or on the face. Without a hair it is a defect on the face but not on the body. When has this been said? If it is small. But if it is large, it is a defect whether it be on the body or on the face. How big is large? Rabban Simeon ben Gamliel says, up to an Italic *as*." Rebbi Eleazar bar Ḥanina said, for example such a Gordianic denar: its measure is half a ubiquitous gold piece. Rebbi Radifa, Rebbi Jonah: Rebbi Jeremiah asked: A bald woman with a row of hair going from one ear to the other? They wanted to understand it from the following: "They added to them for women mouth odor, sweat odor, and a hairless mole." They did not mention baldness. They wanted to conclude that it is not a defect. There came Rebbi Samuel the son of Rebbi Yose ben Rebbi Abun: Rebbi Nasa said, it is a defect. It is listed only if it is ugly for both sexes. But something which is beautiful in one sex but ugly in the other, like a bald pate, even though it is a defect it was not listed. You should know that this is so because a beard is beautiful for a man and a defect for a woman, and we did not state: In addition, for a woman a beard. There are breasts which are beautiful for a woman and a defect for men, and we did not state: In addition, for a man women's breasts.

(fol. 62a) **משנה ו**: הַמְקַדֵּשׁ שְׁתֵּי נָשִׁים בְּשָׁוֶה פְרוּטָה אוֹ אִשָּׁה אַחַת בְּפָחוֹת מִשָּׁוֶה פְרוּטָה אַף עַל פִּי שֶׁשִּׁילַּח סִבְלוֹנוֹת לְאַחַר מִכֵּן אֵינָהּ מְקוּדֶּשֶׁת שֶׁמַּחֲמַת קִידּוּשִׁין הָרִאשׁוֹנִים שִׁילַּח. וְכֵן קָטָן שֶׁקִּידֵּשׁ.

Mishnah 6: Somebody who preliminarily marries two women with the value of a *peruṭah*, or one woman with the value of half a *peruṭah*[129], is not preliminarily married even if afterwards he sent presents[130], since he sent them based on the earlier preliminary marriage. The same holds for an underage boy who contracted a preliminary marriage[131].

129 Even though it is possible to contract a multiple polygamous marriage with a group of women by giving the marriage gift to one of them who acts as the agent for all of them, the gift must be worth as many *perutot* as there are women to be married.

130 Worth much more than a *peruṭah*.

131 If he contracts the preliminary marriage when underage and sends presents to the woman after he came of age he is not preliminarily married.

(62d line 39) **הלכה ו׃** הַמְקַדֵּשׁ שְׁתֵּי נָשִׁים בְּשָׁוֶה פְּרוּטָה כול׳. תַּנֵּי. וְכוּלָּן שֶׁבָּעֲלוּ קָנוּ. רִבִּי שִׁמְעוֹן וְרִבִּי יְהוּדָה אוֹמֵר מִשּׁוּם רִבִּי שִׁמְעוֹן. וְכוּלָּן שֶׁבָּעֲלוּ קָנוּ. שֶׁלֹּא הָיְתָה בְעִילָתוֹ אֶלָּא לְשׁוּם קִידּוּשִׁין הָרִאשׁוֹנִים. אִם קָנוּ. רִבִּי חִייָה בְשֵׁם רִבִּי יוֹחָנָן. קָנוּ לַחוֹמְרִין. רִבִּי חִייָה בְשֵׁם רִבִּי יוֹחָנָן. כָּל־תַּנָּיֵי שֶׁהוּא מַעֲשֶׂה מִתְּחִילָּתוֹ מְקוּדֶּשֶׁת לַחוֹמְרִין. רִבִּי מָנָא בְעָא קוֹמֵי דְרִבִּי יוּדָן. מָאן תַּנָּא. כָּל־תַּנַּאי שֶׁהוּא מַעֲשֶׂה מִתְּחִילָּתוֹ תְּנָייוֹ בָטֵל. דְּלֹא כְרִבִּי שִׁמְעוֹן. רִבִּי יוּדָן בְּשֵׁם רִבִּי יוֹחָנָן. מְקוּדֶּשֶׁת לַחוֹמְרִין. הֵיךְ עֲבִידָא. הֲרֵי אֲנִי מְקַדְּשָׁךְ בִּבְעִילָה עַל מְנָת שֶׁיֵּרְדוּ גְשָׁמִים. יָרְדוּ גְשָׁמִים מְקוּדֶּשֶׁת. וְאִם לָאו אֵינָהּ מְקוּדֶּשֶׁת. רִבִּי חִייָה בְשֵׁם רִבִּי יוֹחָנָן. בְּקִידּוּשֵׁי מִלְוָה לַחוֹמְרִין וּבְקַרְקָעוֹת לֹא קָנָה וּבְמִטַּלְטְלִין אֵין מוֹסְרִין אוֹתוֹ לְמִי שֶׁפָּרַע. בִּיקֵּשׁ לְהַעֲמִיד לוֹ מִקָּחוֹ. נִשְׁמְעִינָהּ מִן הָדָא. וַהֲרֵי לָךְ אֶצְלִי בָהֶן יַיִן. וְיַיִן אֵין לוֹ. הָא אִם יֵשׁ לוֹ יַיִן הֲרֵי זֶה חַייָב. תַּנֵּי רִבִּי חִייָה. אִם יֵשׁ לוֹ יַיִן חַייָב לִיתֵּן לוֹ. רִבִּי שְׁמוּאֵל בַּר רַב יִצְחָק שָׁלֹא אָמַר לְהַמּוֹ. הֲווֹן יָדְעִין דְּהוֹרֵי רִבִּי חִייָה בְשֵׁכ רִבִּי יוֹחָנָן. קִידּוּשֵׁי מִלְוָה לַחוֹמְרִין. וּבְאִישׁ לְרִבִּי זְעִירָא. לָמָּה. בְּגִין דַּהֲווֹן מַחְמְרִין וְקָלִיל עֲלֵיהוֹן. אָמַר רִבִּי יוֹסֵה בֵּירִבִּי בּוּן. בְּקוּלָּא הֲווֹן נְהִיגִין וְאַחְמַר עֲלֵיהוֹן. שֶׁאִם בָּא אַחֵר וְקִידְּשָׁהּ תָּפְסוּ בָהּ קִידּוּשִׁין. אָמַר רִבִּי יוּדָן בֵּירִבִּי חָנָן. עֶרְוָה שֶׁאֵינָהּ עֶרְוָה. תּוֹפֵס אֶת שֶׁאֵינָהּ עֶרְוָה.

Halakhah 6: "If somebody preliminarily marries two women with the value of a *peruṭah*," etc. It was stated[132]: "In all these cases, if they had intercourse they acquired[133]. Rebbi Simeon [ben][134] Jehudah says in the name of Rebbi Simeon: In all these cases, if they had intercourse they did acquire[135] since his intercourse was predicated on the preceding preliminary marriage.[136]" What did they acquire[137]? Rebbi Hiyya in the name of Rebbi Johanan: They acquired for restrictions[138]. Rebbi Hiyya in the name of Rebbi Johanan: With any condition which refers to a preceding action[139], she is preliminarily married for restrictions. Rebbi Mana asked before Rebbi Yudan: Who is the Tanna who stated: "Any condition which refers to a preceding action is invalid"[140]? This does not follow Rebbi Simeon[141]. Rebbi Yudan in the name of Rebbi Johanan: She is preliminarily married for restrictions. How is that: "I am marrying you preliminarily by intercourse on condition that rains should fall.[142]" If rain fell, she is preliminarily married, otherwise she is not preliminarily married. Rebbi Hiyya in the name of Rebbi Johanan: In matters of a preliminary marriage by a loan[143] for restrictions, for real estate it was not acquired[144], for movables one does not deliver him to "Him Who exacted retribution.[145]" If [the buyer] insists on the deal? Let us hear from the following: "You have wine to get from me, when he had no wine.[146]" Therefore, if he had wine he would be obligated to deliver. Rebbi Hiyya stated, if he has wine he is obligated to deliver. Rebbi Samuel ben Rav Isaac did (not)[147] say there[148]: You should know that Rebbi Hiyya instructed following Rebbi Johanan that a preliminary marriage by a loan is for restrictions. Rebbi Ze'ira resented it. Why? Because they were restrictive in practice and he taught them leniency[149]?

Rebbi Yose ben Rebbi Abun said, they were lenient in practice[150] and he taught them to be restrictive, that if another man came and married her preliminarily, his marriage would hold. Rebbi Yudan ben Rebbi Ḥanan said, if there is a doubt between adultery and no adultery, decide on no adultery[151].

132 Tosephta 4:4; Babli *Ketubot* 73b.

133 The invalid marriage was validated retroactively by the couple living together.

134 Reading of the parallel sources. The ms. tradition of the names in the mss. of the Babli is varied and quite uncertain.

135 In the Babylonian sources (Note 132): Did not acquire. Probably the text here should not be emended.

136 Since preliminary marriage is a formal act of acquisition, it needs intention of the acquirer. If there is no intention because the acquirer wrongly thought that he already had acquired, there is no acquisition. This is the reasoning behind the Babylonian statements.

137 Since the argument of R. Simeon is based on generally accepted principles, it is difficult to see what he understands by "acquiring".

138 A single woman can be married to any man not forbidden to her by incest prohibitions. A married woman cannot be married by any other man; if another man gives her a gift for preliminary marriage and she accepts it, these actions have no consequence whatsoever in law. But a woman preliminarily married for restrictions is not married in this sense. As explained later in the Halakhah, if another man performs preliminary marriage with her, his action is potentially valid in law; the woman is forbidden to both men until at least one of them validly divorces her. But for the anonymous Tanna the marriage is unconditionally validated by intercourse.

139 If the preliminary marriage was performed unconditionally and then the husband added a condition, that condition is invalid, as stated later. But in marriage law, the condition is considered valid if it causes any trouble.

140 Mishnah *Baba mesi'a* 7:14. In contract law, an action already completed cannot retroactively be made conditional. If someone married

a woman and after the fact declares that the marriage shall be valid only if she will support him, the marriage is valid but she has no obligation to support her husband.

141 Since (Note 139) he accepts legal consequences of conditions attached after the act.

142 One has to wonder why this marriage should not be invalidated as an idolatrous act or at least as rainmaking by sympathetic magic.

143 Which is invalid for R. Meïr, cf. Note 62. It is decided here that a preliminary marriage for which nothing of value changes hands is valid only as a restriction (Note 138).

144 If a debt be liquidated by handing over real estate without a contract, the deal is invalid.

145 Cf. Chapter 1, Note 106. A contract for sale of movables for which no money changes hands and no action of acquisition is performed is unenforceable. (The entire statement with slight variations is quoted in *Sefer Ha'ittur* 1, לח b, Note 6.)

146 This refers to Mishnah *Baba meṣi'a* 5:1: A person made a contract for later delivery of grain at the then going rate of 25 denars a *kur* (30 *se'ah*). The buyer demanded delivery when the going rate was 30 denars a *kur*, in order to sell the grain and invest the proceeds in wine. The seller told him that he was ready to take the grain at 30 denars and to give him wine instead. If the seller actually has the wine, this is a valid deal. But if the seller has no wine at that moment, the deal would be an illegal circumvention of the prohibition of interest payments.

147 It seems best to delete this word. The emendation of the standard commentaries, to read שלח for שלא does not make sense since שלח אמר "he sent (by letter) said (in person)" is a contradiction in terms.

148 "There" usually refers to Babylonia.

149 They considered preliminary marriage by cancellation of a debt as invalid. R. Samuel ben Rav Isaac gave them a handle to validate the marriage.

150 They considered preliminary marriage by cancellation of a debt as valid. R. Samuel ben Rav Isaac instructed them to consider the marriage only probationary; if another man interferred between preliminary and definitive marriages, a bill of divorce would be required from at least one of the men involved.

151 This is the same statement as the preceding. In a case where it is doubtful whether a woman is married

and therefore immune to all proposals of marriage by another man, or is not married and open to such proposals, one has to decide that she might be open to proposals and eventually require bills of divorce from all parties involved.

(fcl. 62a) **משנה ז**: הַמְקַדֵּשׁ אִשָּׁה וּבִתָּהּ אוֹ אִשָּׁה וַאֲחוֹתָהּ כְּאַחַת אֵינָן מְקוּדָּשׁוֹת. וּמַעֲשֶׂה בְחָמֵשׁ נָשִׁים וּבָהֶן שְׁתֵּי אֲחָיוֹת וְלִיקֵּט אֶחָד כַּלְכָּלָה שֶׁל תְּאֵינִים מִשֶּׁלָּהֶן הָיְתָה וְשֶׁל שְׁבִיעִית הָיְתָה וְאָמַר הֲרֵי כוּלְּכֶם מְקוּדָּשׁוֹת לִי בְּכַלְכָּלָה זוֹ וְקִיבְּלָתָהּ אַחַת מֵהֶן עַל יְדֵי כּוּלָּם וְאָמְרוּ חֲכָמִים אֵין הָאֲחָיוֹת מְקוּדָּשׁוֹת.

Mishnah 7: If somebody preliminarily marries a woman and her daughter[152] or two sisters[153] simultaneously[153], they are not preliminarily married[154]. It happened to five women, among them two sisters, that a man collected a bag of figs from their own property in the Sabbatical year and said: All of you are preliminarily married to me by this bag, and one of them accepted for all of them. Then the Sages said, the sisters are not preliminarily married[156].

152 Forbidden in *Lev.* 18:17.
153 Forbidden in *Lev.* 18:18.
154 If the action was not simultaneous, the first marriage would be valid and the second meaningless because impossible.
155 Since the simultaneous marriage to two closely related women is impossible, it is invalid, and the two women may marry other men without bills of divorce.
156 The invalidity of the act for the two sisters has no influence on the validity for the others. Naturally the woman who acts as recipient cannot be one of the sisters.

(62d line 56) **הלכה ז**: הַמְקַדֵּשׁ אִשָּׁה וּבִתָּהּ כול'. אָמַר רִבִּי חִייָה בַּר בָּא. אַתְּ שְׁמַע מִינָהּ חָמֵשׁ. אַתְּ שְׁמַע מִינָהּ שֶׁחָמֵשׁ נָשִׁים מִתְקַדְּשׁוֹת כְּאַחַת. שֶׁהָאִשָּׁה מְקַבֶּלֶת קִידּוּשֶׁיהָ וְקִידּוּשֵׁי חֲבֵירָתָהּ. וּמְקַדְּשִׁין בִּגְזֵילָה. וּמְקַדְּשִׁין בְּפֵירוֹת עֲבֵירָה. וְאֵין קִידּוּשִׁין תּוֹפְסִין בָּעֲרָיוֹת.

Halakhah 7: "If somebody preliminarily marries a woman and her daughter," etc. Rebbi Ḥiyya bar Abba said, one understands from this five rules: One understands that five women can be preliminarily married simultaneously. That a woman may receive her own wedding gift and that of her companion. And one may use the spoils of robbery for a preliminary marriage[157]. And one may preliminarily marry using produce acquired by a prohibited act[158]. And preliminary marriage is impossible in incest situations.

---

157 Since the Mishnah stated that the figs were the property of the women being married. It also states that this happened in a Sabbatical year. Since the produce of a Sabbatical year is ownerless, the Mishnah seems to contradict itself. One will have to explain that the women collected the figs and acquired them by the act of collection. Then the man came and took them away from them. The Mishnah only implies that a woman may be preliminarily married by objects robbed from herself since by accepting marriage she forgives the robber. It does not imply that objects obtained by robbery can be used to marry an uninvolved woman.

The Babli, 52a, comes to an opposite conclusion. It assumes that the figs grew in the women's orchard and were collected as ownerless produce by the man. Then the conclusion is that in any other year the marriage would have been invalid, even involving the owners of the robbed object.

158 Sabbatical produce can only be used to be eaten under the rules of the Sabbatical. Using such produce for an act of acquisition is illicit. Nevertheless, the act remains valid.

(62d line 59) אָמַר רִבִּי לֶעְזָר. בָּאֲחָיוֹת לֹא קִידֵּשׁ וּבַחַטָּאוֹת כִּיפֵּר. הֵיךְ עֲבִידָא. שָׁחַט שְׁתֵּי חַטָּאוֹת לְשֵׁם חֵטְא אֶחָד הַמִּזְבֵּחַ בּוֹרֵר אֶת הָרָאוּי לוֹ. שְׁתֵּיהֶן אֲסוּרוֹת בַּאֲכִילָה. שָׁחַט שְׁנֵי אֲשָׁמוֹת לְשֵׁם אָשָׁם אֶחָד הַמִּזְבֵּחַ בּוֹרֵר אֶת הָרָאוּי לוֹ. שְׁנֵיהֶן אֲסוּרִין בַּאֲכִילָה. רִבִּי זְעִירָא בְּשֵׁם רִבִּי יוֹחָנָן. שָׁחַט אֶת הָרִאשׁוֹן שֶׁלֹּא לִשְׁמוֹ וְאֶת הַשֵּׁנִי לִשְׁמוֹ כִּיפֵּר. שֶׁאֵינוֹ הָרִאשׁוֹן שֶׁלֹּא לִשְׁמוֹ כָּשֵׁר אֶלָּא מִכֹּחַ שְׁמוֹ הַבָּא אַחֲרָיו. אֲבָל שָׁחַט הָרִאשׁוֹן לִשְׁמוֹ וְהַשֵּׁנִי שֶׁלֹּא לִשְׁמוֹ. אִם כִּיפֵּר הָרִאשׁוֹן עַל מַה הַשֵּׁנִי בָא וּמְכַפֵּר. עַל טוּמְאָה שֶׁאֵירְעָה בֵּין זֶה לָזֶה. וּבִפְסָחִים לֹא כִיפֵּר. שֶׁאֵין הַפֶּסַח בָּא אֶלָּא לַאֲכִילַת בָּשָׂר. וּדְלֹא כְרִבִּי נָתָן. דְּרִבִּי נָתָן אָמַר. יוֹצְאִין בִּזְרִיקָה בְּלֹא אֲכִילָה.

Rebbi Eleazar said, sisters are not preliminarily married but in the case of purification sacrifices it atoned[159]. How is that? If one slaughtered two purification offerings for one transgression[160], the altar selects that which is appropriate[161]; both are forbidden to be eaten[162]. If one slaughtered two reparation offerings for one damage, the altar selects that which is appropriate; both are forbidden to be eaten[163]. Rebbi Ze'ira in the name of Rebbi Johanan: If the first[164] one was slaughtered not for its purpose but the second for its purpose, it did atone since the first, which was not for its purpose, becomes acceptable only through the purpose stated later[165]. But if the first was slaughtered for its purpose but the second not for its purpose: if the first atoned for what may the second atone? For impurity which occured between the first and the second[166]. But for Passover sacrifices it did not atone[167] since the Passover sacrifice is only for the meat to be eaten. This does not follow Rebbi Nathan since Rebbi Nathan said, one fulfills one's duty by sprinkling [the blood] without eating[168].

159 If a person simultaneously slaughters two purification sacrifices for one transgression, he has fulfilled his obligation. (Mishnah *Me'ilah* 1:2 describes this situation: A person dedicated an animal as purification sacrifice. Then this animal was lost, another was dedicated as replacement, and then the first one was found before the second was sacrificed. Each of the animals becomes the replacement of the other.) This statement is nontrivial since as a general rule an animal dedicated as purification sacrifice but whose owner then used another animal for the same purpose can no longer be used for anything.

160 Simultaneously.

161 Expression of Mishnah *Zebaḥim* 9:1. Since both sacrifices have equal standing, there is no reason to prefer one to the other. Only selected parts of the purification offering are given to the altar; the remainder of the meat has to be eaten by the priest (*Lev.* 6:17-23).

162 The priests are commanded to eat the meat of the animal which effects the purification. But in this case it is impossible to determine which animal effects the purification.

163 The rules of reparation sacrifices follow those of purification sacrifices; *Lev.* 7:7.

164 This deals with a separate case, that the animals were slaughtered one after the other.

165 Mishnah *Zebaḥim* 1:1 states that both purification and Passover sacrifices which were slaughtered not for their stated purpose are invalid and cannot be offered to the altar. Normally, a purification offering which is invalidated at the time of slaughter is burned outside the Temple precinct and another sacrifice is required independent of the first. But if the second sacrifice is slaughtered correctly immediately after the first, when its flesh is still in the Temple precinct, then the correct slaughter of the second rehabilitates the first, both sacrifices have their selected parts offered on the altar, and both are forbidden as food to the priests.

166 This answer makes more sense in *Šebuot* 1:4 (33b 1.4) where the relative merit of the purification sacrifices on New Year's day are discussed, one required for the New Moon and one for the holiday. If one sacrifice purifies, what is the use of the second? To atone for impurities which might have occurred in the meantime. In the case discussed here, the second sacrifice is invalid and useless.

167 The Passover sacrifice does not atone. He holds that people who bring a Passover sacrifice which cannot be eaten did not fulfill their duty,

Mishnah *Pesaḥim* 7:4.

168 *Peschim* 7:5 (34b l. 45), Babli 78b.

משנה ח: (fol. 62a) הַמְקַדֵּשׁ בְּחֶלְקוֹ מִקָּדְשֵׁי קָדָשִׁים וּמִקָּדָשִׁים קַלִּים אֵינָהּ מְקוּדֶּשֶׁת. מִמַּעֲשֵׂר שֵׁנִי בֵּין בְּשׁוֹגֵג בֵּין בְּמֵזִיד לֹא קִידֵּשׁ דִּבְרֵי רִבִּי מֵאִיר. רִבִּי יְהוּדָה אוֹמֵר מֵזִיד קִידֵּשׁ שׁוֹגֵג לֹא קִידֵּשׁ. וּבְהֶקְדֵּשׁ בְּמֵזִיד קִידֵּשׁ שׁוֹגֵג לֹא קִידֵּשׁ דִּבְרֵי רִבִּי מֵאִיר. רִבִּי יְהוּדָה אוֹמֵר שׁוֹגֵג קִידֵּשׁ מֵזִיד לֹא קִידֵּשׁ.

Mishnah 8: If somebody uses his portion either from most holy or simply holy sacrifices for preliminary marriage, she is not preliminarily married[169]. From Second Tithe[170] there is no preliminary marriage whether unintentionally[171] or intentionally, the words of Rebbi Meïr[172]. Rebbi Jehudah says, intentionally he performed preliminary marriage[173], unintentionally he did not perform preliminary marriage[174]. From Temple property, intentionally he performed preliminary marriage[175], unintentionally he did not perform preliminary marriage[176], the words of Rebbi Meïr. Rebbi Jehudah says, unintentionally he performed preliminary marriage[177], intentionally[178] he did not perform preliminary marriage.

169 The parts of most holy sacrifices (purification and reparation sacrifices) that are eaten are reserved for male Cohanim in the Temple precinct, off limits to women. The Cohen's part of simple sacrifices (well-being sacrifices) are eaten by the Cohen's family in purity. Since a woman by preliminary marriage becomes "bought by the Cohen's

money", she might eat from these parts. But everybody agrees that sacrificial meat never is the Cohen's property but that the Cohanim "eat from the Almighty's table." Since the Cohen's part is not his property, it cannot be used in a marriage transaction. Cf. *Ma'aser Šeni* 1:2, Note 65.

170 Which is eaten by the farmer's family in Jerusalem; cf. Introduction to Tractate *Ma'aser Šeni*. (First Tithe is profane in the Levite's hand.)

171 At the moment of the transaction neither man nor woman was aware that the gift was one of Second Tithe.

172 He holds that Second Tithe is Heaven's peroperty in the hand of the farmer.

173 In his opinion, Second Tithe is the farmer's property but is reserved for sanctified use. If the farmer intentionally misused Second Tithe as marriage gift, he desecrated it. The tithe becomes profane and the farmer has to replace it in the statutory amount of 125%.

174 If the use was unintentional, the tithe is not desecrated but cannot be used.

175 The intentional use of Temple property for private purposes is sacrilege and desecrates the property, which becomes profane.

176 In R. Meïr's opinion, Temple property becomes profane only by intentional profanation.

177 He extends the rules of *Lev.* 5:14-16 to all Temple property. The inadvertent use of Temple property constitutes larceny which requires a reparation offering and restitution in the amount of 125%, but the object taken becomes profane and, therefore, can be used as marriage gift.

178 Since intentional sin cannot be atoned for by sacrifice (*Num.* 15:30), the rules of *Lev.* 5:14-16 cannot apply.

(62d line 69) **הלכה ח:** הַמְקַדֵּשׁ בְּחֶלְקוֹ כּוֹל׳. רִבִּי לָעֶזֶר אָמַר. דִּבְרֵי הַכֹּל. רִבִּי יוֹחָנָן אָמַר. בְּמַחֲלוֹקֶת. תַּמָּן תַּנִּינָן. הַבְּכוֹר מוֹכְרִין אוֹתוֹ תָּמִים חַי וּבַעַל מוּם וְשָׁחוּט. וּמְקַדְּשִׁין בּוֹ אֶת הָאִשָּׁה.

[181]רִבִּי יְהוּדָה בֶּן פָּזִי בְּשֵׁם רִבִּי יְהוֹשֻׁעַ בֶּן לֵוִי. חַי לֹא שָׁחוּט. וְאָמַר רִבִּי יוּדָה בַּר פָּזִי. רִבִּי מֵאִיר יָלִיף כָּל־הַקֳּדָשִׁים מִן מַעֲשֵׂר בְּהֵמָה. מַה מַעֲשֵׂר בְּהֵמָה אֵין מְקַדְּשִׁין בָּהֶן אֶת הָאִשָּׁה אַף כָּל־הַקֳּדָשִׁים אֵין מְקַדְּשִׁין בָּהֶן אֶת הָאִשָּׁה. רִבִּי

HALAKHAH 8

יוּדָה יָלִיף כָּל־הַקֳּדָשִׁים מִן הַבְּכוֹר. מַה הַבְּכוֹר מְקַדְּשִׁין בּוֹ אֶת הָאִשָּׁה. אַף כָּל־הַקֳּדָשִׁים מְקַדְּשִׁין בָּהֶן אֶת הָאִשָּׁה. מַחְלְפָה שִׁיטָתֵיהּ דְּרַבִּי יוּדָה בֶּן פָּזִי. תַּמָּן הוּא אָמַר. בֵּין חַי בֵּין שָׁחוּט. וְהָכָא הוּא אָמַר. חַי לֹא שָׁחוּט. תַּמָּן בְּשֵׁם גַּרְמֵיהּ בְּרַם הָכָא בְּשֵׁם רִבִּי יְהוֹשֻׁעַ בֶּן לֵוִי. אֲפִילוּ תֵימַר. כָּאן וְכָאן בְּשֵׁם גַּרְמֵיהּ. בִּמְקַדֵּשׁ בְּחַיִּים וּבְרָאוּי לִיפּוֹל לוֹ לְאַחַר שְׁחִיטָה. מַה טַעְמָא דְרַבִּי יְהוֹשֻׁעַ בֶּן לֵוִי. וּבְשָׂרָם יִהְיֶה לָךְ כַּחֲזֵה הַתְּנוּפָה. וּמַאי טַעְמָא דְרַבִּי יוּדָה בֶּן פָּזִי. וְהָיָה לְךָ אֲפִילוּ לְאַחַר שְׁחִיטָה. מַה מְקַיְּים רִבִּי יְהוֹשֻׁעַ בֶּן לֵוִי וְהָיָה לְךָ. רִיבָּה לוֹ הֲנָיָיה אַחֶרֶת. שֶׁיְהֵא נֶאֱכָל לִשְׁנֵי יָמִים וְלַיְלָה אֶחָד.

1 יודה בר | מ יהודה בן   ואמר | מ תמן תנינן המקדש בחלקו מקדשי קדשים קלים אינה מקודשת. אמר   בר | מ בן   In *Ma'aser Šeni*, the texts referring to 2-4 rabbis Meïr and Jehudah are interchanged.   2 מן מעשר | מ ממעשר   3 הקדשים | מ הקדעין   4 כל הקדשים מן הבכור | מ כל הקדש מבכור   5 כל | מ - בן | מ בר   6 לא | מ ולא   7 ברם הכא | מ והכא   8 בחיים | מ בחי   לאחר | מ ולאחר   מה | מ מא׳   9 יודה | מ יודן   10 והיה לך | מ יהיה לך   והיה לך | מ יהיה לך

Rebbi Eleazar said, it is everybody's opinion. Rebbi Johanan said, it is in dispute[179]. There[180], we have stated: "One may sell a firstling unblemished alive, blemished alive or slaughtered, and one may use it for preliminarily marrying a woman."

[181]Rebbi Jehudah bar Pazi in the name of Rebbi Joshua ben Levi: Alive, but not slaughtered. And Rebbi Jehudah bar Pazi said, Rebbi Meïr learns all sacrifices from animal tithe. Just as one may not become betrothed to a woman with animal tithe, so no sacrifices may be used to become betrothed to a woman. Rebbi Jehudah learns all dedicated things from the firstling. Just as one may become betrothed to a woman with a firstling, so all sacrifices may be used to become betrothed to a woman. The opinion of Rebbi Jehudah bar Pazi is inverted There, he says, alive or slaughtered. But here, he says alive, but not slaughtered. There in his

own name, here in the name of Rebbi Joshua ben Levi. Even if you say there and here in his own name; if he becomes betrothed while it is still alive and with what is scheduled to fall to him. After slaughter, what is the reason of Rebbi Joshua ben Levi? (*Num.* 18:18): "Their meat shall be for you, like the breast of weaving." And what is the reason of Rebbi Jehudah ben Pazi? "*Shall be for you*"[182], even after slaughtering. How does Rebbi Joshua ben Levi uphold "*shall be for you*"[182]? He added another *being* that it should be eaten during two days and one night.

179 The statement that the Cohen's share of simple sacrifices may not be used as a marriage gift.

180 Mishnah *Ma'aser Šeni* 1:2, Notes 43-44. The firstling becomes the Cohen's property at the rancher's corral, outside the Temple precinct.

181 From here to the end of the paragraph, the text is from *Ma'aser Šeni* 1:2, Notes 63-69 (מ). The only major addition is a quote of the Mishnah here.

182 The text is misquoted here, correct in *Ma'aser Šeni*.

(63a line 7) תַּמָּן תַּנִּינָן. חַלַּת עַם הָאָרֶץ וְהַמְדוּמָע וְהַלָּקוּחַ בְּכֶסֶף מַעֲשֵׂר שְׁיָרֵי מְנָחוֹת פְּטוּרִין מִן הַדְּמַאי.

תַּנֵּי וְכוּלָּם שֶׁיִּקְרָא שֵׁם לִתְרוּמַת מַעֲשֵׂר אוֹ לְמַעֲשֵׂר שֵׁינִי שֶׁלָּהֶם מַה שֶׁעָשָׂה עָשׂוּי. רִבִּי לָעֲזָר אוֹמֵר. חוּץ מִשְּׁיָרֵי מְנָחוֹת. רִבִּי יִרְמְיָה אָמַר. הַשְׁאָר בְּמַחֲלוֹקֶת. רִבִּי יוֹסֵי בָּעֵי. הַיי דָא מַחֲלוֹקֶת. מַה אֲנָן קַייָמִין. אִין כְּרִבִּי מֵאִיר. הוּא מַעֲשֵׂר שֵׁינִי הוּא שְׁיָרֵי מְנָחוֹת לֹא עָשָׂה כְלוּם. אִין כְּרִבִּי יוּדָה. מַה שֶׁעָשָׂה עָשׂוּי. אָמַר רִבִּי מָנָא. אֲזָלִית לְקַיסָרִין וְשָׁמְעִית רִבִּי חִזְקִיָּה יָתִיב מַתְנֵי. הַמְקַדֵּשׁ בְּחֶלְקוֹ מָקָדְשֵׁי הַקֳּדָשִׁים וּמִקֳּדָשִׁים קַלִּין אֵינָהּ מְקוּדֶּשֶׁת. רִבִּי לָעֲזָר אָמַר. דִּבְרֵי הַכֹּל. רִבִּי יוֹחָנָן אָמַר. בְּמַחֲלוֹקֶת. וְאָמְרִית לֵיהּ. מְנָן שְׁמִיעַ לָךְ הָדָא מִילְּתָא. אָמַר לִי. מֵרִבִּי יִרְמְיָה. וְאָמְרִית. יָאוּת. דְּהוּא שָׁמַע הָדָא דְּרִבִּי לָעֲזָר. רִבִּי לָעֲזָר דִּבְרֵי הַכֹּל הוּא דְּאָמַר. בְּמַחֲלוֹקֶת. רִבִּי יוֹסֵי דְּלָא שְׁמִיעָא לֵיהּ צְרִיכָא הוּא דוּ

אָמַר. הַיי דָא מַחֲלוֹקֶת. אִין כְּרִבִּי מֵאִיר. הִיא מַעֲשֵׂר הִיא שְׁיָרֵי מְנָחוֹת לֹא עָשָׂה כְּלוּם. אִין כְּרִבִּי יוּדָה. מַה שֶּׁעָשָׂה עָשׂוּי.

1 וכולם | ד כולן   שלהם | ד שלחן   3 היי דא | ד היידה   אנן | ד נן   הוא | ד היא
4 שיני | ד -   הוא | ד היא   5 מתני | ד ומתני   6 מקדשי | ד בקדשי   ומקדשים | ד ובקדשים   7 שמיע לך | ד שמע ר׳   אמ׳ | ד ואמ׳   8 מר׳ | ד מן ר׳   יאות | ד יאות
ר׳ ירמיה   ר׳ לעזר דברי | ד דברי   9 הוא | ד -   דו | ־ הוא דו   10 היי דא | ד היידה   מעשר | ד מעשר שיני   לא | ד היא לא

There[183], we have stated: "*Ḥallah* of the *am haärez*, food containing heave, food bought with money of the Second Tithe, and the remainders of flour sacrifices are free from *demay*."

[184]It was stated: "Concerning all of these, if he gave a name to their heave of the tithe or Second Tithe, what he did is done." Rebbi Eleazar said, with the exception of the remainders of flour sacrifices. Rebbi Jeremiah said, the rest is in dispute. Rebbi Yose asked, what dispute? Where are we standing, if according to Rebbi Meïr, both for Second Tithe and for the remainders of flour sacrifices, he did not do anything. If according to Rebbi Jehudah, what he did is done. Rebbi Mana said, I went to Caesarea and heard Rebbi Ḥizqiah who was sitting there, stating: "If [a priest] preliminarily marries by means of his share in the holiest sacrifices or simple holy sacrifices, she is not married." Rebbi Eleazar said, that is everybody's opinion. Rebbi Joḥanan said, it is in dispute. I said to him, from whom did you hear this, and he said, from Rebbi Jeremiah. I said, this explains the matter! Rebbi Jeremiah, who heard that Rebbi Eleazar said, it is everybody's opinion, he says it is in dispute. Rebbi Yose, who did not hear that, asked which dispute? If according to Rebbi Meïr, both for tithe and for the remainders of flour sacrifices, he did not do anything; if according to Rebbi Jehudah, what he did is done.

240 QIDDUŠIN CHAPTER TWO

183 Mishnah *Demay* 1:3, Notes 112-114.

184 This text is from *Demay* 1:3, Notes 183-188.

(63a line 20) כַּד דְּמָךְ רִבִּי מֵאִיר רִבִּי יוּדָה וְאָמַר. אַל יִיכַּנְסוּ תַלְמִידָיו שֶׁלְרִבִּי מֵאִיר כָּאן. דָּחַק סוּמָכוּס וְעָאל. אָמַר. הַמְקַדֵּשׁ בְּקָדְשֵׁי קָדָשִׁים. וְאִשָּׁה נִכְנֶסֶת הִיא לָעֲזָרָה. אָמַר לֵיהּ. בִּמְקַדֵּשׁ עַל יְדֵי שָׁלִיחַ. בְּמָה קִידְשָׁהּ. רִבִּי לָעְזָר אָמַר. בְּגוּפוֹ. רִבִּי יוֹחָנָן אָמַר. בְּטוֹבַת הֲנָייָה שֶׁבּוֹ. אוֹ נאמַר. וְלֹא פְּלִיגִין. מַה דְּאָמַר רִבִּי לָעְזָר בְּגוּפוֹ. בְּחֶזְקַת טוֹבַת הֲנָייָה שֶׁבּוֹ. רִבִּי חִזְקִיָּה רִבִּי בֵּיבַי בְּשֵׁם רִבִּי לָעְזָר. מְקַדְּשִׁין בִּפְרוּטָה שֶׁלְּמַעֲשֵׂר שֵׁינִי.

When Rebbi Meïr expired, Rebbi Jehudah decided and said, Rebbi Meïr's students shall not enter here[185]. Symmachos squeezed by and entered. He said, "Most holy sacrifices for preliminary marriage," how could a woman enter the Temple courtyard? He said to him, if he contracts preliminary marriage through an agent[186]. By what does he contract preliminary marriage? Rebbi Eleazar said, by its body[187]. Rebbi Joḥanan said, by the goodwill created[188]. Or we might say that they do not disagree[189]. When Rebbi Eleazar said, by its body, [he meant] by the expected goodwill from it. Rebbi Ḥizqiah, Rebbi Bevai in the name of Rebbi Eleazar: One may contract preliminary marriage with a *peruṭah* from Second Tithe[190].

185 Babli 52b, *Nazir* 49b. In the version of the Babli, Symmachos quoted R. Meïr's Mishnah in R. Jehudah's school, R. Jehudah objected that most holy sacrifices are distributed at a place reserved to male Cohanim, and R. Yose gave the answer attributed here to R. Jehudah.

Since in the preceding paragraph it was established that R. Jehudah admits the possibility of contracting marriage by the Cohen's part in the sacrifices, the question arises how this is possible for most holy meat. In R. Meïr's Mishnah, most holy sacrifices could be mentioned together with simple sacrifices since all are forbidden.

186   According to the Babli it also could be a transaction between an unmarried Cohen and the Cohen father of an underage girl. Then not even an agent is needed.

187   The meat itself, given from one Cohen to another. Then the question arises whith whom a Cohen possibly could trade most holy meat.

188   The goodwill created by a gift of meat might be worth a *perutah*. Goodwill is immaterial, not subject to the restrictions imposed on sancta.

189   To avoid the question raised in Note 187.

190   Second Tithe is agricultural produce. It may be redeemed by money, which transfers the sanctity from the produce to the coin (*Deut.* 14:25). But only the original produce is called "holy" (*Deut.* 26:13); the replacement is functionally but not intrinsically holy. Therefore, the money may be given as marriage gift to a woman in Jerusalem who may buy food with it for consumption in purity.

(63a line 26) בְּמַעֲשֵׂר שֵׁינִי. רִבִּי אַבָּהוּ בְּשֵׁם רִבִּי יוֹחָנָן. לֹא עָלַת עַל דַּעְתּוֹ לַעֲבוֹר עַל דִּבְרֵי תוֹרָה. אָמַר רִבִּי זְעִירָא. אַחַת לֹא עָלְתָה עַל דַּעְתּוֹ וְאַחַת לֹא עָלְתָה עַל דַּעְתֵּיהּ. אָמַר רִבִּי יוֹנָה. הַמְקֻדָּשׁ לֹא עָלַת עַל דַּעְתּוֹ וּמַעֲשֵׂר שֵׁינִי לֹא עָלַת עַל דַּעְתֵּיהּ. אָמַר רִבִּי אָבִין. הֶקְדֵּשׁ לֹא עָלַת עַל דַּעְתּוֹ וְלֹא עָלַת עַל דַּעְתֵּיהּ. מַעֲשֵׂר שֵׁינִי עָלַת עַל דַּעְתּוֹ וְלֹא עַל דַּעְתֵּיהּ.

"With Second Tithe." Rebbi Abbahu in the name of Rebbi Johanan: He did not intend to transgress the words of the Torah[191]. Rebbi Ze'ira said, in one case he did not intend, in one case she did not intend[192]. Rebbi Jonah said, the sanctified he did not intend[193], Second Tithe she did not intend[194]. Rebbi Abin said, the sanctified neither he nor she did intend[195]; Second tithe he did intend but she did not[194,196].

191   One has to explain why Second Tithe cannot be used as marriage gift in error according to R. Jehudah. If the groom did not intend to acquire the Second Tithe, he cannot give it away.

192   The rules for both Temple

property and Second Tithe can be explained in the same way. R. Jonah and R. Abin try to understand what R. Ze'ira meant.

193 Misappropriation of Temple property is characterized as a sin in *Lev.* 5:15-16. One cannot assume that a man intentionally wants to sin. Therefore, for R. Meïr one has to assume that the marriage is invalid, for R. Jehudah that it is valid. Both will agree that if the groom is interviewed and he insists that he intentionally misused Temple property, then for R. Meïr the marriage is valid, for R. Jehudah it is invalid (Notes 175,177).

194 No woman wants to be married by produce which she will be obligated to bring to Jerusalem before it can be used. According to the undisputed opinion of R. Eleazar (Note 190), the Mishnah must speak of produce which is Second Tithe, not of money for which the tithe was redeemed.

195 Nobody wants to start his marriage with a blatant sin.

196 In the Babli, 53b, this opinion is attributed to R. Joḥanan.

(63a line 30) רִבִּי יוֹסֵה בְשֵׁם רִבִּי פְּדָיָיה. הֶקְדֵּשׁ מֵזִיד יוֹצֵא לַחוּלִין בְּלֹא פִדְיוֹן. וְהָא תַנֵּי. בִּשְׁגָגָה. פְּרָט לַמֵּזִיד. הָדָא דְאַתְּ אָמַר לַחוֹמֶשׁ וּלְקָרְבָּן. הָא לָצֵאת מוֹצִיא. רִבִּי חָמָא בַּר עוּקְבָא בְשֵׁם רִבִּי יוֹסֵי בֶּן חֲנִינָה. מִיעוּט שְׁלָמִים יוֹצְאִין לַחוּלִין בְּלֹא פִדְיוֹן. וְהָא תַנֵּי. מִקָּדְשֵׁי. לֹא כָּל־קָדָשֵׁי. הָדָא דְאַתְּ אָמַר לַחוֹמֶשׁ וּלְקָרְבָּן. הָא לָצֵאת מוֹצִיא.

Rebbi Yose in the name of Rebbi Pedaiah: Intentionally desecrated Temple property becomes profane without redemption[197]. But did we not state[198]: "In error," that excludes intention? That you say for the additional fifth[177] and the sacrifice, but profaned it is[199]. Rebbi Ḥama bar Uqba in the name of Rebbi Yose ben Ḥanina: The excluded well-being offerings[200] become profane without redemption. But did we not state[201]: "From the sancta," not all sancta? That you say for the additional fifth and the sacrifice, but profaned it is[199].

197 This explains why for R. Meïr a marriage effected by intentional misuse of Temple property is valid.

198 *Sifra Wayyiqra Parašah* 11(8), (Babli *Pesaḥim* 32b) referring to *Lev.* 5:15 dealing with larceny committed with sacrifices or Temple property, explicitly restricted to unintentional sin.

199 Since intentional sin is excluded from expiation by sacrifice, the rules of *Lev.* 5:14-16 do not apply.

200 Well-being offerings, which remain the property of the donor and of which only a small part is given to the altar and the priests, is excluded from the rules of *Lev.* 5:14-16, as will be explained immediately following.

201 *Sifra Wayyiqra Pereq* 20(1), referring to *Lev.* 5:15, speaking of larceny committed "*from* the Eternal's sancta". In rabbinic interpretation, prefix מ or מן always implies "some, not all". In this case, the verse is taken to refer to "*the Eternal's* sancta", no part of which is private property This excludes well-being and other simple sacrifices but includes sacrifices given to the priests since these offerings always remain Heaven's property (cf. Note 169).

(63a line 35) תַּמָּן תַּנִּינָן. בְּהֵמָה שֶׁנִּמְצֵאת מִירוּשָׁלַיִם וְעַד מִגְדַּל עֵדֶר לְכָל־רוּחַ. רִבִּי הוֹשַׁעְיָה רַבָּה אָמַר. לָבֹא בִדְמֵיהֶם שָׁנוּ. אָמַר לֵיהּ רִבִּי יוֹחָנָן. וְאוֹמְרִין לוֹ לְאָדָם צֵא וּמְעוֹל בַּקֳּדָשִׁים. אֶלָּא בְּאַחַת הִילְכוּ בָהֶן אַחַר הָרוֹב. אִם רוֹב זְכָרִים עוֹלוֹת. וְאִם רוֹב נְקֵיבוֹת זִבְחֵי שְׁלָמִים. וְאֵין הַשְּׁלָמִים בָּאִין מִן הַזְּכָרִים וּמִן הַנְּקֵיבוֹת. כֵּיצַד הוּא עוֹשֶׂה. מוֹצִיאָן לַחוּלִין וְחוֹזֵר וְעוֹשֶׂה אוֹתָן עוֹלוֹת. וְקַשְׁיָא. יֵשׁ חַטָּאת קְרֵיבָה עוֹלָה. אָמַר רִבִּי חֲנִינָה. תַּנָּאֵי בֵּית דִּין הוּא עַל הַמּוֹתָרוֹת שֶׁיִּיקָרְבוּ עוֹלוֹת. אָמַר רִבִּי יוֹסֵי לְרִבִּי יַעֲקֹב בַּר אָחָא. וְאֵין זֶה מֵזִיד. אָמַר לֵיהּ. מִכֵּיוָן שֶׁתְּנָאֵי בֵּית דִּין הוּא אֵין זֶה מֵזִיד. אָמַר רִבִּי זְעִירָה. כַּמָּה דְאַתְּ אָמַר תַּמָּן. תְּנָאֵי בֵּית דִּין הוּא עַל הָאוֹבְדוֹת שֶׁיִּיקָרְבוּ עוֹלוֹת.

There[202], we have stated: "An animal that is found as from Jerusalem to Migdal-Eder in every direction[203]." The elder Rebbi Hoshaia said, this was taught for their monetary value[204]. Rebbi Joḥanan said to him, does one say to a person, go and commit larceny with sacrifices[205]? But in every case[206] they followed the majority of cases: If most are male, they are elevation offerings, if most are female, well-being offerings. But do not well-being offerings come from males and females? What does he do? He redeems them as profane and then turns them into elevation offerings[207]. This is difficult. Can a purification offering[208] become an elevation offering? Rebbi Ḥanina said, it is a stipulation by the court that all redundant animals should be brought as elevation offerings[209]. Rebbi Yose said to Rebbi Jacob bar Ḥama, is that not intentional [misuse]? He said to him, since it is a stipulation by the court, it is not intentional [misuse]. Rebbi Ze'ira said, as you say there, it is a stipulation by the court that lost animals should be brought as elevation offerings[210].

202 Mishnah Šeqalim 7:4. The present paragraph has a parallel there in Halakhah 7:6 of which, however, it is not a direct copy.

203 If an animal which is a potential sacrifice (cattle, sheep, or goats) is found ownerless near Jerusalem, one may assume that it was dedicated as sacrifice but escaped from its owner. Elevation offerings must be male (*Lev.* 1:2,10); well-being sacrifices can be of either gender. Most well-being offerings were bought from redemption monies of Second Tithe. The Mishnah precribes that male animals be used for elevation offerings, females for well-being offerings.

204 It is impossible to say that a male animal which was found ownerless should be taken as elevation offering since it might have been dedicated as well-being offering. The animal should be redeemed and the redemption money used for an elevation offering. The same argument is given in the Babli, 55a.

205 It is impossible to redeem an unblemished dedicated animal (*Lev.* 27:10). Any redemption is both sinful and ineffective. R. Hoshiah's rule seems to be impossible.

206 The animal itself should be used for what was its most probable dedication.

207 One follows both R. Hoshaia and R. Joḥanan. The animal is first

redeemed and then rededicated; this precludes the sin of freeing a dedicated animal and removes the prior specific dedication. (In the Babli, 55b, R. Joḥanan holds that the redemption of unblemished animals is never possible. He requires that the animal be put out to graze until it develops a blemish; then it can be redeemed and the proceeds used for another sacrifice.)

208   This reading is unacceptable since purification offerings are female (*Lev.* 4:28,32). One must read: "well-being offering." This argument is missing in *Šeqalim*.

209   Therefore, it is part of every dedication of any male animal that, if not needed for its original purpose, it should be used as an elevation offering.

210   It is also part of every dedication of any male animal that, if lost and then found by another person, it should become an elevation offering.

(fol. 62a) **משנה ט**: הַמְקַדֵּשׁ בְּעָרְלָה וּבְכִלְאֵי הַכֶּרֶם וּבְשׁוֹר הַנִּסְקָל וּבְעֶגְלָה עֲרוּפָה וּבְצִיפּוֹרֵי מְצוֹרָע בִּשְׂעַר נָזִיר וּבִפְטֶר חֲמוֹר וּבְבָשָׂר בְּחָלָב וּבְחוּלִין שֶׁנִּשְׁחֲטוּ בָעֲזָרָה אֵינָהּ מְקוּדֶּשֶׁת. מְכָרָן וְקִידֵּשׁ בִּדְמֵיהֶן הֲרֵי זוֹ מְקוּדֶּשֶׁת.

Mishnah 9: If a man performs preliminary marriage using '*orlah*[211], or *kilaim* of a vineyard[212], or an ox sentenced to be stoned[213], or a calf whose neck was broken[214], or the birds of a sufferer from skin disease[215], the hair of a *nazir*[216], or the first-born of a she-ass[217], or meat cooked in milk[218], or profane meat slaughtered in the Temple precinct[219], [the woman] is not preliminarily married. If he sells any of these items[220] and uses their proceeds for preliminary marriage, she is preliminarily married.

211   The fruit of a tree in the first three years after planting whose usufruct is forbidden (*Lev.* 19:23-24; cf. Introduction to Tractate *'Orlah*.) The entire list consists of items forbidden for usufruct. Since marriage is to the man's advantage, items forbidden for usufruct cannot be used as marriage

gifts.

212 While mixtures of seeds are always forbidden (cf. Introduction to Tractate *Kilaim*), only foreign produce in a vineyard is forbidden for usufruct (*Deut.* 22:9).

213 An animal which killed a human (*Ex.* 21:28,29).

214 To atone for an unsolved murder (*Deut.* 21:1-9); cf. Tractate *Sotah*, Chapter 9.

215 The two birds the recovered sufferer from skin disease needs for his purification (*Lev.* 14:1-7).

216 Which must be burned when his sacrifice is cooked, *Num.* 6:18.

217 This is forbidden for usufruct only before it was redeemed by a lamb, or whose neck broken. *Ex.* 13:11-13. The question of the biblical root of the prohibition of usufruct is raised in the Halakhah.

218 *Ex.* 23:19, 34:26, *Deut.* 14:21.

219 Forbidden for usufruct by rabbinic interpretation.

220 While the sale is sinful, the coins received in payment are not forbidden.

(63a line 45) **הלכה ח:** הַמְקַדֵּשׁ בְּעָרְלָה וּבְכִלְאֵי הַכֶּרֶם כול'. פֶּטֶר חֲמוֹר. רִבִּי לְעָזָר אָמַר. מְקַדְּשִׁין בּוֹ אֶת הָאִשָּׁה. רִבִּי יוֹחָנָן אָמַר. אֵין מְקַדְּשִׁין בּוֹ אֶת הָאִשָּׁה. רִבִּי אִימִּי בְשֵׁם רִבִּי לְעָזָר. פֶּטֶר חֲמוֹר מְקַדְּשִׁין בּוֹ אֶת הָאִשָּׁה מִקַּל וָחוֹמֶר. מָה אִם הַבְּכוֹר שֶׁאֵינוֹ מוֹצִיא מִידֵי אִיסּוּרִין בְּחַיָּיו אַתְּ אָמַר. מְקַדְּשִׁין בּוֹ אֶת הָאִשָּׁה. זֶה שֶׁהוּא מוֹצִיא מִידֵי אִיסּוּרִין בְּחַיָּיו לֹא כָל־שֶׁכֵּן. מַה נְפִיק מִן בֵּינֵיהוֹן. עָבַר וּפְדָייוֹ שֶׁלֹּא מִדַּעַת הַבְּעָלִים. רִבִּי לְעָזָר אָמַר. אֵינוֹ פָדוּי. רִבִּי יוֹחָנָן אָמַר. פָּדוּי. מַתְנִיתָא מְסַיְּיעָא לְרִבִּי לְעָזָר וּפְלִיגָא עָלוֹי. מַתְנִיתָא מְסַיְּיעָא לְרִבִּי לְעָזָר. הַגּוֹנֵב פֶּטֶר חֲמוֹר שֶׁלַּחֲבֵירוֹ מְשַׁלֵּם תַּשְׁלוּמֵי כָפֶל. וְסוֹפָא פְלִיגָא עָלוֹי. שֶׁאַף עַל פִּי שֶׁאֵין לוֹ בֶן[225] עַכְשָׁיו יֵשׁ לוֹ בֶן[225] לְאַחַר זְמָן. מַתְנִיתָא פְלִיגָא עַל רִבִּי לְעָזָר. פֶּטֶר חֲמוֹר אֵין מְקַדְּשִׁין בּוֹ אֶת הָאִשָּׁה. פָּתַר לָהּ רִבִּי לְעָזָר לְאַחַר עֲרִיפָה. דְּאָמַר רִבִּי לְעָזָר. הַכֹּל מוֹדִין לְאַחַר עֲרִיפָה שֶׁאֵינוֹ פָדוּי.

Halakhah 9: "If a man performs preliminary marriage using *'orlah*, or *kilaim* of a vineyard," etc. The first-born of a she-ass, Rebbi Eleazar said, may be used to preliminarily marry a woman; Rebbi Johanan said, it may not be used to preliminarily marry a woman. Rebbi Immi in the name of Rebbi Eleazar: The first-born of a she-ass may be used to preliminarily marry a woman by an argument *de minore ad majus*. Since you say that a firstling, whose prohibition cannot be lifted during its lifetime, can be used to preliminarily marry a woman, this one, whose prohibition can be lifted during its lifetime, not so much more[221]? What is the difference between them[222]? If somebody transgressed and redeemed it without the knowledge of its owner[223]. Rebbi Eleazar said, it is not redeemed[224]. Rebbi Johanan said, it is redeemed[224]. A *baraita* supports Rebbi Eleazar and disagrees with him. A *baraita* supports Rebbi Eleazar: [225]If somebody steals the first-born of another person's she-ass, he has to pay double restitution[226]. The end[227] disagrees with him: For even though he has no interest in it now he will later[228]. The Mishnah disagrees with Rebbi Eleazar: One may not use the first-born of a she-ass to preliminarily marry a woman[229]. Rebbi Eleazar explained that, after breaking of [the foal's] neck. For Rebbi Eleazar said, everybody agrees that after its neck was broken it cannot be redeemed[230].

221 The firstlings of cattle, sheep, or goats (the animals admitted to the altar) must be given to a Cohen. If without blemish, the animal must be sacrificed and eaten by Cohanim. If blemished, it remains the property of the Cohen and may be eaten by any Jew. In both cases, the living animal cannot be used for any work. The only use permitted is as sanctified or profane food; as far as use goes it is forbidden during its lifetime and becomes permitted by slaughter. But the firstling of a she-ass is supposed to be redeemed by the gift of a lamb to a Cohen; by this act, the donkey becomes totally profane and can be put to work immediately.

222 What additional differences does one find between Rabbis Eleazar

and Johanan?

223 A third party gave a lamb to a Cohen to redeem the firstborn of the she-ass, without knowledge of the latter's owner.

224 For R. Eleazar the unredeemed donkey is his owner's property; it cannot be redeemed without the owner's knowledge. For R. Johanan the unredeemed donkey is not the owner's money, being forbidden for the latter's usufruct, but it can be redeemed by a third party.

225 Quoted in the Babli, *Bekhorot* 11a. The translation follows the Babli in reading בו "in it" instead of בן "son" of the ms.

226 This implies that the unredeemed firstling represents property value, agreeing with R. Eleazar.

227 The second half of the *baraita* quoted, Note 225.

228 Since by giving a lamb to the Cohen the owner can establish ownership of the donkey. This agrees with R. Johanan's opinion that the unredeemed firstling donkey is not his owner's property.

229 A paraphrase of Mishnah 9.

230 If the owner prefers to break the neck of his firstling donkey rather than give a lamb to a Cohen, R. Eleazar agrees that by this act he has lost his ownership and the carcass is forbidden for any usufruct. The Babli agrees in the name of Babylonian authorities, 57b; *Bekhorot* 10b.

(63a line 57) פֶּטֶר חֲמוֹר אֵין מְקַדְּשִׁין בּוֹ אֶת הָאִשָּׁה. וְרַבִּי שִׁמְעוֹן מַתִּיר. הָדָא פְלִיגָא עַל רבי לְעָזָר בְּתַרְתֵּיי. אִין בְּחַיֵּי דִּפְלִיגָא עֲלוֹי מִן רַבָּנִין. אִין לְאַחַר עֲרִיפָה פְלִיגָא עֲלוֹי מִן רבי שִׁמְעוֹן. רבי חֲנִינָה בְּשֵׁם רבי יוּדָן. תִּיפְתָּר שֶׁמֵּת. עָרְפוֹ אָסוּר בַּהֲנָייָה. וְרַבִּי שִׁמְעוֹן מַתִּיר. עֲרִיפָה עֲרִיפָה. מָה עֲרִיפָה שֶׁנֶּאֶמְרָה לְהַלָּן עוֹרְפוֹ וְקוֹבְרוֹ וְאָסוּר בַּהֲנָייָה. אַף עֲרִיפָה שֶׁנֶּאֶמְרָה כָּאן עוֹרְפוֹ [וְקוֹבְרוֹ] וְאָסוּר בַּהֲנָייָה. עַל דַּעְתֵּיהּ דְּרבי לְעָזָר נִיחָא. בְּחַיָּיו הוּא מַתִּיר צָרִיךְ שֶׁיְּהֵא אָסוּר עַל עֲרִיפָה. עַל דַּעְתֵּיהּ דְּרַבִּי יוֹחָנָן קַשְׁיָא. בְּחַיָּיו הוּא אָסוּר לֹא כָּל־שֶׁכֵּן לְאַחַר עֲרִיפָה. אֲתָא רבי יַעֲקֹב בַּר אָחָא בְּשֵׁם רבי יוֹחָנָן רבי זְעִירָא בְּשֵׁם רַבָּנִין. עַל דְּרַבָּנִין צְרִיכָה. שֶׁלֹּא תֹאמַר. הוֹאִיל וְהִקֵּישָׁתָהּ הַתּוֹרָה עֲרִיפָתוֹ לִפְדִיוֹנוֹ. מַה פִּדְיוֹנוֹ יוֹצֵא לַחוּלִּין אַף עֲרִיפָתוֹ יוֹצֵא לַחוּלִּין. מָצִינוּ דָבָר

שֶׁהֲרָמָתוֹ יוֹצֵא לַחוּלִין וְאָסוּר בַּהֲנָיָיה. הֲתִיבוּן. הֲרֵי טֶבֶל טָבוּל לְמַעֲשֵׂר עָנִי הֲרֵי הוּא וַהֲרָמָתוֹ יוֹצֵא לַחוּלִין. וְאָמַר רִבִּי בָּא רַב הוּנָא בְּשֵׁם רִבִּי. הָאוֹכֵל פֵּירוֹתָיו טְבוּלִים לְמַעֲשֵׂר עָנִי חַיָּיב מִיתָה. רַבָּנִן דְּקַיְסָרִין בְּשֵׁם רִבִּי יִרְמְיָה. כָּךְ מְשִׁיבִין חֲכָמִים לְרִבִּי שִׁמְעוֹן. מָצִינוּ דָּבָר טָעוּן פִּדְיוֹן מוּתָּר בַּהֲנָיָיה. הֲתִיבוּן. הֲרֵי בְכוֹר אָדָם טָעוּן פִּדְיוֹן וּמוּתָּר בַּהֲנָיָיה.

[231]"One may not use the first-born of a she-ass to preliminarily marry a woman, but Rebbi Simeon permits it." That disagrees with Rebbi Eleazar in two respects. If during its lifetime, it disagrees following the rabbis; if after breaking the neck, it disagrees following Rebbi Simeon[232]. Rebbi Ḥanina in the name of Rebbi Yudan: Explain it that it died[233]. If he broke its neck, it is forbidden for usufruct, but Rebbi Simeon permits it. [234]"Breaking the neck, breaking the neck." Since "breaking the neck" mentioned there implies that one has to break its neck, bury it, and it is forbidden for usufruct, so "breaking of the neck" mentioned here implies that one has to break its neck, [bury it,][235] and it is forbidden for usufruct. Following Rebbi Eleazar it is understandable. He permits during its lifetime; he needs an argument to forbid it after the breaking of the neck. Following Rebbi Joḥanan it is difficult. If it is forbidden during its lifetime, not so much more after breaking of its neck? There came Rebbi Jacob bar Aḥa in the name of Rebbi Joḥanan, Rebbi Ze'ira in the name of the rabbis: It is needed following the rabbis, lest you say that since the Torah combined the breaking of its neck with its redemption[236], and its redemption makes it profane, so also the breaking of its neck should make it profane[236a]. Do we find anything whose lifting makes profane and which is forbidden for usufruct[237]? They objected: There is *tevel* containing the tithe of the poor[238] which becomes totally profane by its

lifting; but Rebbi Abba, Rav Huna said in the name of Rebbi[239]: A person eating produce which is *tevel* for the tithe of the poor is guilty of a deadly sin. The rabbis of Caesarea in the name of Rebbi Jeremiah: So the rabbis answer Rebbi Simeon: Do we find anything that needs redemption and is permitted for usufruct[240]? He replied to them: There is the first-born human who needs redemption and is permitted for usufruct[241].

231 This is a new *baraita*; in slightly different formulation it appears in the Babli, *Bekhorot* 10b-11a.

232 The *baraita* does not specify the status of the firstling. It is clear that after redemption the firstling is profane and can be used as a marriage gift. If the *baraita* speaks of the living unredeemed firstling, it contradicts R. Eleazar's statement that it can be given as marriage gift. If it refers to the dead firstling, the assertion that R. Simeon permits its use contradicts the statement that everybody prohibits the dead fistling.

233 It died a natural death before being redeemed. In this version, R. Simeon will agree that usufruct is forbidden after its neck was broken. This is the Babli's explanation, *loc. cit.* Note 230.

234 A new *baraita*, Babli *Bekhorot* 10b; *Mekhilta dR. Ismael Pisḥa* 18 (Horovitz-Rabin p. 71); *Mekhilta dR. Simeon ben Ioḥai* 13:13 (Epstein-Melamed p. 43). Then the comparison is between breaking the neck of the firstling and of the calf which atones for an unsolved murder. Since the calf has to be buried and its grave is forbidden for all usufruct (*Soṭah* 9:5, Note 132) it is clear that the carcass itself is forbidden for all usufruct.

235 Added from all parallel sources and a Genizah fragment.

236 The prohibition of usufruct of the firstling after its neck was broken is far from clear from the biblical text. Redemption by a lamb or breaking the neck are mentioned in the same verse (*Ex.* 13:13, 34:20); one might assume that both follow the same rule. The same explanation is given in the Babli, *Bekhorot* 10b.

236a A Genizah fragment adds here:

לפם כן צרך מימר עריפה ער' וגו'. ר' יעקב בר אחא בש' רב י.. ... שמעון את חכמין.

Therefore it was necessary to say "breaking the neck, breaking the neck." R. Jacob bar Aḥa in the name of Reb[bi] Y[oḥanan] . . . . one undertands this for the Sages.

The text seems to be redundant; its omission in the Leiden text may be original.

237 This challenges R. Joḥanan's position that the living unredeemed firstling is forbidden for usufruct. In comparable cases, untithed produce (ṭevel) or sacrificial animals which developed a blemish, redemption transfers holiness to the redeeming object. But in the case of the donkey both it and the redeeming lamb are totally profane.

238 In general, ṭevel is produce from which either the required heave or the tithe was not taken; its consumption is sinful. The tithe of the poor is due in the third and sixth years of a Sabbatical cycle, when no Second Tithe is due. Its only claim to biblical status is from Deut. 14:28. Second Tithe, which must be eaten near the Sanctuary, has a status of holiness; produce from which Second Tithe was not taken is recognized as ṭevel (Ma'aser Šeni 3:5, Notes 61ff.) But the tithe of the poor is totally profane; produce from which this tithe was not taken is referred to as ṭevel only here.

239 It seems that one should read "Rav" instead of "Rebbi".

240 Any dedicated animals which become disqualified as sacrifices are forbidden for all use before being redeemed.

241 A first-born human male whose father did not redeem him by giving five šeqalim to a Cohen must redeem himself when adult, but nowhere is there any restriction on his earning power before redemption.

(63a line 72) מְכָרָן וְקִידֵּשׁ בִּדְמֵיהֶן מְקוּדָּשׁ. רִבִּי חַגַּיי בְּשֵׁם רִבִּי זְעִירָא. בְּשֶׁאֵין דְּמֵיהֶן. אָמַר רִבִּי חֲנִינָה. זֹאת אוֹמֶרֶת שֶׁאֵין מְקַדְּשִׁין בִּגְזֵילָה.

"If he sells any of these items and uses their proceeds for preliminary marriage, he is married." Rebbi Ḥaggai in the name of Rebbi Ze'ira: Because it is not its proceeds. Rebbi Ḥanina said, this means that one cannot marry preliminarly with [the proceeds of] robbery[242].

242 This paragraph is quoted by Rosh (*Qiddušin* 2, #31) as follows:

רִבִּי חַגַּי בְּשֵׁם רִבִּי זְעִירִי. שֶׁאֵין טוֹפְסִין דְּמֵיהֶן. אָמַר רִבִּי חֲנִינָא. זֹאת אוֹמֶרֶת שֶׁמְקַדְּשִׁין בִּגְזֵילָה.

"Rebbi Ḥaggai in the name of Rebbi Ze'iri: Because [the prohibition of usufruct] is not transferred to its proceeds. Rebbi Ḥanina said, this means that one can marry preliminarly with [the proceeds of] robbery."

However, Ran (*Novellae Baba meṣi'a* 7:1), Rashba (*Novellae ad* 57b), Ritba (*Novellae ad* 56b), and Meïri (*Bet Habeḥira Qiddušin*, ed. A Sopher, p. 261) all read the statement of R. Ḥaggai in the version of the Leiden ms. but that of R. Ḥanina in the version of Rosh. [It seems that most authors did not have access to the Yerushalmi but copied from Ran (R. Nissim Gerondi); they cannot be counted as independent sources.] His arguments and those of the other medieval authorities are discussed in great detail and at length by J. Rosanes (*Mishneh Lammelekh*, Maimonides *Hilkhot Iššut* 5:7)]. In the opinion of the Babli (Rashi *Ḥulin* 4a, '*Avodah zarah* 54a), the prohibition of usufruct is not transferred to the (illegitimate) proceeds except in the cases of idols and Sabbatical produce. However, our ms. sources (including the Constantinople print edition) do not support Ran's reading of R. Ḥanina; one has to accept the ms. reading as it stands.

The statement of R. Ḥaggai is straightforward and was explained by Ran. Since objects forbidden for usufruct are worthless, the money received by the seller was not payment for the object. Since it was necessary to point out that the marriage was valid, it follows that if the money had been given in exchange for an object acquired unlawfully, the marriage would be invalid.

משנה י: הַמְקַדֵּשׁ בִּתְרוּמוֹת וּבְמַעְשְׂרוֹת וּבְמַתָּנוֹת כְּהוּנָה וּבִדְמֵי חַטָּאת וּבְאֶפֶר חַטָּאת הֲרֵי זוֹ מְקוּדֶּשֶׁת וַאֲפִילוּ יִשְׂרָאֵל. (fol. 62a)

Mishnah 10: If a man perform preliminary marriage using heaves[243], or tithes[244], or gifts to priests[245], or money for purification[246], or the ashes of purification[247], she is married even if he is an Israel[248].

243 Which can be consumed only by a Cohen.

244 Which either are given to a Levite, or a poor person, or must be eaten in purity in Jerusalem.

245 From slaughtered profane animals, prescribed in *Deut.* 18:3.

246 It is not clear what this money represents; probably the sums of restitution mentioned in *Lev.* 5:16, *Num.* 5:8; cf. *2K.* 12:17). In the Babli, most independent Mishnah mss., and in the Halakhah one reads מֵי חַטָּאת "purification water", the water used in the purification rite of *Num.* 19.

247 Ashes from the burning of the Red Cow, *Num.* 19. This is very precious material.

248 While an Israel and his wife have no use for most of these items, they can sell them to Cohanim. The items have value and can be used as marriage gifts.

(63a line 74) **הלכה י:** הַמְקַדֵּשׁ בִּתְרוּמוֹת וּבְמַעְשְׂרוֹת כול׳. רִבִּי יוֹסֵי בֶּן חֲנִינָה אָמַר. אָדָם נוֹתֵן מַעְשְׂרוֹתָיו בְּטוֹבַת הֲנָייָה. מַה טַּעַם דְּרִבִּי יוֹסֵי בֶּן חֲנִינָה. וְאִישׁ אֶת קֳדָשָׁיו לוֹ יִהְיוּ. מַה עֲבַד לָהּ רִבִּי יוֹחָנָן. יִתְּנֵם לְכָל־מִי שֶׁיִּרְצֶה.

1 ר׳ | ד דר׳   חנינה | ד חנינא   2 - | נד ור׳ יוחנן אמ׳.   אין אדם נותן מעשרותיו בטובת הנייה ד הנאה   מה | נד מא   חנינה | ד חנינא   3 מה עבד לה ר׳ יוחנן | נ ור׳ יוחנן אמר. לא יהיה   ד ליה

[249]Rebbi Yose ben Rebbi Ḥanina said, a person gives his tithes for the benefit of goodwill. What is the reason of Rebbi Yose ben Rebbi Ḥanina? (*Num.* 5:10) "Everybody shall be the owner of his holy things." How does Rebbi Joḥanan explain this? He may give them to whomever he likes.

249 This text is from *Demay* 6:3, explained there in Notes 59-76 and *Nedarim* 11:3, Note 46. It seems that the text in *Demay* is the original source.

(63b line 2) מַתְנִיתָא פְלִיגָא עַל רִבִּי יוֹסֵי בֶּן חֲנִינָה. קוֹנָם כֹּהֲנִים וּלְוִיִּם נֶהֱנִין לִי. יִטְּלוּ עַל כָּרְחוֹ. פָּתַר לָהּ בְּאוֹמֵר. אִי אֶיפְשִׁי לִיתֵּן מַתָּנָה כָּל־עִיקָּר. תֵּדַע לָךְ שֶׁהוּא כֵן. דְּתַגִּינָן כֹּהֲנִים אֵילוּ לְוִיִּם אֵילוּ נֶהֱנִין לִי. יִטְּלוּ אֲחֵרִים. מַתְנִיתָא פְלִיגָא עַל רִבִּי יוֹחָנָן. הָאָמַר. הֵילָךְ סֶלַע זוֹ וְתֵן בְּכוֹר זֶה לְבֶן בִּתִּי כֹהֵן. פָּתַר לָהּ בְּרוֹצֶה לִיתְּנוֹ לִשְׁנֵי כֹהֲנִים וּבֶן בִּתּוֹ אֶחָד מֵהֶן. וְהוּא אָמַר לוֹ. הֵילָךְ סֶלַע זֶה וְתֵן כּוּלוֹ לְבֶן בִּתִּי כֹהֵן.

1 בן | ג ביר'   חנינה | ד חנינא   3 לך | ג -   4 הא'. הילך | ג אמ' הוא יש' ליש'.   האלך ד אמ' הוא יש' ליש'. הילך   זו | נד זה   5 לשני כהנים | ג לשנים ד לשנים כהנים הילך סלע זה | ג הא לך סלע ד הילך סלע זו   6 כולו | ד כולן

A Mishnah disagrees with Rebbi Yose ben Rebbi Ḥaninah: "A vow that no Cohanim or Levites should have any advantage from me: they should take against his will." He explains it about a person who says, I cannot possibly give them *any* gifts. You should know that this is so, since we have stated: "*These* Cohanim and Levites should [not] have any advantage from me; let others take." A *baraita* disagrees with Rebbi Joḥanan: "One may say, here you have a tetradrachma and give this firstling to my daughter's son, a Cohen." He explains, if he already wanted to give it to two Cohanim and that daughter's son was one of them; then one said, here you have a tetradrachma and give it whole to my daughter's son, a Cohen.

(42d line 3) בְּעוֹן קוֹמֵי רִבִּי זְעִירָא. בְּהָדָא כֹּהֵן לְיִשְׂרָאֵל. אָסוּר. מַה דְּרִבִּי יוֹסֵי אָמַר. לֹא אֲגִיבוֹן. רִבִּי חִזְקִיָּה בְּשֵׁם רִבִּי אָחָא. אָכֵין אָמַר לוֹן. עַל דַּעְתֵּיהּ דְּרִבִּי יוֹסֵי בֶּן חֲנִינָה כֹּהֵן לְיִשְׂרָאֵל לָמָּה הוּא אָסוּר. לֹא מִפְּנֵי מַרְאִית הָעַיִן. אַף רִבִּי יוֹחָנָן אִית לֵיהּ יִשְׂרָאֵל לְיִשְׂרָאֵל אָסוּר מִפְּנֵי מַרְאִית הָעָיִן. וְעוֹד מִן הָדָא דְּתַנֵּי. הַכֹּהֲנִים וְהַלְוִיִּם הַמְסַייְּעִים בַּגְּרָנוֹת אֵין נוֹתְנִין לָהֶן לֹא תְרוּמָה וְלֹא מַעֲשֵׂר. וְאִם נָתַן הֲרֵי זֶה חִילֵּל. וְלֹא יְחַלְּלוּ אֶת קָדְשֵׁי בְּנֵי יִשְׂרָאֵל. וְהֵן מְחַלְּלִין

אוֹתָן. יוֹתֵר מִכֵּן אָמְרוּ. תְּרוּמָתָן אֵינָן תְּרוּמָה וּמַעְשְׂרוֹתָן אֵינָן מַעְשְׂרוֹת וְהֶקְדֵּישָׁן אֵינוֹ הֶקְדֵּשׁ. וַעֲלֵיהֶן אָמַר הַכָּתוּב רָאשֶׁיהָ בְּשׁוֹחַד יִשְׁפּוֹטוּ וְכֹהֲנֶיהָ בִּמְחִיר יוֹרוּ וגו'. וְהַמָּקוֹם מֵבִיא עֲלֵיהֶן שָׁלֹשׁ פּוּרְעָנִיּוֹת. הָדָא הוּא דִכְתִיב לָכֵן בִּגְלַלְכֶם צִיּוֹן שָׂדֶה תֵחָרֵשׁ וִירוּשָׁלַיִם לְעִיִּים תִּהְיֶה וְהַר הַבַּיִת לְבָמוֹת יָעַר.

1 זעירא | נ זעורא   בהדא | נ - ד כהדא   אסור | נ ר' אוסר ד -   דר' | נ ר'   2 לא אגיבון | נ -   אחא | נד אחא אמ'   אכין אמ' לון | נ הכין אגיבון ד הכין אמ' לון   3 בן | נ נ בר   אף | נד אוף   4 ועוד | ד אמ' ר' יוסי ביר' בר'. חילול קדשים יש כאן ותמר מפני מרעית העין. ועוד   5 דתני | נ - ד מן הדא דתני   המסייעים | נד המסייעין   6 חילל ד חילול   7 מעשרות | נ מעשר   8 אמ' הכת' | נ הכת' אמ'   וכהניה במחיר יורו וגו' | נ - ד וכהניה במחיר יבואו   10 תחרש וירוש' לעיים תהיה והר הבית לבמות יער | ו נ תחרש וירוש' לעיין תהיה והר הבית לבמות יער ד תחרש וגו'

They asked before Rebbi Zeïra: a Cohen to an Israel, Rebbi forbids. What does Rebbi Yose say? He did not respond. Rebbi Ḥizqiah in the name of Rebbi Aḥa said, so he said to them: In the opinion of Rebbi Yose ben Rebbi Ḥanina, why is a Cohen to an Israel forbidden, not because it looks badly? Also Rebbi Joḥanan holds that from an Israel to an Israel it is forbidden because it looks badly. In addition, because of the following, as it was stated: "Cohanim and Levites who help at the threshing floor have no right either to heave or to tithe, and if the farmer gave, it is desecrated, as it is said (*Lev.* 22:15): 'They should not desecrate the sanctified things of the Children of Israel,' but they do desecrate them! In addition, they said that their heave is no heave, their tithes are no tithes, their dedications are no dedications, and about them the verse says (*Micha* 3:11): 'Their heads judge for bribes, their priests instruct for hire, etc.' The Omnipresent brings over them three catastrophes; that is what is written (*Micha* 3:12): 'Therefore, because of you Zion will be ploughed over as a field, Jerusalem will be desolate, and the Temple Mount a wooded hill.'

(42d line 13) מַתְנִיתָא פְּלִיגָא עַל רִבִּי יוֹחָנָן. הַמְקַדֵּשׁ בִּתְרוּמוֹת וּבְמַעְשְׂרוֹת וּבְמַתָּנוֹת וּבְמֵי חַטָּאת הֲרֵי זוֹ מְקוּדֶּשֶׁת אַף עַל פִּי יִשְׂרָאֵל. פָּתַר לָהּ בִּתְרוּמָה שֶׁנָּֽפְלָה לוֹ מִשֶּׁלַּאֲבִי אִמּוֹ כֹהֵן.

2 ובמי חטאת | נד ובמי חטאת ובאפר חטאת   3 משלאבי | נ מאבי

A Mishnah disagrees with Rebbi Johanan: " If a man performs preliminary marriage using heaves, or tithes, or gifts to priests, or water for purification, or the ashes of purification, she is married even if he is an Israel." He explains it with heave he inherited from his maternal grandfather, a Cohen.

האומר פרק שלישי

(fol. 63b) **משנה א**: הָאוֹמֵר לַחֲבֵירוֹ צֵא וְקַדֵּשׁ לִי אִשָּׁה פְּלוֹנִית וְהָלַךְ וְקִידְּשָׁהּ לְעַצְמוֹ מְקוּדֶּשֶׁת. וְכֵן הָאוֹמֵר לָאִשָּׁה הֲרֵי אַתְּ מוּקדֶּשֶׁת לִי לְאַחַר שְׁלֹשִׁים יוֹם וּבָא אַחֵר וְקִידְּשָׁהּ בְּתוֹךְ שְׁלֹשִׁים מְקוּדֶּשֶׁת לַשֵּׁנִי. בַּת יִשְׂרָאֵל לַכֹּהֵן תּאכַל בַּתְּרוּמָה. מֵעַכְשָׁיו וּלְאַחַר שְׁלֹשִׁים יוֹם וּבָא אַחֵר וְקִידְּשָׁהּ בְּתוֹךְ שְׁלֹשִׁים מְקוּדֶּשֶׁת וְאֵינָהּ מְקוּדֶּשֶׁת. בַּת יִשְׂרָאֵל לַכֹּהֵן אוֹ בַת כֹּהֵן לְיִשְׂרָאֵל לֹא תּאכַל בַּתְּרוּמָה.

Mishnah 1 If somebody said to another: go and marry me preliminarily to woman X, and [the agent] went and married her preliminarily himself, she is preliminarily married[1]. Also, if somebody said to a woman, you are preliminarily married to me after thirty days and another man married her preliminarily within these thirty days, she is preliminarily married to the second man[2]; as a daughter of an Israel married to a Cohen she may eat heave[3]. From today and after thirty days, and another man married her preliminarily within these thirty days, she is and is not preliminarily married[3]. As a daughter of an Israel married to a Cohen or daughter of a Cohen married to an Israel she may not eat heave[4].

1 A person who accepts agency does not by this act lose the ability to legally act in his own behalf. As long as the agent did not sign a contract which subjects him to a fine unless he execute what he promised, the principal may consider him a trickster but has no legal recourse.

2   At the moment at which the second man married her, she was legally single; his marriage is valid. After thirty days, when the first man's preliminary marriage should enter into force, she already is a married woman. The preliminary marriage of a married woman to another man is nonexistent in law. It is not forbidden; only actions which exist in law can be forbidden.

3   If the groom is a Cohen, she is married to the Cohen; the existence of the first man is irrelevant. But if the first man gave her a wedding gift and said: you are preliminarily married to me now but the mutual legal obligations shall start only after 30 days (which would give the groom 13 months to arrange the definitive wedding), and if within these thirty days another man preliminarily married her unconditionally, neither of the two marriages can be unquestionably valid. Therefore, she needs valid bills of divorce from both men. [In *Giṭṭin* 7:3 (Note 80) Rebbi disagrees and holds that the preliminary marriage of the second man disappears at the end of 30 days; this opinion is adopted by Samuel in the Babli, 59b, but not mentioned in the Yerushalmi *Qidduŝin*.]

4   The daughter of an Israel can eat heave only if she is certainly married to a Cohen; the daughter of a Cohen can eat heave only if she certainly is not married outside the clan.

(63c line 16) **הלכה א:** הָאוֹמֵר לַחֲבֵירוֹ. צֵא וְקַדֵּשׁ לִי אִשָּׁה פְּל' כול'. הֲרֵי זֶה זָרִיז וְנִשְׂכָּר וְנִקְנָה הַמִּקָּח אֶלָּא שֶׁנָּהַג מִנְהַג רַמָּיוּת. אַף לְמִידַּת הַדִּין כֵּן. הָאוֹמֵר לַחֲבֵירוֹ. צֵא וְקַח לִי מִקָּח פְּלוֹנִי. וְהָלַךְ וּלְקָחוֹ לְעַצְמוֹ. הֲרֵי זֶה זָרִיז וְנִשְׂכָּר וְנִקְנָה הַמִּקָּח אֶלָּא שֶׁנָּהַג מִנְהַג רַמָּיוּת. רִבִּי זְעִירָא מֵיקַל לְהוֹן דַּחֲמֵי לְחַבְרֵיהּ זְבִין זְבִינָא וּמַעֲלֶה לֵיהּ עָלוֹי. אָמַר רבי אָבוּן בְּשֵׁם רִבִּי זְעִירָא. אַף לְעוֹשֶׂה עָלוֹי חֲבִילָה רַבָּנִין קָרֵיי עָלוֹי לַמָּס מֵרֵעֵהוּ חָסֶד וְיִרְאַת שַׁדַּי יַעֲזוֹב.

Halakhah 1: "If somebody says to another: go and marry me preliminarily to woman X," etc. He looks out for himself and is rewarded since his acquisition is valid, but he behaved treacherously[5]. The same holds for monetary transactions. If somebody says to another: go and buy for me goods X, and [the agent] went and bought [the merchandise] for himself, he looks out for himself and is rewarded since his acquisition is valid, but he behaved treacherously[6]. Rebbi Ze'ira cursed those who saw another person trying to buy certain goods and outbid him. Rebbi Abun in the name of Rebbi Ze'ira: Also about one who organizes a group against another[7], the rabbis quote: "A person who prevents a good thing coming to his neighbor abandons the fear of the Almighty.[8]"

5 Babli 58b.
6 The Babli, 59a, agrees in general but points out that an agent must have some flexibility in warding off claims by third parties; it might be to the advantage of the principal if the agent acquires for himself rather than let the property fall into hostile hands.
7 S. Lieberman [*Tarbiz* 4 (1937), p. 379] explains that simply by having a group of people showing interest, even if no competing bid ensues, the hand of the seller is strengthened and the buyer forced to increase his bid.
8 *Job* 6:14, interpretation of Targum. (In a Genizah fragment: "The rabbis *of Caesarea* quote.")

(63c line 22) לֹא הוּחְזַק הַשָּׁלִיחַ בָּעֵדִים. הוּא אוֹמֵר. לְעַצְמִי קִידַּשְׁתִּי. וְהִיא אוֹמֶרֶת. לָרִאשׁוֹן. הַשֵּׁינִי כְּאוֹמֵר לָאִשָּׁה. קִידַּשְׁתִּיךְ. וְהִיא אוֹמֶרֶת. לֹא קִידַּשְׁתָּנִי. וְהוּא כְּאוֹמֶרֶת לָרִאשׁוֹן. קִידַּשְׁתָּנִי. וְהוּא אוֹמֵר. לֹא קִידַּשְׁתִּיךְ. אָמְרָה. אֵינִי יוֹדַעַת. חֲזָקָה לַשֵּׁינִי. הוּחְזַק הַשָּׁלִיחַ בָּעֵדִים. הוּא אוֹמֵר. לְעַצְמִי קִידַּשְׁתִּי. וְהִיא אוֹמֶרֶת. לָרִאשׁוֹן. חֲזָקָה לָרִאשׁוֹן. אָמְרָה. אֵינִי יוֹדַעַת. שְׁנֵיהֶן נוֹתְנִין גֵּט. וְאִם רָצוּ אֶחָד נוֹתֵן גֵּט וְאֶחָד כּוֹנֵס.

If the agent was not identified as such by the witnesses[9] and he says, I married her preliminarily for myself, but she says, to the first, the second is like one who says to a woman: I married you preliminarily but she says, you did not marry me preliminarily[10]. Also it is as if she said to the first, you married me preliminarily but he says, I did not marry you preliminarily. If she says, I do not know, the presumption is in favor of the second[11]. If the agent was identified as such by the witnesses and he says, I married her preliminarily for myself, but she says, to the first, the presumption is in favor of the first[12]. If she said, I do not know, both of them give a bill of divorce or, if they so desire, one gives a bill of divorce and the other marries definitively.

9   The witnesses to the preliminary marriage say that they did not know that the male was appointed as agent and, therefore, they did not listen carefully whether the male stated that he was marrying the woman for himself or for a third party.

10   The case treated in Mishnah 11. The party which asserts the existence of the marriage is forbidden to marry the close relatives of the other party. The party which denies the existence of a marriage is not forbidden to marry any close relative of the other party.

11   If the ceremony was not announced as one of marriage by proxy and nobody noticed anything unusual in the formulas being used, it was not a marriage by proxy and the woman is certainly married to the agent.

12   If the agent was announced as a proxy and nobody noticed anything out of the ordinary, it was a marriage by proxy.

(63c line 28) לְפִיכָךְ אִם מֵת הַשֵּׁינִי בְּתוֹךְ שְׁלֹשִׁים יוֹם אוֹ גֵירְשָׁהּ חָלוּ עָלֶיהָ קִידּוּשֵׁי רִאשׁוֹן לְאַחַר שְׁלֹשִׁים יוֹם. מֵת לְאַחַר שְׁלֹשִׁים וְלֹא גֵירֵשׁ לֹא חָלוּ עָלֶיהָ קִידּוּשֵׁי הָרִאשׁוֹן. הָדָא דְּתַנֵּי רִבִּי חִייָה. כָּל־תְּנַאי שֶׁנִּיתְקַיֵּים אַף עַל פִּי שֶׁבָּטַל לְאַחַר מִיכֵּן הֲרֵי זוֹ מְקוּדֶּשֶׁת. וְכָל־תְּנַאי שֶׁבָּטַל בִּשְׁעַת קִידּוּשִׁין אַף עַל פִּי שֶׁמִּיתְקַיֵּים לְאַחַר מִיכֵּן אֵינָהּ מְקוּדֶּשֶׁת.

Therefore[13], if the second died within thirty days or divorced her, the preliminary marriage of the first is activated after thirty days. If he died after thirty [days] without having divorced her, the preliminary marriage of the first is not activated[14]. That is what Rebbi Ḥiyya stated: With any condition which was fulfilled[15], even if later it becomes moot, she is preliminarily married. But with any condition which was not satisfied at the moment of preliminary marriage, even if later it became moot, she is not preliminarily married

13 Referring to the second part of the Mishnah, about the man who stipulated that the preliminary marriage be effective only after 30 days.

14 If the second man was preliminarily married to her at the end of 30 days, the first preliminary marriage would be marriage to an already married woman; it is null and void. It cannot be reactivated even if the second man later dies.

15 At the time of the activation of the preliminary marriage.

(63c line 33) רִבִּי אַבָּהוּ בְּשֵׁם רִבִּי יוֹחָנָן. הֲרֵי זוֹ עוֹלָה לְאַחַר שְׁלֹשִׁים יוֹם. וּמְכָרָהּ בְּתוֹךְ שְׁלֹשִׁים יוֹם. הֲרֵי זוֹ מְכוּרָה וְהֶקְדֵּישָׁהּ הֶקְדֵּשׁ. חָזַר וּלְקָחָהּ בְּתוֹךְ שְׁלֹשִׁים יוֹם חָל עָלֶיהָ הֶקְדֵּישׁ עוֹלָה. לְאַחַר שְׁלֹשִׁים לֹא חָל עָלֶיהָ הֶקְדֵּשׁ עוֹלָה. לֹא דַמְיָיא עוֹלָה לְאִשָּׁה. מַה דַמְיָיא אִשָּׁה לְעוֹלָה. אָמַר רִבִּי חִייָה בַּר אָדָא. תִּיפְתָּר שֶׁמֵּת הַשֵּׁינִי וַהֲוָה לֵיהּ אָח. מִכֵּיוָן שֶׁהִיא זְקוּקָה לְיִיבּוּם לֹא חָלוּ עָלֶיהָ קִידּוּשֵׁי הָרִאשׁוֹן. מַה דַמְיָיא עוֹלָה לְאִשָּׁה. אָמַר רִבִּי מַתַּנְיָה. תִּיפְתָּר שֶׁהִקְדִּישָׁהּ לְבַעֲלַת מוּם קָבוּעַ. רִבִּי בּוּן בַּר חִייָא בְּעָא קוֹמֵי רִבִּי זְעִירָא. תַּמָּן אַתְּ אָמַר. אֲמִירָתִי לַגָּבוֹהַּ כִּמְסִירָתִי לְהֶדְיוֹט. וְהָכָא אַתְּ אָמַר הָכֵין. אָמַר לֵיהּ. תַּמָּן בְּאוֹמֵר. מִכְּבָר. בְּרַם הָכָא בְּאוֹמֵר. לְאַחַר שְׁלֹשִׁים יוֹם.

Rebbi Abbahu in the name of Rebbi Johanan: "This animal shall be an elevation sacrifice after thirty days." If he sold it within the thirty days, it is sold; its dedication sanctifies[16]. If he bought it back within the thirty days, the dedication as elevation sacrifice applies to it. After thirty days, the dedication as elevation sacrifice no longer applies[17]. But an elevation sacrifice cannot be compared to a woman[18]! Could an elevation sacrifice be compared to a woman? Rebbi Ḥiyya bar Ada said, explain it that the second man died[19] but he had a brother. Since she is a candidate for levirate, the preliminary marriage of the first cannot be valid. Could an elevation sacrifice be compared to a woman? Rebbi Mattania said, explain it that he dedicated an animal with a permanent defect.[20] Rebbi Abun bar Ḥiyya asked before Rebbi Ze'ira: There you say, my promise to Heaven is like my delivery to a private person[21], and here, you say so? He answered him: there, immediately, but here if he says, after thirty days[21].

16 Since nobody can dedicate anything which is not his, the first dedication was invalidated by the sale; the buyer may use the animal for any sacrifice, not just as elevation sacrifice (*Nazir* 2:9, Note 120).

17 Since at the end of 30 days the animal was neither his property nor in his possession.

18 As R. Abun bar Ḥiyya notes later in this paragraph, dedications follow rules quite different from acquisitions; it is difficult to understand why the dedicated animal could validly be sold.

19 He died childless. While the widow is not automatically married to the levir, she is prevented from marrying any other man unless she receives *ḥaliṣah* from him. Therefore, the preliminary marriage of the first is void even if the second man, whose preliminary marriage was valid immediately, dies within the thirty days.

20 Then the dedication was not as elevation sacrifice but stipulated that the animal be sold and the money used as elevation sacrifice. In that case, it would not be necessary that the original owner buy the animal back but only that the buyer renounce his property rights before the end of 30 days.

21 Mishnah 1:6. If the animal is immediately delivered to the Temple, it cannot be sold.

22 Mishnah 1:6 does not exclude the case that a dedication (and the corresponding virtual delivery) be deferred.

(63c line 43) רִבִּי אַבָּהוּ בְשֵׁם רִבִּי יוֹחָנָן. הֲרֵי זוֹ עוֹלָה שְׁלֹשִׁים יוֹם. כָּל־שְׁלֹשִׁים הֲרֵי זוֹ עוֹלָה. לְאַחַר שְׁלֹשִׁים יוֹם יָצְאָת לַחוּלִין מֵאֵילֶיהָ. מְעִילָתָהּ מָה הִיא. רִבִּי יוֹחָנָן אָמַר. מְעִילָתָהּ בְּרוּרָה. רִבִּי זְעִירָא רִבִּי הִילָא תְּרֵיהוֹן אָמְרִין. מְעִילָתָהּ סָפֵק. הֲרֵי אַתְּ מְקוּדֶּשֶׁת לִי שְׁלֹשִׁים יוֹם. הֲרֵי זוֹ מְקוּדֶּשֶׁת. מַה בֵּין הֶקְדֵּשׁ וּמַה בֵּין אִשָּׁה. מָצִינוּ הֶקְדֵּשׁ יוֹצֵא בְּלֹא פִדְיוֹן וְלֹא מָצִינוּ אִשָּׁה יוֹצְאָה בְלֹא גֵט. הֵן אַשְׁכַּחְנָן הֶקְדֵּשׁ יוֹצֵא בְלֹא פִדְיוֹן. כְּרִבִּי שִׁמְעוֹן. דְּרִבִּי שִׁמְעוֹן אָמַר. נִכְנָסִין וְלֹא נוֹתְנִין. אָמַר רִבִּי יוֹסֵי בֵּירִבִּי בּוּן. תִּיפְתָּר דִּבְרֵי הַכֹּל בְּשָׂדֶה מִקְנָה. הֲרֵי זוֹ גִיטָּהּ שְׁלֹשִׁים יוֹם. אֵין זֶה גֵט כְּרִיתוּת. אָמַר רִבִּי יִצְחָק בְּרִבִּי לְעָזָר. הָדָא דְאַתְּ אָמַר מְקוּדֶּשֶׁת. בְּשֶׁקִּידְּשָׁהּ בְּכֶסֶף. אֲבָל אִם קִידְּשָׁהּ בִּשְׁטָר הוֹאִיל וְלֹא לָמְדוּ כְתָב קִידוּשִׁין אֶלָא מִגֵּירוּשִׁין. מַה בְּגֵירוּשִׁין אֵינָהּ מְגוֹרֶשֶׁת אַף בְּקִידוּשִׁין אֵינָהּ מְקוּדֶּשֶׁת.

Rebbi Abbahu in the name of Rebbi Johanan: "This shall be an elevation sacrifice for thirty days," it is an elevation sacrifice for thirty days; after thirty days it automatically becomes profane[23]. What is its status regarding larceny[24]? Rebbi Johanan said, the larceny is clear[25]. Rebbi Ze'ira, Rebbi Hila both say, the larceny is in doubt[26]. "You are preliminarily married to me for thirty days," she is preliminarily married[27]. What is the difference between dedication and woman? We find that a dedication can be eliminated without redemption but we do not find that a woman could leave without a divorce document. Where do we find that a dedication can be eliminated without redemption? Following Rebbi Simeon, since Rebbi Simeon says, "they enter without paying.[28]" Rebbi Yose ben Rebbi Abun said, explain it according to everybody regarding a bought field[29]. "This is your bill of divorce for thirty days": it is no bill of divorce[30]. Rebbi Isaac ben R. Eleazar said, when do you say that she is preliminarily married? If he effectuated the preliminary marriage by money. But if he effectuated the preliminary marriage by a document, since marriage documents were inferred from divorce documents[31] and in the case of a divorce she is not divorced, so in the case of a preliminary marriage she is not preliminarily married.

23 A different version, describing an animal designated as (most holy) elevation offering for 30 days and afterwards as (simply holy) well-being offering, is quoted as tannaïtic text in the Babli, *Nedarim* 29a.

24 An animal dedicated as sacrifice is forbidden for all use; it cannot be used for work, nor can it be shorn for its wool. The question is whether illicit use of an animal temporarily declared a sacrifice triggers the penalties spelled out in *Lev.* 5:14-16.

25 Since during the 30 days it is a sacrifice, if it was used then all the penalties are due.

26 If the animal was sacrificed during the thirty days, any prior use was larceny. But if the animal was not sacrificed, then it reverts to profane status and its use was not illegitimate; it would be forbidden to dedicate an animal to atone for the larceny. The prior use was an "evil that cannot be corrected."

27 Permanently, even after 30 days.

28 Mishnah '*Arakhin* 7:4. If a field donated to the Temple was not redeemed before the Jubilee year, it becomes profane property of the Cohanim (*Lev.* 27:21). In R. Simeon's opinion, the reversion to profane status is automatic; the Cohanim to whom it is distributed do not have to redeem it from the Temple treasury.

29 A field which was not a family heirloom but bought from another owner automatically reverts to its hereditary owner in the Jubilee year. Even if in the meantime the field was given to the Temple by the buyer, it reverts without payment (*Lev.* 27:24).

30 Since it is implied that after 30 days there should be no divorce, it is invalid. A divorce must be irrevocable to be valid (*Giṭṭin* 4:8, Note 192). A shortened version of the text is discussed by Ran, *Nedarim* 29a.

31 Chapter 1, Note 21.

(63c line 54) רִבִּי אַבָּהוּ בְּשֵׁם רִבִּי יוֹחָנָן. הֲרֵי זוֹ עוֹלָה לְאַחַר שְׁלֹשִׁים יוֹם. מְכָרָהּ בְּתוֹךְ שְׁלֹשִׁים אֵינָהּ מְכוּרָה. הִקְדִּישָׁהּ לֹא קָדָשָׁה. לֵיי דָא מִילָּה אָמַר לֵיהּ. לְאַחַר שְׁלֹשִׁים. לְשַׁיֵּיר לוֹ גִיזָה וַעֲבוֹדָה. תְּלוֹשׁ מִן הַקַּרְקַע הַזֶּה שֶׁיִּקְנֶה לָךְ לְאַחַר שְׁלֹשִׁים יוֹם. מְכָרוֹ בְּתוֹךְ שְׁלֹשִׁים יוֹם אֵינוֹ מָכוּר. הִקְדִּישׁוֹ לֹא קָדַשׁ. לֵיי דָא מִילָּה אָמַר לֵיהּ לְאַחַר שְׁלֹשִׁים. לְשַׁיֵּיר לוֹ אֲכִילַת פֵּירוֹת. הֵילָךְ סֶלַע זֶה שֶׁתִּתְקַנֶּה לִי שָׂדְךָ לְאַחַר שְׁלֹשִׁים יוֹם. מְכָרָהּ בְּתוֹךְ שְׁלֹשִׁים אֵינָהּ מְכוּרָה. וּמַה בֵּינָהּ לְאִשָּׁה. אֶלָּא מְכָרָהּ הֲרֵי זוֹ מְכוּרָה.

Rebbi Abbahu[32] in the name of Rebbi Johanan: "This animal shall be an elevation sacrifice after thirty days;" if he sold it during the thirty days, it is not sold; its dedication does not sanctify[33]. For which purpose did he say: "after thirty"? To reserve for himself shearing and work[34]. "Pick from this field[35] that it should be acquired by you after thirty days;" if he sold it within thirty days it is not sold, if he[36] dedicated it it is not sanctified. Why did he say, after thirty days? To reserve usufruct for himself[37]. "Here you have this tetradrachma that your field should be mine after thirty days[38];" if he sold it within thirty days it is not sold, if he dedicated it it is not sanctified. What is the difference between this and a woman[39]? But if he sold it, it is sold[40].

32 It seems that this name is incorrect since earlier R. Abbahu stated that the animal may be validly sold (Note 16). Since the name tradition in the first case is confirmed by a parallel, the quote here is the one to be questioned.

33 This Amora holds that even "a delayed promise to Heaven is like an immediate delivery to a private person"

(Note 21).

34 For the first 30 days.

35 This is authorization of transfer of ownership following Mishnah 1:5. Title to the field is transferred immediately even if actual possession by the buyer is deferred.

36 The seller.

37 The seller may harvest the field for the next 30 days.

38 While real estate may be acquired by money (Mishnah 1:5), the language implies that both ownership and possession will be deferred for 30 days.

39 Since it is stated in the Mishnah that money given now for a later acquisition of a woman in preliminary marriage does not prevent her from marrying another man in the meantime.

40 To exclude any sale to a third party, either ownership or possession must have been transferred at the moment of transaction.

(63c line 62) הֵי לָךְ כֶּסֶף זֶה שֶׁיִּקָּנֶה לִי עַבְדְּךָ לְאַחַר שְׁלֹשִׁים. אִית תַּנָּיֵי תַּנֵּי. הָרִאשׁוֹן בְּיוֹם וּבְיוֹמַיִים. וְאִית תַּנָּיֵי תַּנֵּי. הַשֵּׁנִי בְּיוֹם וּבְיוֹמַיִים. אִית תַּנָּיֵי תַּנֵּי. זֶה וָזֶה אֵינוֹ בְּיוֹם וּבְיוֹמַיִים. אִית תַּנָּיֵי תַּנֵּי. זֶה וָזֶה בְּיוֹם וּבְיוֹמַיִים. מָאן דָּמַר. הָרִאשׁוֹן בְּיוֹם וּבְיוֹמַיִים. וּמֵת תַּחַת יָדוֹ. מָאן דְּאָמַר. הַשֵּׁנִי בְּיוֹם וּבְיוֹמַיִים. כִּי כַסְפּוֹ הוּא. מָאן דְּאָמַר. זֶה וָזֶה בְּיוֹם וּבְיוֹמַיִים. הָרִאשׁוֹן וּמֵת תַּחַת יָדוֹ. הַשֵּׁנִי כִּי כַסְפּוֹ הוּא. מָאן דְּאָמַר. זֶה וָזֶה אֵינוֹ בְּיוֹם וּבְיוֹמַיִים. הָרִאשׁוֹן שֶׁאֵינוֹ כַסְפּוֹ וְהַשֵּׁנִי אֵינוֹ מֵת תַּחַת יָדוֹ.

"Here you have money that your slave shall become acquired by me after thirty days.[41]" Some Tannaïm stated: The first [owner] is subject to "a day or two"[42]. But some Tannaïm stated: The second [owner] is subject to "a day or two". Some Tannaïm stated: Neither the first nor the second [owners] are subject to "a day or two". But some Tannaïm stated: Both first and second [owners] are subject to "a day or two". He[43] who says, the first [owner] is subject to "a day or two", "if he dies in his possession[44]." He[45] who says, the second [owner] is subject to "a day or two", "for he is his money[46]." He[47] who says, both first and second [owners] are subject to "a day or two", the first because of "if he dies in his possession," the second because of "for he is his money." He[48] who says, neither the first nor the second [owners] are subject to "a day or two", for he is not the first's money and does not die in the possession of the second.

41 As explained in this paragraph, ownership is transferred immediately but possession is deferred for thirty days.

42 *Ex.* 21:20-21. Killing a slave is murder. But if the slave dies because of a punishment he receives from his owner and lives at least 24 hours after the punishment, the owner's act is not prosecutable.

43 In the Babli, *Baba batra* 50a, R. Meïr.

44 *Ex.* 21:20, the verse which declares the owner guilty of murder if he kills his slave.

45 In the Babli, R. Jehudah.

46 *Ex.* 21:21, the verse which exempts the owner from prosecution if the slave lives for 24 hours. "His money" indicates ownership.

47 In the Babli, R. Yose.

48 In the Babli, R. Eleazar.

(63c line 69) בַּת כֹּהֵן לְיִשְׂרָאֵל תֹּאכַל בַּתְּרוּמָה. אִית תַּנָּיֵי תַּנֵּי. לֹא תֹאכַל בַּתְּרוּמָה. אָמַר רִבִּי הִילָא. מָאן דְּאָמַר. תֹּאכַל בַּתְּרוּמָה. כְּשֶׁהַשֵּׁנִי כֹהֵן. וּמָאן דְּאָמַר. לֹא תֹאכַל בַּתְּרוּמָה. בְּשֶׁאֵין הַשֵּׁנִי כֹהֵן.

"As daughter of an Israel married to a Cohen she may eat heave[49]." Some Tannaïm state: She may not eat heave. Rabbi Hila said, the one who says that she may eat heave refers to the case that the second man is a Cohen, but the one who says that she may not eat heave refers to the case that the second man is not a Cohen.

49 If the first man wanted the preliminary marriage to be valid only after 30 days cf. Note 3.

(63c line 71) מֵעַכְשָׁיו לְאַחַר שְׁלֹשִׁים יוֹם. רִבִּי אַבָּהוּ בְּשֵׁם רִבִּי יוֹחָנָן. אֲפִילוּ קִידּוּשֵׁי מֵאָה תּוֹפְסִין בָּהּ. אָמַר רִבִּי לְעָזָר. לָכֵן צְרִיכָה. אֲפִילוּ קִידְּשָׁהּ הַשֵּׁנִי קִידּוּשִׁין גְּמוּרִין. רִבִּי יִצְחָק בַּר טַבְלַיי בְּעָא קוֹמֵי רִבִּי לְעָזָר. מַה נַּפְשָׁךְ. מַה שֶּׁקָּנְתָה בָּהּ הָרִאשׁוֹן קָנָה וְהַשְּׁאָר הַשֵּׁנִי בָּא וְגוֹמֵר. אָמַר לֵיהּ. וְכִי יֵשׁ נַפְשָׁךְ בַּעֲרָיוֹת. מָהוּ כְדוֹן. כָּל־אִשָּׁה שֶׁאֵינָהּ קְנוּיָה לְאָדָם אֶחָד אֲפִילוּ קִידּוּשֵׁי מֵאָה תּוֹפְסִין בָּהּ.

"From today and after 30 days." Rebbi Abbahu in the name of Rebbi Johanan: Even preliminary marriages of a hundred men apply to her[50]. Rebbi Eleazar said, it was necessary [to state], even if the second preliminarily married her absolutely[51]. Rebbi Isaac bar Tebele asked before Rebbi Eleazar: As you take it[52]; what the first acquired, he acquired; the remainder the second finished[53]. He answered, is this kind of argument applicable to incest prohibitions[54]? How is that? To any woman who is not acquired by one man only, even preliminary marriages of a hundred men apply.

50   This refers to the case where a sequence of men said: "from now and after 30 days," cf. Note 3. In this case, she is married to none of them completely; cf. *Yebamot* 3:5, Notes 102-105 (5:1, end; *Nedarim* 10:6 Note 59); Babli 60a.

51   The interpretation of R. Abbahu is not the only one possible. Since the Mishnah mentions the condition "from now and after 30 days" only for the first man, it is quite possible that the second marries her unconditionally. Then no other man can join the list of suitors but nevertheless the woman is still "married and not married".

52   מַה נַפְשֶׁךָ is a technical term implying that a certain conclusion follows from two mutually exclusive premises.

53   This elliptic statement can be explained as follows (R. Moses Margalit): If the statement of the first groom, "from today and after 30 days", means that he requires 30 days to make up his mind and might annul the preliminary marriage, then it is obvious that the second contracted a valid marriage and the first is eliminated. But if "from today and after 30 days" means that he wants to be married now but his obligations start only after 30 days, the first acquired the right to preliminarily marry the woman after 30 days. If now the second man marries her unconditionally within the thirty days, which the first cannot hinder, his acquisition should have eliminated the option which the first had acquired.

54   Incest and adultery prohibitions are so serious that no kind of intellectual acrobatics is applicable to them.

1) line 63d) חַד תַּלְמִיד בְּעָא קוֹמֵי רִבִּי זְעִירָא. נָתַן לָהּ בְּשַׁחֲרִית עַל מְנָת לְגָרְשָׁהּ בֵּין הָעַרְבָּיִם. חַד דָּוִיד סְבַר מֵימַר. כָּל־שֶׁהוּא קוֹנֶה. אָמַר רִבִּי זְעִירָא. לְאַחַר שְׁלֹשִׁים קוֹנֶה קִנְיָין גָּמוּר. אֲבָל אִם הוֹסִיף בָּהּ הַשֵּׁינִי קִנְיָין גָּמוּר קוֹרֵא אֲנִי עָלֶיהָ לֹא יוּכַל בַּעֲלָהּ הָרִאשׁוֹן אֲשֶׁר שִׁלְּחָהּ לָשׁוּב לְקַחְתָּהּ.

A student asked before Rebbi Ze'ira: If he gave it to her in the morning on condition that he divorce her in the afternoon[55]? A certain David was of the opinion that anything acquires[56]; Rebbi Ze'ira said that after thirty days he acquires absolutely[57]. But if the second one added absolute acquisition, I am reading for her: "Her first husband who had sent her away cannot return to take her back.[58]"

[55] From the following it seems that the question was about a case in which A gave a wedding gift to a woman stating that she should be preliminarily married to him "from now after a specified time" but divorcing her before the end of the stated period. B preliminarily married the same woman after A's conditional marriage but before the divorce. The Mishnah refers to the situation after the end of the 30 day period, when both preliminary marriages are in conflict. That situation may be rectified by at least one divorce. But in the situation described here, the question remains whether a divorce is possible for a marriage which has not yet started.

[56] Therefore, a divorce is possible also for a partial marriage.

[57] He questions the possibility of divorce of a not yet existing marriage.

A Genizah fragment adds a sentence which was lost by the Leiden scribe by homeoteleuton:

ניתגרשה מזה מותר לזה. נית׳ מזה מותר לזה. ניתגרשה משניהן מות״ לאיזו ... בשלא הוסיף בה השיני קנײן גמור.

If she was divorced by the first, she is permitted to the second; if she was divorced by the second, she is permitted to the first. If she was divorced by both of them, she is permitted to anybody [she likes]. If the second did not add absolute acquisition;

The first two sentences are the conclusion of the previous text. The last sentence is the introduction to the following text. The text does not add anything to the understanding of the Leiden text.

58 *Deut.* 24:4. If the second preliminary marriage was unconditional and the second man died, the first who had given a divorce whose validity may be suspect cannot marry the woman, since for the rule that a divorcee married to another man may not be taken back by her first husband, the divorce and the preliminary marriage to the second man was real.

(63d line 5) הָיוּ שְׁנֵיהֶן כֹּהֲנִים שְׁנֵיהֶן אַחִים. שְׁנֵיהֶן אֲסוּרִין. הָיוּ שְׁלֹשָׁה אַחִין וְקִידְּשׁוּהָ שְׁנַיִם מֵהֶן וָמֵתוּ. הָדָא הִיא דְתַנֵּי רִבִּי חִייָה. אֵשֶׁת מֵת אֶחָד מִתְיַיבֶּמֶת וְלֹא אֵשֶׁת שְׁנֵי מֵתִים. הָיוּ שְׁנֵי אַחִים וְקִידְּשׁוּהָ שְׁנֵיהֶן וּמֵת אֶחָד מֵהֶן. הַשֵּׁינִי מָהוּ שֶׁיְּהֵא מוּתָּר בָּהּ. מָה נַפְשָׁךְ. מַה שֶּׁקָּנָה בָהּ קָנָה וְהַשְּׁאָר נָפְלָה לוֹ מֵאֵת אָחִיו. רִבִּי יוּדָן בַּר פָּזִי אָמַר. אָסוּר בָּהּ. אָמַר רִבִּי יוֹסֵי. טַעֲמָא דְּרִבִּי יוּדָה בַּר פָּזִי. כָּל־יְבָמָה שֶׁאֵינָהּ כּוּלָּהּ לִפְנִים צַד הַקַּנוּי שֶׁבָּהּ נִידוֹן מִשּׁוּם עֶרְוָה וְעֶרְוָה פוֹטֶרֶת צָרָתָהּ. אָמַר רִבִּי חֲנִינָה. יָאוּת אָמַר רִבִּי יוּדָה בַּר פָּזִי. כְּלוּם נָפְלָה לוֹ לֹא מֵחֲמַת אָחִיו. לְאָחִיו הִיא אֲסוּרָה לוֹ הִיא מוּתֶּרֶת.

If both were Cohanim or brothers, both are forbidden[59]. If there were three brothers; two of them contracted a preliminary marriage with her and then died. That is what Rebbi Hiyya stated[60]: The wife of one deceased contracts levirate marriage but not the wife of two deceased men. If they were brothers, both contracted a preliminary marriage with her and then one of them died. Is she permitted to the second? As you take it, what he had acquired, he had acquired; the rest he inherits from his brother[61]. Rebbi Jehudah ben Pazi said, she is forbidden to him. Rebbi Yose said, the reason of Rebbi Jehudah ben Pazi is that the aspect acquired in any sister-in-law who is not totally inside [the family] is considered to be under the incest prohibition and an incest prohibition frees the co-wife[62]. Rebbi Hanina said, Rebbi Jehudah ben Pazi said it correctly. Does she not become his because of his brother? To his brother she was forbidden[59]; to him she should be permitted?

59   Here starts a discussion of the statement of the Mishnah that the situation can be resolved if one of the men writes a bill of divorce and the other marries the woman. There are cases in which both must divorce and neither of them can marry: A Cohen may not marry a divorcee; this includes a woman who is divorced without ever being really married. The wife of a brother is prohibited to her brother-in-law except in the case of a required levirate marriage. In the case of the Mishnah, if the two men are brothers, the woman is forbidden to either of them as the brother's wife.

60   *Yebamot* 3:10, Note 137.

61   The argument is that the surviving brother should be allowed to marry both in his own right and as levir.

62   *Yebamot* 2:2, Note 55. The argument of Note 61 is invalid: Levirate is possible only if the brother's marriage was undoubtedly valid.

(63d line 14) בַּת כֹּהֵן לְיִשְׂרָאֵל לֹא תֹאכַל בַּתְּרוּמָה. לָכֵן צְרִיכָה שֶׁאֲפִילוּ הַשֵּׁינִי כֹּהֵן.

"A daughter of a Cohen married to an Israel may not eat heave." This is a necessary statement, even in case the second man is a Cohen[63].

63   The statement of the Mishnah seems to be trivial since the daughter of a Cohen married to an Israel is excluded from heave by biblical decree (*Lev.* 22:12). It is stated here that she is excluded even if the claim of the Israel on her is only one of partial marriage.

(fol. 63b) **משנה ב:** הָאוֹמֵר לָאִשָּׁה הֲרֵי אַתְּ מְקוּדֶּשֶׁת לִי עַל מְנָת שֶׁאֶתֵּן לָךְ מָאתַיִם זוּז הֲרֵי זוֹ מְקוּדֶּשֶׁת וְהוּא יִתֵּן. עַל מְנָת שֶׁאֶתֵּן לֵיךְ מִיכָּן וְעַד שְׁלֹשִׁים יוֹם נָתַן לָהּ בְּתוֹךְ שְׁלֹשִׁים יוֹם מְקוּדֶּשֶׁת וְאִם לָאו אֵינָהּ מְקוּדֶּשֶׁת. עַל מְנָת שֶׁיֵּשׁ לִי מָאתַיִם זוּז הֲרֵי זוֹ מְקוּדֶּשֶׁת וְיֵשׁ לוֹ. עַל מְנָת שֶׁאַרְאֵךְ מָאתַיִם זוּז הֲרֵי זוֹ מְקוּדֶּשֶׁת וְיַרְאֶנָּהּ. וְאִם הֶרְאָהּ עַל שׁוּלְחָנוּ אֵינָהּ מְקוּדֶּשֶׁת.

Mishnah 2: If somebody says to a woman: You are preliminarily married to me on condition that I give you 200 *zuz*[64], she is preliminarily married and he is obligated to give[65]. On condition that I give you within the next 30 days; if he gave her within 30 days she is preliminarily married; otherwise she is not preliminarily married. On condition that I owe 200 *zuz*, she is preliminarily married if he has it. On condition that I show you 200 *zuz*, she is preliminarily married once he shows it to her[66]; but if he showed it on his bank she is not preliminarily married[67].

64 Accadic *zūzum*, the half-sheqel piece, identified with the Roman *denarius*.

65 It is understood that he also gave a *peruṭah*'s worth at the time he contracted the preliminary marriage. There is no time limit set for the liquidation of the claim. However, it seems that if she has to sue him in court for the 200 *zuz*, the preliminary marriage is invalidated.

66 He assures her that she is marrying a person of means; nevertheless it is not sufficient that he prove to her that he has the means; in order to be married she must be shown the actual coins.

67 If he is a banker, handling his depositors' money, he cannot show anything which is not his own capital invested in his business.

(63d line 15) **הלכה ב:** הָאוֹמֵר לָאִשָּׁה. הֲרֵי אַתְּ מְקוּדֶּשֶׁת כול׳. תַּמָּן תַּנִּינָן. הֲרֵי זֶה גִיטֵּיךְ עַל מְנָת שֶׁתִּתְּנִי לִי מָאתַיִם זוּז. הֲרֵי זוֹ מְגוֹרֶשֶׁת וְתִתֵּן. לֹא הִסְפִּיקָה לִיתֵּן עַד שֶׁמֵּת. רַבָּן שִׁמְעוֹן בֶּן גַּמְלִיאֵל אוֹמֵר. נוֹתְנָן לְאָבִיו וּלְאָחִיו וְהִיא

פְּטוּרָה מִן הַחֲלִיצָה וּמִן הַיִּבּוּם. אַף בְּקִידּוּשִׁין כֵּן. הֲרֵי אַתְּ מְקוּדֶּשֶׁת לִי עַל
מְנָת שֶׁאֶתֵּן לֵיךְ מָאתַיִם זוּז. כְּרַבָּן שִׁמְעוֹן בֶּן גַּמְלִיאֵל אָבִיו וְאֶחָיו נוֹתְנִין לָהּ
וְהִיא זְקוּקָה לַחֲלִיצָה וּלְיִיבּוּם.

Halakhah 2: "If somebody says to a woman: You are preliminarily married to me," etc. [68]There, we have stated: "This is your bill of divorce on condition that you give me 200 *zuz*, she is divorced and has to pay. If she did not manage to pay before he died, it was stated: Rabban Simeon ben Gamliel says, she pays his father or his brother and is free from *haliṣah* and levirate marriage. The same holds for preliminary marriage: "You are preliminarily married to me on condition that I give you 200 *zuz*;" if he did not manage to pay before he died, Rabban Simeon ben Gamliel says, his father or his brothers pay and she is subject to *haliṣah* or levirate marriage.

68 This is a reformulation of the first paragraph of *Giṭṭin*, Halakhah 7:5, Notes 116-118. In the Babli, 60b, the rabbis who disagree with Rabban Simeon ben Gamliel hold that the conditional divorcee never is subject to *haliṣah* or levirate marriage.

(63d line 20) רִבִּי אַבָּהוּ בְשֵׁם רִבִּי יוֹחָנָן. סֵדֶר הַסִּימְפּוֹן כָּךְ הוּא. אֲנָא פְּלָן בַּר
פְּלָן מְקַדֵּשׁ לֵיךְ אַנְתְּ פְּלָנִיתָא בַּר פְּלָן עַל מְנָת לִיתֵּן לִיךְ מִיקָּמַת פְּלָן וּמִכְנְסִינִיךְ
לְיוֹם פְּלָן. וְאִין אָתָא יוֹם פְּלָן וְלָא כְּנַסְתִּיךְ לָא יְהֵי לִי כְּלוּם. עִירָא לוֹ אוֹנֶס.
רִבִּי יוֹחָנָן אָמַר. אוֹנְסָא כְּמָאן דְּרָא עֲבַד. רִבִּי שִׁמְעוֹן בֶּן לָקִישׁ אוֹמֵר. אוֹנְסָא
כְּמָאן דַּעֲבַד. עַל דַּעְתֵּיהּ דְּרִבִּי שִׁמְעוֹן בֶּן לָקִישׁ הֵיךְ צָרִיךְ לְמֵיעֲבַד. דְּאִין אָתָא
יוֹם פְּלָן וְלָא הֲוֵיתִי כּוֹנְסָהּ לִי לֹא יְהֵא עֲלַיִיךְ כְּלוּם. רִבִּי יוֹחָנָן דָּמִיךְ פְּקִיד
לִבְנָתֵיהּ דְּיֶהֱווֹן עָבְדָן כְּרִבִּי שִׁמְעוֹן בֶּן לָקִישׁ. אָמַר. שֶׁמָּא יַעֲמוֹד בֵּית דִּין אַחֵר
וְיִסְבּוֹר דִּכְוָותֵיהּ וְנִמְצְאוּ בָנָיו בָּאִין לִידֵי מַמְזֵרוּת.

⁶⁹Rebbi Abbahu in the name of Rebbi Joḥanan: The following is the contract text: "I, X son of Y, contract a preliminary marriage with you, Z, daughter of U, on condition that I give you property A and definitively marry you by day B. If that day should pass without me having taken you in, I shall have no claim on you." If anything intervened beyond his control? Rebbi Joḥanan said, matters beyond his control are as if he were inactive. Rebbi Simeon ben Laqish said, matters outside his control are as if he had acted. In the opinion of Rebbi Simeon ben Laqish, what would be necessary? "If that day should pass without you having taken me in, I shall have no claim on you." When Rebbi Joḥanan was dying, he told his daughters to act following Rebbi Simeon ben Laqish. He said, sometime in the future there might be a court which follows him; then his descendants might be in danger of bastardy.

69 This text is also in *Giṭṭin* 7:6, Notes 132-139; the contract text also in *Eruvin* 3 and later in Halakhah 3. A. Gulak (*Tarbiz* 5, 1934, pp. 126-133) has discussed the text in detail.

The term σύμφωνον "agreement" appears in Egyptian papyri of the Byzantine period (after the middle of the fifth Century C. E.) and later in Justinian's legislation to designate special stipulations within a written contract [R. Taubenschlag (Chapter 1, Note 369) p. 224]. In earlier Greek sources one finds only the adjective σύμφωνος, α, ον "agreeing". Since the authorities quoted in the Talmud belong to the third Century, the term must have been in use in the Hellenistic world long before it appeared in surviving papyri.

As a special stipulation, the *symphōn* contract has to be executed concurrent with the preliminary marriage; otherwise it could not undo the marriage without a divorce. This supplementary contract fulfills the same role as the Alexandrian *Ketubah* (*Yebamot* 15:3, Note 34, and the sources quoted there.)

On the other hand, the delivery of property by the groom as pledge first is documented in Hammurabi's laws; it appears in Roman contracts as *arra* (or *arrha*) *sponsalicia* (*arra* = ἀρραβών = עֲרָבוֹן) only in Byzantine times, clearly under the influence of Eastern usage.

(63d line 29) הִגִּיעַ הַזְּמָן. הוּא אוֹמֵר. נָתַתִּי. וְהִיא אוֹמֶרֶת. לֹא נָטַלְתִּי. אָמַר רִבִּי אָבוּן. מִיכֵּן שֶׁהוּא מְבַקֵּשׁ לְהוֹצִיא סִימְפּוֹן מִיַּד הָאִשָּׁה עָלָיו לְהָבִיא רְאָייָה. הַגַּע עַצְמָךְ דְּלָא הֲוָה סִימְפּוֹן. אָמַר רִבִּי יוֹסֵה. מִיכֵּן שֶׁהוּא מְבַקֵּשׁ לְאוֹסְרָהּ עָלָיו צָרִיךְ לְהָבִיא רְאָייָה שֶׁכָּנְסוּ עַצְמָן בְּתוֹךְ סִימְפּוֹן. אֲתָא עוֹבְדָא קוֹמֵי רִבִּי אַבָּהוּ. אֲמַר לֵיהּ. זֵל הַב. אֲמַר לֵיהּ. רִבִּי. אִשָּׁה לֹא קָנִיתִי וְאַתְּ אֲמַר לִי. אִיזֵיל הַב. אֲמַר רִבִּי אַבָּהוּ. מִיָּמַיי לֹא שָׂחַק בִּי אָדָם אֶלָּא זֶה. חָזַר וְאָמַר. אִין חָזַר בֵּיהּ יִתֵּן. אִין הִיא חַזְרַת70 בָּהּ תִּתֵּן. וְלֹא הָדָא הִיא קַדְמִיָּיתָא. חָזַר וַעֲשָׂאוֹ מַעֲשֵׂה בֵית דִּין.

[71]If the appointed time has arrived[72] and he says, I gave, but she says, I did not receive[73]: Rebbi Abun said, since he tries to wrest the contract from the woman's hand[74], the burden of proof is on him. Think of it, maybe there was no contract[75]? Rebbi Yose said, since he tries to forbid her to anybody, he has to prove that they entered into the contract[76]. A case came before Rebbi Abbahu[77]; he said to him, go and deliver[78]. He answered, Rabbi, I did not acquire a wife and you say to me, go and deliver! Rebbi Abbahu said, it never happened to me that one got the better of me except this one. He rephrased and said: If he changed his mind, he shall deliver. If she changed her mind, she shall deliver[79]. Is that not his former judgment[80]? He rephrased to give it the status of a court document[81].

70 Vocalization of the ms. The standard Livorno vocalization used in this book would require חָזְרַת.

71 The interpretation essentially follows Gulak, Note 69. The paragraph is also discussed by Nachmanides, Nissim Gerondi (Ran), and Yom Tov ben Abraham Išbili (Ritba) in their

Novellae to 60a.

72 And for some reason the engagement was dissolved.

73 The valuable object promised in the additional contract.

74 The text of the contract specifies that the valuable object remain the woman's property even if the marriage be cancelled.

75 If there is no written document in the woman's hand, the burden of proof is on her, not him.

76 If they were married, and therefore she is forbidden to any man in the world except her husband, he has to show that the conditions of the contract were adhered to.

77 In which the *symphōn* stipulations were not satisfied and the marriage did not take place.

78 The woman stated that she did not receive the *symphōn* gift; absent proof to the contrary, she has to be believed.

79 She has to return the gift or prove that she never received it. [Both Hammurabi's codex (§§159-161) and the *Corpus Iuris* (V,1,5) double the value of the *arra* which has to be returned if the woman's party decides not to proceed with the marriage. Talmudic law does not seem to have adopted this clause; it would be difficult to read it into R. Abbahu's decision.]

While the Babli does not know the institution of *symphōn*, A. Gulak sees in the rules of *symphōn* the precursor of the Medieval contracts of promise of marriage.

80 He still insists that the man has to deliver the valuable object if he cannot prove prior delivery.

81 As explained in the next paragraph, the *symphōn* was drawn up by three witnesses who could act as a court. A court document whose genuinness was attested to cannot be attacked in court.

(63d line 36) סֵדֶר סִימְפּוֹן כָּךְ הוּא. עֵד אֶחָד מִשֶּׁל חָתָן וְעֵד אֶחָד מִשֶּׁל כַּלָּה וּשְׁנֵיהֶן בּוֹרְרִין לָהֶן עוֹד אֶחָד כְּדֵי שֶׁיְּהוּ לוֹ שְׁנֵי עֵדִים לָזֶה וּשְׁנֵי עֵדִים לָזֶה. הָדָא דְאַתְּ אָמַר בְּשֶׁאֵין שְׁנֵיהֶן מוֹדִין. אֲבָל אִם הָיוּ שְׁנֵיהֶן מוֹדִין שְׁנֵיהֶן יְכוֹלִין לַעֲקוֹר קִידּוּשִׁין. כְּהָדָא. הוּא אוֹמֵר. בָּעַלְתִּי. וְהִיא אוֹמֶרֶת. לֹא נִבְעַלְתִּי. אַף עַל פִּי שֶׁחָזַר וְאָמַר. לֹא בָעַלְתִּי. לֹא הַכֹּל מִמֶּנּוּ. שֶׁכְּבָר אָמַר מִשָּׁעָה רִאשׁוֹנָה. בָּעַלְתִּי. אֲבָל אִם לֹא אָמַר מִשָּׁעָה רִאשׁוֹנָה. בָּעַלְתִּי. שְׁנֵיהֶן יְכוֹלִין לַעֲקוֹר חֲזָקָה. הִיא

עֵד אֶחָד מִשֶּׁלְחָתָן וְעֵד אֶחָד מִשֶּׁלְּכַלָּה וְהֶחָתָן חָתוּם בִּכְתַב יָדוֹ. רִבִּי אַבָּהוּ אָמַר. סִימְפּוֹן. רִבִּי בָּא אָמַר. קִידּוּשִׁין. אֲנִי אוֹמֵר. לֹא עָמַד וּבִירֵר אֶת הַסִּימְפּוֹן אֶלָּא סָבַר שֶׁהוּא מַתִּיר בַּאֲחוֹתָהּ.

The following is the way of contracting: One witness for the groom and one witness for the bride; these two together select a third in order to have two witnesses for each side[82]. That is, if not both of them agree. But if both of them agree, both may invalidate the preliminary marriage[83]. As, e. g., [84]"if he said, I copulated, but she says, I was not copulated with. Even if he changed his story and then said, I did not copulate, he cannot be believed since from the start he had said, I copulated. But if from the start he said that he had not copulated, the two together can uproot the presumption." If there was one witness for the groom, one witness for the bride, and the groom signed personally: Rebbi Abbahu said, it is a *symphōn*[85], Rebbi Abba said, it is preliminary marriage[86], for I am saying that he did not really intend a *symphōn* but thought that it would permit her sister to him[87].

82 We do not find in any other talmudic document that the witnesses testify for one party. The witnesses are supposed to testify to the genuineness of the document, equally for both sides. Each side chooses one representative and both together choose a third in the constitution of a court of arbitration (Mishnah *Sanhedrin* 3:1). The procedure justifies R. Abbahu's position in the preceding paragraph that every *symphōn* has the status of a court document.

83 If there is a *symphōn*, both parties can agree to call off the marriage. If there is a dispute, the document has to be submitted to the competent local court to determine that the relationship can be terminated without a divorce.

84 This has nothing directly to do with the topic of *symphōn*. The reference is to *Yebamot* 13:16, Notes 133-134: A levirate marriage can be contracted only by sexual relations. If

the sister-in-law was living in the levir's house but claims that he never slept with her, she might be able to force him to give her *ḥalîṣah*. If they both agree, the court must accept their statement even though it may seem unlikely that a man would not sleep with a woman available to him. Similarly in the present case, even though a court will be reluctant to free a preliminarily married woman without a bill of divorce, if both parties agree to the existence of a *symphōn*, the court will have to hold that the preliminary marriage be void since it was conditional and the condition was not fulfilled.

85   Since there are three signatures, as required.

86   The groom may not appear as judge in his own case. Since the formal conditions of *symphōn* are not satisfied, there is no *symphōn* and the preliminary marriage is unconditional.

87   The groom might have wanted a document which would allow him to marry the bride's sister if for some reason the preliminary marriage would end in divorce. But preliminary marriage triggers all incest prohibitions; a *symphōn* is valid only to cancel a preliminary marriage if all rules are carefully observed as required for a court document.

(63d line 46) עַד שֶׁיְּהֵא מִדַּעְתּוֹ וּמִדַּעְתָּהּ. הָיָה מִדַּעְתּוֹ סִימְפּוֹן וּמִדַּעְתָּהּ קִידּוּשִׁין. רִבִּי חֲנִינָה אָמַר. סִימְפּוֹן. רִבִּי חַגַּיי בְּשֵׁם רִבִּי זְעִירָא אָמַר. קִידּוּשִׁין. וַהֲוָה רִבִּי חֲנִינָה מִתְרֵס כֵּלָיו קָבַל רִבִּי חַגַּיי. אָמַר לֵיהּ רִבִּי הִילָא. קַבַּל חַגַּיי. דְּחַגַּיי אִינָשָׁא סָבוֹרָא הוּא. דָּמַר רִבִּי זְעִירָא. בָּאֲדָר קַדְמַייָא דְּמָךְ רִבִּי הִילָא. בָּאֲדָר תִּנְיָינָא אָתָא עוֹבָדָא קוֹמֵי רִבִּי חֲנַנְיָה חַבְרֵיהוֹן דְּרַבָּנִין וּבְעָא מֵיעֲבַד כְּהָדָא דְרִבִּי חַגַּיי. אָמַר לֵיהּ רִבִּי שְׁמוּאֵל בַּר אִימִּי. לֹא יָאוּת הֲוָה רִבִּי הִילָא אָמַר לָךְ. קַבַּל לְחַגַּיי. דְּחַגַּיי אִינָשָׁא סָבוֹרָא הוּא. אָמַר רִבִּי חַגַּיי. מַתְנִיתָא מְסַייְעָא לֵיהּ. קִידַּשְׁתָּנִי. וְהוּא אוֹמֵר. לֹא קִידַּשְׁתִּיךְ. הוּא מוּתָּר בִּקְרוֹבוֹתֶיהָ וְהִיא אֲסוּרָה בִקְרוֹבָיו. הָתִיב רִבִּי בּוֹרְקַי קוֹמֵי רִבִּי מָנָא. וְאִם אַף בְּסִימְפּוֹן כֵּן. אָמַר לֵיהּ. לֵית סִימְפּוֹן סָפֵק. אֶלָּא הוּא סִימְפּוֹן אוֹ קִידּוּשִׁין.

Only if it be with his and her agreement[88]. If it was *symphōn* in his opinion and preliminary marriage in her opinion[89], Rebbi Ḥanina[90] said, it is *symphōn*, Rebbi Haggai in the name of Rebbi Ze'ira said, it is preliminary marriage. Rebbi Hanina was taking up arms against Rebbi Haggai, when Rebbi Hila said to him, accept Haggai, for Haggai is a thinking man; this is what Rebbi Ze'ira said. In the first Adar[91], Rebbi Hila died. In the second Adar, a case came before Rebbi Hananiah, the colleague of the rabbis, and he wanted to rule following Rebbi Haggai. Rebbi Samuel bar Immi told him, Rebbi Hila was wrong when he told you, accept Haggai, for Haggai is a thinking man[92]. Rebbi Haggai said, a Mishnah[93] supports him: "'You married me preliminarily', and he says, 'I did not marry you preliminarily.' He is permitted her relatives but she is forbidden his relatives." Rebbi Borqai asked before Rebbi Mana: Is it the same with *symphōn*[94]? He answered, a *symphōn* is not doubtful but the rules are identical for *symphōn* and[95] preliminary marriage.

88 While preliminary marriage essentially is a unilateral act by the groom where the woman only has a right of refusal but no active role, a *symphōn* is a contract between parties of equal standing.

89 As A. Gulak (*loc. cit.* Note 69) points out, since the disagreement is about the nature of the contract, not its contents, it is clear that even for the woman the preliminary marriage is conditional and will be void if any of the conditions were not satisfied. The difference in the status of the contract is that in case of preliminary marriage, the woman would have to return the *arra* and would have no right unilaterally to cancel the marriage.

90 As shown subsequently in the paragraph, he really is the later R. Hananiah, not the earlier R. Hanina.

91 In an intercalary year, when the 12th month is reduplicated as "second Adar" to make sure that Passover fall after the spring equinox.

92 Since R. Haggai reported R. Ze'ira's opinion, rather than his own.

93 Mishnah 3:11. R. Haggai on his own shows that the Mishnah supports R. Ze'ira since it shows that one party can accept the consequences of preliminary marriage without imposing

the same consequences on the other party. Since (Note 89) the preliminary marriage even in the woman's opinion was conditional, the ability of the groom to unilaterally terminate the relationship is not impaired if one rules following R. Ze'ira.

94 Do the rules of Mishnah 3:11 also apply to *symphōn*?

95 Reading או as או(ה), not או (A. Gulak; cf. also S. Lieberman, ו,או=הוא, *Tarbiz* 4, 1933, pp. 377-378.)

(63d line 56) קִדֵּשׁ בְּתוֹךְ סִימְפוֹן הֲרֵי אֵילוּ קִידּוּשִׁין גְּמוּרִין. גֵּירַשׁ. תַּלְמִידוֹי דְּרִבִּי יוֹנָה אַמְרִין. נָגְעוּ בָהּ גֵּירוּשִׁין. רִבִּי יוֹנָה אָמַר. לֹא נָגְעוּ בָהּ גֵּירוּשִׁין. כַּד דְּמָךְ רִבִּי יוֹנָה עַבְדוֹן תַּלְמִידוֹי דִּכְוָותֵיהּ. אָמְרִין. לְאַחַר שְׁלֹשִׁים יוֹצְאָה בְלֹא גֵּט. וְאַתְּ אָמַר. נָגְעוּ בָהּ גֵּירוּשִׁין. אֶלָּא לֹא נָגְעוּ בָהּ גֵּירוּשִׁין. מֵת מִתּוֹךְ סִימְפוֹן. רִבִּי אַבָּהוּ אָמַר. מוּתֶּרֶת לְהִינָּשֵׂא. רִבִּי בָּא אָמַר. אֲסוּרָה לְהִינָּשֵׂא. רִבִּי מָנָא שָׁאַל לְבֵית אָבוֹי דְּרִבִּי יוֹסֵי. הֵיךְ רַבְּכוֹן נְהִיג עֲבִיד. אָמַר לֵיהּ. כְּדֵי זְמָן מְרוּבָּה הוּא אם.96 תֵּלֵךְ וְתִינָּשֵׂא מִיָּד. כְּדוּ זְמָן מְמוּעָט הוּא אָמַר. מַה בְּכָךְ שֶׁתַּמְתִּין. שָׁלַיח דְּבָרִים בְּתוֹךְ סִימְפוֹן. רִבִּי מָנָא אָמַר. סִימְפוֹן. רִבִּי בָּא אָמַר. קִידּוּשִׁין. וְחָשְׁשִׁין רַבָּנִין לְהָדָא דְּרִבִּי מָנָא.

If he performed a preliminary marriage during the validity of the *symphōn*, this is unconditional preliminary marriage[97]. If he divorced[98], the students of Rebbi Jonah said, divorce touched her[99]; Rebbi Jonah said, divorce did not touch her[100]. When Rebbi Jonah died, his students acted following him. They said, since after 30 [days][101] she would leave without a bill of divorce, how can you say that divorce touched her? But divorce did not touch her. If he died during the time stipulated in the *symphōn*, Rebbi Abbahu said, she is permitted to marry; Rebbi Abba said, she is not permitted to marry[102]. Rebbi Mana asked the family of Rebbi Yose's father: How did your master usually act? He said to him, when it was a long time[103], he said that she should go and marry immediately. If the time was short, he said, what is the hurt if she waits? If he sent things during the validity[104] of the *symphōn*, Rebbi Mana said, [it follows the rules of] *symphōn*; Rebbi Abba said, [it follows the rules of] preliminary marriage. The rabbis take note of Rebbi Mana's opinion[105].

96 Probably this should be אמ׳, to be read אָמַר (*Qorban Ha'edah*).

97 An unnecessary procedure since based on the *symphōn* he could proceed immediately with definitive marriage, retroactively validating the *symphōn* as preliminary marriage. His action overrides the *symphōn*.

98 During the period specified in the *symphōn*. This also is unnecessary since the contract permits each party to declare its unwillingness to proceed with the marriage, thereby eliminating the preliminary marriage.

99 She is forbidden to marry a Cohen.

100 It is as if a man not married to a woman divorces her; she is not touched by that action and free to marry a Cohen.

101 Or any other period specified in the *symphōn* as final term for the definitive marriage.

102 This discussion presupposes the opinion of Rabban Simeon ben Gamliel (Note 68) that the family of a man who dies after conditional preliminary marriage has the option to fulfill the conditions and force the widow to contract levirate marriage with the brother of the deceased. If a *symphōn* follows the rules of conditional preliminary marriage, the woman cannot marry another man without the family of the deceased giving up their option. The widow/bride naturally could exercise her option to invalidate the *symphōn*, but then she will have to return the *arra*.

103 If the end of the period specified in the *symphōn* was far off, to require the woman to wait would be an unreasonable burden on her.

104 In addition to the contractual *arra*, the groom sent additional gifts to his prospective bride. If these are also considered *arra*, the bride keeps them if the marriage does not take place by the action of the groom; if they are engagement presents they have to be returned.

105 If the marriage does not take place, it would be incumbent upon the man to prove in court that the gifts were specifically designated as engagement presents, not *arra*.

משנה ג: עַל מְנָת שֶׁיֵּשׁ לִי בֵּית כּוֹר עָפָר הֲרֵי זוֹ מְקוּדֶּשֶׁת וְיֵשׁ לוֹ. עַל (fol. 63b) מְנָת שֶׁיֵּשׁ לִי בְּמָקוֹם פְּלוֹנִי אִם יֵשׁ לוֹ בְּאוֹתוֹ מָקוֹם מְקוּדֶּשֶׁת וְאִם לָאו אֵינָהּ מְקוּדֶּשֶׁת. עַל מְנָת שֶׁאַרְאֵיךְ בֵּית כּוֹר עָפָר הֲרֵי זוֹ מְקוּדֶּשֶׁת וְיַרְאֶנָּהּ. וְאִם הֶרְאָהּ בַּבִּקְעָה אֵינָהּ מְקוּדֶּשֶׁת. רִבִּי מֵאִיר אוֹמֵר כָּל תְּנַאי שֶׁאֵינוֹ כִּתְנַאי בְּנֵי גָד וּבְנֵי רְאוּבֵן אֵינוֹ תְנַאי שֶׁנֶּאֱמַר וַיֹּאמֶר מֹשֶׁה אֲלֵיהֶם אִם יַעַבְרוּ בְנֵי גָד וּבְנֵי רְאוּבֵן. וְאִם לֹא יַעַבְרוּ חֲלוּצִים אִתְּכֶם וגו'. רִבִּי חֲנַנְיָה בֶּן גַּמְלִיאֵל אוֹמֵר צָרִיךְ הָיָה הַדָּבָר לְאוֹמְרוֹ שֶׁאִילְמָלֵא כֵן יֵשׁ בְּמַשְׁמַע שֶׁאֲפִילוּ בְאֶרֶץ כְּנַעַן לֹא יִנְחָלוּ.

Mishnah 3: "On condition[106] that I possess a *bet kor* of arable land," she is preliminarily married if he owns it. "On condition that I possess it at place X", she is preliminarily married if he owns it at place X, otherwise she is not preliminarily married. "On condition that I shall show you a *bet kor* of arable land," she is preliminarily married and he has to show her[107], but if he showed it in the valley[108] she is not preliminarily married. [109]Rebbi Meïr says, any condition which is not formulated in the manner of the condition imposed on the tribes of Gad and Reuben is invalid[110], as it is said[111]: "Moses said to them, if the tribes of Gad and Reuben cross over ... but if they will not in arms cross over with you, etc." Rebbi Ḥananiah ben Gamliel said, that formulation was necessary[112] for otherwise one would have understood that even in the Land of Canaan they should not inherit.

106 He gives the woman a *peruṭah* as marriage gift and specifies that he preliminarily marries her as owner of a *bet kor*, 30 *bet se'ah* or 75'000 square cubits of agricultural land. If he actually is the owner of the land, she is married immediately; he can show her the title to his land later.

107 Since he said "to show", it means that she has to see it with her own eyes; it is not enough for him to prove his ownership to her.

108 בִּקְעָא everywhere means open agricultural land not easily accessible.

In all these conditions, a claim of ownership is understood.

109 In the independent Mishnah mss. and later in the Halakhah here starts a new Mishnah 4.

110 He requires that a condition spell out (1) what happens if the condition is satisfied, (2) what happens if the condition is not satisfied, and (3) the positive statement has to precede the negative. For him the simple formulation of the Mishnah is unacceptable.

111 *Num.* 32:29-30.

112 The involved formulation of the deed of Transjordan to the tribes of Gad and Reuben was necessary under the circumstances. A simple condition is valid; it is not necessary for a man to say: "Be preliminarily married to me on condition that I possess a *bet kor* of arable land, but be not preliminarily married to me if I do not possess a *bet kor* of arable land."

(63d line 65) **הלכה ג:** עַל מְנָת שֶׁיֵּשׁ לִי בֵּית כּוֹר עָפָר כול'. רִבִּי חֲנַנְיָה בְּרֵיהּ דְּרִבִּי הֵלֵל בְּעָא. אִילוּ מָאן דְּאָמַר. בְּנִי פְלוֹנִי יַעֲשֶׂה דְּבַר פְּלוֹנִי וְיִטּוֹל חֶפֶץ פְּלוֹנִי וּשְׁאָר בָּנַיי יִירְשׁוּ נְכָסַיי. אִין עֲבַד הוּא נְסִיב וְאִין לָא עֲבַד לָא נְסִיב. אוֹ שַׁנְיָיא הִיא דִּכְתִיב לָתֵת לְתִשְׁעַת הַמַּטּוֹת וַחֲצִי הַמַּטֶּה. וַהֲוֵי דוּ אָמַר. בְּנִי פְלוֹנִי יַעֲשֶׂה דְּבַר פְּלוֹנִי וְיִטּוֹל חֵפֶץ פְּלוֹנִי וּשְׁאָר בָּנַיי יִירְשׁוּ נְכָסַיי. אִין עֲבַד הוּא נְסַב וְאִין לָא עֲבַד לָא נְסַב לָא מִיכָּא וְלָא מִיכָּא.

Halakhah 3: "On condition that I possess a *bet kor* of arable land," etc. Rebbi Ḥananiah the son of Rebbi Hillel asked[113]: If somebody said, my son A should perform action X and receive property Y, and the rest of my sons shall inherit my properties; if he performs, he takes, but if he does not perform, he does not take[114]. Or maybe it is a difference since it is written: "To give to Nine and a half tribes.[115]" It is as if he said, my son A should perform action X and receive property Y, and the rest of my sons shall inherit my properties; if he performs, he takes, but if he does not perform, he does not take from here or from there.

113 He asks against R. Ḥanaiah ben Gamliel.
114 This does not disinherit A from sharing with his brothers.
115 *Num.* 34:13. This verse clearly excludes the Transjordan tribes from property in Canaan. Therefore, R. Ḥanaiah ben Gamliel's argument is correct.

(63d line 71) תַּמָּן תַּנִּינָן. מַתְנֶה אָדָם עַל עֵירוּבוֹ. מַתְנֵה מַתְנִיתָא. כֵּינֵי מַתְנִיתָא. מַתְנֶה אָדָם עַל עֵירוּבוֹ. אָמַר רִבִּי אֶלְעָזָר. מָאן תַּנָּא. אִם בָּאוּ וְאִם לֹא בָאוּ. רִבִּי מֵאִיר. הֵיידֵין רִבִּי מֵאִיר. חֲבֵרַייָא אָמְרִין. רִבִּי מֵאִיר דְּקִידּוּשִׁין. דְּתַנֵּי. הָאוֹמֵר לְאִשָּׁה. הֲרֵי אַתְּ מְקוּדֶּשֶׁת עַל מְנָת שֶׁיֵּרְדוּ גְשָׁמִים. יָרְדוּ גְשָׁמִים מְקוּדֶּשֶׁת וְאִם לָאו אֵינָהּ מְקוּדֶּשֶׁת. רִבִּי מֵאִיר אוֹמֵר. בֵּין שֶׁיָּרְדוּ גְשָׁמִים בֵּין שֶׁלֹּא יָרְדוּ גְשָׁמִים מְקוּדֶּשֶׁת עַד שֶׁיִּכְפּוֹל תְּנָייו. הַכֹּל מוֹדִין שֶׁאִם אָמַר. לְאַחַר שֶׁיֵּרְדוּ גְשָׁמִים. יָרְדוּ גְשָׁמִים מְקוּדֶּשֶׁת וְאִם לָאו אֵינָהּ מְקוּדֶּשֶׁת. רִבִּי יוֹסֵי אָמַר. רִבִּי מֵאִיר דְּעֵירוּבִין הִיא. דְּתַנִּינָן תַּמָּן. אִם סָפֵק. רִבִּי מֵאִיר וְרִבִּי יְהוּדָה אוֹמְרִים. הֲרֵי זֶה גַּמָּל חַמָּר. לֹא אָמַר רִבִּי מֵאִיר אֶלָּא לְחוּמְרִין. אָמַר רִבִּי מָנָא. וְיֵאוּת. בְּעֵירוּבוֹ אֵינוֹ קוֹנֶה שֶׁלֹּא זָכָה בּוֹ אֶת עֵירוּבוֹ. כִּבְנֵי עִירוֹ. שֶׁנָּתַן דַּעְתּוֹ לַעֲקוֹר אֶת רַגְלָיו מִבְּנֵי עִירוֹ. וְהָכָא לָרִאשׁוֹן אֵינָהּ מְקוּדֶּשֶׁת שֶׁלֹּא יָרְדוּ גְשָׁמִים. וְלַשֵּׁנִי אֵינָהּ מְקוּדֶּשֶׁת שֶׁלֹּא כָּפַל תְּנָייו. רִבִּי חַגַּי בָּעָא קוֹמֵי רִבִּי יוֹסֵה וְהֵן אִם לֹא כִי לֹא אֶחָד הוּא. אָמַר לֵיהּ. שַׁנְייָא הִיא שֶׁהָיְתָה הָאָרֶץ לִפְנֵיהֶן וְהוּא מְבַקֵּשׁ לְהוֹצִיאָהּ מִיָּדָם.

2 עירובו | ע עירוביו   אלעזר | ע לעזר   ואם | ע אם   היידין | ע היידן   4 על | ע לי על
5 שירדו | ע ירדו   שלא | ע לא   6 יכפול תנייו | ע יכפיל (תניין) [תנאו][116]   אמ' | ע
אמ' לאשה. הרי את מקודשת לי   7 מקודשת | ע מקודשת. ברם כרבנן. בין שירדו בין
שלא ירדו מקודשת[117]   8 היא | ע -   תמן | ע -   9 גמל חמר | ע חמר גמל. ר' יוסי ור'
שמעון אומ'. ספק העירוב כשר   יוסי | ע יוסה   10 קונה | ע -   את עירובו | ע לו
עירובו.   כבני עירו. שנתן דעתו | ע -   12 תנייו | ע הראשון את תניייו   13 וחן | ע
ההן   לא אחד | ע לא חד   שנייא | ע שנייה

[118]There, we have stated: "A person can impose a condition of his *'eruv*.[119]" So is the Mishnah: "A person can impose a condition of his

'eruvin.¹²⁰" Rebbi Eleazar said, who is the Tanna of "if they came", "if they did not come"? Rebbi Meïr¹²¹! Which Rebbi Meïr? The colleagues say, Rebbi Meïr of *Qiddušin*¹²². As it was stated: If somebody say to a woman: You are preliminarily married to me on condition that there will be rain¹²³. If rain fell, she is preliminarily married, otherwise she is not preliminarily married. Rebbi Meïr says, she is preliminarily married whether or not rain fell unless he doubled his condition¹²⁴. Everybody agrees that if he said, after rainfall¹²⁵, if it rained she is preliminarily married, otherwise she is not preliminarily married. Rebbi Yose said, it follows Rebbi Meïr in *Eruvin*, as we have stated there¹²⁶: "If it be in doubt, Rebbi Meïr and Rebbi Jehudah say, he is a camel-donkey driver.¹²⁷" Rebbi Yose said, Rebbi Meïr said this only as a restriction¹²⁸. Rebbi Mana said, that is correct. He cannot acquire his *'eruv* since he is not able to enjoy it. [Why not] like the people of his place? If he had decided to leave his place¹²⁹. And here¹³⁰, she is not preliminarily married to the first, since no rain came. She is not preliminarily married to the second, since [the first] did not double his condition. Rebbi Haggai asked before Rebbi Yose¹³¹: Is this 'if" not a reaction? He answered, there is a difference since the land was in their hand¹³² and he wanted to take it away from them.

116 The scribe wrote תניין for תניי by a slip of the pen which made the י too long; the corrector changed Galilean תניי into Babylonian תנו.
117 The opinion attributed here to the rabbis obviously is R. Meïr's.
118 From here to the end of the Halakhah, the text is also in *Eruvin* 3, 21b line 1 ff.
119 The rabbinic interpretation of the biblical commandment that (*Ex.* 16:29) "nobody shall leave his place of residence on the Seventh Day" is that on the Sabbath one may not go a

distance greater than 2'000 cubits from the boundary of the built-up domain in which one resides. Since by tradition the diameter of the encampment of the Israelites in the desert was 12 *mil*, 24'000 cubits (*Shevi'it* 6:1, Note 28), and certainly the Israelites were able to freely move in their camp on the Sabbath, it is clear that the restriction to 2'000 cubits is purely rabbinical. Therefore, it is open to manipulation. One of the accepted ways of manipulation is for a person to deposit some food, the *'eruv*, at the border of the permitted domain and declare that he intends to consider the place of that food as dwelling for the coming Sabbath. Then he still can move freely in the built-up domain, which is counted only as 4 cubits, but he has an additional 2'000 cubits on the other side of the *'eruv*, but nothing on the opposite side of the built-up area. Mishnah *'Eruvin* 3:5 permits a person to prepare a number of *'eruvin* which are mutually exclusive, and say: "If attackers appear in the East, my *'eruv* in the West shall be active; if they appear in the West, my *'eruv* in the East shall be active; if there is no danger, I shall be like the other inhabitants of my place."

120 Since there are at least two. This remark belongs to *'Eruvin*, not to *Qiddušin*.

121 He will hold that even if there was only one *'eruv*, it has to be spelled out that the *'eruv* shall be invalid if there is no danger; otherwise the person making the *'eruv* can never keep the Sabbath with the other inhabitants of his place.

122 Mishnah *'Eruvin* 3:5 is a direct application of Mishnah *Qiddušin* 3:3 and the *baraita* quoted in the sequel.

123 If a *peruṭah* changed hands and a definite time was given for the duration of the condition.

124 If it was not stated explicitly that there was no marriage without rainfall, the condition is void and the marriage valid unconditionally.

125 If the *peruṭah* is given with the understanding that it is counted as marriage gift when it rained before a fixed date, that explains the modalities of the preliminary marriage, it is not a condition.

126 Mishnah *'Eruvin* 3:4. Somebody put an *'eruv* near the Sabbath boundary. If it was somehow moved and now it is not clear whether it is inside or outside the Sabbath boundary: If it is still within the boundary, the person making it can reach it on the Sabbath and it is valid. If it is outside, it cannot

be reached and is invalid. If it is in doubt, according to rabbis Meïr and Jehudah, the person making it can only move in the domain permitted both if the *'eruv* is valid and if it is invalid.

127 The donkey driver has to go behind his animal; it will not move otherwise. The camel driver has to go in front of his animal and draw it by its bridle; it will not move otherwise. The camel-donkey driver cannot function at all; the usual Babli expression "donkey-camel driver" describes one who cannot move from between the animals as similar to the person with an *'eruv* in doubt who cannot leave the four cubits at which he started the Sabbath.

128 R. Meïr requires a double formulation of a condition only for marriage and divorce, not for *'eruvin*. While this is also the opinion of Rif, most interpreters of the Babli hold that a double formulation is always required. Cf. *Sefer Ha'ittur* I, p. 74 ff.

129 The fact that the person with the *'eruv* in doubt is a donkey-camel driver has nothing to do with the requirement of a double formulation. The *'eruv* cannot be valid if the person cannot reach it on the Sabbath; the person cannot have the domain available to the other residents since he had decided not to be part of the population for the coming Sabbath.

130 A hypothetical case in which a first man contracted a preliminary marriage conditioned upon the timely arrival of rains, when a second man contracted an unconditional preliminary marriage with the same woman before the arrival of rains. Since she was not married when the second man came, it is impossible to say that the latter's preliminary marriage were invalid. It is also impossible to say that it were valid, since the first man's condition was not stated in the double formulation required by R. Meïr; she needs divorces from both men.

131 This question is directed against R. Hanaiah ben Gamliel. What was the necessity of the double formulation in the case of the tribes Gad and Reuben? The question should be asked not for the negative part but for the positive; was it necessary to state that the tribes will get the Transjordan territory if they come to fight in Canaan?

132 They already were in possession; to make this possession conditional needed the involved formulation.

(64a line 10) רִבִּי יוּדָה בַּר סִיסִין רִבִּי יוּדָה בַּר פָּזִי בְשֵׁם רִבִּי אָחָא. יָרְדוּ לְסִימְפוֹן בְּשִׁיטַת רִבִּי מֵאִיר דְּקִידּוּשִׁין. רִבִּי חֲנַנְיָה חֲבֵרִין דְּרַבָּנִין בָּעָא. לָמָּה לִי כְרַבִּי מֵאִיר. אֲפִילוּ כְרַבָּנִין. לֹא כֵן אָמַר רִבִּי אַבָּהוּ בְשֵׁם רִבִּי יוֹחָנָן. סֵדֶר סִימְפוֹן כָּךְ הוּא. אֲנָא פְלָן בַּר פְלָן מְקַדֵּשׁ לִיךְ אַנְתְּ פְּלָנִיתָא בַּת פְּלוֹנִי עַל מְנָת לִיתֵּן לִיךְ מִיקָמַת פְלָן וּמִכְנָסִינָיךְ לְיוֹם פְּלָן. וְאִין אָתָא וְלָא כְנָסְתִּיךְ לָא יְהֵא לִי עָלַיִךְ כְּלוּם. וְיֹאמַר. עַל מְנָת. שֶׁלֹּא לִכְפּוֹל תְּנָיִיו. אִילוּ לֹא כָפַל תְּנָיִיו מִיעָקַר קִידּוּשִׁין. אָמַר רִבִּי יוֹסֵי בֵּירִבִּי בּוּן. בְּכָל־אָתָר אִית לְרִבִּי מֵאִיר מִמַּשְׁמַע לָאו אַתְּ שׁוֹמֵעַ הֵין. וְהָכָא לֵית לֵיהּ. אָמַר רִבִּי מַתַּנְיָה. חוֹמֶר הוּא בַּעֲרָיוֹת.

1 בר סיסין | ע בן שלום   ר' אחא | ע ר' יוחנן   2 ר' חנניה חברין דרבנין בעא | ע ר' ירמיה ר' חנניה חברה דרבנן בעי   למה לי | ע ולמה   3 כרבנין | ע כרבנן   לא | ע לית   4 ליך אנת | ע אותך. את   5 ליתן | ע מיתן   מיקמת | ע מקמת   ליום | ע ביום   אתא | ע אתא יום פלן   6 עליך | ע עלייך   ויאמר | ע ויימר   לכפול | ע יכפיל   7 יוסי | ע יוסה   8 חומר | ע על שם חומר

Rebbi Jehudah bar Sisin[133], Rebbi Jehudah bar Pazy in the name of Rebbi Aḥa. They formulated the *symphōn* according to Rebbi Meïr[134]. Rebbi Ḥananiah, the colleague of the rabbis, asked: Why does it have to follow Rebbi Meïr but not also the rabbis? Did not Rebbi Abbahu say in the name of Rebbi Joḥanan: The following is the contract text: "I, X son of Y, contract a preliminary marriage with you, Z, daughter of U, on condition that I shall give you property A and definitively marry you by day B. If that day should pass without me having taken you in, I shall have no claim on you." Why can he not say "on condition" but not double his stipulation? If he did not double his stipulation, could this eliminate the preliminary marriage[135]? Rebbi Yose ben Rebbi Abun said, everywhere Rebbi Meïr holds that from "no" you infer "yes", except here[136]? Rebbi Mattaniah said, one is more restrictive in matters of incest and adultery.

133 An Amora of this name is not otherwise documented in Talmudic literature. Probably the reading of י "R. Jehudah ben Shalom" is correct.

134 Since it states both that there is preliminary marriage if the conditions are satisfied but none if they are not satisfied.

135 Even the rabbis must require an extra stipulation which will eliminate the preliminary marriage if the conditions are not satisfied.

136 The Babli (*Nedarim* 11a,13b; *Ševu'ot* 36a) emphatically holds that R. Meïr requires a double formulation since he does not infer a positive statement from a negative one. For example, a statement "this shall for me be not profane" implies a dedication for the rabbis but not for R. Meïr.

(fol. 63b) **משנה ד:** הַמְקַדֵּשׁ אֶת הָאִשָּׁה וְאָמַר כְּסָבוּר הָיִיתִי שֶׁהִיא כֹהֶנֶת וַהֲרֵי הִיא לְוִיָּה לְוִיָּה וַהֲרֵי הִיא כֹהֶנֶת עֲנִיָּה וַהֲרֵי הִיא עֲשִׁירָה עֲשִׁירָה וַהֲרֵי הִיא עֲנִיָּה הֲרֵי זוֹ מְקוּדֶּשֶׁת מִפְּנֵי שֶׁלֹּא הִטְעַתּוּ

Mishnah 4: If a person contracts a preliminary marriage with a woman and then says, I was of the opinion that she was a Cohenet but she is a Levite, a Levite but she is a Cohenet, poor but she is rich, rich but she is poor, she is preliminarily married since she did not trick him[137].

137 His relations with other people are not influenced by his erroneous opinions, as long as he alone is responsible for them.

(64a line 20) **הלכה ד**: רִבִּי מֵאִיר אוֹמֵר. כָּל־תְּנַאי כול'. רִבִּי לְעָזָר אוֹמֵר. מְקוּדֶּשֶׁת אֲפִילוּ בְעֵדִים. רִבִּי שְׁמוּאֵל בְּשֵׁם רִבִּי זְעִירָא. מְקוּדֶּשֶׁת לְחוֹמְרִין.

Halakhah 4: [109]"Rebbi Meïr says, any condition," etc. Rebbi Eleazar said, she[138] is preliminarily married as if by witnesses. Rebbi Samuel in the name of Rebbi Ze'ira: She is preliminarily married as a restriction[139].

138 A woman preliminarily married with a condition that was not expressed in double form and was not satisfied. He holds that for R. Meïr she is married unconditionally. In the opinion of Nachmanides (reported in *Sefer Hatterumot* 51:6) the statement does not refer to the preceding Mishnah, but to Mishnah 4: Even if there are witnesses who can testify that the groom told them that he was going to marry a Cohenet, as long as she did nothing to suggest that idea to him, she is validly married.

139 For him R. Meïr agrees that the woman cannot be married if the stipulation was not fulfilled. But he will hold that if a second man married her, she needs a bill of divorce from both of them since both of them have equal claim on her.

(64a line 21) רִבִּי יַעֲקֹב בַּר אָחָא בְּשֵׁם רִבִּי אִימִּי. רְאוּבֵן חַיָּיב לְשִׁמְעוֹן. סָמְכֵיהּ גַּבֵּי לֵוִי. אֵיפַּרְסָן לֵוִי. לֵית רְאוּבֵן חַיָּיב לְשִׁמְעוֹן. הָדָא דְאַתְּ אָמַר. בְּשֶׁלֹּא עָשׂוּ בָהּ עָרְמָה. אֲבָל עָשׂוּ בְהַעֲרָמָה חַיָּיב.

כְּהָדָא חֲזָרְיָיה סָמְכוּן לִתְנָאֵי קְרָיָיה גַּבֵּי זְבוּנָה. קָרַן זְבוּנָה וְאָזַל לֵיהּ. אֲתָא עוֹבְדָא קוֹמֵי רִבִּי מָנָא אָמַר. אִין פְּרִיטִין אִינּוּן פְּשָׁעִין. אִין דֵּינָרִין אִינּוּן כֵּינִי אוֹרְחָא דִזְבוּנָה מְדַדְיָה.

חַד בַּר נַשׁ קָם עִם חַבְרֵיהּ בְּשׁוּקָא. אָמַר לֵיהּ. הַב לִי קִיתוֹנָה דְאִית לִי גַּבָּךְ. אָמַר לֵיהּ. הַב לִי דֵּינָרָא דְאִית לִי גַּבָּךְ. אָמַר לֵיהּ. הַב לִי קִיתוֹנָא וְסַב דֵּינָרָא. אָתָא עוֹבְדָא קוֹמֵי רִבִּי מָנָא. אָמַר לֵיהּ. אַתְּ אוֹדֵית לֵיהּ בְּדֵינָרָא וְהוּא לֹא אוֹדֵי לָךְ בְּקִיתוֹנָא. אֵיזִיל וְהַב לֵיהּ דֵּינָרָא. אָמַר רִבִּי יַעֲקֹב בַּר אָחָא. מוֹדֵי רִבִּי אִימִּי דּוּ אָמַר בְּשֶׁהַדִּין לֹא כֵן אֶלָּא בְּדִיל דְּלָא יִכְפּוֹר בְּקִיתוֹנָה לֹא חִיֵּיב.

חַד בַּר נַשׁ הֲוָה חַיָּיב לְחַבְרֵיהּ מֵאָה דֵינָרִין בְּקַרְטִיס. שָׁלַח חַמְשִׁין גַּבֵּי שְׁלִיחָא. אָמַר לֵיהּ. אִין לָא יְהַב לָךְ קַרְטִיסָא לֹא תִתֵּן לֵיהּ כְּלוּם. אָתָא עוֹבְדָא קוֹמֵי רִבִּי אִימִּי. אָמַר. אֵיזִיל הַב וַאֲנָן יָדְעִין. הַגַּע עַצְמָךְ דְּאָמַר רִבִּי אִימִּי עוֹשִׂין לוֹ מוֹדַע בֵּית דִּין. דְּזָכָה לְחַבְרֵיהּ. רַבָּנִין דְּהָכָא אָמְרִין. דְּזָכָה זָכָה.

12 דמר ‎| G דדמך   אימי ‎| G אמי

Rebbi Jacob bar Aḥa in the name of Rebbi Immi: Reuben owes to Simeon; he transferred [the debt] to Levi[140]. Levi became poor[141]; then Reuben owes nothing to Simeon. That is, if it was not done in bad faith, but if it was done in bad faith, he is obligated.

Similarly, the pedlars directed the village wax chandlers to a merchant. The merchant absconded. The case came before Rebbi Mana, who said, if it is a matter of pennies, they were negligent[142]. If it is a matter of denars, it is the way of merchants to move around.

A person met another in the market place. He said to him, give me the linen which you hold for me. The other responded, give me the denar which you hold for me. The first said, give me the linen and deduct the denar. The case came before Rebbi Mana, who said to him, you admitted that you owe him a denar; he did not admit anything about the linen. Go and give him the denar! Rebbi Jacob bar Aḥa said, Rebbi Immi[143] will agree that this is not the law but that he obligated him lest the other deny his liability for the linen.

A person owed another one 100 denars on a document[144]. He sent 50 with an agent and instructed him: If he does not surrender the document, do not give him anything. The case came before Rebbi Immi. He said, go and give it, for we know. Think of it, Rebbi Immi [might die][145]! One writes for him a proclamation of the court[146].

If one accepts for another person, the rabbis here say, what he accepted, he accepted for the claimant.

140 And Simeon accepted the assignment, thinking that Levi had good credit. The case belongs here because it frees Reuben from liability as long as he did nothing to inflate Levi's credit in Simeon's eyes.

141 Levy and Kohut explain as Greek ἀπορέω, "to become poor".

142 The wax-chandlers should have collected their debt expeditiously; but for a large debt the pedlars remain obligated.

143 One is tempted to read "R. Mana" for "R. Immi".

144 Greek χάρτης, Latin *charta*, "papyrus, roll of papyrus".

145 Reading of the Geniza fragment. It makes more sense than the reading "who said" of L. The emendation of *Pene Moshe*, דמח instead of דמר, is confirmed by the Genizah text as to meaning but not as to formulation.

146 The agent was not empowered to pay the 50 denars without getting the document; the creditor was not willing to give the document for less than full payment. R. Immi told him to deliver the document and receive a court document instead which documented the remaining claim.

(64a line 37) דְּלְמָא. רִבִּי דוֹסְתַּי בֵּירִבִּי יַנַּאי וְרִבִּי יוֹסֵי בֶּן כִּיפָר נַחְתּוֹן לְגַבֵּיהּ לַחֲבִרָיָא תַּמָּן. אִיתְאָמַר עֲלֵיהוֹן לְשָׁנָא בִּישָׁא. הֲווֹן בָּעֲיָין דְּלָא יְהִיוְיָין כְּלוּם. אָתוֹן בָּעֵי מִיפְּקָא מִינְהוֹן. אָמְרִין לוֹן. כְּבָר זַבְנוּן. אָמְרִין לוֹן. וּמִנָּן. אָמְרִין לוֹן. מִנָּן בְּעֵי תְקַמִּינוֹן טָבָאוֹת. אָמְרִין לוֹן. שׁוֹמְרֵי חִנָּם אֲנַחְנוּ. אֲזַלוֹן לְגַבֵּי רִבִּי דוֹסְתַּי בֵּירִבִּי יַנַּאי. אָמַר לוֹן. אָהֵן הוּא כּוּלָּהּ. נַסְבּוֹן לְרִבִּי יוֹסֵי בֶּן כִּיפָר וְכַפְתוֹן וְאַפְקוּן מִינֵּיהּ. כַּד סַלְקוֹן לְהָכָא אָתָא לְגַבֵּי אֲבוֹי. אָמַר לֵיהּ. חָמֵי מָה עָבַד לִי בְּרָךְ. אָמַר לֵיהּ. מָה עָבַד לָךְ. אָמַר לֵיהּ. אִילּוּ אַשְׁוֵי עִימִּי לָא הֲווֹן מַפְקָה מִינָּן כְּלוּם. אָמַר לֵיהּ. מָה עַבְדָּת כֵּן. אָמַר לֵיהּ. רָאִיתִי אוֹתָן בֵּית דִּין שָׁוֶה וְכוֹבָעֵיהֶן אַמָּה וּמַדְבְּרִין מַחֲצָיִין וְיוֹסֵה אֲחִי כָּפוּת וּרְצוּעָה עוֹלָה וְיוֹרֶדֶת. וְאָמַרְתִּי. שֶׁמָּא דּוֹסְתַּי אַחֵר יֵשׁ לְאַבָּא. אָמַר רִבִּי חַגַּי. הָדָא דְּאַתְּ אָמַר בְּהַהוּא דְלָא יָכִיל מִיקְמָה גַּרְמֵיהּ טַבָיוֹת. בְּרַם הַהוּא דְּיָכִיל מִיקְמָה טַבָאוֹת נְסַב לוֹן מִן דֵּין וְיָהַב לְדֵין וְיִמְחוֹל שְׁטָר לְחַבְרֵיהּ. רִבִּי חֲנַנְיָה וְרִבִּי מָנָא. חַד אָמַר מָחִיל. וָחֳרָנָה אָמַר. לָא מָחִיל עַד דַּחֲזַר לֵיהּ שְׁטָרָא.

1 לגביה | ט מיגבי 2 איתאמר | ט ואיתאמרת לשנא בישא | ט לשן ביש הוון בעיין | ט אתון בעיי 3 מינהון | ט מיניה זבנון | ט זבינן ומנן | ט - 4 מנן | ט אנן טבאות | ט טבאת שומרי | ט שומר אזלון | ט אתון 5 אהן הוא | ט ההנו 6 וכפתון | ט ופטרוי חמיי | ט לית את חמי 7 אשוי | ט אשווי 8 מפקה | ט מפקין

HALAKHAH 5

9 מחציין ט מחציים 10 ואמרתי | ט ואמרית דאת אמר | ט דתימר | 11 בהוא | ט בההוא טביות | ט טבאות 12 נסב | ט מיפק דין | ט הדא ויהב | ט ויטלון וימחול | ט דין דמחל 13 מחיל | ט מחל (2 times) דחזר ט דמחל

[147]Rebbi Dositheos ben Rebbi Yannai and Rebbi Yose ben Kipper descended to collect there for the colleagues when they were slandered. They asked but were not given anything. Then they came and wanted to take it back from them. They answered, we already acquired it. They said, we wish for you to accept it in good faith; they answered, we are unpaid trustees. They approached Rebbi Dositheos ben Rebbi Yannai who told them, there it is, all of it. They took Rebbi Yose ben Kipper, whipped him with ropes, and took it from him. When they returned here, he went to his father and told him, look what your son did to me! He asked him, what did he do to you? He answered, if he had taken my position, they could not have taken anything from us. He asked him, why did you act in such a way? He said, I saw that they were a unanimous court, their hats were a cubit wide, they were directing blows, my brother Yose was bound and the whip ascended and descended. I said, does my father have another Dositheos? Rebbi Haggai said, you say that for somebody who cannot give a warranty in good faith. But if somebody gives a warranty in good faith, one takes from this one and gives to the other.

If somebody forgave a bond to another person: Rebbi Hanania and Rebbi Mamal: one said it is forgiven; the other said it is not forgiven unless he handed over the bond.

147 Text and translation are from *Gittin* 1:6, Notes 181-199 (ט). The Genizah text simply refers to the *Gittin* text, reserving less than one line for the entire quote.

(fol. 63b) **משנה ה:** הָאוֹמֵר לָאִשָּׁה הֲרֵי אַתְּ מְקוּדֶּשֶׁת לִי לְאַחַר שֶׁאֶתְגַּיֵּיר אוֹ לְאַחַר שֶׁתִּתְגַּיְירִי לְאַחַר שֶׁאֶשְׁתַּחְרֵר אוֹ לְאַחַר שֶׁתִּשְׁתַּחְרְרִי לְאַחַר שֶׁיָּמוּת בַּעֲלִיךְ אוֹ לְאַחַר שֶׁתָּמוּת אֲחוֹתֵיךְ לְאַחַר שֶׁיַּחֲלוֹץ לֵיךְ יְבָמֵיךְ אֵינָהּ מְקוּדֶּשֶׁת. וְכֵן הָאוֹמֵר לַחֲבֵירוֹ אִם יָלְדָה אִשְׁתְּךָ נְקֵיבָה הֲרֵי הִיא מְקוּדֶּשֶׁת לִי לֹא אָמַר כְּלוּם.

Mishnah 5: If somebody say to a woman: You are preliminarily married to me after I convert, or after you are converted[148], after I am freed, or after you are freed[149], after your husband has died[150], or after your sister has died[151], or after your levir has given you *ḥaliṣah*[152], she is not preliminarily married. Similarly, if somebody say to another, if your wife have a daughter, she shall be preliminarily married to me, he did not say anything[153].

148 While marriage exists for Gentiles, preliminary marriage is a uniquely Jewish institution. If one or both parties are Gentile, no preliminary marriage is possible.

149 A slave cannot marry. Therefore, if one or both parties are servile, no preliminary marriage is possible.

150 A married woman cannot marry another party. A preliminary marriage in anticipation of the husband's death is impossible.

151 If the man was once married to a woman, her sister is forbidden to him during the woman's lifetime. This is the only incest prohibition of *Lev.* 18 for which no criminal penalty is indicated in *Lev.* 20. But *Lev.* 18:18 is read as: "A woman in addition to her sister you are unable take, to be co-wives, to uncover her nakedness in addition to her, during her lifetime." The act of preliminary marriage is here defined as impossible during the sister's lifetime.

152 This Tanna follows the majority interpretation of *Deut.* 25:5, which reads: "If brothers dwell together and one of them die without children, the widow of the deceased *is unable to be an outside man's*." Cf. *Yebamot* 1:1, Notes 93-103; Note 166 below.

153 A marriage contract cannot be concluded as a futures contract on anything which does not yet exist. The Mishnah in the Babli states in addition that if the wife of the prospective father-in-law was visibly pregnant, the

contract is valid. The Halakhah shows that the Yerushalmi clearly holds that a woman is said to exist only from the moment of her birth, not while she still is in her mother's womb.

(64a line 52) **הלכה ה:** הָאוֹמֵר לָאִשָּׁה הֲרֵי אַתְּ מְקוּדֶּשֶׁת לִי כול׳. בְּעוֹן קוֹמֵי רִבִּי יוֹחָנָן. מַה בֵּינָהּ לָאוֹמֵר. הֲרֵי זוֹ תְרוּמָה עַל הַמְחוּבָּרִין הַלָּלוּ שֶׁיִּתָּלֵישׁוּ. אָמַר לוֹן. תַּמָּן יֵשׁ בְּיָדוֹ לִתְלוֹשׁ בְּרַם הָכָא אֵין בְּיָדוֹ לְשַׁחְרֵר. הָתִיב רִבִּי פֵּס. הַגַּע עַצְמָךְ שֶׁהָיְתָה שִׁפְחָתוֹ. אָמַר רִבִּי בָּא בַּר מָמָל. לִכְשֶׁתִּשְׁתַּחְרֵר נִתְלֵית בְּדַעַת אַחֶרֶת.

4 נתלית G | ניתלית

Halakhah 5: "If somebody say to a woman," etc. They asked before Rebbi Joḥanan: What is the difference between this and one who says, "this shall be heave for this standing produce after it has been cut"⁵⁴? He said to them, there, it is in his power to cut; but here, it is not in his power to be freed¹⁵⁵. Rebbi Ephes asked, think of it, if she was his slave girl¹⁵⁶? Rebbi Abba bar Mamal said, "after you are freed", she is made dependent on another person's will¹⁵⁷.

154 It is impossible to give heave from standing grain since the obligation of heave starts only at the end of the harvesting process. Nevertheless, the farmer can set aside a certain amount for heave at the start of the harvest to cover everything he will harvest in the future. Then why is it impossible for somebody who at the moment is unable to contract a preliminary marriage to give a gift which is to become a marriage gift as soon as the obstacle to his contracting is removed? The same question is asked in the Babli, 62a.

155 But it is uniquely in the power of the slave's owner, or, in the case of Gentiles, in the power of the rabbinic court to whom they must apply for conversion.

156 Since it is in his own power to free her. In the Babli, 62b, the question is attributed to R. Abba bar Mamal.

157 In the case of the owner

marrying his own slave girl, it is purely a matter of formulation. By making it conditional, "if you be set free", he abdicates his own power. The Yerushalmi will agree that if the owner simply marries his slave girl, without mentioning her need to be freed, by one action he sets her free and marries her (R. Moses Isserles in *Šulḥan ʿArukh Yore Deaʿ* 267:58). (The classical commentators of the Yerushalmi incorrectly read the Babli's explanation into the Yerushalmi text.)

(64a line 57) דְּלָמָא. רִבִּי הוֹשַׁעְיָה רַבָּא וְרִבִּי יוּדָן נְשִׂיָּיא הֲווֹן יְתִיבִין. אָמְרִין. נֵימָא חֲדָא מִילָה בְּקִידּוּשִׁין. הָאוֹמֵר לָאִשָּׁה. הֵא לֵיךְ פְּרוּטָה זוּ שֶׁתִּתְקַדְּשִׁי לִי לִכְשֶׁאֲגָרְשֵׁךְ. מָהוּ. גָּחֲכוֹן וְקָמוּן לְהוֹן. אָמַר רִבִּי יוֹסֵי. וְלָמָּה גָּחֲכוֹן. לֹא אָמַר רִבִּי בָּא בַּר מָמָל. לִכְשֶׁתִּשְׁתַּחְרֵר נִתְלֵית בְּדַעַת אַחֶרֶת. וְהָכָא לִכְשֶׁתִּתְגָּרֵשׁ נִתְלֵית בְּדַעַת אַחֶרֶת. אִין אַתְּ בְּעָא מַקְשָׁיָיא הָכֵן קָשֵׁי. חַד בַּר נַשׁ הֲוָה אֲזִיל מְקַדְּשָׁא חֲדָא אִיתָא. קְדָמֵיהּ חַבְרִיהּ וַאֲמַר לָהּ. הֲוֵי יָדְעָה דִּהֲהֵן גַּבְרָא דְּהוּא אֲזַל מְקַדְּשָׁתֵיךְ דַּעְתֵּיהּ בִּישָׁא. עָתִיד הוּא מִישְׁבַּק לֵיךְ. אֶלָּא הֵא לֵיךְ פְּרוּטָה זוּ שֶׁתִּתְקַדְּשִׁי בָּהּ לִי לִכְשֶׁאֲגָרְשֵׁךְ. מָהוּ.

2 לאשה G | לאשתו   הא ליך G | הילוך   3 לא G | לא כן   5 אין G | אן   בעא מקשייא G | בעי מקשייה   חוה G | -   6 ידעה G | דעתיך   דהוא אזל G | דיאתי   7 דעתיה בישא G | דעתה בישה   לכשאגרשך G | לכשייגרש   מהו G | מה הוא

The elder Rebbi Hoshaia and Rebbi Jehudah Neśia were sitting together. They said, let us say something on the subject of preliminary marriage. If somebody say to his[158] wife, here you have a *peruṭah* that you should be preliminarily married to me after I have divorced you, what is the rule? They laughed and got up[159]. Rebbi Yose said, why did they laugh? Did not Rebbi Abba bar Mamal say, "after you are freed", she is made dependent on another person's will; and here "after you are divorced," she is made dependent on another's will[160]. If you want to find a difficulty, ask the following: A person went to preliminarily marry a woman. Another person overtook him and said to her, you should know that the man who is coming to preliminarily marry you has a bad mind. In the future he will abandon you. But here you have this *perutah* that you should be preliminarily married to me after he will have[158] divorced you[161]. What is the rule?

158 Translation follows the Genizah text.
159 The Babli, 62b, takes R. Hoshaia's question seriously. Naturally, the answer to the question as stated is simply that the action is invalid since a married woman cannot marry again while married, not even her own husband.
160 In the opinion of the Babli, the reason is that while the husband can divorce her unilaterally, he cannot marry her again against her will. This is the "other will" which is involved here.

161 It was shown in 3:1 that if a man gives a gift for preliminary marriage stipulating that the marriage be valid only after 30 days, and another man came, married, and divorced her within those thirty days, the first man's marriage is valid. The problem naturally is that "30 days" is an objective standard, not depending on another's will; but the clause "if the other man will have divorced you" makes it dependent on another's will and invalidates the preliminary marriage.

(64a line 65) תַּמָּן תַּנִינָן. הֲרֵי נְטִיעוֹת הָאֵילּוּ קָרְבָּן אִם אֵינָן נִקְצָצוֹת. טַלִּית זוֹ קָרְבָּן אִם אֵינָהּ נִשְׂרֶפֶת. וְנִשְׂרָפָה. לְמַפְרֵיעָן קָדְשׁוּ. מָעַל. אִין תֵּימַר. מִיכָּן וְלָבֹא. לֹא מָעַל.

There[162], it was stated: "These orchard trees shall be *qorbān* if they are not cut, this garment shall be *qorbān* if it is not burned." And it was burned. Were they sanctified retroactively? He committed larceny. If you say that it refers to the future, he did not commit larceny.

162 Mishnah *Nedarim* 3:6 and the relevant Halakhah (Notes 110-121). The text here does not make any sense and is not intended to make any sense. The Genizah fragment starts the quote of the Mishnah; the missing part of the line contained an instruction to continue the text in *Nedarim*. The same is intended here. We have a quote of the start of the Mishnah and a few words from the first paragraph of the Halakhah, ending with a complete copy of the last sentence, a sign that the copy now starts in earnest. It is clear that both scribes of the Genizah and the Leiden mss. considered the *Nedarim* text as the original for *Qiddušin*. For the reader's convenience, here is the text omitted by the scribes:

Halakhah 6: "These orchard trees shall be *qorbān*," etc. If he saw the king's cutting crew coming near, if he saw fire coming near, and he said: These orchard trees shall be *qorbān* if they are not cut, this garment shall be *qorbān* if it is not burned or torn. Were they sanctified retroactively or only for the future? What is the difference? If he used them. If you say that they are sanctified retroactively, he committed larceny. If you say that it refers to the future, he did not commit larceny.

(64a, line 68) חִזְקִיָּה אָמַר. פְּדָיָין חָזְרוּ לִקְדוּשָׁתָן. רַבִּי יוֹחָנָן אָמַר. פְּדָיָין פְּדוּיִין. מַתְנִיתָא פְּלִיגָא עַל רַבִּי יוֹחָנָן. אֵין לָהֶן פִּדְיוֹן. פָּתַר לָהּ. לִכְשֶׁקְּצָצוּ אֵין לָהֶן פִּדְיוֹן. אָמַר רִבִּי יוֹסֵי. מָאן דְּאָמַר חִזְקִיָּה בִּשְׁפְּדָיָין הוּא. אֲבָל אִם פְּדָיָין אַחַר פְּקָעָה מֵהֶן קְדוּשָׁתָן. מַחְלְפָה שִׁיטָתֵיהּ דְּרִבִּי יוֹסֵי. תַּמָּן הוּא אוֹמֵר. פְּדָיָין אַחַר פְּקָעָה מֵהֶן קְדוּשָׁתָן. וְהָכָא הוּא אָמַר. נִישָּׂאת לְאַחֵר לֹא פָּקְעוּ מִמֶּנָּה קִידּוּשִׁין. לֹא צְרִיכָא דְלֹא כְשֶׁנָּתַן לָהּ שְׁתֵּי פְרוּטוֹת. אַחַת מִכְּבָר וְאַחַת לִכְשֶׁיְּגָרְשָׁהּ מָהוּ.

2 לחן | נ לה   לכשקצצו | נ לכשיקצצו[163]   3 מאן | נ מה[163]   4 אומר | נ אמ'   5 אחר | נ -   6 צריכא[164] | נ צורכה   כשנתן | נ בשנתן   7 לכשיגרשה | נ לכשיגרשנה[163]

[165]Hizqiah said, if he redeemed them they revert to their sanctity. Rebbi Johanan said, if he redeemed them they are redeemed. The Mishnah disagrees with Rebbi Johanan: "These have no redemption." He

explains thus: After they were cut they do not need redemption. Rebbi Yose said, what Hizqiah said refers to the case that he himself redeemed them. But if another person redeemed them, the sanctity is removed from them. The argument of Rebbi Yose is switched: There, he says that if [another] redeemed them, the sanctity is removed from them, but here, he says that if she was married to another man the *qiddušin* [of the first] were not removed! All that is questionable for him is if he gave her two *peruṭot*, one for the moment and one for after he divorced her; what is the situation?

163 Clearly, the spelling in *Nedarim* is the correct one
164 A Babli word; the Yerushalmi word is in *Nedarim*.
165 *Nedarim* 3:6, Notes 114-121.

(64a, line 75) אָמַר רִבִּי יַנַּאי. נִימְנוּ שְׁלֹשִׁים וְכַמָּה זְקֵנִים. מִנַּיִן שֶׁאֵין קִידּוּשִׁין תּוֹפְסִין בִּיבָמָה. תַּלְמוּד לוֹמַר לֹא תִהְיֶה אֵשֶׁת הַמֵּת הַחוּצָה לְאִישׁ זָר. שֶׁלֹּא יְהֵא בָהּ הֲוָיָיה לְזָר. אָמַר לֵיהּ רִבִּי יוֹחָנָן. וְלָאו מַתְנִיתָהּ הִיא. אוֹ לְאַחַר שֶׁיַּחֲלוֹץ לִיךְ יְבָמֵיךְ. אֵינָהּ מְקוּדֶּשֶׁת. וַהֲוָה רִבִּי יַנַּאי מְקַלֵּס לֵיהּ. הַצָּלִים זָהָב מַכִּיס. בְּנִי אַל יָלִיזוּ מֵעֵינֶיךָ. חֲכַם בְּנִי וְשַׂמַּח לִבִּי וְאָשִׁיבָה חוֹרְפִי דָבָר. תֵּן לְחָכָם וְיֶחְכַּם עוֹד. יִשְׁמַע חָכָם וְיוֹסֶף לֶקַח וגו'. אָמַר לֵיהּ רִבִּי שִׁמְעוֹן בֶּן לָקִישׁ בָּתַר כָּל־אִילֵּין קִילוּסַיָּיא יָכוֹל הוּא פָּתַר לָהּ כְּרִבִּי עֲקִיבָה. דְּרִבִּי עֲקִיבָה אוֹמֵר. יֵשׁ מַמְזֵר בִּיבָמָה.

3 בה | א לה לזר | א אצל אחר ולאו | א ולא 4 והוה | א והה ינאי | א יוחנן
5 ואשיבה חורפי דבר | א - 6 וגו' | א - ליה | א - 7 הוא | א הוא אנא

[166]Rebbi Yannai said: More than 30 Elders voted: from where that *qiddushin* have no legal effect on a sister-in-law? The verse says, "the wife of the deceased may not belong to any outside unrelated man", that she cannot have any existence with an outsider. Rebbi Johanan said to

him, is that not a Mishnah? "Or after your levir will have performed *ḥaliṣah* with you, she is not preliminarily married." And Rebbi Yannai praised him "those who pour out gold from the wallet," "my son, they should not be removed from your eyes," "get wise, my son, and make me happy, that I can answer those who insult me", "give to the wise that he shall become wiser," "let the wise listen that he increase in knowledge." Rebbi Simeon ben Laqish said, after all these praises I can explain it following Rebbi Aqiba since Rebbi Aqiba said that there exists a bastard from a sister-in-law!

166 *Yebamot* 1:1 (א), Notes 95-100. In the Genizah text, the entire paragraph again is only worth one line's mention.

(64b, line 7) שְׁמוּאֵל אוֹמֵר. בַּעֲנִיּוּתֵינוּ צְרִיכָה מִמֶּנּוּ גֵּט. אָמַר רִבִּי יוֹסֵי בֵּירְבִּי בּוּן. מַתְנִיתָא לְאַחַר שֶׁיַחֲלוֹץ לִיךְ יְבָמֵיךְ. אֲבָל אִם אָמַר. לְאַחַר שֶׁיָּמוּת יְבָמֵיךְ. הֲרֵי זוֹ מְקוּדֶּשֶׁת. תַּנֵּי רִבִּי חִייָה. בַּת יוֹמָהּ מִתְקַדֶּשֶׁת בַּכֶּסֶף. בַּת שָׁלֹשׁ שָׁנִים וְיוֹם אֶחָד מִתְקַדֶּשֶׁת בְּבִיאָה. אָמַר רִבִּי מָנָא. מַתְנִיתָא אָמְרָה כֵן. וְכֵן הָאוֹמֵר לַחֲבֵירוֹ אִם יָלְדָה אִשְׁתְּךָ נְקֵיבָה הֲרֵי הִיא מְקוּדֶּשֶׁת לִי. לֹא אָמַר כְּלוּם. מִפְּנֵי שֶׁאֵינָהּ בְּעוֹלָם. הָא אִם הָיְתָה בְּעוֹלָם הֲרֵי זוֹ מְקוּדֶּשֶׁת.

1 יוֹסֵי G | יוסה   2 מתניתא G | מתניתה אמרה   4 מנא מתניתא G | יוסה מתניתה

[167]Samuel said, in our poverty, she needs a bill of divorce from him. Rebbi Yose ben Rebbi Abun said, the Mishnah [said], "after your levir has given you *ḥaliṣah*"; but if he said, "after your levir has died," she is preliminarily married[168]. [169]Rebbi Ḥiyya stated: A one-day-old girl can be preliminarily married by money; a girl of three years and one day can be preliminarily married by intercourse." Rebbi Mana said, the Mishnah implies this: "Similarly, if somebody say to another, if your wife have a

daughter, she shall be preliminarily married to me, he did not say anything," because she does not exist. Therefore, if she does exist, she is preliminarily married.

167 Here starts the discussion of the Mishnah dealing with the widow of a childless man. Samuel disagrees with the Mishnah; his position is accepted in the Babli as practice (*Yebamot* 92b). While the marriage of the widow outside the family without *ḥaliṣah* certainly is sinful, it nowhere in the biblical text is punished as a criminal act; for Samuel this indicates that such a marriage should not be void by biblical standards.

168 He holds that the Mishnah can be explained following Samuel. Even though the marriage by the widow of the childless man outside the family is valid, the marriage conditional on the action of the levir is invalid as explained by R. Abba bar Mamal. Therefore, the marriage conditioned on an act of God is valid, in particular also since after the death of the levir it no longer is sinful.

169 Here starts the discussion of the Mishnah dealing with the newborn girl.

משנה ו: הָאוֹמֵר לָאִשָּׁה הִתְקַדְּשִׁי לִי עַל מְנָת שֶׁאֲדַבֵּר עָלַיִךְ לַשִּׁלְטוֹן (fol. 63b) וְאֶעֱשֶׂה עִמָּךְ כַּפּוֹעֵל דִּיבֶּר עָלֶיהָ לַשִּׁלְטוֹן וְעָשָׂה עִמָּהּ כַּפּוֹעֵל מְקוּדֶּשֶׁת וְאִם לָאו אֵינָהּ מְקוּדֶּשֶׁת. עַל מְנָת שֶׁיִּרְצֶה אַבָּא רָצָה הָאָב מְקוּדֶּשֶׁת וְאִם לָאו אֵינָהּ מְקוּדֶּשֶׁת. מֵת הָאָב הֲרֵי זוֹ מְקוּדֶּשֶׁת. מֵת הַבֵּן מְלַמְּדִין אֶת הָאָב לוֹמַר שֶׁאֵינוֹ רוֹצֶה.

Mishnah 6: If somebody says to a woman, be preliminarily married to me on condition that I speak for you to the government, or work for you as a worker, she is preliminarily married if he did speak for her to the government or did work for her as a worker; otherwise she is not preliminarily married[170]. On condition that my father agree; if the father agreed, she is preliminarily married, otherwise she is not preliminarily married. If the father died, she is preliminarily married[171]; if the son died, one instructs the father to say that he does not agree[172].

170 As the Halakhah explains, there are two possible interpretations of this Mishnah, depending on whether or not a *peruṭah* changes hands at the moment. The problem does not arise in the Babli, which instead of "be preliminarily married to me" reads הרי את מקודשת לי "you are preliminarily married to me"; that language implies that (a) at least a *peruṭah* changes hands at the moment of engagement and (b) the marriage, if valid, is in effect from the moment of giving. Both implications are absent in the Yerushalmi version.

171 One interprets "on condition that my father agree" as "if my father does not object". Since the father died, he can no longer object.

172 If the father has other sons, one tells him to free the woman from the obligation of levirate by rejecting the preliminary marriage.

(64b line 14) **הלכה ו:** הָאוֹמֵר לָאִשָּׁה הִתְקַדְּשִׁי לִי כול׳. רַב אָמַר. וְהוּא שֶׁנָּתַן לָהּ שָׁוֶה פְרוּטָה אֲנָן קַיָּימִין. רִבִּי אִימִּי בְּעֵי קוֹמֵי רִבִּי. וְכָל־הַדְּבָרִים לֹא וְהוּא שֶׁנָּתַן לָהּ שָׁוֶה פְרוּטָה אֲנָן קַיָּימִין. אֶלָּא כֵיְנֵי. בַּמֶּה שֶׁאֲדַבֵּר עָלַיִךְ לַשִּׁלְטוֹן. וְדִבֵּר עָלֶיהָ לַשִּׁלְטוֹן בְּשָׁוֶה פְרוּטָה מְקוּדֶּשֶׁת וְאִם לָאו אֵינָהּ מְקוּדֶּשֶׁת. בַּמֶּה שֶׁאֶעֱשֶׂה עִמָּךְ כַּפּוֹעֵל. וְעָשָׂה עִמָּהּ כַּפּוֹעֵל שָׁוֶה פְרוּטָה מְקוּדֶּשֶׁת וְאִם לָאו אֵינָהּ מְקוּדֶּשֶׁת. רִבִּי בָּא בְשֵׁם רַב. וְהוּא שֶׁיְּיִחֲדָה לוֹ סֶלַע בַּמִּגְדָּל. בַּמֶּה קִידְּשָׁהּ. כְּהַהִיא דְּתַנִּינָן תַּמָּן. כָּל־הַנַּעֲשָׂה דָמִים בְּאַחֵר כֵּיוָן שֶׁזָּכָה זֶה נִתְחַיֵּיב זֶה בַּחֲלִיפָיו.

2 שוה G | שווה   אמי G | אימי   קומי ר׳ | G -   4 ודיבר G | דיבר   בשוה G | שווה
5 ועשה G | עשה   שוה G | שווה   לאו G | לאו   7 כההיא G | כיי

Halakhah 6: "If somebody says to a woman, be preliminarily married to me," etc. Rav said, we deal with the case that he gave her a *perutah*'s worth[173]. Rebbi Immi asked (before Rebbi)[174]: Do we not always deal with the case that he gave her a *perutah*'s worth[175]? But so it is: "By what I shall speak for you to the government; if he did speak for her to the government for a *perutah*'s worth she is preliminarily married, otherwise she is not preliminarily married." "By what I shall work for you as a worker; if he did work for her as a worker for a *perutah*'s worth, she is preliminarily married, otherwise she is not preliminarily married." Rebbi Abba in the name of Rav: Only if she set aside a tetradrachma in her chest for him[176]. With what did he effectuate the preliminary marriage? As we have stated there: "If anything is bartered instead of money, if one party entered in possession, the other is obligated for its trade-in[177]."

173 In the Babli, 53a. the uncontested opinion of R. Simeon ben Laqish.

174 This should be deleted with G.

175 In all preceding cases, if it says "be preliminarily married to me on condition", it was understood that the proposal was accompanied by a marital gift. Then the present Mishnah would be unnecessary. But the new facet of this Mishnah is that preliminary marriage may be effected with lawyer's or worker's fees.

176 The lawyer or the worker have to present the bill for their work; if the bill amounts to at least a *perutah*, she is married by the forgiving of the bill if she had the money to pay. This formulation avoids the problem of the Babli, that marriage cannot be effectuated by forgiving a loan, and the fee due a professional might be considered a loan slowly accreting through delivery of his services.

177 Mishnah 1:6, Note 521. By writing the bill, the lawyer puts a monetary value on his services.

(64b line 22) עַל מְנָת שֶׁיִּרְצֶה אַבָּא רָצָה הָאָב מְקוּדֶּשֶׁת לֹא רָצָה אֵינָהּ מְקוּדֶּשֶׁת. סְתָמוֹ אֵינוֹ רוֹצֶה. מֵת הָאָב הֲרֵי זוֹ מְקוּדֶּשֶׁת. סְתָמוֹ רוֹצֶה. מֵת הַבֵּן מְלַמְּדִין אֶת הָאָב לוֹמַר אֵינוֹ רוֹצֶה. סְתָמוֹ רוֹצֶה. אָמַר רִבִּי יוֹחָנָן לְרִבִּי יַנַּאי. וְאִית מַתְנִיתָא אֲמָרָהּ כֵּן. אָמַר לֵיהּ. וּלְיַנַּאי עֲלִיבָא אַתְּ שָׁאִיל מִילָה בְּקִידּוּשִׁין. חָזַר רִבִּי יַנַּאי וּפָתַר מַתְנִיתָהּ עַל מְנָת שֶׁיִּרְצֶה אַבָּא. רָצָה הָאָב מְקוּדֶּשֶׁת וְאִם לָאו אֵינָהּ מְקוּדֶּשֶׁת. בְּאוֹמֵר עַל מְנָת דּוּ אָמַר. וְהוּא לֹא אָמַר. מֵת הָאָב הֲרֵי זוֹ מְקוּדֶּשֶׁת. כְּמָאן דְּאָמַר. מֵת הַבֵּן מְלַמְּדִין אֶת הָאָב שֶׁיֹּאמַר. אֵינִי רוֹצֶה. כְּמָאן דְּאָמַר. אָמַר רִבִּי זְעִירָא לְרִבִּי יוֹסֵי. יָכִיל רִבִּי יַנַּאי מִיפְתּוֹר מַתְנִיתָהּ הֵיךְ דּוּ בָעֵי. אָמַר לֵיהּ. כֵּן אָמַר רִבִּי שִׁמְעוֹן בֶּן לָקִישׁ. לֹא מִיתְמְנַע רִבִּי מִיכְּלָל בַּאֲתַר חַד וּפָרֵט בַּאֲתַר חַד. אָמַר רִבִּי יוֹסֵי. מַתְנִיתָהּ אֲמָרָהּ כֵּן. עַל מְנָת שֶׁיֵּשׁ לִי בֵּית כּוֹר עָפָר. כְּלָל. בְּמָקוֹם פְּלוֹנִי. פְּרָט.

3 אינו G | איני   יניי G | ינאי   4 ינאי עליבא G | יניי עליבה   שאיל מילה G | שאל מלה   5 ינאי G | יניי   6 דו אמר G | דיאמר   7 כמאן G | כמן   8 זעירא G זעורה   לר' יוסי G קומי ר' יסא   היך דו G | הך דהוא   9 ליה G | לה   מיתמנע G מתמנע   מיכלל G | כלל   יוסי G | יוסה   מתניתי' G | ומתניתהא

"On condition that my father agree; if the father agreed, she is preliminarily married; if the father does not agree, she is not preliminarily married;" silently he does not agree[178]. "If the father died, she is preliminarily married;" silently he agreed[179]. "If the son died, one instructs the father to say that he does not agree;" silently he agreed. Rebbi Joḥanan asked Rebbi Yannai, can the Mishnah say so? He answered him, do you ask wretched Yannai to explain *Qiddušin*? Rebbi Yannai returned and explained the Mishnah: "On condition that my father agree; if the father agreed, she is preliminarily married; otherwise she is not preliminarily married," he said on condition that [the father] express his opinion but he did not[180]. "If the father died, she is preliminarily married;" as if he had given his opinion[181]. "If the son died, one instructs the father to say that he does not agree;" as if he had given his opinion[182]. Rebbi Ze'ira said [before Rebbi Yasa][183]: Can Rebbi Yannai explain the Mishnah as he wishes? He answered him, so says Rebbi Simeon ben Laqish, Rebbi does not refrain from stating generality and detail simultaneously[184]. Rebbi Yose said, the Mishnah states thus: "On condition that I have a *bet kor* of arable land", a generality; "at place X", a detail[185].

178 This is an example of the problem of the undistributed middle, frequently discussed in the Babli but rarely in the Yerushalmi. The Mishnah is silent on the status of the marriage if the father refuses to express an opinion. The formulation "if the father agreed" seems to imply that failure to give a positive reply is a rejection. If the formulation had been "unless the father objects," the father's silence would have signified assent.

179 According to the argument of the preceding Note, if the father died without expressing an opinion, the marriage should be invalid. The second and third clauses of the Mishnah seem to contradict the first.

180 One has to read the first clause as explained in Note 178, that there is no undistributed middle but the son made the validity of the marriage dependent on the explicit acceptation by his father. The father's silence means rejection.

181 If the father died before he had an opportunity to react, the court may assume that he might have assented if he had lived; the woman is married to the extent that if another man married her preliminarily before the first one married her definitively, she would need a bill of divorce from both of them.

182 Even if the father had given his initial consent, if the son died before the definitive marriage the court will instruct the father to refuse to accept the marriage in order not to forbid the woman to a Cohen. This clause has nothing to do with the problem of the undistributed middle.

183 Reading of G. The text of L is unacceptable; R. Ze'ira cannot ask his student's student R. Yose but he can ask his teacher and R. Simeon ben Laqish's

student R. Yasa.

184 The three clauses of this part of the Mishnah refer to three different situations. In the first clause, a very restrictive interpretation is appropriate, in the second a very general one, in the third even a prior acceptance is turned into a rejection. This agrees with the general style of the Mishnah.

185 Mishnah 3:3. The example does not quite fit the problem, but the general thrust is clear.

(fol. 63b) **משנה ז**: קִידַּשְׁתִּי אֶת בִּתִּי וְאֵינִי יוֹדֵעַ לְמִי קִידַּשְׁתִּיהָ וּבָא אֶחָד וְאָמַר אֲנִי קִידַּשְׁתִּיהָ נֶאֱמָן. זֶה אָמַר אֲנִי קִידַּשְׁתִּיהָ וְזֶה אָמַר אֲנִי קִידַּשְׁתִּיהָ שְׁנֵיהֶם נוֹתְנִין גֵּט וְאִם רָצוּ אֶחָד נוֹתֵן גֵּט וְאֶחָד כּוֹנֵס. קִידַּשְׁתִּי אֶת בִּתִּי קִידַּשְׁתִּיהָ וְגֵרַשְׁתִּיהָ כְּשֶׁהִיא קְטַנָּה וַהֲרֵי הִיא קְטַנָּה נֶאֱמָן. קִידַּשְׁתִּיהָ וְגֵרַשְׁתִּיהָ כְּשֶׁהִיא קְטַנָּה וַהֲרֵי הִיא גְדוֹלָה אֵינוֹ נֶאֱמָן. נִשְׁבֵּית וּפְדִיתִיהָ בֵּין שֶׁהִיא קְטַנָּה בֵּין שֶׁהִיא גְדוֹלָה אֵינוֹ נֶאֱמָן.

Mishnah 7: "I preliminarily married off my daughter but I do not know to whom I married her preliminarily," and somebody comes and says, I married her preliminarily, he is believed[186]. This one says, "I married her preliminarily," and that one says, "I married her preliminarily," both give a bill of divorce or, if they so wish, one gives a bill of divorce and the other marries her definitively. "I preliminarily married off my daughter, married her preliminarily and received her bill of divorce while she was underage," and [now] she still is underage, he is believed[187]. "I preliminarily married off my daughter, married her preliminarily and received her bill of divorce while she was underage," and [now] she is an adult, he is not believed[188]. "She had been kidnapped[189] and I ransomed her," he is not believed whether she is underage or adult.

186 Since the father has the right to marry off his underage daughter, if he believes that the person claiming her is his son-in-law, he has the right to marry her to him.

187 Since he has the right to marry his daughter to a man whose intercourse will make her unfit for the priesthood, he can also declare her unfit for the priesthood as divorcee without producing proof.

188 Since he does not have the right to marry off his adult daughter, he cannot declare her ineligible for the priesthood without producing proof.

189 And presumed raped, which forbids her to a Cohen.

(64b line 34) **הלכה ז:** הָאוֹמֵר. קִדַּשְׁתִּי אֶת בִּתִּי סל׳. מָהוּ נֶאֱמָן. שְׁמוּאֵל אָמַר. נֶאֱמָן לִיתֵּן גֵּט. אַסִּי אָמַר נֶאֱמָן לִכְנוֹס. רַב הִינָא בְּשֵׁם רַב אָמַר. נֶאֱמָן לִכְנוֹס. רִבִּי יוֹחָנָן אָמַר נֶאֱמָן לִכְנוֹס וְאֵין לְמֵידִין מִמֶּנּוּ דָּבָר אַחֵר. מָהוּ אֵין לְמֵידִין מִמֶּנּוּ דָּבָר אַחֵר. אַחַת מִשָּׁדוֹתַי מָכַרְתִּי וְאֵינִי יוֹדֵעַ לְמִי מְכַרְתִּיהָ. בָּא אֶחָד וְאָמַר. אֲנִי לְקַחְתִּיהָ לֹא הַכֹּל מִמֶּנּוּ. אַף בְּקִדּוּשִׁין כֵּן. אַחַת מִבְּנוֹתַיי קִדַּשְׁתִּי וְאֵינִי יוֹדֵעַ לְמִי קִדַּשְׁתִּיהָ. וּבָא אֶחָד וְאָמַר. אֲנִי קִדַּשְׁתִּיהָ. לֹא הַכֹּל מִמֶּנּוּ. מַתְנִיתָא פְלִיגָא עַל רַב. הַמֵּבִיא גֵט מִמְּדִינַת הַיָּם וְאָמַר. בְּפָנַיי נִכְתַּב וּבְפָנַיי נֶחְתַּם. לֹא יִשָּׂא אֶת אִשְׁתּוֹ. תַּמָּן חוּחְזָקָה אֵשֶׁת אִישׁ בִּפְנֵי הַכֹּל. בְּרַם הָכָא לֹא חוּחְזָקָה אֵשֶׁת אִישׁ אֶלָא בִּפְנֵי שְׁנַיִם. לִכְשֶׁיָּבוֹאוּ שְׁנַיִם וְיֹאמְרוּ. זֶהוּ שֶׁקִּידֵּשׁ. מַתְנִיתָא פְלִיגָא עַל שְׁמוּאֵל. זֶה אוֹמֵר. אֲנִי קִדַּשְׁתִּיהָ. וְזֶה אוֹמֵר. אֲנִי קִדַּשְׁתִּיהָ. שְׁנֵיהֶן נוֹתְנִין גֵּט. וְאִם רָצוּ אֶחָד נוֹתֵן גֵּט וְאֶחָד כּוֹנֵס. פָּתַר לָהּ בְּאוֹמֵר. לְאֶחָד מִשְּׁנֵי אֵילּוּ קִדַּשְׁתִּיהָ וְאֵינִי יוֹדֵעַ אֵי זֶהוּ. רִבִּי זְעִירָא רִבִּי יוֹסֵי בְּשֵׁם רִבִּי יוֹחָנָן. קָדַם אֶחָד מֵהֶן וְכָנַס מוֹצִיאִין מִיָּדוֹ. הָדָא דְאַתְּ אָמַר בְּשֶׁזֶּה אוֹמֵר. אֲנִי קִדַּשְׁתִּיהָ. וְזֶה אוֹמֵר. אֲנִי קִדַּשְׁתִּיהָ. וְקָדַם וְכָנַס. אֲבָל אִם אָמַר אֲנִי קִדַּשְׁתִּיהָ. וּכְנָסָהּ. וּבָא אַחֵר וְאָמַר. אֲנִי קִדַּשְׁתִּיהָ. לֹא כָל־הֵימֶנּוּ. וְתַגִּי כֵן. אִם מִשֶּׁכְּנָסָהּ בָּא אַחֵר וְאָמַר. אֲנִי קִדַּשְׁתִּיהָ. לֹא כָל־הֵימֶנּוּ.

2 בשם רב אמ׳ | **ב** אמ׳ בשם רב 3 ממנו[190] | **ב** הימינו (2 times) 4 בא | **ב** ובא לקחתיה | **ב** הוא שלקחתיה ממנו | **ב** הימינו 9 זהו | **ב** זה הוא 10 שמואל | **ב** ר׳ יוחנן 12 זהו | **ב** זה הוא 13 יוסי | **ב** יסא[191] מוציאין | **ב** אין מוציאין 14

וכנס | ב אחד מהן וכנס

[192]"If one says, I preliminarily married off my daughter", etc. About what is he trustworthy? Samuel says, he is trusted to give a bill of divorce. Assi said, he is trusted to marry. Rav Huna said in the name of Rav: He is trusted to marry. Rebbi Johanan said, he is trusted to marry but one does not infer anything for another case from this ruling. What means, one does not infer anything for another case from this ruling? I sold one of my fields but I do not remember to whom I sold it. If someone comes and says, I bought it, he is not trusted in any way. In preliminary marriage, the same holds true. "I betrothed one of my daughters but I do not remember to whom I betrothed her. If someone comes and says, I married her preliminarily," he is not trusted in any way. The Mishnah disagrees with Rav: "If somebody brings a bill of divorce from overseas and says, it was written and signed in my presence, he shall not marry that woman." There, she is considered by everybody to be a married woman. Here, she is considered to be a married woman only by two persons. One waits until these two come and say, this is the man who gave her *qiddushin*. The Mishnah disagrees with Samuel: "This one says, I married her preliminarily, and that one says, I married her preliminarily. Both of them give a bill of divorce, but if they agree, one gives a bill of divorce and the other one marries." He explains this, if [the father] says, I did betrothe her to one of these two but I do not remember which one it was. Rebbi Ze'ira, Rebbi Yasa, in the name of Rebbi Johanan: If one of them jumped the gun and married her, one does remove her from him. That is, if this one says, I married her preliminarily, and that one says, I married her preliminarily, and one of them jumped the gun and married

her definitively. But if he said, I married her preliminarily and then married her definitively, and another one comes and says, I married her preliminarily, he is not trusted in any way. It was stated thus: If after the marriage another man comes and says, I married her preliminarily, he is not trusted in any way.

190   The (unetymological) Babylonian version of Galilean דימינו.
191   The correct version, cf. Note 183.
192   *Yebamot* 2:11 (ב) (Notes 184–195). G simply has a note: גרש בסו״ף "One פי׳קא חניינא דיבמות עד לא הכל . . . continues the end of the second Chapter of *Yebamot* as far as "he is not [trusted] in any way."

(fol. 63b) **משנה ח:** מִי שֶׁאָמַר בִּשְׁעַת מִיתָתוֹ יֵשׁ לִי בָנִים נֶאֱמָן. יֵשׁ לִי אַחִים אֵינוֹ נֶאֱמָן.

Mishnah 8: If somebody said when dying, I have children, he is believed[193]; I have brothers, he is not believed[194].

משנה ט: הַמְקַדֵּשׁ אֶת בִּתּוֹ סְתָם אֵין הַבּוֹגְרוֹת בִּכְלָל. מִי שֶׁיֵּשׁ לוֹ שְׁתֵּי כִתֵּי בָנוֹת מִשְּׁתֵּי נָשִׁים וְאָמַר קִידַּשְׁתִּי אֶת בִּתִּי הַגְּדוֹלָה וְאֵינִי יוֹדֵעַ אִם גְּדוֹלָה שֶׁבַּגְּדוֹלוֹת אוֹ גְּדוֹלָה שֶׁבַּקְּטַנּוֹת אוֹ קְטַנָּה שֶׁבַּגְּדוֹלוֹת שֶׁהִיא גְּדוֹלָה מִן הַגְּדוֹלָה שֶׁבַּקְּטַנּוֹת כּוּלָּן אֲסוּרוֹת חוּץ מִן הַקְּטַנָּה שֶׁבַּקְּטַנּוֹת דִּבְרֵי רַבִּי מֵאִיר. רַבִּי יוֹסֵי אוֹמֵר כּוּלָּן מוּתָּרוֹת חוּץ מִן הַגְּדוֹלָה שֶׁבַּגְּדוֹלוֹת.

Mishnah 9: If somebody preliminarily marries off his daughter without mentioning her name, the adult ones are not included[195]. If somebody has two groups of daughters from two wives and he says, I preliminarily married off my older daughter, but he does not know[196] whether the oldest of the older ones, or the oldest of the younger ones, or the youngest of the older ones who is older than the oldest of the younger ones, all are forbidden[197] except the youngest of the younger ones, the words of Rebbi Meïr. Rebbi Yose says, all are permitted except the oldest of the older ones[198].

משנה י: קִידַּשְׁתִּי אֶת בִּתִּי הַקְּטַנָּה וְאֵינִי יוֹדֵעַ אִם קְטַנָּה שֶׁבַּקְּטַנּוֹת אוֹ קְטַנָּה שֶׁבַּגְּדוֹלוֹת אוֹ גְדוֹלָה שֶׁבַּקְּטַנּוֹת שֶׁהִיא קְטַנָּה מִן הַקְּטַנָּה שֶׁבַּגְּדוֹלוֹת כּוּלָּן אֲסוּרוֹת חוּץ מִן הַגְּדוֹלָה שֶׁבַּגְּדוֹלוֹת דִּבְרֵי רִבִּי מֵאִיר. רִבִּי יוֹסֵי אוֹמֵר כּוּלָּן מוּתָּרוֹת חוּץ מִן הַקְּטַנָּה שֶׁבַּקְּטַנּוֹת.

Mishnah 10: I preliminarily married off my younger daughter, but he does not know whether the youngest of the younger ones, or the youngest of the older ones, or the oldest of the younger ones who is younger than the youngest of the older ones, all are forbidden except the oldest of the older ones, the words of Rebbi Meïr. Rebbi Yose says, all are permitted except the youngest of the younger ones.

משנה יא: הָאוֹמֵר לָאִשָּׁה קִידַּשְׁתִּיךְ וְהִיא אוֹמֶרֶת לֹא קִידַּשְׁתַּנִי הוּא אָסוּר בִּקְרוֹבוֹתֶיהָ וְהִיא מוּתֶּרֶת בִּקְרוֹבָיו. הִיא אוֹמֶרֶת קִידַּשְׁתַּנִי וְהוּא אוֹמֵר לֹא קִידַּשְׁתִּיךְ הִיא אֲסוּרָה בִּקְרוֹבָיו וְהוּא מוּתָּר בִּקְרוֹבוֹתֶיהָ.

Mishnah 11: If somebody says to a woman, I married you preliminarily, but she says, you did not marry me preliminarily[199], he is forbidden her relatives[200] but she is permitted his relatives. I she says, you married me preliminarily but he says, I did not marry you preliminarily, she is forbidden his relatives but he is permitted her relatives.

193 His childless widow is free to marry outside the family; she does not have to investigate whether his claim is true. The Torah empowers a father to recognize a son (*Deut.* 21:17); the court is not empowered to require additional proof (cf. Babli *Baba batra* 134b).

194 If he dies childless and had married his wife without telling her that he had brothers, he cannot now subject her to levirate with a brother-in-law she might be unable to locate since her husband's uncorroborated statement cannot undo the *prima facie* presumption created at the time of his marriage (cf. *Ke˒ubot* 1:4, Note 177; 5:5 Note 100; *Gittin* 3:4, Notes 92 ff.)

195 Since the father has no right to marry off his adult daughter. The Babli, 64b, points out that even if the adult daughter appoints her father as agent to find her a husband, the father cannot contract the preliminary marriage without mentioning that he is an agent. Then the name of the principal automatically has to be stated.

196 When he took the money or signed the contract, he did not mention her name and now he does not remember which girl he had in mind when he contracted the marriage.

197 They are forbidden to marry. None of them can marry an outsider for she may already be married. She cannot marry the man her father contracted with for he may be her sister's husband. That man has to write a separate bill of divorce for every girl.

198 Since only she is unequivocally determined by the predicate "old".

199 And there is no witness present to support either of the parties.

200 While in the absence of witnesses he cannot force the woman to be married to him, since he declares himself to be married to her he has to observe all incest prohibitions which would follow from the marriage if it were real.

(64b line 52) **הלכה י:** קִידַּשְׁתִּי אֶת בִּתִּי הַקְּטַנָּה כול׳. קִידַּשְׁתִּי אֶת בִּתִּי. הַקְּטַנּוֹת בִּכְלַל הַגְּדוֹלוֹת אֵינָן בִּכְלָל. נִתְקַדְּשָׁה בִתִּי. אֲפִילוּ קְטַנּוֹת אֵינָן בִּכְלָל. גֵּירַשְׁתִּי אֶת בִּתִּי. הַקְּטַנּוֹת בִּכְלָל וְהַגְּדוֹלוֹת אֵינָן בִּכְלָל. נִתְגָּרְשָׁה בִתִּי. אֲפִילוּ קְטַנּוֹת אֵינָן בִּכְלָל. קִידַּשְׁתִּיהָ לְאֶחָד מִן הַפְּסוּלִין לָהּ. נֶאֱמָן. הִבְעַלְתִּיהָ לְאֶחָד

מִן הַפְּסוּלִין לָהּ. אֵינוֹ נֶאֱמָן. נִשְׁבֵּית וּפְדִיתִיהָ. בֵּין שֶׁהִיא קְטַנָּה וּבֵין שֶׁהִיא גְדוֹלָה אוֹ שֶׁנִּבְעֲלָה לְאֶחָד מִן הַפְּסוּלִין לָהּ. לֹא כָל־הֵימֶינּוּ לְפוֹסְלָהּ.

2 הגדולות G ו הגדולות   נתקדשה G ניתקדשה   3 נתגרשה G ניתגרשה   5
ופדיתיה G ופדיתיהא   בין G בן   ובין G בן   6 לאחד מן G מאחד מכל

Halakhah 10: "I preliminarily married off my younger daughter," etc. "I preliminarily married off my daughter." The underaged are included[201], the adults are excluded[202]. "My daughter was preliminarily married," even the underaged are not included[203]. "I accepted my daughter's bill of divorce," the underaged are included, the adults are excluded. "My daughter was divorced," even the underaged are not included. "I preliminarily married off my daughter to one of those disqualified for her," he is believed. "I made her sleep with one of those disqualified for her," he is not believed. "She had been kidnapped and I ransomed her," whether she is underage or adult or had intercourse with one of those disqualified for her, he is not believed.

201 Since Scripture bases the rules of a criminal procedure on the uncorroborated statement of a father who says "I gave my daughter to this man" (*Deut.* 22:16), it is concluded that his statement concerning a daughter over which he has the power to give her away into marriage has to be accepted by the court without further documentation or corroboration.

202 Since the father has no right to give her away into marriage.

203 The language seems to imply that the father was not involved in the marriage. But an underage girl cannot be legally wedded without her father arranging the marriage. For illegal acts, the father's standing is no different from any other person in the world; one needs two independent witnesses. The father, being his daughter's relative, is automatically disqualified as a witness.

(64b line 59) כֵּינִי מַתְנִיתָה. שֶׁאָמַר בְּשָׁעַת מִיתָתוֹ. יֵשׁ לִי בָנִים. נֶאֱמָן. יֵשׁ לִי אַחִים. אֵינוֹ נֶאֱמָן. רַב אָמַר. מֵאַחַר שֶׁבְּיָדוֹ לְגָרֵשׁ נֶאֱמָן. מִילְתֵיהּ דִּשְׁמוּאֵל אָמְרָה כֵן. חַד פַּרְסָאָה מִידְמַךְ אָמַר לוֹן. הָבוּ לְאִיתְתֵיהּ דְּהַהוּא גַּבְרָא גִּיטָא. אֲמָרוֹן לֵיהּ. וְלָמָּה. בְּגִין הַהוּא אָחוּךְ עֲלִיבָא. כַּד דְּמַךְ אֲתָא עוֹבְדָא קוֹמֵי שְׁמוּאֵל. אָמַר. מֵאַחַר שֶׁיֵּשׁ בְּיָדוֹ לְגָרֵשׁ נֶאֱמָן. רִבִּי יוֹחָנָן אָמַר. אֵינוֹ נֶאֱמָן. נְחַת עוּלָא לְתַמָּן וְאָמַר בְּשֵׁם רִבִּי יוֹחָנָן וְחַבְרוֹן עֲלוֹי. הַגַּע עַצְמָךְ שֶׁהָיָה כֹהֵן.

1 כיני G | כני   שאמר G | מי שאמר   2 מילתיה G | מלתה   3 לאיתתיה G | לאתתה   גיטא G | גטה   4 ליה G | לה

So is the Mishnah: "If somebody said when dying, I have children, he is believed; I have brothers, he is not believed;" Rav said, since it is in his hand to divorce, he is to be believed[204]. The word of Samuel agrees with this. A Persian when dying said to them: Give this man's[205] wife a bill of divorce. They asked him, why? Because of your wretched brother? After he died, the case came before Samuel who said, since it was in his hand to divorce, he is to be believed[206]. Rebbi Johanan said, he is not to be believed. Ulla descended there[207] and said this in the name of Rebbi Johanan; they[208] ganged up on him. Think of it, if he was a Cohen[209]?

204 One is not forced to say that the man married under false pretenses when he did not inform his bride of the existence of a brother; that now he cannot change her situation while maintaining the validity of his marriage, since he could conditionally divorce his wife, the divorce becoming active a moment before his death, and thereby protect her from the complications of levirate (in particular, in this case where the widow would be bound to an unknown brother-in-law whom she might be unable to locate).

205 His own.

206 There is no reason to believe that the bill of divorce was not written and duly delivered. Samuel's decision was that the estate, after payment of the widow's claims, has to be held by a court-appointed trustee for the brother as next of kin.

207 In Babylonia he proclaimed the Babylonian authorities Rav and Samuel to be in error.
208 The Babylonian scholars.
209 This is R. Johanan's and Ulla's argument against Rav and Samuel: Since a Cohen may not give his wife a conditional bill of divorce without forbidding her permanently to himself, and civil law does not make any difference in the personal standing of the parties, the Babylonian argument is invalid; the Mishnah is justified.

In the Babli, *Baba batra* 134b/135a, R. Johanan holds that a man who says that he divorced his wife cannot be believed without corroborating evidence. Then he cannot be believed if unexpectedly he declares to have a brother.

(64b line 66) הָתִיב רַב שֵׁשֶׁת. וְהָא מַתְנִיתָא פְּלִיגָא. קִידַּשְׁתַּנִי. וְהוּא אוֹמֵר לֹא קִידַּשְׁתִּיךְ. הוּא מוּתָּר בִּקְרוֹבוֹתֶיהָ וְהִיא אֲסוּרָה בִּקְרוֹבָיו. אָמְרִין. אָכֵין הֲוָה עוֹבְדָא. שִׁמְעוֹן בַּר בָּא אַייְתֵי גִיטָּא וּנְתָנוֹ לָהּ בְּעֵד אֶחָד. אָתָא עוֹבְדָא קוֹמֵי רִבִּי יוֹחָנָן. אָמַר. אֵין עֵד אֶחָד בְּאֵשֶׁת אִישׁ כְּלוּם. לֹא רִבִּי חִייָה בַּר אַסִּי אָמַר בְּשֵׁם אַסִּי. אֵין עֵד אֶחָד בְּאֵשֶׁת אִישׁ כְּלוּם. רַב אָמַר. הַמְקַדֵּשׁ בְּעֵד אֶחָד לֹא עָשָׂה כְּלוּם. שְׁמוּאֵל אָמַר. הַמְקַדֵּשׁ בְּלֹא שִׁידּוּכִים לוֹקֶה. וְתוֹפְסִין קִידּוּשִׁין. מַר עוּקְבָא בְּשֵׁם שְׁמוּאֵל אָמַר תְּלָת. הַמְקַדֵּשׁ בְּלֹא שִׁידּוּכִין לוֹקֶה. וְהַבָּא עַל אֲרוּסָתוֹ בְּבֵית חָמִיו לוֹקֶה. וְהַמְבַזֶּה שָׁלִיחַ בֵּית דִּין לוֹקֶה.

1 ששת G | שישת   2 בקרובותיה G | בקרובו   אכין הוה G | הכן הווה   3 עובדא G |
עובדה   4 אין G | אן   6 ותופסין G | ותפסו בה   7 מר עוקבא G | ר' נחמיה בר
מר עוקבן   8 שליח G | שלוח

Rav Sheshet objected[210]: Does not the Mishnah disagree? "You married me preliminarily but he says, I did not marry you preliminarily; he is permitted her relatives but she is forbidden his relatives."[211] They said, so did it happen: Simeon bar Abba brought a bill of divorce and delivered it in front of one witness. The case came before Rebbi Johanan, who said, a single witness in marital matters is nothing[212]. Did not Rebbi Hiyya bar Assi in the name of Assi[213] say: a single witness in marital matters is nothing? Rav said, one who performs a preliminary marriage in front of a single witness did not do anything[214]. Samuel said, he who performs a preliminary marriage without prior negotiation is whipped, but the preliminary marriage holds. Mar Uqba in the name of Samuel said three things: He who performs a preliminary marriage without prior negotiation is whipped[215]; one who sleeps with his betrothed in his father-in-law's house[216] is whipped; one who insults the court bailiff[217] is whipped.

210 The language is unusual; how can one object if no statement was yet enunciated? But it is impossible to move the question after the statements of Rav and Samuel because of the concurrent testimony of G (which admittedly is fragmentary at this point.)

211 Mishnah 12; the order of arguments is that of the Mishnah in the Babli.

Rav Sheshet's point is that the case treated in the Mishnah simply cannot happen. Either there are witnesses to the marriage, then there can be no dispute; or there are no witnesses, then there is no marriage.

212 There was no delivery, the woman is not yet divorced. The agent has to take the document back and deliver it anew in front of two witnesses.

213 Unfortunately, these names are missing in G; there is an outside chance that the reference is to Rav Hiyya bar Ashi, student of Rav.

214 In the Babli, 65a, this is a statement of Rav Nahman in the name of Samuel; it is stated explicitly that this holds even if the parties agree.

215 In the Babli, 12b, this is attributed to Rav and rejected as practice in Nahardea, Samuel's place. Probably this means that a betrothal is possible at the second, but not the first, date.

216 As was the custom in Mishnaic times in Judea (*Ketubot* 1:5; Mishnah and Note 208).

217 Who acts in an official capacity.

(64b line 75) **הלכה:** מִי שֶׁיֶּשׁ לוֹ שְׁתֵּי כִיתֵּי בָנוֹת כול'. רַב חָמָא אָמַר. תְּרֵיי מִן תְּרֵיי. אָמַר רִבִּי יַעֲקֹב בַּר אָחָא כְּגוֹן אֲנָא דְאִית לִי תְּרֵיי מִן תְּרֵיי. מַתְנִיתָה בְּשֶׁיֶּשׁ לוֹ שְׁתֵּי כִיתֵּי בָנוֹת מִשְּׁתֵּי נָשִׁים. אֲבָל אֵין לוֹ אֶלָּא כַת אַחַת. אִם אָמַר. גְּדוֹלָה. לֹא קִידֵּשׁ אֶלָּא גְדוֹלָה. וְאִם אָמַר. קְטַנָּה. לֹא קִידֵּשׁ אֶלָּא קְטַנָּה.

Halakhah: "If somebody has two groups of daughters," etc. Rav Ḥama said, two of two[218]. Rebbi Jacob bar Aḥa said, for example I, who have two of two. The Mishnah [speaks of] him who has two groups of daughters from two wives, but if he has only one group and he said, the older, he married off only the oldest; if he said, the younger, he married off only the youngest.

218 Even R. Meïr will agree that if one wife has more than two daughters, the intermediate ones will neither be called "old" or "young" but be specified by name. Therefore, the whole disagreement is about a man who has two daughters each from two wives.

(64c line 4) תַּמָּן תַּנִּינָן. עַד לִפְנֵי הַפֶּסַח. רִבִּי מֵאִיר אוֹמֵר. עַד שֶׁיַּגִּיעַ. רִבִּי יוֹסֵי אוֹמֵר. עַד שֶׁיֵּצֵא. רִבִּי יִרְמִיָה בְּעָא קוֹמֵי רִבִּי זְעִירָה. מַחְלְפָה שִׁיטָתֵיהּ דְּרִבִּי מֵאִיר. מַחְלְפָה שִׁיטָתֵיהּ דְּרִבִּי יוֹסֵי. מַחְלְפָה שִׁיטָתֵיהּ דְּרִבִּי יוֹסֵי. תַּמָּן הוּא אָמַר. עַד שֶׁיֵּצֵא כָּל־רְשׁוּיוֹת הַגְּדוֹלוֹת. עַד שֶׁיֵּצֵא כָּל־רְשׁוּיוֹת הַקְּטַנּוֹת. וְהָכָא אָמַר הָכֵין. אָמַר לֵיהּ. מִשְּׁמֵת בֶּן עַזַּאי וּבֶן זוֹמָא בָּטְלוּ הַשַּׁקְדָּנִים. וְלֹא עָמַד שַׁקָּד עַד שֶׁעָמַד יִרְמִיָה. אָמַר רִבִּי בָּא בְּרֵיהּ דְּרִבִּי חִייָה בַּר וָא. וְהוּא מְקַנְתֵּר לְהוֹן. לֹא כְבָר קַשִּׁיתָהּ הֲרֵי עוֹלָם. לֹא כְבָר קַשִּׁיתָהּ רִבִּי אֶלְעָזָר קוֹמֵי רִבִּי יוֹחָנָן. מַחְלְפָה שִׁיטָתֵיהּ דְּרִבִּי מֵאִיר. וְאָמַר לוֹן. לֵית הִיא מַחְלְפָה. מַתְנִיתָא הִיא דְּמִחְלְפָה. דְּתַנֵּי דְבֵית רִבִּי כֵן. עַד לִפְנֵי הַפֶּסַח. רִבִּי מֵאִיר אוֹמֵר. עַד שֶׁיֵּצֵא. רִבִּי יוֹסֵי אוֹמֵר. עַד שֶׁיַּגִּיעַ. אָמַר לֵיהּ. אֲנָן בָּעֵיי עַד לִפְנֵי וְאַתְּ אָמַר אָכֵן. אָמַר רִבִּי זְעִירָא. לְשׁוֹן נִיוָותִי הוּא. עַד לִפְנֵי פִּיסְחָא. אָמַר רִבִּי אָבִין. הַכֹּל מוֹדִין בַּפֶּסַח שֶׁהוּא מוּתָּר. מַה פְּלִיגִין. בִּפְרָס הַפֶּסַח. הָהֵן אָמַר. עַד שֶׁיֵּצֵא. וְהָהֵין אָמַר. עַד שֶׁיַּגִּיעַ.

2 בעא | נ בעי   2-3 מחלפה שיטתיה דר' מאיר. מחלפה שיטתיה דר' יוסי | נ -   4 אמ' |
נ אומ'   שיצא | נ שיצאו (twice)   גדולות | נ הגדולות (2 times)   5 והכא | נ וכא הוא
6 שקד | נ שוקד   והוא | נ למה הוא   7 לא כבר קשיתה זרי עולם | נ -   קשיתה | נ
קשונתה   8 מאיר | נ יוסי   ואמ' לון | נ אמ' ליה   9 דמחלפה | נ מחלפה   10 אמ'
ליה | נ -   11 אכן | נ אכין   ניוותי | נ ניותי   12 בפרס | נ בפרוס   13 שיצא | נ
שיגיע   שיגיע | נ שיצא

[219]There, we have stated: "'Until before Passover', Rebbi Meïr says, until it comes, Rebbi Yose says, until it passed." Rebbi Jeremiah asked before Rebbi Ze'ira: The opinion of Rebbi Meïr seems inverted; the opinion of Rebbi Yose seems to be inverted. The opinion of Rebbi Yose seems inverted: There, he says "until all the elder possibilities are exhausted, until all the younger possibilities are exhausted," and here, he says so? He said to him: Since Ben Azai and Ben Zoma died, the perseverers disappeared; no perseverer was there until Jeremiah appeared. Rebbi Abba, son of Rebbi Ḥiyya bar Abba, said, why does he needle him? Did not great mountains find this difficult, did not Rebbi Eleazar already ask before Rebbi Joḥanan, does not the opinion of Rebbi Meïr seem to be inverted? He said to him, it is not inverted, the Mishnah is inverted, for in the House of Rebbi they stated: "'Until before Passover', Rebbi Meïr says, until it passed, Rebbi Yose says, until it comes." He said: We ask "until before", and you say so? He said to him, this is a Nabatean expression, "much before Passover'. Rebbi Abin said, everybody agrees that he is permitted on Passover[46]. Where do they disagree? The day before Passover. One of them says, until it passed, the other until it comes.

219 This is essentially *Nedarim*, Halakhah 8:3 (Notes 36-45). In G, the entire reference to this text seems to have been in one missing line.

(64c line 19) **הלכה**: הָאוֹמֵר לָאִשָּׁה כול׳. אָמַר רִבִּי יוֹסֵי. מִסְתַּבְּרָא דְלָא יְהֵוֵי רִבִּי מֵאִיר פְּלִיג הָכָא. אָמַר רִבִּי מָנָא. כָּל־גַּרְמֵיהּ אָמְרָה דְהוּא פְּלִיג. מָה אִין תַּמָּן שֶׁבְּכֻלָּם גְּדוֹלוֹת וּקְטַנּוֹת אַתְּ אָמַר. רִבִּי מֵאִיר פְּלִיג. כָּאן שֶׁבְּכֻלָּם גְּדוֹלוֹת אֵצֶל קְטַנּוֹת וְכֻלָּם קְטַנּוֹת אֵצֶל גְּדוֹלוֹת לֹא כָּל־שֶׁכֵּן שֶׁיְּהֵא רִבִּי מֵאִיר פְּלִיג.

2 גרמיה G | גרמה   4 קטנות G | קטנה   וכלום G | וכולם

Halakhah: "If somebody says to a woman," etc. Rebbi Yossi said, it is reasonable that Rebbi Meïr not disagree in this case[220]. Rebbi Mana said, the entire series implies that he disagrees. Since there, where they are all[221] older and younger[222], you say that Rebbi Meïr disagrees, so here, where all are old compared to young or young compared to old, he certainly disagrees[223].

220 This refers to the next Mishnaiot 12 and 13, where the question is whether the mother or a daughter was being married. There, R. Meïr's name is not mentioned. R. Yose imples that the Mishnah is R. Meïr's.

221 Reading with G כולם for כלים "nothing" of L.

222 The case of two groups of girls from different mothers.

223 R. Mana seems to imply that also in Mishnah 11, and certainly in Mishnaiot 12 and 13, R. Meïr imposes incest restrictions on all parties, including those who deny being parties to a marriage.

(fol. 63b) **משנה יב:** קִידַּשְׁתִּיךְ וְהִיא אוֹמֶרֶת לֹא קִידַּשְׁתָּ אֶלָּא בִתִּי הוּא אָסוּר בִּקְרוֹבוֹת הַגְּדוֹלָה וּגְדוֹלָה מוּתֶּרֶת בִּקְרוֹבָיו. הוּא מוּתָּר בִּקְרוֹבוֹת קְטַנָּה וּקְטַנָּה מוּתֶּרֶת בִּקְרוֹבָיו.

Mishnah 12: "I am preliminarily married to you," but she says, you are only preliminarily married to my daughter; he is forbidden the relatives of the old woman[224], and the old woman is permitted his relatives; he is permitted the relatives of the young woman, and the young woman is permitted his relatives[225].

(fol. 63c) **משנה יג:** קִידַּשְׁתִּי אֶת בִּתֵּךְ וְהִיא אוֹמֶרֶת לֹא קִידַּשְׁתָּ אֶלָּא אוֹתִי הוּא אָסוּר בִּקְרוֹבוֹת קְטַנָּה וּקְטַנָּה מוּתֶּרֶת בִּקְרוֹבָיו. הוּא מוּתָּר בִּקְרוֹבוֹת גְּדוֹלָה וּגְדוֹלָה אֲסוּרָה בִּקְרוֹבָיו.

Mishnah 13: "I am preliminarily married to your daughter," but she says, you are only preliminarily married to me; he is forbidden the relatives of the young woman[224], and the young woman is permitted his relatives; he is permitted the relatives of the old woman, and the old woman is forbidden his relatives.

224 Since he claims marriage with her daughter, he is forbidden the relatives he could not marry had the claim been true (cf. Mishnah *Yebamot* 4:7). While all relatives of the mother's are also relatives of the daughter's, the lists of forbidden unions are different in the two cases.

225 She did not claim being party to a marriage; it was her mother who claimed for herself but the mother's action cannot impair the daughter.

(64c line 24) **הלכה יג:** קִידַּשְׁתִּי אֶת בִּתֵּךְ כול'. רַב חוּנָא אָמַר. מְפַתִּים אוֹתוֹ לִיתֵּן גֵּט וְכוֹפִין אוֹתוֹ לִיתֵּן קְנָס. הַגַּע עַצְמָךְ שֶׁהָיָה חָבֵר וְהָיָה יוֹדֵעַ שֶׁחַיָּיב גֵּט וּקְנָס וְהָלַךְ וְנָשָׂא אֶת אֲחוֹתָהּ. מוֹצִיאִין אֶת הַוַּדַּאי מִפְּנֵי הַסָּפֵק.

Halakhah 13: "I am preliminarily married to your daughter," etc. Rav Huna said, one induces him to give a bill of divorce, and one forces him to pay a fine[226]. Think of it, if he was a Fellow and knew that he would be obligated for a bill of divorce and a fine; if he went and married her sister, would one force the divorce of the certain because of the doubtful[227]?

226 It is not clear from this text to which woman the bill of divorce has to be given. If sense is to be made of the text, one has to read it in the light of the Babli, 65a, where Samuel states that if a woman claims to be preliminarily married to a man, which claim he denies, one has to try to make him give her a bill of divorce to free the woman for marriage to another. In the case of the Mishnah, the bill of divorce would be for the mother; the daughter is not mentioned in the discussion. Rav, the teacher of R. Huna, states that if he gave the bill of divorce on his own initiative, one can force him to pay the divorce settlement required by the law of *ketubah*.

227 Rav Huna's statement is rejected as impractical. Assuming that the man either is reasonably well trained in the law or has access to legal advice, he can avoid being badgered into offering a bill of divorce and then forced to pay a hefty sum by threatening to marry the woman's sister. Since the Mishnah permits him to marry the sister, one cannot ask him to give a divorce to his sister-in-law since by that act he would prohibit his prospective wife to himself. It is in the interest of the woman desiring the bill of divorce to make it clear that she has no monetary claims. (Explanation of D. Fraenckel.)

The last sentence cannot be read as declarative: "one forces the divorce of the certain because of the doubtful", meaning that the man would be barred from marrying the sister because of the unproven claim of the woman, since this would contradict both the Mishnah which permits the woman's relatives to the man, and the general principle that in marriage matters only those statements count which can be backed up by the testimony of two witnesses. The case cannot be compared to *Yebamot* 3:4 where a man is forced to divorce his (rabbinically) preliminarily married wife and give *halîṣah* to her sister.

"Fellow" is used here not in the technical sense of a person observing the laws of ritual purity (cf. Introduction to Tractate *Demay*), but somewhat learned in the law.

(fol. 63c) **משנה יד:** כָּל־מָקוֹם שֶׁיֵּשׁ קִדּוּשִׁין וְאֵין עֲבֵירָה הַוָּלָד הוֹלֵךְ אַחַר הַזָּכָר. וְאֵיזוֹ זוֹ. זוֹ כֹהֶנֶת לְוִיָּה וְיִשְׂרָאֵלִית שֶׁנִּישֵּׂאת לְכֹהֵן לְלֵוִי וּלְיִשְׂרָאֵל. וְכָל־מָקוֹם שֶׁיֵּשׁ קִדּוּשִׁין וְיֵשׁ עֲבֵירָה הַוָּלָד הוֹלֵךְ אַחַר הַפָּגוּם שֶׁבִּשְׁנֵיהֶם. וְאֵיזוֹ זוֹ. זוֹ אַלְמָנָה לְכֹהֵן גָּדוֹל גְּרוּשָׁה וַחֲלוּצָה לְכֹהֵן הֶדְיוֹט מַמְזֶרֶת וּנְתִינָה לְיִשְׂרָאֵל בַּת יִשְׂרָאֵל לְנָתִין וּלְמַמְזֵר.

Mishnah 14: In any case of a not sinful preliminary marriage, the child follows the father[228]. Who is this? A priestly, or Levitic, or Israel woman married to a Cohen, a Levite, or an Israel[229]. And in any case of a sinful preliminary marriage, the child follows the blemished part. Who is this? A widow [married to] a High priest, a divorcee or one who has received *ḥaliṣah* to a common priest[230], a bastard[231] or a Gibeonite[232] to an Israel, the daughter of an Israel to a Gibeonite or a bastard.

משנה טו: וְכָל־מִי שֶׁאֵין לָהּ עָלָיו קִדּוּשִׁין אֲבָל יֵשׁ לָהּ קִדּוּשִׁין עַל אֲחֵרִים הַוָּלָד מַמְזֵר. וְאֵי זוֹ זוֹ. זוֹ הַבָּא עַל אַחַת מִכָּל־הָעֲרָיוֹת שֶׁבַּתּוֹרָה. וְכָל־מִי שֶׁאֵין לָהּ לֹא עָלָיו וְלֹא עַל אֲחֵרִים קִדּוּשִׁין הַוָּלָד כְּמוֹהָ. וְאֵיזוֹ זוֹ. זוֹ וְלַד שִׁפְחָה וְנָכְרִית.

Mishnah 15: In any case where a preliminary marriage with him is impossible but with others is possible, the child is a bastard. Who is this? This is one having sexual relations with any woman forbidden in the Torah because of incest or adultery[233]. And in any case where a preliminary marriage is impossible with anybody, the child follows the mother. Who is this? The child of a slave girl or a Gentile woman[234].

228 The child belongs to the same marriage class (detailed in Mishnah 4:1) as his father.

229 As the Halakhah points out, this list is far from complete; it contains only those cases in which there is absolutely no controversy.

230 The divorcee is forbidden to any Cohen by biblical decree (*Lev.* 21:7); the woman having received

ḥalîṣah is a divorcee only by common practice. The child is "desecrated" in the sense of *Lev.* 21:7; the marriage prohibition is transferred to future generations.

231 Who is forbidden any endogamous marriage, *Deut.* 23:3.

232 Cf. Halakhah 4:1. Notes 46 - 71; *Ketubot* 3:1, Notes 16-19.

233 The child is a bastard in all cases of adultery; in cases of incest only those mentioned as deadly sins in *Lev.* 18,20; cf. Mishnah *Yebamot* 4:13.

234 Since preliminary marriage is a uniquely Jewish institution, Gentiles are automatically excluded since for them only definitive marriage exists (cf. Chapter 1, Notes 33-39.) The Jewish father cannot have any family relationship with his Gentile child: The widow of a man having only had a child with a Gentile woman is the widow of a childless man and subject to levirate marriage: Mishnah *Yebamot* 2:5.

(64c line 27) **הלכה יד:** כָּל־מָקוֹם שֶׁיֵּשׁ קִידּוּשִׁין כול׳. רְבִּי שִׁמְעוֹן בֶּן לָקִישׁ בְּעָא קוֹמֵי רְבִּי יוֹחָנָן. הֲרֵי גֵר שֶׁנָּשָׂא מַמְזֶרֶת הֲרֵי יֵשׁ קִידּוּשִׁין וְאֵין עֲבֵירָה וְהַוָּלָד הוֹלֵךְ אַחַר הַפָּגוּם שֶׁבִּשְׁנֵיהֶן. אָמַר לֵיהּ. בְּכָל־מָקוֹם שֶׁשָּׁנָה רְבִּי פֵּירַשׁ. וְאֵי זֶה זֶה. זֶה כֹּהֶנֶת לְוִיָּה וְיִשְׂרְאֵלִית שֶׁנִּישְׂאוּ לְכֹהֵן לְלֵוִי וּלְיִשְׂרָאֵל. רְבִּי אָבִין שָׁמַע לָהּ מִן דְּבַתְרָהּ. בְּכָל־מָקוֹם שֶׁיֵּשׁ קִידּוּשִׁים וְאֵין עֲבֵירָה הַוָּלָד הוֹלֵךְ אַחַר הַזָּכָר. רְבִּי שִׁמְעוֹן בֶּן לָקִישׁ בְּעָא קוֹמֵי רְבִּי יוֹחָנָן. הֲרֵי גֵר שֶׁנָּשָׂא מַמְזֶרֶת הֲרֵי יֵשׁ קִידּוּשִׁין וְאֵין עֲבֵירָה וְהַוָּלָד הוֹלֵךְ אַחַר הַפָּגוּם שֶׁבִּשְׁנֵיהֶן. אָמַר לֵיהּ. כָּל־מָקוֹם שֶׁשָּׁנָה רְבִּי פֵּירַשׁ. וְאֵי זֶה זֶה. זֶה אַלְמָנָה לְכֹהֵן גָּדוֹל. גְּרוּשָׁה וַחֲלוּצָה לְכֹהֵן הֶדְיוֹט. וּמַמְזֶרֶת וּנְתִינָה לְיִשְׂרָאֵל. וּבַת יִשְׂרָאֵל לְמַמְזֵר וּלְנָתִין. וְיַתְבִינֵיהּ. הֲרֵי חָלָל שֶׁנָּשָׂא לְבַת יִשְׂרָאֵל הֲרֵי קִידּוּשִׁין וְאֵין עֲבֵירָה. הַוָּלָד הוֹלֵךְ אַחַר הַפָּגוּם שֶׁבִּשְׁנֵיהֶן. הֲרֵי הַמַּחֲזִיר גְּרוּשָׁתוֹ מִשֶּׁנִּישֵּׂאת הֲרֵי קִידּוּשִׁין וְאֵין עֲבֵירָה וְהַוָּלָד כָּשֵׁר. דְּאָמַר רְבִּי חִייָה בְּשֵׁם רְבִּי יוֹחָנָן. הַמַּחֲזִיר גְּרוּשָׁתוֹ מִשֶּׁנִּישֵּׂאת בִּתָּהּ כְּשֵׁרָה לִכְהוּנָה. הָה טַעַם. הִיא תּוֹעֵיבָה וְאֵין בָּנֶיהָ תוֹעֵיבִין.

5 הזכר | G הפגום שבשניהם235   10 הרי | G הרי יש   הוולד | G והולד   11 ואין | G ויש   13 היא תועיבה | G כי תועבה היא. היא תועבה   ואין בניה | G אן הוולד

Halakhah 14: "In any case of a not sinful preliminary marriage," etc. Rebbi Simeon ben Laqish asked before Rebbi Johanan: If a proselyte married a bastard girl, there is no sinful preliminary marriage[236], but the child follows the blemished part? He answered, everywhere Rebbi taught, he explained: "Who is this? A priestly, or Levitic, or Israel woman married to a Cohen, a Levite, or an Israel.[237]" Rebbi Abin understood this from the second part: (In any case of a not sinful preliminary marriage, the child follows the father.) [In any case of a sinful preliminary marriage, the child follows the blemished part.][238] Rebbi Simeon ben Laqish asked before Rebbi Johanan: If a proselyte married a bastard girl, there is no sinful preliminary marriage, but the child follows the blemished part? He answered, everywhere Rebbi taught, he explained: "Who is this? A widow [married to] a High priest, a divorcee or one who has received *haliṣah* to a common priest, a bastard or a Gibeonite to an Israel, the daughter of an Israel to a bastard or a Gibeonite.[238]" Could he not have objected to him: In the case of a disqualified priest married to the daughter of an Israel there is no sinful marriage but the child follows the blemished part[239]? In the case of a man taking back his divorcee after she had been remarried, there is (no)[240] sinful marriage but the child is unblemished since Rebbi Hiyya said in the name of Rebbi Johanan: The daughter of a man taking back his divorcee after she had been remarried is enabled for the priesthood. What is the reason? [For she is an abomination,][241] she is an abomination but her children are not an abomination[242].

235 The first half of the line is missing in G but obviously the text must have read וְיֵשׁ עֲבֵירָה instead of וְאֵין עֲבֵירָה.

236 Following the rabbis in Halakhah 4:1 (*Yebamot* 8:2, Note 151), whose opinion is that of R. Yose in the Babli, 72b; for R. Jehudah the marriage would be sinful but not punishable, not included in the list of Mishnah 14 (Maimonides, *Issure Bi'ah* 15:7).

237 He pointedly avoids taking a position about marriages permitted to proselytes.

238 The text in parentheses is from L, the one in brackets from G. It is obvious that the G text is correct.

239 Halakhah 4:6. The question is not answered since the case presents a genuine inconsistency in the Mishnah.

240 Text of L; the interpretation has to follow G.

241 *Deut.* 24:4; quote missing in L; it is in *Yebamot* 4:13, Note 207.

242 The marriage of the remarried divorcee is sinful but not incestuous; the formulation of the Mishnah correctly excludes this case.

(64c line 43) רִבִּי יוֹסֵי בֵּירְבִּי בּוּן בְּשֵׁם רַב. גֵּר וְעֶבֶד מְשׁוּחְרָר וְחָלָל מוּתָּרִין בְּכוֹהֶנֶת. מַאי טַעֲמָה. כְּשֵׁירִין הוּזְהֲרוּ עַל הַפְּסוּלוֹת וּפְסוּלוֹת עַל הַכְּשֵׁירִין. אֲבָל לֹא כְשֵׁירוֹת עַל הַפְּסוּלִין וְלֹא פְסוּלִין עַל הַכְּשֵׁירוֹת וְהָא תָאנֵי. לֹא יָקְחוּ לֹא יָקָחוּ. מְלַמֵּד שֶׁאַף הָאִשָּׁה מוּזְהֶרֶת עַל יְדֵי אִישׁ. סָבְרִין מֵימַר בִּכְשֵׁירוֹת עַל הַפְּסוּלִין וְאֵינָן אֶלָּא בִפְסוּלוֹת עַל הַכְּשֵׁירִים.

²⁴³Rebbi Yose ben Rebbi Abun in the name of Rav: A proselyte, a freedman, and a disqualified priest are permitted priestly wives. What is the reason? Qualified men are warned against disqualified women and disqualified women against qualified men but not qualified women against disqualified men nor disqualified men against qualified women. Did we not state: "they should not take, should not take", which teaches that the woman is warned through the man? They wanted to say, qualified women against disqualified men but it is only disqualified women against qualified men.

243 As noted in G, this paragraph is quoted in *Yebamot* 9:1, explained there in Notes 10-14; a slightly different text.

(64c line 48) חַד גִּיּוּר אֲתָא לְגַבֵּי רִבִּי יוֹסֵא. אָמַר לֵיהּ. מָהוּ מִינְסוֹב מַמְזֶרְתָּא. אָמַר לֵיהּ. שָׁרֵי. חֲזַר וַאֲתָא לְגַבֵּי רִבִּי יוּדָה. אָמַר לַיהּ. שָׁרֵי. אֶלָּא הֱוֵי יָדַע דִּבְנוֹי דְּרַהוּא גַבְרָא מַמְזֵירִין קוֹמֵי שְׁמַיָּיא. חֲזַר וַאֲתָא קוֹמֵי רִבִּי יוֹסֵי. אָמַר לֵיהּ. הֲוֵית יָדַע דְּהוּא כֵן וְלָמָּה שָׁרִית לִי מִן קַדְמִיתָא. אָמַר לֵיהּ. מָה דְשָׁאַלְתְּ לִי אֲגִיבוּנָךְ. אָמַר רִבִּי יוֹסֵה. הָהֵן גִּיּוּרָא מְדַמֵּי לְעַמְרָא גוּפְנָא. אִין בָּעִית לְמִיתְנֵיהּ בְּעַמְרָא שָׁרֵי. בְּכִיתְנָא שָׁרֵי.

1 מינסוב G שנשא   2 ליה G לה   חזר ואתא לגבי G אתה לגבה   3 ממזירין G ממזרין שמייא G שמייה   קומי G לגבה   4 ליה G פה   מה דשאלת לי אגיבונך G דשאלתני אגיבתך   5 החי׳ G הדן   גיורא G גיורה   6 בכיתנא G בכתנה

A proselyte came to Rebbi Yose and asked him, is it permitted to marry a bastard girl? He answered him, it is permitted. He continued and came to Rebbi Jehudah, who answered him, it is permitted[244] but you should know that the children of such a man would be bastards before Heaven[245]. He returned to Rebbi Yose and told him, since you knew that, why did you permit it to me at the start? He replied, I answered you what you asked me[246]. Rebbi Yose said, the proselyte can be compared to cotton[247]. If one wants to use it with wool it is permitted, with linen it is permitted.

244 The language is somewhat difficult since for R. Jehudah proselytes are part of the "Congregation of the Eternal" (*Deut.* 23:3), to whom marriage with bastards is forbidden (*Yebamot* 8:2, Note 151; *Qiddušin* Halakhah 4:1, Note 105). But even R. Jehudah will agree that marriage of a proselyte with a bastard is not punishable.

245 From his point of view, he is obligated to point out the implicit punishment meted out by Heaven for such an illicit union.

246 Since he holds that proselytes are not part of the "Congregation of the Eternal", he is not obligated to point out that the children of the proselyte will remain outside the congregation if he marries a bastard.

247 Which is neutral for the

prohibition of *ša'aṭnez*. While wool and linen cannot be mixed, either one may be mixed with cotton; cf. Introduction to Tractate *Kilaim*.

(64c line 55) נִיחָא בַּת יִשְׂרָאֵל לְמַמְזֵר וּלְנָתִין. דִּכְתִיב לֹא יָבֹא מַמְזֵר בִּקְהַל יי׳. מַה תַּלְמוּד לוֹמַר לֹא יָבוֹא לוֹ. לִפְסוֹל. אָמַר רַבִּי אַבָּהוּ. מָהוּ מַמְזֵר. מוּם זָר. וּפְלִיג עַל הַהוּא דְּאָמַר רִבִּי יוּדָה בַּר פָּזִי. אֱלֹהִים מוֹשִׁיב יְחִידִים בַּיְתָה. אֲפִילוּ מַמְזֵר בְּסוֹף הָעוֹלָם וּמַמְזֶרֶת בְּסוֹף הָעוֹלָם הַקָּדוֹשׁ בָּרוּךְ הוּא מְבִיאָן וּמְזַוְוגָן זֶה בָּזֶה. רַב הוּנָא אָמַר. אֵין מַמְזֵר חָיָיה יוֹתֵר מִשְּׁלֹשִׁים יוֹם. בְּיוֹמוֹי דְּרִבִּי בֶּרֶכְיָה סָלַק חַד בַּבְלָאִי לְהָכָא וַהֲוָה יָדַע בֵּיהּ דְּהוּא מַמְזֵר. אָמַר לֵיהּ. זְכֵה עִימִּי. אָמַר לֵיהּ. לְמָחָר אַתְּ קָאִים בְּצִיבּוּרָא וַאֲנָא עָבִיד לָךְ פְּסִיקָא. אֲתָא יְתִיב וְדָרִישׁ. מִן דַּחֲסִיל מִידְרַשׁ אָמַר לוֹן. אֲחוּנָן. זְכוֹן עִם הָדֵין דְּהוּא מַמְזֵר. מִן דַּאֲזַל לֵיהּ קָהָלָא אָמַר לֵיהּ. רִבִּי. חַיֵי שָׁעָה בְּעִית גַּבָּךְ וְאוֹבְדְתָא חַיִין דְּהַהוּא גַבְרָא. אָמַר לֵיהּ. חַיֶּיךָ. הָהִין יָהֲבִית לָךְ. דְּאָמַר רִבִּי בָּא רַב הוּנָא בְּשֵׁם רַב. אֵין מַמְזֵר חָיָה אֶלָּא שְׁלֹשִׁים יוֹם. אֵימָתַי. בִּזְמַן שֶׁאֵינוֹ מְפוּרְסָם. אֲבָל אִם הָיָה מְפוּרְסָם חַי הוּא.

1 ניחא G | ניחה G | - 2 ר׳ יצחק בר ב..נה ר׳ אחא בשם ר׳ לעזר כתוב לא יבא ממזר ר׳ אבהו מהו G | ר׳ אבהוא מהוא G | אחד בסוף G | בסוף 4 בזה G | לזה 5 רב הונא .... שלשים יום G | - G | ברכיה G | ברכייה 6 בבלאי להכא והווה G | בבליי להכה והוה ביה g | בה ליה. זכה עימי G | רבי זכי עמי 7 ליה | ג לה קאים בציבורא G | קיים בצבורה עביד לך פסיקא G | עבד לר׳ פסיקה אתא G | למחר אתא ודריש G | דרש 8 דחסיל G | דחסל הדין G | ההן גברא ליה G | לה 9 בעית G | בעת ואובדתא G | ואובדתה ליה G | לה 10 ההין יהבית G | חיין יהבת אין G | אן G | חיה G | חייא 11 אלא שלשים G | יתר משלשין אמתי G | אמתיי חיי G | חייא

One understands "the daughter of an Israel to a bastard or a Gibeonite," for it is written: "A bastard shall not come into the Eternal's congregation." Why does the verse say: "*of his* shall not come"? To disqualify[248]. Rebbi Abbu said, what means ממזר? "A strange defect."[249] This disagrees with what Rebbi Jehudah ben Pazi[250] said, "God installs singles[251] as heads of families," even if there is a male bastard at one end of the world and a female bastard at the other, the Holy One, praise to Him, brings them and copulates them with one another. Rav Huna said, a bastard does not live more than thirty days.[252] In the days of Rebbi Berekhiah, a Babylonian immigrated here[253]; he was informed that this was a bastard. He[254] said to him, support me[255]. He[255] told him, tomorrow you will stand up in the community and I shall look for an allowance for you. He came and sat during the sermon. When he[245] finished the sermon, he said, our brothers, support this man for he is a bastard. After the congregation had left, he[254] said to him, rabbi, I requested material support from you but you destroyed this man's life. He[255] answered, by your life, life[256] I gave you for Rebbi Abba, Rav Huna, said in the name of Rav: A bastard lives only thirty days. When? If he is not publicly known. But when he is publicly known, he survives.

248 Marrying a bastard, while sinful, is not punishable. Therefore, one might assume the children of a bastard not to be bastards; they are not conceived in deadly sin. But *Deut.* 23:3 disqualifies the children from marrying in the congregation: "A bastard shall not come into the Eternal's congregation, even the tenth generation *of his* shall not come into the Eternal's congregation."

It seems that G had here another derivation, of which no trace is left in L and *editio princeps*.

249 The word for "bastard" has no etymology in the Pentateuch (following J. Barth, the root is مذر "to be dirty").

250 In *Gen. rabba* 65(2), this is attributed to the Tanna R. Jehudah (bar Ilai).

251 A single person in God's eyes cannot be a bachelor who could find mates all around him; he must be an intrinsic single who has no known marriage partner. This is the bastard who cannot marry a Jewish partner,

and as a Jew is unable to contract marriage with a Gentile (but cf. Halakhah 15).

252 This sentence is missing in G; it is superfluous here but will be quoted later in a fitting context.

253 When at the end of the Fourth Century, Jews usually emigrated from the hostile Christian Roman empire to the more welcoming Persian empire.

254 The bastard.

255 R. Berekhiah.

256 Following the reading of G.

(64c line 68) רִבִּי זְעִירָא כַּד סְלִיק לְהָכָא שְׁמַע קָלִין קַרְיֵי מַמְזֵירָא וּמַמְזֵרְתָּא. אָמַר לוֹן. מַהוּ כֵן. הָא אֲזָלָא הַהִיא דְּרַב הוּנָא. דְּרַב הוּנָא אָמַר. אֵין מַמְזֵר חַי יוֹתֵר מִשְּׁלֹשִׁים יוֹם. אָמַר רִבִּי עוּקְבָא בַּר אָחָא. עִימּוֹ הָיִיתִי כַּד אָמַר רִבִּי בָּא רַב הוּנָא בְּשֵׁם רַב. אֵין מַמְזֵר חַי יוֹתֵר מִשְּׁלֹשִׁים יוֹם. אֵימָתַי. בִּזְמַן שֶׁאֵינוֹ מְפוּרְסָם. אֲבָל אִם הָיָה מְפוּרְסָם חַי הוּא.

1 סליק | ג סלק   קריי | ג קריין   2 אזלא | ג אזעלא   3 אמ' | ג אמ' ליה   עוקבא | ג יעקב   עימו | ג עמך   5 אבל | ג הא   חיה | ג חי

[257]When Rebbi Ze'ira immigrated here, he heard voices call "he-bastard, she-bastard". He said, what is this? There goes that of Rav Huna, since Rav Huna said, no bastard lives more than thirty days. Rebbi Jacob bar Aḥa said to him, I was with you when Rebbi Abba, Rav Huna said in the name of Rav: No bastard lives more than thirty days, when? If he is not publicly known. Therefore, if he is publicly known, he lives.

257 This is from *Yebamot* 8:3, Note 201; an addition to Rav Huna's statement. The text is missing in G.

(64c line 73) תַּנֵּי. גּוֹי וְעֶבֶד הַבָּא עַל בַּת יִשְׂרָאֵל הַוָּלָד מַמְזֵר. רִבִּי שִׁמְעוֹן בֶּן יְהוּדָה אוֹמֵר בְּשֵׁם רִבִּי שִׁמְעוֹן. אֵין הַוָּלָד מַמְזֵר. שֶׁאֵין מַמְזֵר אֶלָּא מֵאִשָּׁה שֶׁהִיא אֲסוּרָה עָלָיו אִיסּוּר עֶרְוָה וְחַיָּיבִין עָלֶיהָ כָּרֵת. וּשְׁנֵיהֶם מִקְרָא אֶחָד דָּרְשׁוּ. לֹא יִקַּח אִישׁ אֶת אֵשֶׁת אָבִיו וְגוֹ'. רִבִּי מֵאִיר דָּרַשׁ. מָה אֵשֶׁת אָבִיו

מְיוּחֶדֶת שֶׁאֵין לוֹ עָלֶיהָ קִידּוּשִׁין.   אֲבָל יֵשׁ לָהּ קִידּוּשִׁין עַל אֲחֵרִים וְהַוָּלָד מַמְזֵר.   אַף כָּל־שֶׁאֵין לָהּ עָלָיו קִידּוּשִׁין הַוָּלָד מַמְזֵר.   רִבִּי שִׁמְעוֹן בֶּן יְהוּדָה דָּרַשׁ.   מָה אֵשֶׁת אָבִיו מְיוּחֶדֶת שֶׁאֵין לָהּ עָלָיו קִידּוּשִׁין.   אֲבָל אִם יֵשׁ לָהּ קִידּוּשִׁין עַל אֲחֵרִים הַוָּלָד מַמְזֵר.   יָצָא גּוֹי וְעֶבֶד שֶׁאֵין לָהּ עָלָיו וְלֹא עַל אֲחֵרִים קִידּוּשִׁין.   הָתִיב רִבִּי שְׁמוּאֵל בַּר אַבָּא עַל הַהִיא תַּנְיָיא קַדְמָיָיא.   הֲרֵי יְבָמָה שֶׁזִּינַת הֲרֵי אֵין לָהּ עָלָיו וְלֹא עַל אֲחֵרִים קִידּוּשִׁין וְהַוָּלָד כָּשֵׁר.   רִבִּי יַנַּאי בְּשֵׁם רִבִּי.   גּוֹי וְעֶבֶד שֶׁבָּאוּ עַל בַּת יִשְׂרָאֵל הַוָּלָד מַמְזֵר.   רִבִּי יוֹחָנָן וְרִבִּי שִׁמְעוֹן בֶּן לָקִישׁ תְּרַייְהוֹן אָמְרִין.   הַוָּלָד מַמְזֵר.   רִבִּי יַעֲקֹב בַּר אָחָא רִבִּי שִׁמְעוֹן בַּר אַבָּא רִבִּי יְהוֹשֻׁעַ בֶּן לֵוִי בְּשֵׁם רִבִּי יַנַּאי בְּרִבִּי.   הַוָּלָד אֵינוֹ כָשֵׁר וְלֹא פָסוּל אֶלָּא מְזוֹהָם.   רִבִּי יוֹנָתָן סָלַק עִם רִבִּי יוּדָה נְשִׂייָא לְחַמְתָא דְגָדֵר.   הוֹרֵי תַמָּן.   הַוָּלָד כָּשֵׁר.   אָמַר רִבִּי זְעִירָא.   הָחֵין וָלָד כָּל־מַה דְהוּא אָזִיל הוּא מִתְעַלֶּה.   רִבִּי עֶבֶד בַּר בְּרֵיהּ עַבְדֵּיהּ כָּשֵׁר.   הוֹרֵי רִבִּי בָּא בַּר זַבְדָּא בְּמָקוֹם כָּל־רַבָּנִין.   הַוָּלָד כָּשֵׁר.   רִבִּי בֵּיבִי אָמַר קוֹמֵי רִבִּי זְעִירָא בְּשֵׁם רִבִּי חֲנִינָה.   הַוָּלָד כָּשֵׁר.   אָמַר רִבִּי זְעִירָא.   אִין מִן הָדָא אֵין לְמֵידִין מַעֲשֶׂה מֵהֲבָרָהּ.   אָמַר רִבִּי חִזְקִיָּה.   אֲנָא יָדַע רֹאשָׁהּ וְסוֹפָהּ.   רִבִּי חָמָא בַּר חֲנִינָה הֲוָה אָזִיל מִיסּוֹק לְחַמְתָה דְגָדֵר.   אָתָא לְגַבֵּי אַבוֹי אָמַר לֵיהּ.   הַב דַּעְתָּךְ דְּאִית תַּמָּן מִן אִינּוּן פְּסוּלַייָא דְּלָא תִפְגַּע בְּהוֹן.

1 הבא G | שבאו   2 בשם G | משׁ'   3 ושניהם G | ר' אבהוא בש"ר יוחנן ושניהן   4 דרשן G | דרשין   מה אשת אביו מיוחדת שאין לו עליה קידושין.   אב̇ל [יש לה קידושין על אחרים והולד ממזר.   אף כל שאין לה) עליו קידושין הולד ממז̇ | G מה אשת אב מיוחדת שא[י]ן לה עליו] קידושין אף [כל שאין] לה עליו קידושין הולד ממזר   7 מה אשת אביו מיוחדת שאין לה עליו קידושין.   אבל אם יש לה קידושין על אחרים הולד ממזר. G | [מה] אשת אב מיוחדת ש[אין לה ל]א עליו ולא על אחרין קידושין הולד ממזר   9 התיב ר' שמואל בר אבא על ההיא תניא קדמייא G | מתיב שמואל בר אבה להדן תנייה קדמייה   10 ר' ינאי בשם ר' | G ר' יניי בש"ר רבי   13 אינו כשר G | לא כשר   15 זעירא G | זעורה   16 זבדא G | זב"ה   במקום G | במקם   17 זעירא | G זעורה   18 הדא אין G | הברה אן   19 הוה אזיל מיסוק G | אזל בעי מסוק   20 אתא G | אתה   ליה G | לה   21 בהון G | בון

It was stated: "If a Gentile or a slave had intercourse with a Jewish woman, the child is a bastard[258]; Rebbi Simeon ben Jehudah says in the name of Rebbi Simeon, the child is not a bastard, for a bastard is only from a woman forbidden to him by an incest prohibition for which the penalty is extirpation[259]." [260]Both of them explained the same verse, "nobody may take his father's wife, etc."[261] Rebbi Meïr explains: Since his father's wife is special in that he cannot have preliminary marriage with her, but she could have preliminary marriage with others, and the child is a bastard, so in all cases in which she cannot have preliminary marriage with him, the child is a bastard[262]. Rebbi Simeon ben Jehudah explains: Since his father's wife is special in that she cannot have preliminary marriage with him, but she could have preliminary marriage with others, and the child is a bastard; this excludes the Gentile and the slave who cannot contract preliminary marriage with her or with others[244]. Rebbi Samuel bar Abba questions that first Tanna: The sister-in-law who whored cannot have preliminary marriage with him or with others[263], but the child is qualified[264]! Rebbi Yannai in the name of Rebbi: If a Gentile or a slave had intercourse with a Jewish woman, the child is a bastard. Rebbi Joḥanan and Rebbi Simeon ben Laqish both say, the child is a bastard. Rebbi Jacob bar Aḥa, Rebbi Simeon bar Abba, Rebbi Joshua ben Levi, in the name of Rebbi (Yannai ben)[265] Rebbi: The child is neither qualified nor disqualified but dirtied[266]. Rebbi Jonathan went with Rebbi Jehudah Neśia to the hot springs of Gadara. There, he instructed: The child is qualified[267]. Rebbi Ze'ira said, this child improves as time goes by. Rebbi declared the child dirtied, his grandson declared him qualified. Rebbi Abba bar Zavda instructed in the name of all rabbis: The child is qualified. Rebbi Bevai said before Rebbi Ze'ira in the name of Rebbi Ḥanina: The child is qualified. Rebbi Ze'ira said, if it is from that, one does not learn from a declaration. Rebbi Ḥizqiah said, I know the story from beginning to end. Rebbi Hama bar Ḥanina went up to the hot springs of Gadara. He visited his father who said to him: Be careful, because there are those who are disqualified[268], lest you injure them.

258 *Yebamot* 7:6 (Note 129), *Ketubot* 3:1 (Note 22), *Giṭin* (Note 123); Babli *Yebamot* 45a. The entire *baraita* in Tosephta 4:15.

259 Mishnah *Yebamot* 4:14.

260 In G, the following is a statement by R. Abbahu in the name of R. Joḥanan.

261 A parallel discussion, among different Tannaïm, is reported in *Yebamot* 4:15 (Notes 211-218). The prohibition of the father's wife (who is not the mother) is repeated in *Deut.* 23:1 from *Lev.* 18:8, 20:11, to be connected with the exclusion of the bastard from endogamous marriage. *Deut.* 23:3. It is understood that a man's child from his father's wife is a bastard. The problem is to discern the legal principle which implies that the child is a bastard.

262 This text, adopted by the *editio princeps*, is the corrector's text. The second clause and a logical connection are missing from the scribe's original text which makes no sense as it stands:

רִבִּי מֵאִיר דָּרַשׁ. מָה אֵשֶׁת אָבִיו מְיוּחֶדֶת שֶׁאֵין לוֹ עָלֶיהָ קִידּוּשִׁין. אֲבָל אִם הָיָה לָהּ עָלָיו קִידוּשִׁין הַוָּלָד מַמְזֵר.

Rebbi Meïr explains: Since his father's wife is special in that he cannot have preliminary marriage with her, but if she could have preliminary marriage with him, the child is a bastard.

Reading of G (lacunae in the text filled in brackets):

רִבִּי מֵאִיר דָּרַשׁ. מָה אֵשֶׁת אָב מְיוּחֶדֶת שֶׁ[אֵין לוֹ עָלֶיהָ] קִידּוּשִׁין הַוָּלָד מַמְזֵר. אֲבָל [כָּל־שֶׁאֵין] לָהּ עָלָיו קִידּוּשִׁין הַוָּלָד מַמְזֵר.

Rebbi Meïr explains: Since his father's wife is special in that he cannot have preliminary marriage with her, so in any case in which she cannot have preliminary marriage with him, the child is a bastard.

It seems that the original text underlying L was the text of G.

263   *Yebamot* 1:1, Notes 93-94. The widow of the childless man is obligated to definitively marry his brother in levirate; by biblical standards this requires no preliminary marriage. By the same token, she is unable to contract preliminary marriage with any other man before being released by *ḥaliṣah* (cf. Halakhah 5, Note 166). Any sexual relations she might have during the time she is waiting for her levir are sinful but neither adulterous nor punishable.

264   To contract marriage "in the Eternal's congregation."

265   There is no R. Yannai ben Rebbi. Later the statement is quoted in the name of R. Gamliel (IV) ben Rebbi. G is illegible at this point.

266   If the child is female, she is not eligible as marriage partner of a Cohen.

267   Even for a Cohen.

268   Children of Jewish women from Gentile fathers.

(64d line 22) אַף עַל גַּב דְּרִבִּי שִׁמְעוֹן בֶּן יְהוּדָה אָמַר מִשּׁוּם רִבִּי שִׁמְעוֹן בֶּן יוֹחַי. גּוֹי וְעֶבֶד שֶׁבָּאוּ עַל בַּת יִשְׂרָאֵל הַוָּלָד כָּשֵׁר.   מוֹדֶה שֶׁאִם הָיְתָה נְקֵיבָה שֶׁהִיא פְּסוּלָה מִן הַכְּהוּנָּה.   אַף עַל גַּב דְּרִבִּי יְהוֹשֻׁעַ אָמַר. הַבָּא עַל אֲחוֹתוֹ הַוָּלָד כָּשֵׁר. מוֹדֶה שֶׁאִם הָיְתָה נְקֵיבָה שֶׁהִיא פְּסוּלָה מִן הַכְּהוּנָּה.   חַד בַּר נַשׁ אָתָא לְגַבֵּיהּ דְּרַב. אָמַר לֵיהּ. בְּנִין דִּילֵידָתֵיהּ אִימֵּיהּ מִן אֲרָמַאי. אָמַר לֵיהּ. כָּשֵׁר. אָמַר לֵיהּ רַב חָמָא בַּר גּוּרְיָא. הֵן דְּעַיְמָךְ מַגְלֵיהּ עַד דְּאָתֵי שְׁמוּאֵל וִיפַסְלִינָךְ. אַף עַל גַּב דְּרַב אָמַר. גּוֹי וְעֶבֶד שֶׁבָּאוּ עַל בַּת יִשְׂרָאֵל הַוָּלָד כָּשֵׁר.   מוֹדֶה שֶׁאִם הָיְתָה נְקֵיבָה שֶׁפְּסוּלָה מִן הַכְּהוּנָּה.

2 מודה | ג מודי   3 אחותו | ג אחות חלוצתו   4 נקיבה | ג הוולד נקיבה   לגביה דרב | ג לגבת רב   5 דילידתיה אימיה | ג דילידת אמא דההוא גברא   6 מגליך | ג רגליך דאתי | ג דייתי   7 מודה | ג מודי

[269]Even though Rebbi Simeon ben Jehudah said in the name of Rebbi Simeon: If a Gentile or a slave came to a daughter of Israel, the child is acceptable; they agree that if she was female, she is blemished for the priesthood. Even though Rebbi Joshua said, the child of him who sleeps

with his sister is acceptable, he agrees that if the child was female she would be blemished for the priesthood. A man came to Rav and said, since the children of this man's mother are from an Aramean? He said, acceptable. Rav Ḥama bar Guria said to him, let your feet carry you away before Samuel comes and declares you blemished. Even though Rav said, if a Gentile or a slave came to a daughter of Israel, the child is acceptable, he agrees that if it was a female, she would be blemished for the priesthood.

259 This paragraph is from *Yebamot* 4:15, Notes 215-218. G only refers to that source.

(64d line 30) אָמַר רְבִּי יַעֲקֹב בַּר אָחָא. תַּנֵּי תַמָּן. הַפּוֹסֵל פּוֹסֵל בִּפְנוּיָה וְהַמַּכְשִׁיר מַכְשִׁיר אֲפִילוּ בְּאֵשֶׁת אִישׁ. רִבִּי תַנְחוּם בַּר פָּפָּא שָׁאַל לְרִבִּי יוֹסֵי תְּרֵין עוֹבְדִין מִן אַלְכְּסַנְדְּרִיאָה. אֶחָד בִּפְנוּיָה וְאֶחָד בְּאֵשֶׁת אִישׁ. בְּאֵשֶׁת אִישׁ שָׁלַח כָּתַב לֵיהּ לֹא יָבֹא מַמְזֵר בִּקְהַל יי. בִּפְנוּיָה שָׁלַח כָּתַב לֵיהּ. מִבַּדִּין אַתֶּם. שֶׁאֵין אַתֶּם מוּזְהָרִין עַל בְּנוֹת יִשְׂרָאֵל הַקְּדוֹשׁוֹת. אָמַר לְרִבִּי מָנָא. סַב וַחֲתִים וְחָתַם. אָמַר לְרִבִּי בְּרֶכְיָה. סַב וַחֲתִים. וְלָא קַבִּיל עֲלוֹי. מִן דְּקָמוֹן קָם רִבִּי מָנָא עִם רִבִּי בְּרֶכְיָה. אָמַר לֵיהּ. לָמָה לֹא חֲתַמְתָּהּ. אָמַר לֵיהּ. לֹא כֵן אָמַר רִבִּי יַעֲקֹב בַּר אָחָא. תַּנֵּי תַמָּן. הַפּוֹסֵל פּוֹסֵל בִּפְנוּיָה וְהַמַּכְשִׁיר מַכְשִׁיר אֲפִילוּ בְּאֵשֶׁת אִישׁ. אָמַר לֵיהּ. בְּרִיךְ רַחֲמָנָא דְּלָא הֲוֵינָא שְׁמִיעַ הָדֵין אוּלְפָנָא. אִילּוּ הֲוֵינָא שְׁמִיעַ הָדֵין אוּלְפָנָא לָא הֲוֵינָא מַחְתִּים וַהֲווֹן אָמְרִין. תַּלְמִידָא פְּלִיג עַל רַבֵּיהּ. אָמַר מַר עוּקְבָן. הָכָא אַתְּ אָמְרַתְּ. הַפּוֹסֵל פּוֹסֵל בִּפְנוּיָה וְהַמַּכְשִׁיר מַכְשִׁיר בִּפְנוּיָה. בְּרַם בְּאֵשֶׁת אִישׁ לֹא אִיתְּמַר כְּלוּם. בְּרוֹמְשָׁא סְלַק בָּעֵי מַחְתִּים. אָמַר לֵיהּ. לֵית הָכָא אֲתָר.

2 אפי' G - .   4 מבדין G ניכרין   5 שאין G שאן   6 וחתים / ג וחתום   9 הדין G החן   10 אילו הוינא G דאילו הווינא   11 רביה G רבה   מר G ר' מר הכא את אמרת G הכן אתאמרת   12 ברומשא G ברומשה

Rebbi Jacob bar Aḥa said: There[270], they state that the one who disqualifies, disqualifies from an unmarried woman, and the one who qualifies, qualifies even from a married woman[271]. Rebbi Tanḥum bar Pappus sent and asked Rebbi Yose about two cases from Alexandria, one involving an unmarried woman, the other a married woman. About the married woman, he wrote him: "A bastard shall not come into the Eternal's congregation.[272]" About the unmarried woman he wrote, be inventive[273], for your are not forewarned about the holy daughters of Israel. He[274] said to Rebbi Mana, take and sign; he signed. He said to Rebbi Berekhiah, take and sign, but he did not agree. After they ended the session Rebbi Mana was standing with Rebbi Berekhiah and asked him, why did you not sign? He answered, did not Rebbi Jacob bar Aḥa say that there, they state that the one who disqualifies, disqualifies from an unmarried woman, and the one who qualifies, qualifies even from a married woman[275]? He said, praised be the Merciful that I had not heard this doctrine, for if I had heard this doctrine I would not have signed and people would have said that the student[276] disagrees with his teacher. Mar Uqban said, here, you say that the one who disqualifies, disqualifies from an unmarried woman, and the one who qualifies, qualifies from an unmarried woman, but about a married woman, nothing was said. The next morning he[277] came and wanted to sign. He[278] said to him, there is no space.

---

270 In Babylonia; Babli *Yebamot* 45b.

271 R. Meïr who declares the child of a Gentile and a Jewish woman a bastard, does so even if the woman was single. R. Simeon ben Jehudah who declares the child qualified does so even if the mother was a Jewish woman married to a Jew. Practice in the Babli is decided according to R.

Simeon ben Jehudah.

272 *Deut.* 23:1. He decided against the Babylonian practice.

273 The expression מבדין is a *hapax legomenon*. It can be derived from Aramaic בדי "to invent a story", or from a multiplicity of Arabic roots. In G one reads "you should recognize that", meaning that both the girl and her child can marry in the congregation. The only argument one has for the text of L is that it is *lectio difficilior*.

274 Rebbi Yose (the Babli, *Yebamot* 45b, is undecided whether it was R. Yose bar Abin or R. Yose bar Zavida) who declared the child of the married woman a bastard and that of the single woman qualified. He collected signatures from the members of his Academy to stress the importance of his decision.

275 How can you qualify the child of the unmarried woman if the child of the married woman is a bastard?

276 R. Mana, the student of R. Yose.

277 R. Berekhiah, who had heard from Mar Uqban that R. Yose decided correctly according to the Galilean tradition.

278 R. Yose, who apparently was offended by R. Berekhiah's behavior. R. Berekhiah was a great preacher but no great authority in law.

(64d line 44) רִבִּי חִיָּיה בַּר בָּא אֲזַל לְצוֹר. אָתָא לְגַבֵּי רִבִּי יוֹחָנָן. אָמַר לֵיהּ. מַה מַּעֲשֶׂה בָא לְיָדֶיךָ. אָמַר לֵיהּ. גֵּר שֶׁמָּל וְלֹא טָבַל. אָמַר לֵיהּ. וְלָמָּה לֹא פָגַעְתָּה בֵּיהּ. אָמַר לֵיהּ רִבִּי יְהוֹשֻׁעַ בֶּן לֵוִי. יָאוּת עֲבַד דְּלָא פְגַע בֵּיהּ. מִחְלְפָה שִׁיטְתֵיהּ דְּרִבִּי יְהוֹשֻׁעַ בֶּן לֵוִי. תַּמָּן רִבִּי יַעֲקֹב בַּר אָחָא רִבִּי שִׁמְעוֹן בַּר בָּא רִבִּי יְהוֹשֻׁעַ בֶּן לֵוִי בְּשֵׁם רִבִּי גַּמְלִיאֵל בְּרִבִּי. הַוָּלָד אֵינוֹ לֹא כָשֵׁר וְלֹא פָסוּל אֶלָּא מְזוּהָם. וְהָכָא הוּא אָמַר הָכֵין. וְלֹא כֵן תַּנֵּי. גֵּר שֶׁמָּל וְלֹא טָבַל טָבַל וְלֹא מָל הַכֹּל הוֹלֵךְ אַחַר הַמִּילָה. דִּבְרֵי רִבִּי אֱלִיעֶזֶר. רִבִּי יְהוֹשֻׁעַ אוֹמֵר. אַף הַטְּבִילָה מְעַכֶּבֶת. אֶלָּא רִבִּי יְהוֹשֻׁעַ בֶּן לֵוִי כְּהָדָא דְתַגֵּי בַּר קַפָּרָא. דְּתַגֵּי בַּר קַפָּרָא. גֵּר שֶׁמָּל וְלֹא טָבַל הֲרֵי זֶה כָשֵׁר. שֶׁאֵין גֵּר שֶׁלֹּא טָבַל לִקְרוּיוֹ. וְקַשְׁיָא. עָלַת לוֹ טוּמְאָה קַלָּה מְטוּמְאָה חֲמוּרָה. אָמַר רִבִּי יוֹסֵי בֵּירִבִּי בּוּן. כֵּיוָן שֶׁזוּ וָזוּ לְשׁוּם קְדוּשַׁת יִשְׂרָאֵל עָלָה לוֹ.

2 בא לידך G | אירע על ידיך   ליה G | לה   3 ביה G | בה   4 שיטתיה G | שטתיה

5 בא G ‎| אבא G ‎| בר' G ‎| ביר' ‎ 6 הכין G ‎| הכן ‎ ולא כן... ‎| מעכבת ‎ - G ‎| 8 כהדא ‎|
G כחדה ‎| קפרא G ‎| קפרה ‎ 9 שלא G ‎| שאינו G ‎| וקשיא ‎| וקישייה ‎ 10 לו G ‎-

Rebbi Hiyya bar Abba went to Tyre. When he came before Rebbi Johanan, he asked him, what case did you handle? He said to him, a proselyte who had been circumcised but had not immersed himself[279]. He asked him, why did you not injure him[280]? Rebbi Joshua ben Levi[281] told him, leave him alone, he acted correctly not to injure him. The argument of Rebbi Joshua ben Levi seems inverted. There, Rebbi Jacob bar Aha, Rebbi Simeon bar Abba, Rebbi Joshua ben Levi, in the name of Rebbi Gamliel ben Rebbi[255]: The child is neither qualified nor disqualified but dirtied[282]. And here, he says so? Did we not state[283]: If a proselyte was circumcised but not immersed, immersed but not circumcised, everything depends on circumcision, the words of Rebbi Eliezer[284]. Rebbi Joshua says, immersion also is necessary[285]. But Rebbi Joshua ben Levi follows what Bar Qappara stated, as Bar Qappara stated: A proselyte who was circumcised but not immersed is qualified since there is no proselyte who did not immerse himself for his emission of semen[286]. Is that not difficult? The cleansing from a minor impurity is counted for him for a major impurity[287]? Rebbi Yose ben Abun said, since either one is for the holiness of Israel, it is counted for him[288].

279 From the context it seems clear that the proselyte had married a Jewish wife and R. Hiyya bar Abba declared the child qualified to marry in the congregation even though his teacher R. Johanan held that the child of a Gentile and a Jewish mother was a bastard.

280 And declare the child a bastard since the father did not complete the process of conversion.

281 Of the generation of R. Johanan's teachers.

282 Then at least R. Hiyya bar Abba

should have declared any female child ineligible for the priesthood.

283 The statement of the *baraita* is missing in G.

284 Circumcision is mentioned in *Ex.* 12:48 as formal requirement for conversion, but nothing else.

285 Since all the Children of Israel, when they were converted to the Jewish faith at Mount Sinai, had to immerse themselves, *Ex.* 19:10.

286 Which is required even for lawful intercourse, *Lev.* 15:16,18.

287 The essence of immersion in water is not the fact of immersion but the intent of the action. The impurity of an emission is minor since it can be remedied immediately. The entrance of a proselyte into the Jewish system of impurity is a major undertaking. How can a routine immersion be the equivalent of a major ceremony?

288 The argument is quoted in the Babli, *Yebamot* 45b, in the name of R. Joshua ben Levi; a similar principle is promulgated by Rav Assi for a woman proselyte who follows the rules of family purity.

(64d line 55) וְאֵי זֶה זֶה. זֶה וְוָלַד שִׁפְחָה וְנָכְרִית. תַּמָּן תַּנִּינָן. חוּץ מִמָּה שֶׁיֵּשׁ לוֹ מִן הַשִּׁפְחָה וּמִן הַנָּכְרִית.

שִׁפְחָה. דִּכְתִיב הָאִשָּׁה וִילָדֶיהָ תִּהְיֶה לַאֲדוֹנֶיהָ. נָכְרִית. רַבִּי יוֹחָנָן בְּשֵׁם רַבִּי שִׁמְעוֹן בֶּן יוֹחַי. כְּתִיב לֹא תִתְחַתֵּן בָּם בִּתְּךָ לֹא תִתֵּן לִבְנוֹ. וּכְתִיב כִּי יָסִיר אֶת בִּנְךָ מֵאַחֲרָי. בִּנְךָ מִיִּשְׂרְאֵלִית קָרוּי בִּנְךָ. וְאֵין בִּנְךָ מִן הַגּוֹיָה קָרוּי בִּנְךָ אֶלָּא בְּנָהּ.

3 דכת׳ | ב -   יוחנן | ב יוחנן אמ׳   4 בתך לא תתן לבנו | ב -   5 מן הגויה | ב מגויה

"Who is this? The child of a slave girl or a Gentile[234]." There[289], we have stated: "Except what he has from a slave girl or a Gentile."

[290]A slave woman: "The woman and her children shall belong to her owner." A Gentile woman. Rebbi Johanan [said] in the name of Rebbi Simeon ben Iohai, it is written: "You shall not conclude marriage with them, your daughter you shall not give to his son". And it is written: "For he will divert your son from following Me." Your son from a Jewish

woman is called your son; but your son from a Gentile woman is not called your son but her son.

יַעֲקֹב אִישׁ כְּפַר נְבוֹרַיָיה אֲזַל לְצוֹר. אַתּוֹן שָׁאֲלוֹן לֵיהּ. מַהוּ מִיגְזוֹר בְּרָהּ דַּאֲרָמִיָּתָא בְּשׁוּבְתָּא. וְסָבַר מִישְׁרֵי לְהוֹן מִן הָדָא וַיִּתְיַלְדוּ עַל מִשְׁפְּחוֹתָם לְבֵית אֲבוֹתָם. שָׁמַע רִבִּי חַגַּיי אָמַר. יֵיתֵי וְיִלְקֵי. אָמַר לֵיהּ. מֵהֵיכָן אַתְּ מַלְקֵינִי. אָמַר לֵיהּ. מִן הָדֵין וְעַתָּה נִכְרוֹת בְּרִית לְהוֹצִיא כָל־הַנָּשִׁים הַנָּכְרִיּוֹת וְהַנּוֹלַד מֵהֶן וגו'. אָמַר לֵיהּ. וּמִן הַקַּבָּלָה אַתְּ מַלְקֵינִי. אָמַר לֵיהּ. וְכַתּוֹרָה יֵעָשֶׂה. אָמַר לֵיהּ. מִן הָדֵין אוֹרִיתָה. אָמַר לֵיהּ. מִן הַהִיא דְּאָמַר רִבִּי יוֹחָנָן בְּשֵׁם רִבִּי שִׁמְעוֹן בֶּן יוֹחַי. לֹא תִתְחַתֵּן בָּם וכול'. אָמַר לֵיהּ. חֲבוֹט חַבְטָךְ דְּהוּא טָבָא בְקַלְטָא.

1 נבורייה | ב נבוריה   שאלון | ב שאלין   מיגזור | ב מיגזר   ברה | ב בריה   2 להון | ב לון   3 וילקי | ב אייתוניה דילקי   מהיכן את | ב מאיכן אתה   4 הדין | ב הדא דכת' להוציא כל הנשים הנכריות והנולד מהן וגו' | ב לאלהינו   6 הדין אוריתה | ב הדא אורייה   7 לא תתחתנן בם וכול' | ב כת' לא תתחתנן בם וכת' כי יסיר את בנך מאחריי. בנך מיש' קרוי בנך ואין בנך מגויה קרוי בנך אלא בנה

Jacob from Kefar Naboraia went to Tyre. They came to ask him, may one circumcise the son of a Gentile woman on the Sabbath? He wanted to permit it from the verse: "They determined their genealogies for their families according to their fathers' houses." Rebbi Ḥaggai heard it and said, he shall come and be whipped. He said to him, for what reason do you whip me? He said, from what is written: "Now we shall make a covenant to send away all foreign women and those born to them, etc". He said, you want to whip me based on tradition? He said, "and it should be done according to the Torah." He said to him, from which teaching? He said, from that which Rebbi Joḥanan said in the name of Rebbi Simeon ben Ioḥai, it is written: "You shall not conclude marriage with them," etc.[291] He said to him, whip your whipping, because it is good to impress.

289 Mishnah *Yebamot* 2:5. As long as the mother is Jewish, there is no difference between legitimate and illegitimate children; but children from a Gentile or servile mother are not their father's children.

290 From here to the end of the Halakhah, the text is from *Yebamot* 2:6 (**ב**), Notes 140-146. G only has a note to continue the text in *Yebamot*, Chapter 2. The story about Jacob from Kefar Naboraia is also in *Gen. rabba* 7(2), *Num. rabba* 19, *Pesiqta rabbati* 14 ed. M. Friedmann 62כ, *Pesiqta dR. Cahana* (Buber) *Parah* Note 99, *Tanḥuma Ḥuqqat* 6, *Tanḥuma Buber Ḥuqqat* 15; *Eccl. rabbati* 7(44).

291 Quoted in the preceding paragraph.

(fol. 63d) **משנה טו:** רִבִּי טַרְפוֹן אוֹמֵר. יְכוֹלִין מַמְזֵרִין לִיטָהֵר. כֵּיצַד. מַמְזֵר שֶׁנָּשָׂא שִׁפְחָה הַוְולָד עֶבֶד. שִׁיחְרְרוֹ נִמְצָא הַבֵּן בֶּן חוֹרִין. רִבִּי אֱלִיעֶזֶר אוֹמֵר. הֲרֵי זֶה עֶבֶד וּמַמְזֵר.

Mishnah 15: Rebbi Tarphon says, bastards can cleanse themselves. How is this? If the bastard married a slave girl, the child is a slave. When he is manumitted, the son is a free person[292]. Rebbi Eliezer said, he is a slave and a bastard[293].

292 Naturally, the son is not legally his father's son and heir; he cannot inherit except by a will. But he will be able to marry in the congregation.

293 In his opinion, manumission of the slave will not remove the stigma of bastardy.

(64d line 68) **הלכה טו:** רִבִּי טַרְפוֹן אוֹמֵר. יְכוֹלִין מַמְזֵרִין לִיטָהֵר כול'. כֵּינֵי מַתְנִיתָה. מַמְזֵר מוּתָּר לוֹ לִישָּׂא שִׁפְחָה. רַב יְהוּדָה בְּשֵׁם שְׁמוּאֵל. הִילְכְתָא כְרִבִּי טַרְפוֹן. רִבִּי שְׁמְלַאי הוֹרֵי בְּאַנְטוֹכִיָא. רִבִּי סִימַאי הוֹרֵי בִּכְפַר סְפּוֹרַיָיא. הֲלָכָה כְרִבִּי טַרְפוֹן.

3 שמלאי G | שמלי   באנטוכיא G | באנטוכייה   סימיי G | סימאי   בכפר ספורייא G | בפרוסף...

Halakhah 15: "Rebbi Tarphon says, bastards can cleanse themselves," etc. So is the Mishnah: A bastard is permitted to marry a slave girl[294]. Rav Jehudah in the name of Samuel: Practice follows Rebbi Tarphon[295]. Rebbi Simlai instructed in Antiochia[296], Rebbi Simai instructed in Kefar Seforaia[297]: Practice follows Rebbi Tarphon.

294 This is not an emendation of the Mishnah, but a logical inference. In general, a Jew is not allowed to sleep with a slave girl since any sexual relations with a person whom he could not marry violate *Deut.* 23:18. But R. Tarphon implies that the informal marriage of a bastard with a slave girl (or a free Gentile woman) has rabbinic blessing since 1) the bastard is precluded from contracting a marriage with members of the congregation and 2) having the possibility of sexual relations is a basic human right (*Gen.* 1:28). The Babli agrees, 69a.

295 Babli, 69a.

296 According to the Babli, his landlord was a bastard; he counseled him how to have marriageable children.

297 The name of the locality cannot be determined either from L (different versions of scribe and corrector) or from G.

(64d line 72) תַּנֵּי מִשֵּׁם רְבִּי מֵאִיר. יֵשׁ אִישׁ וְאִשָּׁה שֶׁמּוֹלִידִין חָמֵשׁ אוּמוֹת. כֵּיצַד. מִי שֶׁיֵּשׁ לוֹ עֶבֶד וְשִׁפְחָה וְהוֹלִידוּ בָנִים הֲרֵי גוֹיִם. נִתְגַּיֵּיר אֶחָד מֵהֶן אֶחָד גֵּר וְאֶחָד גּוֹי. נִתְגַּיֵּיר רַבָּן וְגִייְרוּ לִשְׁנֵי עֲבָדִים וְהוֹלִידוּ בָנִים הֲרֵי אֵילוּ עֲבָדִים. אָמַר רִבִּי זְעִירָא. הָדָא אֲמָרָה. גּוֹי שֶׁבָּא עַל שִׁפְחָה וְהוֹלִיד בֶּן הַוָּלָד עֶבֶד. שִׁיחְרֵר שִׁפְחָה וְהוֹלִידָה בֶן הַוָּלָד מַמְזֵר. וְאַחַר כָּךְ שִׁיחְרֵר הָעֶבֶד וְהוֹלִיד בֶּן הֲרֵי זֶה עֶבֶד מְשׁוּחְרָר. יֵשׁ מוֹכֵר לְאָבִיו לָתֵת לְאִמּוֹ כְּתוּבָּתָהּ. כֵּיצַד. מִי שֶׁיֵּשׁ לוֹ עֶבֶד וְשִׁפְחָה וְהוֹלִיד בֶּן. שִׁיחְרֵר אֶת הַשִּׁפְחָה וּנְשָׂאָהּ וְכָתַב כָּל־נְכָסָיו לִבְנָהּ. זֶהוּ שֶׁהוּא מוֹכֵר אָבִיו לָתֵת לְאִמּוֹ כְּתוּבָּתָהּ.

1 שמולידין G ‎| שהן מולידין   2 מי G | גוי   3 רבן G | ־בו   לשני עבדים G | לשום
עבד   4 זעירא הדא G | זעורה הדה   שפחה G | השפחה   5 כך G | מיכן   העבד |
G את העבד   6 עבד G | בן עבד   יש G יש שהוא   שיש G | שייש   7 את השפחה |
G שפחה

[298]"It was stated in the name of Rebbi Meïr: It can happen that a man and a woman give birth to five nations[299]. How is this? [A Gentile][300] had a male and a female slave who had children: these are Gentiles[301]. If one of them[302] became Jewish, one is a proselyte and one a Gentile. If their master converted and converted them[303] as slaves, [any children] are slaves." Rebbi Ze'ira said, this implies that if a Gentile had intercourse with a slave girl, the child is a slave[304]. "If he manumitted the slave girl and she had a son, the child is a bastard[305]. If afterwards he manumitted the slave and he begat a child, he is a freed slave.[306]" [307]"It can happen that a man sells his father to pay his mother's *ketubah*. How is this? Somebody has a male and a female slave and they have a son. He manumitted the female slave, married her, and willed all his property to her son. That is one who sells his father to pay his mother's *ketubah*."

298 Tosephta 5:11-12; in slightly different form Babli *Yebamot* 99a.

299 A nation is defined here as a group of people following identical marriage rules.

300 Reading of G and Tosephta; implied by L.

301 As far as Jewish marriage laws are concerned, there is no difference between a Gentile free person and a Gentile slave.

302 One of the children.

303 If the parents become slaves in a Jewish household, the children will be slaves under Jewish law.

304 This rule is presupposed everywhere in the Yerushalmi. Since the slave girl cannot marry and is forbidden as sex partner to any free Jew by *Deut.* 23:18, she has the right to freely associate both with slaves and Gentiles. The children of the slave

mother always inherit their mother's status; Mishnah 3:15.

305 Once the woman is freed, if she continuous to live with the slave who was her de-facto husband as a slave, the child is a bastard for R. Meïr (Note 252).

306 Following Mishnah 3:15, there is marriage without sin; the child obtains the status of his father.

307 Tosephta 5:13; Babli *Yebamot* 99a.

(65a line 5) רִבִּי מֵאִיר אוֹמֵר. אֵין מַמְזֵרִין טְהוֹרִין לֶעָתִיד לָבוֹא. שֶׁנֶּאֱמַר וְיָשַׁב מַמְזֵר בְּאַשְׁדּוֹד. מוֹלִיכִין טִינָה אֵצֶל טִינָה וְסָרִיּוֹת אֵצֶל סָרִיּוֹת. רִבִּי יוֹסֵי אוֹמֵר. מַמְזֵרִים טְהוֹרִין לֶעָתִיד לָבוֹא. שֶׁנֶּאֱמַר וְזָרַקְתִּי עֲלֵיכֶם מַיִם טְהוֹרִים וגו׳. אָמַר לוֹ רִבִּי מֵאִיר. וַהֲלֹא אֵינוֹ אוֹמֵר אֶלָּא מִכָּל־טוּמְאוֹתֵיכֶם וּמִכָּל־גִּילּוּלֵיכֶם אַטַהֵר אֶתְכֶם. אָמַר לוֹ רִבִּי יוֹסֵי. אִילּוּ נֶאֱמַר וְכָל־טוּמְאוֹתֵיכֶם וּמִכָּל־גִּילּוּלֵיכֶם וְשָׁתַק הָיִיתִי אוֹמֵר כִּדְבָרֶיךָ. הָא אֵינוֹ אוֹמֵר אַטַהֵר אֶתְכֶם אֶלָּא מִן הַמַּמְזֵירוּת. רִבִּי הוּנָא בְּשֵׁם רַב יוֹסֵף אָמַר. אֵין הֲלָכָה כְּרִבִּי יוֹסֵי לֶעָתִיד לָבוֹא.

2 סריות G | סיריות (twice)   יוֹסֵי G | יוֹסֵה   3 וגו׳ G | וטהרתם   5 יוֹסִי G | יוֹסֵה וכל G | מכל   6 גילוליכם G | גלולכם   7 מן G | אף מן   הונא G | חונה   7 יוֹסִי | יוֹסֵה G   8 לבוא G | לבוא עלובין הן הדורו[ת]

[308]"Rebbi Meïr says, bastards will not be purified in the future, since it is said[309]: 'The bastard will dwell in Ashdod'; one carried garbage to garbage and deviant to deviant. Rebbi Yose says, bastards will be purified in the future, since it is said[310]: "I shall pour upon you pure water [and purify you][283]." Rebbi Meïr said to him, but it says only "from all your impurities and all your abominations I shall purify you." Rebbi Yose said to him, if it had only said, "from all your impurities and all your abominations" and then stopped, I would have agreed with you. But since it adds "I shall purify you[311]", from bastardy. Rebbi Huna said in the name of Rav Joseph, practice in the future will not follow Rebbi Yose[312].

308 Tosephta 5:4, Babli 72b, in different formulation.

309 *Za.* 9:6.

310 *Ez.* 36:25.

311 Quoted in G; the "etc." in L is better talmudic style, not quoting the part of the verse to which one really refers.

312 A repetition not logically necessary.

313 G adds: "The generations are wretched."

עשרה יוחסין פרק רביעי

(fol. 65a) **משנה א:** עֲשָׂרָה יוֹחֲסִין עָלוּ מִבָּבֶל כַּהֲנֵי לְוִיֵּי יִשְׂרְאֵלֵי חֲלָלֵי גֵּירֵי וַחֲרוּרֵי מַמְזִירֵי וּנְתִינֵי שְׁתוּקֵי וַאֲסוּפֵי. כַּהֲנֵי לְוִיֵּי וְיִשְׂרְאֵלֵי מוּתָּרִין לָבוֹא זֶה בָזֶה. לְוִיֵּי וְיִשְׂרְאֵלֵי גֵּירֵי וַחֲרוּרֵי וַחֲלָלֵי מוּתָּרִין לָבוֹא זֶה בָזֶה. גֵּירֵי וַחֲרוּרֵי וּמַמְזִירֵי נְתִינֵי שְׁתוּקֵי וַאֲסוּפֵי מוּתָּרִין לָבוֹא זֶה בָזֶה.

Mishnah 1: Ten marriage classes returned from Babylonia: Priests, Levites, Israel, desecrated priests[1], proselytes, freedmen, bastards[2], dedicated ones[3], silenced ones[4], foundlings. Priests, Levites, and Israel are permitted to marry one another. Levites, Israel, proselytes, freedmen, and desecrated priests are permitted to marry one another[5]. Proselytes, freedmen, bastards, silenced ones, and foundlings are permitted to marry one another.

1 Descendants of the forbidden union of a priest and a divorcee or a prostitute.

2 Descendants of an adulterous or incestuous union involving a deadly sin.

3 Gibeonites, cf. Notes 46 ff.

4 As explained in Mishnah 2, children with a known mother but unknown father.

5 The marriage class of the child being that of the father by Mishnah 3:14.

(65b line 27) **הלכה א:** עֲשָׂרָה יוֹחֲסִין עָלוּ מִבָּבֶל כול'. כַּהֲנֵי לְוִיֵּי וְיִשְׂרְאֵלֵי. עַל שֵׁם וַיַּעֲלוּ מִבְּנֵי יִשְׂרָאֵל וּמִן הַכֹּהֲנִים וְהַלְוִיִּם וְהַמְשֹׁרְרִים וְהַשּׁוֹעֲרִים וְהַנְּתִינִים אֶל יְרוּשָׁלָםִ בִּשְׁנַת שֶׁבַע לְאַרְתַּחְשַׁסְתְּא הַמֶּלֶךְ.

Halakhah 1

Halakhah 1: "Ten marriage classes returned from Babylonia," etc. Priests, Levites, and Israel, as described[6]: "There came of the Children of Israel, and of the priests, the Levites, both the servants[7] and the doorkeepers, and the Temple slaves, to Jerusalem in the seventh year of king Artaxerxes.[8]"

---

6   *Ezra* 7:7.

7   This is clearly a copyist's error; it must read "singers" as in the masoretic text. Even at the end of the Second Temple period, levitic singers and doorkeepers formed two clearly identified classes in the Temple service. All the distinctions in marriage classes here are clearly attributed to Ezra, not to the early returnees under Sheshbazzar and Zerubabel.

8   This quote seems to be missing in G.

(65b line 30) חֲלָלֵי. עַל שֵׁם וּמִבְּנֵי הַכֹּהֲנִים בְּנֵי חֲבַיָּה בְּנֵי הַקּוֹץ אֵלֶּא בִּקְשׁוּ כְתָבָם הַמִּתְיַחֲשִׂים וְלֹא נִמְצָאוּ וַיְגוֹאֲלוּ מִן הַכְּהוּנָה. וַיֹּאמֶר הַתִּרְשָׁתָא לָהֶם. וְלָמָה נִקְרָא שְׁמוֹ הַתִּרְשָׁבָא. שֶׁהִתִּירוּ לוֹ לִשְׁתּוֹת בַּיַּיִן. הַתִּרְשָׁתָא. וַאֲנִי הָיִיתִי מַשְׁקֶה לַמֶּלֶךְ. אֲשֶׁר לֹא יֹאכְלוּ מִקָּדְשֵׁי הַקֳּדָשִׁים. הָא בְקָדְשֵׁי הַגְּבוּל יֹאכְלוּ. אָמַר רְבִּי יוֹסֵי. גְּדוֹלָה הִיא הַחֲזָקָה. מִכֵּיוָן שֶׁהוּחְזְקוּ שָׁם לִהְיוֹת אוֹכְלִין אַף כָּאן אוֹכְלִין. נִיחָא תַּמָּן דִּכְתִיב הַצִּיבִי לָךְ צִיּוּנִים. הָכָא מָה אִית לָךְ. כְּמַאן דְּאָמַר. מֵאֲלֵיהֶן קִיבְּלוּ אֶת הַמַּעְשְׂרוֹת. עַד עֲמוֹד כֹּהֵן לְאוּרִים וְתוּמִּים. וְכִי אוּרִים וְתוּמִּים הָיוּ בְאוֹתָהּ שָׁעָה בַּבַּיִת שֵׁנִי. אֶלָּא כְּאָדָם שֶׁהוּא אוֹמֵר. עַד שֶׁיִּחְיוּ הַמֵּתִים. עַד שֶׁיָּבוֹא בֶּן דָּוִד.

3 ולמה G | נחמייה הוא התרשתא ולמה   שהתירו G | שהיתירו   5 - | G הן יאכלו בקודשי המקדש אם אינן כהנים ברורי[ם]   6 כמאן G | כמן

"Desecrated priest." Following[9] "from the sons of Cohanim, the family Ḥavaya, the family Ḥaqqos ..[10] . they tried to find their genealogical documents; but they were not found and they were freed from priesthood.

And the *tiršata*[11] told them." Why was he called *hattiršata*? Because they permitted him to drink of the wine[12]. *Hatiršata*, "I was the king's cup bearer." "That they should not eat from what was dedicated as holy[13]." Therefore, from outside[14] holy food they might eat? Rebbi Yose said, great is the permanence of the *status quo ante*[15]. Since they were used to eat there[16], they may also eat here. One understands there, as it is written: "Put up signposts for yourself.[17]" What can one say here[18]? Following him who said, they accepted tithes voluntarily[19]. "Until a priest will be appointed for *urim* and *tummim*." But were there any *urim* and *tummim* then, in the Second Temple[20]? But [he is] like a person who says until the dead will be resurrected, until David's son[21] will come.

9   *Ezra* 2:61-63. The verses prove that there were desecrated priests coming from Babylonia, as asserted in the Mishnah.

10   Not mentioned here is the statement that their problem was rooted in the fact that their ancestors 500 years earlier had married the daughters of Barzilai the Gileadite; this is the subject of the following paragraph. The quote then shows that the category of "desecrated priest" is hereditary.

11   The Persian title of the governor, "the one to be feared". The title is applied to Nehemiah in 8:9; therefore, traditionally the appellation is interpreted as a kind of nickname of Nehemiah (as is explicit in G) and as such the Iranian word is read as an Aramaic pun. It is clear from *Neh.* 7 that the title in *Ezra* 2 cannot apply to Nehemiah; it probably refers to Sheshbazzar.

12   As cup-bearer to the Persian monarch, Nehemiah certainly had to taste the wine to make sure it was not poisoned. But drinking Gentile wine is forbidden in rabbinic Judaism. Since Nehemiah shows himself to be strictly orthodox in *Ezra* and *Nehemiah*, the natural assumption is that he had obtained a special dispensation from the religious authorities of the time. The interpretation reads the name הַתִּרְשָׁתָא (which never appears without

initial ה) not as a noun with definite article but a composite הַתֵּר-שָׁתָא "permitted drinker." The explanation is quoted by Rashi, 69b, *s.v.* התרשתא.

13 It seems that the Yerushalmi is in disagreement with the vocalization by the Masoretes. In the Pentateuch, to which the verses clearly are referring, masoretic vocalization strictly differentiates between the noun קָדָשִׁים *"sancta,* sacrifices" and the superlative adjective קָדָשִׁים "most holy". Since the mss. of the Ben-Asher tradition uniformly write קָדָשִׁים in the verse here, it is clear that the masoretic interpretation of the verse forbade *all* holy food to the desecrated priests, whether Temple sacrifices or "outside *sancta*", i. e., heave and tithes. But the Yerushalmi, based on the Mishnaic distinction between קָדְשֵׁי קָדָשִׁים "most holy sacrifices", destined exclusively for the altar and/or legitimate priests in the Temple precinct, קָדָשִׁם קַלִּים "simple sacrifices" (well-being offerings) shared between altar, priests, and the donor's family, and קָדְשֵׁי הַגְּבוּל "outside *sancta*", here reads מִקָּדְשֵׁי הַקֳּדָשִׁים "from most holy sacrifices." This immediately raises the question why desecrated priests are not summarily excluded from all holy food (as they are in rabbinic practice). As far as the fragmentary text of G can be interpreted, this is exactly the question asked, which is missing in L and *editio princeps*: "[If they are genuine priests] they should eat Temple *sancta*; if they are not genuine priests [they should be excluded from all *sancta*]" The Yerushalmi is quoted by Rashi as explanation of the Babli, 69b *s. v.* ואמר להם.

14 Maybe better: "Borderline *sancta*."

15 Cf. *Giṭṭin* 3:4 Note 87. *Ketubot* 5:5 Note 100, *Yebamot* 15:12 Notes 181. An echo of the discussion here is in the Babli, 69b.

16 In Babylonia, an impure country, where heaves and tithes were given to the priests as a remembrance of biblical rules, not a biblical obligation.

17 *Jer.* 31:20. The verse is read as exhortation to symbolically observe in the diaspora also those biblical precepts which are intrinsically bound to the Land (*Threni rabbati* 1:62).

18 Since heave and heave of the tithe in the Land require genuine purity and genuine priests.

19 Cf. Halakhah 1:9, *Ševi'it* 6:1.

20 The *urim wetummim* oracle was never part of the High Priest's vestment in the Second Temple since its nature was unknown.

21 The Messiah.

(65b line 39) אִילֵין בְּנוֹת בַּרְזִילִיי לְשֵׁם שָׁמַיִם נִתְגַּיְירוּ אוֹ שֶׁלֹּא לְשֵׁם שָׁמַיִם נִתְגַּיְירוּ. אִין תֵּימַר. לְשֵׁם שָׁמַיִם נִתְגַּיְירוּ. יֹאכְלוּ בְקָדְשֵׁי הַקֳּדָשִׁים. וְאִין תֵּימַר. שֶׁלֹּא לְשֵׁם שָׁמַיִם נִתְגַּיְירוּ. אֲפִילוּ בְקָדְשֵׁי הַגְּבוּל לֹא יֹאכְלוּ. אֲפִילוּ תֵימַר. לְשׁוּם שָׁמַיִם נִתְגַּיְירוּ. וְגִיּוֹרֶת לֹא כְזוֹנָה הִיא אֵצֶל כְּהוּנָה. פָּתַר לָהּ. לֹא הָיוּ בָנוֹת אֶלָּא בְּנוֹת בָּנוֹת. וְאֵין מִבְּנוֹת בָּנוֹת כְּיִשְׂרָאֵל הֵם. וּכְרַבִּי שִׁמְעוֹן. דְּרַבִּי שִׁמְעוֹן אָמַר. גִּיּוֹרֶת שֶׁנִּתְגַּיְירָה פָּחוֹת מִבַּת שָׁלֹשׁ שָׁנִים וְיוֹם אֶחָד. לֹא הָיָה בָהּ דַּעַת לִטְבּוֹל אוֹ מִשֶּׁהִטְבִּילָה אוֹתָהּ מִכֵּיוָן שֶׁהִיא חוֹזֶרֶת וְטוֹבֶלֶת לְשֵׁם קְדוּשַׁת יִשְׂרָאֵל כָּל אַחַת גִּיּוֹרֶת הִיא וְגִיּוֹרֶת כְּזוֹנָה הִיא אֵצֶל הַכְּהוּנָה.

1 ברזיליי | G ברזלייִ   2 בקדשי הקדשים | G בקודשי המקדש   5 חם | G חן

[22]Did those daughters of Barzilai's[23] convert in the name of Heaven[24] or not[25] in the name of Heaven? If you say that they converted in the name of Heaven should not [their descendants] eat most holy sacrifices? But if you say that they converted not in the name of Heaven, then [their descendants] should not eat even outside *sancta*. Even if you say that they converted in the name of Heaven, is a female proselyte not like a prostitute for the priesthood[26]? Explain it that they were not daughters but daughters of daughters[27]. But if they were daughters of daughters, they are like Israel![28] But following Rebbi Simeon, since Rebbi Simeon said, a proselyte who converted at less that three years and one day of age[29]. She had no intent to immerse herself but [her mother] immersed her; if then later she immerses herself for the holiness of Israel, each of them then becomes a proselyte and a proselyte is like a prostitute for the priesthood[30].

22 Cf. the discussion in pp. 17-20 of Introduction to Talmudic Literature in the first volume, *Berakhot*, of this edition of the Yerushalmi.

23 There seems to be no indication in the Bible that Barzilai was not

Jewish. But in 2S. 17:27 Barzilai the Gileadite is associated with Šobi ben Nahaš from Rabbat Ammon in providing for David's army in his flight from Absalom. Since Šobi is characterized as a Gentile, the implication here is that Barzilai also was a Gentile and this is used to explain why some 500 years later Barzilai's descendants could not serve as priests.

24 I. e., were honest converts to be counted as Jews.

25 A conversion for the only purpose of being able to be married to a Jewish partner is considered to be invalid; the person so converted then remains Gentile. The Babli disagrees; a conversion is valid and irrevocable if it satisfies the minimal legal conditions imposed on the act: *Yebamot* 24b; *Seder Eliahu Rabba* Chap. 29.

26 Lev. 21:7 forbids only a whore, a desecrated woman, and a divorcee as marriage partners to the Cohen. Now the divorcee and the desecrated are Jewish born; they cannot be proselytes. The legal definition of a "whore" is a person who had sexual relations with a man whom she could not possibly marry. Since a Gentile is excluded from preliminary marriage, a Gentile woman who is presumed to have had sexual experience when very young, automatically qualifies as whore under this definition.

27 The daughters of Barzilai married not priests but courtiers of David's court (*1K*. 2:7). Then their children were regular Israelites according to Mishnah 3:14 and could marry priests.

28 Their descendants then would have been genuine priests able to serve in the Temple.

29 This sentence is obviously incomplete; one must add "may marry into the priesthood", cf. *Bikkurim* Halakhah 1:5; Babli *Yebamot* 60b, *Qiddušin* 76b,78a.

30 This explains the attitude of the rabbis who oppose R. Simeon. They agree that by biblical standards, the proselyte toddler could be married to a priest as explained by R. Simeon in *Bikkurim* Halakhah 1:5. But they require a conscious act for a rabbinically valid conversion and this is impossible for a toddler. If later the adolescent girl immerses herself for the impurity of menstruation, this is a conscious act and counts fully as valid conversion (cf. Halakhah 3:14, Note 278.) But at that time, the girl is much older than three years and R. Simeon's argument does not apply. It follows that the daughters of Barzilai, even if

converted as toddlers, were rabbinically prohibited to priests. The priests who married them, presumably for their money and standing at court, therefore created a class of rabbinically desecrated priests who could be barred from Temple *sancta* (in the formulation of G) but not from outside *sancta*.

(65b line 49) הַמִּתְגַּיֵּיר לְשֵׁם אַהֲבָה וְכֵן אִישׁ מִפְּנֵי אִשָּׁה וְכֵן אִשָּׁה מִפְּנֵי אִישׁ וְכֵן גִּירֵי שׁוּלְחַן מְלָכִים וְכֵן גִּירֵי אֲרָיוֹת וְכֵן גִּירֵי מָרְדְּכַי וְאֶסְתֵּר אֵין מְקַבְּלִין אוֹתָן. רַב אָמַר. הֲלָכָה גֵּרִים הֵן וְאֵין דּוֹחִין אוֹתָן כְּדֶרֶךְ שֶׁדּוֹחִין אֶת הַגֵּרִים תְּחִילָּה. אֲבָל מְקַבְּלִין אוֹתָן וּצְרִיכִין קֵירוּב פָּנִים שֶׁמָּא גְיִירוּ לְשֵׁם.
4 פנים שמא | ג פעם שנייה

Any person who converts because of love, i. e., a man because of a woman or a woman because of a man, or proselytes of the king's table[31], or lion proselytes[32], or the proselytes of Mordechai and Esther[33], one does not accept. Rav said, they are proselytes[34]; one does not reject them in the way one has to reject proselytes from the start[35]. But one accepts them; they need to be received in a friendly way; perhaps[36] they became proselytes for God[24].

31 People who convert in order to obtain a government post.

32 The ancestors of the Samaritans who converted because of fear of the lions (*2K*. 17:25 ff.)

33 "And many of the people of the land became Jewish, for the fear of the Jews fell on them" (*Esth*. 8:17).

34 This is rabbinic practice.

35 A person who wants to become Jewish has to be told that he is better off not being a Jew (Babli *Yebamot* 47b) and sent away; he can be accepted only if he comes back.

35 This is the translation of the text of L. The text is problematic since שֶׁמָּא "perhaps" is Babylonian Aramaic. According to G, one has to read: "They have to be approached a second time, to convert them for the name [of Heaven]." While the text of L represents rabbinic practice from the

Middle Ages, the text of G has no echo in rabbinic literature. Therefore, the text of L has to be preferred.

(65b line 53) גֵּירֵי עַל שֵׁם וְכָל־הַנִּבְדָּל מִטּוּמְאַת גּוֹיֵי הָאָרֶץ אֲלֵיהֶם. חֲרוּרֵי עַל שֵׁם וְכָל־הַנְּתִינִים וגו׳. מַמְזֵרֵי. אָמַר רִבִּי סִימוֹן. כְּתִיב. וְאֵלֶּה הָעוֹלִים מִתֵּל מֶלַח תֵּל חַרְשָׁא. מִתֵּל מֶלַח זוֹ בָּבֶל. תֵּל חַרְשָׁא אֵילוּ שְׁתוּקֵי וַאֲסוּפֵי. כְּרוּב אֵילוּ הַמַּמְזֵירִין. רוּבִּין אֵילוּ שֶׁהָלְכוּ אַחַר עֵינֵיהֶן. אַדּוֹן. שֶׁהָיוּ אוֹמְרִים. אֵין דִּין וְאֵין אָדוֹן. רִבִּי חִזְקִיָּה מַפִּיק לִישְׁנֵיהּ. אֵילוּ שֶׁהָלְכוּ אַחַר עֵינֵיהֶן וְאָמְרוּ. אֵין דִּין וְאֵין דַּיָּין. וְאִימֵּר שֶׁהֵימְרוּ לָאֵל בְּמַעֲשֵׂיהֶן הָרָעִים. רִבִּי אַבּוּן בְּשֵׁם רִבִּי פִּינְחָס. פִּירְסְמוּ עַצְמָן כְּאִימְרָא בְחָלוּק. רִבִּי לֵוִי בְּשֵׁם רִבִּי שִׁמְעוֹן בֶּן לָקִישׁ. רְאוּיִים הָיוּ לֵיעָשׂוֹת תֵּל מֶלַח אֶלָּא שֶׁשָּׁתְקָה לָהֶן מִידַּת הַדִּין. תֵּל חַרְשָׁא.

2 וגו׳ | G   ובני עבדי שלמה | G   3 כרוב | G   כרוב אדון   4 אילו | G   אלו | G   רובין | G   רובים   5 לישניה | G   לשנה   אילו שהלכו | G   אלו שהילכו   7 כאימרא | G   כאימרה

[36]"Proselytes," meaning "everyone who separated himself from the impurities of the peoples of the earth to join them.[37]" Freedmen, as in "and all the Gibeonites, etc.[38]" Bastards. Rebbi Simeon said, it is written[39]: "And the following came up from Salt Hill, Ploughing Hill". From Salt Hill, that is Babylon. Ploughing Hill refers to silenced ones and foundlings[40]. Kerub[41] means the bastards; the young are those who go after their eyes[42]; Addon[43], for they were saying, there is no judgment and no Master. Rebbi Ḥizqiah changed the wording: These are those who went after their eyes and said, there is no judgment and no judge. And Immer[44], who rebelled against God by their evil deeds. Rebbi Abbun in the name of Rebbi Phineas: They publicized themselves like the seam of a garment[45]. Rebbi Levi in the name of Rebbi Simeon ben Laqish: They would have been worthy of being turned into a salt hill, but Divine justice was silent for them. Ploughing Hill.

36 One continues to prove that in fact all categories of people enumerated in the Mishnah were among the returnees from the Babylonian captivity.

37 *Ezra* 6:21. In the Babli, 70a, the verse is applied to both proselytes and freedmen.

38 G shows that the reference is to *Ezra* 2:58, *Neh.* 7:60; the freedmen are the "sons of Solomon's servants" mentioned in that verse. In both cases, MT is without initial ו.

39 *Ezra* 2:60 = *Neh.* 7:61. The subject are people for whom it is questionable whether they should be able to contract Jewish marriages. The place names have not been identified. A similar homiletic interpretation of the same verse is in the Babli, 70a.

40 "Ploughing" as metaphor for illicit sexual activity is hinted at in *Jud.* 14:18. In Karaite theory, the forbidden ploughing on the Sabbath (*Ex.* 34:21) is the sex act.

41 As in the interpretation of *Cherubim* as "like youngsters", represented as baby angels, כ is taken as prefix, not part of the root.

42 Cf. *Soṭah* Mishnah 1:8.

43 Reading the place name אַדּוֹן as noun אָדוֹן.

44 Accadic/Aramaic אמר "lamb", homiletically identified with Hebrew המר (in Galilean pronounciation which identified א ה ח ע) "to rebel" (cf. *Ps.* 107:11).

45 Identifying אמר "lamb" and Aramaic/Syriac אִמְרָה (חוּמְרָא) "knot, seam, flounce", in addition to Hebrew אִמְרָה "maxim, saying". The sermon uses *Immer* as acoustic echo of all these meanings.

(65b line 53) תַּנֵּי. רִבִּי אִמִּי בְשֵׁם רִבִּי יְהוֹשֻׁעַ בֶּן לֵוִי. עַל שֵׁם וַיִּתְּנֵם יְהוֹשֻׁעַ בַּיּוֹם הַהוּא חוֹטְבֵי עֵצִים וְשׁוֹאֲבֵי מַיִם לָעֵדָה. נִיחָא לָעֵדָה. וּלְמִזְבֵּחַ לי׳. אֶלָּא תְּלָיָין יְהוֹשֻׁעַ בַּדּוֹפָן. אָמַר. אֲנִי לֹא מְקָרְבָן וְלֹא מְרַחֲקָן. אֶלָּא בְּמִי שֶׁהוּא עָתִיד לִבְנוֹת אֶת בֵּית הַבְּחִירָה וְאֶת שֶׁדַּעְתּוֹ לְקָרֵב יְקָרֵב לְרַחֵק יְרַחֵק. בָּא דָוִד וְרִיחֲקָן. שֶׁנֶּאֱמַר. וְהַגִּבְעוֹנִים לֹא מִבְּנֵי יִשְׂרָאֵל הֵמָּה. וְלָמָּה רִיחֲקָן. עַל שֵׁם וַיְהִי רָעָב בִּימֵי דָוִד שָׁלֹשׁ שָׁנִים שָׁנָה אַחַר שָׁנָה. אָמַר דָוִד. בְּעָוֹן אַרְבָּעָה דְבָרִים הַגְּשָׁמִים נֶעֱצָרִים. בְּעָוֹן עוֹבְדֵי עֲבוֹדָה זָרָה וְגִילּוּי עֲרָיוֹת וּשְׁפִיכוּת דָּמִים וּפוֹסְקִין צְדָקָה בָּרַבִּים וְאֵינָן נוֹתְנִין. בְּעָוֹן עוֹבְדֵי עֲבוֹדָה זָרָה מְנַיָּין. הִשָּׁמְרוּ

לָכֶם פֶּן יִפְתֶּה לְבַבְכֶם וגו׳. מַה כְּתִיב בַּתְרֵיהּ. וְחָרָה אַף יי בָּכֶם וְעָצַר אֶת הַשָּׁמַיִם וגו׳. בַּעֲוֹן מְגַלֵּי עֲרָיוֹת מְנַיִין. וַתֶּחֱנִיפִי אֶרֶץ בִּזְמוֹתַיִךְ וּבְרָעָתֵךְ. מַהוּ עוֹנְשׁוֹ שֶׁלַּדָּבָר. וַיִּמָּנְעוּ רְבִיבִים וּמַלְקוֹשׁ לֹא הָיָה וגו׳. בַּעֲוֹן שׁוֹפְכֵי דָמִים מְנַיִין. כִּי הַדָּם הוּא יַחֲנִיף אֶת הָאָרֶץ. בַּעֲוֹן פּוֹסְקֵי צְדָקָה בָּרַבִּים וְאֵינָן נוֹתְנִין מְנַיִין. נְשִׂיאִים וְרוּחַ וְגֶשֶׁם אָיִן אִישׁ מִתְהַלֵּל בְּמַתַּת שָׁקֶר. בָּדַק דָּוִד בְּכָל־דּוֹרוֹ וְלֹא מָצָא אֶחָד מֵהֶן. הִתְחִיל שׁוֹאֵל בְּאוּרִים וְתוּמִּים. הֲדָא הוּא דִכְתִיב וַיְבַקֵּשׁ דָּוִד אֶת פְּנֵי יי בָּאוּרִים וְתוּמִּים. אָמַר רִבִּי אֶלְעָזָר. כְּתִיב בַּקְּשׁוּ אֶת יי כָּל־עַנְוֵי הָאָרֶץ אֲשֶׁר מִשְׁפָּטוֹ פָּעֲלוּ. מַהוּ אֲשֶׁר מִשְׁפָּטוֹ פָּעֲלוּ. שֶׁהוּא עוֹשֶׂה מִשְׁפָּט וּפָעֳלוֹ כְּאַחַת. וַיֹּאמֶר יי עַל שָׁאוּל וְעַל בֵּית הַדָּמִים. עַל שָׁאוּל שֶׁלֹּא עֲשִׂיתֶם עִמּוֹ חֶסֶד. וְעַל בֵּית הַדָּמִים עַל אֲשֶׁר הֵמִית אֶת הַגִּבְעוֹנִים. שָׁלַח דָּוִד וְקָרָא לָהֶם. מַה לָּכֶם וּלְבֵית שָׁאוּל. אָמְרִין לֵיהּ. עַל אֲשֶׁר הֵמִית מִמֶּנּוּ שִׁבְעָה אֲנָשִׁים. שְׁנֵי חוֹטְבֵי עֵצִים וּשְׁנֵי שׁוֹאֲבֵי מַיִם וְחַזָּן וְסוֹפֵר וְשַׁמָּשׁ. אָמַר לוֹן. מָה אַתּוּן בְּעוּ כְדוֹן. אָמְרוּ לֵיהּ. יוּתַּן לָנוּ שִׁבְעָה אֲנָשִׁים מִבָּנָיו וְהוֹקַעֲנוּם לַיי בְּגִבְעַת שָׁאוּל בְּחִיר יי. אָמַר לוֹן. וּמָה הֲנָייָה לְכוֹן וְאֵינוּן מִתְקַטְלִין. סְבוּ לְכוֹן כְּסַף וּדְהָב. וַהֲווֹן אָמְרִין. אֵין לָנוּ כֶסֶף עִם שָׁאוּל וְעִם בֵּיתוֹ. אָמַר. דִּילְמָא דְּאִינּוּן בְּהָתִין פְּלָגוֹן מִן פְּלַג. נְסַב כָּל־חַד מִינְּהוֹן וַהֲוָה מְפַייֵס לֵיהּ קוֹמֵי גַרְמֵיהּ וַהֲוָה אָמַר לֵיהּ. מָה הֲנָייָה אִית לָךְ דְּאִינוּן מִתְקַטְלִין. סַב לָךְ דְּהָב וּכְסָף. וְהוּא אָמַר. אֵין לָנוּ כֶסֶף עִם שָׁאוּל וְעִם בֵּיתוֹ. בְּאוֹתָהּ שָׁעָה אָמַר דָּוִד. שָׁלשׁ מַתָּנוֹת טוֹבוֹת נָתַן הַקָּדוֹשׁ לְיִשְׂרָאֵל. רַחֲמָנִין וּבוֹיְישָׁנִין וְגוֹמְכֵי חֲסָדִים. רַחֲמָנִין מְנַיִין. וְנָתַן לְךָ רַחֲמִים. בּוֹיְישָׁנִין מְנַיִין. וּבַעֲבוּר תִּהְיֶה יִרְאָתוֹ עַל פְּנֵיכֶם. זֶה סִימָן לְבוֹיְישָׁן שֶׁאֵינוֹ חוֹטֵא. וְכָל־שֶׁאֵין כּוֹ בּוֹשֶׁת פָּנִים בָּרִיא דָּבָר שֶׁלֹּא עָמְדוּ אֲבוֹתָיו עַל הַר סִינַי. וְגוֹמְלֵי חֲסָדִים מְנַיִין. וְשָׁמַר יי אֱלֹהֶיךָ לְךָ אֶת הַבְּרִית וְאֶת הַחֶסֶד. וְאִילּוּ אֵין בָּהֶן אֶחָד מֵהֶן. מִיַּד עָמַד וְרִיחֲקָן. שֶׁנֶּאֱמַר וְהַגִּבְעוֹנִים לֹא מִבְּנֵי יִשְׂרָאֵל הֵמָּה. אַף עֶזְרָא רִיחֲקָן. שֶׁנֶּאֱמַר וְהַנְּתִינִים יוֹשְׁבִים בָּעוֹפֶל. אַף לֶעָתִיד לָבוֹא הַקָּדוֹשׁ בָּרוּךְ הוּא מְרַחֲקָן. דִּכְתִיב וְהָעוֹבֵר אֶת הָעִיר יְאַבְּדוּהוּ.

בעוון 9 בכם ועצר את השמים וגו' - |G בעוון | G 10 בעוון | G 11 בעוון | G
12 את הארץ G| אף על הארץ[46] בעוון | G ברבים | G ברבין | G מהן | 14 G|
מהם הדא G| הדה 15 אלעזר | G לעזר בקשו | G כתוב בקשו | 16 מהו | G -
18 דוד | G דויד וקרא | G ואמר 19 ולבית | G בבית 20 שואבי | G שאבי | 21
מבניו והוקענום בגבעת שאול בחיר לי' | G וגו' 22 מתקטלין | G מקטלין סבו | G
סבון 23 דילמ' | G דלמה דאינון | G דאנון פלגון | G פלגין 24 מן פלג | G
מפלג ליה | G לה קומי גרמיה | G קומה נפשה והוה | G והווה ליה | G לה 25
אית - G| דאינון מתקטלין | G ואנון מקטלין 26 אין לי כת' | G אן לי כתב דוד | G
דויד שלש | G שלוש 27 ובויישנין | G ובוישנין חסדים | G חסדין 28 זה | G
וזה 29 בריא | G ברי חסדים | G חסדין שנא' | G -[47] 33 והעובר את
האיר יאבדוהו | G והעובד ה[עי]ר יובדוהו

[48]["The dedicated ones"][49]. Rebbi Immi in the name of Rebbi Joshua ben Levi, because of: "At that moment Joshua *dedicated them* as hewers of wood and drawers of water for the congregation.[50]" One understands "for the congregation." But "for the Eternal's altar"[51]? But Joshua kept them in limbo. He said, I shall not include nor exclude them. But he who sometime in the future will build the Temple, if he wants to include them he may include, exclude them he may exclude. David came and excluded them as it is said[52]: "But the Gibeonites are not part of the Children of Israel." Why did he exclude them? Because "[53]there was a famine in David's time, three years year after year." David said, for four sins[54] the rains are locked away. For the sins of foreign worship, incest and adultery, murder, and the sins of those who publicly promise money for welfare but do not pay. From where for the sin of foreign worship? "[55]Beware, lest you be seduced" etc. What is written afterwards? "The Eternal's rage will be inflamed against you and he locks the sky, etc." From where for the sins of the incestuous and adulterers? "[56]You distorted the Land by your immorality and your evil deeds." What is the

punishment? "Rainshowers were withheld, there was no late rain," etc. From where because of the murderers? "[57]Because blood will distort the Land." From where for the sins of those who publicly promise money for welfare but do not pay? "[58]Clouds and wind but no rain means the man who prides himself by lying gifts." David checked his entire generation and did not find one of these. He turned to ask the *urim* and *tummim*. That is what is written: "[53]David asked before the Eternal" by *urim* and *tummim*.[59] Rebbi Eleazar said, "Ask the Eternal, all the meek of the Land, who execute His Law.[60]" What means "Whose Law is Work"? He enforces His Law and this is His Action[61]. "[53]The Eternal said, because of Saul and the House of blood guilt." "Because of Saul," whom you did not grant the last favor, "and because of the House of blood guilt, for he had killed the Gibeonites." David sent and called them, what is between you and the house of Saul? They told him, because he killed seven of our men, two hewers of wood, two drawers of water, a religious leader, a scribe, and a beadle. He asked them, what do you want now? They said to him: "[62]May there be given to us seven men of his sons and we shall hang them before the Eternal on the hill of Saul, the elected of the Eternal." He said to them, what use is it for you that they be killed? Take silver and gold for yourselves! But they answered, [63]"there is no money for us from Saul and his house." He said, maybe they are afraid[64]; he separated them and spoke to each one separately, trying to mollify him by himself, and asked him: What use is it for you that they be killed? Take gold and silver! But he said, "there is no money for us from Saul and his house." It is written "for me"[65]. At this moment, David said that the Holy One gave three good gifts to Israel: They are merciful, decent, and charitable⁶⁶. From where that they are merciful? "He gave you mercy⁶⁷." From where that they are decent? "That His fear should be on your faces.⁶⁸" This is a sign, for a decent person does not sin. About anybody indecent it is clear that his ancestors did not stand on Mount Sinai. From where that they are charitable? "The Eternal, your God, kept for you covenant and charity.⁶⁹" But these, nothing of this in found in them. Immediately he went to exclude them as it is said: "But the Gibeonites are not of the Children of Israel.⁵²" And Ezra also excluded them, as it is said: "And the dedicated ones dwelt in the Ophel.⁷⁰" Also in the future the Holy One, praise to Him, will exclude them as it is written: "One crossing the city they cause to be lost.⁷¹"

46 There seems to be no verse to which this quote would apply.

47 In this paragraph, all the notes "as it is said" are additions by the corrector of L.

48 To this and the following paragraph there exists an almost parallel text in *Sanhedrin* 6:9 (ו), an enlarged version in the Babli *Yebamot* 78b-79a and *Num. rabba* 8(4), and a shortened version in *Midrash Samuel* 28[5].

49 Reading of G; in L: "It was stated". The following text deals with the identity of "the dedicated ones", their exclusion from the Jewish marriage community, and proof that they were among the returnees from Babylon.

50 *Jos.* 9:27.

51 This is also mentioned in *Jos.* 9:27, but the service in the Tabernacle is reserved for priests and Levites. The statement is interpreted to mean that their status will only be determined when the Eternal's altar is given its permanent place.

52 2*S.* 21:2.

53 2*S.* 21:1.

54 In ו "three" and this also seems to be the reading underlying the Babli's version and *Pirqe R. Eliezer* Chapter 17. The number is 4 in *Ta'anit* 3:3 (66c l. 29).

55 *Deut.* 11:16-17.

56 *Jer.* 3:2-3. While the prophet obviously speaks of Baal worship, all

his imagery is that of sexual transgressions. Quoted in the name of R. Jehudah in *Sifra Qedošim Pereq* 7(4).

57   *Num.* 35:33.

58   *Prov.* 25:14. In the name of different Amoraim in the Babli, *Ta'anit* 8b, *Midrash Prov.* 25(14).

59   In MT, there is a lacuna in *2S.* 21:1 between "David asked before the Eternal," and "The Eternal said, because of Saul and the House of blood guilt." It is explained that he asked by applying the *urim and tummim* oracle. In the Babli and the sources dependent on it, R. Eleazar explains that "asking *before* the Eternal" means applying the *urim and tummim* oracle since in *Num.* 27:21 it says, "*before* Eleazar the priest he shall stand and ask the *urim and tummim*."

60   *Zeph.* 2:3. The homily is slightly more explicit in the Babli, where it is credited to R. Simeon ben Laqish. It addresses a seeming inconsistency in *2S.* 21:1 where God's answer is that the famine is a punishment for two crimes, the first "about Saul" and the second "about the House of blood guilt because he killed the Gibeonites." The verse of the prophet is read to mean that even at the moment a person is judged for his misdeeds his "works", his good deeds, are mentioned in the Heavenly court. But here the sin "about Saul" was not Saul's but David's and the entire people's since they let him be buried in Transjordan and did not bring him to his proper burial in his ancestral land until prodded by the absence of rain (*2S.* 21:14, where the coming of rain is described as a direct consequence of the proper burials given to Saul and Jonathan.)

61   While the Babli certainly reads with the Masoretes עָלָיו, it might be that the Yerushalmi reads עָלָיו.

62   *2S.* 21:6.

63   *2S.* 21:4.

64   In]: They are afraid one in front of the other (to accept blood money).

65   In *2S.* 21:4, the *Ketib* is "for me" but the *Qere* "for us". The homily explains both readings; both are correct.

66   In addition to the sources mentioned in Note 48, the following is also in *Midrash Psalms* 1,17.

67   *Deut.* 13:18.

68   *Ex.* 20:20.

69   *Deut.* 7:12.

70   *Neh.* 3:26, 11:21. The emphasis is on their dwelling separately.

71   This quote (as well as the version of G) is clearly corrupt; it tele-

scopes a quote and its interpretation into one sentence. The correct text is in ג:

וְהָעוֹבֵד הָעִיר יַעֲבְדוּהוּ מִכֹּל שִׁבְטֵי יִשְׂרָאֵל.
יַאֲבִידוּהוּ מִכֹּל שִׁבְטֵי יִשְׂרָאֵל.

(*Ez.* 48:19) "The city worker will cultivate it, from all the tribes of Israel." (Interpretation) 'He will cause him to be lost from all the tribes of Israel.'

Ezechiel, in his description of the future Israel, gives Jerusalem a strip of land from the Meditteranean to the Dead Sea, which will be cultivated by the Temple workers to provide food for the city. The verse is taken out of context and, in Galilean dialect, ע and א are identified, changing "cultivate" into "getting lost". The city worker is the dedicated one.

(65c line 34) כְּתִיב וַיֹּאמֶר הַמֶּלֶךְ אֲנִי אֶתֵּן. וַיִּקַּח הַמֶּלֶךְ אֶת שְׁנֵי בְּנֵי רִצְפָּה בַת אַיָּה אֲשֶׁר יָלְדָה לְשָׁאוּל אֶת אַדְמוֹנִי וְאֶת מְפִיבוֹשֶׁת וְגו'. וּלְמִיכַל בַּת שָׁאוּל לֹא הָיָה לָהּ וָלֶד עַד יוֹם מוֹתָהּ. וְאַתְּ אָמַר אָכֵן. אָמוֹר מֵעַתָּה. בְּנֵי מֵירַב הָיוּ וְגִידְּלָתָן מִיכַל וְנִקְרְעוּ עַל שְׁמָהּ. וַיִּתְּנֵם בְּיַד הַגִּבְעוֹנִים וַיּוֹקִיעוּם בָּהָר לִפְנֵי י"י וַיִּפְּלוּ שְׁבַעְתָּם יָחַד. חָסֵר יו"ד. זֶה מְפִיבוֹשֶׁת בֶּן יְהוֹנָתָן בֶּן שָׁאוּל שֶׁהוּא אָדָם גָּדוֹל בַּתּוֹרָה וְנָתַן דָּוִד עֵינָיו בּוֹ לְהַצִּילוֹ מִיָּדָם. אָמַר דָּוִד. הֲרֵינִי מַעֲבִירָן לִפְנֵי הַמִּזְבֵּחַ וְכָל־מִי שֶׁהַמִּזְבֵּחַ קוֹלְטוֹ הֲרֵי הוּא שֶׁלִּי. וְהֶעֱבִירָן לִפְנֵי הַמִּזְבֵּחַ וְנִתְפַּלֵּל עָלָיו וְהָלַךְ הַמִּזְבֵּחַ וְקָלְטוֹ. הָדָא הוּא דִּכְתִיב אֶקְרָא אֶל אֱלֹהִים עֶלְיוֹן לָאֵל גּוֹמֵר עָלָי. שֶׁהִסְכִּים הַקָּדוֹשׁ בָּרוּךְ הוּא עִם דָּוִד. וְהֵמָּה הוּמְתוּ בִּימֵי קָצִיר בָּרִאשׁוֹנִים כְּתִיב קְצִיר שְׂעוֹרִים. וַתִּקַּח רִצְפָּה בַת אַיָּה אֶת הַשַּׂק וַתַּטֵּהוּ לָהּ עַל הַצּוּר. מַהוּ עַל הַצּוּר. אָמַר רִבִּי הוֹשַׁעְיָה. שֶׁהָיְתָה אוֹמֶרֶת הַצּוּר תָּמִים פָּעֳלוֹ. רִבִּי אַבָּא בַּר זְמִינָא בְּשֵׁם רִבִּי הוֹשַׁעְיָה. גָּדוֹל הוּא קִידּוּשׁ הַשֵּׁם מֵחִילּוּל הַשֵּׁם. בְּחִילּוּל הַשֵּׁם מַה כָּתוּב לֹא תָלִין נִבְלָתוֹ עַל הָעֵץ. וּבְקִידּוּשׁ הַשֵּׁם כָּתוּב מִתְּחִילַת הַקָּצִיר עַד נִתַּךְ מַיִם עֲלֵיהֶם. מְלַמֵּד שֶׁהָיוּ תְּלוּיִין מִשִּׁשָּׁה עָשָׂר בְּנִיסָן עַד שִׁבְעָה עָשָׂר בְּמַרְחֶשְׁוָן. וְהָיוּ הָעוֹבְרִים וְהַשָּׁבִים אוֹמְרִים. מָה חָטְאוּ אֵילּוּ שֶׁנִּשְׁתַּנֵּית עֲלֵיהֶן מִידַּת הַדִּין. וְהָיוּ אוֹמְרִים. עַל שֶׁפָּשְׁטוּ יְדֵיהֶן בַּגֵּרִים גְּרוּרִין. אָמְרוּ. מָה אֵילּוּ שֶׁלֹּא נִתְגַּיְּירוּ לְשֵׁם שָׁמַיִם רָאוּ הֵיאַךְ תָּבַע הַקָּדוֹשׁ בָּרוּךְ הוּא אֶת דָּמָן. הַמִּתְגַּיֵּיר לְשֵׁם שָׁמַיִם עַל אַחַת כַּמָּה וְכַמָּה. אֵין אֱלוֹהַּ כֵּאלֹהֵיכֶם וְאֵין

אוּמָה כְּאוּמַתְכֶם. וְאֵין לָנוּ לְהִידָּבֵק אֶלָּא בָּכֶם. הַרְבֵּה גֵרִים נִתְגַּייְרוּ בְּאוֹתָהּ שָׁעָה. הָדָא הוּא דִכְתִיב וַיִּסְפֹּר שְׁלֹמֹה אֶת כָּל־הָאֲנָשִׁים הַגֵּרִים וַיַּעַשׂ מֵהֶם שִׁבְעִים אֶלֶף נֹשֵׂא סַבָּל וּשְׁמֹנִים אֶלֶף חֹצֵב בָּהָר.

2 אשר ילדה לשאול את אדמוני ואת מפיבושת G | וגו'   4 הגבעונים ויוקיעום בהר ויפלו שבעתם יחד G | וגו'   5 שבעתם G | שבעתים   חסר יו"ד G | כתב חסיר חד[72] שהוא אדם G | שהיה אדן   6 מידם G | מידן   7 והעבירן G | העבירן   ונתפלל G | וניתפלל   9 גומר עלי G | וגו'   שהסכים G | לי שהסכים   11 מהו G | מה הוא 12 ר' G | רב   14 מתחילת הקציר עד G | והוו תליוב עד   16 שנישתנית G | שנישתניח[73]

It is written: "The King said, I shall give[73]." "The King took the two sons of Rișpah bat Ayah whom she had born to Saul, Admoni and Mephiboshet[74]," etc. "Michal, Saul's daughter, did not have a child until the day of her death,[75]" and you say so? Say now that they were sons of Merab but Michal raised them, so they were named after her. "He gave them into the hand of the Gibeonites who hanged them on the mountain before the Eternal; all seven fell together.[76]" Defective without י[77]. That refers to Mephiboshet ben Jonathan ben Saul, who was great in the Torah and David intended to save him from their hand. David said, I let them pass by the altar and anyone received by the altar will be mine. He let each pass by the altar, prayed for him, and the altar moved and received him. This is what is written: "I shall call to the Most High God, to the Power Who has the ultimate decision about me[78]!" For the Holy One, praise to Him, agreed with David. "[76]They were killed on the first days of harvest;" it is written "the barley harvest." "Rișpah bat Ayah took a sack and laid it out on the rock.[79]" What means: 'On the rock"? Rebbi Hoshaia said, she was reciting: "The rock, perfect is His action[80]." Rebbi Abba bar Zamina in the name of Rebbi Hoshaia: Sanctification of the

Name is greater than desecration of the Name. Referring to desecration of the Name it is written: "Do not leave his corpse on the gallows overnight.[81]" But referring to sanctification of the Name it is written: "From the start of harvest until water was poured on them.[79]" This teaches that they were hanging from the sixteenth of Nisan[82] to the seventeenth of Marḥeshwan[83]. The passers-by were saying: How did these people sin that the rules of justice were changed for them? They were answered: Because these had attacked attached[84] proselytes. They would say that even for those who did not convert for the sake of Heaven, the Eternal avenged their blood; if one would convert for the sake of Heaven not so much more? There is no Power like your God and no people like your people. Many converts were converted at that time; that is what is written[85]: "Solomon counted all proselytes and appointed from them 70'000 carriers and 80'000 hewers of stone in the mountains."

72 A similar text is in ו .

73 Here ends the Genizah fragment.

73 2S. 20:6.

74 2S. 20:8. In the MT ארמני, not אדמוני. The verse ends: "And the five sons of Mikhal, Saul's daughter, which she had borne to Adriel ben Barzilai from Meḥolah." Adriel's wife was Merab, Saul's elder daughter (1S. 18:19).

75 2S. 6:23. In the opinion of the Yerushalmi (Sukkah 5:4, 55c l. 22; Sanhedrin 2:4, 20b l. 57) she died in childbirth. In the opinion of the Babli (Sanhedrin 21a) she earlier had a child in Hebron.

76 2S. 20:9.

77 In the MT, the word is written with an extra י , שבעתים, correctly spelled in G and ו . The correct text seems to that of G and ו : "One is missing", referring to Mephiboshet ben Jonathan.

78 Ps. 57:3.

79 2S. 20:10.

80 Deut. 32:4, the verse which opens the traditional burial service called צִדּוּק הַדִּין "justification of the (Divine) judgment." This is alluded to

not only here (and in the sources mentioned in Note 48) but also in the Babli, 'Avodah zarah 18a.

81 *Deut.* 21:23.

82 The first day of the barley harvest, *Lev.* 23:14.

83 The year is declared one of draught if the rains did not start by the 17th of *Marḥeshwan* (Mishnah *Ta'anit* 1:4).

84 The word was changed by the corrector. Probably one should read with אֲרוּרִים ן "cursed", *Jos.* 9:33.

85 *2Chr.* 2:16-17.

(65c line 59) רַב הוּנָא אָמַר. בִּימֵי רִבִּי לֶעְזָר בֶּן עֲזַרְיָה בִּיקְשׁוּ לְקָרְבָן. רִבִּי אַבָּהוּ מַפִּיךְ לִישָׁנָא. בִּימֵי רִבִּי לֶעְזָר. אָמְרוּ. מִי מְטַהֵר חֶלְקוֹ שֶׁל מִזְבֵּחַ. הָדָא אֶמְרָה יְהוֹשֻׁעַ רִיחֲקָן. אֲפִילוּ תֵימָא יְהוֹשֻׁעַ רִיחֲקָן. כְּלוּם רִיחֲקָן אֶלָּא פְּסוּלֵי מִשְׁפָּחָה. אִין תֵּימַר. מִשּׁוּם פְּסוּלֵי עֲבֵירוֹת. מֵעַתָּה הַבָּא עַל הַגִּתִּינָה לֹא יְהֵא לָהּ קְנָס. וְהָתַנִּינָן. הַבָּא עַל הַגִּתִּינָה יֵשׁ לָהּ קְנָס. אָמַר רִבִּי אֶלְעָזָר. אֵירְרָן כְּנָחָשׁ. שֶׁנֶּאֱמַר וְעַתָּה אֲרוּרִים אַתֶּם. וְכָתוּב וַיֹּאמֶר אִישׁ יִשְׂרָאֵל אֶל הַחִוִּי. וְכִי חִוִּי הָיוּ. אֶלָּא שֶׁעָשׂוּ מַעֲשֵׂה חִוִּי. אָמַר. יוֹדֵעַ אֲנִי שֶׁאָמַר הַקָּדוֹשׁ בָּרוּךְ הוּא כִּי בַּיּוֹם אֲכָלְךָ מִמֶּנּוּ מוֹת תָּמוּת. אֶלָּא הֲרֵינִי הוֹלֵךְ וּמְרַמֶּה בָהֶן וְהֵן אוֹכְלִין וְנֶעֱנָשִׁין וַאֲנִי יוֹרֵשׁ אֶת הָאָרֶץ לְעַצְמִי. כָּךְ עָשׂוּ אֵילּוּ. אָמְרוּ. יוֹדְעִין אֲנַחְנוּ שֶׁהַקָּדוֹשׁ בָּרוּךְ הוּא אָמַר לְיִשְׂרָאֵל כִּי הַחֲרֵם תַּחֲרִימֵם הַחִתִּי וְהָאֱמֹרִי וְהַפְּרִזִּי כַּאֲשֶׁר צִוְּךָ יי אֱלֹהֶיךָ. וְכָתוּב לֹא תִכְרוֹת לָהֶם בְּרִית. הֲרֵי אָנוּ הוֹלְכִין וּמְרַמִּין בָּהֶן וְהֵם כּוֹרְתִין עִמָּנוּ בְּרִית. מַה נַפְשָׁךְ. יַהַרְגוּ אוֹתָנוּ עָבְרוּ עַל הַשְּׁבוּעָה. יְקַיְּימוּ אוֹתָנוּ עָבְרוּ עַל הַגְּזֵירָה. בֵּין כָּךְ וּבֵין כָּךְ הֵן נֶעֱנָשִׁין וְאָנוּ יוֹרְשִׁין הָאָרֶץ.

Rav Huna said that in the days of Rebbi Eleazar ben Azariah they tried to include them[86]. Rebbi Abbahu inverts the wording: In the days of Rebbi Eleazar they said, who could purify the altar's part[87]? That implies that Joshua excluded them. He excluded them only as disqualified for marriage. If you would say, disqualified (because of sins)[88] then the rapist of a Gibeonite girl should not have to pay the fine, but we have stated[89]: The rapist of a Gibeonite girl has to pay the fine." Rebbi Eleazar said, he cursed them as a snake, as it is said: "But now you are cursed⁹⁰." And it is written: "The people of Israel said to the Ḥiwwite.⁹¹" But were they Ḥiwwites⁹²? They acted like the snake⁹³ which said, I know that the Holy One, praise to Him, did say "because on the day you eat from it, you will die a death⁹⁴." I shall go and trick them so that they eat and will be punished and I shall inherit the earth for myself. So these people acted; they said, we know that the Holy One, praise to Him, said to Israel: "You shall certainly ban them, the Hittite, the Emorite, and the Perizite, as the Eternal, your God, has commanded you⁹⁵" And it is written: "You shall not conclude a covenant with them.⁹⁶" We shall go and trick them that they conclude a covenant with us. As you take it, if they kill us, they violate their oath. If they let us live, they violated the [divine] decision. In any case, they will be punished and we shall inherit the Land.

86   To permit marriage with Gibeonites.

87   R. Eleazar ben Azariah vetoed the admission of Gibeonites into the Jewish marriage pool by arguing that *Jos.* 9:23,27 implies that Joshua made the Gibeonites Temple slaves, in addition to their being the people's slaves by *Jos.* 9:21. Now the servitude to the people had certainly lapsed. The "dedicated ones" returned from Babylonia as free men and one had to assume that already in the time of the Judges they had regularly been manumitted in this respect. But nobody could manumit Temple slaves, and marriage with slaves was impossible. In this version, the exlusion of Gibeonites from the Jewish marriage pool is a legal necessity which cannot be changed.

88   It seems that one should read with the parallel in *Ketubot* 3:1 (27a l. 59), Notes 16-19, עבדות "slavery" instead of עבירות "sins".

89   Implied by Mishnah *Ketubot* 3:1. The same Mishnah states that the statutory fine is not applicable to the rape of a virgin slave girl. If Gibeonites were excluded as Temple slaves, they should be classified with slaves in matters of the fine (and be

excluded from marriage in all its forms.) Cf. Tosafot *Yebamot* 79a, s.v. ונחינים. It follows that R. Abbahu's argument is rejected.

90   *Jos.* 9:23.

91   *Jos.* 9:7.

92   In *2S.* 20:2, they are described as Emorites.

93   In Aramaic חִוְיָא. The name of Eve, חַוָּה, instead of the Hebrew חַיָה, hints at her relationship with the snake.

94   *Gen.* 2:17.

95   Misquoted from *Deut.* 20:17.

96   *Deut.* 7:2.

(65c line 74) רַב נַחְמָן בַּר יַעֲקֹב אָמַר. מְקַבְּלִין גֵּרִים מִן הַקַּרְדּוּיִים וּמִן הַתַּדְמוֹרִיִּים. רִבִּי אַבָּהוּ בְּשֵׁם רִבִּי יוֹחָנָן. מַתְנִיתָא אָמְרָה כֵּן שֶׁגִּיּוּרֵי תַדְמוֹר כְּשֵׁירִין. דְּתַנִּינָן תַּמָּן כָּל־הַכְּתָמִים הַבָּאִין מֵרֶקֶם טְהוֹרִין. הָא גִירֵי תַדְמוֹר כְּשֵׁירִין.

1 הקרד״יים | א הקרדויין   3 דתנינן תמן | א תמן תנינן   טהורין | א טהורים

⁹⁷Rav Nahman bar Jacob said, one accepts proselytes from Kurds and Palmyrenians. Rebbi Abbahu in the name of Rebbi Johanan: A Mishnah said that the proselytes from Palmyra are acceptable. There, we have stated: "All stains coming from Petra are pure." Therefore, the proselytes from Palmyra are acceptable.

97   This paragraph and the next are from *Yebamot* 1:6, Notes 229-242 (א). The full comparison of the texts of the next paragraph is given there.

(65d line 3) רִבִּי יַעֲקֹב בַּר אָחָא אָמַר שְׁמוּעֲתָא. רִבִּי חֲנִינָה וְרִבִּי יְהוֹשֻׁעַ בֶּן לֵוִי חַד מַכְשִׁיר וְחַד מְקַבֵּל. מָאן דְּמַכְשִׁיר מְקַבֵּל וּמָאן דִּמְקַבֵּל לֹא מַכְשִׁיר. רִבִּי יוֹסֵה בֵּירִבִּי בּוּן בְּשֵׁם רַב נַחְמָן. בָּבֶל לְיוּחֲסִין עַד נָהָר יְזָק. רִבִּי יוֹסֵי בֵּירִבִּי בּוּן אָמַר. רַב וּשְׁמוּאֵל. חַד אָמַר עַד נָהָר יְזָק. וְחַד אָמַר. עַד נָהַרְיוֹאָנִי. אָמַר רַב יְהוּדָה. בֵּין הַנְּהָרוֹת כְּגוֹלָה לְיוּחֲסִין. רִבִּי חֲנִינָה בֶּן בְּרוֹקָא בְּשֵׁם רַב יְהוּדָה. בְּנֵי מֵישָׁא לֹא חָשׁוּ לָהֶם אֶלָּא מִשּׁוּם סְפֵק חֲלָלוֹת. כֹּהֲנִים שֶׁשָּׁם לֹא הִקְפִּידוּ עַל הַגְּרוּשׁוֹת. תַּמָּן אָמְרִין. מֵישָׁא מֵתָה מָדַי חוֹלָה. עֵילָם וְגַבְבַּיי גּוֹסְסוֹת. חֲבִיל יַמָּא הָכִילְתָּא דְּבָבֶל. שְׁנַיָּיא וְגַבְבַּיָּא וְצַרְרַיָּיא תְּכִילְתָּא דַּחֲבִיל יָמָא.

Rebbi Jacob bar Aḥa presented traditions: Of Rebbi Ḥanina and Rebbi Joshua ben Levi, one declares permissible and the other admits. He who declares permissible admits. But he who admits does not declare admissible. Rebbi Yose ben Rebbi Abun in the name of Rebbi Naḥman: Babylonia, as far as family pedigree is concerned, extends up to the *yzq* canal. Rebbi Yose ben Rebbi Abun said, of Rav and Samuel, one said up to the *yzq* canal, the other said up to the *Wani* canal. Rav Jehudah said, between the rivers is like Nahardea as far as family pedigree is concerned. Rebbi Ḥanina ben Beroqa in the name of Rav Jehudah: The people of Moesia are questionable only because of doubts of desecrated women. The Cohanim amongst them did not care about divorcees. There they said, Moesia is dead, Media sick, Elam and *gbby* dying. The maritime district is the purple-blue of Babylonia. *Šny', gbby', and ṣrry* are purple-blue of the maritime district.

(65d line 13) רִבִּי יַעֲקֹב בַּר אָחָא בְּשֵׁם רִבִּי יֹאשִׁיָּה. דּוֹר אֶחָד עָשָׂר שֶׁבְּמַמְזֵר כְּרִבִּי שִׁמְעוֹן כָּשֵׁר. דְּלֹא דָרַשׁ עֲשִׂירִי עֲשִׂירִי. תַּנֵּי. רִבִּי אֶלְעָזָר בֵּירִבִּי שִׁמְעוֹן אוֹמֵר. דּוֹר אֶחָד עָשָׂר שֶׁבְּמַמְזֵר זְכָרִים אֲסוּרִין וּנְקֵיבוֹת מוּתָּרוֹת. רִבִּי שְׁמוּאֵל בְּרֵיהּ דְּרִבִּי יוֹסֵי בֵּירִבִּי בּוּן. אַתְיָא דְּרִבִּי אֶלְעָזָר בֵּירִבִּי שִׁמְעוֹן כְּרִבִּי מֵאִיר. כְּמָה דְרִבִּי מֵאִיר אָמַר. גְּזֵירָה שָׁוָה בְּמָקוֹם שֶׁבָּאַת. כֵּן רִבִּי לֶעָזָר בֵּירִבִּי שִׁמְעוֹן אָמַר. גְּזֵירָה שָׁוָה בְּמָקוֹם שֶׁבָּאַת. מַה לְהַלָּן זְכָרִים אֲסוּרִין וּנְקֵיבוֹת מוּתָּרוֹת. אוֹף הָכָא זְכָרִים אֲסוּרִין וּנְקֵיבוֹת מוּתָּרוֹת. מֵעַתָּה אֲפִילוּ מִיָּד. בִּלְבַד מֵעֲשִׂירִי וּלְמַעֲלָה.

1 יאשיה | ג יושיא   2 דלא | ג ולא   עשירי עשירי | ג עשירי   3 ונקיבות | ג נקיבות - | ג   אף הכא זכרים אסורין נקיבות מותרות   4 בון | ג בון אמ'   אלעזר ג לעזר   5 שבאת | ג שכתוב   לעזר | ג -   6 אמ' | ג אומ'   שבאת | ג שכתוב   7 ונקיבות | ג נקיבות   8 ולמעלה | ג ולמעלן

⁹⁸Rebbi Jacob bar Aḥa in the name of Rebbi Josia: The eleventh generation of bastards is qualified following Rebbi Simeon; he does not use [the principle of *gezerah šawah* for] "the tenth, the tenth." It was stated: Rebbi Eleazar ben Rebbi Simeon says, in the eleventh generation of bastards, the males are forbidden but the females permitted. Rebbi Samuel ben Rebbi Yose ben Rebbi Abun said, it turns out that Rebbi Eleazar ben Rebbi Simeon follows the argument of Rebbi Meïr. As Rebbi Meïr said, a *gezerah šawah* is as if written in a verse, so Rebbi Eleazar ben Rebbi Simeon says, a *gezerah šawah* is as if written in a verse. Here also, the males are forbidden but the females permitted. In that case, even immediately? Only from the tenth onward.

98   The following four paragraphs are from *Yebamot* 8:3, Notes 193-212.

(65d line 13) שָׁאֲלוּ אֶת רִבִּי אֱלִיעֶזֶר. דּוֹר אֶחָד עָשָׂר שֶׁבְּמַמְזֵר מָהוּ. אָמַר לָהֶן. הָבִיאוּ לִי דוֹר שְׁלִישִׁי וַאֲנִי מְטַהֲרוֹ. מַאי טַעֲמָא דְּרִבִּי אֱלִיעֶזֶר. דְּלָא חַיי. וְאַתְיָיא דְּרִבִּי לִיעֶזֶר כְּרִבִּי חֲנִינָה. דְּאָמַר רִבִּי חֲנִינָה. אַחַת לְס׳ לְע׳ שָׁנָה הַקָּדוֹשׁ בָּרוּךְ הוּא מֵבִיא דֶּבֶר בָּעוֹלָם וּמְכַלֶּה אֶת הַמַּמְזִירִים וְנוֹטֵל עִמָּהֶן כְּשֵׁירִים שֶׁלֹּא לְפַרְסֵם לַחַטָּאִים. וְאַתְיָיא כְּהָדָא דְּאָמַר רִבִּי לֵוִי בְּשֵׁם רִבִּי שִׁמְעוֹן בֶּן לָקִישׁ. בְּמָקוֹם אֲשֶׁר תִּשְׁחֵט הָעוֹלָה תִּשְׁחֵט הַחַטָּאת לִפְנֵי י׳. שֶׁלֹּא לְפַרְסֵם אֶת הַחַטָּאִים. וְגַם הוּא חָכָם וַיָּבֵא רָע. לֹא מִסְתַּבְּרָה דְּלֹא וְגַם הוּא חָכָם וַיָּבֵא טוֹב. אֶלָּא לְלַמְּדָךְ שֶׁאֲפִילוּ רָעָה שֶׁהַקָּדוֹשׁ בָּרוּךְ הוּא מֵבִיא לָעוֹלָם בְּחָכְמָה הוּא מְבִיאָהּ. וְאֶת דְּבָרָיו לֹא הֵסִיר וְקָם עַל בֵּית מְרֵעִים וְעַל עֶזְרַת פּוֹעֲלֵי אָוֶן. רַב הוּנָה אָמַר. אֵין מַמְזֵר חַי יוֹתֵר מִשְּׁלֹשִׁים יוֹם. רִבִּי זְעִירָא כַּד סְלַק לְהָכָא שְׁמַע קָלִין קַרְיֵי. מַמְזִירָא וּמַמְזֶרְתָּא. אָמַר לוֹן. מָהוּ כֵן. הָא אַזְלָא הַהִיא דְּרַב הוּנָא. דְּרַב הוּנָא אָמַר. אֵין מַמְזֵר חָיָה יוֹתֵר מִל׳ יוֹם. אָמַר לֵיהּ רִבִּי יַעֲקֹב בַּר אֲחָא. עִמָּךְ הָיִיתִי כַּד אָמַר רִבִּי אַבָּא רַב הוּנָא בְּשֵׁם רַב. אֵין מַמְזֵר חַי יוֹתֵר מִל׳ יוֹם. אֵימָתַי. בִּזְמַן שֶׁאֵינוֹ מְפוּרְסָם. הָא אִם הָיָה מְפוּרְסָם חַי הוּא.

2 מאי | ג ומה   חיי | ג הוה   3 ואתייא | ג אתייא   לט לע׳ | ג לששים ולשבעים   4
את הממזירין | ג ממזיריהן   עמהן כשירים | ג את הכשירין עמהן   5 לחטאים | ג את
חטאיהן   ואתייא | ג ואייתינא   כההיא | ג כיי   דאמ' | ג דמר   7 וגם | ג ומה טע'.
8 שהקב״ה מביא לעולם | ג שמביא הקב״ה בעולם   9 וקם | ג כל כך למה. וקם   10 -
| ג ואתייא כההיא דאמ' ר' לוי בשם ר' שמעון בן לקיש. במקום אשר תשחט העולה תשחט
החטאת לפני ל׳.   שלא לפרסן את החטאים[99]   חיי | ג חי   11 קריי | ג קריין   אזלא |
ג אזילא   12 חיה | ג חי   ל | ג שלשים   13 אבא | ג בא   14 מל | ג משלשים
חיי | ג חי

They asked Rebbi Eliezer, what is the status of the eleventh generation of a bastard? He said to them, bring to me a third generation and I shall declare him pure, for he would not live[196]. Rebbi Eliezer parallels Rebbi Ḥanina? As Rebbi Ḥanina said, once every sixty to seventy years the Holy One, praise to Him, brings a plague into the world to eliminate the bastards and he takes the qualified ones with them in order not to publicize the sinners. This parallels what Rebbi Levi said in the name of Rebbi Simeon ben Laqish: "In the place where the ascent offering has its throat cut before the Eternal, the purification sacrifice has its throat cut," in order not to publicize the sinners. "Also He is wise and brings evil;" could one better understand "also He is wise and brings good"? But to teach you that even the evil that the Holy One, praise to Him, brings to the world, He brings in wisdom. "His word He did not remove, He overcomes the house of evildoers and accomplices of workers of iniquity."[99]

[100]Rav Huna said, no bastard lives more than thirty days. When Rebbi Ze'ira immigrated here, he heard voices call "he-bastard, she-bastard". He said, what is this? There goes that of Rav Huna, since Rav Huna said, no bastard lives more than thirty days. Rebbi Jacob bar Aḥa said to him, I was with you when Rebbi Abba, Rav Huna said in the name of Rav: No

bastard lives more than thirty days, when? If it is unknown. Therefore, if it is known, he lives.

99 In *Yebamot*, the statement of R. Levi in the name of R. Simeon ben Laqish is repeated here.

100 Cf. Chapter 3:14, Notes 242-247.

(65d line 36) רִבִּי יָסָא בְּשֵׁם רִבִּי יוֹחָנָן. אַף לְעָתִיד לָבֹא אֵין הַקָּדוֹשׁ בָּרוּךְ הוּא נִזְקַק אֶלָּא לְשֵׁבֶט לֵוִי. מָה טַעֲמָא. וְיָשַׁב מְצָרֵף וּמְטַהֵר כֶּסֶף וְטִהַר אֶת בְּנֵי לֵוִי וְזִיקַּק אוֹתָם כוֹל'. אָמַר רִבִּי זְעִירָא. כְּאָדָם שֶׁהוּא שׁוֹתֶה בְּכוֹס נָקִי. אָמַר רִבִּי הוֹשַׁעְיָה. בְּגִין דְּלֵית אֲנָן לְוִיִּים נַפְסִיד. אָמַר רִבִּי חֲנִינָה בְּרֵיהּ דְּרִבִּי אַבָּהוּ. אַף לְעָתִיד לָבוֹא הַקָּדוֹשׁ בָּרוּךְ הוּא עוֹשֶׂה עִמָּהֶן צְדָקָה. מַה טַעֲמָא. וְהָיוּ לַיְיָ מַגִּישֵׁי מִנְחָה בִּצְדָקָה.

2 לשבט לוי | ג לשבטו שללוי מה | ג מאי 3 וזיקק | ג וזקק כול' | ג וגו' זעירא | ג זעורא יי | ג רב 4 דלית אנן | ג דאנן 5 מה | ג ומה

Rebbi Yasa in the name of Rebbi Johanan: In the future, the Holy One, praise to Him, will only deal with the tribe of Levi. What is the reason? "The refiner will sit, the purifier of silver, and will refine them," etc. Rebbi Ze'ira said, like a man who only drinks from a clean cup. Rebbi Hoshaia said, because we are not[101] Levites, should we lose? Rebbi Hanina the son of Rebbi Abbahu said, also in the future, the Holy One, praise to Him, will deal with them charitably. What is the reason? "They will be for the Eternal presenters of an offering in charity."

101 In *Yebamot*: "we are". According to the Babli, he was a Cohen, therefore also a Levite.

(65d line 42) אָמַר רִבִּי יוֹחָנָן. כָּל־מִשְׁפָּחָה שֶׁנִּשְׁתַּקַּע בָּהּ פְּסִיל אֵין מְדַקְדְּקִין אַחֲרֶיהָ. אָמַר רִבִּי שִׁמְעוֹן בֶּן לָקִישׁ. מַתְנִיתָא אָמְרָה כֵן. מִשְׁפַּחַת בְּנֵי צְרִיפָה

הָיְתָה בְּעֵבֶר הַיַּרְדֵּן וְרִיחֲקָהּ בֶּן צִיּוֹן בִּזְרוֹעַ. וְעוֹד אַחֶרֶת הָיְתָה שָׁם וְקֵירְבוּהָ בְּנֵי צִיּוֹן בִּזְרוֹעַ. וְלֹא בִיקְשׁוּ חֲכָמִים לְפַרְסְמָן. אֲבָל חֲכָמִים מוֹסְרִין אוֹתָן לִבְנֵיהֶן וְתַלְמִידֵיהֶן פַּעֲמַיִּים בַּשָּׁבוּעַ. אָמַר רִבִּי יוֹחָנָן. הָעֲבוֹדָה שֶׁאָנוּ מַכִּירָן. וּמַה נַּעֲשָׂה וְנִשְׁתַּקְעוּ בָהֶן גְּדוֹלֵי הַדּוֹר. אָמַר רִבִּי יְהוֹשֻׁעַ בֶּן לֵוִי. חֲמֵשֶׁת אֲלָפִים עֲבָדִים הָיוּ לְפַשְׁחוּר בֶּן אִמֵּר וְכוּלָּם נִשְׁתַּקְעוּ בִכְהוּנָּה גְדוֹלָה. הֵן הֵן עַזֵּי פָנִים שֶׁבַּכְּהוּנָּה. אָמַר רִבִּי אֶלְעָזָר. עִיקַּר טִירוֹנִיָּיא שֶׁבָּהֶן וְעַמְּךָ כִּמְרִיבֵי כֹהֵן. אָמַר רִבִּי אַבָּהוּ שְׁלֹשׁ עֶשְׂרֵה עֲיָירוֹת נִשְׁתַּקְעוּ בַּכּוּתִיים בִּימֵי שָׁמָד. אָמְרִין הָדָא עדן דמשאה מִנֵּיהוֹן.

2 בני | ג בית 3-4 וקירבוה בני ציון | ג וקרבה בן ציון 4 ולא | ג אע״פ כן לא 5 ותלמידיהן | ג ולתלמידיהן שאנו | ג שאיני ומה נעשה | ג - 7 היו | ג היו לו אמר | ג אימר - | ג הכהן וכולם | ג וכלן 8 אלעזר | ג לעזר 9 בכותיים | ג בכותים שמר | ג השמד 10 עדן דמשאה מנהון | ג עירו דמושהן מיניהון

Rebbi Joḥanan said, one does not investigate a family in which a family disqualification has disappeared. Rebbi Simeon ben Laqish said, a Mishnah says so: "There was a family Bene Ṣerifa in Transjordan who were forcibly distanced by Ben Ṣion. Another [family] was there who were forcibly integrated by the people of Ṣion.[102]" Nevertheless, the Sages did not want to make their names public. But the Sages transmit them to their sons and students two times in a Week. Rebbi Joḥanan said, by the Temple service, I know them and the leading personalities of the generation have disappeared in them. Rebbi Joshua ben Levi said, Pashḥur ben Immer had 5000 slaves, and their traces have disappeared in the high priesthood. These are the insolent in the priesthood. Rebbi Eleazar said, their main training: "Your people is like quarrelsome priests." Rebbi Abbahu said, Samaritans disappeared in thirteen villages in the times of [persecution][103]. They said, עדן דמשאה [104] is one of them.

102 The text of ג "by Ben Ṣion" is confirmed by all sources of Mishnah *Idiut* 8:7.

103 The translation follows ג which alone makes sense.

104 This place is unidentified, just as is the corresponding one in ג.

(65d line 53) אָמַר רִבִּי חֲנִינָה. מַתְנִיתָא דְלָא כְרִבִּי יוּדָה. דְּרִבִּי יוּדָה אָמַר. אַרְבַּע קְהִילּוֹת הֵן. קְהַל כֹּהֲנִים קְהַל לְוִיִּים קְהַל יִשְׂרָאֵל קְהַל גֵּרִים. מְתִיבִין לְרִבִּי יְהוּדָה. וְהָכְתִיב לֹא יָבֹא פְצוּעַ דַּכָּא וּכְרוּת שָׁפְכָה בִּקְהַל יי׳. פְּסוּלֵי גוּף אִינּוּן. וְהָכְתִיב בָּנִים אֲשֶׁר יִוָּלְדוּ לָהֶם דּוֹר שְׁלִישִׁי יָבֹא לָהֶם בִּקְהַל יי׳. בַּעֲשֵׂה אִינּוּן. וְרַבָּנִין אָמְרִין. שְׁלֹשָׁה קְהִילּוֹת הֵן. קְהַל כֹּהֲנִים קְהַל לְוִיִּים קְהַל יִשְׂרָאֵל. לֹא יָבֹא. לֹא יָבֹא. לֹא יָבֹא.

1 חנינה | ג חיננא   2 ארבע | ג ארבעה   הן | ג אינון קהל   3 לר' יהודה | ג דר' יודה וכרות שפכה בקהל יי' | ג -   פסולי | ג פסול   4 יוולדו | ג יולדו   בקהל יי' | ג -   5 הן | ג אינון

[105]Rebbi Ḥanina said, the Mishnah does not follow Rebbi Jehudah, since Rebbi Jehudah said that four congregations are called "congregation", the congregation of Cohanim, the congregation of Levites, the congregation of Israelites, the congregation of converts. They objected to Rebbi Jehudah, but is it not written, "one injured in his testicles or with amputated urethra should not come into the Eternal's congregation"? That refers to bodily blemishes. But is it not written, "children that will be born to them in the third generation may enter the Eternal's congregation"? That is a positive commandment. But the rabbis said, there are three congregations, the congregation of Cohanim, the congregation of Levites, the congregation of Israelites; "they shall not come, they shall not come, they shall not come."

105 This text is from *Yebamot* 8:2, explained there in Notes 150-155.

(fol. 65a) **משנה ב**: וְאֵי זֶהוּ שְׁתוּקֵי. כָּל־שֶׁהוּא מַכִּיר אֶת אִמּוֹ וְאֵינוֹ מַכִּיר אֶת אָבִיו. וַאֲסוּפֵי כָּל־שֶׁנֶּאֱסַף מִן הַשּׁוּק וְאֵינוֹ מַכִּיר לֹא אֶת אָבִיו וְלֹא אֶת אִמּוֹ. אַבָּא שָׁאוּל הָיָה קוֹרֵא לִשְׁתוּקֵי בְּדוּקֵי.

Mishnah 2: What is a silenced one? Anyone who knows his mother but not his father. But a foundling is one collected from the public domain who knows neither his father nor his mother. Abba Shaul called the silenced one "investigated one".

(65d line 59) **הלכה ב**: וְאֵי זֶהוּ שְׁתוּקֵי כול'. מָהוּ בְּדוּקֵי. בְּדוֹק אַחֲרָיו.

Halakhah 2: "What is a silenced one," etc. What means "investigated one"? Investigate him[106]!

106 One has to apply the rules detailed in *Ketubot* 1:8,9 to determine whether or not the child is to be treated as a bastard. In the interpretation of the Babli, 74a, Abba Shaul holds that the unmarried mother is to be believed if she states that the child is not the result of an incestuous relationship.

(65d line 60) אֲחוֵי דְּרִבִּי יְהוּדָה בַּר זַבְדִּי בְּשֵׁם רִבִּי. תִּינוֹק כָּל־זְמַן שֶׁהוּא מוּשְׁלָךְ בַּשּׁוּק אוֹ אָבִיו אוֹ אִמּוֹ מְעִידִין עָלָיו. נֶאֱסַף מִן הַשּׁוּק צָרִיךְ שְׁנֵי עֵדִים. אָבִיו וְאִמּוֹ כִּשְׁנֵי עֵדִים הֵן. רַבָּנִין דְּקַיְסָרִין בְּשֵׁם רַב חִסְדָּא. הָדָא דְּאַתְּ אָמַר בְּתִינוֹק שֶׁאֵינוֹ מַרְגִּיעַ. אֲבָל בְּתִינוֹק שֶׁהוּא מַרְגִּיעַ צָרִיךְ שְׁנֵי עֵדִים. וְאָבִיו וְאִמּוֹ כִּשְׁתֵּי עֵדִים הֵן. וְאַתְיָא כְּהַהִיא דְּאָמַר רִבִּי יַנַּאי. עֲגָלִים וְסַיָּיחִין הַמְקַפְּצִין אֵין לָהֶן חֲזָקָה.

The brother of Rebbi Jehudah bar Zavdi in the name of [Rav][107]: As long as a baby lies in the public domain, either his father or his mother can testify about him[108]. Once he was collected from the public domain, one needs two witnesses; its father and mother are like two witnesses[109].

The rabbis of Caesarea in the name of Rav Hisda[110]: That is, if the baby is not moving. But a baby which is moving needs two witnesses; its father and mother are like two witnesses. This parallels what Rebbi Yannai said: property rights on jumping calves and lambs cannot be proven by possession[111].

107 This is the reading later in the Halakhah, in *Baba batra* 3:1, and in the Babli, 73b, against the reading here 'ר meaning "Rebbi".

108 As long as the baby was not taken up, it is not called a foundling and one of the parents is empowered to declare it his child and not a bastard.

109 Once it is designated a foundling, it needs two witnesses to admit it to the Jewish marriage pool. If two people declare that they are its parents, they really disqualify themselves as witnesses since close relatives cannot testify. Nevertheless, they are admitted *as if* they were true and independent witnesses.

110 In *Baba batra* 3:1, the rule is attributed directly to Rav Hisda. This may support S. Lieberman's contention that Tractate *Neziqin* was edited by the rabbis of Caesarea.

In the Babli, 73b, Rava restricts this rule to years of famine or similar situations where the parents may be expected to be unable to care for their child.

111 If the ownership of an independently moving calf or lamb is in dispute, one cannot say that the person in whose herd it is at the moment is in possession and any other claimant has to bear the burden of proof since the animal could have wandered with the herd; the situations of both the person in possession and the claimant are equal and ownership has to be proven independently.

(65d line 60) רִבִּי בָּא בְשֵׁם רַב חִסְדָּא. שְׁלֹשָׁה הֵן שֶׁהֵן נֶאֱמָנִין עַל אָתָר. חַיָּה וּשְׁיָּירָה וְהַמְטַהֶרֶת חֲבֵרוֹתֶיהָ. חַיָּה. וַתִּקַּח הַמְיַלֶּדֶת וַתִּקְשֹׁר עַל שָׁנִי לֵאמֹר זֶה יָצָא רִאשׁוֹנָה. וּשְׁיָּירָה. כַּהֲהִיא דְּאָמַר רִבִּי אַבָּא אַחֲוֵי דִיהוּדָה בַּר זַבְדִּי בְּשֵׁם רַב. תִּינוֹק כָּל־זְמַן שֶׁהוּא מוּשְׁלָךְ לַשּׁוּק אוֹ אָבִיו אוֹ אִמּוֹ מְעִידִין עָלָיו. נֶאֱסַף מִן הַשּׁוּק צָרִיךְ שְׁנֵי עֵדִים. אָבִיו וְאִמּוֹ כִּשְׁנֵי עֵדִים הֵן. וְהַמְטַהֶרֶת חֲבֵרוֹתֶיהָ.

כַּהֲהִיא דְּתַנִּינָן תַּמָּן. שָׁלֹשׁ נָשִׁים יְשֵׁינוֹת בְּמִטָּה אַחַת. נִמְצָא דָם תַּחַת אַחַת מֵהֶן כּוּלָּן טְמֵיאוֹת. בָּדְקָה אַחַת מֵהֶן וְנִמְצֵאת טְמֵיאָה הִיא טְמֵיאָה וּשְׁתַּיִם טְהוֹרוֹת. אָמַר רִבִּי בָּא. וּבִלְבַד מֵעֵת לָעֵת.

[112]Rebbi Abba in the name of Rav Ḥisda: Three are trustworthy immediately[113]: a midwife, a caravan, and the one who purifies her colleagues. A midwife: "The midwife took and wound a red string [around his hand] to indicate that this one was born first[114]." A caravan, as Rebbi Abba, the brother of Rebbi Jehudah bar Zavdi said in the name of Rav: As long as a baby lies in the public domain, either its father or its mother can testify about him. Once it was collected from the public domain, one needs two witnesses; its father and mother are like two witnesses. The one who purifies her colleagues, as we have stated there[115]: "Three women sleep on one bed. If blood was found under one of them, all three are impure[116]. If one of them checked herself out and found herself impure[116], she is impure and the other two are pure." Rebbi Abba said, only within 24 hours[117].

112 The same statements are in the Babli, 73b.

113 They are trustworthy *only* immediately; after some time they must be treated under the rules which require two independent witnesses.

114 *Gen.* 38:28, quoted incompletely. In a multiple birth, the midwife has the authority to determine which child was born first, which may determine inheritance rights. The Babli empowers the midwife to testify who is whose child in case several women give birth in the same room.

115 Mishnah *Niddah* 9:4.

116 In the impurity of menstruation.

117 The Babli emphatically disagrees and requires that the checking be done immediately upon leaving the bed.

(fol. 65a) **משנה ג**: כָּל־הָאֲסוּרִין לָבוֹא בַקָּהָל מוּתָּרִין לָבוֹא זֶה בָזֶה וְרִבִּי יְהוּדָה אוֹסֵר. רִבִּי אֱלְעָזֶר אוֹמֵר וַדָּאָן בְּוַדָּאָן מוּתָּר וַדָּאָן בִּסְפֵיקָן וּסְפֵיקָן בְּוַדָּאָן וּסְפֵיקָן בִּסְפֵיקָן אָסוּר. וְאִילּוּ הֵן הַסְּפֵיקוֹת שְׁתוּקִי אֲסוּפִי וְכוּתִי.

Mishnah 3: Any who are forbidden to marry in the congregation are permitted to marry one another[118] but Rebbi Jehudah forbids. Rebbi Eliezer says, certain with certain are permitted, certain with questionable, questionable with certain[119], and questionable with questionable are forbidden. The following are questionable: the silenced one, the foundling, and the Samaritan[120].

118 Even a bastard who is certainly forbidden may marry a foundling whose status is only questionable, as already stated in Mishnah 1.

119 This clause was inserted only as a memory help; "certain with questionable" is the same as "questionable with certain"; it does not make any difference who is the male and who the female.

120 Who are Jewish but do not follow the rabbinic rules of marriage and divorce. The child of a Samaritan divorcee from a second husband might be a bastard by rabbinic rules.

(65d line 74) **הלכה ג**: כָּל־הָאֲסוּרִין לָבוֹא בַקָּהָל כול'. רִבִּי יִרְמְיָה אָמַר. כְּלָלָא. פְּצוּעַ דַּכָּא יִשְׂרָאֵל מוּתָּר לוֹ לִישָּׂא מַמְזֶרֶת. אָמַר רִבִּי יוֹסֵי. וּבִלְבַד פְּסוּל מִשְׁפָּחָה. הָא פְּסוּל גּוּף לֹא. חֵיילֵיהּ דְּרִבִּי יוֹסֵי מִן הָדָא. דְּאָמַר רִבִּי חִלְקִיָּה רִבִּי סִימוֹן בְּשֵׁם רִבִּי יְהוֹשֻׁעַ בֶּן לֵוִי. לֹא שָׁנוּ אֶלָּא פְּצוּעַ דַּכָּא יִשְׂרָאֵל. אֲבָל פְּצוּעַ דַּכָּא כֹהֵן כְּמָה דְּאַתְּ אָמַר תַּמָּן. כֹּהֵן בָּרוּר אָסוּר לוֹ לִישָּׂא גִיּוֹרֶת. אַף הָכָא יִשְׂרָאֵל בָּרוּר אָסוּר לוֹ לִישָּׂא מַמְזֶרֶת.

2 ובלבד | ג בלבד   3 לא | ג לא בדא   5 כהן ברור אסור | ג אם כהן ברור הוא פסול   6 לו | ג -

[121]Rebbi Jeremiah said, as a matter of principle, an Israel with an injured testicle may marry a female bastard. Rebbi Yose said, it applies

only to family disabilities, not to bodily defects. The strength of Rebbi Yose comes from the statement of Rebbi Ḥilqiah, Rebbi Simon in the name of Rebbi Joshua ben Levi: One did state this only for an Israel with an injured testicle, but not a Cohen, since, as you say there, if he is certainly a Cohen he is forbidden to marry a convert; here also, he is certainly an Israel and forbidden to marry a female bastard.

121   The entire Halakhah is from *Yebamot* 8:2, Notes 136-155 (ג).

(66a line 6) נִשְׁמְעִינָהּ מִן הָדָא. דְּאָמַר רִבִּי אִימִי תַּנֵּי רִבִּי יַעֲקֹב גְּבוּלָיָיא קוֹמֵי רִבִּי יוֹחָנָן רִבִּי יִצְחָק בַּר טְבְלַיי בְּשֵׁם רִבִּי שִׁמְעוֹן בֶּן לָקִישׁ. דִּבְרֵי רִבִּי יְהוּדָה. מַמְזֵר לֹא יִשָּׂא מַמְזֶרֶת כְּדֵי שֶׁיִּכְלוּ מַמְזֵירִין מִן הָעוֹלָם. וְדִכְוָותָהּ עַמּוֹנִי לֹא יִשָּׂא עֲמוֹנִית. אָמַר רִבִּי יוֹסֵי בֵּירִבִּי בּוּן. עַל דְּרַבָּנִין צְרִיכָה. אֵין יִסְבּוֹר רִבִּי יְהוּדָה גֵּירִים פְּסוּלִים בְּקָהָל לִי אִינּוּן. לִישָּׂא עֲמוֹנִית אֵינוֹ יָכוֹל שֶׁהוּא קָהָל לִי אֶצְלוֹ. לִישָּׂא מִצְרִית אֵינוֹ יָכוֹל שֶׁהוּא קָהָל לִי אֶצְלָהּ. אָמַר רִבִּי מַתַּנְיָה. מְשַׁחְרְרִין שִׁפְחָה וּמַשִּׂיאִין לוֹ. וְדִכְוָותָהּ מִצְרִי לֹא יִשָּׂא מִצְרִית. נִשְׁמְעִינָהּ מִן הָדָא. תַּנֵּי רִבִּי אַבָּהוּ קוֹמֵי רִבִּי יוֹחָנָן. אָמַר רִבִּי יְהוּדָה. בִּנְיָמִין גֵּר מִצְרִי הָיָה מִתַּלְמִידֵי רִבִּי עֲקִיבָה. אָמַר. אֲנִי גֵּר מִצְרִי נָשׂוּי גִּיּוֹרֶת מִצְרִית. בָּנַי בֵּן גֵּר מִצְרִי וַאֲנִי מַשִּׂיאוֹ לְגִיּוֹרֶת מִצְרִית. וְנִמְצָא בֶּן בְּנִי כָשֵׁר לָבֹא בְּקָהָל. אָמַר לוֹ רִבִּי עֲקִיבָא. לֹא בְנִי. אֶלָּא אַף אַתָּה הַשִּׂיאוֹ לְבַת גִּיּוֹרֶת מִצְרִית כְּדֵי שֶׁיִּהוּ שְׁלֹשָׁה דוֹרוֹת מִיכָּן וּשְׁלֹשָׁה דוֹרוֹת מִיכָּן.

1 - | ג על דעתיה דר' יודה ממזר לא ישא ממזרת   דאמ' | ג דמר   גבולייא | ג גבליא   3 יכלו | ג יתכלו   4 צריכה¹²² | ג נצרכה   אין | ג דאין   5 יהודה | ג יודה   גירים | ג גירין   פסולים | ג פסולין   בקהל | ג קהל   6 אצלו | ג אצלה   מתנייה | ג מתניה   7 שפחה ומשיאין לו | ג לו שפחה   8 יהודה | ג יודה   9 מתלמידי ר' | ג מתלמידיו   שלר'   גיורת | ג לגיורת   10 ונמצא | ג נמצא   לבא¹²³ | ג לבוא   11 עקיבא¹²³ | ג עקיבה

[In the opinion of Rebbi Jehudah, may a male bastard not marry a female bastard?]¹²⁴ Let us hear from the following, as Rebbi Immi said, Rebbi Jacob from Gebal stated before Rebbi Johanan, Rebbi Isaac bar Tevele in the name of Rebbi Simeon ben Laqish: Rebbi Jehudah stated that a male bastard should not marry a female bastard so that bastards should disappear from the world. Similarly, is an Ammonite man forbidden to marry an Ammonite woman? Was that needed for the rabbis? For if Rebbi Jehudah thought that this disqualified converts from any of the Eternal's congregations, then [the Ammonite] could not marry an Ammonite woman since for her he would be of the Eternal's congregation. He could not marry an Egyptian woman since for her he would be of the Eternal's congregation. Rebbi Mattania said, one frees a slave girl and marries her to him. Similarly, could an Egyptian man not marry an Egyptian woman? Let us hear from the following, as Rebbi Abbahu stated before Rebbi Johanan: "Rebbi Jehudah said, Benjamin, an Egyptian convert, was a student of Rebbi Aqiba. He said, I am an Egyptian convert married to an Egyptian convert. My son is an Egyptian convert; I shall marry him to an Egyptian convert so that my grandson will be qualified to marry into the congregation. Rebbi Aqiba said to him, my son, it is not so. But you marry him to the daughter of an Egyptian woman convert so that there should be three generations on either side."

122 A Babylonian expression; א has the correct Yerushalmi version.

123 Text inserted by the corrector, Babylonian spelling.

124 Missing here, added from א.

Since the paragraph is the answer to the question asked in this sentence, it is clear that א is the source and the text here the copy.

(66a line 19) רַב יְהוּדָה בְּשֵׁם רַב. הֲלָכָה כְּרִבִּי לְעֵזֶר דִּבְרֵי חֲכָמִים. רִבִּי יִרְמְיָה בְּשֵׁם רִבִּי שְׁמוּאֵל בַּר רַב יִצְחָק. לֹא יָבֹא מַמְזֵר בִּקְהַל יי. בְּקָהָל בָּרוּר אֵינוֹ בָא. בָּא הוּא בִקְהַל סָפֵק.

2 לא | ג כת׳ לא

Rav Jehudah in the name of Rav: Practice follows Rebbi Eliezer. The words of the Sages? Rebbi Jeremiah in the name of Rebbi Samuel bar Rav Isaac: "No bastard shall marry into the Eternal's congregation". He cannot marry into a congregation which is certain. He may marry if the membership in the congregation is questionable.

(66a line 21) תַּמָּן תַּנִּינָן. סָפֵק בֶּן תִּשְׁעָה לָרִאשׁוֹן סָפֵק בֶּן שִׁבְעָה לָאַחֲרוֹן יוֹצִיא וְהַוָּלָד כָּשֵׁר וְחַיָּיבִין אָשָׁם תָּלוּי. תַּנֵּי. הָרִאשׁוֹן כָּשֵׁר לִהְיוֹת כֹּהֵן וְהַשֵּׁנִי מַמְזֵר בְּסָפֵק. רִבִּי אֶלְעָזֶר בֶּן יַעֲקֹב אוֹמֵר. אֵין מַמְזֵר בְּסָפֵק. מוֹדֶה רִבִּי אֶלְעָזֶר בֶּן יַעֲקֹב בִּסְפֵק כּוּתִים וּבִסְפֵק חֲלָלִים. כְּהַהִיא דְתַנִּינָן תַּמָּן. עֲשָׂרָה יוּחֲסִין עָלוּ מִבָּבֶל. עַל דַּעְתֵּיהּ דְּרִבִּי אֱלִיעֶזֶר בֶּן יַעֲקֹב שְׁמוֹנָה. עַל דַּעְתִּין דְּרַבָּן גַּמְלִיאֵל וְרִבִּי אֶלְעָזֶר תִּשְׁעָה. עַל דַּעְתִּין דְּרַבָּנִין עֲשָׂרָה.

1 תשעה | ג תשע 2 אשם | ג באשם כהן | ג כהן גדול 3 אליעזר | ג ליעזר 5 אליעזר | ג ליעזר 6 דרבנין | ג דרבנן אליעזר | ג ליעזר

There, we have stated: "If it is doubtful whether [the child is] a nine-months' child of the first [brother] or a seven-months' of the second, he has to divorce her, the child is legitimate, and they are obligated for a reparation offering for a possible sin." It was stated: "The first son could be [High][125] Priest, any second son possibly is a bastard. Rebbi Eliezer ben Jacob said, there is no such thing as a possible bastard." Rebbi Eliezer ben Jacob agrees in cases of doubt of Samaritans and desecrated persons. This refers to what we have stated there: "Ten classes returned from Babylonia." In the opinion of Rebbi Eliezer ben Jacob, eight. In the opinion of Rabban Gamliel and Rebbi Eliezer, nine. In the opinion of the rabbis, ten.

125 Missing from the text here but necessary. If the male child is legitimate and his father a Cohen, he is a Cohen. The emphasis is on the fact that the child in theory could be High Priest.

(fol. 65a) **משנה ד:** הַנּוֹשֵׂא אִשָּׁה כֹהֶנֶת צָרִיךְ לִבְדּוֹק אַחֲרֶיהָ אַרְבַּע אִימָהוֹת שֶׁהֵן שְׁמֹנֶה אִמָּהּ וְאֵם אִמָּהּ וְאֵם אֲבִי אִמָּהּ וְאִמָּהּ וּלְוִיָּה וְיִשְׂרְאֵלִית מוֹסִיפִין עוֹד אַחַת.

Mishnah 4: One who comes to marry a woman from a priestly family[126] has to check four mothers who are eight: Her mother, and her maternal grandmother, her mother's paternal grandmother and great-grandmother[127]. But for a levitic or Israel woman one adds another generation[128].

126 Since only in priestly families the women may become disqualified, the Cohen who wants to be sure that his descendants will be qualified to serve in the Temple is asked to verify that in generations back no divorcee or otherwise disqualified woman married into his fiancée's family.

127 The list is obviously incomplete; the Mishnah in the Babli and the independent Mishnah mss. add the paternal grandmother and the latter's mother and mother-in-law. The list is quite uneven; looking at the bride's family tree we denote by *f* a female to be checked, by *m* a male:

```
        f     f
        |     |
        f  f  f
        |  |  |
        f  m  f  m
        |  /  |  /
        f     m
        |  /
        f
        |  /
       bride
```

The positions mentioned in the Yerushalmi Mishnah are underlined.

128 Even though priestly disqualifications do not apply to these women.

(66a line 28) **הלכה ד:** הַנּוֹשֵׂא אִשָּׁה כֹּהֶנֶת כול׳. אָמַר רִבִּי יוֹחָנָן. דְּרִבִּי מֵאִיר הִיא. דְּתַנֵּי. אֵי זוֹ הִיא עִיסָּה כְּשֵׁירָה. כָּל־שֶׁאֵין בָּהּ לֹא חָלָל וְלֹא מַמְזֵר וְלֹא נָתִין. רִבִּי מֵאִיר אוֹמֵר. כָּל־שֶׁאֵין בָּהּ אַחַת מִכָּל־אֵילוּ בִּתָּהּ כְּשֵׁירָה לִכְהוּנָּה. אֲבָל מִשְׁפָּחָה שֶׁנִּשְׁתַּקַּע בָּהּ פְּסוּל. רִבִּי מֵאִיר אוֹמֵר. בּוֹדֵק עַד אַרְבַּע אִימָּהוֹת וּמַשִּׂיא. וַחֲכָמִים אוֹמְרִים. בּוֹדֵק לְעוֹלָם. רַב אָמַר. זוֹ דִבְרֵי רִבִּי מֵאִיר. אֲבָל חֲכָמִים אוֹמְרִים. בּוֹדֵק מֵאֵי זוֹ מִשְׁפָּחָה מַשִּׂיאִין לִכְהוּנָּה וּמַשִּׂיא. בְּיַד מִי הוּא בוֹדֵק. רִבִּי חַגַּיי בְּשֵׁם רִבִּי יֹאשִׁיָּה. בּוֹדֵק בְּיַד קְרוֹבוֹתָיו. רִבִּי חָמָא אַתָא סַבָּא אֲמַר לֵיהּ. מַשִּׂיאִין לִכְהוּנָּה מִן הָדָא זַרְעִיתָא. אֲמַר לֵיהּ. אִין. וְאַסִּיב עַל פּוּמֵיהּ. רַב אֲמַר לְחִייָה בְּרֵיהּ. נָחוֹת דְּרַג וְסַב אִיתָּא. אֲמַר רִבִּי אִידֵי שְׁכִיחָה הָא מִילְּתָא בְּפוּמְהוֹן דְּרַבָּנָן. וְאִם לֹא נִטְמְאָה הָאִשָּׁה וּטְהוֹרָה הִיא. מִכֵּיוָן שֶׁלֹּא נִטְמְאָה טְהוֹרָה. וְלֹא כִיהוּדָה בֶּן פַּפּוֹס שֶׁנּוֹעֵל דֶּלֶת בִּפְנֵי אִשְׁתּוֹ. אָמְרוּ לֵיהּ. נְהוּגִין הֲווֹן אַבְהָתָךְ עֲבָדִין כֵּן. חַד כֹּהֵן אֲתָא לְגַבֵּי רִבִּי יוֹחָנָן. אֲמַר לֵיהּ. עַבְדִּית מַתְנִיתָהּ. נָשָׂאתִי אִשָּׁה וּבָדַקְתִּי אַחֲרֶיהָ אַרְבָּעָה אִימָּהוֹת שֶׁהֵן שְׁמוֹנֶה. אֲמַר לֵיהּ. אֵין הוּא עִיקְּרָא לָקִי מִן רֵאשָׁה מָאן מוֹדַע לָךְ.

Halakhah 4: "One who comes to marry a woman from a priestly family," etc. Rebbi Joḥanan said, this is Rebbi Meïr's, as we have stated[129]:

"What is qualified dough[130]? Anyone about whom there is [no suspicion of descent from] a desecrated one, a bastard, or a Gibeonite. Rebbi Meïr says, the daughter of any woman not tainted with any of these is qualified for the priesthood. But about a family in which a disability had disappeared, Rebbi Meïr says he checks up to four mothers and marries, but the Sages say, he checks forever.[131]" Rav said, these[132] are the words of Rebbi Meïr, but the Sages say, he checks from which family one marries into the priesthood and marries[133]. Through whom does he check? Rebbi Haggai in the name of Rebbi Josia: He checks through his female relatives[134]. To Rebbi Hama came an old man[135]; he asked him: Does one marry into the priesthood from this family? He answered: yes, and he[136] was making a match based on this information. Rav said to his son Hiyya: Descend a degree to marry a wife[137]. Rebbi Idi said, the following is a frequent saying of the rabbis: "If the woman was not impure but she is pure.[138]" If she was not impure, she is pure[139]. Not like Pappos ben Jehudah who locks the door before his wife[140]. One said to him, did your forefathers act like this[141]? A Cohen came to Rebbi Johanan and said to him: I acted on the Mishnah when I married a woman from a priestly family and checked after her four mothers which are eight. He said to him, if the origin was defective, who would inform you[142]?

---

129   *Ketubot* 1:9 (Notes 248-254); a slightly different version in the Tosephta 5:2, Babli *Ketubot* 14a.

130   As dough is kneaded from different ingredients, so a dough woman is descended from both more and less qualified sources; cf. *Ketubot* 1:9 Note 251. [For "mixture of dough" used as simile for lineage, perhaps also cf. Swiss-German expression *vom Teig* "from the dough", meaning "from (the best) families". (E.G.)]

131   Until he finds the source of the trouble.

132   The interpretation of the position of the Sages.

133   All women in a family from whom one married into the priesthood are qualified unless her personal disqualification be known. In the Babli, 76b, Rav's statement is stronger: A presumption of legitimacy applies to all families (unless anything derogatory be known).

134   Testimony by females is close to be hearsay evidence, but sufficient to qualify a marriage. The language of the statement is derived from Mishnah *Ketubot* 1:9, dealing with a woman's bodily defects.

135   Interpretation of *Pene Moshe*. *Qorban Ha'eda* reads: Rebbi saw an old man coming. Both interpretations are possible; in neither case is the text idiomatic Aramaic.

136   R. Hama.

137   Rav had married a noble woman and relative who gave him a hard time.

138   *Num.* 5:28.

139   They reject the Mishnah and hold that anybody can marry any woman about whose family nothing derogatory is known.

140   Cf. *Soṭah* 1:7, Note 260. He did not permit his wife to talk to any male except himself.

141   Jews do not lock up their wives in a harem; *Soṭah* 1:7; Babli *Giṭṭin* 90a.

142   If there was a problem a few generations earlier, would you know? Note that the Cohen quotes the Mishnah in Hebrew, claiming the status of a learned person, but R. Joḥanan answers him in Aramaic, demoting him to the unlearned class since he followed the Mishnah.

(66a line 43) לְוִיִּים וְיִשְׂרְאֵלִים מוֹסִיפִין עָלֶיהָ עוֹד אַחַת. וְלֹא נִמְצֵאת מַחְמִיר בְּיִשְׂרָאֵל יוֹתֵר מִן הַכֹּהֲנִים. אָמַר רִבִּי יוֹסֵי בֵּירִבִּי בּוּן. אַחַת זוֹ וְאַחַת זוֹ קְנָס קָנְסוּ חֲכָמִים בָּהֶן שֶׁיְּהֵא אָדָם דָּבֵק בְּשִׁבְטוֹ וּבְמִשְׁפַּחְתּוֹ.

"But for Levites or Israel one adds another generation[143]." Does it not turn out that one is more stringent for an Israel than for a Cohen? [144]Rebbi Yose ben Abun said, in both cases[145] the Sages demanded a fine so that everybody should cling to his tribe and family.

143 This quote is different from the Mishnah which speaks of a Cohen marrying a non-priestly wife whereas here one refers to a non-priest marrying a priestly wife. The Tosephta, 5:4, straddles the issue, mentioning לְוִיָּה וְיִשְׂרְאֵלִים "a Levite (f. singular) and Israels (m. plural)"

144 In a different situation R. Yose ben R. Abun gives the same explanation in *Ketubot* 1:5, end. He seems to think that in Herodian times and later the priests had a tendency to develop into a separate caste.

145 Both the cases mentioned in the Mishnah and the one mentioned in the quote.

(fol. 65a) **משנה ה:** אֵין בּוֹדְקִין מִן הַמִּזְבֵּחַ וּלְמַעְלָה וְלֹא מִן הַדּוּכָן וּלְמַעְלָה. וְכָל־מִי שֶׁהוּחְזְקוּ אֲבוֹתָיו מְשׁוֹטְרֵי הָרַבִּים וְגַבָּאֵי צְדָקָה מַשִּׂיאִין לִכְהוּנָּה וְאֵינוֹ צָרִיךְ לִבְדּוֹק אַחֲרֵיהֶן. רַבִּי יוֹסֵי אוֹמֵר אַף מִי שֶׁהָיָה חָתוּם עַד בְּאַרְכֵי הַיְשָׁנָה שֶׁלְצִיפּוֹרִי. רִבִּי חֲנִינָה בֶּן אַנְטִיגוֹנוֹס אוֹמֵר אַף מִי שֶׁהָיָה מוּכְתָּב בְּאִיסְטְרַטְיָא שֶׁל מֶלֶךְ.

Mishnah 5: One does not investigate from the altar[146] and before, or from the podium[147] and before[148]. From every family whose ancestors were known as public officials and welfare administrators one marries into the priesthood; no investigation is necessary. Rebbi Yose says, also anybody signing as witness in the ancient archive[149] of Sepphoris. Rebbi Hanina ben Antigonos says, also anyone who ever was registered in the king's army[150].

146 The daughters of priests accepted for service in the Temple are automatically qualified to be married by priests.

147 The same holds for daughters of Levitic men accepted as singers in the Temple. One has to assume that the same holds for Levites serving in other

functions in the Temple.

148 The Babylonian Mishnah adds: "Nor from the Synhedrion and before." This addition is unnecessary since it is implied by the next sentence.

149 Greek ἀρχεῖον. It seems that only select families were admitted to be notaries to certify deeds in Sepphoris.

150 Greek στρατιά.

(66a line 46) **הלכה ה:** אֵין בּוֹדְקִין מִן לֹא הַמִּזְבֵּחַ וּלְמַעְלָה כול'. כְּתִיב שׂוֹם תָּשִׂים עָלֶיךָ מֶלֶךְ. אֵין לִי אֶלָּא מֶלֶךְ. מְנַיִין לְרַבּוֹת שׁוֹטְרֵי הָרַבִּים וְגַבָּאֵי צְדָקָה וְסוֹפְרֵי דַיָּינִין וּמַכִּין בִּרְצוּעָה מְנַיִין. תַּלְמוּד לוֹמַר מִקֶּרֶב אָחִיךָ תָּשִׂים עָלֶיךָ מֶלֶךְ. כָּל־שֶׁתְּמַנֵּיהוּ עָלֶיךָ לֹא יְהֵא אֶלָּא מִן הַבְּרוּרִין שֶׁבְּאַחֶיךָ. רִבִּי שְׁמוּאֵל בַּר נַחְמָן בְּשֵׁם רִבִּי יוֹנָתָן. וְהִתְיַיחְשָׂם בַּצָּבָא בַּמִּלְחָמָה. זְכוּת יַחֲסֵיהֶם עוֹמֶדֶת לָהֶם בַּמִּלְחָמָה. עַד כְּדוֹן מִן הַקַּבָּלָה. מִדִּבְרֵי תוֹרָה. לֹא יָבֹא מַמְזֵר בִּקְהַל יְיָ. לֹא יָבֹא פְצוּעַ דַּכָּא וגו'. מַה כְּתִיב בַּתְרֵיהּ. כִּי תֵצֵא מַחֲנֶה עַל אוֹיְבֶיךָ וגו'.

Halakhah 5: "One does not investigate from the altar and before," etc. It is written[151]: "You certainly shall put a king over you." This refers not only to a king; from where to add public officials, administrators of welfare, clerks of the court, and those who whip with a lash[152]; from where? The verse says, "from amidst your brothers you shall appoint a king over you[151]," anybody whom you appoint over you shall only be from the select among your brethren[153]. Rebbi Samuel bar Naḥman in the name of Rebbi Jonathan: "Their distinguished lineage in the army in war.[154]" The merit of their lineage supports them in war. So far from tradition[155]; from the words of the Torah? "No bastard shall come into the Eternal's congregation[156]." "No person injured in his testicles shall come[157], etc." What is written afterwards? "When you encamp against your enemies, etc.[158]"

151 *Deut.* 17:15.

152 Employees of the criminal court.

153 He can be called your brother only if he belongs to your marriage group. Therefore, anybody whose daughter cannot be married by anybody, including priests, is excluded from public office. In the Babli, 76b, it is inferred from this argument that only children of a Jewish mother can be appointed to public office.

154 *1Chr.* 7:40. This refers to the statement of R. Hanina ben Antigonos and a hypothetical army of the Messiah. In the Babli, 76b, "the king's army" is interpreted as David's army as described in *1Chr.*

155 Prophets and Hagiographs, which do not have standing as sources of the law.

156 *Deut.* 23:3.

157 *Deut.* 23:2. The spelling supports the Yemenite tradition.

158 *Deut.* 23:10, directly after the end of the rules of exclusion from endogamous marriage. It is explicit in the Babli (*Yebamot* 4a) that the order of verses in *Deut.* is important for the correct interpretation. The implication is that only persons of impeccable lineage should be admitted to the Eternal's army.

משנה ו: בַּת חָלָל זָכָר פְּסוּלָה מִן הַכְּהוּנָּה לְעוֹלָם. יִשְׂרָאֵל שֶׁנָּשָׂא חֲלָלָה בִּתּוֹ כְּשֵׁירָה לַכְּהוּנָה. חָלָל שֶׁנָּשָׂא בַת יִשְׂרָאֵל בִּתּוֹ פְּסוּלָה לַכְּהוּנָה. רַבִּי יְהוּדָה אוֹמֵר בַּת גֵּר זָכָר כְּבַת חָלָל זָכָר. רַבִּי אֱלִיעֶזֶר בֶּן יַעֲקֹב אוֹמֵר. יִשְׂרָאֵל שֶׁנָּשָׂא גִיּוֹרֶת בִּתּוֹ כְּשֵׁירָה לַכְּהוּנָה וְגֵר שֶׁנָּשָׂא בַת יִשְׂרָאֵל בִּתּוֹ כְּשֵׁירָה לַכְּהוּנָה. אֲבָל גֵּר שֶׁנָּשָׂא גִיּוֹרֶת בִּתּוֹ פְּסוּלָה לַכְּהוּנָה. אֶחָד גֵּרִים וְאֶחָד עֲבָדִים מְשׁוּחְרָרִין וַאֲפִילוּ עַד עֲשָׂרָה דוֹרוֹת עַד שֶׁתְּהֵא אִמּוֹ מִיִּשְׂרָאֵל. רַבִּי יוֹסֵי אוֹמֵר אַף גֵּר שֶׁנָּשָׂא גִיּוֹרֶת בִּתּוֹ כְּשֵׁירָה לַכְּהוּנָה. (fol. 65a)

Mishnah 6: The daughter of a male desecrated priest[1] is always disqualified for the priesthood. The daughter of an Israel who married a desecrated woman is qualified for the priesthood[159]. The daughter of a desecrated priest who married an Israel woman is disqualified for the priesthood. Rebbi Jehudah says, the daughter of a male proselyte is like the daughter of a desecrated priest[160]. Rebbi Eliezer ben Jacob said, the daughter of an Israel who married a proselyte is qualified for the priesthood and the daughter of a proselyte who married an Israel woman is qualified for the priesthood, but the daughter of a proselyte who married a proselyte is disqualified for the priesthood[161], both proselytes and freedmen, even for ten generations, unless the mother be from Israel. Rebbi Yose says, even the daughter of a proselyte who married a proselyte is qualified for the priesthood[162].

159 Desecrated priests and their descendants can marry Israel or Levite partners without sin. According to Mishnah 3:14, the children have the status of the male, qualified Israel for an Israel father and desecrated priest for a desecrated father.

160 This statement has no basis in the Torah; it accepts as law *Ez.* 44:22 which instructs priests to marry only "virgins from the seed of Israel and widows of priests."

161 Even if she was conceived after both partners became Jewish. He accepts as "seed of Israel" the child of either a male or a female Israel.

162 If they married after conversion, as Jews, their children are "the seed of Israel".

(66a line 54) **הלכה ו:** בַּת חָלָל זָכָר כול'. רַב הַמְנוּנָא בְּשֵׁם רַב. בַּת. בַּת בַּת. לְעוֹלָם. רִבִּי יוֹחָנָן בְּשֵׁם רִבִּי יִשְׁמָעֵאל. בְּעַמָּיו. מַה בְּעַמָּיו שֶׁנֶּאֱמַר לְהַלָּן זְכָרִים אֲסוּרִין וּנְקֵיבוֹת מוּתָּרוֹת. אַף בְּעַמָּיו שֶׁנֶּאֱמַר כָּאן זְכָרִים אֲסוּרִין וּנְקֵיבוֹת מוּתָּרוֹת. מַה נָפַק מִבֵּינֵיהוֹן. כֹּהֵן שֶׁבָּא עַל הַגְּרוּשָׁה וְהוֹלִיד בֵּן וְהָלַךְ הַבֵּן וְהוֹלִיד בֵּן וּבַת. עַל דַּעְתֵּיהּ דְּרַב בֵּן וּבַת בֵּן וּבֵן בַּת וּבַת אֲסוּרָה. עַל דַּעְתֵּיהּ דְּרִבִּי יוֹחָנָן בַּת בֵּן אֲסוּרָה וּבַת בַּת מוּתֶּרֶת. מַתְנִיתָא פְלִיגָא עַל רַב. יִשְׂרָאֵל שֶׁנָּשָׂא חֲלָלָה בִּתּוֹ כְּשֵׁירָה לַכְּהוּנָּה. פָּתַר לָהּ חֲלָלָה מִבָּנָהּ. מַתְנִיתָא פְלִיגָא עַל

רִבִּי יוֹחָנָן. רִבִּי יְהוּדָה אוֹמֵר. בַּת גֵּר זָכָר כְּבַת חָלָל זָכָר. פָּתַר לָהּ. לֹא בָא רִבִּי יוּדָה אֶלָּא לְהוֹסִיף. אִילוּ אָמַר. בַּת חָלָל כְּבַת גֵּר. יֵאוּת.

"The daughter of a desecrated priest," etc. Rav Hamnuna in the name of Rav: Daughter, daughter's daughter, forever[153]. Rebbi Johanan in the name of Rebbi Ismael: "In his clans." Since by "in his clans" said there males are forbidden and females permitted, so by "in his clans" said here males are forbidden and females permitted[164]. What is the difference between them[165]? A Cohen who came to a divorcee and fathered a son; the son went and fathered a son and a daughter. In the opinion of Rav the son, the son's daughter, the daughter's son, and the daughter are forbidden[166]. In the opinion of Rebbi Johanan the son's daughter is forbidden, the daughter's son is permitted[167]. The Mishnah disagrees with Rav: "The daughter of an Israel who married a desecrated woman is qualified for the priesthood." He explains it, a broomstick desecrated one[168]. The Mishnah disagrees with Rebbi Johanan: "Rebbi Jehudah says, the daughter of a male proselyte is like the daughter of a desecrated priest.[169]" He explains that Rebbi Jehudah only comes to add[170]. If he had said that the daughter of a desecrated priest is like the daughter of a male proselyte, you would have had a point.

163   All descendants of a desecrated priest are desecrated, both male and female, for all generations.

164   In *Lev.* 21:1 it is stated that a Cohen may not defile himself by impurity "in his clans". A female member of a priestly family is under no such constraint. It is claimed that in v. 4, in which a Cohen is warned not to enter a marriage which would desecrate him, the expression "in his clans" similarly frees female members of a priestly family from the disability of desecration.

165   Rav and R. Johanan.

166   In fact, all descendants in all

degrees are desecrated.

167 Following the Mishnah, if she married an Israel or a Levite.

168 Rav will hold to his position that all descendants of a desecrated priest remain desecrated and the females forbidden to the priesthood. But he notes that there is a category of desecrated women who are not descendants of desecrated priests, viz., women having had sexual relations with men whom they could not have married (such as women raped by Gentiles.) He will agree that the daughter of such a woman, whom he calls חֲלָלָה מְבֻנָּה "broomstick desecrated", born as a regular Jew and married to an Israel, is qualified for the priesthood. (Explanation of *Qorban ha'edah*.)

Since חֲלָלָה מְבֻנָּה does not make much sense, one might read חֲלָלָה מִבִּיאָה "desecrated by intercourse."

169 Since R. Jehudah holds that Ez. 44:22 prohibits the daughter of a proselyte from an Israel mother to the priesthood, how could he agree that the daughter of a desecrated woman from an Israel is qualified for the priesthood?

170 He does not disagree with the anonymous Tanna; he only comes to add rules about proselytes not mentioned by the anonymous Tanna.

(66a line 64) דְּלָמָה. רִבִּי הוֹשַׁעְיָה רבָּא וְרִבִּי יוּדָן נְשִׂיָּיא הֲווֹן יָתְבִין. רְהִיט רִבִּי יוֹחָנָן וּלְחִישׁ לְרִבִּי הוֹשַׁעְיָה בְּאוּדְנֵיהּ. פְּצוּעַ דַּכָּא כֹּהֵן מַהוּ שֶׁיִּשָּׂא בַת גֵּרִים. אָמַר לֵיהּ. מָה אָמַר לָךְ. אָמַר לֵיהּ. אָמַר לִי מִילָּה דְּנַגָּר בַּר נַגָּרִין לֹא מְפָרֵיק לֵיהּ. לֹא אָמַר לִי גִּיוֹרֶת שֶׁהִיא כְזוֹנָה אֶצְלוֹ וְלֹא בַת יִשְׂרָאֵל שֶׁהִיא מְחַלְּלָה. לֹא אָמַר לִי אֶלָּא בַת גֵּרִים. וּבַת גֵּרִים לֹא כְיִשְׂרָאֵל הִיא. פָּתַר לָהּ כְּרִבִּי יוּדָה. אָמַר. בַּת גֵּר זָכָר כְּבַת חָלָל זָכָר.

1 רבא | ג רובה   יתבין | ג יתיבין   רהיט | ג רהט   2 ולחיש | ג ולחש   לר' הושיה באודניה | ג באודנא דר' הושיה רובה   3 אמ' לי | ג -   4 מחללה | ג כחללה   5 אמ' | ג דר' יודה אמ'

[171]Example. The elder Rebbi Hoshaia and Rebbi Judah Neśia were sitting together. Rebbi Johanan ran und whispered into Rebbi Hoshaia's ear: May a Cohen who is injured in his testicles marry the daughter of

converts? He asked him, what did he tell you? He answered, a question which a carpenter, son of carpenters, cannot resolve. He did not ask me about a convert, since she is like a whore for him. He did not ask about an Israelite daughter, whom he will desecrate. He asked only about the daughter of converts! Is the daughter of converts not an Israel? You have to explain it following Rebbi Jehudah, who said, the daughter of a male convert has the status of the daughter of a desecrated male.

171 From here to the end of the Halakhah, the text is from *Yebamot* 8:2 (ב), explained in Notes 156-164; partially from *Bikkurim* 1:5 (ד), Notes 87-106. The Leiden ms. in *Bikkurim* only notes the first few words and then writes "one continues this in *Qiddušin* 4:7." The full text was added by someone who prepared the ms. for the Venice printer; that text must have come from another ms. since not all deviations from L can be explained by copyists' errors.

(66a line 70) כֹּהֵן שֶׁבָּא עַל הַגְּרוּשָׁה וְהוֹלִיד בַּת. בַּת בַּת מָה הִיא. רִבִּי חֲנַנְיָה וְרִבִּי מָנָא. חַד אָמַר כְּשֵׁירָה וְחַד אָמַר פְּסוּלָה. מָתִיב מָאן דְּאָמַר כְּשֵׁירָה לְמָאן דְּאָמַר פְּסוּלָה. בַּת חָלָל זָכָר אֵינָהּ פְּסוּלָה. וַחֲלָלָה מִבְּנָהּ אֵינָהּ פְּסוּלָה מִשֵּׁם מַה הִיא פְּסוּלָה.

[172]If a Cohen had intercourse with a divorcee and fathered a daughter, what is the status of the daughter's daughter[173]? Rebbi Hanania and Rebbi Mana, one said she is qualified[174], the other said she is disqualified[175]. The one who said that she is qualified asked the one who said that she is disqualified: Is the daughter of a male desecrated priest not disqualified[176]? Is the broomstick desecrated one not disqualified[177]? Why is she disqualified[178]?

172 This paragraph is not a copy of the corresponding paragraph in *Yebamot* (גּ Note 171).
173 Assuming the mother was married to an Israel.
174 Following R. Johanan.
175 Following Rav.
176 This is explicit in the Mishnah.
177 Mishnah *Yebamot* 6:5.
178 Since she is qualified by Mishnah 3:14, she does not appear in any list of disqualified women. (Cf. Note 168.)

(66a line 74) רִבִּי אֱלִיעֶזֶר בֶּן יַעֲקֹב אוֹמֵר כול׳. תַּמָּן תַּנִּינָן. רִבִּי אֱלִיעֶזֶר בֶּן יַעֲקֹב אוֹמֵר. הָאִשָּׁה בַת גֵּרִים לֹא תִינָּשֵׂא לִכְהוּנָּה עַד שֶׁתְּהֵא אִמָּהּ מִיִּשְׂרָאֵל. וְכוּלְּהוּ מִקְרָא אֶחָד דָּרְשׁוּ. כִּי אִם בְּתוּלוֹת מִזֶּרַע בֵּית יִשְׂרָאֵל. רִבִּי יוּדָה אוֹמֵר עַד שֶׁיְּהֵא אָבִיהָ מִיִּשְׂרָאֵל. רִבִּי לִיעֶזֶר בֶּן יַעֲקֹב אוֹמֵר. עַד שֶׁיְּהֵא אוֹ אָבִיהָ אוֹ אִמָּהּ מִיִּשְׂרָאֵל. רִבִּי יוֹסֵי אוֹמֵר עַד שֶׁיִּיוָּלְדוּ בִקְדוּשַׁת יִשְׂרָאֵל. רִבִּי שִׁמְעוֹן אוֹמֵר עַד שֶׁיָּבוֹאוּ בְתוּלִים בִּקְדוּשַׁת יִשְׂרָאֵל. תַּנֵּי בְשֵׁם רִבִּי שִׁמְעוֹן. גִּיּוֹרֶת שֶׁנִּתְגַּיְיְרָה פְחוּתָה מִבַּת שָׁלֹשׁ שָׁנִים וְיוֹם אֶחָד כְּשֵׁירָה לִכְהוּנָּה. מַה טַעַם. וְכָל־הַטַּף בַּנָּשִׁים אֲשֶׁר לֹא יָדְעוּ מִשְׁכַּב זָכָר הַחֲיוּ לָכֶם. וּפִינְחָס עִמָּהֶן. מָה עָבְדִין לֵיהּ רַבָּנִין. הַחֲיוּ לָכֶם. לַעֲבָדִים וְלִשְׁפָחוֹת.

3 וכולהו | ר וכולהון   דרשו | ר הן דורשין   יודה | ר יהודה   4 אביה | ר אמה   ליעזר בן יעקב | ר אלעזר   עד שיהא | ר -   5 מיש׳ | ר -   שיוולדו | ר שיולדו   6 שיבואו | ר שיביאו   7 שנתגייירה פחותה מבת שלש שנים ויום אחד | ר פחותה מבת שלש שנים ויום אחד שנתגייירה   מה טע׳ | ר שנא׳   9 מה עבדין ליה רבנין | ר ורבנין

"Rebbi Eliezer ben Jacob says," etc. There, we have stated: "Rebbi Eliezer ben Jacob says, the daughter of proselytes should not marry into the priesthood unless her mother be from Israel" They all interpret the same verse (*Ez.* 44:22): "Only virgins from the seed of the House of Israel." Rebbi Jehudah says, unless his father be from Israel. Rebbi Eliezer ben Jacob says, either her father or her mother. Rebbi Yose says, unless they are born in the holiness of Israel. Rebbi Simeon says, unless they grow the hymen in the holiness of Israel. It was stated in the name of Rebbi Simeon: "A girl which became a proselyte being less than three years and one day of age is acceptable for the priesthood since it was said (*Num.* 31:18): 'All the female children unfit for sleeping with a male you shall let live for yourselves,' and Phineas was with them." How do the rabbis explain? You shall let live as slaves and slave girls for yourselves.

(6Eb line 9) רִבִּי יוֹסֵה רִבִּי יָסָא בְּשֵׁם רִבִּי יוֹחָנָן רִבִּי יוֹנָה רִבִּי חִייָה בְּשֵׁם רִבִּי יוֹחָנָן. הֲלָכָה כְּרִבִּי יוֹסֵה. חָנִין בַּר בָּא בְּשֵׁם רַב. הֲלָכָה כְּרִבִּי יוֹסֵי. וְהַכֹּהֲנִים נָהֲגוּ כְּרִבִּי אֱלְעָזֶר בֶּן יַעֲקֹב. חַד כֹּהֵן נְסַב בַּת גֵּרִים. אֲתָא עוֹבְדָא קוֹמֵי רִבִּי אֲבָהוּ וְאַרְבְּעֵיהּ אֲסַפְסְלֵיהּ. אָמַר לֵיהּ רִבִּי בֵּיבַי. לֹא כֵן אַלְפָן רִבִּי. הֲלָכָה כְּרִבִּי יוֹסֵי. אָמַר לֵיהּ. וְלֹא נָהֲגוּ הַכֹּהֲנִים כְּרִבִּי אֱלְעָזֶר בֶּן יַעֲקֹב. אָמַר לֵיהּ. רִבִּי. וְעַל הַמִּנְהָג לוֹקִין. אָמַר לֵיהּ אֵין כֵּינִי אַתְּ חֲמֵי מְפַייֵיס וַאֲנָא מוֹקִים לֵיהּ. מִן דְּקַיְימֵי אָמַר לֵיהּ. הוֹאִיל וְהוּתְּרָה הָרְצוּעָה אַף אֲנִי מוּתָּר בָּהּ.

1 ר' יוסד | ר - יסא | ר יסה ר' יונה ר' חייה בשם ר' יוחנן | ר - 2 חנין בר בא בשם רב הלכה כר' יוסי | ר - והכהנים | ר כוהנים 3 נהגו | ר נהגו סלסול בעצמן 4 על ספסילא | ר אספסליה ר' | ר רב אלפן | ר אלפון 5 נהגו כהנים | ר כהנים נהגו סלסול בעצמן בן יעקב | ר - ר' | ר - 6 המנהג | ר מנהג כיני | ר כך ואנא | ר לי ואנא מן | ר מה דקיימי | ᵛ דק' ᵛ דקיימא

Rebbi Yose, Rebbi Yasa in the name of Rebbi Johanan; Rebbi Jonah, Rebbi Hiyya in the name of Rebbi Johanan: Practice follows Rebbi Yose. Hanin bar Abba in the name of Rav: Practice follows Rebbi Yose, but Cohanim are used to follow Rebbi Eliezer ben Jacob. A Cohen married the daughter of proselytes. The case came before Rebbi Abbahu who let him kneel before the low bench. Rebbi Bevai said to him, did the Rabbi not teach us that practice follows Rebbi Yose? He answered, but are not Cohanim used to follow Rebbi Eliezer ben Jacob? He retorted, Rebbi, does one whip because of what one is used to do? He said to him, if you look at it in such a way, you have appeased me and I shall let him get up. After he got up, he said to him, since the lash was withdrawn I am permitted to have her.

(66b line 16) רִבִּי יַעֲקֹב בַּר אִידִי בְּשֵׁם רִבִּי יְהוֹשֻׁעַ בֶּן לֵוִי. מַעֲשֶׂה בְּשִׁפְחָה בְּדָרוֹם שֶׁהָיוּ קוֹרִין עָלֶיהָ עִרְעֵר וְשָׁלַח רִבִּי אֶת רוֹמִינוֹס לְבוֹדְקָהּ. וּבָדַק וּמָצָא שֶׁנִּתְגַּיְּירָה זְקֵינָתָהּ פְּחוּתָה מִבַּת שָׁלֹשׁ שָׁנִים וְיוֹם אֶחָד וְהִכְשִׁירָהּ לִכְהוּנָה. רַב הוֹשַׁעְיָה אָמַר. כְּרִבִּי שִׁמְעוֹן הִכְשִׁירוּהּ. אָמַר רִבִּי זְעִירָא. דִּבְרֵי הַכֹּל הִיא. הָכָא דְּאָמַר רִבִּי זְעִירָא בְּשֵׁם רַב אָדָא בַּר אַחֲוָה רִבִּי יוּדָן מַטֵּי בָהּ בְּשֵׁם רַב רִבִּי אַבָּהוּ בְּשֵׁם רִבִּי יוֹחָנָן. וָלָד בּוֹגֶרֶת כָּשֵׁר שֶׁהוּא בְּלֹא תַעֲשֶׂה שֶׁהוּא מִכֹּחַ עֲשֵׂה. וְהוּא אִשָּׁה בִּבְתוּלֶיהָ יִקַּח לֹא בּוֹגֶרֶת. כָּל־לֹא תַעֲשֶׂה שֶׁהוּא בָּא מִכֹּחַ עֲשֵׂה עֲשֵׂה הוּא. וְדִכְוָותָהּ כִּי אִם בְּתוּלָה מֵעַמָּיו יִקַּח אִשָּׁה. לֹא גִיּוֹרֶת. כָּל־לֹא תַעֲשֶׂה שֶׁהוּא בָּא מִכֹּחַ עֲשֵׂה עֲשֵׂה הוּא. הָתִיב רִבִּי הוֹשַׁעְיָה. הֲרֵי דּוֹר שֵׁנִי שֶׁלְּמִצְרִי הֲרֵי הוּא בְּלֹא תַעֲשֶׂה שֶׁהוּא בָּא מִכֹּחַ עֲשֵׂה. עֲשֵׂה הוּא. חָזַר רִבִּי הוֹשַׁעְיָה וְאָמַר. לֹא דוֹמֶה עֲשֶׂה שֶׁבְּיִשְׂרָאֵל לַעֲשֵׂה שֶׁבַּכֹּהֲנִים. עֲשֵׂה שֶׁבְּיִשְׂרָאֵל אָסוּר בַּכֹּל. עֲשֵׂה שֶׁבַּכֹּהֲנִים אָסוּר בַּכֹּהֲנִים וּמוּתָּר בִּלְוִיִּים וּבְיִשְׂרָאֵל.

1 שפחה | ג משפחה   בדרום | ג אחת ברודוס   2 רומינוס | ג רומנוס   לבודקה | ר לבודקן   3 זקינתה | ג זקנתה   פחותתה | ג פחות   4 הכשירוה | גר הכשירה   5 זעירא | ג זעירה   אחוה | ג אחווה   יודן | ר יודא   רב. ר' אבהו | ר ר' אבהו   6 ולד | ר ולד   שהוא | שבא   עשה | ר עשה עשה   7 לא בוגרת | ר - ג ולא בוגרת   שהוא בא | גר שבא   8 לא | גר ולא   גיורת | ג בוגרת   9 שהוא בא | גר שבא   הושעיה | ר הושעיא   שלמצרי | ג למצרי   הרי הוא | ג שהוא   10 שהוא בא | ר שבא   11 דומה | ר דמי   שבישי' | ר ביש'   12 בלויים | ר בלוים

Rebbi Jacob bar Idi in the name of Rebbi Joshua ben Levi: It happened that a family in the South had a bad reputation. Rebbi sent Romanus to investigate them. He investigated and found that a grandmother had been converted at less than three years and a day of age, and he declared them fit for the priesthood. Rav Hoshaia said, he declared them fit following Rebbi Simeon Rebbi Ze'ira said, here it is everybody's opinion since Rebbi Ze'ira said in the name of Rav Ada bar Ahava, Rebbi Judan brings it in the name of Rebbi Abbahu in the name of Rebbi Johanan: The child of an adult is fit since it is a prohibition deduced from a positive commandment. (*Lev.* 21:13) "But he shall take a wife in her virginity." Any prohibition deduced from a positive commandment is a positive commandment. Analogously, (*Lev.* 21:14) "only a virgin from amidst his people he shall take as wife," not a proselyte. Is any prohibition deduced from a positive commandment a positive commandment? Rebbi Hoshaia objected: But the second generation of an Egyptian is a prohibition deduced from a positive commandment! Rebbi Hoshaia turned around and said, a positive commandment for Israel cannot be compared to a positive commandment for Cohanim. A positive commandment for Israel implies a prohibition for everybody. A positive commandment for Cohanim implies a prohibition for Cohanim but a permission for Levites and Israel.

(Col. 65a) **משנה ז**: הָאוֹמֵר בְּנִי זֶה מַמְזֵר אֵינוֹ נֶאֱמָן. וַאֲפִילוּ שְׁנֵיהֶן אוֹמְרִין עַל הָעוּבָּר שֶׁבְּמֵעֶיהָ מַמְזֵר הוּא אֵינָן נֶאֱמָנִין. רַבִּי יְהוּדָה אוֹמֵר נֶאֱמָנִין.

Mishnah 7: If somebody says, this my son is a bastard, he cannot be believed[179]. Even if both of them say about the fetus in her belly that he is a bastard, they cannot be believed[180]. Rebbi Jehudah says, they are believed[181].

179 Since a father is a relative of his wife's child, he is unable to testify about him.

180 Both parents agree. They cannot testify even before the child's birth when the child does not yet have a personality in the legal sense that the formal rules of testimony would be applicable to him.

181 Even the father alone is able to declare his son illegitimate by the power invested in him by *Deut.* 21:17.

(66b line 30) **הלכה ז:** הָאוֹמֵר בְּנִי זֶה מַמְזֵר אֵינוֹ נֶאֱמָן כול'. תַּמָּן תַּנִּינָן. הָאוֹמֵר. בְּנִי זֶה. נֶאֱמָן. רִבִּי אַבָּהוּ בְּשֵׁם רִבִּי יוֹחָנָן. לָתֵת לוֹ אֲבָל לֹא לִיקַח מִמֶּנּוּ. אָמַר רִבִּי יוֹסֵי. וְלָא מַתְנִיתָא הִיא. אֲפִילוּ שְׁנֵיהֶן אוֹמְרִין עַל הָעוֹבֵר שֶׁבְּמֵעֶיהָ מַמְזֵר הוּא אֵינָם נֶאֱמָנִין. דִּילְמָא עַל דְּרִבִּי יְהוּדָה אִתְאָמְרַת. דְּרִבִּי יוּדָה אוֹמֵר. נֶאֱמָנִין עָלֶיהָ. רִבִּי אַבָּהוּ בְּשֵׁם רִבִּי יוֹחָנָן. לָתֵת לוֹ אֲבָל לֹא לִיקַח מִמֶּנּוּ. אָמַר רִבִּי חִזְקִיָּה. עוֹד הִיא מַתְנִיתָא. כִּי אֶת הַבְּכוֹר בֶּן הַשְּׂנוּאָה יַכִּיר. הָיוּ מַחֲזִיקִים בּוֹ שֶׁהוּא בְנוֹ וּבִשְׁעַת מִיתָתוֹ אָמַר. אֵינוֹ בְנוֹ. אֵינוֹ נֶאֱמָן. שֶׁאֵינוֹ בְנוֹ וּבִשְׁעַת מִיתָתוֹ אָמַר. בְּנִי הוּא. נֶאֱמָן. אִית תַּנָּיֵי תַּנֵּי. עַל קַדְמְיָיתָא נֶאֱמָן. רִבִּי חִזְקִיָּה רִבִּי זְרִיקָן בְּשֵׁם רִבִּי הוּנָא. הָיוּ מַחֲזִיקִין אוֹתוֹ שֶׁהוּא מִשְׁפַּחְתּוֹ נֶאֱמָן. הָיָה עוֹמֵד בְּצַד הַמּוּכְסִין וְאָמַר. בְּנִי הוּא. וְחָזַר וְאָמַר עַבְדִּי הוּא. נֶאֱמָן. עַבְדִּי הוּא. וְחָזַר וְאָמַר בְּנִי הוּא. אֵינוֹ נֶאֱמָן. אִית תַּנָּיֵי תַּנֵּי. נֶאֱמָן. אָמַר רִבִּי מָנָא. בְּגִין אִילֵּין כּוּתָאֵי דְּינוּן מְשַׁעְבְּדִין בִּבְנֵיהֶן.

Halakhah 7: "If somebody says, this my son is a bastard, he cannot be believed," etc. There, we have stated[182]: "If somebody said, this is my son, he is to be believed." Rebbi Abbahu in the name of Rebbi Johanan: To give him[183], but not to take from him. Rebbi Yose said, is that not the Mishnah: "Even if both of them say about the fetus in her belly that he is a bastard, they cannot be believed"[184]? Maybe it[185] was said following Rebbi Jehudah, for Rebbi Jehudah said, they can be believed; Rebbi Abbahu in the name of Rebbi Johanan: To give him, but not to take from him. Rebbi Ḥizqiah said, still it is a *baraita*: "For he has to recognize the firstborn, the son of the hated one.[186]" If they[187] maintained that he was his son but at the moment of his death he said that he was not his son, he cannot be believed[188]. That he was not his son but at the moment of his death he said that he was his son, he is believed[189]. Some Tannaïm state on the first case that he is believed. Rebbi Hisqiah, Rebbi Zeriqan in the name of Rebbi Huna: If they maintained that he was from his slave girl, he is believed[190]. If he was standing next to the customs collectors[191] and said, he is my son, but later he said, he is my slave, he is believed[192]. He is my slave, but later he said, he is my son, he is not believed[193]. Some Tannaïm state, he is believed. Rebbi Mana said, because of those Samaritans[194] who use their sons as slaves.

182 Mishnah *Baba batra* 8:8, dealing with rights of inheritance.

183 Make him a legal heir.

184 The Mishnah makes the statement of R. Johanan superfluous.

185 The statement of R. Abbahu in the name of R. Johanan.

186 *Deut.* 21:17. Quoting a verse is obviously not quoting a *baraita*. Probably the *baraita* quoted in the Babli, 78b, *Sifry Deut.* 217 is meant: "'For he has to recognize the firstborn, the son of the hated one;' he has to make him recognized by others; this implies that a person is believed if he says, this son of mine is the firstborn. Rebbi Jehudah says, just as a man is believed if he says, this son of mine is the firstborn, so he is believed if he says that he is the son of a divorcee or one who had received *ḥaliṣah*, but the Sages say, he is not believed."

187 The parents.

188 Once a person has obtained public recognition as a son, the presumption of permanence of the *status quo ante* requires valid testimony by two independent witnesses to change that status; cf. *Giṭṭin* Chapter 3.

189 Since the dying person also could have given an unrelated person a part of his estate.

190 If the father acknowledged that he had fathered the child with his slave girl and everybody assumed that he had manumitted the pregnant girl in

order to be the legal father of the child but on his deathbed he acknowledged that he never manumitted the girl and, therefore, his child is not his child in Jewish law (Mishnah *Yebamot* 2:5), he must be believed since his statement now is compatible with his earlier statements.

191 When he would have to pay customs duty for the importation of a slave but not for an accompanying son.

192 We believe him that he was cheating on the customs.

193 Nobody pays custom duties which he is not obligated for.

194 In *Baba batra*: The Nabateans.

(66b line 43) תַּנֵּי. נֶאֱמָן עַל הַגָּדוֹל וְאֵינוֹ נֶאֱמָן עַל הַקָּטָן. אִי זֶהוּ גָדוֹל. רִבִּי זְעִירָא אָמַר. כָּל־שֶׁיֵּשׁ לוֹ אִשָּׁה וּבָנִים. רִבִּי אַבָּהוּ. כָּל־שֶׁיֵּשׁ לוֹ אִשָּׁה. מַתְנִיתָא פְלִיגָא עַל רִבִּי אַבָּהוּ. גֵּר שֶׁמָּל וְלֹא טָבַל וְהָיוּ לוֹ בָנִים וְאָמַר. מַלְתִּי וְלֹא טָבַלְתִּי. נֶאֱמָן וּמַטְבִּילִין אוֹתוֹ בַּשַּׁבָּת. מִשֵּׁם מֵהַנְכָּיָיה. דִּבְרֵי רַב יוּדָה. מָה עֲבַד לַהּ רִבִּי אַבָּהוּ. פָּתַר לָהּ. מִשּׁוּם מַה בְכָךְ.

It was stated[195]: He is believed about the adult but is not believed about the young[196]. Who is adult? Rebbi Ze'ira said, any one who has a wife and children; Rebbi Abbahu, any one who has a wife[197]. A *baraita*[198] disagrees with Rebbi Abbahu: A proselyte who was circumcised but did not immerse himself[199] but has children; if he said, I was circumcised but did not immerse, he is believed and one immerses him even on the Sabbath because of parsimony[200], the words of Rav[201] Jehudah. What does Rebbi Abbahu do with this[202]? He explains it, because who cares[203]?

195 According to the Tosephta, 5:5, the author of this statement is R. Jehudah.

196 It is clear that this sentence is corrupt and one must read: He is believed about the young but is not believed about the adult. Even R. Jehudah will agree that the Torah gives the father only the right to recognize or to refuse to recognize his child; the moment other people are involved, the usual rules of judicial

proof must apply. Since the father does not have the right to declare his grandchildren as bastards he has lost the right to declare his child a bastard the moment the child has children.

197 Since by declaring his son a bastard, the father would forbid the son to his daughter-in-law; he would infringe upon the rights of a third party and cannot be believed.

198 Also quoted in the Babli, *Yebamot* 47b.

199 He is Jewish for R. Jehudah but still Gentile for R. Yose.

200 To avoid problems with handling food when he or his family are present. Since for R. Yose, immersion of a circumcised proselyte changes him from Gentile to Jew, this could not be done on the Sabbath. One has to assume that the father admitted that he never was immersed only after he and his children already were known as Jews. Then he can no longer testify to disqualify his children from prospective Jewish marriages; he must be accepted as a Jew.

201 This certainly must read "Rebbi" since the Babylonian Amora Rav Jehudah cannot be the author of a *baraita*.

202 Since the *baraita* implies that one immerses him on the Sabbath only because he has children; does this not prove R. Ze'ira's point?

203 Since the author of the *baraita* is R. Jehudah for whom immersion is unnecessary, there is no problem of Sabbath desecration involved and he will agree that in order to satisfy even the followers of R. Yose, the proselyte should immerse himself at the first opportunity. This explanation is attributed to R. Jehudah himself in the Babli, *loc. cit.*

(fol. 65a) **משנה ח:** מִי שֶׁנָּתַן רְשׁוּת לִשְׁלוּחוֹ לְקַדֵּשׁ אֶת בִּתּוֹ וְהָלַךְ הוּא וְקִידְּשָׁהּ אִם שֶׁלּוֹ קָדְמוּ קִידּוּשָׁיו קִידּוּשִׁין וְאִם שֶׁלִּשְׁלוּחוֹ קָדַם קִידּוּשָׁיו קִידּוּשִׁין וְאִם אֵינוֹ יָדוּעַ שְׁנֵיהֶן נוֹתְנִין גֵּט וְאִם רָצוּ אֶחָד נוֹתֵן גֵּט וְאֶחָד כּוֹנֵס.

Mishnah 8: If somebody empowered his agent to contract preliminary marriage for his daughter and then went himself and contracted for her, if he was first, his preliminary marriage is valid[204], but if his agent was first, that preliminary marriage is valid[205]. If precedence cannot be established, both give a bill of divorce or, if they agree, one gives a bill of divorce and one marries definitively.

[204] Appointing an agent does not abolish the intrinsic right of a father to contract for his underage daughter's marriage (to a different person).

[205] If the father himself would marry his daughter successively to two different men, the second marriage would be nonexistent. The actions of father and agent can be considered as if all were actions of the father himself.

(66b line 49) **הלכה ח:** מִי שֶׁנָּתַן רְשׁוּת לִשְׁלוּחוֹ כול'. תַּנֵּי. אִישׁ וְאִשָּׁה שֶׁבָּאוּ מִמְּדִינַת הַיָּם. הוּא אוֹמֵר. אִשְׁתִּי הִיא. וְהִיא אוֹמֶרֶת. בַּעֲלִי הוּא. אֵין הוֹרְגִין עֲלֵיהֶן מִשּׁוּם אֵשֶׁת אִישׁ. הוּחְזְקוּ. הוֹרְגִין עֲלֵיהֶן מִשּׁוּם אֵשֶׁת אִישׁ. עַד כַּמָּה הִיא חֲזָקָה. רִבִּי יוֹנָה רִבִּי בָּא רִבִּי חִייָה בְּשֵׁם רִבִּי יוֹחָנָן. עַד שְׁלֹשִׁים יוֹם. תַּמָּן תַּנִּינָן. תִּינוֹק שֶׁנִּמְצָא בְיַד הָעִיסָּה וּבָצֵק בְּיָדוֹ. רִבִּי מֵאִיר מְטַהֵר וַחֲכָמִים מְטַמְּאִין. שֶׁדֶּרֶךְ תִּינוֹק לְטַפֵּחַ בָּעִיסָּה. וְשׂוֹרְפִין עַל הַחֲזָקוֹת. רִבִּי יוֹסֵי בְּשֵׁם רִבִּי זְעִירָא. אִיתְפַּלְגוֹן רִבִּי יוֹחָנָן וְרִבִּי שִׁמְעוֹן בֶּן לָקִישׁ. רִבִּי יוֹחָנָן אָמַר. הוֹרְגִין עַל הַחֲזָקוֹת. וְרִבִּי שִׁמְעוֹן בֶּן לָקִישׁ אָמַר. אֵין הוֹרְגִין עַל הַחֲזָקוֹת. רִבִּי יוֹסֵי בֵּירִבִּי בּוּן בְּשֵׁם רִבִּי זְעִירָא. כָּל־עַמָּא מוֹדַיי שֶׁהוֹרְגִין עַל הַחֲזָקוֹת. מַה פְלִיגִין. בַּשְׂרֵיפָה. רִבִּי יוֹחָנָן אָמַר. הוֹרְגִין עַל הַחֲזָקוֹת וְאֵין שׂוֹרְפִין עַל הַחֲזָקוֹת. רִבִּי שִׁמְעוֹן בֶּן לָקִישׁ אָמַר. כְּשֵׁם שֶׁהוֹרְגִין עַל הַחֲזָקוֹת כָּךְ שׂוֹרְפִין עַל הַחֲזָקוֹת. וּמְנַיְין שֶׁהוֹרְגִין עַל הַחֲזָקוֹת. רִבִּי שְׁמוּאֵל בְּרֵיהּ דְּרִבִּי יוֹסֵי בֵּירִבִּי בּוּן אָמַר. כָּתוּב וּמַכֵּה אָבִיו וְאִמּוֹ מוֹת יוּמָת. וְכִי דָבָר בָּרִיא הוּא שֶׁזֶּה הוּא אָבִיו. וַהֲלֹא חֲזָקָה הִיא שֶׁהוּא אָבִיו. וְאַתְּ אָמַר. הוֹרְגִין. אַף הָכָא הוֹרְגִין.

[206] **Halakhah 8:** "If somebody empowered his agent," etc. It was stated: "If a man and a woman come from overseas; he says, she is my wife, and

she says, he is my husband. One will not execute anybody because of her being a married woman[207]. If they become generally known[208], one will execute because of her being a married woman." How long does it take to be generally known? Rebbi Jonah, Rebbi Abba, Rebbi Hiyya in the name of Rebbi Johanan: Up to thirty days[209]. There[210], we have stated: "A toddler who is found near cake-dough with a piece of dough in his hand[211], Rebbi Meïr declares pure[212] but the Sages declare it impure, for toddlers will slap their hands on cake-dough[213]." Does one burn because of general knowledge[214]? Rebbi Yose in the name of Rebbi Ze'ira: Rebbi Johanan and Rebbi Simeon ben Laqish disagree. Rebbi Johanan said, one executes because of general knowledge. Rebbi Simeon ben Laqish said, one does not execute because of general knowledge. Rebbi Yose ben Rebbi Abun in the name of Rebbi Ze'ira: Everybody agrees that one executes because of general knowledge. Where do they disagree? About burning. Rebbi Johanan said, one executes because of general knowledge but one does not burn because of general knowledge[215]. Rebbi Simeon ben Laqish said, since one executes because of general knowledge, one also burns because of general knowledge. And from where that one executes because of general knowledge? Rebbi Samuel, the son of Rebbi Yose ben Rebbi Abun said, it is written[216]: "He who hits his father or his mother shall be put to death." But is it certain that this one is his father? Is it not only general knowledge that he is his father[217]? But it says, one executes. So here also[218] one executes.

206 In the ms. but not in *editio princeps*, Halakhah 8 follows Halakhah 10. The theme of Halakhah 8 agrees better with Mishnah 10 than with Mishnah 8.

207 If somebody commits adultery

with the woman, he cannot be prosecuted in the absence of proof (by witnesses or documents) that the woman actually is a wife, not a concubine.

208 Public knowledge creates *prima facie* evidence which is valid as long as it is not rebutted by legal proof to the contrary; cf. *Ketubot* 5:5, Note 100.

209 Once a couple has lived in town as husband and wife for thirty days, adultery by another man with the wife is a capital crime since it seems unlikely that she would be able to prove that she is not married. Once *prima facie* evidence is established, husband and wife are barred from testifying in the matter since they are presumed related to each other.

210 Mishnah *Ṭahorot* 3:8.

211 The dough is supposed to be made in the purity of heave. The toddler is assumed to be impure unless he was immersed in a *miqweh* and then watched every moment lest he touch anything which would make him impure. If the toddler took the cake dough by himself, the cake dough is impure. If it is known that he was handed the piece of dough by a pure adult, the rest of the cake dough remains pure.

212 R. Meïr is reluctant to accept that anything which happens most of the time happens all the time unless the contrary be known. Since some toddlers do not touch anything impure and some toddlers do not play with dough if they see it, it is not said that the cake dough has to be impure.

213 The cake dough is impure by *prima facie* evidence unless proven to be otherwise.

214 If the cake dough was made of heave material.

215 Babli 80a; cf. also *Demay* 6:6, Note 138.

216 *Ex.* 21:15.

217 This is not really a proof since fatherhood is not only a matter of public knowledge but also of probability since "most intercourse of an adulteress is still with her husband" (*Soṭah*, Yerushalmi 1:7 Note 265, Babli 27a; Tosephta *Yebamot* 12:8.)

218 In the matter of the couple who married at another place and declare themselves husband and wife; Babli 80a.

(fol. 65a) **משנה ט:** וְכֵן הָאִשָּׁה שֶׁנָּתְנָה רְשׁוּת לִשְׁלוּחָהּ לְקַדְּשָׁהּ וְהָלְכָה וְקִידְּשָׁה אֶת עַצְמָהּ אִם שֶׁלָּהּ קָדְמוּ קִידּוּשֶׁיהָ קִידּוּשִׁין וְאִם שֶׁלִּשְׁלוּחָהּ קָדַם קִידּוּשָׁיו קִידּוּשִׁין וְאִם אֵינוֹ יָדוּעַ שְׁנֵיהֶן נוֹתְנִין גֵּט וְאִם רָצוּ אֶחָד נוֹתֵן גֵּט וְאֶחָד כּוֹנֵס.

Mishnah 9: Similarly, if a woman empowered her agent to contract preliminary marriage for her and then went and contracted for herself, if she was first, her preliminary marriage is valid[204], but if her agent's was first, that preliminary marriage is valid[205]. If precedence cannot be established, both give a bill of divorce or, if they agree, one gives a bill of divorce and one marries definitively.

(66b line 49) **הלכה ט:** וְכֵן הָאִשָּׁה שֶׁנָּתְנָה רְשׁוּת כול׳. וְלֵית הָדָא פְּלִיגָא עַל רִבִּי יוֹחָנָן. דְּרִבִּי יוֹחָנָן אָמַר. אָדָם מְבַטֵּל שְׁלִיחוּתוֹ בִּדְבָרִים. פָּתַר לָהּ. מִשּׁוּם חוּמְרָא דַעֲרָיוֹת. רִבִּי יוֹסֵה בֵּירְבִּי בּוּן שָׁמַע לָהּ מִן דְּבַתְרָהּ. וְכֵן הָאִשָּׁה שֶׁנָּתְנָה רְשׁוּת לִשְׁלוּחָהּ לְקַדְּשָׁהּ וְהָלְכָה הִיא וְקִידְּשָׁה אֶת עַצְמָהּ. וְלֵית הָדָא פְּלִיגָא עַל רִבִּי יוֹחָנָן. דְּרִבִּי יוֹחָנָן אָמַר. אָדָם מְבַטֵּל שְׁלִיחוּתוֹ בִּדְבָרִים. פָּתַר לָהּ. מִשּׁוּם חוּמְרָא הוּא בָּעֲרָיוֹת.

Halakhah 9: "Similarly, if a woman empowered her agent," etc. [219]Does this not disagree with Rebbi Johanan, since Rebbi Johanan said that a person invalidates agency by a declaration? He explains it by the stringency of the rules of adultery and incest. Rebbi Yose ben Rebbi Abun understood this from the latter part: "Similarly, if a woman empowered her agent to contract preliminary marriage for her and then went and contracted for herself." Does this not disagree with Rebbi Johanan, since Rebbi Johanan said that a person invalidates agency by a declaration? He explains it by the stringency of the rules of adultery and incest.

219 Since the argument is repeated for Mishnah 9, it is clear that the Halakhah refers both to Mishnah 8 and Mishnah 9. The statement of R. Johanan is in *Gittin* 4:1, see Notes 2-3 there for explanation.

(fol. 65a) **משנה י**: מִי שֶׁיָּצָא הוּא וְאִשְׁתּוֹ לִמְדִינַת הַיָּם וּבָא הוּא וְאִשְׁתּוֹ וּבָנָיו וְאָמַר אִשָּׁה שֶׁיָּצָאת עִמִּי לִמְדִינַת הַיָּם הֲרֵי הִיא זוֹ וְאֵילּוּ בָנֶיהָ אֵינוֹ צָרִיךְ לְהָבִיא רְאָיָה לֹא עַל הָאִשָּׁה וְלֹא עַל הַבָּנִים. מֵתָה וְאֵילּוּ בָנֶיהָ צָרִיךְ לְהָבִיא רְאָיָה עַל הַבָּנִים וְאֵינוֹ מֵבִיא רְאָיָה עַל הָאִשָּׁה.

אִשָּׁה נָשָׂאתִי בִּמְדִינַת הַיָּם הֲרֵי הִיא זוֹ וְאֵילּוּ בָנֶיהָ מֵבִיא רְאָיָה עַל הָאִשָּׁה וְאֵינוֹ צָרִיךְ לְהָבִיא רְאָיָה עַל בָּנֶיהָ. מֵתָה וְאֵילּוּ בָנֶיהָ צָרִיךְ לְהָבִיא רְאָיָה עַל הָאִשָּׁה וְעַל הַבָּנִים.

Mishnah 10: If somebody left for overseas together with his wife; he returns with his wife and her children and says, "the wife with whom I left for overseas is this one and those are her children,"[220] he does not have to bring proof either about the wife[221] or the children. "She died and those are her children," he has to bring proof about the children[222] but not about the wife.

"I married a wife overseas, this is she and those are her children," he has to bring proof about the wife[223] but not about her children. "She died and those are her children," he has bring proof both about the wife and about the children.

220 A Cohen who wants to find matches for his children as members of the priestly clan.

221 Even if nobody recognizes her anymore.

222 That they are the children of his legal wife.

223 That she is of those whom he legally could marry.

(66b line 70) **הלכה י:** מִי שֶׁיָּצָא הוּא וְאִשְׁתּוֹ לִמְדִינַת הַיָּם כול'. רִבִּי אַבָּהוּ בְּשֵׁם רִבִּי יוֹחָנָן. אִישׁ וְאִשְׁתּוֹ עָשׂוּ אוֹתָן כִּשְׁנֵי עֵדִים. חֲזָקָה אֵין אִשָּׁה שׁוֹתֶקֶת עַל בְּנֵי חֲבֵירָתָהּ. רִבִּי אָבוּן שָׁמַע לָהּ מִן דְּבַתְרָהּ. אִשָּׁה נָשָׂאתִי בִּמְדִינַת הַיָּם הֲרֵי זוֹ וְאֵילּוּ בָנֶיהָ. רִבִּי אַבָּהוּ בְּשֵׁם רִבִּי יוֹחָנָן. אִישׁ וְאִשְׁתּוֹ עָשׂוּ אוֹתָן כִּשְׁנֵי עֵדִים. חֲזָקָה אֵין אִשָּׁה שׁוֹתֶקֶת עַל בְּנֵי חֲבֵירָתָהּ.

Halakhah 10: "If somebody left for overseas together with his wife," etc. Rebbi Abbahu in the name of Rebbi Johanan: They considered a man and his wife as two witnesses[224] since it is general knowledge that a woman will not be silent about another woman's children. Rebbi Abun referred this to the later statement: "I married a wife overseas, this is she and those are her children;" Rebbi Abbahu in the name of Rebbi Johanan: They considered a man and his wife as two witnesses since it is general knowledge that a woman will not be silent about another woman's children[225].

224 In order to let a person marry a Jewish partner, the court will need to have either generally accepted knowledge that the person is Jewish and is not a bastard, or to require testimony to this effect. A man and his wife are really barred from testifying about their children but since a woman is not supposed to raise another woman's children as her own, her assertion can be believed.

225 Therefore, once the foreign woman has been accepted as his legitimate wife, no proof is needed about the children. In the language of the Tosephta (5:8): "A woman is believed if she says: These are my children."

(66b line 75) **הלכה יא:** אִשָּׁה נָשָׂאתִי בִּמְדִינַת הַיָּם. תַּנֵּי. הֵבִיא רְאָייָה עַל הַגְּדוֹלִים יָבִיא רְאָייָה עַל הַקְּטַנִּים. לְיֵי דָא מִילָּה. אָמַר רִבִּי יוֹנָה. אֲנִי אוֹמֵר שֶׁמָּה נִתְגָּרְשָׁה בֵּינְתַיִם.

Halakhah 11: ""I married a wife overseas." It was stated: If he brought proof about the older ones[226], he still has to bring proof about the younger ones. Why? Rebbi Jonah said, I say that perhaps she was divorced in the meantime[227].

226 If the wife had died.

227 They could be children of the same woman but the older ones would be priests, the younger ones desecrated as children of a divorcee married to a priest. The Babli, 79b, disagrees and holds that once the wife has been found acceptable for the priesthood, no proof about her children is needed. It refers "older" and "younger" to children from different mothers.

(fol. 65a) **משנה יא:** לֹא יִתְיַיחֵד אִישׁ אֶחָד עִם שְׁתֵּי נָשִׁים אֲבָל אִשָּׁה אַחַת מִתְיַיחֶדֶת עִם שְׁתֵּי אֲנָשִׁים. רִבִּי שִׁמְעוֹן אוֹמֵר מִתְיַיחֵד עִם שְׁתֵּי נָשִׁים בִּזְמַן שֶׁאִשְׁתּוֹ עִמּוֹ וְיָשֵׁן עִמָּהֶן בְּפוּנְדָּקִי מִפְּנֵי שֶׁאִשְׁתּוֹ מְשַׁמַּרְתּוֹ. מִתְיַיחֵד אָדָם עִם אִמּוֹ וְעִם בִּתּוֹ וְיָשֵׁן עִמָּהֶן בְּקֵירוּב בָּשָׂר. וְאִם הִגְדִּילוּ זֶה יָשֵׁן בִּכְסוּתוֹ וְזֶה יָשֵׁן בִּכְסוּתוֹ.

Mishnah 11: One man should not be alone with two women[228] but one woman may be alone with two men. Rebbi Simeon says, he may be alone with two women as long as his wife is with him; he can sleep with them in a hostelry[229] because his wife will watch over him. A man can be alone with his mother or his daughter and sleep with them with their skins touching; once they grew up each one sleeps in his garment.

וְלֹא יְלַמֵּד רַוָּוק סוֹפְרִים וְלֹא תְלַמֵּד אִשָּׁה סוֹפְרִים. רִבִּי אֱלִיעֶזֶר אוֹמֵר אַף מִי שֶׁאֵין לוֹ אִשָּׁה לֹא יְלַמֵּד סוֹפְרִים.

And a bachelor shall not be a school teacher[230]; a woman shall not be a school teacher. Rebbi Eliezer says, also a man without a wife shall not be a school teacher.[231]

רִבִּי יְהוּדָה אוֹמֵר לֹא יִרְעֶה רַוָּק אֶת הַבְּהֵמָה. וְלֹא יִישְׁנוּ שְׁנֵי רַוָּקִים בְּטַלִּית אַחַת וַחֲכָמִים מַתִּירִים.

Rebbi Jehudah says, a bachelor shall not be a shepherd and two bachelors shall not sleep under one cover, but the Sages permit[232].

כָּל־שֶׁאֲסָקוֹ עִם הַנָּשִׁים לֹא יִתְיַחֵד עִם הַנָּשִׁים לְעוֹלָם. וְלֹא יְלַמֵּד אָדָם אֶת בְּנוֹ אוּמָנוּת בֵּין הַנָּשִׁים.

Anybody whose occupation is with women should never be alone with women. And a man should not teach his son a craft for women.

רִבִּי מֵאִיר אוֹמֵר לְעוֹלָם יִשְׁתַּדֵּל אָדָם לְלַמֵּד אֶת בְּנוֹ אוּמָנוּת נְקִיָּה וְיִתְפַּלֵּל לְמִי שֶׁהָעוֹשֶׁר שֶׁלּוֹ שֶׁאֵין לָךְ אוּמָנוּת שֶׁאֵין בָּהּ עֲנִיּוּת וַעֲשִׁירוּת. שֶׁאֵין עֲנִיּוּת מִן הָאוּמָנוּת וְאֵין עֲשִׁירוּת מִן הָאוּמָנוּת. רִבִּי שִׁמְעוֹן בֶּן אֶלְעָזָר אוֹמֵר רָאִיתָ מִיָּמֶיךָ חַיָּה וָעוֹף שֶׁיֵּשׁ לָהֶן אוּמָנוּת וְהֵן מִתְפַּרְנְסִין שֶׁלֹּא בְצַעַר וַהֲלֹא לֹא נִבְרְאוּ אֶלָּא לְשַׁמְּשֵׁנִי וְכָךְ מִתְפַּרְנְסִין שֶׁלֹּא בְצַעַר. וַאֲנִי נִבְרֵאתִי לְשַׁמֵּשׁ אֶת קוֹנִי אֵינוֹ דִין שֶׁאֶתְפַּרְנֵס שֶׁלֹּא בְצַעַר אֶלָּא שֶׁהֲרֵיעוֹתִי אֶת מַעֲשַׂי וְקִפַּחְתִּי אֶת פַּרְנָסָתִי.

Rebbi Meïr says that a man should try to teach his son a clean and easy trade and pray to Him to Whom riches and properties belong since there is no trade in which poverty and riches are not found, for neither poverty nor riches come from the trade. Rebbi Simeon[233] ben Eleazar says, did you ever see a wild animal or a bird which had a trade? And they sustain themselves without pain. But they were created only to serve me and sustain themselves without pain, and I was created to serve my Maker, it should be logical that I should be able to sustain myself without pain; only I worsened my deeds and destroyed my sustenance.

(fol. 65a) אַבָּא גּוּרְיוֹן אִישׁ צַיְידָן אוֹמֵר מִשׁוּם אַבָּא שָׁאוּל. לֹא יְלַמֵּד אָדָם אֶת בְּנוֹ חַמָּר גַּמָּל סַפָּן קַדָּר סַפָּר רוֹעֶה וְחֶנְוָנִי שֶׁאוּמְנָתָן אוּמָנוּת לִיסְטִין. רִבִּי יְהוּדָה אוֹמֵר מִשְּׁמוֹ הַחַמָּרִין רוּבָּן רְשָׁעִים. הַגַּמָּלִין רוּבָּן כְּשֵׁירִים. הַסַּפָּנִין רוּבָּן חֲסִידִים. טוֹב שֶׁבָּרוֹפְאִים לְגֵיהִנָּם. כָּשֵׁר שֶׁבַּטַּבָּחִים שׁוּתָפוֹ שֶׁלַּעֲמָלֵק.

Abba Gorion from Sidon says in the name of Abba Shaul[234]: A man should not teach his son to be a donkey driver, a camel driver, a hairdresser, a sailor, a potter, a shepherd, or a grocer, since their occupations are those of robbers. Rebbi Jehudah says in the latter's name: Most donkey drivers are wicked[235], most camel drivers are in order[236], most sailors are pious; the best of physicians goes to hell[237], the qualified among the butchers is an associate of Amaleq[238].

228 In a locked room.

229 Where everybody sleeps in the same room.

230 Because of the mothers of the schoolchildren.

231 If he is married but his wife lives at another place, he is considered unmarried in this respect.

232 They hold that Jews never engage in bestiality or homosexual acts.

233 This list is different in different Mishnah mss. It seems that both "hairdresser" and "potter" should be deleted and replaced by קָרָן or קָרָר "teamster". But the text could also be a conflation of two different texts, one denigrating trades that have a reputation of dishonesty and one that serves women (Babli 82a) like jewelers, hairdressers, etc. For a better text cf. below, 66c l. 26.

234 In the Babli: Abba Guria.

235 They are always hitting their animal.

236 Camels will walk by themselves a certain number of steps and have to be led gently.

237 He will be punished for every patient of his who dies because he did not give him the best of care.

238 He is a professional killer.

(66c line 1) **הלכה יא:** לא יִתְיַיחֵד אִישׁ אֶחָד עִם שְׁתֵּי נָשִׁים כול'. אָמַר רִבִּי אָבִין. בַּמֶּה דְבָרִים אֲמוּרִים. בִּכְשֵׁירִין. אֲבָל בִּפְרוּצִין לֹא תִתְיַיחֵד אֲפִילוּ בְּמֵאָה אִישׁ. תַּנֵּי. בֶּן יוֹמוֹ שֶׁמֵּת הֲרֵי הוּא לְאָבִיו וּלְאִמּוֹ וּלְכָל־קְרוֹבָיו כְּחָתָן שָׁלֵם. לֹא סוֹף דָּבָר בֶּן יוֹמוֹ חַי אֶלָּא אֲפִילוּ יָצָא רֹאשׁוֹ וְרוּבּוֹ בַּחַיִּים. וְיוֹצֵא בַחֵיק וְנִקְבַּר בְּאִשָּׁה אַחַת וּבִשְׁנֵי אֲנָשִׁים. אַבָּא שָׁאוּל אוֹמֵר. אַף בְּאִישׁ אֶחָד וּבִשְׁתֵּי נָשִׁים. מִסְתַּבְּרָא רִבִּי שִׁמְעוֹן מוֹדֵי לְאַבָּא שָׁאוּל. אַבָּא שָׁאוּל לֹא מוֹדֵי לְרִבִּי שִׁמְעוֹן. שֶׁאֵין יֵצֶר הָרָע מָצוּי בְּבֵית הַקְּבָרוֹת.

Halakhah 11: "One man should not be alone with two women," etc. Rebbi Abun said, when has this been said[239]? With decent men. But with profligates she should not be alone even with a hundred men[240]. It was stated[241]: A one day old child who died is for his father, his mother, and all his relatives like one fully grown[242]. Not only if he died when one day old but even if he was alive when his head and most of his body were born[243]. He is carried out at the bosom[244] and buried by one woman and two men; Abba Shaul says even one man and two women. It is obvious that Rebbi Simeon will agree with Abba Shaul but Abba Shaul does not need to agree with Rebbi Simeon since there is no sexual desire in the cemetery[245].

239 That a woman can be alone with two men.
240 In the Babli, 80b, this is a statement of Rav Jehudah in the name of Rav.
241 A similar text is quoted in the Babli, 80b.
242 They have to observe all the rules of the impurity of the dead and of mourning.
243 From the moment his life is independent and it is no longer permitted to destroy the fetus to save the mother's life (Mishnah *Ahilut* 7:6).
244 He does not need a bier and ten adults like a grown-up. Since he died before he had occasion to sin, his soul is pure and ready to enter Paradise without human intercession.
245 In all other situations, Abba

Shaul agrees with the anonymous Tanna. In the Babli, Abba Shaul's statement is rejected by reference to a story which R. Ḥananel (quoted by Tosaphot *s.v.* כי) identifies as that of The Widow of Ephesus.

(66c line 9) רִבִּי יוֹחָנָן בְּשֵׁם רִבִּי שִׁמְעוֹן בֶּן יוֹחַי. כִּי יְסִיתְךָ אָחִיךָ בֶן אִמֶּךָ אוֹ בִנְךָ אוֹ בִתְּךָ אוֹ אֵשֶׁת חֵיקֶךָ. אִמְּךָ בַּסֵּתֶר. בִּתְּךָ בַּסֵּתֶר. מִתְיַיחֵד אָדָם עִם אִמּוֹ וְדָר עִמָּהּ. עִם בִּתּוֹ וְדָר עִמָּהּ. עִם אֲחוֹתוֹ וְאֵינוֹ דָר עִמָּהּ. וְיָשֵׁן עִמָּהֶן בְּקֵירוּב בָּשָׂר. תַּנֵּי רִבִּי חֲלַפְתָּא בֶּן שָׁאוּל. הַבַּת אֵצֶל הָאָב עַד בַּת שָׁלֹשׁ שָׁנִים וְיוֹם אֶחָד. הַבֵּן אֵצֶל הָאֵם עַד בֶּן תֵּשַׁע שָׁנִים וְיוֹם אֶחָד. הִגְדִּילוּ זֶה יָשֵׁן בִּכְסוּתוֹ וְזֶה יָשֵׁן בִּכְסוּתוֹ. תַּנֵּי. שְׁנַיִם שֶׁהָיוּ יְשֵׁינִים בְּמִטָּה אַחַת זֶה מִתְכַּסֶּה בִּכְסוּת עַצְמוֹ וְקוֹרֵא וְזֶה מִתְכַּסֶּה בִּכְסוּת עַצְמוֹ וְקוֹרֵא. אִם הָיוּ בְנוֹ וּבִתּוֹ קְטַנִּים מוּתָּר. תַּמָּן אָמְרִין. אִישׁ וְאִשְׁתּוֹ מוּתָּר. רִבִּי יַעֲקֹב בַּר אָחָא בְּשֵׁם רִבִּי לֶעְזָר. לְאִישׁ וְאִשָּׁה נִצְרָכָה.

7 קטנים G | הקטנים

Rebbi Joḥanan in the name of Rebbi Simeon ben Ioḥai[246]: "If your brother, your mother's son, or your son, or your daughter incites you[247]". "Your mother in secret," "your daughter in secret." A man can be alone with his mother and live with her[248], with his daughter and live with her, with his sister and does not live with her, and sleep with them with their skins touching. Rebbi Ḥalaphta ben Shaul stated: The daughter with her father up to the age of three years and one day[249]; the son with his mother up to the age of nine years and one day[250]. If they get older, each one sleeps in his own clothing. It was stated[251]: If two people sleep in the same bed, each one covers himself with his own garment and recites {the *Šemaʿ*}[252]; if his son or daughter were small it is permitted. There, they say: A man with his wife is permitted[253]. Rebbi Jacob bar Aḥa in the name of Rebbi Eleazar: A man with his wife is problematic[254].

| 246 So also in *Soṭah* 1:1, Note 38. In the Babli 80b, R. Joḥanan in the name of R. Ismael, in *Sanhedrin* 21b, *Avodah zarah* 36b, in the name of R. Simeon ben Yoṣadaq. The latter attribution probably is the correct one; in these two quotes also the verse correctly is called "a hint", not a proof.

247 *Deut.* 13:7. As usual, the reference is to the part of the verse not quoted; in this case that the inciting happens "in secret".

248 In a one-room apartment.

249 The day she becomes nubile.

250 Before that day, his sex act has no legal consequences (Mishnah *Yebamot* 10:6).

251 Similar statements are in *Berakhot* 24a.

252 Which, as a holy text, it is forbidden to recite in the presence of nudity.

253 Even if both are naked under the same bedsheet, since "his wife is part of his body" (Babli *Berakhot* 24a).

254 Even if his wife is part of his body, he could recite the Šemaʿ while lying close to her only if she would not represent a sexual attraction to him. This is not a desirable situation.

(66c line 18) פִּסְקָא. וְלֹא יְלַמֵּד רַוָּוק סוֹפְרִים וְלֹא תְלַמֵּד אִשָּׁה סוֹפְרִים כול'. תַּנֵּי. רִבִּי אֶלְעָזָר אוֹמֵר. אַף מִי שֶׁיֵּשׁ לוֹ אִשָּׁה וּבָנִים וְאֵינָן עִמּוֹ בְּאוֹתוֹ מָקוֹם לֹא יְלַמֵּד סוֹפְרִים. רִבִּי יוּדָן בֵּירִבִּי יִשְׁמָעֵאל עֲבַד חַד מַתְנַיָּין הָכֵן.

3 הכן G | דכן

New paragraph. "And a bachelor shall not be a school teacher; a woman shall not be a school teacher, etc." It was stated: Rebbi Eliezer says, also a man with a wife and children shall not be a school teacher if they are not with him at that place. Rebbi Yudan ben Rebbi Ismael acted accordingly in the case of a Mishnah teacher.

(66c line 22) פִּסְקָא. רִבִּי יְהוּדָה אוֹמֵר לֹא יִרְעֶה רַוָּוק אֶת הַבְּהֵמָה וְלֹא יָשְׁנוּ שְׁנֵי רַוָּוקִים בְּטַלִּית אֶחָד וַחֲכָמִים מַתִּירִים. יָאוּת אָמַר רִבִּי יוּדָה. מָה טַעְמָא דְּרַבָּנִין. חַס וְשָׁלוֹם לֹא נֶחְשְׁדוּ יִשְׂרָאֵל לֹא עַל הַזָּכוּר וְלֹא עַל הַבְּהֵמָה. וְהָתַנִּינָן. לֹא יְלַמֵּד רַוָּוק סוֹפְרִים. מִשּׁוּם שֶׁאִמּוֹ בָּאָה עִמּוֹ וַאֲחוֹתוֹ בָּאָה עִמּוֹ.

2-1 פסקא. ...מתירים | G - | 4 רווק | G רבק   סופרים | G סופרין

New paragraph. "Rebbi Jehudah says, a bachelor shall not be a shepherd and two bachelors shall not sleep under one cover, but the Sages permit." Does not Rebbi Jehudah say it correctly? What is the rabbi's reason? Perish the thought! Jews are not suspected either with males or with animals. But did we not state: "A bachelor shall not be a school teacher"[255]? Because his mother or his sister will come with him[256].

255 Suspecting the unmarried school teacher to be a pedophile with young males.

256 He is only suspected to be susceptible to the lure of heterosexual relations. The same argument is in the Babli, 82a, where also it is indicated that a female school teacher is not suspected of being attracted to her male students but to their fathers.

(66c line 26) פִּסְקָא. לֹא יְלַמֵּד אָדָם אֶת בְּנוֹ אוּמָּנוּת בֵּין הַנָּשִׁים כול'. תַּנֵּי. לֹא יְלַמֵּד אָדָם אֶת בְּנוֹ חַמָּר וְגַמָּל וְסַפָּן קַדָּר קָרָר רוֹעֶה חֶנְוָנִי מִפְּנֵי שֶׁאוּמְּנוּתָן אוּמָנוּת לִיסְטִין.

2 וספן | G -   קרר | G -

New paragraph. "A man should not teach his son a craft for women," etc. It was stated: A man should not teach his son to be a donkey driver, a camel driver, a sailor, a potter, a teamster, a shepherd, or a grocer, since their occupations are those of robbers[233].

(66c line 29) פִּסְקָא. אַבָּא אוֹרְיָין אִישׁ צַיְידָן אוֹמֵר מִשּׁוּם אַבָּא שָׁאוּל כול'. רוֹב חַמָּרִים רְשָׁעִים. רוֹב גַּמָּלִין כְּשֵׁירִין. רוֹב סַפָּנִין חֲסִידִים. רוֹב מַמְזֵירִין פִּקְחִין. רוֹב עֲבָדִים נָאִים. רוֹב בְּנֵי אָבוֹת בּוֹיְישָׁנִים. רוֹב בָּנִים דּוֹמִין לַאֲחֵי הָאֵם. כָּשֵׁר שֶׁבָּרוֹפְאִים לְגֵיהִנָּם. הַכָּשֵׁר שֶׁבַּטַּבָּחִים שׁוּתָף עֲמָלֵק. תַּנֵּי רִבִּי שִׁמְעוֹן בֶּן יוֹחַי. הַכָּשֵׁר שֶׁבַּגּוֹיִם הֲרוֹג. הַטּוֹב שֶׁבַּנְּחָשִׁים רְצַץ אֶת מוֹחוֹ. הַכְּשֵׁירָה שֶׁבַּנָּשִׁים בַּעֲלַת כְּשָׁפִים. אַשְׁרֵי מִי שֶׁעוֹשֶׂה רְצוֹן הַמָּקוֹם.

2 רוב ספנין חסידים | G רובן של ספנים חסידין   2-3 רוב ממזירון ... האם - G | 4
כשר G | הטוב   5 יוחיי G | יוחיי   שבנחשים G | שבנחשין   3 רוב בני אבות
בויישנים G | רובן של בני אבות בוישנין   רוב בנים G | רובן שלבנים

New paragraph. Abba Orion from Sidon says in the name of Abba Shaul[234]: Most donkey drivers are wicked[235], most camel drivers are in order[236], most sailors are pious, most bastards are intelligent, most slaves are beautiful, most sons look like their mother's brothers. The qualified physicians go to hell[237], the qualified among the butchers is an associate of Amaleq[238]. Rebbi Simeon ben Iohai stated: Kill the best of Gentiles[257], smash the head of the best of snakes; the best qualified among women is a sorceress. Blessed is he who does the will of the Omnipresent.

257 He spent 14 years in a cave on the run from the Roman government. In *Mekhilta dR. Ismael, Bešallaḥ* 1; *Mekhilta dR. Simeon bar Iohai* p. 51; *Tanḥuma Bešallaḥ* 8, his proof is from *Ex.* 14:7, where Pharao mobilized 600 chariots and it is argued that the horses to draw the chariots must have belonged to "those who feared the word of the Eternal" (*Ex.* 9:20); but that verse refers only to domestic animals which at that time did not include horses used only by the military.

(66d line 1) רִבִּי מֵאִיר אוֹמֵר. מִכָּל־מָקוֹם אָדָם מִתְפַּרְנַס. אַשְׁרֵי מִי שֶׁרוֹאֶה אֶת הוֹרָיו בְּאוּמָנוּת מְעוּלָה. אוֹי לוֹ לְמִי שֶׁרוֹאֶה אֶת הוֹרָיו בְּאוּמָנוּת פְּגוּמָה.
2 אוי G | אי   פגומה G | בזויה

Rebbi Meïr says[258]: A person can earn his livelihood from anywhere. Blessed is he who sees his parents in an esteemed trade; woe to him who sees his parents in a degrading[259] trade.

258 Cf. Tosephta 5:14.   259 In G: despised.

(66d line 3) פִּיסְקָא. רִבִּי מֵאִיר אוֹמֵר לְעוֹלָם יִשְׁתַּדֵּל אָדָם לְלַמֵּד אֶת בְּנוֹ אוּמָנוּת נְקִיָּה כול'. מַה יַעֲשֶׂה אָדָם. יִשְׁתַּדֵּל וִילַמֵּד אֶת בְּנוֹ אוּמָנוּת קְטַנָּה וְיִתְפַּלֵּל וִיבַקֵּשׁ רַחֲמִים מִמִּי שֶׁהָעוֹשֶׁר שֶׁלּוֹ. שֶׁאֵין לָךְ אוּמָנוּת שֶׁאֵין בָּהּ עֲנִיִּים וַעֲשִׁירִים. אֶלָּא הַכֹּל לְפִי זְכוּת הָאָדָם. רִבִּי שִׁמְעוֹן בֶּן אֶלְעָזָר מִשּׁוּם רִבִּי מֵאִיר. רָאִיתָ מִיָּמֶיךָ אֲרִי סַבָּל. אֲרִי קַיָּיץ. זְאֵב מוֹכֵר קְדֵירוֹת. וְהֵן שׁוּעָל חֶנְוָנִי. מִתְפַּרְנְסִין בְּלֹא צַעַר. וְלָמָה נִבְרָאוּ. לְשַׁמְּשֵׁנִי. וַאֲנִי נִבְרֵאתִי לְשַׁמֵּשׁ אֶת קוֹנִי. וַהֲרֵי הַדְּבָרִים קַל וְחוֹמֶר. וּמָה אִם אֵילּוּ שֶׁנִּבְרְאוּ לְשַׁמְּשֵׁנִי כָּךְ הֵן מִתְפַּרְנְסִין בְּלֹא צַעַר. אֲנִי שֶׁנִּבְרֵאתִי לְשַׁמֵּשׁ אֶת קוֹנִי אֵינוֹ דִין שֶׁאֱהֵא מִתְפַּרְנֵס בְּלֹא צַעַר. וּמִי גָרַם לִי לִהְיוֹת מִתְפַּרְנֵס בְּצַעַר. הֱוֵי אוֹמֵר. חֲטָאַיי. עַל שֶׁהֲרֵיעוֹתִי מַעֲשַׂיי קִיפַּחְתִּי פַּרְנָסָתִי.

2 וילמד G | שלמד   את בנו G | לו   3 ויבקש רחמים G | ליהיות מתפרנס ממנה ורוח ... בה ענייים ועשירים G | בו עניין ועשירין   5 ארי קייץ G | צבי קייץ   חנווני G | חנוני   קדירות G | קדרות   והן G | והרי הן   7 והרי דהברים קל וחומר ומה G | מה   אילו | G אלו שנבראו G | שניבראו   8 שנבראתי G | שניבראתי   קוני | G קונייי   בלא צער G | שלא   9 קיפחתי פרנסתי G | וקיפחתי פרסיי

New paragraph. "Rebbi Meïr says that a man should try to teach his son a clean trade," etc. What should a man do? A person should try and teach his son an unassuming trade and pray for mercy to Him to Whom riches belong since there is no trade in which poor and rich people are not found, for everything depends on a person's merit. [260]Rebbi Simeon ben Eleazar in the name of Rebbi Meïr: Did you ever see a lion porter, a (lion) [deer][261] maker of fig cakes, a fox grocer, a wolf selling pots? And they sustain themselves without pain. Why were they created? Only to serve me, and I was created to serve my Maker. Is it not an argument *de minore ad maius*? Since they were created to serve me and sustain themselves so without pain, should it not be logical that I, who was created to serve my Maker, should be able to sustain myself without pain?

What caused me to have to sustain myself with pain? One has to say, my sins. Because I worsened my deeds and destroyed my sustenance.

260 Tosephta 5:15, Babli 32b.
261 Reading of G and the parallel sources.

(fol. 65b) **משנה יב:** רִבִּי נְהוֹרַאי אוֹמֵר. מֵנִיחַ אֲנִי כָּל־אוּמָנִיּוֹת שֶׁבָּעוֹלָם וְאֵינִי מְלַמֵּד אֶת בְּנִי אֶלָּא תוֹרָה. שֶׁאָדָם אוֹכֵל מִשְׂכָרָהּ בָּעוֹלָם הַזֶּה וְהַקֶּרֶן קַיֶּמֶת לָעוֹלָם הַבָּא וּשְׁאָר אוּמָנִיּוֹת אֵינָן כֵּן. שֶׁאִם נִכְנַס אָדָם לִידֵי חֹלִי אוֹ לִידֵי זִקְנָה אוֹ לִידֵי מִידָּה שֶׁל יִסּוּרִין וְאֵינוֹ יָכוֹל לַעֲסוֹק בִּמְלַאכְתּוֹ הֲרֵי הוּא מֵת וּמוּטָל בָּרָעָב. אֲבָל הַתּוֹרָה אֵינָהּ כֵּן אֶלָּא מְשַׁמַּרְתּוּ מִכָּל־רַע בְּנַעֲרוּתוֹ וְנוֹתֶנֶת לוֹ אַחֲרִית וְתִקְוָה בְּזִקְנוּתוֹ. בְּנַעֲרוּתוֹ מַה הוּא אוֹמֵר. וְקוֹוֵי יְיָ יַחֲלִיפוּ כֹחַ יַעֲלוּ אֵבֶר כַּנְּשָׁרִים יָרוּצוּ וְלֹא יִיגָעוּ יֵלְכוּ וְלֹא יִיעָפוּ. בְּזִקְנוּתוֹ מַה הוּא אוֹמֵר. עוֹד יְנוּבוּן בְּשֵׂיבָה דְּשֵׁנִים וְרַעֲנַנִּים יִהְיוּ. וְכֵן הוּא אוֹמֵר בְּאַבְרָהָם אָבִינוּ עָלָיו הַשָּׁלוֹם. וְאַבְרָהָם זָקֵן בָּא בַּיָּמִים וַיְיָ בֵּרַךְ אֶת אַבְרָהָם בַּכֹּל. מָצִינוּ שֶׁעָשָׂה אַבְרָהָם אָבִינוּ אֶת כָּל־הַתּוֹרָה כֻּלָּהּ עַד שֶׁלֹּא נִיתְּנָה שֶׁנֶּאֱמַר עֵקֶב אֲשֶׁר שָׁמַע אַבְרָהָם בְּקוֹלִי וַיִּשְׁמֹר מִשְׁמַרְתִּי מִצְוֹתַי חֻקּוֹתַי וְתוֹרֹתָי.

Mishnah 12: Rebbi Nehorai says: I am leaving aside all trades in the world and teach my son only Torah[262], for a man eats from its rewards in this world and the capital remains for the future world. But with other trades it is not so, for if a person is afflicted with sickness, or old age, or a measure of suffering, and cannot continue in his trade, he dies, abandoned, from hunger. But the Torah is different, it guards him from all evil in his youth and gives him a future and hope in his old age. What does it say about his youth? "Those who trust in the Eternal will renew strength, they rise on wings like an eagle, they run without effort, they walk without tiring.[263]" What does it say about his old age? "They still bear fruit in old age, fat and invigorated they will be.[264]" So it says about our father Abraham, peace on him: "Abraham was old, came into days, and the Eternal blessed Abraham with everything.[265]" We find that our father Abraham kept the entire Torah before it was given, as it is said: "As a reward because Abraham listened to My voice and kept My watch, My commandments, My laws, and My teachings.[266]"

262   This really is frowned upon,   264   *Ps.* 92:15.
Mishnah *Avot* 2:2, 4:5.   265   *Gen.* 24:1.
263   *Is.* 40:31.   266   *Gen.* 26:5.

(66d line 14) **הלכה יב**: רִבִּי נְהוֹרַיי אוֹמֵר. מַנִּיחַ אֲנִי כָּל־אוּמָנִיוֹת שֶׁבָּעוֹלָם וְאֵינִי מְלַמֵּד אֶת בְּנִי אֶלָּא תוֹרָה. שֶׁכָּל אוּמָנוּת אֵינוֹ עוֹמֶדֶת לוֹ לְאָדָם אֶלָּא בִּימֵי נַעֲרוּת בִּזְמַן שֶׁכּוֹחוֹ עָלָיו. אֲבָל אִם בָּא בִּידֵי חוֹלִי אוֹ נִכְנַס לִידֵי זִקְנָה אוֹ לְמִידָה שֶׁלַּיִּיסוּרִין וְאֵינוּ יָכוֹל לַעֲשׂוֹת מְלָאכָה הֲרֵי הוּא מֵת בְּרָעָב. אֲבָל הַתּוֹרָה אֵינָהּ כֵּן אֶלָּא מְכַבַּדְתּוֹ וּמְשַׁמְּרַתּוֹ מִכָּל־רַע בְּנַעֲרוּתוֹ. וְנוֹתֶנֶת לוֹ אַחֲרִית וְתִקְוָה בְּזִקְנוּתוֹ. בְּנַעֲרוּתוֹ מַה הוּא אוֹמֵר. וְקוֹיֵי יי יַחֲלִיפוּ כֹחַ יַעֲלוּ אֵבֶר כַּנְּשָׁרִים יָרוּצוּ וְלֹא יִיעָפוּ יֵלְכוּ וְלֹא יִיגָעוּ. וּבְזִקְנוּתוֹ מַה הוּא אוֹמֵר. עוֹד יְנוּבוּן בְּשֵׂיבָה דְּשֵׁנִים וְרַעֲנַנִּים יִהְיוּ. וְכֵן אַתָּה מוֹצֵא בְּאַבְרָהָם אָבִינוּ שֶׁשִּׁימֵּר אֶת הַתּוֹרָה עַד שֶׁלֹּא בָּאת לָעוֹלָם. שֶׁנֶּאֱמַר עֵקֶב אֲשֶׁר שָׁמַע אַבְרָהָם בְּקוֹלִי וַיִּשְׁמוֹר מִשְׁמַרְתִּי מִצְוֹתַי חֻקּוֹתַי וְתוֹרוֹתָי. אַף גִּידְּלוֹ וּבֵירְכוֹ בְּנַעֲרוּתוֹ וְנָתַן לוֹ אַחֲרִית וְתִקְוָה בְּזִקְנוּתוֹ. בְּנַעֲרוּתוֹ מַהוּ אוֹמֵר. וְאַבְרָהָם כָּבֵד מְאוֹד בַּמִּקְנֶה בַּכֶּסֶף וּבַזָּהָב. וּבְזִקְנוּתוֹ מַהוּ אוֹמֵר. וְאַבְרָהָם זָקֵן בָּא בַּיָּמִים וַיי בֵּרַךְ אֶת אַבְרָהָם בַּכֹּל.

1 ר' נהוריי או' | G אמ' ר' נהוריי   2 שכל אומנות אינו עומדת לאדם | G לפי שכל אומניות שבעולם אינן עומדות לאדן   3 או נכנס לידי זקנה או למידה שלייסורין | G או למידת יסורין   4 ואינו יכול לעשות מלאכה הרי | G אינו יכול לעמוד בהן והרי

5 מכבדתו G | מחבבתו ומגדלתו ומכבדתו | - G שהמקום בר' חו' מחבב 'מגדל ומשמר את
הזקנים בזיק[נתם]   6 יעלו אבר כנשרים ירוצו ולא ייגעו ילכו ולא ייעפו | G וגו'   7
בזקנותו מ"ה הוא | G ובזייקנותן יהיו | G וגו'   ששימר | G .. לו
המקום ובירכו לפי ששימר   9 לעולם | G -   שנא' | G הדה הוא דכת'   11 מהו | G
מה   במקנה בכסף ובזהב | G וגו'   12 מהו | G מה הוא

Halakhah 12: [267]"Rebbi Nehorai says: I am leaving aside all trades in the world and teach my son only Torah." For all trades support a person only in his youth as long as he is in possession of his powers. But if a person is afflicted with sickness or a measure of suffering, and cannot continue working, he dies from hunger. But the Torah is different, it honors him and guards him from all evil in his youth and gives him a future and hope in his old age[268]. What does it say about his youth? "Those who trust in the Eternal will renew strength, they rise on wings like an eagle, they run without effort, they walk without tiring.[263]" What does it say about his old age? "They still bear fruit in old age, fat and invigorated they will be.[264]" So you find about the patriarch Abraham who kept the Torah before it came into the world[269], as it is said: "As a reward because Abraham listened to My voice and kept My watch, My commandments, My laws, and My teachings.[266]" Also it made him great and blessed him in his youth and gave him a future and hope in his old age. What does it say about his youth? "Abraham was very wealthy with livestock, silver, and gold." And about his old age, what does it say? "Abraham was old, came into days, and the Eternal blessed Abraham with everything.[265]"

267 Tosephta 5:16-17; a shortened version in the Babli, 82b, and *Masekhet Sopherim* 17:1.

268 G has here an amplification that looks redundant.

269 G lacks "into the world". The

text of L should be interpreted as "came into *this* world", not excluding the doctrine of pre-existence of the Torah in the abstract prior to Creation.

(66d line 28) רִבִּי חִזְקִיָה רִבִּי כֹהֵן בְּשֵׁם רַב. אָסוּר לָדוּר בְּעִיר שָׁאֵין בָּהּ לֹא רוֹפֵא וְלֹא מֶרְחָץ וְלֹא בֵית דִּין מַכִּין וְחוֹבְשִׁין. אָמַר רִבִּי יוֹסֵי בֵּירִבִּי בּוּן. אַף אָסוּר לָדוּר בְּעִיר שָׁאֵין בָּהּ גִּינּוֹנִיתָא שֶׁל יָרָק. רִבִּי חִזְקִיָה רִבִּי כֹהֵן בְּשֵׁם רַב. עָתִיד אָדָם לִיתֵּן דִּין וְחֶשְׁבּוֹן עַל כָּל־מַה שֶׁרָאַת עֵינוֹ וְלֹא אָכַל. רִבִּי לָעְזָר חֲשַׁשׁ לְהָדָא שְׁמוּעֲתָא וּמַצְמִית לֵיהּ פְּרִיטִין וַאֲכִיל בְּהוֹן מִכָּל־מִילָה חֲדָא בְשַׁתָּא.

Rebbi Ḥizqiah, Rebbi Cohen in the name of Rav. It is forbidden to dwell in a city which has neither a medical man, nor a public bath, nor a court lashing and jailing[270]. Rebbi Yose ben Rebbi Abun said, also it is forbidden to dwell in a city which has no vegetable garden[271]. Rebbi Ḥizqiah, Rebbi Cohen in the name of Rav: Every person will have to justify himself for everything his eye saw and which he did not eat[272]. Rebbi Eleazar took note of this statement and saved coins from which he ate every kind once a year.

270 A different version is in the Babli, *Sanhedrin* 17b.

271 In the Babli, this is a Tannaïtic statement attributed to R. Aqiba. A diet without fruit and vegetables is unhealthy.

272 Since asceticism is sinful; cf. *Nedarim* 1:1, Note 95.

Indices

Sigla

Parallel Texts from Yerushalmi Tractates

Yebamot Chapter 1		א	Ma'aśer Šeni		מ
Yebamot Chapter	2	ב	Pesaḥim		ס
Yebamot, other Chapters		ג	Nedarim		נ
Demay		ד	Sanhedrin		ן
Yebamot, Chapter 5		ה	Soṭah		ס
Šebuot		ו	'Erubin		ע
'Avodah zarah		ז	Qiddušin		ק
Ḥallah		ח	Bikkurim		ר
Giṭṭin		ט	Šabbat		ש
Yebamot, Chapter 10		י	Ševi'it		ש
Ketubot		כ	Berakhot		ת
'Orlah		ל			

Manuscript text and *editio princeps*

Ashkenazic Text (Sussman)	A
Genizah Texts	G
Leiden manuscript	L
Rome manuscript Zera'im-Soṭah	R
Editio princeps	V

Index of Biblical Quotations

Gen. 1:28	340	23:9	92	12:3	191,192
2:17	363	23:13	9	12:4	169
2:24	19	24:1	412	12:6	191
9:6	18	26:5	412	12:21	117
15:19	179	38:28	372	12:44	169
17:11	151			12:48	337
20:12	19	Ex. 5:16	253	13:13	117,151,250

Ex. 18:18	67	14:14	88	18:11	201		
19:10	337	14:19	85	18:15	117		
20:12	162	15:16	337	18:20	84		
20:20	357	17:13	85	27:21	357		
21:2	45,46,49,54	18:5	17	30:14	284		
21:3	88	18:17,18	231	31:18	389		
21:4	45,46	19:3	162	35:33	357		
21:5	35,46,49,80,88	19:20	5,43,49				
21:6	45,46,195,82,88	19:23	175	Deut. 4:9	151		
21:7	26,27,77	19:24	245	4:10	155		
21:8	64	19:27	149	5:16	165		
21:10-11	10,26,27,48,63	20:18	19	6:13	162		
		21:1	149,173,385	7:2	363		
21:17	163	21:5	173	7:12	357		
21:20-21	267	21:7	321,322	11:16	176,356		
21:25	186	21:13	391	11:17	356		
21:26	101	21:14	391	11:18	176		
21:28	246	22:12	271	11:19	151		
21:35	124	22:19	132	11:26	187		
22:3	124	23:14	361	11:28	187		
22:6	29	23:46	90	12:1	175		
22:8	26,29,125	24:19	162	13:7	407		
22:16	198	25:17	97	13:18	357		
22:30	117	25:26	60	14:1	173,174		
23:13	104	25:27	84	14:2	173		
23:18	24	25:31-43	45,46,58	14:25	241		
34:7	186	25:40	58,59	14:28	251		
34:21	352	25:46	15	15:12-18	45,46,48,49		
34:25	24	25:47-54	46				
		25:48	59	15:17	80,89		
Lev. 1:2	244	25:50	50,51	17:3	170		
1:4	149,195	25:52	51,58	17:15	383		
2:6	149	25:53	58,59,62.82	18:3	252		
4:28	245	25:54	60,89	19:15	17		
5:14-16	236,242,264	27:10	195	20:17	363		
		27:19	148	21:1-9	246		
5:23	124	27:21	264	21:17	311,392,393		
5:26	29			21:23	361		
6:8	149	Num. 3:40	117	22:9	246		
7:7	234	5:8	252	22:24	3		
8:23	88	5:28	380	23:1	331,335		
12:3	151	6:23	85	23:2	383		
13:42	173	9:13	169	23:3	322,325,331,383		
14:1-7	246	15:30	236	23:10	383		

INDEX OF BIBLICAL QUOTATIONS

Deut. 23:18	340,341	2K. 12:17	253	4:23	165		
23:29	92	17:25	349	13:6	187		
24:1	3,9,39,85	25:30	153	13:21	187		
24:4	270,324			17:19	44		
24:30	39	Is. 5:14	186	25:14	357		
25:5	39,294	40:31	412	30:17	165		
30:5	177						
30:15-20	187	Jer. 3:2-3	356	Job 6:14	259		
32:4	360	30:60	179	33:23	186		
		31:20	347				
		32:44	91	Ru. 1:4	4		
Jos. 9:7	363			4:7	126		
9:21	362	Ez. 36:25	343				
9:23	362,363	44:22	384,386,388	Eccl. 4:12	181		
9:27	352,362	48:19	358	10:1	186		
9:33	361						
		Hos.5:5	153	Esth. 8:17	350		
Jud. 14:18	352	Micah 7:18	186				
21:23	4	Soph. 2:3	357	Ezra 2:58,60	352		
		Za. 9:6	343	2:61-63	346		
1S. 18:19	360	Mal. 2:6	20	6:21	352		
				7:7	345		
2S. 3:29	153	Ps. 1:1	183				
6:23	360	24:1	147	Neh. 3:26	357		
17:19	43	37:25	153	7:60-61	352		
17:27	349	39:7	155	8:9	346		
20:2	363	57:3	360	8:17	177		
20:6	360	62:13	186	10:1	17:8		
20:8	360	85:3	188	10:37	178		
20:9	360	90:16	153	11:21	357		
20:10	360	92:15	412				
21:1-2	356,357	107:11	352	1Chr. 7:40	383		
21:4	357	112:2	153				
21:6	357	119:1,3	183	2Chr. 2:16-17	361		
21:14	357			24:24	153		
		Prov. 3:9	162,163	26:21	153		
1K. 12:18	153	3:34	187,188	35:23	153		
		3:35	187				

Index of Talmudical Quotations

Babylonian Talmud

Berakhot 24a	407	Ketubot 14a	379	18b	79		
		31a	138	19a	64		
Šabbat 91a	138	46b	64	19b	65,66,77,78		
104a	188	47a	11	21b	83,86		
		63b	56	22b	87,90,95		
Erubin 15b	11	67a	145	23b	101,104,105		
		73b	229	26a	91,129,131,132		
Pesaḥim 12b	24			27a	129		
32b	243	Nedarim 11a	289	27b	139		
91a/b	169,170	29a	264	28a	142		
		36a	191	28b	147,148		
Roš Haššanah 17a	186	61a	54	29a	151		
17b	186			30b	151		
		Nazir 12b	195	31b	153		
Yoma 38b	188	49b	240	33b	167		
86b	188			35b	173		
		Gittin 20a	23	36a	173		
Sukkah 25a	11	21b	11	39b	182		
		23b	99	43a	193		
Beṣah 37b	143	25a	143	45a	201		
		40a	106	45b	202		
Ta'anit 8b	357	42a	107	46a	198		
		42b	101	47a	68,208,213		
Mo'ed Qaṭan 28b	153	90a	380	48a	217		
				49a	217,218,219		
Yebamot 4a	383	Qiddušin 2a	9	50a	220		
24b	349	4a	63	52a	232		
45a	331	5a	11,12	52b	240		
45b	335,337	8a	51,213	53b	242		
47b	350,395	8b	211	55a	244		
54b	19	11b	29	58b	259		
60b	349	12a	27	59a	206,259		
78b	356	12b	213,315	59b	258		
79a	363	13a	211,213	60a	268		
92b	301	14b	48	60b	273		
99a	341,342	15a	57	62a	295		
		15b	60	62b	295,297		
Soṭah 16b	85	16a	48,58	63a	303		
27a	398	16b	56,81	64b	311		
		17b	80,81	65a	315,320		

INDEX OF TALMUDICAL QUOTATIONS

Qiddušin 69a	340	52b	136	36b	407
69b	347	53a	136	72a	112
72b	324,343	55a	136		
73b	371,372	86a	138	Zebaḥim 22a	30
76b	349,380,383	86b	137		
78a	206,235,349	92b	132	Menaḥot 37a	117
78b	206,393	100a	93	43a	167
79b	402	126a	121	79b	24
80a	398	128a	95,123	93b	195
80b	405,407	134b	311,314	112b	24
82a	404,408	135b	132		
82b	411,412	152a	132	Hulin 13a	132
90b	186				
91b	169	Sanhedrin 17b	414	Keritut 11a	44,45
		21a	360	24b	24
Baba Qama 11a	124	21b	407		
11b	117	48b	153	Bekhorot 10b	250
12a	95	57b	16,17,19	11a	248,250
27b	132	71b	19	13a	90
46b	132	72a	138	50a	92
51b	114	78a	117	52b	143
52a	113	111a	186		
69b	143			Temurah 2a	195
		Šebuot 36a	289	24b	24
Bab Meṣiʻa 8b	110	39b	29	25a	105
9b	110	40b	29	25b	99,108
47a	126,147				
		Abodah Zarah 18a		Arakhin 30a	58
Baba Batra 50a	267		361		

Jerusalem Talmud

Berakhot 2:3	151	Ševiʻit 6:1	176,347	Orlah 3:8	180
3:3	163	10:3	46		
				Bikkurim 1:5	349,387
Peah 1:1	153,185,186	Terumot 7:1	138		
3:8	134			Šabbat 1:2	155
		Maʻaser Šeni 1:2	236,238		
Deamy 1:3	240	3:5	251	Erubin 3	285
6:3	115,253	4:4	104	7	104
6:6	398				
6:12	210	Hallah 4:12	171	Pesaḥim 1:4	24
				8:1	169,192

420 INDICES

Sukkah 5:4	360	6:2	193	4:5	43		
		9:5	250	4:8	264		
Ta'aniot 1:4	361			5:6	207		
3:3	356	Ketubot 1:4	311	6:2	197		
		1:5	315,381	6:4	220		
Mo'ed Qaṭan 2:3	208	1:9	379	7:3	258		
		2:1	26	7:5	273		
Yebamot 1:1	294,300,	2:11	127	7:6	274		
	332	3:1	92,138,322,331,	8:1	116		
1:2	190		362	9:7	203,208		
1:6	32,78,363	3:6	10				
2:1	41	4:2	66	Nazir 2:9	262		
2:2	271	4:3	78				
2:4	216	4:13	121	Baba Qama 3:4	138		
2:11	309	5:3	202				
3:5	268	5:5	14,89,347,398	Baba Meṣi'a 4:1	145		
3:10	271	5:10	77	4:2	214		
4:2	19	6:1	97	6:3	206		
4:13	324	6:7	37	7:14	77		
4:15	82,331,333	7:9	145,223				
5:1	41	9:3	95	Baba Batra 3:1	110,136,		
7:6	331	9:5	120		371		
8:2	324,325,369,374,			8:5	132		
	387	Nedarim 1:1	414				
8:3	328,365	3:6	298,299	Sanhedrin 6:9	356		
9:1	324	8:3	317	10:1	185,186		
10:14	69	10:6	268				
13:16	277	11:3	253	Šebuot 1:4	234		
15:3	274	11:5	100	6:1	26		
15:12	347			6:5	96		
		Giṭṭin 1:6	191,293				
Soṭah 1:1	407	2:6	105	Abodah Zarah 5:10			
1:7	380,398	3:4	311,347		112		
2:5	139	4:1	400				
3:1	174	4:3	46	Niddah 2:5	29		
3:4	17	4:4	207	3:4	117		

Mishnah

Ma'aser Šeni 1:2	238	Erubin 3:4	286	8:1	169
4:8	38	3:5	286	Šeqalim 1:6	143
Orlah 3:8	175	Pesaḥim 6:1	169	1:7	142
		7:4	235	7:4	244

INDEX OF TALMUDICAL QUOTATIONS

Yebamot 2:5	322,394	4:1	142		
2:6	339	4:2	214	Zebaḥim 1:1	234
3:4	320	4:3,4	37	5:8	191
4:13	322	5:1	230	9:1	234
4:15	331	7:14	77	Hulin 1:7	142
5:1	41	8:4	104	6:6	85
6:5	388	Baba Batra 3:1	95	Bekhorot 6:1	83
10:6	407	5:9	137	9:3	142
Soṭah 1:8	352	8:8	393	Arakhin 7:1	57
Ketubot 1:9	380	Sanhedrin 1:4	17	7:4	264
3:1	362	7:15	10	Me'ilah 1:2	234
5:9,10	56	Makkot 3:17	182		
7:8	220	Šebuot 6:7	125	Nega'im 4:5-6	173
Nedarim 3:6	298	Idiut 2:9	153	14:4	86
Giṭṭin 2:3	85	4:7	34	Ahilut 7:6	405
		8:7	369	Tahorot 3:8	398
Baba Qama 9:6	206	Abot 2:2	412	7:1	114
Baba Meṣi'a 1:5	100	4:5	412	Niddah 9:4	372

Tosephta

Peah 2:10	136	2:7-9	213	5:15	411
		2:8	211	5:16-17	413
Pesaḥim 2:22	170	3:1	68,206		
8:10	169	4:4	229	Baba Qama 4:3	147
		4:15	331	9:19	138
Yebamot 12:8	398	5:2	379,381	Baba Batra 2:12	129
Qiddušin 1:5	95	5:4	343		
1:9	147,148	5:5	394	Arakhin 4:4	147
1:11	151	5:8	401		
1:14	186	5:11	341	Tahorot 7:1	114
1:17	181	5:13	342	8:1	1134
2:3	217	5:14	409		

Midrashim

Gen. rabba	8,16,18,	Tanḥuma Buber	143	Mekhilta dR. Ismael	
	19,21,327,339	Midrash Shemuel	153,356		26,63,79,80,82,83,84,87,
Num. rabba	153,339,	Midrash Prov.	357		88,89,101,151,153,169,
	356	Pesiqta Rabbati	8,339		191,195,250,409
Thr. rabba	153,347	Pesiqta dR. Cahana		Mekhilta dR. Simeon b.	
Eccl. rabba	339		339		Iohai
Tanḥuma	153,339				11,29,48,54,56,63,64,75,

Mekhilta dR. Simeon b. Iohai	78,79,80,82,84,86,88,89, 101,169,195,250,408	Sifry Num..	117	Soferim	413
		Sifr Deut.	11,12,48, 81,83,85,86,88,170,173, 393	Avadim	56,81
Sifra	17,29,57,58,59,60, 81,85,86,89,90,173,195, 243,357	Onqelos	186	Eliahu rabba	349
				Pirke R. Eliezer	352
		Pseudo-Jonathan	186	Wehizhir	63

Rabbinic Literature

Braua, S.Z.	65,75		252,234	Rashba	23,66,193,252
Eliahu Wilna	186	Margalit M. (Pene Moshe)	198,268,292,380	Rashi	252,347
Fraenckel, D.	(Qorban Ha'edah) 54,63,193, 198,281,320,380,386	Meïri	252	Ritba	252,275
				Rosanes, J.	252
		Midrash Haggadol	86, 88	Rosh	252
Ibn Ezra	186			Sefer Hatterumot	290
Isserles, M.	296	Nachmanides	275,290	Sefer Ha'ittur	129,230, 287
Maimonides	65,193.	Ran	22,252,275		

Index of Greek, Latin, and Hebrew Words

ἀπορέω	292	ὠνή	129	אשם	2
ἀρχεῖον	382			חרף	43,44
βῶλοι	123	Arra, arrha	275	לקח	1
στατιά	382	Boloe	123	נשׂא	2
σύμφωνον	274	Catella	123	פרע	186
χάρτης	292	Centenarius	92	שום	122
Χάρυβδις	44				

Author Index

Aquila	44		48	Milgram, J.	29
Assaf, S.	166	Gulak, A.	274,275, 279,280	Sperber, D.	34
Barth J.	327			Sussnman, J.	i,6,48
Epstein, J.N.	30	Lieberman, S.	259,280, 371	Taubenschlag, R.	99,129, 191,274
Ginzberg, L.	6				
Guggenheimer, H.		Melamed, E.Z.	30		

Subject Index

Arra, arrha	276 ff.	Divorce, conditional	273
Abortion	18	Gentile	21
Accounting, heavenly	182,188	without marriage	269
Acquisition, of ownerless property	110,132	Documents, interpretation of	132
Action, not words	211	*Dedrans*	34
Agency, direct	191	Dough	379
indirect	191	*Dupondius*	33
Agent	257,259		
as witness	193	Eligible	383
Agio	143	Emancitation, partial	99,108
Allotment	64	*'Eruv*	286
price of	67,74,75	Estate	122
renunciation	77	distribution	122,143
Animal, lost	244	Existence, of human	295
Asceticism	414		
Assarius	8	Fellow	320
Assignment of credit	291	Firstborn	393
		Firstlings	247,248
Banker's agio	38	Forbidden acts	258
Bastard	322,334	Foundling	371
Bes	35	Freedom, forced	46,59
Bet kor	282		
Betrothed	1,2,7	Gentile slave, find of	100
Broomstick desecrated	386	freedom of	90
Burden of proof	145	land of	97
		manumission	89,97ff.
Camel-donkey driver	287	ownerless	89
Chattel Mortgage	95	Gift, by deed	129,132
Cherubim	371	unannounced	104
Claim, multiple	208	Girl, adolescent	63,80
Codex Hammurabi	276	adult	63
Coins, tolerance	37	Greivance procedure	166
Congregation	325		
Contract, reneging on	214	Half-obolus	27
Conversion	337,395	*Hazaqah*, acquisition by	14
Corpus iuris	276	permanence	15
Court of arbitration	277	Heave	295
Cross-breeding	175	Hebrew slave, allowance of	81
		bought from Gentile	61
Deaf-mute	97	freed by Jubilee	57
Dedication	262	pierced	46,80,83
Deed, testamentary	132	sick	56

Herd, of multiple owners	142,143	repudiation	198
		sinful	321
Incest, Gentile	19	states of	1
Indictments, multiple	138	stipulation	78
Inheritance of levir	121	Marriageable, family	380
Intercourse, Gentile	19	Marriages, simultaneous	35,42,227,231
perverse	10,19	Midwife, authority of	372
		Mina	58
Jesus	173	Minor, transaction of	97
Jubilee and Sabbatical	54	Mortgage	123
		Mount Sinai, presence at	155
Land, right of redemption	62	Murder, of a slave	267
Law, applicable	19		
Legal tender	142	Nakedness	17
Liability, for error	206	New Testament	3
of borrower	104		
of thief	124	Obligations, of men	150
transfer of	145	of women	148,149
Libra	92	*Obolus*	33
		'Omer	175
Manumission	3	*'Orlah*	245
bill of	105	Ownership	95,109
by proxy	105	Ownership. of animals	371
testamentary	107		
Marriage, acquisition	7	Passover, on the Sabbath	169
by document	22	subscription	192
by proxy	4,251	Passover sacrifice, multiple	235
by remission of debt	205	*Paterna potestas*, on adult daughter	
by robbery	232		307,311
by sanctum	235	of underage daughter	307,312
claim of	319	on son	311,395
classes	344	Permanence of *status quo ante*	393
conditional	229	*Peruṭah*	3,8
definitive	2,3	Piercing	87
delayed	257 ff.	"Ploughing"	352
Gentile	16	Possession, by Temple	147
impossible	321	in barter	141,142
levirate	8	of animals	108 ff.
of bastard	340	of movables	95,112,126,138
of Hebrew slave	45,82,88	of real estate	95
of underage girl	52,63,65,75,198,	undisturbed	49
	199,200,201	Prefix, partitive	243
preliminary	2	Preliminary marriage, conditional	303
probationary	230	impossible	294,332

Priest, desecrated	346,384,385	Skin disease	173
Prima facie evidence	398,401	Slave girl, Hebrew	10,26
Promise, to Heaven	141	Slave woman, in will	106
Property, of Heaven	243	Slave, Gentile	3,89
Prophetic text	91,93	Hebrew	3,27,45
Proselyte, without heirs	15,110,136,137	Stipulations, in contracts	283
		Strangling	18
Quadrans	33	*Symphon*	274 ff.
Real estate, claim to	96	Theft, of the Sabbath	138
Roman Law	3	Tithe of the poor	251
		Title guarantee	95,125
Sabbath boundary, biblical	286	Tooth and Eye	101
rabbinic	286	Transfer, by deed	131
Sacrifice, temporary	264	conditional	129
Sacrifices, goodwill	241	of title	265
multiple	234	Trial by oath	125
Sale, defered	230		
without action	230	Underage girl, emancipated	79,202
Samaritans	373	Undistributed middle	305
Second Passover	171	Usufruct, prohibited	24
Semis	33,34		
Šeqel	38	Wife, acquisition by	100
Servant, indentured	46	rebellious	56
Sex act	19	Wine, Gentile	346
Shaving hair	86	sold to Gentile	112
Sin, intentional	236	*Zuz*	38,272

www.ingramcontent.com/pod-product-compliance
Lightning Source LLC
Chambersburg PA
CBHW030516230426
43665CB00010B/634